Volume 7
Reformed Catholic
Problem of the Forged Catholicism
Warning against Idolatry

PRACTICAL WORKS
Volume 8
Discourse on Conscience
Three Books on Cases of Conscience
Treatise Whether a Man is in Damnation or Grace
A Case of Conscience
Grain of Mustard Seed

Volume 9
True Manner of Knowing Christ Crucified
True Gain
Exhortation to Repentance: Zephaniah 2:1–2
Nature and Practice of Repentance
Combat of the Flesh and Spirit
Man's Imagination
Direction for Government of the Tongue
Damned Art of Witchcraft
Resolution to Countrymen on Prognostication

Volume 10
Treatise on How to Live Well in All Estates
Treatise on Vocations
Right Manner of Erecting and Ordering a Family
Calling of the Ministry
Manner and Method of Preaching
Christian Equity
Death's Knell
Treatise on Dying Well

"On the broad shoulders of William Perkins, epoch-making pioneer, stood the entire school of seventeenth-century Puritan pastors and divines, yet the Puritan reprint industry has steadily bypassed him. Now, however, he begins to reappear, admirably edited, and at last this yawning gap is being filled. Profound thanks to the publisher and heartfelt praise to God have become due."
—J. I. Packer, Board of Governors' Professor of Theology, Regent College, Vancouver, British Columbia

"Without a doubt, the Puritans were theological titans. The Puritan theological tradition did not emerge out of a vacuum. It was shaped by leaders and theologians who set the trajectory of the movement and shaped its commitments. William Perkins was one of those men. Perkins's contribution to Puritan theology is inestimable, and this new reprint of his collected works is a much-awaited addition to all who are still shaped and influenced by the Puritans and their commitment to the centrality of the grace of God found only in Jesus Christ. Even now, every true gospel minister stands in debt to Perkins, and in his shadow."
—R. Albert Mohler Jr., president, The Southern Baptist Theological Seminary

"The list of those influenced by the ministry of William Perkins reads like a veritable Who's Who of the Puritan Brotherhood and far beyond. This reprinting of his works, so long unobtainable except by a few, is therefore a publishing event of the first magnitude."
—Sinclair B. Ferguson, Chancellor's Professor of Systematic Theology, Reformed Theological Seminary; Teaching Fellow, Ligonier Ministries

"The father of Elizabethan Puritanism, Perkins presided over a dynasty of faith. The scope of his work is wide, yet on every topic he treats one discovers erudition and deep reflection. He was the first in an amazing line of ministers at Cambridge University's main church. A pastor to pastors, he wrote a bestseller on counseling, was a formative figure in the development of Reformed orthodoxy, and a judicious reformer within the Church of England. I am delighted to see Perkins's works made available again for a wide audience."
—Michael Horton, J. Gresham Machen Professor of Theology and Apologetics, Westminster Seminary California

"William Perkins was a most remarkable Christian. In his relatively short life he was a great preacher, pastor, and theologian. His prolific writings were foundational to the whole English Puritan enterprise and a profound influence beyond his own time and borders. His works have become rare, and their

republication must be a source of real joy and blessing to all serious Christians. Perkins is the first Puritan we should read."
—W. Robert Godfrey, president emeritus, Westminster Seminary California

"Relatively few in the church's history have left a written legacy of enduring value beyond their own time. Perkins is surely among that select group. Reformation Heritage Books is to be commended for its commitment to making his *Works* available in this projected series, beginning with this volume."
—Richard B. Gaffin Jr., professor of biblical and systematic theology emeritus, Westminster Theological Seminary

"Christians have heard about William Perkins, especially that he was an extraordinary preacher whose sermons made a deep impression on Cambridge and that they were still impacting the town in the decades that followed Perkins's death at a mere forty-four years of age in 1602. He was at the heart of the revival of truth and holy living that made the Reformation a glorious work of God. He was the outstanding Puritan theologian of his time, but most of us have not had the opportunity to study his works because of their rarity. After more than three hundred years, this ignorance is going to be ended with the remarkable appearance during the next decade of the complete works of this man of God. We are looking forward to their appearance very much. There will be sufficient gaps between their publication to ensure a sincere attempt at imbibing the truths of each volume, and then we face the challenge of translating Perkins's teaching into flesh-and-blood living."
—Geoff Thomas, pastor emeritus, Alfred Place Baptist Church, Aberystwyth, Wales

The Works of
WILLIAM PERKINS

The Works of
WILLIAM PERKINS

VOLUME 9

A Declaration of the True Manner of Knowing Christ Crucified
The True Gain
A Faithful and Plain Exposition upon Zephaniah 2:1–2
The Nature and Practice of Repentance
The Combat of the Flesh and Spirit
A Treatise of Man's Imaginations
A Direction for Government of the Tongue
A Discourse of the Damned Art of Witchcraft
A Resolution to Country Man on Prognostication

EDITED BY J. STEPHEN YUILLE

General editors:
Joel R. Beeke and Derek W. H. Thomas

REFORMATION HERITAGE BOOKS
Grand Rapids, Michigan

The Works of William Perkins, Volume 9
© 2020 by Reformation Heritage Books

Reformation Heritage Books
2965 Leonard St. NE
Grand Rapids, MI 49525
616-977-0889
orders@heritagebooks.org
www.heritagebooks.org

Printed in the United States of America
25 26 27 28 29 30/10 9 8 7 6 5 4 3 2

ISBN 978-1-60178-764-4 (vol. 9)
ISBN 978-1-60178-765-1 (vol. 9) epub

Library of Congress Cataloging-in-Publication Data

Perkins, William, 1558-1602.
 [Works]
 The works of William Perkins / edited by J. Stephen Yuille ; general editors: Joel R. Beeke and Derek W. H. Thomas.
    pages cm
 Includes bibliographical references and index.
 ISBN 978-1-60178-360-8 (v. 1 : alk. paper) 1. Puritans. 2. Theology—Early works to 1800. I. Yuille, J. Stephen, 1968- editor. II. Beeke, Joel R., 1952- editor. III. Thomas, Derek, 1953- editor. IV. Title.
 BX9315.P47 2014
 230—dc23
                                2014037122

For additional Reformed literature, request a free book list from Reformation Heritage Books at the above regular or e-mail address.

Contents

General Preface ix

Preface to Volume 9 xi

A Declaration of the True Manner of Knowing Christ Crucified 1

The True Gain 23

A Faithful and Plain Exposition upon Zephaniah 2:1–2 79

The Nature and Practice of Repentance 125

The Combat of the Flesh and Spirit 169

A Treatise of Man's Imaginations 181

A Direction for the Government of the Tongue 253

A Discourse of the Damned Art of Witchcraft 293

A Resolution to Country Man on Prognostication 405

Scripture Index 439

Subject Index 455

General Preface

William Perkins (1558–1602), often called "the father of Puritanism," was a master preacher and teacher of Reformed, experiential theology. He left an indelible mark upon the English Puritan movement, and his writings were translated into Dutch, German, French, Hungarian, and other European languages. Today he is best known for his writings on predestination, but he also wrote prolifically on many doctrinal and practical subjects, including extended expositions of Scripture. The 1631 edition of his English *Works* filled over two thousand large pages of small print in three folio volumes.

It is puzzling why his full *Works* have not been in print since the early seventeenth century, especially given the flood of Puritan works reprinted in the mid-nineteenth and late twentieth centuries. Ian Breward did much to promote the study of Perkins, but Breward's now rare, single-volume compilation of the *Work of William Perkins* (1970) could only present samplings of Perkins's writings. We are extremely pleased that this lacuna is being filled, as it has been a dream of many years to see the writings of this Reformed theologian made accessible again to the public, including laymen, pastors, and scholars.

Reformation Heritage Books is publishing Perkins's *Works* in a newly typeset format with spelling and capitalization conformed to modern American standards. The old forms ("thou dost") are changed to the modern equivalent ("you do"), except in Scripture quotations and references to deity. Punctuation has also been modernized. However, the original words are left intact, not changed into modern synonyms, and the original word order retained even when it differs from modern syntax. Pronouns are capitalized when referring to God. Some archaic terms and obscure references are explained in the editor's footnotes.

As was common in his day, Perkins did not use quotation marks to distinguish a direct quotation from an indirect quotation, summary, or paraphrase, but simply put all citations in italics (as he also did with proper names). We have removed such italics and followed the general principle of placing citations in quotation marks even if they may not be direct and exact quotations. Perkins generally quoted the Geneva Bible, but rather than conforming his quotations to any particular translation of Scripture, we have left them in his words. Scripture references in the margins are brought into the text and enclosed in square brackets. Parenthetical Scripture references in general are abbreviated and punctuated according to the modern custom (as in Rom. 8:1), sometimes corrected, and sometimes moved to the end of the clause instead of its beginning. Other notes from the margins are placed in footnotes and labeled, "In the margin." Where multiple sets of parentheses were nested within each other, the inward parentheses have been changed to square brackets. Otherwise, square brackets indicate words added by the editor. An introduction to each volume by its editor orients the reader to its contents.

The projected *Works of William Perkins* will include ten volumes, including four volumes of biblical exposition, three volumes of doctrinal and polemical treatises, and three volumes of ethical and practical writings. A breakdown of each volume's contents may be found inside the cover of this book.

If it be asked what the center of Perkins's theology was, then we hesitate to answer, for students of historical theology know that this is a perilous question to ask regarding any person. However, we may do well to end this preface by repeating what Perkins said at the conclusion of his influential manual on preaching, "The sum of the sum: preach one Christ by Christ to the praise of Christ."

—Joel R. Beeke and Derek W. H. Thomas

Preface to Volume 9 of William Perkins's *Works*

More than a century ago, B. B. Warfield encouraged the students at Princeton Seminary to remember "that intellectual training alone will never make a true minister, that the heart has rights which the head must respect, and that it behooves us above everything to remember that the ministry is a spiritual office."[1] Warfield's exhortation was fueled by his conviction that preparation for ministry must include the training of the heart, hand, and head—that is, it must incorporate the "devotional, practical, and intellectual."[2] Four centuries earlier, William Perkins communicated the same message to his students at Cambridge. A preacher, said he, must possess "not only the knowledge of divine things flowing in his brain but engraved on his heart and printed in his soul by the spiritual finger of God."[3]

This was Perkins's desire, not only for prospective pastors, but for every follower of Christ. It stemmed from his conviction that Christianity is—above all else—a religion of the heart. "Saving knowledge in religion is experimental," wrote Perkins, "and he that is truly founded upon Christ feels the power and efficacy of His death and resurrection, effectually causing the death of sin, and the life of grace which both appear by new obedience."[4]

Much has been written on Perkins's experiential piety—namely, his overwhelming sense of man's depravity and his corresponding deep appreciation for God's sovereignty in salvation; his unwavering quest for an assurance rooted in

---

1. B. B. Warfield, "Spiritual Culture in the Theological Seminary," in *The Princeton Theological Review* 2 (1904): 65.

2. Warfield, "Spiritual Culture," 67. Warfield went on to encourage the students to guard and nurture their devotional life. He prescribed the reading of Puritan literature as particularly useful for cultivating piety, because it is "marked by intense devotion to duty and strong insistence on personal holiness." "Spiritual Culture," 80.

3. William Perkins, *The Art of Prophesying; or, A treatise concerning the sacred and only true manner and method of preaching*, in *The Whole Works of that Famous and Worthy Minister of Christ in the University of Cambridge, M. William Perkins*, 3 vols. (London: John Legate, 1631), 2:672.

4. William Perkins, *A Godly and Learned Exposition Upon Christ's Sermon in the Mount*, in *The Works of that Famous and Worthy Minister of Christ in the University of Cambridge, M. William Perkins*, 3 vols. (London: John Haviland, 1631), 3:259–60.

Christ and confirmed by the active testimony of the Holy Spirit in the believer's life; his unassailable conviction that the faith that brings people into union with Christ is that which issues forth in a life of obedience; his unquenchable desire for a heart-felt appropriation of God's truth as opposed to mere intellectual assent; and his steadfast commitment to the Word and sacraments as the means by which God's Spirit works in God's people.

Without question, these motifs were foundational to the development of Perkins's experiential piety, yet they by no means exhaust the subject. This is confirmed in the present volume, which brings together eight of Perkins's lesser known works and, by so doing, introduces the reader to other important facets of his religion of the heart.

The first work is *A Declaration of the True Manner of Knowing Christ Crucified*, published in 1596. Perkins wrote it—as the title suggests—to demonstrate what it means to know "Christ crucified."[5] He was driven by concern for those who placed their hopes in a mere theoretical knowledge of Christ—what he described as "a knowledge swimming in the brain."[6] For Perkins, true knowledge "alters and disposes the affections." It is, first, to feel "our sins" so profoundly that we dislike "ourselves and our past lives" and seek "conformity with Christ in all good duties." It is, second, to comprehend the Father's love in giving "His own dear Son to death" and the Son's goodness in loving "His enemies more than Himself" to such a degree that our hearts are "inflamed to love God."[7]

For Perkins, we cultivate such "lively, powerful, and operative knowledge" by following three steps.[8] The first is "consideration," whereby we see Christ as He is "revealed in the history of the gospel" and "offered in the ministry of the Word and sacraments." This sight makes us feel our need of Him and correspondingly long for Him. The second step is "application," whereby we recognize that Christ was crucified for us, meaning He stood in our "very room and place" while our "very personal and particular sins were imputed and applied to Him." The third step is "affection," whereby we are "carried to Christ," esteeming Him at "so high a price" that all else pales in comparison.[9]

---

5. William Perkins, *A Declaration of the True Manner of Knowing Christ Crucified*, in *The Whole Works of that Famous and Worthy Minister of Christ in the University of Cambridge, M. William Perkins*, 3 vols. (London: John Legate, 1631), 1:625.

6. *True Manner*, 1:627.

7. *True Manner*, 1:627.

8. *True Manner*, 1:626–27.

9. For Perkins, when we know Christ in this way, "all the blessings of God, whether spiritual or temporal…are conveyed unto us from the Father by Christ." This includes: (1) Christ's merit which is "the value and price of His death and passion whereby man is perfectly reconciled to God"; (2) Christ's virtue, which is "the power of His Godhead whereby He creates new hearts in all them who believe in Him, and makes them new creatures"; and (3) Christ's example, whereby

For these three steps to produce their desired effect, Perkins was convinced that we must meditate on "the passion of Christ."[10] We do so, not by means of "the wooden crucifix after the popish manner," but by means of "the preaching of the Word and in the sacraments."[11] As we hear of Christ agonizing in the garden, we think of our sins that "brought such bloody and grievous pains upon Him." As we hear of Him bound and led away, we remember our sins that "brought Him into the power of His enemies, and were the very bonds wherewith He was tied." As we hear of His condemnation, we consider "the wrath and fury of God against sin, and…His great and infinite mercy to sinners." As we hear of Christ clothed in purple and crowned with thorns, we behold "the everlasting shame that is due unto us." As we hear of Him naked upon the cross, we remember that He covered our deformity "with His most precious and rich nakedness." As we hear of His cry from the cross, we think of "how He suffered the pangs and torments of hell as our pledge and surety." As we hear of His death, we consider that "our sins were the cause of it." As we hear of the trembling of the earth, we think of how we "deserved to be swallowed by the earth and to go down into the pit alive rather than to have any part in the merit of Christ crucified."[12]

By applying ourselves to this "history of the passion of Christ," we move purposefully and deliberately through the three steps of "consideration," "application," and "affection," until our knowledge becomes "lively, powerful, and

---

He becomes a "pattern of all good duties, to which we ought to conform ourselves." *True Manner*, 1:627–28.

10. *True Manner*, 1:630.

11. *True Manner*, 1:632. Perkins's emphasis on beholding Christ's passion raises the interesting question of his relationship to Ignatian spirituality. Perkins and Ignatius of Loyola (1491–1556) share some similarities in terms of their subject matter and their common concern to stir the affections. For his part, Ignatius writes, "For it is not knowing much, but realizing and relishing things interiorly, that contents and satisfies the soul." Ignatius, *The Spiritual Exercises of St. Ignatius of Loyola*, trans. E. Mullan (New York: P. J. Kennedy & Sons, 1914), second annotation. Perkins would agree. However, their respective approaches to meditation are markedly different. Perkins stresses the three faculties of the soul, whereas Ignatius depends primarily upon sense data in order to stimulate the imagination. This tendency in Ignatius is evident, for example, in his meditations on hell. He writes of the need "to see with the sight of the imagination the great fires, and the souls as bodies in fire," "to hear with the ears wailings, howlings, cries," "to smell with the smell smoke, sulphur, dregs and putrid things," "to taste with the taste bitter things," and "to touch with the touch; that is to say, how the fires touch and burn the souls." *The Spiritual Exercises*, fifth exercise. To arrive at this experience, he encourages his readers "to chastise the flesh" (i.e., give it sensible pain) by "wearing haircloth or cords or iron chains next to the flesh, by scourging or wounding oneself, and by other kinds of austerity." Such an approach is completely foreign to Perkins, who is primarily concerned with exciting the affections via the understanding.

12. *True Manner*, 1:633.

operative."[13] For Perkins, it is only when our affections are thus engaged that we truly know "Christ crucified."

Perkins's Christ-centered piety remains the focus of his second work: *The True Gain: More in Worth than All the Goods in the World*, published in 1601. According to Perkins, he wrote it to explain an "infallible truth"—namely, Christ "in the act of our reconciliation with God admits neither deputy nor partner."[14] His text is Philippians 3:7–9, where the apostle Paul declares, "But what things were gain to me, those I counted loss for Christ. Yea doubtless, and I count all things but loss for the excellency of the knowledge of Christ Jesus my Lord: for whom I have suffered the loss of all things, and do count them but dung, that I may win Christ, and be found in him, not having mine own righteousness, which is of the law, but that which is through the faith of Christ, the righteousness which is of God by faith."

By way of exposition, Perkins divides the text into two parts. In the first, he considers Paul's losses: (1) his "privileges," "virtues," and "works" before his conversion; and (2) his "virtues" (e.g., hope, fear, love) and "works of grace" after his conversion.[15] For Perkins, Paul's example affords a simple (yet profound) doctrine—in short, we must come to Christ without any "virtues or works" of our own and we must esteem ourselves to be "wretched and miserable" sinners while simply praying, "Lord, be merciful to me a sinner" (Luke 18:13).[16]

In the second part of his exposition, Perkins considers Paul's gain: "the whole Christ...according to both natures."[17] To gain Christ is to gain His Godhead "in respect of virtue and operation showed in (or upon) the manhood of Christ," and it is to gain His manhood which is "really communicated to the faith of the believing heart." In this manner Christ is said "to be made unto us of God, wisdom, righteousness, sanctification, and redemption" (1 Cor.

---

13. For an introduction to some of the issues surrounding the Puritan meditative tradition, see F. L. Huntley, *Bishop Joseph Hall and Protestant Meditation in Seventeenth Century England: A Study with the Texts of the Art of Divine Meditation (1606) and Occasional Meditations (1633)* (Binghamton: Centre for Medieval and Early Renaissance Studies, 1981); U. Milo Kauffman, *The Pilgrim's Progress and Traditions in Puritan Meditation* (New Haven: Yale University Press, 1966); and Louis Martz, *The Poetry of Meditation: A Study in English Religious Literature of the Seventeenth Century* (New Haven: Yale University Press, 1962).

14. William Perkins, *The True Gain: More in Worth than All the Goods in the World*, in *The Whole Works of that Famous and Worthy Minister of Christ in the University of Cambridge, M. William Perkins*, 3 vols. (London: John Legate, 1631), 1:645.

15. *True Gain*, 1:648–49.

16. *True Gain*, 1:652. Perkins adds, "Works may be considered either as causes of salvation or only as a way directing thereto. If they are considered as causes, they are not necessary, but in this respect they are dung. If they are respected as a way leading and directing to eternal life, they are indeed necessary thus and not otherwise." *True Gain*, 1:649.

17. Perkins describes this as "the ancient and catholic doctrine." *True Gain*, 1:653.

1:30). Christ is our wisdom because "from His wisdom there is wisdom derived in some measure to all who are mystically united to Him." Christ is our justice "because that justice which is in the manhood…whereby He obeyed His Father's will and suffered all things to be suffered for us…is imputed to us and accounted ours." Christ is our sanctification because from "this holiness of His our holiness is derived and springs as a fruit." And Christ is our redemption because He "lives in the estate of exaltation and glory…not only for Himself, but also for us, that we, being partakers thereof, may live together with Him."[18]

Given Christ's inestimable worth, we (like Paul) desire to be found in Christ—that is, "to be taken out of the first Adam and to be united unto Christ as His very flesh or as a true member of His mystical body."[19] By this union we gain the righteousness of Christ. "A sinner stands just before the tribunal seat of God," writes Perkins, "not by the justice of the law, but by the justice of faith, which is the obedience of Christ, without any works of ours."[20] We also gain fellowship with Christ, meaning we "grow more and more in holy experience of the endless love of God."[21] Finally, we gain "the reward of eternal life."[22]

According to Perkins, the means by which we become "a true member of His mystical body" (thereby gaining Him) is faith alone.[23] Recognizing that this assertion is "scandalous" to some, he affirms that faith is the only "instrument" by which we receive what is "given by the Father, procured by the Son, [and] applied by the Holy Spirit." However, when it comes to a "way" to eternal life, faith is not alone, but is accompanied by other works and virtues. "If we speak of the way to life," says Perkins, "then we are not saved only by faith. For though faith is the only instrument to apprehend Christ, yet it is not the only way to life. Repentance also is the way, yea all virtues and all works are the way."[24]

---

18. *True Gain*, 1:654.

19. *True Gain*, 1:655–57. Perkins affirms that we must follow four rules when seeking to understand this mystery: (1) "The whole person of him who believes is united to the whole person of Christ." (2) "We are first joined to the flesh of Christ and by His flesh to His Godhead. For that which brings us to have fellowship with God joins us to God." (3) "This union stands not in imagination but is a true and real conjunction." (4) "The bond of this conjunction is one and the same Spirit, being both in Christ and us, first in Christ and then in us." *True Gain*, 1:658.

20. *True Gain*, 1:659.

21. *True Gain*, 1:663.

22. *True Gain*, 1:667.

23. Perkins describes faith as "a special gift of God whereby we believe Christ and His benefits to be ours.… Now God gives Christ in the Word and sacraments. And in them He does (as it were) open His hand and reach forth all the blessings of Christ unto us. We must not, therefore, imagine to find Christ where and how we list, but we must seek Him in the Word and sacraments, and there we must receive Him if we desire to receive Him aright." *True Gain*, 1:662. The closest Perkins comes to the five solas is when he declares, "We are justified and accepted of God to eternal life through grace alone by faith alone for Christ alone." *True Gain*, 1:663.

24. *True Gain*, 1:650.

This discussion of the "way to life" brings us to the third work in this volume: *A Faithful and Plain Exposition upon Zephaniah 2:1–2*, published posthumously in 1606. Perkins originally preached this sermon at Stourbridge Fair in Cambridge.[25] As the title indicates, he took Zephaniah's warning to the nation of Israel as his chief text: "Search yourselves, even search you, O nation, not worthy to be beloved: before the decree come forth, and you be as chaff that passeth on a day."[26] In his sermon, Perkins unpacked five principal points: (1) what we should do—search; (2) what we should search—ourselves; (3) who should search—we; (4) why we should repent—God's decree of judgment threatens us; and (5) why we should repent immediately—the execution of God's decree is imminent.

In short, the prospect of God's impending judgment calls for a careful searching of our lives. Perkins describes this as "a principal duty in repentance, even the beginning and foundation of all true grace."[27] To ensure success, he lays out three rules. First, we must know that we have "sinned in the sin of Adam"; that is to say, his sin in eating the forbidden fruit is our sin and, therefore, we stand condemned in God's sight.[28] Second, we must know that "the seeds of all sins" are by nature in us.[29] Third, we must know that we are "by nature the child[ren] of wrath and God's enem[ies]."[30] With this foundation in place, Perkins speaks directly to his audience, rebuking them for (among other things) their contempt of religion and godliness, their dishonest business dealings,

---

25. William Crashaw, "The Epistle Dedicatory," in William Perkins, *A Faithful and Plain Exposition upon Zephaniah 2:1–2*, in *The Whole Works of that Famous and Worthy Minister of Christ in the University of Cambridge, M. William Perkins*, 3 vols. (London: John Haviland, 1631), vol. 3. Stourbridge Fair was held annually on Stourbridge Common in Cambridge. Originally, it ran for two days, but in Perkins's day it lasted from August 24 to September 29. The 1589 charter states that it "far surpassed the greatest of and most celebrated fairs of all England; whence great benefits had resulted to the merchants of the whole kingdom, who resorted thereto, and there quickly sold their wares and merchandises to purchasers coming from all parts of the realm." For more on this, see Alison Taylor, *Cambridge: The Hidden History* (Stroud: Tempus Publishing, 1999); and Tania McIntosh, *The Decline of Stourbridge Fair 1770–1934* (Leicester: University of Leicester, 1998). Of note, Stourbridge Fair was the inspiration for John Bunyan's "Vanity Fair" in *The Pilgrim's Progress*.

26. I have provided the text as Perkins cited it in his treatise. The KJV reads: "Gather yourselves together, yea, gather together, O nation not desired; before the decree bring forth, before the day pass as the chaff, before the fierce anger of the LORD come upon you, before the day of the LORD's anger come upon you."

27. *A Faithful and Plain Exposition*, 3:414.

28. *A Faithful and Plain Exposition*, 3:415.

29. Perkins adds, "If God did not thus moderate and restrain the natures of men, but suffer them to break out to the full, there would then be no order, but all confusion in the world." *A Faithful and Plain Exposition*, 3:415–16.

30. *A Faithful and Plain Exposition*, 3:416.

and their blatant abuse of the Sabbath.[31] Because of their lack of repentance, God's decree of judgment is about to fall on them. "And if you would escape the rigor of that judgment," he warns, "enter now into judgment with yourself and search yourself!"[32]

Perkins stays with the theme of repentance in his fourth work: *Two Treatises: The Nature and Practice of Repentance; and The Combat of the Flesh and Spirit*, published in 1593.[33] While the previous work is essentially an earnest exhortation to repent, these two treatises provide a systematic explanation of the doctrine of repentance. Perkins walks the reader through its "nature," "cause," "parts," "degrees," "motives," "contraries," and "corruptions." His entire discussion is governed by his view of repentance as "a work of grace arising from a godly sorrow, whereby a man turns from all his sins unto God, and brings forth fruit worthy [of] amendment of life."[34] Perkins's definition is carefully

---

31. This work is the best example of Perkins's "plain" style of preaching. While certainly not void of rhetorical devices, his sermon is for the most part unadorned. While stressing the efficacy of God's Word preached in the power of the Holy Spirit, Perkins was at the same time committed to a method of preaching that was marked by clarity and simplicity, and fueled by a familiar acquaintance with eternal realities, because he viewed this as the principal means by which to instruct the mind and incline the heart. For more on this, see J. Stephen Yuille, "A Simple Method: William Perkins and the Shaping of the Protestant Pulpit," *Puritan Reformed Journal* 9, no. 1 (2017): 215–30.

32. *A Faithful and Plain Exposition*, 3:427.

33. William Perkins, *Two Treatises: The Nature and Practice of Repentance; and The Combat of the Flesh and Spirit*, in *The Whole Works of that Famous and Worthy Minister of Christ in the University of Cambridge*, M. William Perkins, 3 vols. (London: John Legate, 1631), vol. 1. Perkins's emphasis on repentance raises the issue of how he understood it in relation to faith. He clarifies, "Some may object that repentance goes before all grace because it is preached first.…The answer hereto may be this: If we respect the order of nature, there are other graces of God which go before repentance, because a man's conscience must in some sort be settled touching his reconciliation with God in Christ before he can begin to repent. Wherefore, justification and sanctification in order of nature go before repentance. But if we respect time, grace and repentance are both together. As soon as there is fire, it is hot. And as soon as a man is regenerate, he repents. If we respect the outward manifestation of these two, repentance goes before all other graces because it first of all appears outwardly. Regeneration is like the sap of the tree that lies hid within the bark. Repentance is like the bud that speedily shows itself before either blossom, leaf, or fruit appear. Yea, all other graces of the heart, which are needful to salvation, are made manifest by repentance. And for this cause repentance (as I take it) is preached first." *Two Treatises*, 1:455.

34. *Two Treatises*, 1:455. Perkins acknowledges that "divines" understand repentance differently. He remarks, "Some make it a fruit of faith containing two parts (mortification and vivification); some make faith a part of it by dividing it into contrition, faith, [and] new obedience; [and] some make it all one with regeneration. The difference is not in the substance of doctrine, but in the logical manner of handling it. And the difference of handling arises from the divers acceptation of repentance. It is taken [in] two ways: generally and particularly. [It is taken] generally for the whole conversion of a sinner, and so it may contain contrition, faith, [and] new obedience under it, and be confounded with regeneration. It is taken particularly for the renovation of the life and behavior, and so it is a fruit of faith. And I only follow this sense

worded so as to address what he perceived to be the prevalence of "counterfeit" repentance. Far too many rested in their "ceremonial" repentance ("an outward show") or "desperate" repentance ("a horror of conscience").[35] Yet, these lacked one essential ingredient in Perkins's estimation, namely, "godly" sorrow.

When we experience "the wrath of God and other miseries," we often experience a measure of "worldly" sorrow. But "godly" sorrow is quite different, since it does not arise from an apprehension of the negative effects of sin but of the very nature of sin. When this "disposition" takes root, we see sin as the greatest evil and we sorrow because of it. Perkins elaborates, "If there were no conscience to accuse, no devil to terrify, no judge to arraign and condemn, no hell to torment, yet he would be humbled and brought to his knees for his sins because he has offended a loving, merciful, and longsuffering God."[36]

The "principal cause" of such "godly" sorrow (and, therefore, of repentance) is the Holy Spirit. By the ministry of the Word, He enables us to gain some "knowledge" of the law of God, the judgment of God, and the guilt of sin. He then assists us in our application of this knowledge to ourselves, thereby producing "fear and sorrow" in respect of God's judgment against sinners.[37] At this point, the Holy Spirit enables us to see God's mercy in the offer of the gospel. Once we apply this to ourselves, we experience joy (as we see our sins pardoned in Christ) and sorrow (as we see how much our sins displease Christ). The end result is repentance, whereby we resolve within ourselves "to sin no more as [we have] done, but to live in newness of life."[38]

For Perkins, this work of repentance continues throughout the believer's life. This is necessitated by the internal combat between the flesh and the spirit (Gal. 5:17). He defines the "spirit" as "a created quality of holiness" which the Holy Spirit produces in the soul (i.e., the mind, affections, and will), and the "flesh" as "the natural corruption" of the soul whereby it is inclined "to that which is against the law."[39] These two are mingled together in each of the faculties of the soul. Thus, the whole of each is partly flesh and partly spirit.[40]

---

in this treatise." "To the Reader," in *Two Treatises*. Perkins acknowledges that Calvin speaks of repentance in the "general" sense—that is, of the whole conversion of a sinner. He provides the following marginal note: Calvin Inst. l. 3. c. 3. par. 9.

35. *Two Treatises*, 1:468. Perkins believes that Saul typifies "ceremonial" repentance, while Judas typifies "desperate" repentance.

36. *Two Treatises*, 1:455.

37. For an analysis of Perkins's use of the law and gospel in preaching, see J. Stephen Yuille, "Ready to Receive: Humbling and Softening in William Perkins's Preparation of the Heart," *Puritan Reformed Journal* 5:2 (2013): 91–106.

38. *Two Treatises*, 1:456.

39. *Two Treatises*, 1:469.

40. *Two Treatises*, 1:469–70.

They fight with each other by "lusting"—that is, "stirring up motions and incli-nations in the heart, either to good or evil."[41] The lusting of the flesh is "to engender evil motions and passions of self-love, envy, pride, unbelief, anger, etc.," and "to hinder, quench, and overwhelm the good motions of the spirit." The lusting of the spirit is "to beget good meditations, motions, inclinations, and desires in the mind, will, and affections" and "to hinder and suppress the bad motions and suggestions of the flesh."

For Perkins, this internal combat is "the estate" of all believers in this life. We are not free from "evil cogitations," "rebellious inclinations," or "slips in life and conversation"; rather, we feel ourselves "laden with the corruptions of [our] vile and rebellious nature." For this reason, we "bewail them from [our] heart, and with might and main fight against them by the grace of God's Spirit."[42] In a word, we repent.

Central to Perkins's doctrine of repentance is his view of the mind as the principal faculty of the soul—a theme he takes up in his fifth work: *A Treatise of Man's Imaginations, showing his natural evil thoughts, his want of good thoughts, and the way to reform them*, published posthumously in 1607. Perkins's text is Genesis 8:21, "And the Lord smelled a sweet savour; and the Lord said in his heart, I will not again curse the ground any more for man's sake; for the imagi-nation of man's heart is evil from his youth; neither will I again smite any more every thing living, as I have done." For Perkins, the "whole meaning" of this text is summed up as follows: "The mind and understanding part of man is naturally so corrupt that as soon as he can use reason, he does nothing but imagine that which is wicked and against the law of God."[43] This corruption is evident in man's thoughts concerning God, his neighbor, and himself.[44]

Perkins prescribes a number of rules for reforming these evil thoughts. First, we must bring all our thoughts "into the obedience of God." Second, we must keep our hearts by watching and guarding them (Prov. 4:23). Third, we must fix our minds on heaven, "where Christ sits at the right hand of His Father." Fourth, "we must labor to be assured in our hearts by God's Spirit of our particular reconciliation with God in Christ." Fifth, we must give ourselves to "spiritual consideration."[45]

---

41. *Two Treatises*, 1:470.

42. *Two Treatises*, 1:474.

43. William Perkins, *A Treatise of Man's Imaginations, showing his natural evil thoughts, his want of good thoughts, and the way to reform them*, in *The Whole Works of that Famous and Worthy Minister of Christ in the University of Cambridge, M. William Perkins*, 3 vols. (London: John Legate, 1631), 2:458.

44. *Man's Imaginations*, 2:459–73.

45. *Man's Imaginations*, 2:477–78. Perkins explains in great detail what we should "consider" concerning God and ourselves. *Man's Imaginations*, 2:479–83.

This last point is crucial to an accurate understanding of Perkins's piety. He never speaks of the Holy Spirit directly touching our soul; moreover, he never contrasts the work of the Holy Spirit and the exercise of the mind. On the contrary, for Perkins, the Holy Spirit works through the mind to edify and sanctify us. This means that we must seek to grow in our knowledge of the truth and in our "spiritual consideration" of the same. Such "consideration" entails "any action of the mind, renewed and sanctified, whereby it does seriously think on those things which may further salvation."[46] This is the means by which the Holy Spirit produces repentance in our lives. "If we give our minds thereunto in a constant course," says Perkins, "we shall undoubtedly find by good experience that evil thoughts shall not prevail against us, but being reformed in our cogitation we shall send out of our minds as from a cleansed fountain such streams of good words and works, through the whole course of our lives, as shall redound to the glory of our God, the good of our brethren, and the consolation of our own souls, through Jesus Christ our Lord, to whom with the Father and the Holy Spirit, be praise in His church for evermore."[47]

In this discussion it becomes apparent that, for Perkins, the mind is "the principal part of the soul."[48] In making this assertion, he is not suggesting that the will necessarily follows the dictates of the mind.[49] He does not believe that the mind is the efficient cause of the will's choice. Rather, in referring to the mind as the supreme faculty of the soul, he means: (1) that (as created in the

---

46. *Man's Imaginations*, 2:478.

47. *Man's Imaginations*, 2:483.

48. *Man's Imaginations*, 2:475. This perspective echoes John Calvin, who states, "Let the office…of understanding be to distinguish between objects, as each seems worthy of approval or disapproval; while that of the will, to choose and follow what the understanding pronounces good, but to reject and flee what it disapproves." *Institutes of the Christian Religion*, in The Library of Christian Classics, ed. J. T. McNeill, trans. Ford Lewis Battles (Philadelphia: Westminster Press, 1960), 1.15.7. Here, Calvin describes the proper functioning of the soul as the mind directing the will. There is no suggestion, however, that the will necessarily follows the mind. On the contrary, he writes, "It will not be enough for the mind to be illuminated by the Spirit of God unless the heart is also strengthened and supported by his power. In this matter the Schoolmen go completely astray, who in considering faith identify it with a bare and simple assent arising out of knowledge, and leave out confidence and assurance of heart." Calvin, *Institutes*, 3.2.33.

49. Norman Fiering identifies three competing perspectives on the relationship between the mind and the will: (1) According to Scholastic intellectualism (or Aristotelian and Thomist intellectualism), the will always follows the mind. This idea is based upon the notion that no one can will evil as evil. In other words, the soul is always inclined toward what it perceives to be good. (2) According to Scholastic voluntarism, the will is divided, in that there is a conflict between the relative and absolute judgment. (3) According to Augustinian voluntarism, the will does not necessarily follow the mind. Therefore, sinful nature is primarily a matter of perverse will, not intellectual error. Norman Fiering, *Moral Philosophy at Seventeenth-Century Harvard: A Discipline in Tradition* (Chapel Hill, N.C.: University of North Carolina Press, 1981), 111–18.

image of God) the will ought to follow the mind; (2) that the knowledge of God always begins in the mind; and (3) that the will cannot choose that which is unknown to the mind. In his discussion, Perkins clearly distinguishes between temporal priority and causal priority,[50] remarking, "The mind must first conceive before the will can desire, or the affections be delighted, or the members of the body practice anything."[51]

According to Perkins, the fall inverted the psychological priority within each of us. In innocence, we were intellectual beings, with the mind informing the will. As a result of the fall, we became voluntarist beings with the corrupted will now driving the darkened mind. By regeneration, however, the temporal priority of the mind is restored. It behooves us, therefore, to engage in "spiritual consideration" whereby God's Spirit impresses God's truth successively upon the three faculties of the soul—instructing the mind, inflaming the affections, and inclining the will.

When the faculties are thus engaged, the alteration in life is plain for all to see. Perkins insists that one of the most significant changes occurs in relation to the tongue. He takes up this subject in the sixth work: *A Direction for the Government of the Tongue according to God's Word*, published in 1593. In the introduction, Perkins bemoans the "lamentable and fearful" abuse of the tongue in his day, and says that it causes "manifold sins against God and innumerable scandals and grievances to our brethren."[52] He is convinced that the only way to tame the tongue is by means of a "pure" heart. "If the fountain is

---

50. There are two main schools of thought surrounding intellectualism and voluntarism. According to Richard Muller, these terms refer to "the two faculties of soul, intellect and will, and to the question of the priority of the one over the other, intellectualism indicates a priority of intellect, voluntarism a priority of the will." "*Fides* and *Cognitio* in Relation to the Problem of Intellect and Will in the Theology of John Calvin," *Calvin Theological Journal* 25 (Nov. 1990): 211. Intellectualism identifies the mind as the causal faculty in the soul's approval of good whereas voluntarism identifies the will (inclination and choice). Does the will necessarily follow the intellect's proposal of the good, or does the will possess the ability to deny the known good? For overviews of the historical development of the views surrounding the relationship between the mind and the will, see Hannah Arendt, *Two/Willing* in *The Life of the Mind* (New York: Harcourt, 1971); and Vernon Bourke, *Will in Western Thought: An Historico-Critical Survey* (New York: Sheed and Ward, 1964).

51. *Man's Imaginations*, 2:477. Elsewhere, Perkins comments, "The mind must approve and give assent, before the will can choose or will: and when the mind has not power to conceive or give assent, there the will has no power to will." *A Reformed Catholic; or, A declaration showing how near we may come to the present Church of Rome in sundry points of religion, and wherein we must forever depart from them*, in *The Whole Works of that Famous and Worthy Minister of Christ in the University of Cambridge, M. William Perkins*, 3 vols. (London: John Legate, 1631), 1:553.

52. William Perkins, "To the Reader," in *A Direction for the Government of the Tongue according to God's Word* in *The Whole Works of that Famous and Worthy Minister of Christ in the University of Cambridge, M. William Perkins*, 3 vols. (London: John Legate, 1631), vol. 1.

defiled," says he, "the streams that issue thence cannot be clean (Matt. 15:19)."[53] For this reason, Perkins encourages us to "get" a pure heart by examining our lives for sin, confessing our sin to God, and seeking pardon in the name of Christ. When God pardons, He stretches forth His "mighty hand" (whereby He made us) to make us a new creature—"to create a new heart in [us], to renew a right spirit in [us], and to establish [us] by His free Spirit."

Having obtained a pure heart, we must now be diligent to "keep" it. This is done by applying "Christ crucified with all His merits." By faith we must spread ourselves "upon the cross of Christ," applying our hands and feet "to His pierced hands and feet," and applying our "wretched heart to Christ's bleeding heart." As we do, we will feel ourselves "warmed by the heat of God's Spirit, and sin from day to day crucified with Christ, and [our] dead heart quickened and revived." By means of this application, God's tender mercy in Christ compels us to "endeavor to keep [our] heart and life unblameable, so that [we] do not offend Him hereafter in word or deed."[54]

From all this it is evident that Perkins has no place for a truncated gospel— a Christ who fails to transform. While excluding good works from justification, he most certainly does not exclude them from the Christian's life. The instrument by which we lay hold of Christ is faith alone (without any works). However, when we speak of the way of salvation, good works are absolutely essential. In short, there must be a transformation in word and deed.

The seventh work in this volume is *A Discourse of the Damned Art of Witchcraft*, published posthumously in 1608. Perkins was driven to preach this series of sermons by his concern over the prevalence of witchcraft in his day.[55] "Witchcraft is a rife and common sin," he writes, "and very many are entangled with it, being either practitioners thereof in their own persons, or at the least yielding to seek for help and counsel of such as practice it."[56] To address the

---

53. *Government of the Tongue*, 1:440.

54. *Government of the Tongue*, 1:440.

55. For more on this, see Peter Elmer, *Witchcraft, Witch-Hunting, and Politics in Early Modern England* (Oxford: University Press, 2016); Malcolm Gaskill, *Witchfinders: A Seventeenth-Century English Tragedy* (Cambridge: Harvard Univ. Press, 2005); Nathan Johnstone, *The Devil and Demonism in Early Modern England* (Cambridge: University Press, 2006); Alan Macfarlane, *Witchcraft in Tudor and Stuart England: A Regional and Comparative Study* (London: Routledge, 1999); Darren Oldridge, *The Devil in Early Modern England* (Stroud: Sutton Publishing, 2000); and J. A. Sharpe, *Instruments of Darkness: Witchcraft in Early Modern England* (Philadelphia: University of Pennsylvania Press, 1996).

56. William Perkins, *A Discourse of the Damned Art of Witchcraft, so far forth as it is revealed in the Scriptures and manifested by true experience*, in *The Whole Works of that Famous and Worthy Minister of Christ in the University of Cambridge, M. William Perkins*, 3 vols. (London: John Haviland, 1631), 3:607.

prevalence of this sin, he chooses to expound Exodus 22:18, "Thou shalt not suffer a witch to live."

Perkins begins by defining his terms. Witchcraft, says he, "is a wicked art, serving for the working of wonders, by the assistance of the devil, so far forth as God shall in justice permit."[57] This "wicked art" consists primarily of "divination," "enchantment," and "juggling." As for the "witch," Perkins defines him or her as "a magician who either by open or secret league, wittingly and willingly, consents to use the aid and assistance of the devil in the working of wonders."[58]

Having instructed his readers as to the nature of witchcraft and the character of witches, Perkins arrives at his main point—namely, "All witches, being thoroughly convicted by the magistrate, ought according to the law of Moses to be put to death."[59] Witchcraft is particularly deserving of death because of its obvious association with the devil. Perkins explains, "Now let it be observed of what horrible impiety they stand guilty before God, who join in confederacy with Satan. Hereby they renounce the Lord who made them, they make no more account of His favor and protection, they do quite cut themselves off from the covenant made with Him in baptism, from the communion of the saints, from the true worship and service of God. And on the contrary they give themselves unto Satan, as their god, whom they continually fear and serve. Thus, they are become the most detestable enemies to God and His people that can be."[60]

Perkins defends his position on the basis of his understanding of the law. First, he believes Moses's judicial law is perpetual because it is moral. It is made "moral" by the sentence of death and, therefore, it "binds all men in all ages."[61] Second, Perkins believes that Moses's judicial law is perpetual because it is natural. Treason is punishable by death "in all countries and kingdoms, among all people in every age." It follows, for Perkins, that witchcraft is punishable by death because it is treason against "God Himself, the King of kings."[62] Third, Perkins believes that witchcraft is a form of idolatry and, therefore, punishable by death (Deut. 17:3–5). Fourth, Perkins believes that witchcraft is a form of seduction and, therefore, punishable by death (Deut. 13:6–9).

---

57. *Damned Art of Witchcraft*, 3:607.

58. *Damned Art of Witchcraft*, 3:636.

59. *Damned Art of Witchcraft*, 3:650. Perkins's insistence that witches be put to death might pose a problem for some readers. Even more disconcerting is his belief that torture ("the rack or some other violent means") may "lawfully and with good conscience be used" to force a confession. *Damned Art of Witchcraft*, 3:643. Perkins does limit its use to exceptional cases of obstinacy; nevertheless, the fact that he makes any allowance at all is problematic.

60. *Damned Art of Witchcraft*, 3:639.

61. *Damned Art of Witchcraft*, 3:651.

62. *Damned Art of Witchcraft*, 3:651.

While providing a fascinating glimpse into an era steeped in folk religion and superstition, this treatise's most lasting significance is its reminder that believers are the victims of the devil's continual assaults. Our vulnerability to attack necessitates prudence in distancing ourselves from all forms of witchcraft, vigilance in keeping watch over our hearts, and diligence in practicing those disciplines by which we can resist the devil's schemes.

The final work in this volume is *A Resolution to the Country Man, Proving It Utterly Unlawful to Buy or Use Our Yearly Prognostications*.[63] The reader will in all likelihood find this treatise to be tedious and even somewhat superfluous, but its subject matter was a serious enough problem in Perkins's day to merit his attention. He was well acquainted with the practice of making prognostications based on the stars, stating that he had "long studied this art" in hopes of learning its "secrets." But eventually God showed him its "profaneness."[64] For this reason, Perkins takes it upon himself to rebuke the prognosticator for his "manifold untruths and impieties," "profane speeches and actions," and "tricks of deceit." While the actual content of this treatise will not generate much interest among pastors or theologians, it might prove otherwise for the historian who will undoubtedly glean some insight into the nature and practice of prognostications in the sixteenth century, and a better understanding of the prominent place they occupied in English society.

When William Crashaw arrived as a young student at Cambridge in 1591,[65] Perkins was well installed in his lectureship at Great St. Andrew's Church (1584–1602) and in his fellowship at Christ's College (1584–1595). Crashaw immediately fell under Perkins's ministerial influence, and it is likely that he was among those students who sought his spiritual counsel on Sunday afternoons. After Perkins's death in 1602, Crashaw supervised the publication of several of Perkins's works. He observed in a preface to one of these: "The scope of all his godly endeavors was to teach Christ Jesus and Him crucified, and [he] much labored to move all men to repentance."[66] This ministerial emphasis is confirmed in the present volume, which brings together several important motifs in Perkins's preaching and writing—namely, what it means to look to

---

63. William Perkins, *A Resolution to the Country Man, Proving It Utterly Unlawful to Buy or Use Our Yearly Prognostications* in *The Whole Works of that Famous and Worthy Minister of Christ in the University of Cambridge, M. William Perkins*, 3 vols. (London: John Haviland, 1631), vol. 3.

64. "To the Reader," in *Prognostications*.

65. William Crashaw (1572–1626) completed his M.A. in 1595 and B.D. in 1603. He ministered at several churches in London. For a brief biographical sketch, see *Dictionary of National Biography*, ed. S. Lee (London: Smith, Elder, & Co., 1909).

66. William Crashaw, "The Epistle Dedicatory," in Perkins, *A Faithful and Plain Exposition upon Zephaniah 2:1–2*.

Christ, repent of sin, renew the mind, tame the tongue, and combat the devil. Each occupies an important place in Perkins's experiential piety—what he himself described as "the more sincere profession of religion."[67]

—J. Stephen Yuille
Vice President of Academics, Heritage College
& Seminary, Cambridge, Ontario
Associate Professor of Biblical Spirituality,
The Southern Baptist Theological Seminary,
Louisville, Kentucky

---

67. *Man's Imaginations*, 2:472. Here, Perkins acknowledges that opponents use the term "Puritanism" in a derogatory fashion to describe this "sincere profession of religion."

A Declaration of the True Manner of Knowing Christ Crucified

"God forbid that I should rejoice, but in the cross of our Lord Jesus Christ" (Gal. 6:14).

Printed by John Legate,
Printer to the University of Cambridge.

1596

To the Reader

It is the common sin of men at this day, and that in the very places of learning, that Christ crucified is not known as He ought. The right knowledge of [Christ] is not to make often mention of His death and passion and to call Him our Savior, or to handle the whole mystery of God incarnate soundly and learnedly, though that is a worthy gift of God. But [it is], first of all, by the consideration of the passion to be touched with an inward and a lively feeling of our sins, for which our Redeemer suffered the pangs of hell, and to grow to a thorough dislike of ourselves and our past lives for them, and from the ground of the heart to purpose a reformation and a conformity with Christ in all good duties that concern man. [It is,] second, in the passion, as in a mirror, to behold, and (in beholding) to labor to comprehend the length, breadth, height, [and] depth of the love of the Father who gave His own dear Son to death, and the goodness of the Son who loved His enemies more than Himself, that our hearts might be rooted and grounded in the same love, and be further inflamed to love God again.

To further this true manner of knowing Christ crucified, I have penned these few lines. Read them at your leisure, and have care to put them in practice; otherwise, you are but an enemy of the cross of Christ, though you profess His name ever so much.

William Perkins
January 5, 1596

The Right Knowledge of Christ Crucified

It is the most excellent and worthy part of divine wisdom to know Christ crucified. The prophet Isaiah says, "The knowledge of thy righteous servant (that is, Christ crucified) shall justify many" [Isa. 53:11]. And Christ Himself says, "This is eternal life to know thee the only God, and whom thou hast sent Jesus Christ" [John 17:3]. And Paul says, "I have decreed to know nothing among you but Jesus Christ and him crucified" [1 Cor. 2:2]. Again, "God forbid that I should rejoice in anything but in the cross of our Lord Jesus Christ" [Gal. 6:14]. Again, "I think all things but loss for the excellent knowledge sake of Christ Jesus my Lord, and do judge them but dung that I might win Christ" [Phil. 3:8].

In the right way of knowing Christ crucified, two points must be considered: (1) how man for his part is to know Christ; [and] (2) how [Christ] is to be known of man.

Point 1

Touching the first, man must know Christ, not generally and confusedly, but by a lively, powerful, and operative knowledge, for otherwise the devils themselves know Christ. In this knowledge three things are required.

The first is notice or consideration, whereby you must conceive in mind, understand, and seriously bethink yourself of Christ as He is revealed in the history of the gospel, and as He is offered to your particular person in the ministry of the Word and sacraments. And that this consideration may not be dead and idle in you, two things must be done. First, you must labor to feel yourself to stand in need of Christ crucified, yea, to stand in excessive need even of the very least drop of His blood for the washing away of your sins. And unless you thoroughly feel yourself to want all that goodness and grace that is in Christ, and that you even stand in extreme need of His passion, you shall never learn or teach Christ in deed and truth. The second thing is with the understanding of the doctrine of Christ to join thirsting, whereby man in his very soul and spirit longs after the participation of Christ, and says in this case, as Samson said, "Give me water, I die for thirst" [Judg. 15:18].

The second part of knowledge is application, whereby you must know and believe not only that Christ was crucified but that He was crucified for you; for you, I say, in particular. Here two rules must be remembered and practiced. First, that Christ on the cross was your pledge and surety in particular; that He then stood in your very room and place in which you yourself in your own person should have stood; that your very personal and particular sins were imputed and applied to Him; that He stood guilty as a malefactor for them, and suffered the very pangs of hell; and that His sufferings are as much in acceptation with God as if you had borne the curse of the law in your own person eternally. The holding and believing of this point is the very foundation of religion as also of the church of God. Therefore, in any wise, be careful to apply Christ crucified to yourself. And as Elisha, when he would revive the child of the Shunamite, went up and lay upon him, and put his mouth upon his mouth, and his hands upon his hands, and his eyes upon his eyes, and stretched himself upon him [2 Kings 4:34], even so, if you would be revived to everlasting life, you must by faith (as it were) set yourself upon the cross of Christ, and apply your hands to His hands, your feet to His feet, and your sinful heart to His bleeding heart, and content not yourself with Thomas to put your finger into His side, but even dive and plunge yourself wholly, both body and soul, into the wounds and blood of Christ. This will make you to cry with Thomas and say, "My Lord, my God."[1] And this is to be crucified with Christ. And yet, do not content yourself with this, but by faith also descend with Christ from the cross to the grave, and bury yourself in the very burial of Christ. And then, look as the dead soldier tumbled into the grave of Elisha was made alive at the very touching of his body [2 Kings 13:21], so shall you by a spiritual touching of Christ, dead and buried, be quickened to everlasting life. The second rule is that Christ crucified is yours, being really given you by God the Father, even as truly as houses and land are given by earthly fathers to their children. You must firmly hold and believe this, and hence it is that the benefits of Christ are before God ours indeed for our justification and salvation.

The third part in lively knowledge is that by all the affections of our hearts we must be carried to Christ and (as it were) transformed into Him. Whereas He gave Himself wholly for us, we can do no less than bestow our hearts upon Him. We must, therefore, love Him above all, following the martyr, Ignatius, who said that Christ "his love was crucified." We must value Him at so high a price that He must be unto us better than ten thousand worlds; yea, all things which we enjoy must be but as "dross and dung" unto us in respect of Him. Lastly, all our joy, rejoicing, comfort, and confidence must be placed in Him.

---

1. John 20:28.

And that thus much is required in knowledge appears by the common rule of expounding Scripture, that words of knowledge imply affection. And, indeed, it is but a knowledge swimming in the brain which does not alter and dispose the affection and the whole man.

Thus much of our knowledge.

Point 2

Now follows the second point: how Christ is to be known. He must not be known barely as God, or as man, or as a Jew born in the tribe of Judah, or as a terrible and just Judge, but as He is our Redeemer and the very price of our redemption. And in this respect, He must be considered as the common "treasury" and "storehouse" of God's church, as Paul testifies when he says, "In him are all the treasures of knowledge and wisdom hid" [Col. 2:3]. And again, "Blessed be God, which hath blessed us with all spiritual blessings in Christ" [Eph. 1:3]. And Saint John says that "of his fullness we receive grace for grace" [John 1:16]. Here, then, let us mark that all the blessings of God, whether spiritual or temporal, all (I say) without exception, are conveyed unto us from the Father by Christ. And so, they must be received by us and not otherwise. That this point may be further cleared, the benefits which we receive from Christ are to be handled, and the manner of knowing them. The benefits of Christ are three: His merit, His virtue, [and] His example.

Christ's Merit

The merit of Christ is the value and price of His death and passion whereby man is perfectly reconciled to God. This reconciliation has two parts: (1) remission of sins, and (2) acceptation to everlasting life.[2]

Remission of sins is the removing or the abolishing both of the guilt and punishment of man's sins. By guilt I understand a subjection or obligation to punishment, according to the order of divine justice. And the punishment of sin is the malediction or curse of the whole law, which is the suffering of the first and second death.[3]

Acceptation to everlasting life is a giving of right and title to the kingdom of heaven, and that for the merit of Christ's imputed obedience.[4]

Now this benefit of reconciliation must be known, not by conceit and imagination nor by carnal presumption, but by the inward testimony of God's Spirit certifying our consciences thereof, who for this cause is called the "Spirit of revelation" [Eph. 1:17]. And that we may attain to infallible assistance of this

---

2. This paragraph break is not in the original.
3. This paragraph break is not in the original.
4. This paragraph break is not in the original.

benefit, we must call to mind the promises of the gospel touching remission of sins and everlasting life. This being done, we must further strive and endeavor by the assurance of God's Spirit to apply them to ourselves, and to believe that they belong unto us. And we must also put ourselves often to all the exercises of invocation and true repentance. For in and by our crying unto heaven to God for reconciliation comes the assurance thereof, as Scripture and Christian experience make manifest. And if it so falls out that any man in temptation apprehends and feels nothing but the furious indignation and wrath of God, against all reason and feeling he must hold to the merit of Christ, and know a point of religion hard to be learned, that God is a most loving Father to them who have care to serve Him even at that instant when He shows Himself a most fierce and terrible enemy.

From the benefit of reconciliation proceed four benefits.

Benefit 1. First, that excellent "peace of God" that passes all understanding, which has six parts. The first is peace with God and the blessed Trinity. "Being justified we have peace with God" (Rom. 5:1). The second [is] peace with the good angels. "Ye shall see the angels of God ascending and descending upon the Son of man" (John 1:51). And angels, like armies of soldiers, encamp about the servants of God and, as nurses, bear them in their arms so that they are neither hurt by the devil and his angels nor by his instruments. It proceeds from this that they, being in Christ, are partakers of His merits. The third is peace with all such as fear God and believe in Christ. This Isaiah foretold when he said that "the wolves shall dwell with the lamb, and the leopard lie with the kid, and the calf and the lion and a fat beast together, and that a little child should lead them" (Isa. 11:6). The fourth is peace with a man's own self, when the conscience washed in the blood of Christ ceases to accuse and terrify, and when the will, affections, and inclinations of the whole man are obedient to the mind enlightened by the Spirit and Word of God. "Let the peace of God rule in your hearts" (Col. 3:15). The fifth is peace with enemies and that [in] two ways: first, in that such as believe in Christ seek to have peace with all men, hurting none, but doing good to all; [and,] second, in that God restrains the malice of enemies and inclines their hearts to be peaceable. Thus, God brought Daniel "into love and favor with the chief of the eunuchs" [Dan. 1:9]. The last is peace with all creatures in heaven and earth, in that they serve for man's salvation. "Thou shalt walk upon the lion and the asp: the young lion and the dragon shalt thou tread under foot" (Ps. 91:13). "And in that day will I make a covenant for them with the beasts of the field, and with the fowls of heaven" (Hos. 2:18). Now this benefit of peace is known partly by the testimony of the Spirit and partly by a daily experience thereof.

Benefit 2. The second benefit is a recovery of that right and title which man has to all creatures in heaven and earth and all temporal blessings, which right Adam lost to himself and every one of his posterity. "Whether it be the world, or life, or death: whether they be things present, or things to come, all are yours" (1 Cor. 3:22). Now the right way of knowing this one benefit is this: when God vouchsafes meat, drink, apparel, houses, lands, etc., we must not barely consider them as blessings of God, for that very heathen men, which know not Christ, can do. But we must acknowledge and esteem them as blessings proceeding from the special love of God the Father, whereby He loves us in Christ, and procured unto us by the merit of Christ crucified. And we must labor in this point to be settled and persuaded. And as often as we see and use the creatures of God for our own benefit, this point should come to our minds. Blessings conceived apart from Christ are misconceived; whatsoever they are in themselves they are not blessings to us but in and by Christ's merit.[5]

Therefore, this order must be observed touching earthly blessings. First, we must have part in the merit of Christ. And then, second, by means of that merit [we have] right before God and comfortable use of the things we enjoy. All men who have and use the creatures of God otherwise, as gifts of God but not by Christ, use them but as flat usurpers and thieves. For this cause, it is not sufficient for us generally and confusedly to know Christ to be our Redeemer, but we must learn to see, know, and acknowledge Him in every particular gift and blessing of God. If men, using the creatures of meat and drink, could, when they behold them, withal by the eye of faith, behold in them the merit of Christ's passion, there would not be so much excess and riot, so much surfeiting and drunkenness as there is. And if men could consider their houses and lands, etc., as blessings to them, and that by the fountain of blessing, the merits of Christ, there should not be so much fraud and deceit, so much injustice and oppression in bargaining as there is.

That which I have now said of meats, drinks, [and] apparel, must likewise be understood of gentry and nobility, in as much as noble birth without new birth in Christ is but an earthly vanity.[6] The same may be said of physic, sleep, health, liberty, yea, of the very breathing in the air. And to go yet further, in our recreations Christ must be known. For all recreation stands in the use of indifferent things, and the holy use of all indifferent things is purchased unto us by the blood of Christ. For this cause, it is very meet that Christian men and women should with their earthly recreations join spiritual meditation of the death of Christ, and from the one take occasion to bethink themselves of the

---

5. This paragraph break is not in the original.
6. In the margin: Consider Col. 2:10; 3:11.

other. If this were practiced, there should not be so many unlawful sports and delights, and so much abuse of lawful recreation, as there is.

Benefit 3. The third benefit is that all crosses, afflictions, and judgments whatsoever cease to be curses and punishments to them who are in Christ, and are only means of correction or trial, because His death has taken away, not some few parts, but all, and every part, of the curse of the whole law. Now in all crosses Christ is to be known by us on this manner. We must judge of our afflictions as chastisements or trials, proceeding not from a revenging Judge but from the hand of a bountiful and loving Father. And, therefore, they must be conceived in and with the merit of Christ. And if we do otherwise regard them, we take them as curses and punishments of sin. And hence it follows that subjection to God's hand in all crosses is a mark and badge of the true church.

Benefit 4. The last benefit is that death is properly no death, but a rest or sleep. Death, therefore, must be known and considered, not as it is set forth in the law, but as it is altered and changed by the death of Christ. And when death comes, we must then look upon it through Christ's death, as through a glass. And thus, it will appear to be but a passage from this life to everlasting life.

Thus much of the merit of Christ crucified.

Christ's Virtue

Now follows His virtue, which is the power of His Godhead whereby He creates new hearts in all them who believe in Him, and makes them new creatures. This virtue is double.

The first is the power of His death whereby He freed Himself from the punishment and imputation of our sins. And the same virtue serves to mortify and crucify the corruptions of our minds, wills, [and] affections, even as a corrosive does waste and consume the rotten and dead flesh in any part of man's body.

The second is the virtue of Christ's resurrection, which is also the power of His Godhead whereby He raised Himself from death to life. And the very same power serves to raise those who belong to Christ from their sins in this life and from the grave in the day of the last judgment.[7]

Now the knowledge of this double virtue must not only be speculative (that is, barely conceived in the brain), but it must be experimental, because we ought to have experience of it in our hearts and lives. And we should labor by all possible means to feel the power of Christ's death killing and mortifying our sins, and the virtue of His resurrection in the putting of spiritual life into

---

7. This paragraph break is not in the original.

us, that we might be able to say that we live not, but that Christ lives in us. This was one of the most excellent and principal things which Paul sought for, who says, "I have counted all things loss and do judge them to be dung…that I may know him and the virtue of his resurrection" (Phil. 3:8, 10). And he says that this is the right way to know and learn Christ, "to cast off the old man which is corrupt through deceivable lusts…and to put on the new man which is created in righteousness and true holiness" (Eph. 4:22, 24).

Christ's Example

The third benefit is the example of Christ. We deceive ourselves if we think that He is only to be known of us as a Redeemer and not as a spectacle and pattern of all good duties, to which we ought to conform ourselves. Good men indeed, who have been (or in present are) upon the earth the servants of God, must be followed by us. But they must be followed not otherwise than they follow Christ, and Christ must be followed in the practice of every good duty that may concern us without exception, simply and absolutely (1 Cor. 11:1).

Our conformity with Christ stands either in the framing of our inward and spiritual life or in the practice of outward and moral duties.

Point 1. Conformity in spiritual life is not by doing that which Christ did upon the cross and afterwards, but doing of the like by a certain kind of imitation. And it has four parts.[8]

The first is a spiritual oblation. For as Christ, in the garden and upon the cross, by prayer made with strong cries and tears, presented and resigned Himself up to be a sacrifice of propitiation to the justice of His Father for man's sin, so we must also in prayer present and resign ourselves (our souls, bodies, understanding, will, memory, affections), and all we have, to the service of God in the general calling of a Christian, and in the particular callings in which He has placed us. Take an example in David. "Sacrifice and burnt offering," says he, "thou wouldest not, but ears thou hast pierced unto me; then said I, lo, I come: I desire to do thy will, O God; yea thy law is within my heart" (Ps. 40:6–7).

The second is conformity in the cross [in] two ways. First, as He bore His own cross to the place of execution, so we must (as good disciples of Christ) deny ourselves, take up all the crosses and afflictions that the hand of God shall lay upon us, [even] if it is every day, and follow Him.[9] Again, we must become like unto Him in the crucifying and mortifying the mass and body of sin which we carry about us. "They which are Christ's have crucified the flesh with the

---

8. The paragraph breaks (marking these "four parts") are not in the original.

9. *Works* (1631) does not include this phrase: "if it is every day, and follow Him."

affections and lusts thereof" (Gal. 5:24). We must do as the Jews did, we must set up the crosses and gibbets whereon we are to fasten and hang this flesh of ours, that is, the sin and corruption that cleaves and sticks unto us, and by the sword of the Spirit wound it even to death. This being done, we must yet go further, and labor by experience to see and feel the very death of it, and to lay it (as it were) in a grave never to rise again. And, therefore, we should daily cast new moulds[10] upon it.

The third is a spiritual resurrection whereby we should by God's grace use means that we may every day more and more come out of our sins, as out of a loathsome grave, to live unto God in newness of life, as Christ arose from His grave. And because it is a hard matter for a man to come out of the grave (or rather dungeon) of his sins, this work cannot be done at once but by degrees, as God shall give grace. Considering we lie by nature dead in our sins and stink in them as loathsome carrion, first we must begin to stir ourselves as a man who comes out of a swoon, awakened by the word and voice of Christ sounding in our deaf ears. Second, we must raise up our minds to a better state and condition, as we usually raise up our bodies. After this, we must put out of the grave first one hand [and] then the other. This done, we must do our endeavor (as it were) upon our knees, at the least to put one foot out of this sepulcher of sin, the rather when we see ourselves to have one foot of the body in the grave of the earth, that in the day of judgment we may be wholly delivered from all bonds of corruption.

The fourth part is a spiritual ascension into heaven by a continual elevation of the heart and mind to Christ sitting at the right hand of the Father. As Paul says, "Have your conversation in heaven" (Phil. 3:20). And, "If ye be risen with Christ, seek things that are above" (Col. 3:1).

Point 2. Conformity in moral duties is either general or special. General is to be holy as He is holy. "Those whom he knew before he hath predestinated to be like the image of his Son" (Rom. 9:29), that is, not only in the cross but also in holiness and glory. "He which hath this hope purifieth himself even as he is pure" (1 John 3:3). Special conformity is chiefly in four virtues: faith, love, meekness, [and] humility.

[First,] we must be like Him in faith. For as He, when He apprehended the wrath of God, and the very pangs of hell were upon Him, wholly stayed Himself upon the aid, help, protection, and good pleasure of His Father, even to the last, so we must by a true and lively faith depend wholly on God's mercy in Christ (as it were) with both our hands in peace, trouble, life, and in the very

---

10. *Mould:* dirt or moss.

pangs of death. And we must not in any way let our hold go, [even] though we should feel ourselves descend to hell.

[Second,] we must be like Him in meekness. "Learn of me that I am meek and lowly" (Matt. 11:29). His meekness showed itself in the patient bearing of all injuries and abuses offered by the hands of sinful and wretched men, and in the suffering of the curse of the law, without grudging or repining, and with submission to His Father's will in all things. Now the more we follow Him herein, the more shall we be conformable to Him in His death and passion (Phil. 3:10).

Third, He must be our example in love. He loved His enemies more than Himself. "Walk in love even as Christ loved us, and hath given himself for us an oblation and sacrifice of sweet smelling savor unto God" (Eph. 5:2). We ought to show the same love by doing service to all men in the compass of our callings and by being all things to all men (as Paul was) that we might do them all the good we can both for body and soul (1 Cor. 9:19).

Lastly, we must follow Christ in humility, whereof He is a wonderful spectacle, in that, being God, He became man for us. And of a man [He] became a worm that is trodden under foot, that He might save man. "Let the same mind be in you that was in Jesus Christ, who being in the form of God, humbled himself and became obedient to the death, even to the death of the cross" (Phil. 2:5).

And here we must observe that the example of Christ has something more in it than any other example has or can have. For it does not only show us what we ought to do (as the examples of other men do) but it is a remedy against many vices and a motive to many good duties.

First of all, the serious consideration of this, that the very Son of God Himself suffered all the pains and torments of hell on the cross for our sins, is the proper and most effectual means to stir up our hearts to a godly sorrow for them. And that this thing may come to pass, every man must be settled without doubt that he was the man that crucified Christ; that he is to be blamed as well as Judas, Herod, Pontius Pilate, and the Jews; and that his sins were the nails, spears, and thorns that pierced Him. When this meditation begins to take place, bitterness of spirit with wailing and mourning takes place in like manner. "And they shall look upon him whom they have pierced, and they shall lament for him as one lamenteth for his only son" (Zech. 12:10). Peter, in his first sermon, struck the Jews as with a thunderclap from heaven when he said unto them, "Ye have crucified the Lord of glory," so as at the same time three thousand men were pricked in their hearts, and said, "Men and brethren, what shall we do to be saved?" (Acts 2:37). Again, if Christ shed His heart blood for our sins, and if our sins made Him sweat water and blood, oh then, why should not we ourselves shed bitter tears, and why should not our hearts bleed for them? He who finds himself so dull and hardened that the passion of Christ does not humble him is in a lamentable case, for there is no faith in the death of Christ effectual in him as yet.

Second, the meditation of the passion of Christ is a most notable means to breed repentance and reformation of life in time to come. For when we begin to think that Christ crucified, by suffering the first and second death, has procured unto us remission of all our past sins, and freed us from hell, death, and damnation, then, if there is but a spark of grace in us, we begin to be of another mind and to reason thus with ourselves: What? Has the Lord been thus merciful to me, [though] I am but a firebrand of hell, as to free me from deserved destruction and to receive me to favor in Christ? Yea, no doubt, He has. His name be blessed therefore. I will not, therefore, sin any more as I have done, but ever hereafter endeavor to keep myself from every evil way. And thus faith purifies both heart and life.

Third, when you are in any pain of body or sickness, think how light these are compared to the agony and bloody sweat, to the crown of thorns and nails, of Christ. When you are wronged in word or deed by any man, turn your eye to the cross, consider how meekly He suffered all abuses for the most part in silence, and prayed for them who crucified Him. When you are tempted with pride or vainglory, consider how (for your proper sins) Christ was despised and mocked and condemned among thieves. When anger and desire of revenge inflame your heart, think how Christ gave Himself to death to save His enemies, even then when they did most cruelly [mis]treat Him and shed His blood. And by these meditations, especially if they are mingled with faith, your mind shall be eased.

A Threefold Knowledge
Thus, we see how Christ crucified is to be known. And hence arises a threefold knowledge: the first of God; the second of our neighbors; [and] the third of ourselves.

Point 1
Touching the first, if we would know the true God aright, and know Him to our salvation, we must know Him only in Christ crucified. God in Himself and His own majesty is invisible, not only to the eyes of the body, but also to the very minds of men. And He is revealed to us only in Christ, in whom He is to be seen as in a glass. For in Christ He sets forth and gives His justice, goodness, wisdom, and Himself wholly unto us. For this cause, He is called the "brightness of the glory, and the engraven form of the person of the Father" (Heb. 1:3)

and "the image of the invisible God" (Col. 1:15). Therefore, we must not know God and seek Him anywhere else but in Christ. And whatsoever out of Christ comes unto us in the name of God is a flat idol of man's brain.

Point 2

As for our neighbors, those especially who are of God's church, they are to be known of us in this manner. When we are to do any duty unto them, we must not barely respect their persons, but Christ crucified in them and they in Christ. When Saul persecuted such as called on the name of Christ, He then from heaven cried, "Saul, Saul, why persecutest thou me?" [Acts 9:4]. Here then let this be marked, that when the poor comes to us for relief, it is Christ who comes to our doors and says, "I am hungry. I am thirsty. I am naked." And let the bowels of compassion be in us toward them as toward Christ, unless we will hear that fearful sentence in the day of judgment: "Go ye cursed into hell… I was hungry, and ye fed me not: I was naked, and ye did not clothe me…" (Matt. 25:41–42).

Point 3

Third, the right knowledge of ourselves arises from the knowledge of Christ crucified, in whom and by whom we come to know five special things of ourselves.

The first [is] how grievous our sins are, and therefore how miserable we are in regard of them. If we consider our offences in themselves, and as they are in us, we may soon be deceived, because the conscience being corrupted often errs in giving testimony, and by that means makes sin to appear less than it is indeed. But if sin is considered in the death and passion of Christ, whereof it was the cause, and the vileness thereof measured by the unspeakable torments endured by the Son of God, and if the greatness of the offence of man is esteemed by the endless satisfaction made to the justice of God, the least sin that is will appear to be a sin indeed, and that most grievous and ugly. Therefore, Christ crucified must be used by us as a mirror or looking glass, in which we may fully take a view of our wretchedness and misery, and what we are by nature. For such as the passion of Christ was in the eyes of men, such is our passion or condition in the eyes of God. And that which wicked men did to Christ, the same do sin and Satan to our very soul.

The second point is that men, believing in Christ, are not their own or lords of themselves, but wholly (both body and soul) belong to Christ, in that they are given to Him by God the Father, and He has purchased them with His own blood. "Ye are Christ's, and Christ [is] God's" (1 Cor. 3:23). Hence, it comes to pass (which is not to be forgotten) that Christ esteems all the crosses and afflictions of His people as His own proper afflictions. Hence again, we must learn to give up ourselves both in body and soul to the honor and service of Christ, whose we are.

The third is that every true believer (not as he is a man, but as he is a new man or a Christian) has his being and subsisting from Christ. "We are members of his body, of His flesh, and of His bone" (Eph. 5:30). In these words, Paul alludes to the speech of Adam, "Thou art bone of my bone, and flesh of my flesh" (Gen. 2:23), and thereby he teaches that as Eve was made of a rib taken out of the side of Adam, so does the whole church of God, and every man regenerate, spring and arise out of the blood that streamed from the heart and side of Christ crucified.

The fourth is that all good works done by us proceed from the virtue and merit of Christ crucified. He is the cause of them in us, and we are the causes of them in and by Him. "Without me," says He, "ye can do nothing" (John 15:5). And, "Every branch that beareth not fruit in me," mark well He says, "in me, he taketh away" (John 15:2).

The fifth point is that we owe unto Christ an endless debt. For He was crucified only as our surety and pledge, and in the spectacle of His passion we must consider ourselves as the chief debtors, and that the very discharge of our debt (that is, the sins which are inherent in us) were the proper cause of all the endless pains and torments that Christ endured, that He might set us (most miserable bankrupts) at liberty from hell, death, and damnation. For His unspeakable goodness, if we do but once think of it seriously, we must needs confess that we owe ourselves (our souls and bodies), and all that we have, as a debt due unto Him. And so soon as any man begins to know Christ crucified, he knows his own debt and thinks of the payment of it.

Thus, we see how Christ is to be known.

Examination

Now we shall not need to make much examination whether this manner of knowing and acknowledging of Christ take any place in the world or not, for very few there are who know Him as they ought. The Turk, even at this very day, knows Him not but as He was a prophet. The Jew scorns His cross and passion. The popish churches, though in word they confess Him, yet they do not know Him as they ought. The friars and Jesuits in their sermons at this day commonly use the passion as a means to stir up pity and compassion toward Christ who, being so righteous a man, was so hardly intreated, and to inflame their hearers to a hatred of the Jews, and Judas, and Pontius Pilate, who put our blessed Savior to death. But all this may be done in any other history. And the service of God, which in that church stands now in force by the canons of the

Council of Trent, defaces Christ crucified, in that the passions of martyrs are made meritorious, the very wood of the cross their only help, and the virgin Mary the "queen of heaven" and a "mother of mercy," who in remission of sins may command her Son. And they give religious adoration to dumb crucifixes made by the hand and art of man.

The common Protestant likewise comes short herein for three causes. First, whereas in word they acknowledge Him to be their Savior, who has redeemed them from their evil conversation, yet in deed they make Him a patron of their sins.[11] The thief makes Him the receiver, the murderer makes Him his refuge, the adulterer (be it spoken with reverence to His majesty) makes Him the bawd.[12] For generally men walk on in their evil ways, some living in this sin, some in that, and yet for all this they persuade themselves that God is merciful and that Christ has freed them from death and damnation. Thus, Christ, who came to abolish sin, is made a maintainer thereof, and the common pack-horse of the world to bear every man's burden.[13]

Second, men are content to take knowledge of the merit of Christ's passion for the remission of their sins, but in the mean season the virtue of Christ's death in the mortifying of sin, and the blessed example of His passion, which ought to be followed and expressed in our lives and conversations, is little or nothing regarded.[14]

Third, men usually content themselves generally and confusedly to know Christ to be their Redeemer, never once seeking in every particular estate and condition of life, and in every particular blessing of God, to feel the benefit of His passion. What is the cause that almost all the world lives in security, almost never touched for their horrible sins? Surely, the reason is because they did never yet seriously consider that Christ in the garden lay groveling upon the earth, sweating water and blood, for their offences. Again, all such as by fraud and oppression, or any kind of hard dealing, suck the blood of poor men, never yet knew that their sins drew out the heart blood of Christ. And proud men and women, who are puffed up by reason of their attire, which is the badge of their shame, and never cease hunting after strange fashions, do not consider that Christ was not crucified in gay attire, but naked, that He might bear the whole shame and curse of the law for us. These and such like, whatsoever they say in word, if we respect the tenor of their lives, are flat enemies of the cross of Christ, and tread His precious blood under their feet.

---

11. In the margin: Calvin on Gal. 6:2.
12. *Bawd:* a person who keeps a house of prostitution.
13. This paragraph break is not in the original.
14. This paragraph break is not in the original.

Now then, considering this so weighty and special point of religion is so much neglected, O man or woman, high or low, young or old, if you have been wanting this way, begin for very shame to learn and (learning truly) to know Christ crucified. And that you may attain to this, behold Him often, not in the wooden crucifix after the popish manner, but in the preaching of the Word and in the sacraments, in which you shall see Him crucified before your eyes (Gal. 3:1). Desire not here upon earth to behold Him with the bodily eye, but look upon Him with the eye of true and lively faith, applying Him and His merits to yourself as your own, and that with a broken and bruised heart, as the poor Israelites, stung with fiery serpents even to death, beheld the brazen serpent. Again, you must look upon Him first of all as a glass or spectacle, in which you shall see God's glory greater in your redemption than in your creation. In the creation God's infinite wisdom, power, and goodness appeared; in your redemption by the passion of Christ His endless justice and mercy [appeared]. In the creation you are a member of the first Adam and bear his image; in your redemption you are a member of the second Adam. In the first, you are endued with natural life; in the second with spiritual. In the first, you have in the person of Eve your beginning of the rib of Adam; in the second, you have your beginning as you are born of God, out of the blood of Christ. Lastly, in the first, God gave life by commanding that to be which was not; in the second, He gives not by life but by death, even of His own Son. This is the mystery into which the angels themselves desire to look (1 Peter 1:12).[15]

Second, you must behold Him as the full price of your redemption and perfect reconciliation with God, and pray earnestly to God that He would seal up the same in your very conscience by His Holy Spirit.[16]

Third, you must behold Christ as an example, to whom you must conform yourself by regeneration. For this cause, give diligence that you may by experience say that you are dead and crucified and buried with Christ, and that you rise again with Him to newness of life; that He enlightens your mind and by degrees reforms your will and affections, and gives you both the will and the deed in every good thing. And that you may not fail in your knowledge, read the history of Christ's passion, observe all the parts and circumstances thereof, and apply them to yourself for your full conversion.[17]

When you read that Christ went to the garden, as His custom was, where the Jews might soon attack Him, consider that He went willingly to the death of the cross for your sins, and not of constraint, and that, therefore, you (for your part) should do Him all service freely and frankly (Ps. 110:3).

---

15. This paragraph break is not in the original.

16. This paragraph break is not in the original.

17. The paragraph breaks (from here to the final paragraph) are not in the original.

When you hear that in His agony His soul was heavy unto death, know it was for your sins, and that you should much more conceive heaviness of heart for the same. Again, [know] that this sorrow of His is joy and rejoicing unto you, if you will believe in Him. Therefore, Paul says, "I say again, rejoice in the Lord."[18]

When you read that in the garden He prayed, lying groveling on His face, sweating water and blood, begin to think seriously what an unspeakable measure of God's wrath was upon your blessed Savior, that did prostrate His body upon the earth and cause the blood to follow. And think that your sins must needs be most heinous that brought such bloody and grievous pains upon Him. Also, think it a very shame for you to carry your head to heaven with haughty looks, to wallow in your pleasures, and to draw the innocent blood of your poor brethren by oppression and deceit, for whom Christ sweat water and blood. And take an occasion from Christ's agony to lay aside the pride of your heart, to be ashamed of yourself, to grieve in heart, yea, even to bleed for your own offences, casting down and humbling yourself with Ezra, saying, "O my God, I am confounded and ashamed to lift up mine eyes unto thee, my God, for my iniquities are increased and my trespass is grown up into heaven" (Ezra 9:6).

When you read that Christ was taken and bound, think that your very sins brought Him into the power of His enemies, and were the very bonds wherewith He was tied. Think that you should have been bound in the very same manner unless He had been a surety and pledge for you. Think also that you in the self same manner are bound and tied with the chains of your own sins, and that by nature your will, affections, and whole spirit are tied and chained to the will of the devil, so as you cannot do anything but that which he wills. Lastly, think and believe that the bonds of Christ serve to purchase your liberty from hell, death, and damnation.

When you hear that He was brought before Annas and Caiaphas, think it was meet that your surety and pledge, who was to suffer the condemnation due unto you, should by the high priest, as by the mouth of God, be condemned. And wonder at this, that the very coessential and eternal Son of God, even the very sovereign Judge of the world, stands to be judged, and that by wicked men. Persuade yourself that this so great confusion comes of your sins. Whereupon, being further amazed at your fearful estate, humble yourself in dust and ashes, and pray God so to soften your stony heart that you may turn to Him, and by true faith lay hold on Christ who has thus exceedingly abased Himself, that His ignominy may be your glory and His arraignment your perfect absolution.

---

18. Phil. 4:4.

When you read that Barabbas, the murderer, was preferred before Christ, though He exceeded both men and angels in holiness, think it was to manifest His innocency, and that your very sins pulled upon Him this shameful reproach. And [think] that for your cause He was esteemed worse than Barabbas. Think of yourself as a most heinous and wretched sinner, and (as Paul says) the "head of all sinners" (1 Tim. 1:15).

When you read that He was openly and judicially condemned to the cursed death of the cross, consider what is the wrath and fury of God against sin, and what is His great and infinite mercy to sinners. And in this spectacle look upon yourself, and with groans of heart cry out, "O good God, what set Thee here before my eyes? I, even I, have sinned. I am guilty and worthy of damnation. Whence comes this change, that Thy blessed Son is in my room, but of Thy unspeakable mercy? Wretch that I am, how have I forgotten myself, and Thee also, my God? O Son of God, how long hast Thou abased Thyself for me? Therefore, give me grace, O God, that beholding my own estate in the person of my Savior thus condemned, I may detest and loath my sins that are the cause thereof, and by a lively faith embrace that absolution which Thou offerest me in Him, who was condemned in my stead and room. O Jesus Christ, Savior of the world, give me Thy holy and blessed Spirit that I may judge myself, and be as vile and base in my own eyes as Thou wert vile before the Jews. Also, unite me unto Thee by the same Spirit, that in Thee I may be as worthy to be accepted before God as I am worthy in myself to be detested for my sins."

When you read that He was clad in purple and crowned with thorns, mocked and spit upon, behold the everlasting shame that is due unto you, and be ashamed of yourself, and in this point conform yourself to Christ, and be content (as He was) to be reproached, abused, and despised, so it is for a good cause.

When you read that, before His crucifying, He was stripped of all His clothes, think it was that He, being naked, might bear your shame on the cross, and with His most precious and rich nakedness cover your deformity.

When you read the complaint of Christ, that He was forsaken by His Father, consider how He suffered the pangs and torments of hell as your pledge and surety. Learn by His unspeakable torments what a fearful thing it is to sin against God, and begin to renounce yourself and detest your sins, and to walk as a child of light, according to the measure of grace received.

When you come to die, set before your eyes Christ in the midst of all His torments on the cross. In beholding this spectacle to your endless comfort, you shall see a paradise in the midst of hell: God the Father reconciled unto you, your Savior reaching out His hands unto you to receive your soul unto Him, and His cross as a ladder to advance it to eternal glory. Whereas He cried aloud with a strong voice at the point of death, it was to show that He died willingly without violence or constraint from any creature, and that if it had so pleased Him, He could have freed Himself from death, and have cast His very enemies to the very bottom of hell.

When you read that He commended His soul into the hands of His Father, consider that your soul also (so be it you will believe in Him) is delivered up into the hands of God, and shall be preserved against the rage and malice of all your enemies, and hereupon you may be bold to commend your spirit into the hands of God the Father.

When you read of His death, consider that your sins were the cause of it, and that you should have suffered the same eternally, unless the Son of God had come in your room. Again, consider His death as a ransom, and apprehend the same by faith, as the means of your life. For by death Christ has wounded both the first and second death, and has made His cross to be a throne or tribunal seat of judgment against all His and your enemies.

When you read of the trembling of the earth at the death of Christ, think with yourself it did in its kind (as it were) groan under the burden of sins of men in the world. And by its motion it signified that even you and the rest deserved to be swallowed by the earth and to go down into the pit alive rather than to have any part in the merit of Christ crucified.

When you read of His burial, think it was to ratify His death, and to vanquish death even in its own den. Apply this burial to yourself, and believe that it serves to make your grave a bed of down, and to free your body from corruption. Lastly, pray to God that you may feel the power of the Spirit of Christ, weakening and consuming the body of sin, even as a dead corpse rots in the grave, till it is resolved to dust.

When you have thus perused and applied to yourself the history of the passion of Christ, go yet further and labor by faith to see Christ crucified in all the works of God either in you or upon you. Behold Him at your table in meat and drink, which is (as it were) a lively sermon and a daily pledge of the mercy of God in Christ. Behold Him in all your afflictions, as your partner who pities your case, and has compassion on you. Behold Him in your most dangerous temptations in which the devil thunders damnation. Behold Him, I say, as a mighty Samson bearing away the gates of His enemies upon His own shoulders, and killing more by death than by life, crucifying the devil, even then when He is crucified, by death killing death, by entrance into the grave opening the grave and giving life to the dead, and in the house of death spoiling him of all his strength and power. Behold Him in all the afflictions of your brethren, as though He Himself were naked, hungry, sick, harborless, and do unto them all the good you can, as to Christ Himself.

If you would behold God Himself, look upon Him in Christ crucified, who is the engraven image of the Father's person. And know it to be a terrible thing in the time of the trouble of your conscience to think of God without Christ, in whose face the glory of God in His endless mercy is to be seen (2 Cor. 4:6). If you would come to God for grace, comfort, salvation, for any blessing, come first to Christ hanging, bleeding, dying upon the cross, without whom there is no hearing God, no helping God, no saving God, no God to you at all. In a word, let Christ be all things without exception unto you (Col. 3:11). For when you pray for any blessing, either temporal or spiritual, be it whatsoever it will be or can be, you must ask it at the hands of God the Father by the merit and mediation of Christ crucified. Now look, as we ask blessings at God's hand, so we must receive them from Him. And as they are received, so we must possess and use them daily, namely as gifts of God procured to us by the merit of Christ. For this very cause, these gifts must be wholly employed to the honor of Christ.

FINIS

The True Gain:
More in Worth than All the Goods in the World

"But the things which were advantage to me,
the same I accounted loss for Christ" (Phil. 3:7).

Printed by John Legate,
Printer to the University of Cambridge.

1601

The Epistle Dedicatory

To the Right Worshipful, Sir Edward Denny, knight.

It is a conclusion of our religion, worthy to be considered, that Christ alone is our Mediator, Justifier, Propitiator, Savior, by works and merits which He Himself wrought within Himself, and not by any works or merits which He works in us by His Spirit. The Scripture says thus much in express words. "Justified freely by the redemption that is in Christ Jesus" (Rom. 3:24). "He hath by himself purged our sins" (Heb. 1:3). "He was made sin for us that we should be made the righteousness of God in him" (2 Cor. 5:21). "In him are ye complete" (Col. 3:10). "By his own blood he entered once into the holy place, and obtained eternal redemption" (Heb. 9:12). Again, Christ is said to "purge our consciences from dead works by his blood" because He "offered himself by his eternal Spirit without spot to his Father" (v. 14). And common reason tells us as much. For if men are mystically united to Christ, and by this union receive the Spirit of Christ, and by the Spirit do good works, and consequently merit eternal life, they are then become partners with Christ, and are received into fellowship with Him in the work of man's redemption. Whereas He, in the act of our reconciliation with God, admits neither deputy nor partner.

This conclusion, being thus of infallible truth, serves greatly to exalt the grace of God, abase nature, and beat down the pride of all justiciary[1] persons and religions. And for the further explaining of it serves this treatise following, which I present to your Worship. And the reason of my doing is this. I remember, almost two years ago, in speech you entered into commendations of that golden text (Phil. 3:7), and withal gave signification of your desire that something might be set down whereby you might be brought to a further understanding of that place of Scripture. Therefore, to satisfy your desire, I have here penned a short exposition of it. And I have further presumed to publish it in your name, desiring it may be a testimony of a thankful mind for your love and favor toward me.

---

1. *Justiciary:* that which relates to justification or redemption before God.

Thus wishing to your Worship continuance and increase of love to the holy Word of God, I take my leave.

Your Worship's in all duty to command,
William Perkins
January 20, 1601

The text (Phil. 3:7) contains a comparison of unequals.

Protasis, the first part: "I count all things dung for Christ." Here consider:

> What things are dung: "all things."
>> Virtues and works before his conversion.
>> Virtues and works after his conversion.

> How they are dung, showed by a gradation:
>> I account all things loss.
>> I deprive myself of them.
>> I account them dung.

Apodosis, the second part: "Christ is my gain." Here consider:

> The amplification by a gradation.
>> I esteem the knowledge of Christ an excellent thing.
>> I desire to gain Christ.
>> I desire to be found in Christ in the day of judgment.

> The degrees of gain in Christ.
>> Justice by the faith of Christ.
>> Fellowship with Christ in the virtue of His resurrection and death.
>> Attainment to the resurrection of the dead.

"But the things which were advantage to me, the same I accounted loss for Christ. Yea, doubtless I count all things but loss, for the excellent knowledge of Christ Jesus my Lord, for whom I have counted all things loss, and do judge them to be dung, that I might win Christ, and be found in him" (Phil. 3:7–8).

The scope of these words is this. In the second verse, Paul admonishes the Philippians to take heed of certain counterfeit apostles who joined Christ and circumcision in the cause of their salvation, and put confidence in the flesh, that is, in the outward works of the ceremonial and moral law. And that this admonition might take the better place, he uses two reasons. The first, propounded in verse 3, is this: true circumcision is to worship God in spirit, to rejoice in Christ, and not to put any confidence in the flesh. The second reason is framed thus: if any man might put confidence in outward things, then I much more, but not I, therefore no man. The proposition (or first part of the reason) is propounded in verse 4 and confirmed in verses 5–6. The second part (or assumption), "but I do not put confidence in outward things," is confirmed in verses 7–8 thus: all things are loss to me in respect of Christ, therefore I put no confidence in anything out of Christ. And this is the very drift of the former words.

In the second place, the proper[1] sense and meaning of this portion of Scripture is to be considered. And, for this cause, we are to be advertised of sundry things in the words themselves.[2]

First of all, let it be observed that in verse 7 Paul says, in the time past, "I have counted all things loss," and in the next verse [he says,] in the time present, "I do count all things loss." The former speech is meant of that time in which he was first called to the knowledge of Christ. The second is spoken of the time when he had long continued an apostle of Christ and wrote this epistle to the Philippians. This distinction of times in one and the same word makes much to the clearing of the doctrine that shall afterwards be delivered.

Second, whereas in our translation it is said, "for whom I have counted all things loss" (v. 8), the words are too scant, and do not fully express the meaning of the Holy Spirit. For the words fully translated signify, "I have made all things loss," or "I have cast away all things," or "I have deprived myself of all things for

---

1. *Works* (1631) reads "former" instead of "proper."
2. This paragraph break is not in the original.

Christ." And whereas Paul had said before, "I count all things loss," his meaning is to amplify his own words by saying, "I deprive myself of all things, and judge them dung for Christ."

Third, the word translated "dung" signifies such things in the entrails of beasts as, being unfit for man's use, are cast to dogs. And by it Paul signifies that he did not only esteem all things as losses, and deprive himself of them, but also cast them away with loathing in a mind never to seek the recovery of them.

Lastly, it must be known that Paul in these verses uses a similitude borrowed from the merchant man. And it may be framed in this manner. The merchant, in hope of a treasure, is content to esteem his commodities no commodities but losses; yea, he is further content to cast them out into the sea, and to esteem them as things cast to dogs, so that he may obtain his intended treasure. So, says Paul, do I count all my former prerogatives as loss, and [I] am content to deprive myself of them, yea, to loathe them as dung, for the obtaining of Christ.

Furthermore, the sum and substance of the words is a comparison of things unequal, and it may be formed thus: all things are loss to me for Christ, and Christ is my gain.

Part 1

The Protasis

The first part of the comparison is of Paul's losses. And it is amplified two ways.

Point 1: What things are losses to Paul

First, he sets down what things are his loss, and they are of two sorts: first, privileges, virtues, and works before his conversion when he was a Pharisee; [and, second,] privileges, virtues, and works after his conversion when he was an apostle of Christ. The first are mentioned in verse 7, [and] the second in verse 8. Second, Paul sets down how all things are losses to him by a gradation, thus: "I count all things loss. I deprive myself of them. I count them dung."

The second part of the comparison is of Paul's gain. And it is amplified by a contrary gradation, thus: "I esteem the knowledge of Christ an excellent thing. I desire to gain Christ. And I desire to be found in him." Of these points in order.

Losses before his conversion
And first of Paul's losses before his conversion, in these words: "For the things that were vantage to me, I counted loss for Christ."

That these things may be well known, let us yet more narrowly search the meaning of these words. The things that were [an] [ad]vantage to Paul are of three sorts. First, his privileges, that he was born a Jew (that is, a member of the church), and again, that he was circumcised and brought up in the straight sect of the Pharisees. Second, his virtues, namely his justice and zeal in his religion. Third, his works, whereby he for outward carriage observed the ceremonial and moral law without reproof. And all these things are called his advantages because he put his confidence in them and thought to merit everlasting life thereby when he was a Pharisee. He adds further that he counted these advantages to be his loss, because so soon as he knew Christ his confidence ceased, his former merits were no merits but as things lost and cast away, yet not simply but for Christ, that is, that he might gain Christ and be found in Christ, as he expounds himself in the following words.

The Use

The meaning thus laid down, sundry things may be learned. The first [is] that it was a heresy of the Pharisees to put [their] confidence in their works, and to think that they could merit eternal life by them. For here Paul says that, being a Pharisee, works were his gain and advantage in the cause of his salvation. And hence we learn what to judge of the popish religion which teaches in substance the very same doctrine of confidence in works and of the merit of salvation thereby. And, therefore, the papists of our time are the children of the old Pharisees, reviving and renewing the old heresy touching merit with new and fresh colors. If they allege that they ascribe merit to the works, not of the ceremonial but of the moral law, and to works, not of nature but of grace, I answer that the Pharisees did the same, as the Pharisee acknowledges in his prayer when he says, "I thank thee, O Lord, I am not as other men" [Luke 18:11].

Second, in Paul's example, being a Pharisee, we learn that it is the pride and arrogance of man's nature to be something within himself, and to erect up something unto himself to be his righteousness and a means of his salvation, out of Christ. "The just," says Habakkuk, "lives by his faith, but he whose soul is not right in him puffs up himself" [Hab. 2:4], or builds towers of defense to himself by vain confidence out of God. The prodigal son must have his part alone by himself from his father. Paul says of the Jews that they established their own righteousness and would not be subject to the righteousness of God [Rom. 10:3]. This being so, let us learn to see and detest this pride in ourselves. For where it reigns and takes place, there Christ is not truly acknowledged. And when men begin to know Christ, this hidden and spiritual pride gives place. And further, by this we learn not to marvel that Turks and Jews deny Christ, and that papists in the cause of their salvation, beside the passion of Christ, foist in something of their own, namely their own merits and satisfactions. For it is the proud nature of man to set up himself in whole or in part, and to rely himself upon something of his own out of Christ. No marvel then that such as are otherwise learned and wise live and die in the opinion of justification by their own works.

Third, whereas Paul accounts things of advantage to be his loss, we learn that no privileges out of Christ minister true comfort or true happiness. It is a privilege to have known Christ and to have eaten and drunk with Him, but of such Christ says, "Depart from me, I know you not" [Luke 13:27]. It is a privilege to be of the kindred of our Savior Christ, but it is of no moment, for Christ says, "Who is my mother and brethren? He that doth the will of my Father is my brother, sister, and mother" [Mark 3:35]. It is a privilege that the virgin Mary was the mother of Christ, but if she had not as well borne Him in her heart by faith as she bore Him in her womb, she had not been saved. It is a privilege to prophesy in the name of Christ, but of such Christ says, "Depart from me ye workers of iniquity" (Matt. 7:23). Lastly, it is a privilege to be endued with all kinds of learning, of arts and tongues, but alas, all is nothing; for if a man had all wit, wisdom, and learning, and could speak in all matters with the tongue of men and angels, unless he is found in Christ he is no better in the sight of God than a damned wretch.[1]

This being so, we must learn, first of all, to moderate our care and our affections for worldly profits, honors, [and] pleasures, and our principal care must evermore be cast on Christ. Second, such persons as live an honest and civil life, and stand upon this, that they are no thieves, no murderers, no adulterers, no blasphemers, but in outward duties show love to God and man, they must, I say, take heed lest they deceive themselves, building upon false grounds. For though civil honesty is a thing commendable before men, yet it is not sufficient to save us before God. And Paul, who was a straight observer of the law, after he came to the knowledge of Christ, counted all his moral obedience, in which he had formerly trusted, but loss and dung for Christ.

Fourth, it has been the doctrine of the popish church these many years that before a man can be in Christ and be justified, he must first of all prepare and dispose himself to receive his justification, and that when he is sufficiently disposed, he does merit of congruity that God should infuse righteousness whereby of a sinner he is made no sinner and righteous before God. But I demand of the patrons of this doctrine whether, when the works of preparation are done, the doer is in Christ or out of Christ? If he is in Christ, he is also justified before he is justified.[2] If he is as yet out of Christ, Paul has given the sentence that the said works are to be esteemed as loss, and that the merit of congruity is no meat for them who desire to feed on Christ, but rather food for dogs.

Lastly, hence we learn how Christ is to be received by us. Such as would truly come to Christ and receive Him must make losses of all things. They must come naked and emptied of all their own righteousness. As men in a shipwreck cast out their commodities, and when there is no remedy leave their ship and betake themselves to the sea, and thus come swimming to the shore, even so must all men first forsake all and then come to Christ. Beggars, that they may obtain their alms, come in their rags, unfolding [their] legs and arms so that their sores and botches may be seen. Benhadad, king of Syria, that he might recover the favor of the king of Israel, casts off his crown and royal robes. He and his men come in sackcloth with halters about their heads. And thus he obtains his desire. In like manner coming to Christ, we must lay aside all

---

1. 1 Cor. 13:1–3.

2. *Works* (1631) does not include the phrase "before he is justified."

opinion of our own goodness, and, in abasing of ourselves, follow [the] beggar's fashions, and with Benhadad clothe ourselves with signs of guiltiness and confusion of face. We must first be annihilated and utterly, in respect of goodness, be made nothing in ourselves, so that we may be what we are out of ourselves in Christ. There is no entering into the kingdom of heaven except we receive it and Christ as a little child in all meekness and humility. For there must be nothing in us to receive Christ but mere faith resting on mere mercy. Let all such think on this, as desire to be in Christ, and to receive true comfort by Him.

Thus much of Paul's losses before his conversion.

Losses after his conversion

Now come to be considered the things which were his losses after his conversion. And they are set down in the following words: "Doubtless I do think all things losses for the excellent knowledge of Jesus Christ my Lord." But that these losses may be the better known, let us a little consider the meaning of the words.[3]

Whereas before Paul had said that therefore he counted things that had been his advantage to be loss unto him for Christ, some man might haply think this is but rash judgment in Paul. Therefore, to cut off this surmise, he says, "Doubtless I count all things loss," that is, that I may not be thought to speak rashly, I say more, that I do now account all things loss, and I speak it confidently, as being resolved [in] what I say. When he says, "I do count," he speaks in the time present of himself as being not only a Christian but also an apostle of Christ. And when he says, "all things," the general speech must be observed, for he excepts nothing pertaining to him but his knowledge and faith in Christ. Here, therefore, we must first of all understand the privilege of an apostle. Second, [we must understand] all inward and Christian virtues, as hope, fear, love of God, good conscience, etc., for of all the inward gifts none is excepted but faith (as I have said). Third, here we must understand works not of nature but of grace, done and effected by the Spirit of God in us, for in the following verse he does reject his own righteousness which is of the law. Now he says of all these, that they are his losses for Christ.

But how are they losses? The speech must warily be understood, lest it be offensive. They are losses not in respect of godly conversation, for they are the causes thereof, and they are means of showing our thankfulness to God and love to man. Now then, they are losses only in respect of justification and salvation, when they are reputed and maintained as meritorious causes thereof either in whole or in part. Though when they are rightly used and applied, they are the excellent gifts of God, yet when they are brought into the act of

------

3. This paragraph break is not in the original.

justification and salvation they become as losses and dung. And this I take to be the meaning of these words. To the like purpose the prophet Isaiah says in the name of the whole church, confessing his sins, "All our righteousness is as a cloth utterly to be cast away" [Isa. 64:6]. And Paul to the Galatians: "If righteousness be by the law, Christ died without cause (or, in vain)" [Gal. 2:21]; that is, if the righteousness of the law is our advantage, Christ must be our loss; and, on the contrary, if He is our advantage, the righteousness of the law must be our loss.

This doctrine of Paul, that all virtues and works (both of nature and grace) are losses in the case of our salvation, sounds not in man's reason, and there are many things brought to the contrary.[4]

First, it is alleged that God does accept and crown our works, and therefore that they are not losses. I answer: God does (as it were) keep a double court: one of justice [and] the other of mercy. In the court of justice, He gives judgment by the law, and accurses every man who does not continue in all things written in the law to do them. In this court nothing can stand but the passion and righteousness of Christ, and for the best works that we can do, we may not look for any acceptation or reward, but use the plea of David, "Enter not, O Lord, into judgment with thy servant, for no flesh shall be justified in thy sight."[5] Now in the court of grace and mercy, God has to deal with His own children who stand before Him justified and reconciled by Christ. And the obedience of such He accepts in this court, and mercifully rewards, though otherwise it is imperfect, yet not for the merit thereof, but for the merit and worthiness of Christ. Thus then, good works in rigor of justice are worthy [of] condemnation and are accepted by mercy procured by the merit of Christ.[6]

Second, it is alleged that works are necessary to salvation, and therefore not to be reputed losses. I answer: works may be considered either as causes of salvation or only as a way directing thereto. If they are considered as causes, they are not necessary, but in this respect they are dung. If they are respected as a way leading and directing to eternal life, they are indeed necessary thus and not otherwise.[7]

Third, it is objected that the law requires works and the law must be satisfied, and therefore he who is justified must be justified by works. The answer is that whosoever is justified and saved is justified and saved by works. But works must be distinguished. Some are personal works done in and by ourselves. These neither justify nor save any man, but in the case of salvation are

---

4. This paragraph break is not in the original.
5. Ps. 143:2.
6. This paragraph break is not in the original.
7. This paragraph break is not in the original.

loss and dung. Besides these, there are works that are out of us, wrought in and by the person of our Savior Christ, namely the works of obedience in satisfying and fulfilling the law. These indeed are the works which justify and save us, and none that proceed from us. To this effect Paul says "that we are justified freely by the redemption that is in Christ" [Rom. 3:24].[8]

Lastly, it is alleged that if all virtues are loss for Christ, then faith itself [is loss]. I answer: faith must diversely be considered. First of all, [it must be considered] as a virtue working and bringing forth many good fruits in us. And thus it is to be reputed loss as all other virtues are. Second, it must be considered, not as a virtue, but as an instrument or hand, not to give or work anything, but to apprehend and receive Christ and His benefits. And thus it is no loss, but is a thing excepted in this text. Now then, we see that the doctrine of Paul is manifest: that all virtues and works, both of nature and grace, are mere losses in the cause of our justification and salvation.

The Use

Hence sundry things may be learned. The first [is] that the most holy works of holy men cannot justify or merit eternal life. When they are brought within the act of justification as causes, Paul says they are but loss and as offals[9] to be cast to dogs. Let this be noted and remembered forever against all justiciary papists who, if they would but seriously consider this one text, might be far better resolved than they are.

Second, hence the doctrine of our church is plainly gathered, namely, that we are saved and justified by faith alone. For all things except our knowledge and faith in Christ are made as dung. And that this doctrine may not be scandalous, sundry things must be remembered. The first is the right meaning of the doctrine, which is, that there is nothing within us that is any cause (either efficient, material, formal, or final) of justification but faith. The second [is] that faith is no principal cause but only an instrument. The third [is] that faith is no instrument to procure or work our justification and salvation, but an instrument to receive or to apprehend our justification given by the Father, procured by the Son, applied by the Holy Spirit. The last [is] that faith must be considered as a cause, or else as a way of salvation. If as an internal cause in us, it only justifies and consequently saves us. If as a way, it does not save alone. For other virtues and works, though they are no causes, yet they are ways to eternal life as well as faith. Here then, when papists make outcries against us, saying that we look to be saved by faith alone, the true and plain answer to them is that we

---

8. This paragraph break is not in the original.
9. *Offals:* animal entrails used as food.

consider faith two ways. First, as a cause within us, not meriting any way, but instrumentally apprehending pardon in Christ and applying it to us for our eternal happiness. And, second, faith may be considered as a way in which we are to walk for the attainment of everlasting life.[10]

In the first sense alone faith justifies and saves, and nothing else within us. To this do the learned fathers agree. Basil says, "This is perfect rejoicing in God, when a man is not puffed up for his own justice, but acknowledges that he wants justice, and that he is justified by faith alone in Christ."[11] Hilary: "That is remitted of Christ by faith, which the law could not loosen, for faith alone justifies."[12] Ambrose: "They are justified freely which do nothing, nor repay like for like, are justified by faith alone, through the gift of God."[13] Again, in his commentary upon the epistle to the Corinthians: "This is appointed of God, that he who believes in Christ should be saved without works, by faith alone receiving remission of sins."[14] Jerome: "God justifieth by faith alone."[15]

Nevertheless, if we speak of the way to life, then we are not saved only by faith. For though faith is the only instrument to apprehend Christ, yet it is not the only way to life. Repentance also is the way, yea, all virtues and all works are the way. In this sense, affliction is said to "work unto us" a more excellent weight of glory [2 Cor. 4:17],[16] not as a cause, but as a way giving direction. And mothers are said to be saved "by bearing of children" [1 Tim. 2:15], not as by a cause, but as by a straight and narrow way. Again, Abraham's faith went not alone, but had a kind of cooperation with his works [James 2:22]; faith and works both being considered as a way to happiness or as marks in a way. In this sense the fathers have ascribed salvation to many things, not as to causes but as to ways. Bernard said well that works are "the way to the kingdom of heaven and not the causes of reigning."[17] Lactantius says, "Great is the help of repentance, which, whosoever takes away, cuts off to himself the way of life."[18] Chrysostom: "Some by watching, by sleeping on the bare ground, by toiling their bodies with daily labor do blot out their sins: but you may obtain the same by a more easy way, that is, by forgiving."[19] Thus many hundreds [of] places of

---

10. This paragraph break is not in the original.

11. In the margin: Hom. de humil. *Fide sola in Christum se justificari.*

12. In the margin: In Matt. 9.

13. In the margin: In cap. 3 ad Rom. *Nihil operates.*

14. In the margin: In 1 Cor. 1.

15. In the margin: In Rom. 10.

16. In the margin: katergazetαι.

17. In the margin: Libro de gratia & lib. arbitrio. *Via regni non causa regnandi.*

18. In the margin: Epit. divin. institut. c. 9.

19. In the margin: Homil. 38 in John.

the fathers are to be understood, when they ascribe remission of sins to martyrdom, fasting, prayer, works of mercy, and such like.

Third, here is laid down the foundation of true humility. For if all our virtues and works are losses in the case of our salvation, then all boasting is excluded, and we are to take nothing to ourselves but shame and confusion and give all glory to God. Yea, the more our virtues and works, if we place any confidence in them, the greater are our losses.

Point 2: How things are losses to Paul

Thus we see what things are losses to Paul. In the next place let us consider how they are losses. This Paul sets down by a gradation thus: "I count them loss. I make them my losses. I count them as dung." This gradation is nothing else but a repetition of one and the same thing enlarged and amplified in speech. Now repetitions in Scripture are not idle and vain, as they are oftentimes in the writings of men, but they commonly signify two things, namely the certainty and the necessity of the thing repeated. And, therefore, in this place they signify the certainty and the necessity of Paul's losses.

Their Certainty

They are certain because he who will be saved by Christ must certainly endure these losses without recovery. The foundation of this certainty lies in an impossibility of merit by any works of man. I make this manifest by five reasons.

The first is this. It is a principal part of Christian inherent righteousness to have and keep a good conscience. Now Paul expressly excludes it from justification, saying, "I know nothing by myself, yet I am not thereby justified" (1 Cor. 4:4).

The second is this. Paul says, "We are not saved by works" (Eph. 2:9). Now he means no other works but such as follow faith and are done by the Spirit of God. And this appears by the reasons which he uses: "that we are created to good works" and "that they are ordained that we should walk in them."

The third [is this]. Before a work can merit, it must please God. Before the work pleases God, the worker must please Him. Before the worker pleases Him, he must be reconciled to God and perfectly justified. Justification, therefore, goes in order before good works, and for this cause works cannot be brought within the act of justification as causes. Good works make not good men in whole or in part. But men, first of all made good by the goodness of Christ imputed, make good works by their goodness.

The fourth is this. The humanity of Christ is the most excellent of all creatures in heaven and earth, yet, being considered by itself, it cannot possibly merit at God's hand. In a work properly meritorious there are three conditions.

First, the doer thereof must do it by himself and not by another, for then the praise is his by whom he does it and not his own. Second, the work to be done must not be a debt or duty, for then the doer deserves nothing. Third, there must be a proportion between the work and the reward of eternal life. Now, the manhood of Christ, considered apart by itself, cannot perform these three conditions. For it does what it does by the Spirit of God, whereby it was conceived and is filled without measure. Again, it is a creature and, therefore, whatsoever it is, has, or can be, it owes all to God. Lastly, it cannot do a work proportional to eternal glory, because it takes all of God and can give nothing to Him. If then it is demanded, how this manhood of Christ merits in our behalf, I answer, not by itself, but by means of the personal union whereby it is exalted and preferred into the unity of the second person, the eternal Word of the Father. Hence it is that Christ merits. None can merit of God but God. Now then, if Christ merits only in this regard, no mere creature (man or angel) can possibly merit by any work.

The fifth reason is this. There are two kinds of transgression of the law. One [is] when a work is directly against the law. The other is when that is done which the law requires, but not in that manner and perfection the law requires. The second kind of transgression is in every good work which is done by men upon earth. Now where any transgression is, there must be pardon. Where pardon is, there is no merit.

That this doctrine of the certainty of our losses may yet the better be cleared, I will set down the supposed grounds of merit, and discover their weakness[es]. They are two.[20]

The first is the promise that God has made to works, whereby He has bound Himself to reward them with eternal glory. I answer that this very promise is made of the good pleasure and mere good will of God, and of the same goodness it is that any man is a doer of any good work, either by nature or grace. Therefore, if a man could fulfill the whole law, he should not merit at God's hand. Thus says the Lord: "That he will shew mercy upon thousands of them that love him and keep his commandments" (Exod. 20:6).[21]

The second ground is that virtue of meriting is derived from Christ, the Head, to His members by divine influence. I answer [that] it is an impossible thing. For the virtue of meriting is in Christ, not simply as He is man, but as He is in one person God and man. The work which merits is done or acted even by the manhood, but the merit of the work is from the Godhead, or from the excellency of the person. Now then, if this virtue is in Christ, not as He is man,

---

20. This paragraph break is not in the original.
21. This paragraph break is not in the original.

but in respect He is man-God or God-man, it cannot be derived to us who are but men, unless every believer should be deified, and made of a mere man God-man, which is impossible. Therefore, there is no capability or possibility of merit in the work of any mere man or creature whatsoever.[22]

For this cause the true church of God [has] ever detested human merit. The merit of congruity before justification is a Pelagian conceit and was never maintained by the orthodox fathers. Stapleton confesses thus much: "The merit of congruity in respect of the first grace was of old hissed out.[23] Neither was it ever admitted by the better sort of schoolmen, as of Thomas in his *Summe* and his latter writings, nor of his followers."[24] And the merit of condignity,[25] whereby works are said of their own dignity, and that properly, to deserve the increase of the first justification and eternal life was not received by the learned in the church for more than a 1,000 years after Christ. Radulfus Ardens,[26] a very learned man in his time, says thus: "Seeing by one grace we come to another, they are called merits and that improperly."[27] For as Augustine witnesses, "God crowns only his own grace in us." Again, "No man may think that God is bound as it were by a bargain to repay that which He has promised. For as God is free to promise, so He is free in respect of repaying, especially considering that merits as well as rewards are His grace. For God crowns nothing else in us but His grace, because if He would deal with us in extremity,[28] none living should be justified in His sight. And hereupon the apostle, who labored more than all, says, 'I think that the afflictions of this time are not worthy the glory that shall be revealed.' Therefore, this covenant or bargain is nothing else but a voluntary promise."[29] After him, Anselm says, "If a man should serve God a thousand years, and that most zealously, he should not worthily deserve to be in the kingdom of heaven so much as half a day."[30] Saint Bernard says, "Touching eternal life, we know that the sufferings of this time are not worthy of the glory to come; no not if one man should suffer all. For the merits of men are not such that eternal life may be due for them, or that God should do some injury if He gave it not. For to let pass that all merits are the gifts of God, and so man is rather debtor to God for them than God to man, what are all merit[s]

---

22. This paragraph break is not in the original.

23. *Hiss out*: to silence or drive away.

24. In the margin: De orig. pecc. l. 1. c. 4.

25. In the margin: *Meritum a condigno.*

26. Radulfus Ardens (died c. 1200) was a French theologian, known for his *Summa de vitiis et virtutibus* (14 volumes). He served as a chaplain to Richard I.

27. In the margin: In Dominica 18 post. Trin. in An. 1050. *Merita dicuntur at improprie..*

28. In the margin: *Districte agere.*

29. In the margin: In Dominica Septuagesimæ.

30. In the margin: De mensuratione crucis an. 1080. *Non meretur ex condigno.*

to so great a glory? Lastly, who is better than the prophet, to whom the Lord gives so worthy a testimony, saying, 'I have found a man according to mine own heart,' for all that he had need to say to God, 'Enter not into judgment with thy servant.'"[31]

Again, in the process of time, when the merit of condignity had taken place, it was not generally received. For it was rejected by sundry schoolmen and others, as of Gregory of Arimine, of Durand, of Waldensis, of Burgensis, and Scotus. Wherefore, to conclude, it now appears to be an infallible certainty that he who desires to be saved by Christ must endure the loss of all his works and virtues whatsoever in the cause of his own justification.

Now then, if this doctrine is so certain and infallible (as it is), then we must also be settled in this point without doubting, that the present Church of Rome errs grievously, in that it magnifies the merit of works. Yea, in this regard, it reverses the very foundation of true religion. For if they make advantage in the matter of salvation by their works, Christ must needs upon infallible certainty be their loss, because Paul makes all works loss, that Christ may be advantage. Therefore, far be it from us all to have any dealing or contract of society with that church, lest we become partakers of her dangerous and fearful losses.

Again, in that all virtues and works of grace are but losses for Christ, we must not only in our first conversion, but ever afterward though we are justified and sanctified even in the pang of death by mere faith, rest on the mere mercy of God and apprehend [a] naked Christ, that is, Christ severed in the case of salvation from all respect of all virtues and works whatsoever. For there is nothing that may be opposed to the severe judgment of God but merely Christ. If we do presume to oppose any of our doings to the sentence of the law, hell, death, condemnation, we are sure to go by the losses.

Thus much of the certainty of Paul's losses.

Their Necessity

Now follows the necessity of them. They are necessary in as much as without them no man can have part in Christ. For the merit of our virtues and good works and the grace of God in Christ cannot stand together. Yea, they are [as] contrary as fire and water, and one overthrows the other in the cause of justification and salvation. To signify this contrariety, Paul says, "If election be of grace, it is not of works" [Rom. 11:6]. And if it is of works, it is not of grace. And again, "If ye be justified by the law, ye are abolished from Christ" [Gal. 5:4]. And to the same purpose, Ambrose says, "Grace is wholly received or wholly lost." And Augustine: "It is [in] no way grace what is not freely given every

---

31. In the margin: Bern. de Annunc. Virg. serm. 1. an. 1140.

way." Hence it follows that the present religion of the Church of Rome abolishes Christ, in as much as it maintains and magnifies the merit of good works.[32]

And this may be gathered by the very doctrine of that church. For it teaches that men must be saved by their prayers, fasting, alms, pilgrimages, building of churches, chapels, bridges, etc. What then shall the passion of Christ do? Whereto serves it? They answer that it frees us from death, and gives to our works the merit of eternal life, and makes them meritoriously to increase our justification. Hence, it follows that Christ is no more but the first cause of our salvation, and that we ourselves are secondary causes under Him and with Him. And thus He is made of a Savior no Savior. For either He must be a full and perfect Savior in Himself or no Savior.[33]

Second, by the former necessity we learn that whosoever will be saved by the merit of Christ must come unto Him without virtues or works of his own, nor carrying in [his] heart so much as the least confidence in them, esteeming himself to be a most vile, wretched, and miserable sinner, as the Publican did, who prayed, "Lord, be merciful to me, a sinner."

---

32. This paragraph break is not in the original.

33. *Works* (1626) does not include the phrase, "For either He must be a full and perfect Savior in Himself or no Savior."

The Apodosis

Hitherto of Paul's losses. Now follows the second part of the comparison, touching Paul's gain: "But Christ is my gain." [This is] a sentence to be remembered, and to be written in the tables of our heart forever. And the reason thereof is manifest. Christ, our Mediator, God and man, is the only fountain of all good things that are (or can be) thought on, whether spiritual or temporal. Saint John says, "Of his fullness we receive grace for grace" [John 1:16]. Again, Paul says, "In him all the treasures of knowledge and wisdom are hid" [Col. 2:3]. And, "Ye are complete in him" [Col. 3:10]. And he calls Christ "our ransom (or counter-price)" [1 Tim. 2:6]. And as he makes Adam the root of all evil in mankind, so he makes Christ the root of all grace and goodness. For the better clearing of this doctrine, two points are to be handled. When Christ is our gain? And how?[1]

Point 1: When Christ is our gain

Touching the time when, I set down three things: (1) He is our gain in this life; (2) He is our gain in death; and (3) He is our gain after death.

In Life

To return to the first, He is our gain in life if we turn from our evil ways and believe in Him, in as much as He has gained for us many benefits, which I will reduce to ten heads.[2]

The first is pardon of sin without term of time, whether past, present, or to come. Yet, we must here remember that pardon of sin is not given absolutely whether men repent or not, but upon condition of repentance.

The second is the imputation of Christ's obedience in fulfilling the law for our justification before God. From the former benefit arises our freedom from hell and from the law, in respect of the curse thereof. And from the second arises a right to eternal life, whereof the possession is reserved to the life to come.

---

1. This paragraph break is not in the original.
2. The paragraph breaks for the ten "heads" are not in the original.

The third is our adoption whereby we are the children of God and brethren of Christ. And hence we have a right of lordship or dominion over the whole world and all things contained therein, whether in heaven or in earth. This right was lost by Adam and is now restored by Christ. Indeed, wicked men and infidels have and use the things of this life at their wills, and that by God's permission, but yet they receive and enjoy them not otherwise than children of traitors do the goods of their parents, who peradventure are suffered to take benefit of some part of them for the preserving of their lives, though title and interest to them is not restored.

The fourth is the ministry, that is, the presence, aid, and protection of the good angels [Heb. 1:14].

The fifth gain or benefit is that all the miseries and calamities of this life cease to be curses, and are made blessings, being turned to the good of them who are to be saved by Christ [Rom. 8:28].

The sixth is the mortification of original sin, with all the parts thereof, by the virtue of the death of Christ.

The seventh is a spiritual life, whereby we live not, but Christ lives in us, making us partakers of His anointing, and thereby enabling us to live as prophets, priests, [and] kings. Prophets, to teach and make confession of our faith in Christ; priests, to dedicate and present our bodies and souls to God for the service of His majesty; [and] kings, to bear rule and dominion over the corruptions and lusts of our hearts.

The eighth gain is that Christ presents all our prayers and good works to His Father in His own name, and thus by His own intercession makes them acceptable unto Him.

The ninth gain is the presence of His Spirit. For when Christ ascended, He took with Him our pawn,[3] namely our flesh, and left with us His own pawn, the presence of the Comforter, to supply His own presence, to guide, comfort, and to assure us of our adoption and salvation [John 16:7].

The tenth and last is perseverance in having and holding the former gains. For thus says the Lord: "I will put my fear into their hearts, that they shall not depart from me" (Jer. 32:40). And it must be remembered that these words are not spoken only in general to the church, but also in singular to every true member thereof, because they are the words of the covenant. Again, David says that "the righteous man is like a tree planted by the water's side, whose leaf never withereth" (Ps. 1:3) who therefore always has [the] sap of grace in the heart to the end.

---

3. *Pawn:* deposit as security.

In Death

Second, as Christ is our gain in life, so He is also our gain in death, in as much as He has taken away the sting of death, and has changed the condition of it by making it of the gate of hell to be the way to eternal life.

After Death

Third, He is our gain after death [in] three ways. Our first gain is the resurrection of our bodies to eternal life in the day of judgment. The second is a privilege to judge the world [1 Cor. 6:2]. For, first of all, judgment shall pass upon the godly. [Once this is] done, they shall be taken up to Christ, and there as witnesses and approvers of His sentence of condemnation, judge together with Him the wicked world. The third is the eternal retribution in which God shall be all in all, first in Christ, and then in all the members of Christ, and that forever and ever.

Point 2: How Christ is our gain

The next point to be handled is how Christ is our gain. For the answering of this, two questions are to be opened.

Question 1

The first is [this]: according to what nature is Christ our gain? I answer, following the ancient and catholic doctrine, that [the] whole Christ is our gain according to both natures.[4] The Godhead of Christ profits no sinner without the manhood, nor the manhood without the Godhead. And as Leo says, each nature works that which is proper unto it, having communication with the other.[5] Again, God may be considered two ways: God absolute or God made man. God absolute (that is, God absolutely considered without respect to Christ) is indeed a fountain of righteousness and life, but this fountain is closed, sealed up, and not to be attained unto, because our sins make a separation between God and us. And God thus considered is a majesty full of terror to all sinful men. But God considered as He was made man and manifested in our flesh is also a fountain of goodness, yea, the same fountain opened, unsealed, and flowing forth to all mankind. Hence it is that Christ is called the light of the world, the bread and water of life, the way, the truth, [and] the life.[6]

Here again, we must remember to make a difference or distinction of the natures of Christ. For the Godhead of Christ is our gain, not in respect of

---

4. In the margin: August. hom. de ovibus c. 12. *Humana divinitas & divina humanitas mediatrix est.*

5. In the margin: Leo epist.. 10.

6. This paragraph break is not in the original.

essence, but in respect of virtue and operation showed in (or upon) the manhood of Christ, whereby it makes things which were done and suffered in the said manhood apt and sufficient to appease God's anger and to merit eternal life for us. As for the manhood, it is not only in effect and operation, but also really communicated to the faith of the believing heart. And hereupon it is (as it were) a treasure and storehouse of all the rich graces of God that serve to justify, save, or any way to enrich the elect of all ages and times through the whole world.[7]

If any doubt of this, let them consider three things of this most glorious manhood. The first is the grace of personal union whereby it is received into the unity of the second person, and has no being or subsisting, but only in the substance thereof. And hence it is truly termed the humanity of the Son of God, or of the Word. The second is that this manhood has in it all fullness of grace [John 3:34], commonly called in the schools habitual grace.[8] Now this fullness of grace contains in it all the gifts of the Holy Spirit, and that in the highest degree of perfection. It has, therefore, in it gifts more for number and greater for measure than all men and angels have. The third is that it receives this excellency of gifts and graces, not for itself, but that it may be (as it were) a pipe or conduit to convey the same graces to all the elect. Our salvation and life depends on the fullness of the Godhead which is in Christ. Nevertheless, it is not conveyed unto us but in the flesh and by the flesh of Christ. Christ signifies thus much, when He says, "My flesh is meat indeed"; "Except ye eat the flesh of the Son of man and drink his blood, ye have no life in you"; and "He which eateth my flesh abideth in me and I in him" (John 6:51–55). And John the Baptist says, "Of his fullness we receive grace for grace" (John 1:16). The Supper of the Lord is ordained for the increase and continuance of grace and life. And of it Paul says, "The bread which we break is a fellowship or communion with the very body of Christ" (1 Cor. 10:16).[9]

On this manner Christ is said "to be made unto us of God, wisdom, righteousness, sanctification, redemption" (1 Cor. 1:30). [He is our] wisdom, not because the essential wisdom of the Godhead is given to us, for that is infinite and incommunicable; neither again because He is the author of our wisdom, giving us knowledge of our salvation as the Father and Holy Spirit do; nor because He is the matter of our wisdom, the knowledge of whom is eternal life; but for a higher cause than all these. Our Mediator, the man Jesus Christ, who is also God, is a head unto us and a root of our wisdom. For He was anointed with the Spirit of wisdom in the assumed manhood, not privately for Himself,

---

7. This paragraph break is not in the original.

8. *Works* (1631) does not include the phrase: "commonly called in the schools habitual grace."

9. This paragraph break is not in the original.

but that we also who believe might be partakers of the same anointing, and that wisdom from Him by His flesh might be conveyed unto us. Therefore, from His wisdom there is wisdom derived in some measure to all who are mystically united to Him, as light in one candle is derived to a hundred, or as heat is derived from heat.[10]

He is our justice, not only because He is the author and giver of our justice, with the Father and the Holy Spirit; neither because the essential justice of Christ is given to us, for then we should all be deified; but because that justice which is in the manhood, consisting partly in the purity of nature and partly in the purity of action, whereby He obeyed His Father's will and suffered all things to be suffered for us, this justice (I say) is imputed to us and accounted ours, according to the tenor of the covenant, as if it were inherent in us.[11]

He is our sanctification, not only because the sanctity or holiness of the Godhead is communicated to us, but because He was sanctified in His manhood above all men and angels. And from this holiness of His, our holiness is derived and springs as a fruit, as the corruption in Adam's posterity is derived from the corruption of Adam. Christ says, "For their sakes sanctify I myself, that they also may be sanctified through the truth" (John 17:19). Cyril says, "As God, He gives Himself the Spirit; as man He receives it; which He does not for Himself but for us, that the grace of sanctification out of Him first received might pass to all mankind."[12] Again, he says, "That the body of our Lord, being sanctified by the virtue of the Word joined to it, is made so effectual for mystical benediction that it can send forth His sanctification into us."[13]

Lastly, Christ is our redemption (or life) in this manner. In the person of the Mediator, being one and the same, there is a double life. One [is] uncreated and essential, agreeing to Christ as He is God. And this life is not given to us at all, save in respect of the efficacy thereof. For in God we live, move, and have our being. The other is the created life of the manhood, and it is either natural, or spiritual. Natural is that wherewith He lived in the estate of humiliation by ordinary means as all other men do. Spiritual is that whereby He now especially lives in the estate of exaltation and glory. And He lives this life, not only for Himself, but also for us, that we, being partakers thereof, may live together with Him [Rom. 6:8]. Thus, the ancient church has taught: the flesh of Christ united to the Word is made quickening flesh that it might further quicken those who are united to it with spiritual life.[14]

---

10. This paragraph break is not in the original.

11. This paragraph break is not in the original.

12. In the margin: Cyril in John lib. 11. c. 25.

13. In the margin: Lib. 11. c. 22.

14. In the margin: Cyril in John l. 3. c. 37 & 4. 12. 14 & l. 10. 13.

Question 2

The next question is: In what estate is Christ our gain? The estate of Christ is twofold: the estate of humiliation from His birth to His death; and the estate of exaltation in His resurrection, ascension, and His sitting at the right hand of God. In the first estate He works and procures our gain. Christ lying basely in the manger, and crucified ignominiously on the cross, gained our deliverance from hell and a right to everlasting life. In the second estate He communicates to us the gain before named, and by degrees puts us in possession of it. And for this end, He now sits at the right hand of God and makes request for us.

The Use

The use of this doctrine, that Christ is our gain, is manifold.

First, it shows that we in ourselves are poor and altogether destitute of all spiritual good things. For to this end is Christ our gain, that He may supply our want, and fill them with graces who are otherwise empty and even hunger-starved.

Second, it teaches that men do in vain seek for so much as the least drop of goodness out of Christ who alone is the storehouse of all good things. Heaven and earth, men and angels, and all things are but as nothing to us, if by them we seek to enjoy anything out of Christ; yea, God is no God to us without Christ.

Third, we learn to detest the treasury which the Church of Rome maintains and magnifies. It is (as it were) a chest in which is contained, not only the overplus of the merits of Christ, but also of martyrs and saints, to be dispensed in pardons at the pope's pleasure. But Christ alone is our full and perfect gain, and therefore in Him there is an all-sufficient treasury of the church. And, as Paul says, "In him we are complete" (Col. 2:10). As for the merits of martyrs and saints, they bring no advantage to the people of God, but are indeed matter for the dunghill.

Fourth, if Christ is our treasure and gain, our hearts must be set on Him. Our minds [are usually] upon our penny, and we hunger after gain. Let us, therefore, hunger after Christ. He is our penny and He is our gain. Nay, we must above all pleasures, honors, [and] profits, love Him and rejoice in Him; yea, we should be swallowed up with love of Him.

Lastly, here is matter of comfort. In the loss of goods and friends, and all calamities of this life, we may not be dismayed. All the losses of this life are but petty losses so long as we have Christ for our gain. Nothing can be wanting unto us in the midst of all our losses and miseries so long as we receive of His fullness, who is the fountain of goodness never dried up.

The Degrees of Paul's Desire

To proceed further, the second part of the comparison, "Christ is my gain," is amplified by a gradation in this manner: "I esteem the knowledge of Christ Jesus my Lord an excellent thing. I desire to gain Christ. I desire to be found in Christ." Of these in order.[15]

Degree 1

By the knowledge of Christ, we are to understand the doctrine of the gospel, or the doctrine of the person and offices of Christ, conceived and known by us. To this knowledge an excellency is ascribed, of which I will speak a little. This excellency appears partly in the matter (and contents) and partly in the effects thereof.

The Matter. Touching the matter, it is full of excellent mysteries, which Paul reduces to six heads in 1 Timothy 3:16.[16]

The first is the incarnation of the Son of God in these words: "God made manifest in the flesh." And here two wonders offer themselves to be considered. First, whereas Adam's flesh and Adam's sin are inseparably joined together in respect of all that nature can do, yet did the Son of God take unto Him man's nature and flesh without man's sin because He was conceived of a virgin by the operation of the Holy Spirit. Whereas if He had been conceived by natural generation, He had with Adam's flesh taken Adam's corruption. The other wonder in the incarnation of Christ is that the flesh of man is united to the person of the Son of God, and thence has its subsistence, otherwise having no subsistence of its own. The like example is not to be found in the world again, saving that we have some resemblance thereof in the plant called mistletoe, which has no root of its own, but grows as a branch of the oak or some other tree, and has its life and sap from the root thereof.

The second mystery in the knowledge of Christ is the justification of Christ in these words: "justified in the Spirit." And it was in this manner. Christ, made man, became our surety and was subject to the law for us. Hereupon our sins were imputed to Him, and the punishment due thereto laid upon Him, that is, the first death with the pains of the second, yea, further, death in the grave had dominion over Him. After all this, by His Spirit (or power of the Godhead) He raised Himself from death, and thereby acquitted Himself of our sins. And this acquittal (or absolution) is His justification whereby He declares Himself to be a perfectly righteous Savior. For if He had not satisfied the wrath of God to the

---

15. This paragraph break is not in the original.
16. The paragraph breaks for the six "heads" are not in the original.

full and brought perfect righteousness, He had never risen again, considering He was judged and condemned for our sins.

The third mystery is "the sight of angels," who desired to look into the incarnation of Christ, in which they saw three things as Luke testifies. First, that it was a means to manifest "the glory of God." Second, that it brought "peace" and good success to men upon earth. Third, that it was a means to reveal "the goodwill of God" to the world [Luke 2:14].

The fourth is the "preaching of Christ to the Gentiles." This appears to be a great mystery because the knowledge of Christ was kept secret from the nations for the space of more than 4,000 years [Rom. 16:25]. For from the creation to Moses, the church of God was shut up in a little family. From Moses to Christ, it was included within the precincts of Jewry, which was not so much as the fourth part of England.

The fifth mystery is the "conversion of the world" to the faith of Christ. And this is so much the greater wonder because this conversion was wrought by the preaching of the gospel, which is flat against the natural reason and will of man, and therefore unfit to persuade. And the preachers hereof were simple and silly men to see to. And some of them who were converted were the very Jews who crucified Christ.

The last mystery is the "ascension of Christ into glory." The greatness of this mystery appears in two things. The first [is] that Christ's ascension was a real and full opening of the kingdom of heaven, which had formerly been shut by our sins. The second [is] that the ascension of Christ was no personal or private ascension, for He ascended in the room and stead of all the elect, and they ascended together in and with Him, and now after a sort are together in and with Him in glory.

Thus, we see the excellency of the knowledge of Christ in respect of the mysteries contained therein.

The Effects. The like excellency appears in the effects thereof, which are two: the knowledge of God and of ourselves.

For the first, by the knowledge of Christ we know God aright. Hence, Christ is called "the brightness of the glory of the Father" and "the engraven image of his person" (Heb. 1:3), and "the image of the invisible God" (Col. 1:15). And Paul says notably that when God shines in our hearts by the light of the gospel, "his glory is to be seen in the face of Christ" (2 Cor. 4:6). The wisdom, power, and goodness of God is made manifest in Christ, and that more fully than ever it was in the creation. In the creation Adam, being but a mere man, was our head, but in the estate of grace Christ (God and man) is our head. By creation we receive but a natural life to be continued by food, [but] by Christ we receive a spiritual [life] to be preserved eternally without food by the operation of the Spirit. As the spouse of Adam was bone of his bone and flesh of his flesh, so is the spouse of Christ bone of His bone and flesh of His flesh, and that in [a] more excellent manner because every particular man as he is born anew, and the whole catholic church (the true spouse of Christ), springs and arises out of the merit and efficacy of the blood that distilled out of the heart and side of Christ. In the creation God makes life from nothing, but by Christ He draws our life forth of death and changes death itself into life. Again, in the law the justice of God is set down and revealed, [but] in Christ we see more, namely perfect justice and perfect mercy, revealed to the full; yea, (which is a wonder) justice and mercy reconciled. Lastly, in Christ we see the length, the breadth, the height, [and] the depth of the love of God,[17] in that God vouchsafes to love the elect with the very same love wherewith He loves Christ [John 17:23].

As by Christ we know God, so also by Christ we know ourselves. And that in this manner. First, we must consider that in the passion He took our person upon Him, and that upon the cross He stood in our place, room, and stead. Second, we are to consider the greatness of His agony and passion set forth unto us, especially by five things. The first is the testimony of the evangelists, who say in emphatical words that He was "full of sorrow" and "grievously troubled" [Matt. 26:37–38]. The second [is] His complaint "that his soul was heavy unto the death" and "that he was forsaken of the Father." The third [is] His prayer with strong cries: "save me from this hour" [and] "let this cup pass." The fourth [is] the coming of an angel to comfort Him. The last [is] His sweat of water and thick (or clotted) blood. Now in Christ thus considered, we see the greatness of God's anger against us for our sins. We see the greatness of our sins. We see the vileness of our persons. We see the hardness of our hearts, who never so much as sigh for our offences for which the Son of God sweat water and blood. We see our unthankfulness, who little respect or regard this work of Christ. Lastly, we see our duty, that we are to be thoroughly touched with true repentance, and to humble ourselves (as it were) to the very pit of hell. For if the Son of God mourns and cries for our sins imputed, we are much more to cry and bleed in our hearts for them, seeing they are ours properly, and by them we have pierced Christ [Zech. 12:10].

And thus the excellency of the knowledge of Christ is manifest.

Hence we learn sundry things. First, if the knowledge of Christ is so excellent, we may not marvel that by the malice of the devil it has been corrupted many hundreds [of] years in the Romish church. It teaches that the gospel is nothing

---

17. Eph. 3:18.

else in effect but the law of Moses perfected. Now if this were so, Christ doubtless died in vain, and we might place our hope in our own righteousness, and the promise of eternal life by Christ should be of no effect. For the law never justifies before God, till it is perfectly kept. If men could perform this condition of perfection, there would be little need of Christ or the gospel.

Second, if this knowledge is of such excellency, it must be learned of us, and that in [a] special manner. If we lend the understanding and memory to other inferior learning, we are to apply the whole man to this. The mind must learn it by opening itself to conceive it. The memory must learn it by storing it up. The will and affections must learn it by resigning and conforming themselves in their kind unto it. Thus, Paul teaches that "to learn Christ, as the truth is in Christ, is to put off the old man and to put on the new man, which after God is created in righteousness and holiness" [Eph. 4:21–22].

Third, by this we learn to value and prize the knowledge of Christ above all things in the world. The angels of God themselves desire to profit in this knowledge. David, who in the darkness of the Old Testament, desired to be a doorkeeper in the house of God [Ps. 84:10], if he were now living on earth would be content with an office a thousand-fold more base that he might enjoy this clear light of the knowledge of Christ. But alas, there are no such Davids nowadays. It is our fault, and the fault of our times, that this knowledge is of little or no value and account among men. And little fruit thereof [is] to be seen. And, therefore, it is to be feared that God will take this treasure of knowledge from us, and send strong illusions to believe lies, because it is little or nothing loved [2 Thess. 2:11].

Paul yet further commends this knowledge in that he calls it "the knowledge of Christ, his Lord." Now He is our Lord [in] four ways: first, by the right of donation (because all the elect are given to Him by the Father in the eternal counsel of election); second, by creation; third, by the right of redemption; [and,] fourth, by right of headship, in that as a living head He gives sense and spiritual life to all who believe in Him. And Paul calls Christ "his Lord" because he believed his own election, in which he was given to Christ, his creation and redemption by Him, and his mystical conjunction with Him as with his head. And here Paul, in his example, teaches us two things.

The first [is] how we should know Christ and the doctrine of the gospel. For the right knowledge whereof there is required, besides general understanding of Christ and His benefits with general assent, a special application thereof. It is not sufficient to believe the election, redemption, justification, [and] glorification of God's people. But we must go further, and believe the very same things in ourselves. The reason may be taken from the contents of the gospel. For it contains two parts: the first is a promise in which Christ with all His benefits is offered and propounded unto us; [and] the second is a commandment to apply the said promise and the substance thereof to ourselves, and that by our faith [1 John 3:23]. And he who takes away this second part overthrows half the gospel of Christ. Here is the foundation of saving knowledge which justifies and brings eternal life, and the foundation of special faith [Isa. 53:11; John 17:3].

The second thing to be learned in Paul's example is that we are to resign ourselves (our bodies and souls) and to render all subjection to Christ. For in that he calls Him Lord, he professes himself to be the servant of Christ. The end of all preaching is to bring not only our words and deeds but also our secret thoughts in subjection [un]to Him [2 Cor. 10:5]. And the end why Christ sits in glory at the right hand of the Father is that every knee may bow unto Him, of things in heaven and earth. It behooves us, therefore, to live and carry ourselves in our places as true and unfeigned servants of Christ.

Degree 2

The second degree in Paul's gradation is that "he desires to gain Christ." Now to gain Christ is nothing else but to make Christ his gain, as appears by the opposition of the words. For he says, "he had deprived himself of all things (that is, made all things his loss) that he might gain Christ." And He is made our gain if two things are done. First, He must be made ours, that is, your Christ (or my Christ) in particular. Second, we must put our confidence in Him.

For the first, that Christ may be ours, a double consent is required: God's consent to give Christ, and our consent to receive Him. God's consent that Christ shall be ours is given in the revelation of the promise touching the woman's seed, made to our first parents, in the continual renewing of the said promise to our forefathers, in the incarnation and birth of Christ, in His passion, in the preaching of the gospel, in the administration of both the sacraments, baptism and the Lord's Supper. Our consent to receive Christ is given when we begin to believe in Him, yea, when we begin to be touched in our hearts for our sins and to hunger and thirst after Christ. And thus, by the concurrence of these two consents Christ is really made ours. And further yet, that He may be not only ours but also our gain, we must set and fix the whole confidence of our hearts upon Him alone for the forgiveness of our sins and the salvation of our souls. For where the gain is, there must the heart be. When riches increase, we may not set our hearts on them, because though they are good things, yet they are not our gain or treasure. Now Christ is not only a good thing unto us, but our gain and the very fountain of all good things. And, therefore, we must bestow our hearts on Him.

Hence, we learn that the popish religion teaches wickedness, for it maintains that we are not only to believe in God but also in the church.[18] It maintains a hope and confidence in saints, especially in the virgin Mary.[19] Lastly, it maintains a confidence in our own works [as long as] it is (as they say) in sobriety.[20] This is to make the creature our gain and to put down Christ our Redeemer.

Again, Paul had said in the former chapter that Christ was his gain both in life and death [Phil. 1:21] and yet now he says that "he still desires to gain Christ." And by his example we learn that in this life our affections must never be satisfied and filled with the desire of Christ till we have the full fruition of Him. Naturally our desires are insatiable in respect of riches, honors, [and] pleasures, but we must learn to moderate and stint ourselves in seeking earthly things, being content with the portion that God does allot us; and the insatiableness of our affections must be directed and turned upon Christ. The woman in the gospel, who had the bloody issue, desired but to touch the hem of His garment. We must go further, not only to touch Him, but also by our faith to lay hold on Him (as it were) with both the hands and to hang upon Him. Thomas desired for his contentation[21] but to put his finger into His side. We must set before our eyes Christ crucified and His precious blood (as it were) distilling afresh from His hands, feet, and side. And we must not only touch His blood, but sprinkle ourselves with it, yea, dip and (as it were) dive ourselves into it, body, soul, and all.

Degree 3

The third and last degree in Paul's gradation is that "he desires to be found in Christ." And here his desire is twofold: the first [is] "to be in Christ"; [and] the second [is] "to be found of God" in the day of judgment.

The first, to be in Christ, is to be taken out of the first Adam and to be united unto Christ as His very flesh or as a true member of His mystical body. Now this incorporation and union into Christ is a mystery, and for the better understanding of it four rules must be observed.

The first [is] that not only our souls are united to the soul or Godhead of Christ, but also that the whole person of him who believes is united to the whole person of Christ, for the Redeemer and they who are redeemed are united together. And Christ, God and man, redeemed us, not only in soul but also in body. Therefore, we believers have our whole persons united to the

---

18. In the margin: Remenses in Rom. 10:14.

19. In the margin: Thomas Becket in Maria spem totam ponit post Christum. Matth. Paris in Henrico. 2.

20. In the margin: Bellarm. tom. 3. de justific. l. 5. c. 7.

21. *Contentation*: contentment.

whole person of Christ. And Saint Paul says that "our very bodies are the members of Christ" (1 Cor. 6:15). And Christ Himself says that "we must eat his flesh and drink his blood, that we may be in him and he in us" (John 6:56).

The second rule is touching the order of this union: that we are first joined to the flesh of Christ and by His flesh to His Godhead. For that which brings us to have fellowship with God joins us to God. Now by the flesh of Christ we have our fellowship with God. It is as the veil of the temple whereby the high priest entered into the holy of holies and into the presence of God [Heb. 10:20]. Again, it serves as a pipe or conduit to derive the efficacy and operation of the Godhead unto us.

The third rule is that this union stands not in imagination but is a true and real conjunction. Neither does the distance of place (we being on earth and the flesh of Christ in heaven) hinder this union. The mind is united after a sort to the thing it minds. After the contract of marriage, two distinct persons, being a thousand miles asunder, remain one flesh. If nature affords thus much, why may not the like be found in the conjunction that is above nature?

The last rule is that the bond of this conjunction is one and the same Spirit, being both in Christ and us, first in Christ and then in us. Saint John teaches this, saying, "that Christ dwells in us by his Spirit given unto us" (1 John 3:24). Again, this Spirit works in us faith, which also knits us to Christ who, as Paul says, "dwells in our hearts by faith" (Eph. 3:17). And by this we further see that distance of place hinders not this union. The Spirit of God, being infinite, may dwell both in Christ and us. And our faith, though it is seated within our hearts, yet it can reach forth itself and apprehend Christ in heaven.

The second desire of Paul is that he "may be found of God to be in Christ," that is, that God would respect him as a member of Christ and accept him into His favor eternally for Christ. For the better understanding of this, the order that God uses in showing His love must be observed. First of all, He begins His love in Christ, whom He loves simply for Himself. Then, from Christ He descends to them who are united to Christ, considering them even as parts of Christ, whom also He loves, yet not simply but respectively in and for Christ. He who looks upon things of divers kinds through a green glass beholds them all to be green. Even so, they whom God respects in and for Christ are loved by God as He is loved, and righteous as He is righteous. And this is the thing which Paul desires, that in the day of judgment he may be thus respected.

Hence we learn that God will make an examination of all our hearts, lives, and works, in the day of judgment. For this finding, which Paul mentions, presupposes that God sees and observes our ways, and will one day certainly discover them, knowing even now certainly whether we are in Christ or not. For this cause, we are to call ourselves to an account, yea, to a straight account, for God will find out whatsoever is amiss, though we have skill to make fair shows before men. And we are withal to amend ourselves. Solomon, upon this ground, dissuades the young man from fornication: "Why shouldest thou my son take delight in a strange woman, seeing the ways of men are before the eyes of God, and he pondereth all their paths?" (Prov. 5:20–21). To this purpose the Jews have a saying worth our marking. "Write," say they, "three things in your heart, and you shall never sin: there is an eye that sees you, an ear that hears you, and a hand that writes all your sayings and doings in a book." And the cause of our manifold sins is that men falsely think that God neither sees nor hears them. Thus says David of his enemies: "They brag in their talk, and swords are in their lips, for, say they, who heareth us?" (Ps. 59:7).

Again, here we see Paul's care, yea, the pitch of all his desires and his principal forecast, that he might be found of God in the day of judgment to be a member of Christ. The like must be our care and forecast now in the time of this life. Yea, this must be the care of all cares, that we may be knit to Christ and so accepted of God when we shall rise to judgment. Christ bids us, "Watch and pray that we may stand before the Son of man" (Luke 21:36). And we cannot do this, unless we are incorporated into Christ. We are bidden first to seek the kingdom of heaven, and that is indeed to be in Christ. To be wise and circumspect in many matters, and yet to want forecast to compass our main and principal good, is the greatest folly of all. What is the fault of the foolish virgins? They were virgins as the wise; they carried the burning lamps of Christian profession. Likewise, they had oil, that is, the oil of grace. But, alas, they had not oil enough to furnish their lamps. Their fault was that they wanted forecast to furnish themselves with sufficient oil. And there is never sufficiency of oil till we are true and lively members of Christ. And this was their damnable folly, that they contented themselves with the name and profession of Christ, and had not a serious and special care indeed to be members of Christ.[22]

Therefore, let us now diligently endeavor to be that in this life which we desire to be found of God in the day of judgment. There are three judgments which we are to undergo: the judgment of men, of ourselves, and of God. The first two we may falsify, [but] the third we cannot. For we may deceive men, and we may deceive ourselves, but we cannot [deceive] God. It is the foundation of all good things to be engrafted into Christ, and for this cause all the forecast of our heads, all other cares and studies, should give place that this might be accomplished. Some man may hereupon demand what he should do that he might be in Christ? I answer, two things. First, he must break off all his sins, and turn unto God. Second, he must pray earnestly, even unto the death, that his

---

22. This paragraph break is not in the original.

heart may be knit to Christ. Again, it may be demanded, How it may be known of us that we are in Christ? Saint John answers, "Hereby we know that he dwelleth in us, by the Spirit which he hath given us" (1 John 4:13). And we may know that we have the Spirit of Christ if the same mind, inclination, and disposition, the like love of God and man, the like meekness, patience, and obedience are in us which were in Christ. For the same fruits argue the same Spirit.

The Degrees of Paul's Gains

"Not having mine own righteousness, which is of the law, but that which is of the faith of Christ" (v. 9). The apostle, having taught in general terms that Christ is his gain, here begins to declare the same in more particular sort. For he sets down a threefold gain which he desired to obtain of Christ. The first is "the righteousness of Christ." The second is "inward fellowship with Him." The third is "the resurrection of the body" to eternal glory.

Degree 1

Now this righteousness of Christ, which Paul makes his first gain, is handled in verse 9. For the better knowledge whereof, I will first open the meaning of the words. And first of all, it must be known that they are an exposition of the words which went before. For whereas Paul had desired to be found in Christ, now he shows his own meaning, that he desired therein nothing else but that he might be accepted by God for Christ's sake, and be esteemed righteous in His righteousness. And that this righteousness may be the better discerned, he sets down two sorts of justice: the one he refuses [and] the other he desires and chooses.

The righteousness refused, he calls "his own," because it is within him and it is exercised by the powers of his soul, namely his mind, will, [and] affections. He says further, it is "of the law," that is, of the works which the law requires. For, as Paul says, "the righteousness of the law is this, he that doth these things shall live therein" [Rom. 10:5].

Again, of the justice desired, he says it is "by the faith of Christ," that is, it arises of the obedience of Christ apprehended by faith. For in this manner to the Romans, he puts the faith of Christ for faith in the blood of Christ [Rom. 3:22, 25]. And whereas some man might haply say that even this righteousness is ours as the former, Paul adds further that "it is of God," wholly and only, and not of us either in whole or in part, being freely given by Him upon our faith, that is, when we believe.

In these few words Paul couches many weighty points of doctrine. I will distinctly propound them one by one.[23]

---

23. This paragraph break is not in the original.

Doctrine 1. First of all, he makes a double justice: one of the law [and] the other of the gospel. Yea, he opposes them as contraries in the case of justification. And that they may the better be conceived, he describes them severally.[24]

Touching the justice of the law, he sets it down by two things. First, he says it is within us, because it is nothing else but a conformity of heart and life to the will of God, revealed in the said law. And the law knows not the righteousness which is without us. Second, he notes the matter of it, that it consists of such virtues and works as the law prescribes.[25]

Now the justice of the gospel is likewise set forth by four things. First, it is not in us, but forth of us, because Paul opposes it to the righteousness which is ours, and within us. Second, Paul sets down the matter of it, or the person in whom it is, namely Christ. Of whom Jeremiah says, "Jehovah is our righteousness" [Jer. 23:6]. And Christ must be considered two ways: as God and as Mediator. According to these two respects He has a double righteousness. One as God, and that is infinite, and therefore incommunicable. The other as Mediator, [and that] is the obedience of Christ which He performed in His manhood, consisting of two parts: His sufferings in life and death, and His fulfilling of the law for us. And this very obedience, which is in Christ and not in us, is the very matter of the justice of the gospel. Third, Paul sets down the means whereby this justice is made ours, and that is faith, which does rest on Christ, and apply His obedience to us. Lastly, Paul sets down the author of this justice, and that is God, who of His grace and mercy freely gives Christ and His obedience unto us, when we believe. Out of these four points a definition of the justice of the gospel may be framed thus: it is the righteousness of the Mediator, namely the obedience of Christ, given us freely by God and received by our faith.

By this distinction of legal and evangelical justice, we learn the difference of the law and the gospel. The law promises life upon the condition of our works, or obedience performed according to the tenor of the law. The gospel requires not the condition of merit or of any work to be done on our parts in the case of our justification, but only prescribes us to believe in Christ and to rest on His obedience as our justice before the tribunal of God. Second, by this we learn that the Church of Rome, and the learned therein, are ignorant of the right difference between the law and the gospel. For they teach that the righteousness, which stands in our inherent virtues and works done by us, is required for justification as well in the gospel as in the law. And [they teach] that the difference lies only in this: that the law is more dark and without grace, [while] the gospel [is] more plain, having also the grace of God annexed unto it

---

24. This paragraph break is not in the original.
25. This paragraph break is not in the original.

to enable us in our own persons to do that which both law and gospel require. But this is indeed to make a confusion of the law and gospel, and to abolish the distinction of the twofold justice before named, which may not be.

Doctrine 2. The second point of doctrine delivered by Paul is that a sinner stands just before the tribunal seat of God, not by the justice of the law, but by the justice of faith, which is the obedience of Christ, without any works of ours. And because this point of doctrine is of great moment, and is withal oppugned by many, I will further confirm it by some special reasons.[26]

First of all, in the justification of a sinner God manifests His mercy and justice to the full. For, as Paul says, "he justifieth freely by his grace" [Rom. 3:24], and, in justifying "he is not only a justifier but also just" [v. 26]. Now this concurrence of mercy and justice is nowhere to be found but in the obedience of Christ, performed by Him in our room and stead. As for all Christian virtues and works of godly men, they are by mercy accepted by God, but they do not satisfy the justice of God according to the tenor of the law.[27]

Second, Paul in the epistle to the Romans, considering Abraham not as an idolater unconverted but as a believer, yea, as the father of all the faithful, says that then "he was justified without works" [Rom. 4:1], and that his faith (that is, the Messiah apprehended by his faith) was counted unto him for righteousness, long after his conversion. Now, as he who is a pattern for us to follow is justified, so must we be justified and not otherwise.[28]

Third, as by Adam's disobedience we are made sinners, so by Christ's obedience we are made righteous [Rom. 5:19]. But we are made sinners by Adam's disobedience imputed to us,[29] therefore we are made just by the obedience of Christ imputed. Bernard used this reason: "Whom another man's fault defiled, another man's water washed. Yet in calling it another man's fault, I do not deny it to be ours; otherwise, it could not defile us. But it is another man's because, we all not knowing of it, sinned in Adam. It is ours because we have sinned, though in another, and it is imputed to us by the just judgment of God, though it is secret. Yet, that you may not complain, O man, against the disobedience of Adam, there is given you the obedience of Christ, that being sold for naught, you may be redeemed for naught."[30] Again, the doctrine of imputed justice he teaches expressly, saying, "All are dead, that the satisfaction of one might be

---

26. This paragraph break is not in the original.
27. This paragraph break is not in the original.
28. This paragraph break is not in the original.
29. In the margin: Lira upon Rom. 5. & Bellar. de grat. ami. 1. 5. c. 17.
30. In the margin: In Dominica. 1. Epiph. serm. 1.

imputed to all, as he alone bore the sins of all."[31] Again, "Death is put to flight by the death of Christ, and the righteousness of Christ is imputed to us."[32]

Fourth, Paul says, "Christ is made unto us of God, justice" [1 Cor. 1:30], that is, justice imputed. For in the next words he says He is "made our sanctification," that is, our justice, not imputed but inherent.[33]

Fifth, as Christ was made sin, so we are made the justice of God. But Christ was made our sin not by any conveyance of any corruption into His most holy heart, but by imputation. We, therefore, are made the justice of God by like imputation. And lest any man should yet surmise that this justice is not imputed, but infused into us, Paul says, "We are made the justice of God in him" [2 Cor. 5:21], that is, in Christ. Hence, it follows manifestly that there is no virtue or work within us which justifies before God, and that our justice, whereby we are just in the sight of God and accepted to life eternal, is out of us, and placed in Christ. Thus much have the fathers observed upon this text of Paul. Augustine says that Christ was made sin that we might be made justice, not our justice but God's justice, neither in us but in Him, as He declared sin not to be His but ours, not placed in Him but in us.[34] Jerome says [that] Christ, being offered for us, took the name of sin that we might be made the righteousness of God in Him, "not ours nor in us." In the same manner speak Theophylact, Anselm, Sedulius presbyter, and others.[35]

Lastly, man, considered as a creature before his fall, owed unto God the fulfilling of the law, which as a certain tribute was daily to be paid unto Him. After the fall, he doubled his debt, because he then became debtor to God of a satisfaction due for the breach of the law. Now the payment of this double debt is our righteousness. But where may we find a sufficient payment for this debt? We ourselves by our sins daily increase the said debt. And our own works, though proceeding of faith, are no convenient payment, because we cannot by one debt pay another. And if we shall search through heaven and earth, there is nothing to be found that may stand for payment with God but the obedience of the Redeemer, which He has presented and laid down before the throne of the Almighty as an endless treasure to make payment on our behalf. And because the said obedience is a satisfaction for our unrighteousness, it is also our justice in the acceptation of God.[36]

---

31. In the margin: Epist. 150.
32. In the margin: Ad milites temp. c. 11.
33. This paragraph break is not in the original.
34. In the margin: Enchir. c. 41. & de verbis Apost. serm. 6.
35. This paragraph break is not in the original.
36. This paragraph break is not in the original.

By these and other reasons, it appears that nothing can absolve us before God and procure the right of eternal life but only the obedience of the Mediator Christ, God and man, and that without any virtue or work of ours.

Hence, it follows that the present Church of Rome corrupts the article of justification by mingling things together, which can no more be compounded and mingled together than fire and water, namely, the justice of the gospel with the justice of the law. For it makes a double justification. The first contains two parts: pardon of sin by the death of Christ, and the infused habit of charity. The second is by works, which (they say) do meritoriously increase the first justification and procure eternal life. Here we see the sovereign medicine of the gospel, namely remission of sins, tempered with the poison of the law. For though virtues and works prescribed in the law have their place as good gifts of God in our lives and conversations, yet when they are set up higher and brought within the circle of justification as meritorious causes they are put quite out of their place and are no better than poison, and hereupon [they] are termed by Paul, loss and dung.[37]

But such as desire to be termed Catholics allege for themselves against us that the obedience of Christ (that is, the righteousness of another) cannot possibly be our righteousness. I answer that the justice of another may be our justice, if it is really made ours. And this is true in Christ. For when we begin to believe in Him, though our persons remain evermore distinct and unconfounded, yet we are made one with Him, and according to the tenor of the evangelical covenant, we are given to Him and He to us, so as we may truly say "Christ is mine" as we can truly say "this house or this land is mine." Now if Christ is ours, then His obedience is not only His but ours also. [It is] His because it is in Him. [It is] ours because with Him it is given us by God.[38]

Again, they allege that when Paul refuses the righteousness of the law, he means nothing else but the works of the law which are performed by the strength of nature, and that he does not exclude the works of grace. I answer, it is false. For he speaks of himself in the time present when he was a Christian apostle; and, therefore, he excludes all righteousness of his own, which he had by the law even when he was an apostle. And the objection, "What then? Shall we sin that grace may abound?" [Rom. 6:1], cannot be inferred upon justification by works of grace, but upon a justification by the obedience of Christ imputed to us without all works of our own.

Again, that we are justified, not by the justice of the law, but by the justice of faith, here is the foundation of our comfort. For hereupon, if we are tempted

---

37. This paragraph break is not in the original.
38. This paragraph break is not in the original.

in the time of this life, we may oppose this justice against the tempter. If Satan pleads against us that we are sinners, and therefore subject to eternal damnation, let us answer him that the obedience of Christ has freed us from this damnation. If he pleads further that we never fulfilled the law and consequently that we have no right to eternal life, we must answer him that Christ fulfilled the law for us. If he shall vex and upbraid us with the consideration of our manifold wants and corruptions, let us tell him that as long as we turn unto God from all our evil ways, bewail our corruptions, and believe in Christ, all our wants are covered in His obedience. Again, if in the time of death, the fear and apprehension of the judgment and anger of God terrify us, we are to oppose this obedience of our Mediator to the judgment of God, and to put it between God's anger and us. Yea, we are to rest upon it, and to enfold and wrap our souls in it, and thus to present them to God. Isaiah the prophet says that the Messiah is "a place of refuge (shelter or shade) against the tempest (or burning heat of the wrath of God)" [Isa. 32:2]. And Paul says, "he is our propitiatory" [Rom. 3:25], to signify that as the propitiatory covered the ark and the law in the ark, which is the hand-writing against us, from the presence of God, so Christ covers our sins, and puts Himself between us and the indignation of His Father.

Doctrine 3. The third and last point of doctrine here delivered by Paul is that faith is the means to receive and obtain the obedience of Christ for our justice. That this may the better be conceived, four points are to be handled. (1) What this faith is? (2) How it is a means to obtain justice? (3) Whether alone by itself or by the help of other virtues? (4) When and how long it is the only means?

For the first, faith is a special gift of God whereby we believe Christ and His benefits to be ours. In the first place, I say it is a gift of God because it comes wholly from God and not from the mind or will of man. Thus, Paul says, "It is given you for Christ to believe in him" [Phil. 1:29]. And Christ our Savior says to two of His disciples: "O foolish and slow of heart to believe" [Luke 24:25]. If it is objected that when we first believe we then believe willingly, I answer [that] it is indeed so. Yet, this willingness is not in us by nature but by grace, because when God gives unto us the gift of faith, He gives us also to will to believe. None comes to Christ but he [who] is drawn by the Father. And to be drawn is when the unwilling will is changed, and by the power of God made a willing will.[39]

I add further that faith in the Messiah is a special gift for two causes. First, because it is a gift above not only corrupted [nature] but also above the first created nature. For it was never in man's nature by creation. Adam never had

---

39. This paragraph break is not in the original.

it. Neither did the moral law reveal it unto us, because it never knew this faith. Nevertheless, other virtues (as love of God and man, fear of God, etc.) are revealed by the law, and were in man's nature by creation. Again, whereas all other gifts of God are given to them who are ingrafted into Christ, faith is given to them who are to be ingrafted,[40] because it is the ingrafting, and therefore cannot be given to them who are already in Christ, but to them who are to be in Christ. Further, I say that by faith we believe Christ and His benefits to be ours. For this is the property of faith whereby it differs from all other graces of God. When Thomas had put his finger into the side of Christ, he said, "My Lord, and my God." To whom Christ replied, "Because thou hast seen, thou hast believed" [John 20:28–29]. Here we see that this is faith: to believe Christ to be our Lord and our God. Paul says, "I live by the faith of Christ." Now what he means by faith he shows in the next words: "who hath loved me and given himself for me" [Gal. 2:20].

If any man shall demand upon what grounds (because we are not to go by imagination) I say he is to conceive a faith that Christ is his Christ, I answer [that] the grounds are two. The first is the commandment of God to believe Christ and His benefits to be ours. "This is his commandment, that ye believe in the name of his Son Jesus Christ" (1 John 3:23). Now to believe in Christ is to put our confidence in Him. And we can put no confidence in Him unless we are first assured that He with His benefits is ours. And whatsoever we ask in prayer, we are commanded to believe that it shall be given unto us [Mark 11:24]. Now above all things we are to ask that Christ and His benefits may be given unto us by God. This, therefore, we must believe. The second ground is this: we must consider the manner that God uses in propounding the promise of grace unto us, for He does not only set it forth unto us in a general sort, but He also uses meet and convenient means to apply it to the persons of men. First of all, He confirms it by oath, so that we ourselves might the better apply it and reap sure consolation thereby [Heb. 6:18]. Second, God gives unto us the Spirit of adoption, who bears witness to our consciences of such things as God has given unto us in particular and are only in general manner propounded in the promise. And this testimony must be certain in itself, and also plainly known unto us, else it is no testimony. Third, both the sacraments are seals of the promise, in the lawful use whereof God offers, yea, exhibits, Christ unto us, and does (as it were) write our names within the promise, so that we might not doubt. Now then look, as God gives the promise, so we must by faith receive it. But God gives the promise and withal applies it; we therefore must receive the promise and by faith apply it to ourselves. If any man shall say that he cannot

---

40. In the margin: *Non insitis, sed mierendis.*

conceive a special faith upon these grounds by reason of his unbelief, I answer that he must strive against his unbelief and endeavor to believe by desiring, asking, seeking, [and] knocking. And God will accept the will to believe for faith itself, so be it there is an honest heart touched with sorrow for past sins and a purpose to sin no more.

That we may yet better know what faith is, understand that there are two kinds of false faith, like indeed to true faith and yet no faith at all. The first is when a man conceives in his heart a strong persuasion that Christ is his Savior, and yet carries in the same heart a purpose to sin and makes no change or amendment of his life. This persuasion is nothing but presumption, and a counterfeit of true faith whose property is to purify the heart and to show itself in the exercises of invocation and true repentance. The second is when men conceive a strong persuasion that Christ is their Savior, and yet for all this condemn and despise the ministry of the Word and sacraments. This also is another counterfeit. For true faith is conceived, cherished, and confirmed by the use of the Word and sacraments. And we must there seek Christ where God will give Him unto us. Now God gives Christ in the Word and sacraments. And in them He does (as it were) open His hand and reach forth all the blessings of Christ unto us. We must not, therefore, imagine to find Christ where and how we list, but we must seek Him in the Word and sacraments, and there we must receive Him if we desire to receive Him aright.

The second point to be considered is how faith is a means to justice? I answer thus. Faith does not justify as it is an excellent work of God in us, for then all virtues might be means of justification as well as faith. It does not justify as it is an excellent virtue in itself, because it is imperfect and mingled with unbelief. It does not justify as a means to prepare and dispose us to our justification, for so soon as we begin to believe in Christ we are justified without any disposition or preparation coming between faith and justification.[41] Lastly, it does not justify as it contains in it all other virtues and good works, as the kernel contains the tree with all its branches. For then it should be a part, yea, the principal part, of our justice, whereas Saint Paul distinguishes justice and faith, saying that "our righteousness is of God upon faith," and not "for faith" but "by faith." Now then, faith justifies as it is an instrument or hand to apprehend or receive the benefits of Christ for ours. And this apprehension is made when we do indeed believe Christ and His benefits to be ours. And lest any should imagine that the very action of faith in apprehending Christ justifies, we are to understand that faith does not apprehend by power from itself but by virtue of

---

41. In the margin: Chrysost. hom. 7 in Rom. *Quam primum homo credidit, confestim simul justificatus est.*

the covenant. If a man believes the kingdom of France to be his, it is not therefore his. Yet, if he believes Christ and the kingdom of heaven by Christ to be his, it is his indeed, not simply because he believes but because he believes upon commandment and promise. For in the tenor of the covenant, God promises to impute the obedience of Christ unto us for our righteousness if we believe.

The third point is whether faith alone is the means to obtain the justice of Christ for us or not? I answer, it is the only means without the help of any other virtue or work. For Paul here teaches that faith apprehends Christ for righteousness "without the law," that is, without anything that the law requires at our hands. And here by this exclusive particle, "without the law," he teaches three things. The first [is] that nothing within us is an efficient or meritorious cause, either principal or less principal, in whole or in part, of our justification or reconciliation with God. The second [is] that nothing within us is an instrument or means to apply the obedience of Christ unto us but faith which is ordained by God to be a hand to receive the free favor of God in the merit of Christ. The third [is] that our renovation or sanctification is no matter, form, or part of our justification, but that it wholly stands in the imputation of the justice of Christ. In a word, Paul utterly excludes all things that are within us, whether by nature or by grace, from the act of justification, so that in this article only grace, only Christ, only faith, [and] only mercy in pardon of sin, may reign.[42]

It may be here objected that Abraham was justified, not by faith alone, but by works, as Saint James teaches [James 2:21]. I answer [that] there is a double justification: one of the person whereby a man or a sinner is made no sinner; [and] the second is the justification of the faith of the person whereby faith is declared to be true faith. And this second is by works. And Saint James speaks of it, as appears in verse 18, where he says, "Show me thy faith by thy works." And whereas he says that "Abraham our father was justified by works," his meaning is that Abraham by works justified himself to be a true believer, yea, the father of all the faithful. And his faith was made perfect by works, that is, declared or justified to be a true faith [v. 22].

The fourth or last point is when and how long faith alone justifies? I answer, not only in the beginning of our conversion, but also in the continuance and final accomplishment thereof. For here Paul desires in the day of judgment to stand before God only by the justice of faith without his own justice of the law. And Paul brings in Abraham (as I have noted before) in the very midst of godly conversation and holy obedience to be justified without any works by his faith in the Messiah [Rom. 4:2–3]. And Paul avouches three things of faith: (1) by it "we have access" to the grace of God; (2) by it we "stand in the same

---

42. This paragraph break is not in the original.

grace"; [and] (3) by it "we rejoice under the hope of glory" [Rom. 5:2]. Thus then, we see there is only one way of justification, namely that we are justified and accepted of God to life eternal through grace alone by faith alone for Christ alone in the beginning, middle, and end of our conversion. And here is plainly discovered the error of the Church of Rome. It makes a double justification: the first [is] whereby a sinner is made of an evil man a just man, and this (they say) is by faith alone; [and] the second is whereby a man of a just man is made more just, and this (they say) is by faith and works together. But [they speak] falsely, as I have shown.

By all this which has been said, we see how righteousness comes by and upon the faith of Christ. And hence we learn that it stands us in hand to prove whether we have faith or not, because where [there] is no faith, there is no justice. Second, our duty is to labor for such a faith that can and does justify itself to be true faith, by works of love to God and men. Third, we must by this faith rest and wholly rely ourselves on the obedience of Christ both in life and death, yea, whatsoever does befall us. Though God should reach out His hand and destroy us, we must still rest upon Him.

Second, if our justice is forth of us, and we must by faith trust God for it, then much more must we trust Him for health, wealth, liberty, peace, food, raiment, and for all the things of this life. And if we cannot trust Him in the less, we shall never trust Him in the principal. Therefore, it is our part to walk in the duties of our callings, and to obey God therein, and for the success of our labors to trust Him upon His Word; yea, when all worldly helps and succors fail, to trust Him still. If we cannot trust Him for our temporal life, we shall never trust Him for our salvation.

Degree 2
The second gain, which Paul desires, is fellowship with Christ. In verse 10 it is first set forth generally, and then by its parts. Generally in these words: "that I may know him." Here it must be remembered that knowledge is twofold: knowledge by faith and [knowledge] by experience. Knowledge by faith is to be assured of Christ and His benefits, though it is against all human reason, hope, and experience. Of this Christ says, "It is eternal life to know thee the only God" [John 17:3]. Knowledge by experience is to have a sense and feeling of our inward fellowship with Christ, and upon often observation of His goodness to grow more and more in experience of His love. Now this knowledge is here meant, and not the first, which was before mentioned in verse 8. And, therefore, Paul's desire is that he may grow more and more in holy experience of the endless love of God and fellowship with Christ.

The parts of this desired communion are two: fellowship with Christ in His resurrection, and fellowship with Him in His death.

Christ's Resurrection

The former is expressed in these words: "and the virtue of his resurrection." And for the better conceiving of it, we are to consider what the resurrection of Christ is? And what is the virtue thereof?

What it is? That the resurrection of Christ may be rightly conceived, five points are to be scanned.[43]

The first [concerns] the person of Him who arose, and that was Christ, God and man. Indeed, the body alone did properly rise, and not the soul or Godhead. Yet, by reason of the union of the two natures in the unity of one person, [the] whole Christ arose, or God Himself (made man) arose. This commends unto us the excellency of Christ's resurrection, and makes it to be the foundation unto us of our resurrection.

The second point is for whom He arose? He arose not as a private person for Himself alone, but He arose in our room and stead, and that for us; so as when He arose all the elect arose with Him and in Him. Thus says Paul, that the Ephesians "were raised together with him" [Eph. 2:6]. His resurrection, therefore, was public. And this is the ground of our comfort.

The third point is when He arose? He arose then, when He lay in bondage under death, and that in the grave, which is (as it were) the castle and hold of death. When Peter says that "God loosed the sorrows of death,"[44] he signifies that Christ was made captive for a time to the first death and to the sorrows of the second. Now in the midst of this captivity and bondage, He raised Himself. And this argues that His resurrection is a full victory and conquest over death and all our spiritual enemies.

The fourth point is that He arose by His own power, as He says of Himself, "I have power to lay down my life, and to take it up again" [John 10:18]. If this had not been, though He had risen a thousand times by the power of another, He had not been a perfect Redeemer.

The last point is wherein stands the resurrection of Christ? *Answer:* It consists in three actions of Christ. The first is the reuniting of His body to His soul, both [of] which were severed for a time, though neither of them was severed from the Godhead. The second action is the change of His natural life, which He led in the estate of humiliation, into a heavenly and spiritual life without infirmities, and not maintained by food as before. For we find not that after His resurrection He ever took meat for necessity, but only upon occasion, to manifest the truth of His manhood. And this life He took unto Himself that He

---

43. The paragraph breaks for these "five points" are not in the original.
44. Acts 2:24.

might convey it to all who should believe in Him. The third action is His coming forth of the grave whereby death itself did (as it were) acknowledge Him to be a conqueror, and that it had no title or interest in Him.

These five things considered, the article of Christ's resurrection shall be rightly understood.

What is its virtue? Touching the virtue of Christ's resurrection, it is nothing else but the power of His Godhead, or the power of His Spirit, whereby He raised Himself mightily from death to life, and that on our behalf. The excellency of it may be known by the effects, which are eight in number.[45]

The first [is] that by it He showed Himself to be the true and perfect Savior of the world. For it was foretold of the Messiah that He should die and rise again (Ps. 16:10; Matt. 12:40). And all this was accordingly accomplished by the virtue of Christ's resurrection.

The second effect is that by it He showed Himself to be the true and natural Son of God. Paul says, "He was declared mightily to be the Son of God, by the Spirit of holiness in his rising from the dead" [Rom. 1:4].

The third effect is that by this virtue He declared Himself to have made a full and perfect satisfaction for the sins of the world, for if He had not satisfied to the full, He had not risen again. And Paul says, "If Christ be not risen we are yet in our sins" [1 Cor. 15:17]. On the contrary then, seeing He is risen, such as believe in Him are not in their sins. Again, "Who shall condemn us? it is Christ which is dead, yea or rather which is risen again" [Rom. 8:34].

The fourth effect is justification, as Paul testifies, "He died for our sins, and rose again for our justification" [Rom. 4:25]. And that was in this manner: when He was upon the cross, He stood there in our room, having our sins imputed unto Him, and when He arose from death He acquitted and justified Himself from our sins, and ceased to be any more a reputed sinner for us. And thus, all that do or shall believe in Him are in Him acquitted, absolved, and justified from all their sins. If any demands how they who lived in the time of the Old Testament, before the resurrection of Christ, could be justified thereby, considering the effect must follow the cause, I answer that they were justified by the future resurrection of Christ, which, though it followed in time, yet did the value and virtue thereof reach even to the beginning of the world.

The fifth effect is the conferring and bestowing of all such gifts and graces as He had merited and procured for us by His death and passion. Thus, Christ testifies that the giving of the Spirit in large and plentiful manner was reserved to the glorification of Christ [John 7:39], which began in His resurrection. And

---

45. The paragraph breaks for these "eight effects" are not in the original.

the preaching of repentance and remission of sins is reserved till after His resurrection [Luke 24:47]. And Saint Peter says that the elect are "regenerate to a lively hope by the resurrection of Christ" [1 Peter 1:3]. By reason of this bestowing of graces and gifts, the resurrection of Christ is the beginning of a new and spiritual world which the Holy Spirit calls "the world to come" [Heb. 2:5], in which shall be a new heaven and a new earth, as Isaiah speaks [Isa. 65:17], and a peculiar people of God, zealous of good works, keeping an eternal Sabbath unto God. This one effect alone sufficiently declares the excellency of this virtue of Christ.

The sixth effect is vivification, which is a raising of us from the death of sin to newness of life. And the reason hereof is plain. For Christ in His resurrection put away His natural life, which with our nature He received from Adam, and took unto Him a spiritual life, that He might communicate the said life to all who believe in Him. Again, as the first Adam makes us like himself in sin and death, so Christ, the second Adam, renews us and makes us like to Himself in righteousness and life. And the head quickened with spiritual life will not suffer the members to remain in the death of sin.

The seventh effect is to preserve safe and sound the gifts and graces which He has procured by His death and bestowed on them who believe. And He does this by the virtue of His resurrection. For to this end He has conquered all our spiritual enemies and does by His power conquer them still in us, so as none shall be able to take His sheep out of His hands.

The last effect is to raise the body from the grave in the day of judgment to eternal glory. If it is objected that the wicked are also raised then by the power of Christ [Rom. 8:11], I answer that the power of Christ is twofold: one is the power of judgment [and] the other [is] a power of a Savior. By the first, Christ, as a Judge, raises the ungodly, that He may execute on them the curse denounced from the beginning of the world: "at what time thou shalt eat the forbidden fruit, thou shalt die the death" [Gen. 2:17]. The second power is here termed the power of Christ's resurrection. And it belongs to Him as He is our Savior, and by it He will raise to eternal life all those who by the bond of the Spirit are mystically united to Him. For by means of this union this raising power shall flow from the head to the dead bodies of them who are in Christ.

Thus we see what the virtue here mentioned is and what Paul desires, namely that he may have experience of these effects in himself.

The Use
The use of the doctrine follows. First of all, in that Christ arose for us, and in that His resurrection is of endless efficacy, here is the foundation of all our spiritual comfort. For by this virtue of Christ's resurrection from death to life, all

our spiritual enemies are conquered and subdued, and by the said virtue does He daily more and more subdue them in us. Upon this ground Christ said, "Ye shall have affliction in the world: but be of good comfort, I have overcome the world" [John 16:33]. And this victory is for us, and it is made ours by our faith, as John says, "This is the victory which overcomes the world, even your faith" [1 John 5:4]. Are you then terrified and afraid with the conscience of your sins, the cruelty of tyrants, the rage of the world, the pains of hell, the pangs of death, the temptations of the devil? Be not dismayed, but by your faith rest on Christ who arose again from death to life for you, and thereby showed Himself to be a Rock for you to rest on, and to be the Lion of the tribe of Judah. And thus you shall find certain remedy against all the troubles and miseries of life and death.

Second, here we are taught to rise with Christ from our sins, and to live unto God in newness of life. And for this end to pray that we may feel the virtue of Christ's resurrection to change and renew us. Great are the benefits which we reap by this virtue, and we are to show ourselves thankful to God for them, which we can do no [other] way but by newness of life. Again, the end why Christ rose for us was that we might rise from our sins and corruptions in which we lie buried as in a grave to a new spiritual life [Rom. 6:4]. And the reward is great to them who make this happy change. For he who is "partaker of the first resurrection shall never see the second death" (Rev. 20:6). As on the contrary, he who never rises from his own sins and evil ways shall certainly feel and endure the second death.[46]

And further, it must be known that the virtue of Christ's resurrection and the merit of His death are inseparably joined together. And, therefore, he who finds not the virtue of Christ to raise him to a holy and spiritual life acceptable to God, falsely persuades himself of the merit of His death in the remission of his sins. Christ, by rising, put under His feet all our enemies, and led captivity captive, even sin itself. It is, therefore, a shame for us to walk in the ways of sin and to make ourselves slaves and captives to it. Christ, by rising from death, made Himself a principal leader and guide to eternal life [Acts 3:15]. What wickedness, then, it is to walk in the ways of our own heart, and not to follow this heavenly guide. The care and purpose to keep a good conscience is a certain fruit and effect of Christ's resurrection. Thus, Saint Peter says that the effect of our baptism is the stipulation of a good conscience by the resurrection of Christ (1 Peter 3:21). Here the word which I translate "stipulation"[47] signifies an interrogation upon an interrogation. For the minister in the name of God demands whether we renounce the world, the flesh, and the devil, and take the

---

46. This paragraph break is not in the original.
47. In the margin: ἐπερώτημα.

true God for our God. And we, upon this demand, do further in our hearts demand of God whether He will vouchsafe to accept us, being wretched sinners, for His servants. And thus we make profession of our mind and desire.[48]

When Christ arose, by the virtue of His resurrection the earth trembled, and thereby this brute creature in his kind professed his subjection and homage to Christ who rose again. If then we believe that Christ arose from death for us, much more should our hearts tremble and we yield ourselves in subjection to Him in all spiritual obedience. Some man may say, "You bid us rise from our sins as Christ rose to the glory of His Father, whereas this is wholly God's work in us, and not ours." I answer, it is indeed so. Yet, we can use the outward means of hearing and reading, and if we have any spark of grace we can ask and desire the Spirit of God who works this in us. Again, exhortations, admonitions, and such like, are means appointed by God whereby He works in us the thing which He requires and commands. Wherefore, let us listen to the voice of Christ. "Awake thou that sleepest, stand up from the dead, and Christ shall give thee life" [Eph. 5:14]. And worldly cares must not hinder us in this work, for as Paul says, they who are risen with Christ must seek the things that are above [Col. 3:1].

Again, here we are taught that we may not content ourselves if we know Christ in the brain and can speak well of Him with a glib tongue. We must go yet further, and by all means labor that we taste and feel by experience how good and sweet a Savior Christ is unto us, so that our hearts may be rooted and grounded in His love. This is the thing which Paul aimed at. We must also seek it by all possible means to attain unto.

Christ's Death

To proceed, that we may have [a] right knowledge of our communion with Christ in His death, two points are to be handled.[49]

The first is: What are the sufferings of Christ? I answer, not only the sufferings which He endured in His own person, but also those which are endured by His members. Thus, Saul, persecuting the church, is said to persecute Christ Himself [Acts 9:4]. And Paul says that "he fulfilled the rest of the afflictions of Christ in his own flesh" (Col. 1:24). And whereas the Lord said of the people of Israel, "I have brought my son out of Egypt" (Hos. 11:1), it is applied by Saint Matthew to Christ Himself. Yet, here it must be remembered that if the members of Christ suffer either civil or ecclesiastical punishments for evil doing, they are not the sufferings of Christ. For when Saint Peter had said, "Rejoice in

---

48. This paragraph break is not in the original.
49. This paragraph break is not in the original.

that you are partakers of the sufferings of Christ," he adds further, "Let no man suffer as an evil doer," opposing the one kind of sufferings to the other (1 Peter 4:13–15). Therefore, our sufferings are then to be accounted the sufferings of Christ when they are for [a] good cause and for the name of Christ.

For the second point, fellowship with Christ in His death is either within us or without us. That within us is called the mortification of the flesh or the crucifying of the affections and the lusts thereof. The other, without us, is the mortification of the outward man by manifold afflictions, and of this Paul speaks in this place. And it may be thus described out of this text: fellowship with Christ in His death is nothing but a conformity in us to His sufferings and death. And it is a thing worthy [of] our consideration to search wherein stands this conformity. For there is no conformity between our sufferings and the sufferings of Christ in two respects. For, first of all, God poured forth on Christ the whole malediction of the law due to our sins, and by this means [He] showed upon Him justice without mercy. Contrariwise, in our afflictions God moderates His anger, and in justice [He] remembers mercy, because He lays no more upon us than we are able to bear [1 Cor. 10:13]. Second, Christ's sufferings are a redemption and satisfaction to God's justice for our sins. Ours are not so, because before God we stand but as private persons, and for this cause the sufferings of one man cannot satisfy for another, and there is no proportion between our sufferings and the glory which shall be revealed. And Christ says of Himself, "I have tread the wine-press alone" (Isa. 63:3).

Now this conformity stands (as I take it) properly in the manner of suffering, and that in four things.[50]

First of all, Christ suffered for a just and righteous cause, for He suffered as our Redeemer, the righteous for the unrighteous. And so, we must likewise suffer for righteousness's sake [Matt. 5:10].

Second, Christ in suffering was a mirror of all patience and meekness [1 Peter 2:21]. And we in our sufferings must show the like patience. And that we are not deceived herein, our patience must have three properties. (1) It must be voluntary, that is, we must willingly and quietly renounce our own wills, and subject ourselves in our sufferings to the will of God. Patience perforce is no patience. (2) It must not be mercenary, that is, we must suffer not for by-respects (as for praise or profit) but for the glory of God, and that we may show our obedience to Him. Hence, it appears that the patience of the papist, who suffers in way of satisfaction, is not right patience. (3) Our patience must be constant. If we endure afflictions for a brunt, and afterwards begin to grudge

---

50. The paragraph breaks for these "four things" are not in the original.

and repine, casting off the yoke of Christ, we fail in our patience. Further, if it is demanded whether the affections of grief and sorrow may stand with patience, I answer, yea, for Christian religion does not abolish these affections, but only moderates them, and brings them in subjection to the will of God when we lie under the cross.

The third point wherein stands our conformity with the sufferings of Christ is this: Christ learned obedience by the things which He suffered (Heb. 5:8), not because He was a sinner but because, being righteous, He had experience of obedience. And we likewise in our sufferings must be more careful to take the fruit thereof than to have them taken away. And their fruit is to learn obedience thereby, especially to the commandments of faith and repentance. When Job was afflicted by God, not for his sins, but that He might make a trial of his faith and patience, he nevertheless in the end took an occasion thereby to renew his old repentance [Job 42:6]. And Paul says that he received in his own flesh the sentence of death that he might learn by faith to trust in God alone [2 Cor. 1:9].

Lastly, Christ's sufferings were even to death itself. Even so, we must resist sin, fighting against it to the shedding of our blood [Heb. 12:4]. Faith and good conscience are things more precious than the very blood of our hearts. And, therefore, if need be, we must conform ourselves to Christ, even in the pains of death.

This is that conformity of which Paul speaks here, which he also magnifies as a special gain. And there are many reasons thereof. First of all, this conformity is a mark of God's child. For "if we obediently endure afflictions," God in them and by them offers Himself as a Father unto us [Heb. 12:7]. Second, it is a sign that the Spirit of God dwells in us. As Peter says, "If ye be railed upon for the name of Christ, the Spirit of glory and of God resteth upon you" (1 Peter 4:14). Third, the grace of God is most of all manifested in afflictions, in which God seems most of all in man's reason to withdraw His grace. "God's power is made manifest in weakness" [2 Cor. 12:9]. "Afflictions bring forth patience" [Rom. 5:3], not of themselves, but because then the love of God is shed abroad in our hearts [Rom. 5:5]. Hope of eternal life shows itself most in the patient bearing of afflictions [Rom. 15:4]. In peace and ease natural life reigns. Contrariwise, in our sufferings natural life decays, and the spiritual life of Christ apparently shows itself. Lastly, this conformity with Christ is the right and beaten way to eternal life [2 Cor. 4:11]. "By many tribulations we must enter into the kingdom of heaven" [Acts 14:22]. That we may reign and live with Christ, we must first die with Him [2 Tim. 2:11]. The estate of humiliation is the way to the estate of exaltation and glory, first in Him and then in us.

The Use

The use of this doctrine follows. Here we see what, for this life, is the condition of all true believers, namely, that after they are made partakers of Christ and His benefits by the virtue of His resurrection, they must also be made conformable to His death. The commandment of our Savior Christ to them who will be His disciples is "to deny themselves and to take up their own crosses every day" (Luke 9:23). And there are three weighty causes why God will have it so. (1) That He may correct past sins [2 Corinthians 12]. (2) That He may prevent sins to come [1 Corinthians 11]. (3) That He may prove what is in our hearts.

Second, we learn, by this which has been said, to comfort ourselves in our sufferings. For in them Christ and we are partners, and He vouchsafes to make us His fellows. Hence, it follows that all our afflictions are well known to Christ, and that they are laid on us with His consent. And for this cause we should frame ourselves to bear them with all meekness. And hence again, we learn that He, being our partner, will help us to bear them, either by moderating the weight of them or by ending them for our good.

Lastly, here we learn that our afflictions are either blessings or benefits. And we may discern them to be such, though not by the light of reason, yet by the eye of faith, because they are means to make us conformable to our Head, Christ Jesus. Benefits of God are of two sorts: positive and privative. Positive, whereby God bestows something on us. Privative, whereby God takes away a blessing and covertly gives another. Benefits of this kind are afflictions. Of the two, these are the rifer[51] for the time of this life, and the other for the life to come. And, therefore, while we live in this world, our duty is with Paul to labor to attain to this conformity with the sufferings of Christ, when upon any occasion we shall be afflicted, for then we shall be fashioned like unto Him, and reap much comfort thereby.

Thus much of the second gain.

Degree 3

Now follows the third in these words: "If by any means, I may attain to the resurrection of the dead." The word "resurrection" here signifies the reward of eternal life, the antecedent being put for the consequent. For to rise again of itself is no gain, considering it is common both to good and bad, but eternal life that follows is the reward. And the form of speech, "if by any means," does not signify or imply any doubting in Paul of his own resurrection to life, for he was persuaded that nothing should separate him from Christ, and it is an article of our and Paul's faith to believe the resurrection of the body to eternal life [Rom. 8;

---

51. *Rifer*: more prevalent.

2 Tim. 1:12]. Wherefore, it signifies properly a difficulty to obtain the gain desired, and an earnest affection in Paul to obtain the same. And when he says, "by any means," we must know that there are three ways or means to come to eternal life. One is by peaceable life and death. The other is by a life laden with many afflictions. The third is by a violent, cruel, and bloody end. And Paul's mind and desire is to obtain the crown of eternal glory by any of these ways, and if not by the first or second, yet by the third. In these words four things are to be considered.

Point 1. The first is the gain itself, and that is the reward of eternal glory. And that we may the more with Paul be stirred up to a desire thereof, I will stand a while to declare the excellency and the conditions of it. It is nothing else but a certain estate of life in which all the promises of God are in and by Christ accomplished unto us in heaven. And it will the better be conceived by the answering of three questions: (1) What shall cease in this estate? (2) What shall we have? (3) What shall we do?

For the first, seven things shall cease. The first is the execution of the mediatorship of Christ, or of the offices of a king, priest, [and] prophet. Thus much teaches Paul when he says that Christ in the last day "must give up his kingdom to his Father" (1 Cor. 15:24). And though the execution shall then cease, yet nothing shall be wanting to them who believe, because then shall be the full and eternal fruition of all the benefits of our redemption. Second, then shall cease all callings in family, church, and commonwealth, because Christ shall then put down all power, rule, and authority (1 Cor. 15:24). In this blessed estate, there shall not be magistrate and people, master and servant, husband and wife, parents and children, pastor and people, but all such outward distinctions of persons shall cease, and we shall be as the angels of God. Third, all virtues that pertain to us (as we are pilgrims here upon earth) shall have an end, as faith, hope, [and] patience, because the things believed and hoped for shall then be obtained. Withal that part of invocation called petition shall cease, as also the preaching and hearing of the Word and the use of sacraments [1 Cor. 13:13]. The fourth thing that shall cease is original sin with the fruits thereof, because no unclean thing may enter into the heavenly Jerusalem. Fifth, then shall cease all miseries and sorrows, all infirmities of body and mind [Rev. 21:4], for then all defects of eyes, arms, and legs, shall be restored. The sixth thing that shall cease is natural life with the means thereof, as meat, drink, clothing, physic, [and] recreation. For then our bodies shall be spiritual, that is, immediately and eternally preserved by the operation of the Spirit of God, as now the body of Christ is in heaven. The last thing to be abolished is the vanity of the creatures, especially of heaven and earth, which in the last judgment shall again be restored to their former excellency [Acts 3:21].

The second question is: What shall we have and enjoy in this estate? I answer, three things. The first is immediate and eternal fellowship with God the Father, Son, and Holy Spirit [1 Cor. 15:28]. For in this happy estate the tabernacle of God shall be with men, as Saint John says [Rev. 21:3]. And God shall be all things that heart can wish to all the elect. Augustine says notably, "There shall be exceeding peace in us, and among us, and with God Himself. Because we shall see Him, and enjoy Him always and everywhere. Therefore, blessed shall that life be for the thing which we shall enjoy, for we shall enjoy God Himself, all other means ceasing. For the measure of enjoying Him, for we shall fully enjoy Him. For the time, for we shall eternally enjoy Him. For the certainty, whereby we shall know that it shall be so. For the place, for we shall enjoy Him in heaven. Lastly, for the companions joined with us, for they shall be the elect."[52] From this fruition of God shall arise endless and unspeakable joy. "In thy presence is fullness of joy, at thy right hand are pleasures for evermore" (Ps. 16:11). In the transfiguration of Christ, which was but a shadow of the eternal glory, Peter was ravished with joy and delight [Matthew 17]. The joy, therefore, which shall be in heaven must needs be unspeakable. The second thing which shall be enjoyed is glory both in mind and body. In mind, because we shall then be partakers of the divine, not essence (for then we should be deified), but nature, that is, divine virtues and qualities [2 Peter 1:4], more excellent than those which God bestowed on Adam, though of the same kind. The glory of the body is to be changed and made like the glorious body of Christ [Phil. 3:21]. The third thing is dominion and lordship over heaven and earth, which lordship once lost by Adam shall then fully be restored. He who overcomes "shall possess all things" (Rev. 21:7).

The third question is: What shall we do? I answer briefly. [We shall] keep an eternal Sabbath in praising of God and giving thanks unto Him.

And thus by the consideration of these things, we may take a taste of the excellency of this third and last gain.

Point 2. The second point here to be considered is the difficulty of obtaining this desired gain of eternal life. And the reason is plain, for the way to eternal life is full of impediments, which I reduce to four heads. First of all, in this way we are to fight, not with flesh and blood, but with principalities and powers in spiritual things seeking the destruction of our souls [Eph. 6:12]. Second, there are within us innumerable lusts that compass us round about, press us down,

---

52. In the margin: Sermon de Temp. 148.

and draw us away to the broad way of destruction [Heb. 12:1; James 1:14]. Third, this way lies full of offences, partly in doctrines [and] partly in evil examples, all tending to this end, either to make us fall or to go out of the way. Lastly, it is beset with manifold tribulations from the beginning to the end [Rom. 8:35].[53]

Hence, we learn that we must give all diligence that we may attain to the reward of glory. And, therefore, we must struggle, strive, and wrestle to enter in at the strait gate [Matt. 7:13]. The principal gain, and the hardness to obtain it, requires our principal study and labor. Therefore, they deal wickedly who use no means but (as they say) leave all to God, thinking it the easiest matter in the world to win the kingdom of heaven. The like is their fault who profess religion in a slack and negligent manner, being neither hot nor cold.

Point 3. The third point is Paul's mind and desire of eternal life. If it is said that wicked men have the like desire, as for example Balaam, I answer [that] in Paul there was an endeavor answerable to his desire, as appears in Acts 24:16, where he says, "that he waited for the resurrection of the just and unjust," and that in the mean season "he labored to keep a good conscience before God and men." Now this desire in the ungodly is barren and yields not its fruit. Again, Paul, being justified, still desires to attain to full fellowship with Christ and to conformity with Him in glory. The like desire, with the like endeavor, should be in us.

Point 4. The last point is Paul's courage and fortitude. He is content to endure any kind of death, yea, cruel death, so [that] he may obtain this third and last gain. And thus, it is verified [that] which he says, "that God *had given him* the spirit, not of fearfulness, but of courage" (2 Tim. 1:7). The courage of Moses was the same. [He] was content to endure afflictions with the people of God, that he might win the recompense of reward [Heb. 11:26]. The courage of the martyrs was the same. [They] "were racked and would not be delivered, that they might obtain a better resurrection" [v. 35]. We likewise, walking in the way to eternal life, must take the like courage unto us in all dangers. For this cause, we must pray unto God to give us the Spirit of courage. And we must always attend upon the calling and commandment of God, making it the stay and foundation of our courage. And we must yet further stay ourselves on the promise of God's presence and protection, so long as we obey Him.[54]

If it is alleged that we are by nature fearful in dangers, and therefore incapable of courage, I answer [that] there is a threefold fear. The first is fear of nature, when man's nature fears, flies, and eschews that which is hurtful unto it. This

---

53. This paragraph break is not in the original.
54. This paragraph break is not in the original.

fear was in Christ, whose soul was heavy unto death [Heb. 5:7], who also feared the cursed death which He endured. And, therefore, this fear of itself is no sin, and it may stand with true fortitude. The second fear is that which arises from the corruption of nature, when a man fears without cause or without measure. Without cause, as when the disciples feared Christ walking upon the sea, or when they feared drowning, Christ lying asleep in the ship. Without measure, as when men, distrusting God, neglect their callings in time of danger, and the duty of invocation, flying to unlawful means of deliverance. Now this second fear is an enemy unto all true courage. The third fear is when perils and death are indeed feared, but yet fear is ordered by faith in the mercy and providence of God, by hope [and] invocation, and it is joined with obedience to God in the time of danger. This is a proceeding of grace, and it may well stand with courage, and it serves to order the two former fears, the one of nature [and] the other of distrust.

Trin-uni Deo gloria

A Faithful and Plain Exposition upon Zephaniah 2:1–2

By that reverend and judicious divine, M. William Perkins.

Containing a powerful exhortation to repentance, as also the manner how men in repentance are to search themselves.

Published by a preacher of the Word.

With a Preface prefixed, touching the publishing of M. Perkins's works. And a catalogue of all such particulars thereof, as are to be expected.

The fifth impression

"He that hideth his sins shall not prosper. But he that confesseth and forsaketh them, shall find mercy" (Prov. 28:13).

Printed by T. C. for William Welby
London
1609

The Epistle Dedicatory

To the Right Worshipful, my very worthy and Christian friend, Sir William Gee, Knight, one of his majesty's honorable Council in the north, Recorder of the towns of Beverley and Hull, and one of his majesty's Justices of Peace in the east-riding of the county of York, a true friend of learning and piety; and to the virtuous and religious Lady, his wife; grace and peace from God, etc.

Among the many reasons (worshipful sir) which have persuaded me that popery cannot be the true religion, this is not the least: the insufficiency of their doctrine of faith and repentance. These two things, though they are the chief and principal points in religion, and so necessary that he who does not but know and practice them aright can never be saved, yet I dare avouch that the faith and repentance of the Romish church, as they are taught by many of the best approved papists,[1] are no better than such a faith and such a repentance as a hypocrite and a very reprobate may attain unto. Indeed, to insist upon repentance only (they make many fair flourishes),[2] they call it penance, make it a sacrament, and say it is a board that saves a man after shipwreck, and write great volumes about it and of *Confession* and of *Cases of Conscience* (as you, good sir, in your own reading, know better than I), and yet alas, when all is done, it is but a shadow of repentance.[3]

And, indeed, how can they teach aright the doctrine of repentance, who err so foully in setting down the justice of God and the vileness of sin? A man must know these two points, else he will never repent. But popery misconceives the justice of God, teaching it not to be infinite in as much as it needs not an infinite satisfaction, and [it] misconceives the nature of sin, teaching every sin not to be damnable nor to offend God's infinite justice. Erring (I say) in these two, how is it possible they should conceive aright the nature of repentance by which a man seeing his sins, their foulness [and] their punishment, and his own misery by them, confesses them, bewails them, fearing God's justice, flies from it, and craves forgiveness of His mercy, and lastly purposes and endeavors to leave

---

1. In the margin: Canit. in Catechis. Costerus in Enchir.
2. In the margin: Corradus, Navarus, Loper Sairus, Graffus, Hallus, and many others.
3. This paragraph break is not in the original.

them all and to lead a new life? The serious consideration hereof has often made me wonder why many popish treatises, being in some sort exhortations to repentance, should be so accounted of as they are by some. For though I confess there are in some of them good and wholesome meditations and many motives to mortification and good life, yet I would gladly learn of any man but this one thing, how those exhortations can be pithy, powerful, sound, or any way sufficient to move a man to repentance, when as not those books nor all popery are able to teach a man sufficiently what true repentance is.

If any man replies, "I will therefore learn the doctrine out of the Protestants' books and use the papists for exhortation only," I then answer: Is it not a more compendious and convenient, and a less scandalous course, to seek exhortations out of such writers as do teach the doctrine aright? Nay, I doubt how it is possible to find powerful exhortation to repentance in any papist, who errs in the doctrine. The reason is manifest, because doctrine is the ground of exhortation. And if the doctrine is unsound, how can the exhortation be any better? Let us, therefore, leave these muddy puddles, and set[4] our water at the fountain. [Let us get] the water of life at the fountain of life: I mean the doctrine of faith and repentance at the written Word of God and at such men's writings as are grounded thereupon and agreeable thereunto.

Now among those many instruments of God[5] who have labored with profit in this great point of religion (namely, repentance), drawing their doctrine out of the breasts of the two Testaments of God's book, I may well say (to say no more) that this man of God, Master Perkins, deserves to have his place. His labors while he lived, and his yet living labors, what they deserve I had rather others should proclaim than I once name, who profess myself to be one of those many who may truly say that by the grace of God, and His good means principally, I am what I am. But leaving him in that glorious mansion, which Christ the Lord of the harvest has prepared for him and now given him, I return to myself, and do humbly praise the Lord of heaven, who gave me my time in the university in those happy days wherein (besides many worthy men of God, whereof some are fallen asleep and some remain alive unto this day) this holy man did spend himself like a candle, to give light unto others.

The scope of all his godly endeavors was to teach Christ Jesus and Him crucified, and [he] much labored to move all men to repentance, that as our knowledge has made popery ashamed of their ignorance, so our holy lives might honor our holy profession. And as repentance was one of the principal

---

4. *Set*: get.
5. In the margin: Deering, Greenham, Bradford, and many.

ends, both of his continual preaching and writing, so especially and purposely he has twice dealt in that argument.

First, in his *Treatise of Repentance*, published [in] 1592, wherein briefly (as his manner was), but soundly, pithily, and feelingly, he lays down the doctrine and the very nature of repentance. And after the positive doctrine, he touches some of the principal controversies and difficulties in that doctrine. But afterwards, thinking with himself that he had not seriously and forcibly enough urged so great and necessary a lesson as repentance is, therefore shortly after, being desired and called to the duty of preaching in that great and general assembly at Stourbridge Fair, he thought it a fit time for this necessary and general exhortation to repentance, to the intent that as we were taught the doctrine of repentance in the former treatise, so in these sermons we might be stirred up to the practice of it. And certainly (good sir), I judge there could have been no matter more fit for that assembly than an exhortation to repentance. For as the audience was great and general, of all sorts, sexes, ages, and callings of men, and assembled out of many corners of this kingdom, so is this doctrine general for all. Some doctrines are for parents, some for children, some for scholars, some for tradesmen, some for men, some for women, but repentance is for all. Without it, it may be said of all and everyone of age (no one excepted): "no repentance, no salvation."

These sermons, being in my hands, and not delivered to me from hand to hand, but taken with this hand of mine, from his own mouth, were thought worthy for the excellency and fit for the generality of the matter, to be offered to the public view.[6]

And now these firstfruits of my labors in another man's vineyard, as also all that hereafter do or may follow, I humbly consecrate to the blessed spouse of Christ Jesus, the holy church of God on earth, and namely to the Church of England, our beloved mother, who may rejoice that she was the mother of such a son, who in few years[7] did so much good to the public cause of religion, as the

---

6. The 1609 edition includes the following: "I have also other works of his in my hands, of which (being many) I confess myself to be but the keeper for the time, taking myself bound to keep them safely, to the benefit of God's church, of whose treasure upon earth I make no question, but they are a part. And I heartily desire you (my good friends) and all other faithful Christians to solicit the Lord in prayer for me that I may faithfully discharge myself of that great charge which in this respect lies upon me, and that His grace and blessing may be on me and all others who are to be employed in this service, wherein (had the Lord so pleased) we could heartily have wished never to have been employed, but that his life might have eased us of the labor, and that as I begin with this, so I (or some other better able, which I rather desire) may go forward, undertaking the weight of this great burden, and not faint till he has made a faithful account to the church of God, of all the jewels delivered to our trust." It is deleted from *Works* (1631), vol. 3.

7. In the margin: Master Perkins [was] but forty years old at his death.

wickedness of many years shall not be able to wear out. But first of all, and especially, I present the same unto you (my very worshipful and Christian friends) who (I must needs say) are very worthy of it in many respects.

First, for the matter itself, which is repentance, [I] myself am able to testify that you are not hearers but doers, ripe in knowledge, and rife in the practice of repentance, insomuch as I dare from the testimony of my conscience, and in the word of a minister pronounce of you, that as you have heard and known this doctrine of repentance, so blessed are you, for you do it.

And second, for him who was the author hereof (whose mouth spoke it from the feeling of his soul, and whose soul is now bound up in the bundle of life), I know and cannot in good conscience conceal the great delight you have always had in the reading of his books, the reverend opinion you had of him [while] living, and how heavily and passionately you took his death and departure. Therefore, to cheer you up in want of him, I send you here this little book, his own child, begotten in his life time, but born after his death. Observe it well, and you shall find it not unlike the father, yea, you shall discern in it the father's spirit, and it doubts not but to find entertainment with them of whom the father was so well respected.

And for myself, I spare to rehearse what interest you have in me and all my labors. It is no more than you worthily deserve and shall have in me forever. You are the fairest flowers in this garden, which in this place I (after others) have planted for the Lord (or, rather, God by us), and [you are] two principal pearls in that crown which at the last day I hope for from the Lord my God, whose Word at my mouth you have received with much reverence and with such profit, as if I had the like success of my labors in others, I should then never have cause to say with the prophet, "I have labored in vain, and spent my strength in vain,"[8] but my judgment is with the Lord, and my work with my God.

And if I knew you not to be such as take more delight in doing well than in hearing of it, I would prove at large what I have spoken of you. Yet give me leave to say that which without open wrong I may not conceal, that besides your care, knowledge, and godly zeal to religion and other duties of the first table to God Himself, your charity and piety to the needy distressed Christians at home and abroad, your merciful dealing with them who are in your power, your benevolence to learning and namely to some in the university, do all proclaim to the world your due praises. These I (knowing well your modesties) do spare once to name. Neither would I have said thus much, were it not for this cold and barren age wherein we live, that so, when our preaching cannot move, yet your

---

8. Isa. 49:4.

godly examples might stir up. Pardon me, therefore, I pray you, and think it not wrong to you, which is a benefit to God's church. But go forward in the strength of the Lord your God and hold on in that happy course you have begun. "Be faithful unto the end" and "The Lord will give you the crown of life" [Rev. 2:10]. "Faithful is he which hath promised, who will also do it" [1 Thess. 5:24].

Proceed (good sir) to honor learning in yourself and others, and religion especially, which is the principal learning. And proceed both of you to practice religion in your own persons and in your family. Hold on to shine before your family, and among the people where you dwell, in zeal and holiness. Hold on hereby still to shame popery, to stop your enemies' mouths, to honor that holy religion which you profess, to gain comfort of good conscience to yourselves and assurance of eternal reward, and lastly to encourage me in those painful duties which lie upon me. For I openly profess that your religious zeal and love of the truth, with many other good helps, are principal encouragements in my ministry and special motives unto me to undertake the charge of publication of so many of the works of this deceased holy man, as may not in better manner be done by others. But I keep you too long from this holy exhortation following. I, therefore, send you to it, and it to you, and from you to the church of God. For I dare not make it privately yours and mine, wherein the whole church has interest as well as we. It was preached in the field, but it is worthy to be admitted into our hearts. I found it in the open field, but upon diligent view, finding it to be God's corn, and a parcel of His holy and immortal seed, therefore I brought it home, as good corn deserves. And as it is God's corn, so in you I desire all holy Christians to lay it up in God's garners, that is, in their hearts and souls.

And thus, committing this little volume to your reading, the matter to your practice, you and yours to the blessed favor of that God whom you serve, and myself and my endeavors to your hearty love and holy prayers, I take my leave.

From my study. August 7, 1605.
Yours in Christ Jesus, ever assured.
William Crashawe

To the Reader

To the Christian Reader, and especially to all such as have any copies of the works of Master Perkins, or intend to [bring] any of them [to] the press.

For as much as there has been lately signification made of divers of Master Perkins's works hereafter to be printed in an epistle to the reader premised before the treatise of *Callings*, and that signification, being but general, might peradventure give occasion to some to set out some particulars (without the consent of Master Perkins's assignees) as imperfectly as are these two books, entitled, *The Reformation of Covetousness* and *The Practice of Faith*, justly and truly (for ought that I see) censured in the aforesaid epistle. It is, therefore, now thought good to mention the particular treatises, and works of his, which shall hereafter (if God will) be published, for the benefit of God's church. I do, therefore, hereby make known to all, whom it any way may concern, that there were found in the study of the deceased, and are in the hands of his executors (or assignees) and preparing for the press,

1. His expositions on the Epistle to the Galatians.
2. On the Epistle of Jude.
3. His book of the Cases of Conscience.
4. His treatises: (1) Of Witchcraft. (2) Of Callings.

All these he had perused himself, and made them ready for the press, according to which copies by himself so corrected, some of them already are, and the rest will be published in due time. And hereupon we desire all men who have copies of them, not to offer that wrong to that worthy man of God, as to publish any of their own, seeing the copies hereof which are to be printed, are of his own correcting. But rather if they can help to make any of them more perfect by their copies, they may therein do a good work to the benefit of many and much comfort to themselves.

And further, I do hereby make known that I have in my hands at this present of his works, taken from his mouth with my own hand, hereafter (if God will) to be published, with the allowance of our church and for the benefit of his children, these particulars,

1. His expositions or Readings on Psalm 101.
2. On Psalm 32.

3. On Hebrews 11.

4. On Revelation 1–3.

5. On Matthew 5–7.

6. His confutation of Canisius, his little Popish Catechism.

7. His treatises: (1) Of Imaginations, out of Genesis 8:2. (2) Of Temptations, out of Matthew 4. (3) Of Christian Equity, out of Philippians 4:3. (4) Of the Callings of the Ministry, out of two places of Scripture. (5) Of Repentance, out of Zephaniah 2:1.

Besides many other particular sermons, and short discourses made upon several and special occasions, of all which some are already published by others and some by myself. And all the rest that remain, as they are the jewels of God's church, so did I willingly dedicate them to the public and general good, judging it were a foul sin in me, or any other, to impropriate[1] to our sins or our own private use the labors of this or any other learned man, which are in my opinion parts of the treasury of the militant church. And as it were wrong to the church if I should conceal them, so doubtless were it to him and his children if I should publish them for mine own alone and not for their benefit. If I do, I think it may be justly said unto me, or whosoever does so, "Your money perish with you." And what herein I have said for myself, I know I may boldly and safely say for his executors or assignees, who have or had in their hands, any of those which were found in his study. In the publishing of all which, as we do intend to deal truly with the Christian reader, and not to commit anything to the press which has not either been written or corrected by the author himself, or faithfully penned according to the truest copies, taken from his own mouth, and since by others of sufficiency and integrity, diligently perused. Some purpose to refer them to the benefit of the author's wife and children, as much as may be, wishing that upon this caveat, men would not be so hasty (as some have been) to commend to the world their imperfect notes, upon a base desire of a little gain, both to hinder the common good of the church, and to defraud the said parties of their private benefit, to whom in all equity and conscience, it does principally appertain. And desiring all who have any perfect copies of such as are in my own hands, that they would either help me with theirs, or rather take mine to help them. That by our joint power and our forces laid together, the walls of this worthy building may go up the fairer and the faster. And so, I commend them all to God's blessing, who endeavor to commend themselves and their labors to God and to His church.

Your brother in the Lord,
W. C.

____

1. *Impropriate*: transfer.

An Exhortation to Repentance

Search yourselves, even search you, O nation, not worthy to be beloved:
before the decree come forth, and you be as chaff that passeth on a day.
—Zephaniah 2:1–2

The prophet, in the first chapter of this prophecy, rebukes the Jews for three notable crimes: idolatry, fraud, and cruelty. In this second [chapter], he exhorts them to repentance, and withal reproves some of their special sins. In the first three verses, he propounds the doctrine of repentance, and adds some special reasons to move and stir them up to the practice of it. In propounding the doctrine of repentance, he directs it to two sorts of men: first, to the obstinate and impenitent Jews (vv. 1–2); [and], second, to the better sort of them (v. 3). So that, the sum and substance of these first two verses is a brief and summary propounding of the doctrine of repentance to the obstinate Jews.

The words contain in them five points touching the doctrine of repentance. (1) The duty to be performed: "search" (v. 1). (2) Who must be searched: "yourselves" (v. 1). (3) Who must do it: "the Jews," who are further described to be a "nation not worthy to be beloved of God" (v. 1). (4) The time limiting them when to repent: "before the decree come forth" (v. 2); that is, before God puts in execution the judgments which are already decreed and appointed for them. (5) A forcible reason urging them to do it, which lies hid and is necessarily implied in the fourth point; namely, that "there is a decree against them" (v. 2). It wants nothing but execution, which also shall come unless they repent, whereby they shall be fanned. And if they shall be found to be chaff, they shall fly away with the wind of God's justice. Of all these points in order.

Point 1

For the first, the Holy Spirit says, "Search yourselves." The words are commonly read thus: "Gather yourselves." Though this is good, for in repentance a man gathers himself and all his wits together, which afore were dispersed and wandered up and down in vanity, yet I rather allow their translation who read thus:

"Search (or fan) yourselves." But either of them may stand because the word in the original does comprehend both significations. Yet it seems that to search (or sift) fits this place better, considering the same manner of speech is afterwards continued in the word "chaff." So that the meaning of the Holy Spirit seems to be this: "Search, try, and fan yourselves, lest you are found [to be] light chaff, and so fly away and are consumed before the justice of God."

Observation 1

Concerning this duty of searching, let us observe, first, that the Holy Spirit, urging the Jews to repent, uses not the word repentance, but bids them search themselves. Yet [He] means [that] He would have them to repent, giving us to understand that no man can have true and sound repentance but he who has first of all searched and examined himself. And this stands with good reason, for no man can repent, who first of all does not know himself and his own wretchedness. But no man can see into himself nor know himself, but he who does diligently search himself. So that the beginning of all grace is for a man to search, try, and fan himself, that thereby he may know what is in himself, so that, upon the search, seeing his fearful and damnable estate, he may forsake himself and his own ways, and turn to the Lord. The Holy Spirit speaks thus in the hearts of holy men: "Let us search and try our ways" [Lam. 3:40]. And mark what follows: "and turn again to the Lord." As though there were no turning again unto the Lord but after a searching of ourselves. With this testimony of the Holy Spirit agrees the testimony of all holy men's consciences, who all know that the first beginning of their turning unto the Lord was a searching of themselves. Let any repentant sinner ask his conscience, and call to mind his first calling and conversion, and he will remember that the first thing in his repentance was this: that he searched into himself and looked narrowly into his ways, and, finding his ways dangerous and his case fearful, [he] did thereupon resolve to take a new course and turn to the Lord for pardon and mercy and for grace to enter into more holy and more comfortable courses.

The man who passes upon ridges of mountains and sides of hills, or who goes over a narrow bridge or some dangerous and steep rocks, at midnight, fears not because he sees no danger. But bring the same man, in the morning, and let him see the narrow bridge he went over in the night, under which runs a violent stream and a bottomless gulf, and the dangerous mountains and rocks he passed over, and he will wonder at his own boldness and shrink for fear to think of it, and [he] will by no means venture the same way again. For now he sees the height of the mountains, the steepness of the hills, the cragginess of the rocks, the fearful downfall, and the furious violence of the stream underneath, and thereby sees the extreme danger which afore he saw not. Therefore, he wonders and rejoices that he has escaped so great a danger, and [he] will by no means be drawn to go that way in the day which he went most carelessly in the darkness of the night, but [he] seeks another way (though it should be far about). So, a sinner in his first estate, which is natural and corrupt (as we are bred and born), has a veil before his face, so that he sees nothing. He sees not the wrath of God and the curse due for sin (hell and damnation), seeking to devour him, although (living always in sin) he walks in the very jaws of hell itself. And because he sees not this fearful danger, therefore, he refuses no sin at all, but rushes securely into all manner of sin. The night of impenitency and the mist of ignorance so blinds his eyes that he sees not the narrow bridge of this life, from which, if he slides, he falls immediately into the bottomless pit of hell.

But when as God's Spirit has by the light of God's Word opened his eyes and touched his heart to consider his estate, then he sees the frail bridge of this narrow life, and how little a step there is between him and damnation. Then he sees hell open, due for his sins, and himself in the highway to it: sin being the craggy rock [and] hell the gaping gulf under it; this life being the narrow bridge and damnation the stream that runs under it.

Then he wonders at his miserable estate, admires the mercy of God in keeping him from falling into the bottom of hell, wonders at the presumptuous boldness of his corruption, which so securely plodded on toward destruction, and being ashamed of himself and his ways, he turns his heart to the God who saved him from these dangers, and [he] sets himself into more holy ways and more comfortable courses, and confesses that ignorance made him bold and blindness made him so presumptuous. But now he sees the danger, and will by no means go the same way again. And thus, the searching and seeing into the foulness of sin, and the danger thereof, is the first beginning of repentance and the first step into grace.

This doctrine teaches us what faith and repentance are generally in the world. All men say they believe and have repented long ago; but try it well, and we shall find in the body of our nation but a lip-faith and a lip-repentance. For even when they say so, they are blind and ignorant of their own estate and know not themselves. [They say] that because they are baptized and live in the church, therefore they are in God's favor and in very good estate, when as they never yet were reconciled to God, and are so far from it that they never yet saw any sins in themselves whereof they should repent. As a man travelling in the night sees no danger but plods on without fear, so the most part of our common people, in the night of their ignorance, think and presume they love and fear God, and love their neighbor, and that they have ever done so. Nay, it is the common opinion that a man may do so by nature, and that he is not worthy to live who does not love God with all his heart and believe in Jesus Christ. But alas, poor simple souls, they never knew what sin was, [they] never searched nor saw into their own hearts with the light of God's law, for if they had, they should have seen such a sea of corruption that then they would confess it to be the hardest thing in the world to love God, to believe in Christ, and [to] forsake sin. It is, therefore, manifest that they have not yet begun to believe or repent, nor have entered into the first step of grace which leads to repentance, for they have not learned this lesson, which the prophet teaches, that is, to "search themselves."

Observation 2

Furthermore, let us in the second place observe better the signification of the word. It signifies to search narrowly, as a man would do for a piece of gold or a precious jewel which is lost in a great house, or as a man may search for gold in a mine of the earth where is much earth and but very little gold ore.

Here we may learn that in true repentance and conversion we must not search so only as to find the gross and palpable sins of our lives, but so as we may find those sins which the world accounts lesser sins, and espy[1] our secret faults and privy corruptions. Some corruptions seem more near akin of our nature, and therein men hope to be excused when they forsake many other greater sins. But a true penitent sinner must search for such, so as a good magistrate searches for a lurking traitor who is conveyed into some close and secret corner. And he must ransack his heart for such corruptions, as wherein his heart takes special delight, and [he] must think that no sin can be so small but it is too great to be spared, and that every sin (great or little) must be searched for, as being all traitors to God's majesty.

But alas, the practice of the world is far otherwise. Great sins are little sins; little sins are no sins. Nay, after a little custom, great sins are also little or nothing, and so at last men make no bones of gross and grievous sins. And for the most part, men search so superficially that they scarce find anything to be sins. Such excuses are made, such distinctions are devised, such mitigations, such qualifications, such colors are cast upon all sins, as now up and down the world gross sins are called into question, whether they are sins or not, and the greater transgressions of the law are counted small matters, necessary evils, or inconveniences, tolerated to avoid other evils. And what is he counted but a curious and precise fool, who stands upon them. Ignorance after thirty-five years [of] preaching is counted no sin; blind devotion in God's service [is] no sin; lip-labor in praying, vain and customable swearing, mocking of religion and the professors thereof, no sin; profaning of the Sabbath, condemning of preachers,

---

1. *Espy:* see.

abusing of parents, no sin; pride in apparel, superfluity in meats, beastly and ordinary drunkenness, fornication, no sins. Nay, deceits, cozenages, oppressing usury, notorious bribery, and covetousness (that mother sin), are counted no sins: These beams are made but motes by profane men. And they are so minced and carved, or there is some such necessity of them or some such other flourish or varnish must be cast upon them, as that they are little or none at all. Alas, alas, is not that a simple and a silly search where such blocks (as these are) lie unspied? What are mole-hills when such mountains are not seen? Motes will be little regarded where such beams are not discerned.[2]

But it is clear that, therefore, there is no true trial nor diligent search made. For a true convert will search his heart for all and [he] will spare none. He deals in searching his own heart as a good justice of [the] peace in searching for traitors or seminary priests. He seeks not superficially but most exactly, and leaves never a corner unsought; and he thinks great sins to be infinite and little sins [to be] great, and judges no sin so small but that it deserves the anger of God. And, therefore, he wonders at the mercy of God, who throws us not all down to hell in a moment. And he cries out with holy Jeremiah: "It is the Lord's mercy that we are not consumed" [Lam. 3:22]. Away then with this superficial and hypocritical search, where so many sins are spared and not found out. It is pharisaical, for even so the Pharisee, when he came into the temple to reckon with God, and to tell what traitors he had found (that is, what sins upon good search he had espied), he returns his precept, all is well, he has found never a one, but [he] begins to thank God that he was so good, and so good, and not so ill, and so ill, nor yet like the publican. The world is full of Pharisees; not only the popish church, but even our church swarms with these superficial search-ers who cannot (because they will not) find any sin to present unto God. Men think, in the country, a church officer hazards his oath if he presents all well, and finds no fault in his parish to present as punishable to the ordinary. For men think it impossible that there should be none in a whole parish. Then how does that man hazard his own soul, who, being made overseer and searcher of his heart, finds nothing in it to present to the Lord. For it is not easier to espy outward and actual transgressions in a whole parish than it is to find a heap of corruptions in a man's heart, if a man will search into the bottom of it with the light of God's law. Therefore, when the Lord comes and keeps His visitation, what shall become of such a man but to undergo the strict and severe search of the Almighty, because he would not search himself?

Our bodies and lives are free from Spanish inquisition (which is one of the last props which Satan has lent the pope, wherewith to uphold his declining

---

2. This paragraph break is not in the original.

kingdom), and the Lord grant we may be ever free from it. But in the meantime, it might put us in mind how to deal with our corrupt hearts and unmortified affections, even to erect an inquisition over them, to lay in wait for them, to search them narrowly, and to use them roughly; yea, to set our hearts upon the rack of God's law, so that it may confess the secret wickedness of it. For the papists do not think us Protestants greater enemies to their superstitions than the inward corruptions of our hearts are to our salvation. Therefore, it may be a godly policy for every man even to erect an inquisition over his own heart and conscience, and not to spare his most secret and dearest sins, and such as are nearest allied to his own nature. For that is the true search here commanded by the prophet and practiced by all godly and holy men: when a man purposes to find all that are, and to espy even all his sins. For a godly man is never satisfied in his search, but still, the more he finds, he suspects the more are still behind. And, therefore, he continues searching his own heart all his life long. Therefore, let every professor look to it between God and his conscience, that he dallies not with himself in this case. For if he does, then when God comes with His privy search, his hypocrisy shall be discovered, and his nakedness shall be laid open in the view of men and angels, to his eternal confusion.

Observation 3

Third, "search," says the prophet, but, not so content, he forces it again, "even search you." In this repeating and urging this exhortation, the Holy Spirit gives them and us to understand that the true searching of a man's heart and life is a duty of great moment and special necessity. Therefore, he leaves it not after once naming it, but enforces it the second time, as being no matter of indifferency but of great necessity, thereby showing that it is a principal duty in repentance, even the beginning and foundation of all true grace.

And further, it is a means also to prevent God's judgments. For when men search not themselves, then God sends the fire of afflictions and crosses to try and search them. But when they search themselves, then God spares to search them by His just judgments.

Now in that this duty of searching is both the beginning of all true grace and the means to stay God's judgments, and therefore is so pithily and forcibly urged by the Holy Spirit, it must teach us all a necessary lesson; namely, to make great conscience of searching ourselves. First, because God has so commanded, and we are to make conscience of obedience to every commandment. Second, because we shall reap two so great commodities thereby: (1) we shall lay a sure foundation for the good work of grace in us; and (2) we shall stay the hand of God and His judgments from being executed upon us.[3]

Let us, therefore, hearken to this counsel of the Holy Spirit. Let us take the fan of the law, and therewith search and winnow our hearts and lives: our hearts for secret and hidden corruptions; [and] our lives for committing of evil and omitting of good. Do with your hearts as men do with their wheat; they will not suffer their corn to lie long in the chaff lest the chaff hurt it, but [they] commit it to the fan so that the wind may separate them. So, the graces of God in our hearts are but corn, our sins and corruptions are chaff. Look well, and you shall find in yourself much chaff, and but little corn. Let not then the chaff lie too long mingled with the corn, lest it corrupt the corn. Let not your sins lie mingled with the grace of God in you. If you do, they will choke it in the end, and so deprive you of all grace. Therefore, rip up your heart, and look into your life, and when you have sinned, enter into yourself, ask your conscience what you have done, and be not quiet till you have found out your sin and the foulness of it. And never think that you know anything in religion till you know what is in your own heart and what are in your special and priviest corruptions. And look into your own faults, not with a partial eye, but with a censorious and strait judgment. Spare sin in no man, but especially condemn it in yourself.

But alas, these times of ours cry out of another state, for even Jeremiah's case is ours. We may complain as he did, "No man repents him of his wickedness, saying, what have I done?"[4] The same is the sore of our people, and the sickness of all nations, that every man runs on in his sins, from sin to sin carelessly, even as the bard[5] horse into the battle. But how rare a thing is it to find a man who daily searches himself, and examines how he lives and how the case stands between God and himself, and that when he has done amiss enters into the closet of his heart and strikes himself upon the breast and disputes the case with himself, saying; "What have I done?" Oh, what is this, that I have done against God, against His church, and against my own soul?

The want of this is that which the prophet complains of in that place, not as though it were sufficient thus to do in a man's own conscience, but because it is a good beginning and a step to further grace. For if a man did thus seriously deal with his conscience after his sin, his conscience would shape him such an answer, and would tell him so roundly what he had done, that he would take heed how he did the same again, and look more narrowly and warily to himself all the days of his life. Seeing, therefore, it is so necessary a duty, let every one

---

3. This paragraph break is not in the original.

4. Jer. 8:6.

5. *Bard:* body armour for war horses.

of us endeavor the practice of it, namely, to rip and ransack our hearts, and to search our ways unto the bottom.

Now for our better instruction and furtherance in the performance hereof, you must know that this search is to be made by the law of God, for nothing else but God's law can help us. And let us see that which we must search for, for if we search by any means, we may seek and search long enough ere we find anything that will be matter of repentance. Ask the devil, he will tell you all is well, you are in an excellent estate, God loves you, and you are sure of heaven. The devil always sings this song for the most part till a man comes to die, for then he appears in his colors, but till then he labors to sing and lull all men to sleep in the cradle of security. Ask your own flesh, and your own hearts and natures, and they will answer and say that all is well and safe, and that we have believed and loved and feared God all our days. Ask the world and men in the world, and they will answer [that] all is well. And they will say further that you are a right good fellow and are worth twenty of these curious fools who stick upon points and stand upon circumstances, as swearing, drinking, good fellowship, and gaming, and such other nice and circumstantial points. Thus will worldly men answer, for your profane course is acceptable to them because thereby you approve the same in them.

Nay, go further, and ask all human learning in the world, and it cannot tell you what one sin is nor what it is to offend God. So that, there remains only the law of God, the light whereof will disclose the darkness of our hearts, and the justice whereof will reveal the unrighteousness and the perverseness of our natures. Therefore, to the law of God we must fly to help us in this search.

And yet, for our better help in this duty, and that there may be nothing wanting to that soul that seeks God, we are further to know that if we will search ourselves by the law profitably, we must mark three rules, the truth whereof unless we know, acknowledge, and feel, we shall never see our own estate nor profit by this search, but plod on from sin to sin until we plunge into hell.

Rule 1

The first rule is that every man, who came from Adam, sinned in the sin of Adam. You must, therefore, know that his sin in eating the forbidden fruit was your sin, and [that] you sinned therein as well as he (though you were then unborn), and that you are guilty of it before God, and must answer for it to God's justice, unless Christ does it for you.

The reason hereof is because we are his seed and posterity. We were then in his loins. He was the father of us all. And [he] was not a private man as we are now, but a public person, the pledge of all mankind, and [he] bore the person of us all at that time. Therefore, what he did then, he did it for himself and for us. What covenant God made with him was made for himself and us. What God promised him and he to God, he promised for himself and for us. What he received for himself and for us, and what he gained or lost by his fall, he gained and lost for us as for himself. He lost the favor of God and original purity; therefore, he lost it for all his posterity. Guiltiness and God's anger and corruption of nature, which he gained, he got for us all as well as for himself. If we doubt of this point, it is proved by the apostle, when the Holy Spirit says, "Sin entered by one man, and death by sin: and that sin went over all, and that it went over all them which sinned not in the like transgression with Adam" (Rom. 5:14) (that is, even our children), who as they are born are born not only tainted with original corruption but guilty also of Adam's sin. This is a most certain truth, though it [may] seem strange, for few men think of it, that ever they shall answer for Adam's sin. And, therefore, if any object, what reason is there that I answer for another man's sin? I answer, true, if it had been Adam's sin alone, but it was his and yours also, for he was your father, and stood in your room. And you also, since you were born, have confirmed what he did.

Now, therefore, though not one of many thinks seriously thereof (namely, that he should stand guilty of a sin committed five thousand years before he was born), yet seeing it is most true both in Scripture and good reason, let every man subscribe in his conscience to this truth. And let this be your first resolution in this search, that you stand guilty of Adam's transgression.

Rule 2

The second rule to be known is that all sins are in every man; more plainly, that in every man by nature are the seeds of all sins, and that not in the worst but in the best natured men. Make choice of the best man and the greatest sin, and that worst sin is to be found in that best man. If any doubt of this, let him consider what original sin is, namely, corruption of the powers of our souls, and that not of some (or in part) but of all and wholly. This corruption has two parts. First, a want, not of some, but of all good inclination, a want of all goodness. Second, a deprivation and proneness, not to some, but to all evil; and not a proneness only, but original sin infuses into every man's heart the seed of all corruption.

Many men stand much upon their good meaning and upright heart, and brag of a good nature. But they are foully deceived, for take the most civil man upon the earth, and the seeds of all sins in the world are in him by nature. But to explain this point fully, observe these two clauses.

First, I say not the practice of all sins, but the seeds. For all men practice not all sin. The seeds are in their nature, but the practice is restrained, sometimes by education, sometimes by good and wholesome laws, sometimes the constitution of men's bodies denies the practice of some sins, sometimes the country a man dwells in, or [the] calling a man lives in, keeps him from the practice of some sins. And a general and limiting grace of God always restrains the nature of all men from running into many sins. If God should take His hand away, and leave every man to his nature, we should see that every man would practice any sin in the world; yea, even the greatest sins that ever we heard to be done in the world. All men who know themselves know this to be true, and the more a man knows his own heart, the more he sees that his heart is a sea of all wickedness, and that it is the mercy and grace of God that he has not fallen into the mightiest and most monstrous sins in the world.

Second, I say by nature. For I know by good education and by grace it is otherwise. Grace rectifies nature, but that is no thanks to nature, for it is as evil and corrupt still, being severed from grace. And, therefore, nature must be fully abolished afore man come[s] to heaven. And yet (though all this is true) I say not that sin breaks out in all natures alike, though all natures are alike corrupt. For the course of nature is restrained in some more than others by the means afore said. But this is the truth, that whereas some are not so angry, some not so wanton, some not so cruel, some not so covetous, some not so ambitious, etc. as others, it comes not from any goodness of nature in them, above the other originally, but from God's hand, which tempers, restrains, and moderates every man's nature as He sees good.

And if God did not thus moderate and restrain the natures of men, but suffer them to break out to the full, there would then be no order, but all confusion in the world. Therefore (especially for His church's quietness, so also for the preservation of public peace and the upholding of society in the world between man and man), the Lord holds a hand over every man's nature, and keeps everyone in a certain compass limited by the wisdom of His power. If the Lord should take away His restraining hand, all societies and commonwealths would be turned upside down, because every man by the universal corruption of his nature would break out into every sin. I end this point by appealing to the testimony of the consciences of all men, and especially of the best and holiest men, of whom I would ask this question: whether they find not in their natures an inclination even to the foulest sins in the world, if shame, or fear, or else the grace of God, restrained them not? So that, the best men do know well enough what ado[6] they have with their corrupt natures, to keep them within the compass of obedience.

Nay, I yet add further, the nature of men, and of all men, is so corrupt since Adam that even the seed of the sin against the Holy Spirit, and a proneness to

---

6. *Ado*: fuss or trouble.

it, is in the nature of every man (though not one man among many thousands does commit that sin). For, seeing in that sin there is a heap or sea of all sins gathered together, he therefore that has in his nature the seed of all sins has also the seed of it.

And again, seeing that all evils tend to a perfection, as well as grace does, what reason therefore is there but we may safely think that the devil would hale[7] everyone to that height of sin, if it were not that the powerful hand of God prevented him? He will neither suffer wicked men, nor the devil himself, to be so wicked as they could and would be.

The use of this second rule is notable. For in this searching of ourselves, it shows us what we are without all color or deceit, and [it] fully discovers unto us the ugliness of our natures. And it may teach us all how to think and esteem of ourselves when we hear of Cain's unnatural murder [Genesis 4], Pharaoh's unnatural cruelty [Exodus 1], the Sodomites' unnatural lust [Genesis 18], Ahithophel's devilish policy [2 Sam. 15–16], Sennacherib's horrible blasphemy [Isaiah 38], Judas's monstrous treason, [or] Julian's fearful apostasy. When we hear of the fearful murders, treasons, perjuries, sins against nature, blasphemies, apostasies, witchcrafts, and the other horrible sins of the world, let us then return into ourselves and look homewards, even into our own hearts, and everyone confess that these should have been even your sins also, if God's grace had not prevented you.

This will humble you, and make you think vilely and basely of yourself, and so consequently bring you to repentance and true amendment. And the very reason why men repent not nor amend their ways is because they are Pharisees by nature and think highly of themselves and of their own natures and their natural inclinations. This will be a harsh and a strange doctrine to them. Oh, they have excellent natures, and they cannot endure such and such sins, and they thank God [that] they are not as ill as others. But let all such men know [that] they must cease magnifying nature and learn to magnify God's grace. Let them know that nature in them, is in the root as much corrupt as in the worst man in the world, and every man's heart is a bottomless fountain of all sin. Therefore, praise not your nature but God's grace and mercy in giving you so good a nature; or, rather, [in] so well restraining and rectifying your nature. And stay not there, but desire of the Lord that as He has given you a better tempered nature than to other men, so also He would bestow on you His special and saving grace; and as He has kept you from the fearful sins of others (you being as ill naturally as they), so He would also lead you into the way of salvation, which else the best nature in the world can never attain unto.

---

7. *hale:* drag

Rule 3

The third rule to be known and practiced of him who will truly search himself is that every man born of Adam is by nature the child of wrath and God's enemy. This is true of all without exception; high or low, rich or poor, noble or simple, born in the visible church or without. And further, by being [an] enemy of God, he is therefore born subject to hell, to damnation, and to all other curses. So that look, as a convicted traitor stands thereby in his prince's high displeasure and is sure of death without special pardon, so stands every man when he is born, convicted of high treason against God, in his high disfavor, and is in danger of hell, which is the fulfilling of the wrath of God.[8]

Thus, David confesses of himself: "I was born in iniquity, and in sin hath my mother conceived me."[9] If "in sin," then in God's wrath and under the danger of damnation. If any ask, how or why this is so? I answer, the truth (as also the equity) of this third rule depends on the two former [rules]. Because every man is born guilty of Adam's great sin, and also tainted originally with all corruption and a proneness of all sin, therefore it follows in equity and justice that every man is born under the wrath and curse of God.

This point is a plain and evident truth, yet men in the world think not so, and it is the cause why men repent not of their sins. For most men think that by nature they are in God's favor and, therefore, they need not so sue for it in humiliation and repentance, but only live civilly and do not open wrong and all is well. Whereas (alas) there is no condemned traitor more out of his prince's favor, nor surer of death without a pardon, than all we [who] are out of God's favor, and sure of damnation, unless we procure God's favor again by faith and repentance.

For the better opening of this third rule, and the manifesting of the truth, let us know further that the curse of God, under the which we all are born, is threefold.

The first is a bondage under Satan. It is a certain truth that every man as he is born of his parents, and till he repents, is a slave of Satan: man or woman, high or low, Satan is his lord and master. He sits as judge in his heart. And in this sense Satan is the king of the nations and god of the world. Men will in words defy Satan and not name him without defiance, and spit at him, and yet (alas) he is in their hearts. They spit him out of their mouths, but he is lower. They should also spit him out of their hearts, and that is true defiance indeed. For alas, he lodges in your heart, and there he makes his throne and reigns until the Spirit of regeneration dispossesses him. And till then, no servant is

---

8. This paragraph break is not in the original.
9. Ps. 51:5.

so subject to his master, no slave to his lord, as is the heart of man by nature unto Satan, the prince of darkness. Nay, our bondage is more fearful than the slavery of any poor Christian in the Spaniards' or in the Turks' galleys. For their bodies are but in bondage and at command and under punishment, but our best part, our heart, our conscience, our soul itself, is captivated unto him and under his command, who is the king of cruelty and confusion, and lord of hell, whose commandments are injustice, whose service is sin, and whose hire is damnation.

The second part of the curse of the first death (or the death of the body) is a separation of the soul and body asunder for a time, namely, till the last judgment. This death is duly and justly the punishment of anyone for the least sin. Therefore, how due and just a punishment upon that horrible heap of sinfulness which is in every man's nature! And it is a most terrible curse. For it is the very gate of hell, and the downfall of damnation unto all men, but such as by faith and repentance do get their death sanctified by the death of Christ. Unto such men indeed it is no curse but a gracious and glorious blessing, for it is altered by Christ's death. But unto all men by nature, and who repent not, it is the heavy curse of God's wrath and the very downfall into the gulf of hell.

The third part of the curse, under which every man is born, is the second death: the death of soul and body, which is the eternal want of God's presence, and the accomplishment of His wrath, and an apprehension and feeling of that wrath seizing on body, soul, and conscience. The first curse was a spiritual death, the death of the soul. The second [was] a temporal death, the death of the body. The third is an eternal death, a death both of soul and body together, and forever. This eternal death is the curse of all curses, the misery of all miseries, and [the] torment of all torments. And I show it thus. Oftentimes when your tooth aches, and sometimes when your head aches, or [you are] in the pain of the stone or colic, you would give all that you have in the world to be eased of that pain; nay, in the extremity of some fits many will wish themselves even out of the world. Now, if the pain of one tooth can so far distemper mind and body that it cannot be relieved with all the pleasures of this life, oh then, what a torment shall that be when not one kind of pain but the whole vial of God's wrath shall be poured, not on one member, but on the whole soul, body, and conscience; and that not for a time under hope of better, but eternally without hope of relief; and that not in this world where there are comforts, helps, and remedies, but in that ugly and darksome place of torments; and that not among living men who might mitigate your pain or else bemoan you and bewail it with you, but with the devils and damned spirits which will now laugh at your destruction and solace themselves in your misery, and will rejoice, as you did serve them in earth so now in hell to be your tormenters! It may be, therefore (by the way), a good warning and wisdom to us all, when we feel the extremity of some bodily pain to consider with ourselves, and say, "Oh then, what shall be my misery and torment if I repent not?" When not [only] one member, but soul, body, and conscience, shall be racked and tormented in the feeling and apprehension of the anger of the Lord of hosts.

In these three points stands that curse and wrath of God, under which every man is born. And these do answer to the three degrees of sin which are in us. For as the first two rules taught us, there is in every man by nature, till he repents, a threefold guiltiness: first, a guiltiness of Adam's sin; second, the taint of original and universal corruption; [and], third, a pollution by many outrageous actual sins. In the first of these, every man is equally guilty. In the second, every man is equally corrupt. But in third, everyone keeps that compass within which the Lord will keep them by His limiting power.

Now as in our guiltiness of Adam's sin, sin has its beginning; in original sin, its continuance; in actual sin its perfection; so answerable hereunto, the wrath of God (which always stands opposite to sin) is begun in leaving us by nature to the slavery of Satan, continued by death, and accomplished in damnation.

And now, I commend these three rules to the careful and Christian consideration of you all, certifying [to] you from God that as you can never be saved unless you repent, nor repent unless you search yourselves (as here the prophet bids), so you can never search yourselves aright till you are persuaded and resolved of these three rules, and of the truth of them all, even in your hearts and consciences. First, that you are guilty of Adam's sin. Second, that you are prone by nature to all evil in the world. Third, that for these you are subject to the wrath of God and to all the curses of His wrath.[10]

But when you are in heart and conscience resolved that these are true, then you are a fit scholar for this lesson of the prophet: "search thyself." For when you go thus prepared unto this search and esteem of yourself, as the three rules have described you, then if you search into yourself, you will find yourself and your estate to be such as will cause you to repent, return, and take a new course. Therefore, what the prophet said to those Jews, I say unto you also: My brethren of this realm of England, who are now here gathered together, out of so many countries and quarters of this realm, yea, in the name of the same God I cry unto you: "Search, O search yourselves." And think it not a matter indifferent to do or not to do. But know it, that God commands you, as ever you will come to salvation, "Search yourselves." And the rather because by these three rules you see how much chaff of corruption is in your nature, and what need therefore it has to be searched into and fanned by repentance. Be well assured, you man,

---

10. This paragraph break is not in the original.

whatsoever you are, there is so much chaff in you that if you search not and fan it not out, you will prove nothing but chaff at the last day, and so be blown away with the wind of God's justice into hell. Take hold, therefore, of this exhortation, and defer it not.

You will not suffer your wheat to lie too long in the chaff for fear of hurting it. Is it then safe to suffer the chaff of your sins and corruptions to lie cankering and rotting in your heart? Be sure that that little portion of grace, which you attain unto by living in the church and under the ministry of the Word of God, will be putrefied and clean corrupted with the chaff of your sins. Therefore, again and again, I exhort you to make conscience of this duty. Search into yourselves, fan out this chaff, this presumption of ours, and high esteeming of our own nature, and conceits of God's favor before we have it, so that this chaff being blown away, the Lord may then bestow upon us soundness of grace and the foundation of all goodness, which is a holy and humble heart.

Salvation is such a building as the foundation thereof had need to be sure and strong. Ignorance, blindness, and presumption, are not sufficient foundations for such a building. Therefore, as no man will build a strong house upon any earth, but he will first search it lest it prove sandy and so overthrow all, so a wise Christian will not build his salvation upon fancies and conceits and natural presumptions, but will "search" and look into his heart, and finding these to be sandy and rotten, and therefore too weak for the foundation of so glorious a building, will refuse them all, and labor to furnish his heart with such sound grace as whereupon he may trust so weighty a work as the salvation of his soul. Again, if you will stand in the day of trial, then search your heart betimes, and discern between chaff and wheat. You see that chaff flies away before the wind, but good corn endures the fan and the fury of the wind. So, in the day of trial, temptation, sickness, or open persecution, the chaff of natural presumption, and outward formality in religion, will fly away. And it must be the penitent, humbled, and believing heart, which must then abide it out, and endure the fan of temptations and persecutions.

And to conclude, let not the devil deceive you in making you imagine or hope to please God, and yet to let your corruptions lie unseen and your sins unsearched out, lest thereby you mar all. For you do not lay up wheat in your garners until it is purged from the chaff. So, think not to store up any saving knowledge, or any other grace of God in your heart, until the chaff of vanity is first blown away, so that the holy graces of God may be laid up in the garners of your soul.[11]

---

11. This paragraph break is not in the original.

And, therefore, without question (to speak one word to touch our common professors in the very sore of their souls) all knowledge that is stored up in these impure and unsearched hearts is even as wheat laid up in the chaff, which is (a thousand to one) sure to be eaten up by the chaff, so that, when the winnowing time of trial and persecutions comes, I fear that such men will (for all their knowledge) shrink aside and betray the truth, their knowledge then proving [to be] no better than chaff because it was laid up in an unholy heart. If, therefore, you would stand and endure, when popery, persecution, or temptations come; if you would abide the fury of the fan of temptations, now then exercise your heart with the fan of God's law, search and ransack it, purge out the chaff of corruption, and store up knowledge in a holy heart and a good conscience. And that will abide the violence of all temptations. Yea, when God suffers the devil to do with us as he did with Peter, to winnow us like wheat, to sift and try us as he did Job with the furious wind of all his malice, the knowledge that will prove wheat will abide the wind, and gold will abide the fire. It will be thus glorious in the end if we follow this holy prophet's counsel and search our hearts.

And thus much for the first point (namely, this duty of searching here commanded), in which we have stayed the longer because it is the foundation of all the rest. And this being well laid, the whole building will go up the faster.

Point 2

Now we come to the second general point here laid down; that is, whom we must search? The prophet answers, "yourselves"; not other men, but yourselves. This search, so urged and enforced by the prophet, must not be of other men's hearts and lives, but of our own. Our own [hearts] are our charge, and not other men's [hearts]. And therein is the saying true, which else is most false, "Every man for himself." For as every soul must be saved by itself, so must it believe, repent, and search itself.

The duty, therefore, here commanded is for every man who would have his soul to be saved, to search it and reform it, and leave others to be searched by themselves. Here the Holy Spirit meets with the common corruption of this world, and that is that men are eagle-eyed to see into the lives of other men, but to look into their own hearts and lives they are blinder than moles. They can see motes in other men's lives but discern not beams in their own. Whereby it comes to pass that they stumble and fall foully, for the eyes of most men are set upon others, and not upon themselves. And thereupon it is that an evil man, seeing other men and not himself, thinks best of himself, and worst of other men. But contrariwise, a good man, seeing himself, and not other men, thinks worst of himself, and better of other men. An evil man looks outward and judges other men, but a good man looks homeward and judges himself. And, in judging, [he] condemns himself far above other men, and that because by searching into his own heart and ways he knows that by himself which he knows not by any man in the world besides.

So then, we must not search other men but ourselves. Our own hearts and our own lives are our charge and burden. The lives of other men concern us not, being private men, further than to follow them being good or [to] take heed of them being evil. But to search or be inquisitive into them is no duty commanded us, but rather a foul and base vice forbidden by God. Indeed, magistrates in their people, pastors in their congregations, and householders in their families, are to search. But they can search only for criminal causes or open actual sins. But this searching must be of our hearts, which no man can search but ourselves only. Few men have a calling to enquire into other men's lives, but every man has a calling to search into himself. But (alas) men do far otherwise. They suffer themselves to rot in their own sins and erect an inquisition over other men's lives. And it is to be seen in daily experience that those men who are the great[est] searchers and priers into other men, are the neglecters and forgetters of themselves. And, contrariwise, they who do narrowly search themselves and their own ways, and look into the corners of their own hearts, do find so much work to do with themselves that they little busy themselves with other men. And thus much may suffice for that point.

It follows: "O nation not worthy to be beloved."

Point 3

The third point: who must search? The Jews, who are here termed a "nation not worthy to be beloved." And yet, for all that, they are bid to search themselves, so that upon their repentance they might be beloved, where we may see the unspeakable love of God and His wonderful mercy, offering grace unto such men as are altogether unworthy of it. God's children are by nature like other men, and God finds nothing in them [that causes Him] to respect them above others. But even of His own mercy, [He] makes them worthy, who of themselves are not. Therefore, how worthy is that God to have all the love of our hearts, who loved us when we were not worthy to be beloved?

But let us examine more particularly why God does call the Jews a "nation not worthy to be beloved." I answer, God had blessed them above other nations. He gave them His covenant of grace, and thereby made them His people, and [He] committed to their trust His holy Word and oracles (Rom. 3:2). But He dealt not so with other nations, neither had the heathen knowledge of His laws. Beside all this, they had a better land than others about them. It flowed with milk and honey (that is, with all commodities and delights). And though their country was but little, yet [they] themselves so populous and so powerful that, while they pleased God, no enemy durst set upon them.

Thus, for soul and body they were every way a nation blessed of God, a people beloved of God above all others. Now how did this people (thus beloved of their God) requite His love, which they had no more deserved than any other nation? Certainly, as they deserved it not afore they had it, so they requited it not when they had it. But [they] requited this love of God with sin, rebellion, and disobedience. They tempted Him. They provoked Him to wrath. They presumed of His mercy, and [they] proved a most stubborn and stiff-necked people, a froward generation. Moses partly saw this in his own experience, and better discerned it in the spirit of prophecy and, therefore, wondering at their wickedness, he cried out, "Do you thus requite the Lord, O foolish people and unwise?"[12] "Thus," that is, with sin and disobedience, which is the only means to displease the Lord and to provoke Him to wrath. For this cause, they are worthily called a foolish and unkind people by Moses, and here by the prophet, "a nation not worthy to be beloved," namely, for their unthankfulness and unkindness. This was such as they not only were slack and careless in performance of such duties as God required, but even multiplied their sins and committed those foul rebellions which His soul hated.

And the prophet, here in this chapter, notes three (from among many) of their great sins for which they were a "nation not worthy to be beloved": covetousness, cruelty, and deceit. All these were the more heinous and intolerable because they were the sins of their princes, rulers, and priests, who should have been lights and examples to the rest.

Now although every sin in itself is of that ill desert as it is able to cast us out of God's favor and deprive us of His love, yet, behold, here God complains, not upon a little cause, but for wonderful and exceeding unthankfulness and unkindness in them, who of all others should have loved the Lord.

As a man cares not for hard usage from him whom he esteems not, but a little unkindness does greatly grieve a man from him who is loved and respected, so is it with the Lord our God. He loved not the Gentiles as He did the Jews, neither was He so bountiful unto them [Psalm 147]. And, therefore (as we may see), though they lived always in ignorance, and continued always in disobedience, yet the text says [that] God regarded not the time of that ignorance [Acts 17:30]. But when as the Jews, His own people, whom He chose out of all people, and bestowed His love upon them, and made His covenant of grace with them, when they became unkind, unthankful, forgetful, stubborn, and rebellious, that caused the Lord even to complain of that indignity, and to

---

12. Deut. 32:6.

cry out by Moses, "Do ye thus requite the Lord, O foolish people and unwise?" And hereby the prophet: "O nation not worthy to be beloved." And, therefore, there is no man, but if he asks what he thinks of this nation of the Jews, he will answer that they are a most vile and wicked people, a froward generation, and that they are worthy to taste deeply of all God's plagues, who so far abused His love and mercy.

But what, does this belong to them alone? And is Israel a nation not worthy to be beloved? Nay, I may cry out with as good cause: O England, a nation not worthy to be beloved! For, God has been as good a God to us as He was to them. And we have been as unkind a people to Him as they were to Him. But that I may be free from discrediting our nation and from defiling my own nest, let us prove both these points and lay them open to the view of the world.

First, therefore, the same mercies (and far greater) have been poured and heaped upon us. He has called us out of the darkness; first from heathenism, and then from popery. He has confirmed His covenant of grace and salvation with us. He has imparted His treasures of His Word and sacraments to us. His holy Word has never [been] better preached, and the mysteries thereof never more plainly opened, since the time of the apostles. And as we have religion, so we have it under a religious prince, whereby it comes to pass that these blessings of salvation we enjoy not in secret or by stealth, but we have it countenanced by authority. So that, religion is not barely allowed but even (as it were) thrust upon men. Beside all this, we have a land also that flows with milk and honey. It is plentiful in all good things. We have liberty and peace under a peaceable prince, and [we have] the companions of peace: prosperity, plenty, health, wealth, corn, wool, gold, silver, abundance of all things, that may please the heart of man. Thus has God deserved the love of England.

Second, but now England, how have you requited this kindness of the Lord? Certainly, even with a great measure of unkindness; that is, with more and greater sins than ever Israel did. So that, if Moses spoke true of them, then may our Moses much more truly cry out against England: "Do you thus requite the Lord, you foolish people?" And if this prophet said thus of Israel for three sins, then may it be said of England for three hundred sins: "(O England) a nation not worthy to be beloved!" For you have multiplied your transgressions above those of Israel, even as though you had resolved with[in] yourself [that] the more God's kindness is heaped on you, the more to multiply your sins against Him. For you, England, as you have requited the Lord with sins, so not with a few sins, or small sins, or sins which hardly could have been prevented, for that had been a matter of some excuse or not of so great complaint. But your sins are many and grievous and capital and, which is worst of all, willful and affected, even as though God had deserved evil from us and that, therefore, we ought maliciously to requite Him.

If any man makes doubt of this and, therefore, thinks I speak too hardly of our church, I will then deal plainly and particularly, and rip up the sores of our nation, so that they may be healed to the bottom. The common sins of England, whereby the Lord is requited, are these:

First, ignorance of God's will and worship. I speak not of that compelled ignorance in many corners of our land, which is to be pitied because they want the means, but [of] willful and affected ignorance. Men are ignorant even because they will be ignorant. Means of knowledge were never so plentiful, and yet gross ignorance [was] never more [plentiful]. Is not he willfully blind who will not open his eyes in the light? And can there be any darkness at noonday but it must be willful? But our nation is dark and blind in the sunshine of the gospel, and grossly ignorant when the gospel beats their ears and light shines round about them. So as if they closed not their eyes and stopped not their ears, they could not but both hear and see. Who would look for ignorance after thirty-five years [of] preaching? And yet, many are as ignorant as if they had been born and brought up under popery. So that, our people are as evil as those in the days of Christ, of whom the Holy Spirit says, "Light is come into the world, but men love darkness more than light."[13] So, knowledge is come into England, but many Englishmen love darkness better than knowledge. Alas, how many thousands have we in our church who know no more in religion than they hear in common talk of all men; and which is worse, they think it sufficient also; and which is worst of all, whereas they might have more, they will not, but care not for it?

The second main sin of England is contempt of Christian religion. Religion has been among us these thirty-five years, but the more it is published the more it is condemned and reproached by many, insomuch as there is not the simplest fellow in a country town who, although he knows not one point of religion, yet he can mock and scorn such as are more religious than he is. This is one of the moths of England that eats up religion. This is grievous in whomsoever, but most intolerable in two sorts of men. First, in them who are altogether ignorant, that they should mock they know not what. A pitiful thing to hear one, who himself cannot give the meaning of one petition in the Lord's prayer, to upbraid other men because they are too forward. But it is the worst of all when men of knowledge, and such as live civilly, and would be counted good Christians and indeed of the better sort, cannot abide to see others go a little before them. But if they do, presently they are hypocrites and dissemblers.

---

13. John 3:19.

Thus, not profaneness nor wickedness, but even religion itself is a byword, a mocking stock, and matter of reproach. So that, in England at this day the man or woman who begins to profess religion and to serve God must resolve with himself to sustain mocks and injuries, even as though he lived among the enemies of religion and not among professors. And as religion increases and spreads itself, so does the number of these mockers. O what a cursed sin is this! To condemn the greatest favor that God can give us, that is, His holy religion, for which we should rather praise Him all the days of our lives. All that God can give a man in this world is His gospel. What then can God give to be regarded when His gospel is condemned?

This sin was never among the Jews. They indeed regarded it not so as it deserved, but who did ever make a mock and a scorn of it but England? O England, how can you answer this? God sends you the most precious jewel that He can send to a nation. And you scorn it, and them who bring it, and them who receive it, even as though it were no blessing but a curse. So that, as Christ says to the Jews, "For which of my good works do you stone me?" [John 10:32], so may the Lord say to England: "I have given you a fruitful land, a blessed prince, gold and silver, peace and liberty, plenty and prosperity. For which of these (O England) do you condemn My religion?" The least of these deserves love, but England has a better than all these, that is, His gospel, the Word of salvation. And yet, that also is condemned (as being worth nothing) and those who confess it, and those who bring it, and consequently, God Himself who gave it. If England had no more sins but this, this deserves that it should be said of us that we are a "nation not worthy to be beloved" above all nations. For some nations would have religion that they might love it, but they cannot have it. Some have it and love it not. But in no nation is it made a mocking-stock but in England. And where are those men but in England who (like the dog in the manger) will neither entertain religion themselves nor suffer them who would. Let us in time take heed of this sin as a sin that cries to God to avenge so vile a dishonor done to His majesty. Neither is there any sin that more certainly foreshows, and more forcibly hastens, the removing of the gospel from us. For high time is it to cease loving where love procures disdain, and to stay giving where gifts are scorned.

Carry home this lesson to your great towns and cities where you dwell,[14] for in these populous places are these great mockers. For where God has His professors, the devil has his mockers. And repent betimes of this sin, for hold on in mocking, and be sure that God (who will not be mocked) will remove His

---

14. In the margin: There were then present inhabitants of London, York, Cambridge, Oxford, Norwich, Bristow, Ipswich, Colchester, Worchester, Hull, Lin, Manchester, Kendal, Coventry, Nottingham, Northampton, Bath, Lincoln, Derby, Leicester, Chester, Newcastle, and of many other most populous cities and towns of England.

gospel from you. But if you leave this sin and entertain the gospel (as it worthily deserves), then be sure of it that God will continue the gospel to you and your posterity after you in the face of all your enemies round about you.

The third common sin of England is blasphemy, many ways but especially in vain swearing, false swearing, forswearing, and the abuse of all the names and titles of the Lord God. This sin is general, even over the whole land, especially in fairs and markets where men for a little gain will not care to call the Lord of hosts to be witness to a lie, and the God of truth to testify an untruth.

And which is worst of all, God's holy name is used in vain oaths and ordinary talk, when men have no cause to swear at all. So that, it is most lamentable to see and observe that the name of any man of honor or worship is used more reverently and less abused than that fearful and glorious name, the Lord our God.

The fourth general and great sin is profanation of the Sabbath. A common sin everywhere, and yet so great a sin that, where it reigns in that country, congregation, family, man or woman, there is no fear of God nor any true grace in them. For the keeping of the Sabbath is the maintaining, increasing, and publishing of religion.

The fifth sin of our nation is evil dealing in bargaining between man and man. How hard a thing it is to find an honest, simple, plain dealing man, and that even in such great assemblies as this is! I fear present experience will testify. You are now many thousands gathered together, some to buy, some to sell, some to exchange. Remember that I have told you [that] an honest hearted and plain dealing man is hard to find. Therefore, labor to approve yourselves sincere hearted men. Remember the counsel of the Holy Spirit: "Let no man oppress or defraud his brother in bargaining: for the Lord is the avenger of all such things."[15] These sins are general and as universal as a canker, and so are the sins [against] the sixth, seventh, and eighth commandments (though they are not altogether so common as these are): adulterers, adulteresses, usuries, briberies, extortions, [and] cozenages. They are a burden under which our earth groans. And they cry against us to heaven, so that upon as good or much better cause may it be said to us as to the Jews: "O nation not worthy to be beloved."

Look at the outward face of our church, at the signs of God's love which are among us, and at God's dealing with us. And behold, we are a beautiful church, a glorious nation, a nation to be admired and wondered at. But look at the lives of our ordinary professors, look at our sins and at our requiting of God's love, and we are a people of Sodom, as full of iniquities as they were, whose sins were so many, so rife, and so ripe, that at the last they will even bring down fire and

---

15. 1 Thess. 4:6.

brimstone or some other strange judgment upon us, if repentance does not prevent it or the cries and prayers of holy men stay not God's hand. So then, let us all here assembled grant and confess that we are a nation so far from being worthy to be beloved as that we are most worthy to be hated and to have all the wrath of God poured upon us.

Now then, are we so? And shall we continue so still? Nay, that is the worst and most wretched of all. Then, let everyone of us learn this duty, enter into ourselves, search our hearts and lives, that they may lie open to our own sight, to the confusion of us in ourselves, that in God by repentance we may be raised up.

Our sins lie open before the face of God, and stink in His presence and cry for vengeance, before the face of God's angels who bewail it, and before the face of the devil who rejoices in our confusions. And shall they lie hid only to ourselves? Now then, if we would have them hidden from God, and stop the cry that they make against us, and keep them from Satan who accuses us for them, we must so search ourselves that they may lie open unto our own hearts. Remember your sins, and God will forget them. Lay them open before your own face, and God will hide them from His. Write them up for your own self, and God will blot them out of His remembrance. But if, contrariwise, you hide them, then assure yourself [that] the more you hide and bury them, the more open do they lie in the face of God. And then what will follow but that they will all be disclosed at the last day to your eternal confusion? Therefore, again and again, I exhort you in the name of God, search yourselves, find out your sins, confess them to God freely and ingenuously, confess their deserts to be hell and damnation, humble your hearts to God, cry and call for pardon as for life and death, purpose and promise to leave them, begin a new course of life, believe steadfastly, and doubt not but of pardon and forgiveness in the blood of Christ, continue in that faith, and that new course of life. So may England prevent God's judgments, and quench that great action of unkindness which God has against them, and become a nation as worthy (upon their faith and repentance) in Christ to be beloved. As for their peace and prosperity, they have been of all nations of the earth admired.

Hitherto of the third general point.

Point 4

The fourth general point in this exhortation is [the] time limited them when they should search: "before the decree come forth." As though the prophet should say, "Israel, repent before God executes His judgments on you." For behold the gracious dealing of God: man sins [and] his sins deserve plagues, but God presently plagues not, but defers it. He puts a time between the sin and the punishment (ordinarily). He does this to show His mercy unto mankind, because He would not destroy them if they would amend. Therefore, after the sin, He smites not presently, but puts off His punishment, that in the meantime man may repent. Here the prophet compares the Lord to a mother, for as she conceives the fruit in her womb, and bears it a long time ere she brings it out, so the Lord, after a man sins, or a people sins, conceives (that is, ordains and decrees) a judgment for it, but He keeps it up, and all that while He bears it. But as she, when her time is come, then travails and brings forth, so when the time that God has appointed is come, and still sin [is] not repented of, then His justice travails to be delivered of that judgment which mercy has kept up so long a time.[16]

Thus, the old world had 120 years given them for time of repentance. All that while God was in conceiving. At last, when their sins were ripe, and [there was] no hope of amendment, then God travailed and brought forth a fearful birth, namely, the universal flood, to wash away and take revenge upon the universal iniquities of those times.[17]

So many hundreds [of] years He gave unto the Jews. He was long in conceiving their destruction, and oftentimes He had it at the bringing forth, as in the captivity of Babylon and under Antiochus, yet His mercy stayed it. And still He travailed longer, telling them here by the prophet that yet the decree is not come forth (though it is conceived). But at last, when Israel would not repent, but grew worse and worse (as in Christ's time), then He could contain [it] no longer, but travailed indeed, and though it is with grief, yet He has brought forth. And what? A most fearful birth, even an utter desolation of that kingdom and country, of their city and temple, and a dispersion of this nation over all the world. But as a woman at last is delivered with danger and difficulty, with pain and sorrow, so the Lord long conceives but at last brings forth His judgments. Yet it is with grief and unwillingness, and He is loath (as it were) and much grieved to execute His most just judgments on those who have professed His name. He often touched the Jews a little and, as being unwilling to smite them, He drew back His hand again. But at last, when their sins did so increase and were so strong that they even did wring out by violence His plagues from Him, then with much bewailing of their great misery (as we may see in Christ weeping for them) He executes His judgments on them. But as they are long a coming, so when they come forth they were the heavier. As a child, the more fullness of time he has, is the greater, the livelier, and the stronger, so God's judgments; the longer God defers them and is in conceiving them, the heavier they are when they come. That is manifest in the Jews, once His own people,

---

16. This paragraph break is not in the original.
17. This paragraph break is not in the original.

for He has destroyed their land with an irrecoverable destruction, and smitten their posterity with a blindness of mind till this hour, so that to this day when the Old Testament is read the veil is over their eyes, so that they cannot see the light of Christ Jesus, but [they] plod on in fearful and palpable blindness.

This doctrine has special use to our church, to teach us to look to ourselves betimes, and try our own ways, and turn to the Lord, for we cannot tell how far off His judgments are. In reason they have been so long deferred, and yet been so justly deserved of us. Certainly, God has been long in conceiving judgments and plagues for the sins of England, and often has God's hand been upon us, by war, famine, pestilence, [and] inundations. And yet, it has been pulled back again. And His sword has been put up into its sheath. And God has stayed its birth, even in the very travail. And we have escaped, even as a man whose neck has been upon the block, and the ax held up to strike. So then, yet the day is not come, yet we have time. Happy [are] we that ever we saw this day, if now we have grace to repent and search our hearts, for then we shall stay His judgment decreed, that it shall never come forth against us! But if we defer to repent, put off from day to day, and lie rotting still in our sins, then know and be assured that as the decree is established so it must needs come forth, and the stroke stricken, repentance is too late. Therefore, what He said to the Jews I say unto us: "Search yourself, O England (a nation not worthy to be beloved), before the decree comes forth, which is already passed against you." Thus much for the fourth point.

Point 5

Fifth, now follows the last point: the reason of all. Why should we search ourselves? The reason is included in the fourth point: "For there is a decree come forth against thee." And although the execution is defeated, and though God is unwilling to take it out, yet without repentance it is most certain [that] it shall come forth and be executed at the last. In one word, this is the reason: Repent, or else certainly God will take vengeance. But (man's heart will say) is this true? Or rather, these are but words to frighten men and keep them in awe. I answer, for proof and experience hereof, never go further than this place, and [a] present example we have in hand. The prophet bids them to "search, search, and repent," else as certainly as there was a judgment conceived, so certainly it should be executed upon them. They would not hear nor search nor repent. But what followed? Let all men judge whether God is not true to His Word to them or not. Yea, alas, who sees not that God has travailed indeed, and has brought forth a fearful judgment on them, and has made them for these 1,500 years the gazing-stock, the byword, and the amazement of all the world?

It was thus threatened to the Jews, and it is thus performed. And, certainly, it has been threatened thus, and it shall be performed thus, to you, O England, except you prevent the judgments that are coming. O, happy England, that I may say unto you, it is yet but coming! For, as for the miserable Jews, (alas) it is come already upon them. To those poor souls it can be said no more, "Repent before the decree come forth." For it is now past. But you are happy, for your day is not yet come, yet I may say unto you, "Repent before the decree come forth." And, O happy England, that you may hear this word "before" sounding in your ears![18]

Therefore, my beloved brethren who are here assembled out of (almost) every corner of this kingdom, hear my words, and carry them home with you into all countries. God is the same God still, as just and as jealous as ever He was. Our sins are as ill, nay, much viler than the Jews' [sins] were. How can it be then? But that must fall to us that fell to them. Therefore, the zeal of God's glory and my desire of your salvation make me that I dare not flatter but tell you the truth; that is, that out of all question, if we search not ourselves and repent, there is a general judgment in preparing for us. Certainly, the decree is out, and what can stop the execution of it but repentance? God has long spared, and He has been long in travailing; therefore (though nothing can be said in way of prophecy), I am in my conscience persuaded to fear, and that out of infallible grounds of the Word of God, that a plague and a judgment, and that most fearful, hangs over England, and that it is already pronounced upon this nation, and shall be as certainly executed without a visible reformation. And because I may seem to speak somewhat large, give me leave to give you the reasons inducing me hereunto.

Reason 1

First, the gospel has been preached these thirty-five years, and is daily more and more, so that the light thereof never shone more gloriously since the primitive church. Yet, for all this, there is a general ignorance, general of all people, general of all points, yea, as though there were no preaching at all. Yea, when popery was newly banished, there was more knowledge in many than is now in the body of our nation. And the more it is preached, the more ignorant are many, the more blind, and the more hardened (even as a stithy,[19] the more it is beaten upon, the harder it is). So they, the more they hear the gospel, the less they esteem it and the more they condemn it. And the more God calls, the deafer they are. And the more they are commanded, the more they disobey.

---

18. This paragraph break is not in the original.
19. *Stithy*: forge or anvil.

We preachers may cry till our lungs fly out or be spent within us, and men are moved no more than stones. Oh alas, what is this, or what can this be, but a fearful sign of destruction? Will any man endure always to be mocked? Then how long has God been mocked? Will any man endure to stand knocking continually? If then God has stood knocking at our hearts thirty-five years, is it not now time [for Him] to be gone unless we open presently?

But if we will know what this argues, to condemn the gospel and not repent when the Word is so abundantly preached, read the story of Eli's wicked sons. He spoke unto them and gave them godly counsel, "but they hearkened not unto the voice of their father" [1 Sam. 2:25]. But some will say that [this] is not [a] great matter [and] not to hear their father [is] a common thing. But mark what follows: "They would not hear their father, because the Lord would destroy them"—a fearful thing. Even so it is with a nation or a people. Are they taught, and are they worse and worse? Take heed: If Eli's sons obey not, it is because God will destroy them.

If, therefore, Eli and many Elis have spoken to England, and England hears not, obeys not, [and] repents not, take heed the Lord in heaven say not, "England will not hear the voice of the prophets because I will destroy it." Let no man say [that] we take upon us to prophesy. We only give warning and show the danger by example of the like.

Reason 2
My second reason is this: one judgment executed, and not working repentance, is always a forerunner of another. That rule is certain, and an evident truth, and needs no proving. Now, we have been visited with famines, earthquakes, pestilences, inundations, thunder and lightning in winter, and most strange and unseasonable weather. But alas, all these have taken no effect. Where is the humiliation, repentance, and reformation which they have wrought? Therefore, it must needs be [that] there remains behind a greater judgment. Men may be so mad to think these to be ordinary things, and to come by course of nature and ordinary causes, but certainly they are the shaking of the rod and forerunners of a great judgment unless repentance cuts off their course. For look, as one cloud follows another till the sun consumes them, so one judgment hastens after another, and repentance is the only sun which must dispel them.

Reason 3
Third, it stands with the justice of God, according as He has revealed it in the Scripture, especially in Deuteronomy 28. Out of the whole chapter, it must needs be gathered as a rule: "I will curse that people that break my laws." Now we may not deny but this land of ours is for abundance of sin a people of Sodom.

All kinds of sins, in all estates of men, rage and reign every day more and more. Therefore, I conclude that unless we repent and so dissolve this cloud of judgment that hangs over our heads, it cannot be but [that] a most fearful tempest is to come at the last. And when it is come, it will be too late to wish they had done it. Therefore, in the bowels of Christ Jesus, let this be to entreat and exhort you all to search and look into yourselves, so that repenting and changing your ways you may get the sword again into its sheath, which is already drawn out but yet has not stricken home, and may quench the wrath which is already kindled but yet burns not out as it will do if by repentance we quench it not. And do this, everyone, as you tender the salvation of your own souls, and the continuance of the gospel to this glorious nation, and the peace and prosperous state of this church and commonwealth. For let men make what causes they will, it is certainly sinfulness that overturns kingdoms and changes states, as all these kingdoms and states have felt, which have continued finally to contemn the gospel.

It follows: "And you be as chaff, that passeth on a day."

The Meaning

The prophet proceeds and describes more plainly the manner and state of that plague which God will send upon them. The meaning was partly opened before, to be in effect thus much: search yourselves lest God take His fan and try you because you would not try yourselves, and, finding you upon the trial not sound wheat but light chaff, blow you to hell with the wind of His wrath. The metaphor, which the prophet uses, is this: he compares the Lord to a husbandman, great and rich, [and] the whole world is His corn field. Several nations (as ours for one) are His heaps of corn. But the heaps of corn are full of chaff, that is, these particular churches are full of hypocrites. Now a wise husbandman lets corn and chaff lie together no longer than till the wind does blow, and then he appoints his fanning time to sever his corn from his chaff, and to blow away his chaff, and lay up his corn. So God, the great and wise Husbandman, will not let the chaff lie forever among the wheat. He has, therefore, appointed His fanning times when to blow the chaff into hell and to gather His wheat into heavenly garners.

Now God's winnowing times are two. The one is at the last day, after this life. And that is God's great winnowing day of all His corn (that is, of all men) when the bad shall be severed from the good forever, never to be mingled again with them, but by the strong and powerful fan of His last and final judgment to be blown into hell. The wind of His wrath, at that day, shall be stronger to blow them all away than all the wind in the world to blow away one handful of light chaff.

God's other fanning time is in this world, and that is also double. The one is when the Word is preached. The preaching of the Word is one of God's fans, for when the gospel is preached to a nation or congregation, it fans them and tries them and purges them, and so serves them that a man may see a manifest difference of the chaff and the wheat, that is, of the godly man and the wicked man. This preaching of the gospel does John the Baptist expressly call a fan, where the Holy Spirit pursues this whole metaphor most plainly. Speaking of Christ, he says, "Whose fan is in his hand, and he will throughly purge his floor, and gather his wheat into his garner, but the chaff he will burn with fire unquenchable."[20] The wind of this fan of the Word preached is so strong that it severs the chaff from the wheat, that is, good professors from hypocrites in the visible church, and blows so strongly upon the wicked that it brings them to the beginning of hell even in this world. For it so works upon the conscience, as if it cannot convert them, it strikes them with fear, terror and torment, either in life or at death, which torment of conscience is the very flashes of hell-fire.

But, when this first fan of the Word will not serve to bring men to repentance (for the Word preached does not confound a man actually, but only pronounce the sentence and thereby strike the conscience), then God has another fan, and that is the fan of His judgments. And that fanning (or winnowing) time is when He executes His vengeance and His judgments on a nation. This is His latter fan, when the first will not prevail. This is His powerful and strong fan driven about with the wind of His wrath. This fan went over the old world, and swept them all away, and went over the nation of the Jews, and we see they are no more.

These three fans of God make a threefold separation of the chaff from the wheat, that is, of the wicked from the elect. With the fan of His Word, which is powerful, He severs them in all affection and disposition, and makes a distinction of them, so as generally the wheat is known to be wheat and chaff discerned to be chaff by the preaching of the Word. But though the tare is known to be tare, yet both grow together, so that the Word only severs them in affection, and sets several notes of distinction upon them both.

But then the second fan of His judgments is more violent, for thereby He severs them asunder in soul, gathering the godly as His wheat into the heavens, and blowing the souls of the wicked into hell. But yet, the bodies of them both lie together, as partakers of the same judgment so subject to the same corruption, and are all lodged in the same grave of the earth, and death has like dominion over them all.

---

20. Matt. 3:12.

But afterwards, at the last day, at God's great harvest and great winnowing time, He then with the wind of His power severs them asunder in soul and body (wheat from the chaff, sheep from the goats), and separates them, never to be mingled again forever and ever. And then with the wind of His wrath, He blows the chaff into unquenchable fire, and with His loving favor gathers His wheat into the everlasting and glorious garners of heaven.

So then, the first severs them in affection; the second in soul for a time; [and] the third actually in soul and body forever and ever.

Now of these three winnowing times, the Holy Spirit speaks here properly of the second; namely, the fan of God's judgments. So that, the meaning of the metaphor is this: search yourselves and repent betimes, lest God come upon you with some fearful judgments because you have so long contemned the fan of the Word, and, finding you too light to abide the trial, [He] does take you away in the judgment and cast you into hell. For as sure as the fan of the Word has made difference of you who are chaff and who are wheat, so sure shall the fan of His judgments blow away the chaff to hell and damnation. Thus much for the meaning.

Now for the use.

The Use

For us in England the case stands thus: our church doubtless is God's corn field, and we are the corn heap of God, and those Brownists and sectaries are blind and besotted, who cannot see that the Church of England is a godly heap of God's corn. But withal, we must confess [that] we are full of chaff, that is, of profane and wicked hypocrites, whose hearts and minds abound in sins and rebellions. And many of our best professors are also too full of chaff (that is, of corruptions), and do give themselves too much liberty in many sins. But alas, the pure wheat, how thin is it scattered? How hard to find a man (at least a family) who dedicates himself to the Lord in holy and sincere obedience, and labors to make conscience of all sins. Now, therefore, seeing we are God's corn field, and we have some pure wheat among much chaff, therefore God will winnow us to find out the corn. If He has but one corn of wheat in a handful of chaff, but one good man of many, He will stir all the heap for those few corns. He will not care to blow all the chaff to hell to find out those few corns of wheat, to lay them up in heaven. So that, out of all question, England being so full of chaff, must look to be winnowed.

Now for the first fan of His Word, it has been used in this land these thirty-five years, and that as powerfully and as plentifully as anywhere in the world. And yet, (alas) many are more godless, more ignorant, more profane than ever they were, yea, wickedness grows and the chaff increases above the wheat. Be sure, therefore, that God will bring His second fan upon us because we will not suffer the first (the mild and gentle fan of His Word) to try and search us. Therefore, He will bring the fearful fan of His judgments, and with it He will blow soul and body into hell with our sins and corruptions which we would not suffer the fan of God's Word to blow from us. The first has so long blown in vain that the second must needs come unto us, and it has already begun to blow. Three or four blasts have blown over us: famine, pestilence, earthquakes, fire, water, [and] wind have so blown some of us that they have taken away a great number of us.[21]

For us that remain, this only remains, that we strengthen ourselves by grace to be able to stand against the next blast. For it will come, and when it comes no wealth nor worldly thing can enable us to endure it. Only faith and repentance and the grace of God will stand at that day. Now, therefore, in that so fearful a fanning abides us, seeing it is so near (as appears by the blasts already passed over us, which are nothing but the forerunners of a greater tempest) what should be our care (except we care not to be blown body and soul into hell) but to labor to eschew this fearful fan of God's wrath, or, at least, if it comes upon us, that it may not blow us to hell but hasten us to heaven? If your heart is touched to ask how this may be, I answer you, only to follow the prophet's advice in this place by searching and trying ourselves. The way to escape God's trial is to try yourself, and [the way] to escape God's judgment [is] to be a judge to your own soul. And so, the way to escape the fearful fan of God is to fan your own heart by the law of God. For whomsoever the first fan (that is, the Word of God) does work upon, these men are never blown away with the fan of God's judgments. Oh then, entertain the Word of God into your heart, submit your soul unto it, let it pierce and try and ransack your heart, and lay before you your wretched estate by your sins. And when you see your nakedness and misery, confess it, bewail it, and be humbled for it, cry and call for mercy and forgiveness, pray against your special sins, strive to purge them out as the poison of your soul, crave grace from God for all your sins. If you see any sins more welcome to your nature, dearer unto you, and which more prevail against you than others do, pray against these sins, and strive against them above all. And endeavor that by the fan of God's Word they may be blown away from you. When you have done this, mark what will come of it. When you have fanned yourself, God will not fan you. But when the fan of His judgment comes and blows so strongly upon the wicked, then the Lord, finding you already fanned and cleansed by His Word, will spare you, and His judgment shall either blow

---

21. In the margin: In the plague at London there died almost 2,000 a week in 1592. But in 1603 there died 3,300 in a week.

over you and pass by you untouched (as over Lot in the destruction of Sodom) or else shall fan out all your corruptions and blow you up to heaven to be laid up as pure wheat in the heavenly garners and mansions of glory, which Christ ascended to prepare for you.

Now then, among those many businesses with which this world does cumber every one of us (all which shall perish with the world itself), let us good brethren spare some time for this great business. Martha may be cumbered about many things, but "this is that one thing which is necessary."[22] Therefore, whatsoever is done, let not this be undone. Once a day, put yourself and your life under the fan of God's law, try yourself (what you are) and your life (how you live). Once a day, keep a court in your conscience, call your thoughts, your words, and your deeds to their trial. Let the Ten Commandments pass upon them. And your sins and corruptions, which you find to be chaff, blow them away by repentance. So shall you remain pure and clean wheat, fit for the house and church of God in this world, and for His kingdom in heaven. But, if we will not do this, then alas, what will follow? My heart grieves to utter it, but I must unless I should be a false prophet, and therefore I will. Our long peace, plenty, and ease, have bred great sins, so great that they reach to heaven and provoke God's majesty to His face, and so strong that they will violently draw down judgments from God upon us. When they come, they will be so powerful and so violent that they will blow us away like chaff and bring this kingdom to some miserable ruin. Oh, therefore, how happy are we if we can entertain this doctrine and practice it. For, in so doing, we shall prevent God's judgments, we shall continue the gospel to this land, and preserve this glorious nation from being destroyed or dis-peopled by some fearful judgment.

Beloved, you come hither to this place,[23] purposely to buy and sell, and thereby to better your estates in this world. How happy then are you, if besides the good markets you make for your bodies and estates, you learn also how to make yourselves abide the trial of God's judgments, and how to be made pure corn, fit to replenish the garners of heaven, and how to continue God's favor and the gospel to this nation. If you go away with this lesson, you have a jewel worth more than [if] you should go home possessed of all the huge riches of this fair. You call this and such like times "fair times," but if you learn this lesson right, then you may say that this was the fairest day indeed that ever shone upon you since you were born. This precious jewel, of which I have spoken all this while, I here offer unto you. Everyone brings hither something to be sold. This is the merchandise that I bring and set to sale unto you. Whatever

---

22. Luke 10:42.
23. In the margin: At Sturbridge Fair.

commodity any of you brings, it is from some quarter of this land, but all is from the earth. But this, that I bring, is from heaven, and all the earth cannot yield it. And as it is from heaven, so it is of a heavenly virtue, and will work that which all the wealth in this fair is not able to do. Therefore, cast not to buy the basest, and let pass the best of all, and never allege that it is above your compass, and [that], being a jewel, it is too dear and costly for you. For I offer it freely unto you, and to every one of you. I pronounce unto you from the Lord that here this blessed doctrine is offered unto you all in His name, freely, "and that you may buy it without money."[24]

Happy is that day when you, coming so far to buy things for your body, and paying so dear for them, do meet with so precious a jewel, the virtue whereof is to save your soul, and [you] pay nothing for it! You may hereafter rejoice, and say, "I went to buy and sell, and to help my body, but I have also learned to save my soul. I went thither to help to maintain my own estate, but I have learned to help to maintain England in prosperity." For assuredly, if we would all of us learn this lesson, and practice it, we might assure ourselves of the glorious prosperity of England to continue from generation to generation. Whereas, alas, if we continue and go forward in our sins and impenitency, it is greatly to be feared that neither the gospel nor this peace will reach to our posterity.[25]

Therefore, now to make an end, I once again, and lastly, commend this doctrine to you all and every one of you. For this merchandise, that I bring, is of that nature that, though some take it, yet there is also enough for everyone. And I commend it unto you even from the very mouth of God Himself. Think of it, I charge you, as ever you look to appear before the face of Christ Jesus, the great Judge, at the last day. And if you would escape the rigor of that judgment, enter now into judgment with yourself and search yourself. If you will not now receive this doctrine, then it shall at the last day be a bill of indictment against you, for if it saves you not, it shall condemn you. Think of it, therefore, seriously, as a matter that concerns your soul and body, yea, and your posterity and this whole realm, all which shall smart for it if we repent not.[26]

And if the body of our people, and those whose hearts are wedded to this world, will not entertain this doctrine, then I turn unto you who fear the Lord, and to you I direct my last warning: Search, O search, and try your hearts and lives, renew and revive your faith and repentance, that if judgments do come and blow upon this nation, and drive the gospel from it, and it into hell, that yet you may have a testimony to your consciences that you did not pull down this general calamity, but for your parts labored to have prevented it by your

---

24. Rev. 22:17.
25. This paragraph break is not in the original.
26. This paragraph break is not in the original.

earnest prayers and hearty repentance. So that, the ensuing posterity may not curse you, but speak reverently of you, and praise God for you, and wish that all had done as you did. For then had they enjoyed this goodly land, and all God's blessings with it, as we (their forefathers) did before them. And so shall our names not rot, but flourish among the posterities to come, who shall be partakers of the desolation. And when we have renewed our repentance, let us then, every one of us, deal with the Lord by earnest prayer for this church and nation, that the Lord would show His mercy upon it, and continue unto it this peace and the gospel. It is nothing with the Lord to do it. His powerful hand is not shortened. He can continue our peace. When the papists look for hurly-burlies,[27] He can continue the gospel. When they hope to set up their idolatry again, let us therefore ply the Lord with our prayers, and with Moses set ourselves in the breach, and pray for the ignorance of the multitude, and bewail their sins, who bewail not their own. So did Noah, Daniel, and Job, in their ages, and prayed for the people in general calamities. Let us all be Noahs, Daniels, and Jobs, in our generations. If we do thus, then when judgments come, we shall either turn them away from our nation, or at the least we shall deliver our own souls.

Let us now turn to the Lord in prayer. And because it cannot be hoped but that this our general sinfulness must needs end with some heavy judgment, let us desire the Lord still to defer our deserved punishments, and still to spare us, and to give us time and leisure to repent. So that, entering into ourselves, and searching our hearts, and turning to the Lord, we may turn away His imminent judgments, and so that when His wrath does burn out indeed, we may then be counted worthy in Christ to escape those things which must needs come upon the world. Amen.

William Perkins

"Let us search and try our ways, and turn again to the Lord" (Lam. 3:40).

Trin-uni Deo gloria

FINIS

---

27. *Hurly-burlies:* upheaval.

Two Treatises:

1. The Nature and Practice of Repentance
2. The Combat of the Flesh and Spirit

A second edition corrected

Printed by John Legate,
Printer to the University of Cambridge
1600

To the Reader

God has bestowed on us great prosperity and peace, with plenty of all temporal blessings that [a] heart can wish, for many years in this land.

Prosperity abused has been the occasion of many grievous sins against the first and second table, especially of atheism, neglect of God's worship, contempt of the Word, profanation of the Sabbath, abuse of the sacraments, etc.

These and such like sins have long called down for judgments from heaven upon us, and the rather because the preaching of the Word has little prevailed to bring us to any amendment of life. Whereupon God has now begun to cause His judgments to seize upon us, especially by plague and pestilence, and that in the very principal part of this land, whereby He Himself does (as Job says) "round us in the ear" and preach repentance to us [Job 36:15].

Wherefore, it stands us now (if ever) in hand to look about us, and if we have not repented, to begin to repent, [and] if we have in former time repented, to do it more earnestly.

If [it] is so that we shall harden our hearts both against His Word and judgments, and put far from us the evil day, we must needs undoubtedly look for judgments far more terrible than ever we felt as yet, if not eternal destruction. Let us be advised by the old world, who made light of Noah's warning, and were drowned in the flood; by Lot's sons-in-law, who took their father's counsel for mockery and were burnt with fire and brimstone from heaven; [and] by the foolish virgins, who were sleeping when they should have been furnishing their lamps, and were shut from the marriage of the lamb.

And to direct you somewhat in the practice of repentance, I have penned this small treatise. Use it for your benefit, and see you are a doer of it, unless you will be a willful murderer and shed the blood of your own soul.

And whereas there have been published heretofore in English two sermons on repentance, one by M. Bradford, martyr, [and] the other by M. Arthur Dent (sermons indeed which have done much good), my meaning is not to add thereunto or teach any other doctrine, but only to renew and revive the memory of that which they have taught.

Neither let it trouble you that the principal divines of this age, whom I follow in this treatise, may seem to be at difference in treating of repentance. For some make it a fruit of faith containing two parts (mortification and vivification);

some make faith a part of it by dividing it into contrition, faith, [and] new obedience;[1] [and] some make it all one with regeneration.[2] The difference is not in the substance of doctrine, but in the logical manner of handling it. And the difference of handling arises from the divers acceptation of repentance. It is taken [in] two ways: generally and particularly. [It is taken] generally for the whole conversion of a sinner, and so it may contain contrition, faith, [and] new obedience under it, and be confounded with regeneration. It is taken particularly for the renovation of the life and behavior, and so it is a fruit of faith. And I only follow this sense in this treatise.

I have added hereto a few lines of the combat between the flesh and the spirit because repentance and this combat are joined together, and the one is not practiced without the other, as appears by resolving Psalm 51.

Spirit: "Have mercy on me, O God, according to thy loving kindness" [v. 1].

Flesh. Yea, but your adultery comprehends infinite sins. Therefore, look for no pardon.

Spirit. "According to the multitude of thy compassions put away mine iniquities."

Flesh. This sin has taken such deep place in you that it will be hardly pardoned.

Spirit. "Wash me throughly from mine iniquities, and cleanse me from my sin" [v. 2].

Flesh. Your special trespass is against man.

Spirit. "Against thee, against thee only have I sinned" [v. 4].

Flesh. Except this one sin your life is unblameable.

Spirit. "Behold I was born in iniquity" [v. 5].

Yea, the best man that is, in the practice of godliness, often appears to be unlike himself. And the cause is this spiritual combat. The flesh sometimes makes him wail and mourn and go drooping, presently after the Spirit puts into him (as we say) the heart of grass,[3] and makes him triumph against the flesh, the devil, [and] the world. Moses was courageous at the Red Sea, but he failed at the waters of strife [Exod. 14:13; Num. 20:11–12]. Job first praises God, and afterwards blasphemes [Job 1:21; 3:1]. David is often fainting in misery, yet by and by revived (Pss. 6:1, 8; 10:17; 41:9–11). Wherefore, there is good cause why

---

1. In the margin: Melanct. loc. com.

2. In the margin: Calv. Inst. l. 3. c. 3. par. 9.

3. The meaning of this expression is unclear.

the consideration of repentance and the combat should go together: that no man, after he has begun to repent, might dream of ease to his flesh as though we should go to heaven in beds of down, but rather that we might be resolved that when we begin to do anything pleasing unto God, then we must look for nothing but continual molestations from our vile and wicked natures.

Written *anno* 1593, the 17 of November, which is the coronation day of our dread sovereign Queen Elizabeth, whose reign God long continue!

William Perkins

Chapter 1

What Repentance Is

Repentance is a work of grace arising from a godly sorrow, whereby a man turns from all his sins unto God and brings forth fruit worthy [of] amendment of life.

A work

I call repentance a work, because it seems not to be a quality, virtue, or habit, but an action of a repentant sinner. This appears by the sermons of the prophets and apostles, which run in this tenor: "Repent," "Turn to God," "Amend your lives," etc. Whereby they intimate that repentance is a work to be done.

A work of grace

Again, repentance is not every kind of work, but a work of grace, because it cannot be practiced by any, but by such as are in the estate of grace. [The] reasons are these: First, no man can repent unless he first hates sin and loves righteousness. And no one can hate sin unless he is sanctified. And he who is sanctified is justified. And he who is justified must needs have that faith which unites him to Christ and makes him bone of His bone and flesh of His flesh. Wherefore, he who repents is justified and sanctified, and made a member of Christ by faith. Second, he who turns to God must first of all be turned to God, and after we are turned then we repent. "Surely after I was converted, I repented: and after that I was instructed, I smote upon my thigh: I was ashamed, yea, even confounded, because I did bear the reproach of my youth" (Jer. 31:19).

Some may object that repentance goes before all grace because it is preached first. The first sermon that ever was made was of repentance, preached by God Himself in Paradise to our first parents. And ever since, the sermons of all the prophets and apostles, and of all faithful ministers, have had repentance for their beginning and scope. The answer hereto may be this: If we respect the order of nature, there are other graces of God which go before repentance, because a man's conscience must in some sort be settled touching his reconciliation with God in Christ before he can begin to repent. Wherefore, justification and sanctification in order of nature go before repentance. But if we respect time, grace and repentance are both together. As soon as there is fire, it is hot. And as soon as a man is regenerate, he repents. If we respect the outward manifestation of these two, repentance goes before all other graces because it first of all appears outwardly. Regeneration is like the sap of the tree that lies hid within the bark. Repentance is like the bud that speedily shows itself before either blossom, leaf, or fruit appear. Yea, all other graces of the heart, which are needful to salvation, are made manifest by repentance. And for this cause repentance (as I take it) is preached first.

Arising from a godly sorrow

I add further that repentance arises from a godly sorrow in the heart. As Paul teaches, "Godly sorrow causeth repentance unto salvation never to be repented of" (2 Cor. 7:10). It is called a "godly sorrow" (or, a sorrow according to God), so that it may be distinguished from worldly sorrow which is a grief arising from the apprehension of the wrath of God and other miseries (as fear of men, loss of good name, calamities in goods and other things) which in this life follow as punishments of sin. Whereas the godly sorrow causes grief for sin because it is sin, and it makes any man in whom it is to be of this disposition and mind: that if there were no conscience to accuse, no devil to terrify, no judge to arraign and condemn, no hell to torment, yet he would be humbled and brought to his knees for his sins because he has offended a loving, merciful, and longsuffering God.

Whereby a man turns to God

Further I say that repentance stands in turning again to God. At the first, man was made a goodly creature in the image of God, having fellowship with Him, whereby he dwelt in God and God in him. By sin there is a partition made between God and man [Isa. 59:2], who is alienated and estranged from God [Eph. 4:18], and is become the child of wrath, a firebrand of hell, the prodigal child going from his father into a far country, the straying (nay, the lost) sheep. Now, when men have grace to repent, then they begin to renew this fellowship and turn again to God. And the very essence (or nature) of repentance consists in this turning. Paul does seem to intimate this when he says that he showed both to Jew and Gentile "that they should repent and turn to God, and do works worthy amendment of life" (Acts 26:20). In these words, he sets down unto us a full description of repentance.

Whereby a man turns from sin

Again, I say that repentance is a turning from sin because it does not abolish or change the substance of body or soul, or any of the faculties thereof, either in whole or in part, but [it] only rectifies and amends them by removing the corruption. It turns the sadness of melancholy to godly sorrow, choler to good zeal, softness of nature to meekness of spirit, madness and lightness to Christian mirth. It reforms every man according to his natural constitution, not abolishing it, but redressing the fault of it.

Whereby a man turns from all sin

Further, I put down that repentance is a turning from all sin to God, so that I may exclude many false turnings. The first [is] when a man turns from God to sin, as when a Protestant becomes a papist, Arian, or Familist. The second [is] when a man turns from one sin to another, as when the riotous person leaves his prodigality and gives himself to the practice of covetousness. This can be no repentance because it is a going from one extreme to another, whereas repentance is to leave the extremes and keep the mean. The third is when a man does not turn from sin, but sin turns from him and leaves him, as when the drunkard leaves drunkenness because his stomach is decayed, the fornicator his uncleanness because the strength of nature fails him, [and] the quarreler his fighting because he is maimed in leg or arm. The last is when men turn from many sins but will not turn from all. Herod did many things at the advertisement of John Baptist, but [he] could not be brought to leave incest in having his brother Philip's wife. This repentance is nothing. For as he who is truly regenerate is wholly in body, soul, and spirit regenerate, so he who truly repents, turns from all sin and turns wholly to God.

Neither is this to trouble any [who say] that they cannot know all their sins, for sound repentance for one special sin brings with it repentance of all sin. And as God requires particular repentance for known sins, so He accepts a general repentance for such as are unknown.

To proceed further, the conversion of a sinner in repentance has three parts. The first [is] a purpose and resolution in the mind. The second [is] an inclination in the will and affections. The third [is] an endeavor in life and conversation to abandon and leave all his former sins, and to employ himself in obedience to God's commandments.

Brings forth fruit worthy amendment of life

Lastly, this repentance must bring forth fruit worthy amendment of life because it cannot be known to be sincere unless it brings forth fruit. Repentant sinners are "trees of righteousness" of God's own planting [Isa. 61:3]. And they grow by the waters that "flow out of the sanctuary," and therefore they must bear fruit that may "serve for meat, and leaf for medicine" [Ezek. 47:12]. Otherwise, the axe of God's judgment is laid to their roots to stock them up [Matt. 3:10].

Chapter 2

The Cause of Repentance

The principal cause of repentance is the Spirit of God. As Paul says, "Instructing them with meekness that are contrary minded, proving if God at any time will give them repentance" (2 Tim. 2:25). And Jeremiah [says,] "Convert thou me, and I shall be converted" (Jer. 31:18).

The instrument of the Holy Spirit in working repentance is the ministry of the gospel only and not the law. [The] reasons hereof are these: First, faith is engendered by the preaching, not of the law, but of the gospel, as Paul says, "The gospel is the power of God to salvation to all that believe from faith to faith" (Rom. 1:16). Therefore, repentance which follows faith as a fruit thereof must needs come only by the preaching of the gospel. Second, the law is the "ministry of death and damnation" [2 Cor. 3:7] because it shows a man his wretched estate but shows him no remedy. Therefore, it cannot be an instrumental cause of that repentance which is effectual to salvation. Third, the doctrine of repentance is a part of the gospel, which appears in this, that the preaching of repentance and the preaching of the gospel are put one for another [Luke 9:6 with Mark 6:12]. And our Savior Christ divides the gospel into two parts: the preaching of repentance and [the] remission of sins in His name [Luke 24:47]. Fourth, that part of the Word which works repentance must reveal the nature of it and set out the promise of life which belongs unto it. But the law neither reveals faith nor repentance. This is a proper work of the gospel. If it is said that the law is a schoolmaster to bring us to Christ, the answer is [that] it brings men to Christ, not by teaching the way or by alluring them, but by forcing or urging them.[1]

Neither do we abolish the law in ascribing the work of repentance to the gospel only. For though it is no cause yet it is an occasion of true repentance, because it represents unto the eye of the soul our damnable estate and smites the conscience with doleful terrors and fears, which though they are not tokens of grace (for they are in their own nature the very gates and downfall to the pit of hell) yet they are certain occasions of receiving grace. The physician is sometimes constrained to recover the health of his patient by casting him into

---

1. In the margin: *Urgendo non alliciendo.*

some fits of an ague. So man, because he is deadly sick of the disease of sin, must be cast into some fits of legal terrors by the ministry of the law so that he may recover his former estate and come to everlasting life.

Repentance is also furthered by calamities which in this case often come in the room and stead of the law. Joseph's brethren, when they were in distress in Egypt, said one to another: "We have verily sinned against our brother in that we saw the anguish of his soul when he besought us, and we would not hear him: therefore is this trouble come upon us" (Gen. 42:21). And the Lord says, "I will go and return to my place till they acknowledge their fault and seek me; in their affliction will they seek me diligently" (Hos. 5:15). And the Israelites say, "My soul had them (namely afflictions) in remembrance, and is humbled in me" (Lam. 3:20). [See the] example of Manasseh: "And when he was in tribulation, he prayed to the Lord his God, and humbled himself greatly" (2 Chron. 33:12). And David says, "It is good for me that I have been afflicted, that I might learn thy statutes" (Ps. 119:71).

Chapter 3

How Repentance Is Wrought

Repentance is wrought in the heart by certain steps and degrees.

First of all, a man must have knowledge of four things; namely, of the law of God, of sin against the law, of the guilt of sin, and of the judgment of God against sin, which is the eternal wrath of God.

Then, in the second place, must follow the application of the former knowledge to a man's own person by the work of the conscience assisted by the Holy Spirit, who for that cause is called the "spirit of bondage" [Rom. 8:15]. And this application is made in a form of reasoning, called a practical syllogism, in this manner:

"The breaker of the law is guilty of eternal death," says the mind.

"But I am a breaker of the law of God," says the conscience as a witness and an accuser.

"Therefore, I am guilty of eternal death," says the same conscience as a judge.

Third, from this application thus made arises fear and sorrow in respect of God's judgments against sin, commonly called the sting of the conscience (or penitence) and the compunction of heart [Acts 2:37]. Now this compunction, unless it is delayed by the comforts of the gospel, brings men to desperation and to eternal damnation. Therefore, he who will repent to everlasting life must go four steps further.

First, he must have knowledge of the gospel, and enter into a serious consideration of the mercy of God revealed therein.

Second, then must follow the application of the former knowledge by the conscience, renewed and assisted by the Spirit of adoption, in this manner:

"He who is guilty of eternal death, if he denies himself, and puts his affiance in the death of Christ, shall have righteousness and eternal life," says the mind enlightened by the knowledge of the gospel.

"But I, being guilty of eternal death, deny myself and put all my affiance in the death of Christ," says the conscience renewed by the Spirit of adoption.

"Therefore, I shall have righteousness and everlasting life by Christ."

Third, after this application, there follows joy and sorrow: joy, because a man's sins are pardoned in Christ; [and] sorrow, because a man by his sins has displeased Him who has been so loving and merciful a God unto him.

Lastly, after this godly sorrow follows repentance, called a transmentation[1] (or, turning of the mind), whereby a man determines and resolves with[in] himself to sin no more as he has done, but to live in newness of life.

---

1. *Transmentation:* a mental transfiguration.

The Parts of Repentance

Repentance has two parts: mortification, and rising to newness of life.

Part 1

Mortification is the first part of repentance, which concerns turning from sin.

Men turn from sin when they do not only abstain from actual sin, but also use all means whereby they may both weaken and suppress the corruption of nature. Surgeons, when they must cut off any part of the body, usually lay plasters to it to mortify it. So that, being without sense and feeling, it may be cut off with less pain. In the same manner, we are to use all helps and remedies prescribed in the Word which serve to weaken or kill sin, so that in death it may be abolished.

And it must not seem strange that I say we must use means to mortify our own sins. For howsoever by nature we cannot do anything acceptable to God, yet being quickened and moved by the Holy Spirit, we stir and move ourselves to do that which is truly good.[1] And, therefore, repentant sinners have grace in them whereby they mortify their own sins. Paul says, "I beat down my body and bring it into subjection" [1 Cor. 9:27]. And, "They which are Christ's have crucified the flesh with the affections and the lusts thereof" [Gal. 5:24]. And, "Mortify therefore your earthly members, fornication, uncleanness, the inordinate affection, evil concupiscence, and covetousness" [Col. 3:5]. And, "If any man purge himself from these, he shall be a vessel unto honor" [2 Tim. 2:21]. And Saint John says, "Every one which hath this hope in him, purgeth himself, even as he is pure" [1 John 3:3]. And, "He which is begotten of God preserveth himself, and the wicked one toucheth him not" [1 John 5:18].

Mortification has three parts: a purpose in mind, an inclination in will, and an endeavor in life and conversation to leave all sin.

---

1. In the margin: *Acti agimus.*

Part 2

Rising to newness of life is the second part of repentance, concerning sincere obedience to God. And it also has three parts.

The first two are a resolution in the mind and an inclination (or lust) in the will to obey God in all things. Barnabas exhorts them of Antioch: "that with purpose of heart they would cleave unto the Lord" [Acts 11:23]. [There] are many examples of these in Scripture. Joshua: "If it seem evil unto you to serve the Lord, choose you this day whom you will serve, whether the gods which your fathers served, or the gods of the Amorites...but I and my household will serve the Lord" [Josh. 24:15]. David: "O Lord, thou art my portion, I have determined to keep thy commandments" [Ps. 119:57]. And, "I have sworn, and will perform it, that I will keep thy righteous judgments" [v. 106]. And, "When thou saidst, Seek my face, mine heart answered unto thee, O Lord, I will seek thy face" [Ps. 27:8]. And, "I have applied mine heart to fulfill thy statutes always even to the end" [Ps. 119:112].

The third part is an endeavor in life and conversation to obey God. [See the] example of Paul: "And herein I take pains to have always a clear conscience towards God and towards men" [Acts 24:16]. Of David: "I have respect to all thy commandments" [Ps. 119:6]. And, "I have chosen the very way of truth, and thy judgments have I laid before me" [v. 30]. And, "I have cleaved to thy testimonies" [v. 31]. And, "Direct me in the path of thy commandments: for therein is my delight" [v. 35].

No man must here think that a repentant sinner fulfills the law in his obedience, for their best works are faulty before God. And whereas the faithful in [the] Scriptures are said to be perfect, we must know that there are two degrees of perfection: perfection in substance, and perfection in the highest degree. Perfection in substance is when a man does sincerely endeavor to perform perfect obedience to God, not in some but in all His commandments. And this is the only perfection that any man can have in this life. A Christian man's perfection is to bewail his imperfection. His obedience consists in the good will more than in the work, and [it] is to be measured by the affection more than by the effect.

Chapter 5

The Degrees of Repentance

Repentance has two degrees. It is either ordinary or extraordinary.

Ordinary repentance is that which every Christian is to perform every day. For as men fall daily either more or less, so the graces of God are proportionally weakened day by day. Wherefore, the continual reparation thereof must be made by a daily renewing of repentance. A Christian man is the temple and house of God's Spirit. He must, therefore, once a day sweep it, that it may be fit to entertain so worthy a guest.

Extraordinary repentance is the same in nature with the former. It differs only from it in degree and measure of grace. And this is to be put in practice when men fall into any enormous, capital, or grievous offences, whereby they do very grievously wound their own consciences, and give great offence to the church. Of this sort was the repentance of Peter when he went forth and wept bitterly, and David's repentance after he had committed adultery and murdered Uriah.

Chapter 6

The Persons Who Must Repent

Men are of two sorts: the natural man and the regenerate [man]. Repentance is needful for both.

[It is needful] for the natural man, that he may be brought from his sins, and the image of God renewed in him. Some may say that many natural men live civilly, abstaining from all outrageous behavior, and therefore need no repentance. I grant indeed they do so. Yet, repentance must go withal. For civil life without grace in Christ is nothing else in God's sight but a beautiful abomination. The Pharisees were civil, yet Christ says of them, "Except your righteousness exceed the righteousness of the scribes and Pharisees, ye shall not see the kingdom of heaven" [Matt. 5:20].

Repentance is also required in the regenerate because they have many unknown and privy corruptions in them which must be mortified. And sometimes they fall grievously. And, therefore, that they may rise again, they must be daily practiced in the spiritual exercises of repentance.

Chapter 7

The Practice of Repentance

In the practice of repentance four special duties are required.

Duty 1

The first is a diligent and serious examination of the conscience by the laws and commandments of God for all manner of sins, both original and actual. [See the] example of the children of Israel: "Wherefore is the living man sorrowful? man suffereth for his sin: let us search and try our ways, and turn again to the Lord" [Lam. 3:39–40]. Of David: "I considered my ways, and turned my feet to thy testimonies" [Ps. 119:59].

Touching original sin, it must be well remembered that one man has not only one part of original sin and another man another, one man this corruption [and] another that, but [that] every man as he received from Adam the whole nature of man so also he received original sin wholly. And, therefore, every man (not one excepted, saving Christ who was extraordinarily sanctified by the Holy Spirit in the womb of the virgin) has in him from his parents the corruption and seed of all sin, which is a natural disposition and proneness to commit any sin whatsoever. Take a view and consider all the horrible sins that are practiced in any part of the world, either against the first or second table. Whatsoever they are, the spawn and seed of them all is even in that man who is thought to be [the] best disposed by nature. Some may say that experience shows the contrary, because among men who want all manner of religion, some are more civil and orderly [and] some more lewdly disposed. I answer that this comes to pass, not because some men are by nature less wicked than others, but because God by His providence does limit and restrain men's corruptions more or less, which He does for the good of mankind. For if men might be wholly left to themselves, corruption would so exceedingly break out into all manner of sins that there should be no living in the world.

In examination of actual sins, three rules must be followed. The first [is] that we must search out, not only our gross sins, but even the very thoughts of our hearts. For repentance is not only a change of the speech, apparel, and outward behavior, but also of the inward and secret thoughts of the heart.

Therefore, the prophet Joel bids the Jews [to] "rend their hearts and not their garments" [Joel 2:13]. And Paul tells the Ephesians that they must "be renewed in the spirit of their minds" [Eph. 4:23]. And Peter bids Simon Magus to repent and pray God "that the thoughts of his heart may be forgiven him" [Acts 8:22]. The second [is] that the very circumstances of sins done must be considered, as the time when, the place where, and the manner how, as namely whether they were done of ignorance or knowledge, of weakness or presumption or obstinate malice. Third, in examination it is very meet and convenient that we pass through all the commandments of the moral law, laying them as most absolute rules to our hearts and lives. And by this means we shall be able to make large bills and catalogues of all our sins, even from the very cradle to any part of our age following, as the servants of God have always done [Job 9:3; Ps. 19:12]. Thus, it will come to pass that we shall plainly see our wretched estate, and acknowledge that our sins are in number as the hairs of our head and as the sands by the sea shore.

A direction for examination of the conscience
First Commandment: "Thou shalt have none other gods, etc." He breaks this commandment:

Who knows not the true God (Jer. 4:22).

Who denies God in his heart by denying His presence, justice, mercy, etc. (Ps. 14:5).

Who hates God, and shows it by disobedience (Exod. 20:5; Rom. 1:30).

Who does not fear God and stand in awe of Him.

Who fears men or other creatures more than God (Matt. 10:28; Rev. 2:10).

Who lives securely in open sins, not fearing God's Word or judgments (1 Thess. 5:6–7).

Who is sorrowful for his sins only in respect of the punishment (2 Cor. 7:10).

Who fears God by men's traditions (Isa. 29:13).

Who does not believe God's Word, but calls the canonical Scripture into question.

Who despairs of God's mercy.

Who has a dead faith without works (James 2:20).

Who puts his confidence in the devil and his works, as seekers to wizards do.

Who loves the creatures (as riches and honor) and his own filthy pleasures more than God (Eph. 5:5).

Who puts confidence in his strength, wisdom, riches, physicians (2 Chron. 16:9, 12).

Who is impatient under the cross (Matt. 10:38).

Who tempts God (Matt. 4:7).

Who seeks for the things of this life more than for God's kingdom (Matt. 6:33).

Who murmurs against God (1 Cor. 10:10).

Who disputes and holds there is no God.

Who holds and maintains opinions against the ancient faith set down in the writings of the prophets and apostles. As did the Manicheans, Donatists, Arians, Anabaptists, etc.

Who so holds one religion as he is ready to follow another (1 Kings 18:21).

Who is full of presumption of God's mercy (Isa. 7:12).

Who falls away from the known truth (2 Peter 2:20).

Who adds to canonical Scripture (Deut. 12:28).

Second Commandment: "Thou shalt make to thyself no graven image, etc." He breaks this commandment:

Who represents God in an image (Exod. 32:6–8).

Who worships God in (or at) images, as crucifixes and such like (2 Kings 18:4).

Who kneels down before an image.

Who is bodily present at mass, keeping his heart to God (1 Cor. 8:9).

Who retains the monuments of idolatry (Exod. 23:13).

Who marries with infidels or such like (Gen. 6:2).

Who makes leagues of amity with such (2 Chron. 18:1).

Who worships God according to his own fantasy (Col. 2:23).

Who worships God with lip-service (Isa. 29:13), as our common people do who place all the service of God in pattering and mumbling over the Creed, Ten Commandments, prayers, and the Lord's prayer, without knowledge of the meaning.

Who has the power of godliness but denies the force of it (2 Tim. 3:5).

Who gives worship to creatures, as saints and angels (Ps. 115:8).

Who refuses to hear the preaching of the gospel (Luke 14:19).

Who negligently worships God (Rev. 3:16).

Who omits invocation of God's name (Isa. 64:7).

Who hears sermons, but when he is reproved, rails and rages and profits nothing (Amos 5:10).

Who changes the worship of God in whole or in part (Deut. 12:32).

Who makes either open or secret leagues with the devil (Ps. 58:6).

Who uses witchcraft, sorcery, or enchantments (Deut. 18:11; Lev. 19:26).

Who consults with wizards (Lev. 20:6).

Who wears amulets or characters about his neck, and puts confidence in them.

Who hinders schools of religion and good learning (Ps. 74:6–7).

Who seeks not (within the compass of his calling) the good estate of God's church, but seeks his own things (Ps. 132:3–4).

Third Commandment: "Thou shalt not take the name of the Lord, etc." He breaks this commandment:

Who does irreverently use God's titles in his talk (Phil. 2:10).

Who swears to do a thing lawful and good, and yet does it not (Matt. 5:23).

Who swears rashly (Jer. 4:2).

Who uses customable swearing in his common talk (Matt. 5:37).

Who blasphemes the name of God (Lev. 24:16).

Who swears falsely (John 8:44).

Who swears against piety and honesty.

Who uses cursing and banning.

Who finds fault with the creatures of God (1 Cor. 10:3).

Who swears by the creatures (Matt. 5:34–35).

Who uses lots in sporting (Prov. 16:33; 18:13).

Who makes and uses charms of herbs and other things (Deut. 18:11).

Who makes jests of the sentences and phrases of Scripture (Isa. 66:2).

Who uses figure casting (Isa. 47:13).

Who does lightly regard God's judgments (Heb. 3:16).

Who, living dissolutely in religion, makes God's name evil spoken of (2 Sam. 12:13; 1 Peter 3:15).

Who makes a vow of continency or of anything not in his power.

Who makes a lawful vow and keeps it not (Deut. 23:21).

Who receives blessings from God and is not thankful (Luke 17:8).

Who teaches the truth but does not practice it (Matt. 23:2).

Fourth Commandment: "Remember the Sabbath day to, etc." He breaks this commandment:

Who labors in the servile works of his ordinary calling (Neh. 13:15).

Who travels abroad on his ordinary business (Exod. 16:24).

Who keeps fairs and markets on this day (Neh. 13:15).

Who works harvest work on this day (Exod. 34:21).

Who uses sports and recreations causing distraction (1 Cor. 10:7).

Who spends the day in idleness (Isa. 58:13).

Who keeps the Sabbath only in outward fashion (Isa. 1:13).

Who profanes it by gluttony and drunkenness.

Who gives servants liberty to do what they list.

Who brings not his family to the congregation to hear God's Word and to receive the sacraments.

Who sanctifies not the Sabbath in his family privately by reading the Word, by conference on that which has been heard in the congregation, and by prayer.

Fifth Commandment: "Honor thy father, etc." He breaks this commandment:

Who thinks but a thought in his mind tending to the dishonor and contempt of his neighbor.

Who mocks or reviles or beats his superiors (Gen. 9:22).

Who disobeys their lawful commandments (Rom. 1:30).

Who is unthankful to parents and will not relieve them if need be (2 Tim. 3:2).

Who disobeys God to obey them (Acts 4:19).

Who exalts himself above the magistrate (2 Thess. 2:4).

Who serves his master with eye service (Col. 3:22).

Who governs his family and those who are under him negligently (1 Tim. 3:4).

Who is slack in punishing faults (1 Sam. 2:23).

Who is too rigorous in speeches and punishments (Eph. 6:9).

Who marries without parents' consent.

Who chooses his calling without parents' consent (Numbers 30).

Who thinks better of himself than of others (Rom. 11:10).

Who despises aged persons (Lev. 19:32).

Sixth Commandment: "Thou shalt not kill." He breaks this commandment:

Who thinks but a thought in his heart tending to the hurt of his neighbor's life.

Who bears malice to another (1 John 3:15).

Who is given to hastiness (Matt. 5:22).

Who uses inward fretting and grudging (James 3:14).

Who is froward of nature, hard to please (Rom. 1:31).

Who is full of rancor and bitterness (Eph. 4:31).

Who derides and scorns others (Gen. 21:9; Gal. 4:29).

Who uses bitter words and railings (Prov. 12:18).

Who uses contending by words or deeds (Gal. 5:20).

Who uses chiding and crying out (Eph. 4:31).

Who is given to make complaints of his neighbor in all places (James 5:9).

Who is a fighter (James 4:1).

Who hurts or maims his neighbor's body (Exod. 21:24).

Who will not forgive an offence (Matt. 5:23).

Who will forgive but not forget.

Who does fare well himself, but gives not alms to relieve the poor (Luke 16:19).

Who uses cruelty in punishing malefactors (Deut. 25:2–3).

Who denies the servants or laborers wages (James 5:4).

Who holds back the pledge (Ezek. 18:7).

Who sells by divers weights and measures.

Who removes the landmark (Prov. 22:28).

Who gives his goods upon usury, which is simply to bind a man to return both the principal and the increase, only for the loan (Ezek. 18:8).

Who by his looseness of life is an occasion why others sin.

Who moves contention and debate (Rom. 1:29).

Who, being a minister, teaches erroneously.

Who teaches slackly (Jer. 48:10).

Who teaches not all (1 Tim. 3:2).

Who hinders men's salvation [in] any way (Matt. 23:13).

Who seeks private revenge.

Seventh Commandment: "Thou shalt not commit, etc." He breaks this commandment:

Who thinks an unchaste thought tending to adultery or to any sin of that kind.

Who looks on a woman to lust after her (Matt. 5:28).

Who commits incest (Lev. 18:22).

Who commits sodomy (1 Cor. 6:9).

Who commits fornication with married or single or contracted folks (Deut. 22:22).

Who uses [the] marriage bed intemperately.

Who lies with a menstruous woman (Ezek. 18:6).

Who uses wantonness (1 Cor. 6:9).

Who uses occasions and provocations to lusts (Gal. 5:9).

Who is given to idleness.

Who wears wanton and light attire (1 Tim. 2:9; 1 Peter 3:3).

Who uses light talk and reading of love-books (1 Cor. 15:35).[1]

---

1. It is unclear what reference Perkins intends.

Who frequents lascivious places (Eph. 5:3).

Who delights in wanton pictures (1 Thess. 5:23).

Who uses the mixed dancing of men and women (Mark 6:22).

Who keeps company with light and suspected persons (Prov. 7:22).

Who neglects to dispose his children in marriage in convenient time (1 Cor. 7:37).

Who makes marriages of young children.

Who punishes adultery with small punishments.

Who marries more wives than one at once (Gen. 2:24).

Who loves his pleasures more than God (2 Tim. 3:4).

Who takes care to fulfill the lusts of the flesh (Rom. 13:14).

Who maintains and frequents stewes[2] (Deut. 23:17).

Who is given to drunkenness and surfeiting (Eph. 5:18).

Who gives himself to wine, sleep, and ease (Prov. 20:13).

Who, for the avoiding of fornication, marries not (1 Cor. 7:2).

Who puts away his wife for other causes than fornication (Matt. 19:9).

Eighth Commandment: "Thou shalt not steal." He breaks this commandment:

Who thinks but a thought tending to the least hindrance of his neighbor's welfare and good estate.

Who lives in no calling (2 Thess. 3:11).

Who neglects his calling (Jer. 48:10).

Who spends his wealth in riot, and provides not for his family (1 Tim. 5:8).

Who is not content with his estate, but seeks to be rich (1 Tim. 6:10).

Who sells the goods of the church or buys them (Mal. 3:8).

Who sells such things as are means to further idolatry or any other sin.

Who uses powdering, starching, blowing, dark shops, to set a gloss on his wares and make them more sellable.

Who conceals the fault of his wares.

Who uses false weights and measures (Lev. 19:35).

---

2. *Stew*: brothel.

Who uses words of deceit (Prov. 20:14).

Who takes more for his wares than the just price (Matt. 7:12).

Who oppresses his tenants by racking his rents (Hab. 2:9).

Who uses engrossing of wares.

Who raises the price, only in consideration of a day of payment.

Who either gives or takes bribes (Isa. 1:16; Ps. 82:2).

Who writes letters of affection in wrong suits.

Who holds back things borrowed (Ezek. 18:7).

Who holds back things found or pawned (Lev. 6:3).

Who, being lusty, lives by begging.

Who relieves such (2 Thess. 3:10).

Who, for gain, defends bad causes and delays suits in law.

Who lays burdens on the people without measure (Isa. 1:23; Ezek. 22:27).

Who spends the church's goods in riot (1 Tim. 6:9).

Who makes merchandise of God's Word and sacraments (Micah 3:11; 2 Cor. 2:17).

Who gets goods by gaming.

Who gets his living by casting of figures and by plays (Eph. 4:28).

Who is rash in suretyship (Prov. 11:15; 17:18).

Who steals men's children to dispose them in marriage (1 Tim. 1:10).

Who takes by stealth the least pin, though it is for the best end.

Who is a receiver of things stolen, and gives consent to the fact any way (Rom. 1:31).

Who uses deceit in bargaining (1 Thess. 4:6).

Who restores not things evil gotten (Ezek. 33:15).

Who keeps back goods given to the church (Acts 5:3).

Who waits for a dearth to sell his things dearer (Amos 8:5).

Ninth Commandment: "Thou shalt not bear, etc." He breaks this commandment:

Who does but conceive a thought of disgrace against his neighbor.

Who envies at the prosperity of his neighbor (1 Tim. 6:4).

Who seeks only his own good report.

Who is suspicious (1 Cor. 13:5).

Who gives hard and rash sentence against others (Matt. 7:1).

Who takes men's sayings and doings in worse part (Matt. 26:60).

Who accuses one falsely (1 Kings 21:13).

Who makes or reports tales openly or in a whispering manner (Lev. 19:16).

Who receives tales (Exod. 23:1).

Who speaks the truth of malice (Ps. 52:1–2).

Who blazes abroad men's infirmities (Matt. 18:17).

Who uses quipping and taunting (Eph. 5:4).

Who uses flattery (Prov. 26:19).

Who lies though it is for ever so good an end (Zech. 13:3).

Who defends an evil cause and impugns the contrary.

Who writes or spread libels.

Tenth Commandment: "Thou shalt not lust." He breaks this commandment:

Who thinks an evil thought against his neighbor though he means not to do it.

Who conceives some inward delight in some evil motion, though he gives not consent to practice it.

Sins directly against the gospel
He sins against the gospel:

Who denies, either directly or by consequent, that Christ is come in the flesh (1 John 4:3, 8).

Who treads underfoot the blood of Christ (Heb. 10:29).

Who believes not the remission of his own sins and acceptation to everlasting life (1 John 3:23).

Who repents not, but hardens himself in all his bad ways (Rom. 2:4–5; Jer. 8:6).

Duty 2

Thus much of examination. Now follows the second duty, which is confession of sin unto God, which is very necessary. For the right way to have our sins covered before God is to uncover and acknowledge them unto Him. For He will justify us, if we condemn ourselves. He will pardon us, if we, as being our own enemies, accuse ourselves. He forgets our sins, if we remember them. When we are vile in our own eyes, we are precious in His. And when we are lost to ourselves, we are found by Him.

That confession may be rightly performed, a notable duty is to be put in practice in it; namely, the arraignment of a repentant sinner whereby he "judges himself that he may not be judged of the Lord" [1 Cor. 11:31]. This arraignment has three special points in it.

First of all, he must bring himself forth to the bar of God's judgment. He does this when he sets himself in the presence of God, as though even now the day of judgment were [here]. As Saint Jerome did, who always thought with[in] himself that he heard this voice sounding in his ears: "Rise you dead and come to judgment."

Second, he must put up an indictment against himself by accusing himself before God, by acknowledging his known sins particularly and his unknown generally, without any excuse or extenuation or defense or hiding of the least of them. Example of David: "I know mine iniquity and my sin is ever before me: against thee, against thee only have I sinned, and done this evil in thy sight… behold, I was born in iniquity, and in sin hath my mother conceived me" [Ps. 51:3–5]. And, "I have sinned greatly, because I have done this thing: but now, I beseech thee, remove the iniquity of thy servant: for I have done very foolishly" [1 Chron. 21:8]. Of Ezra: "O my God, I am ashamed and confounded to lift up mine eyes unto thee, my God: for our iniquities are increased over our heads, and our trespass is grown up unto heaven" [Ezra 9:6].

Third, he must with heaviness of heart, as a judge upon the bench, give sentence against himself, acknowledging that he is worthy of everlasting hell, death, and damnation. As the prodigal child: "Father, I have sinned against heaven, and against thee, and am not worthy to be called thy child" [Luke 15:18–19]. And Daniel: "We have sinned and committed iniquity, and have done wickedly: yea, we have rebelled and have departed from thy precepts, and from thy judgments…O Lord, righteousness belongeth unto thee, and unto us open shame" [Dan. 9:5–7]. Of Job: "Behold, I am vile, what shall I answer thee. I will lay my hand upon my mouth" [Job 39:36]. And, "I abhor myself, and I repent in dust and ashes" [Job 42:6]. Of the publican: "Who standing afar off, would not lift up so much as his eyes to heaven, but smote his breast, saying, Lord be merciful to me a sinner" [Luke 18:13].

As for confession of sin to men, it is not to be used but in two cases. First, when some offence is done to our neighbor [Matt. 5:24]. Second, when ease and comfort is sought for in trouble of conscience [James 5:16].

Duty 3

The third duty in the practice of repentance is deprecation, whereby we pray to God for the pardon of the sins which have been confessed with contrition of heart, with earnestness and constancy, as for the weightiest matter in the world. And here we must remember to behave ourselves to God as the poor prisoner does at the bar, who when the judge is about to give sentence, cries unto him for favor as for life and death. And we must do as the cripple or leprous man in the way: sit down, unfold our legs and arms, and show the sores of our sins, crying to God continually as they do ("Look with your eye, and pity with your heart"), so that we may find mercy at God's hands, as they get alms at the hands of passengers. Thus, Hosea instructs the people: "O Israel, return unto the Lord thy God: for thou hast fallen by thine iniquity: take unto you words, and turn unto the Lord, and say unto him, Take away all iniquity and receive us graciously: for we will render thee the calves of our lips" (Hos. 14:1–2). Of Daniel: "We do not present our supplication before thee for our own righteousness, but for thy great tender mercies. O Lord hear, O Lord forgive, O Lord consider and do it: defer not for thine own name's sake, O my God" [Dan. 9:18–19]. Of David: "Have mercy upon me, O God, according to thy loving kindness: according to the multitude of thy compassions put away mine iniquities" [Ps. 51:2].

Duty 4

The last duty is to pray to God for grace and strength, whereby we may be enabled to walk in newness of life. Of David: "Behold, I desire thy commandments, quicken me in thy righteousness" (Ps. 119:40). And, "Teach me to do thy will, for thou art my God: let thy good Spirit lead me into the land of righteousness" (Ps. 143:10).

Chapter 8

Legal Motives to Repentance

Motives to repentance are either legal or evangelical. Legal are such as are borrowed from the law. And they are especially three.

Motive 1

The first is the misery and cursed estate of every impenitent sinner in this life by reason of his sins. His misery (that I may express it to the conceit[1] of the simplest) is sevenfold: (1) within him; (2) before him; (3) behind him; (4) on his right hand; (5) on his left hand; (6) over his head; [and] (7) under his feet.

Within him

His misery within is twofold.

The first is a guilty conscience, which is a very hell unto the ungodly man. For he is like a silly prisoner, and the conscience [is] like a jailer who follows him at the heels and dogs him wherever he goes, to the end [that] he may see and observe all his sayings and doings. It is like a registrar who always sits with the pen in his hand, to record and enroll all his wickedness for everlasting memory. It is a little judge who sits in the middle of a man, even in his very heart, to arraign him in this life for his sins, as he shall be arraigned at the last day of judgment. Therefore, the pangs, terrors, and fears of all impenitent persons are (as it were) certain flashings of the flames of the fire of hell. The guilty conscience makes a man like him who lies on a bed that is too straight, and the covering too short [Isa. 28:20], who would with all his heart sleep but cannot. Belshazzar, when he was in the midst of his mirth, seeing the hand writing upon the wall, was smitten with great fear, so as "his countenance changed, and his knees smote together" [Dan. 5:6].

The second evil within a man is the fearful slavery and bondage under the power of Satan, the prince of darkness, in that his mind, will, and affections are so knit and glued to the will of the devil that he can do nothing but obey

---

1. *Conceit:* understanding.

him and rebel against God. And hence, Satan is called the prince of this world [2 Cor. 4:4], who keeps the hold of the heart as an armed captain keeps a sconce[2] or castle with watch and ward.

Before him

The misery before man is a dangerous snare which the devil lays for the destruction of the soul. I say it is dangerous because he is in setting of it twenty or forty years, before he strikes, when as (God knows) men do little think of it [2 Tim. 2:25]. It is made of three cords. With the first he brings men into his snare. And that he does by covering the misery and the poison of sin, and by painting out to the eye of the mind the deceitful profits and pleasures thereof. With the second he hopples[3] and ensnares them. For after a man is drawn into this or that sin, the devil has so sugared it over with fine delights that he cannot but needs must live and lie in it. By the third he draws the snare and endeavors with all his might to break the neck of the soul. For when he sees a fit opportunity, especially in grievous calamities and in the hour of death, he takes away the vizard[4] of sin, and shows the face of it in the true form, as ugly as himself. Then withal he begins (as we say) to show his horns. Then he rages in terrifying and accusing, that the soul of man may be swallowed up by the gulf of final despair.

Behind him

The misery behind him is past sins. The Lord says to Cain, "If thou doest not well, sin lieth at the door" [Gen. 4:7]. Here sin is compared to a wild beast which follows a man wherever he goes and lies lurking at his heels. And though for a time it may seem to be hurtless, because it lies asleep, yet at length, unless men repent, it will rise up, seize on them, and rend out the very throats of their souls. Job in his affliction says, "Thou writest bitter things against me, and makest me possess the sins of my youth" (Job 13:26). And David prays, "Forgive me the sins of my youth" (Ps. 25:7). If the memory of past sins is a trouble to the godly man, oh what a rack, what a gibbet, will it be to the heart of him who wants grace?

On the right hand

The misery on the right hand is prosperity and ease, which by reason of man's sins is an occasion of many judgments. In it, men practiced the horrible sins of Sodom [Ezek. 16:49]. It puffs up the heart with devilish pride, so as men shall think themselves to be as God Himself, as did Sennacherib, Nebuchadnezzar,

---

2. *Sconce:* hiding place.
3. *Hopple:* fetter.
4. *Vizard:* mask or disguise.

Antiochus, Alexander, Herod, [and] Domitian. It steals away man's heart from God and quenches the sparks of grace. As the Lord complains of the Israelites: "I spoke unto thee when thou wast in prosperity: but thou saidst, I will not hear: this hath been thy manner from thy youth" (Jer. 22:21). It is like the ivy that embraces the tree and winds round about it, but yet draws out the juice of it. Hence it is that many turn it to an occasion of their destruction. Solomon says, "The prosperity of fools destroyeth them" (Prov. 1:32). When the milt[5] swells, the rest of the body pines away, and when the heart is puffed with pride, the whole man is in danger of destruction. The sheep that goes in the best pasture, soonest comes to the slaughter house. And the ungodly man fats himself with continual prosperity that he may the sooner come to his own damnation (Rom. 1:32).

On the left hand

The misery on the left hand is adversity, which stands in all manner of losses and calamities in goods, friends, good name, and such like. Of this read at large [in] Deuteronomy 28. The misery over his head is the wrath of God, which He testifies in all manner of judgments from heaven, in danger of which every impenitent sinner is every hour. And the danger is very great. The Scripture says, "It is a fearful thing to fall into the hands of the living God" (Heb. 10:31). He has "store houses" full of all manner of judgments [Deut. 32:34]. And they "watch" for secure sinners, so that they cannot escape [Ezek. 7:6]. God's wrath is a fire making havoc and bringing to naught whatsoever it lights on. Yea, because He is slow to anger, [it is] therefore more terrible. As a man, therefore, stays his hand for a time that he may lift it higher and fetch a deeper blow. When the dumb creatures melt as wax and vanish away at His presence when He is angry, as the huge mountains and rocks do [Nahum 1:4, 5, 9; Psalm 97]; frail man must never look to stand. If the roaring of a lion makes men afraid, and the voice of thunder is terrible, oh, how exceedingly should all be astonished at the threatenings of God!

Under his feet

The misery under his feet is hell-fire, for every man, till he repents, is in as great danger of damnation as the apprehended traitor of hanging, drawing, and quartering. A man, walking in his way, falls into a deep dungeon that is full of ugly serpents and noisome beasts. In his fall he catches hold of a twig of a tree that grows at the mouth of the dungeon and hangs by it. Afterwards, there comes a beast, both lean and hunger-bitten, which, having cropped the whole

---

5. *Milt*: spleen.

tree, is ever and anon knapping[6] at the twig on which he hangs. Now, what is the danger of this man? Surely, he is likely to fall into the pit over which he hangs. Well, this man is every penitent sinner. The pit is hell, prepared for the devil and his angels. The twig is the brickle[7] and frail life of man. The hunger-bitten beast is death, that is ready every hour to knap[8] our life asunder. The danger is fearful. For man, hanging (as it were) over the mouth of hell, when life is ended, unless he uses good means before he dies, he then falls to the very bottom of it.

If this is the misery wherewith the careless man is sieged and compassed about every way, and that for his sins, why do men lie in the dead sleep of security? Oh, it stands them in hand to take up the voice of bitter lamentation, and for their offences to howl after the manner of dragons. If men could weep nothing but tears of blood for their sins, if they could die a thousand times in one day for very grief, they could never be grieved enough for their sins.

Motive 2

The second motive to draw men to repentance is the consideration of the wretched estate of an impenitent sinner in his death, which is nothing but the wages[9] and allowance that he receives for his sins [Rom. 6:23]; and it is the very suburbs (or rather the gates) of hell. Saint Paul compares death to a scorpion who carries a "sting" in its tail, which is sin [1 Cor. 15:55–56]. Now then, when impenitent and profane persons die, then this scorpion comes and grips them with its legs and stabs them at the heart with its sting. Wherefore, the best thing is, before death comes, to use means to pull out the sting of death. And nothing will do it but the blood of Christ. Let men, therefore, break off their sins by repentance. Let them come to the throne of grace and cry. Yea, let them fill heaven and earth with cries for mercy. Oh! Pray, pray, pray for the pardon of your own personal and particular sins. If you obtain but one drop of God's special mercy in Christ, all danger is past. For death has lost its sting, and then a man without danger may put an ugly serpent in his bosom.

Motive 3

The third motive is the consideration of his estate after death. When the day of the last judgment shall be, he must be brought and set before the tribunal seat of Christ. He shall not be able to escape or hide himself. Then, the books shall be brought out, and all his sins shall be discovered before God's saints and

---

6. *Knapping:* striking or breaking.
7. *Brickle:* brittle.
8. *Knap:* break with a quick blow.
9. In the margin: ὀψώνια.

angels. The devil, and his own conscience, shall accuse him. None shall be [an] advocate to plead his cause. He himself shall be speechless. He shall at length hear the dreadful sentence of damnation: "Go ye cursed into hell prepared for the devil and his angels."[10] This thing might move the vilest atheist in the world to leave his wicked ways and come to amendment of life. We see the strongest thief that is, when he is led in the way from the prison to the bar, leaves his thieving and behaves himself orderly. And, indeed, if he would then cut a purse, it would be high time that he was hanged. All men by nature are traitors and malefactors against God. While we live in this world, we are in the way going to the bar of God's judgment. The wheel of the heavens turns one bout[11] every day, and winds up somewhat of the thread of our life. Whether we sleep or wake, we are always coming nearer our end. Wherefore, let all men daily humble themselves for their sins, and pray unto God that He would be reconciled unto them in Christ. And let them endeavor themselves in obedience to all God's commandments, both in their lives and callings.

Again, after the last judgment, there remains eternal death appointed for him who stands in these three things: (1) a separation from all joy and comfort of the presence of God; (2) eternal fellowship with the devil and his angels; [and] (3) the feeling of the horrible wrath of God, which shall seize upon body, soul, and conscience, and shall feed on them as fire does on pitch and brimstone, and torment them as a worm crawling in the body and gnawing on the heart. They shall always be dying and never dead, always in woe and never in ease. And this death is the more grievous because it is everlasting. Suppose the whole world to be a mountain of sand, and that a bird must carry from it but one mouthful of sand every thousand years. Many innumerable thousands of years will be expired before she will have carried away the whole mountain. Well, if a man should stay in torment so long, and then have an end of his woe, it would be some comfort. But when the bird shall have carried away the mountain a thousand times, alas, alas, a man shall be as far from the end of his anguish and torment as ever he was. This consideration may serve as an iron scourge to drive men from their wicked lives.[12]

Chrysostom would have men in their meetings in taverns and feasts to talk of hell, so that by often thinking on it they might avoid it. A grave and chaste matron, being moved to commit folly with a lewd ruffian, after long discourse, she called for a pan of burning coals, requesting him for her sake to hold his finger in them but one hour. He answered that it was an unkind request. To which she replied that, seeing he would not hold so much as one finger in a

---

10. Matt. 25:41.

11. *Bout:* a period of activity.

12. This paragraph break is not in the original.

few coals for one small hour, she could not yield to do the things for which she should be tormented body and soul in hell-fire forever. And so, all men should reason with themselves when they are about to sin. None will be brought to do a thing that may make so much as their finger or tooth to ache. If a man is but to snuff a candle, he will first spit on his finger, because he cannot abide the heat of a small and tender flame. Therefore, we ought to have great care to leave our sins whereby we bring endless torment to body and soul in hell-fire, to which our fire is but ice in comparison.

Chapter 9

Evangelical Motives to Repentance

Evangelical motives are especially two.

Motive 1

The first is taken from the consideration of man's redemption. He who redeemed mankind is God Himself, as Paul says, "God was in Christ, reconciling the world to himself" (2 Cor. 5:19). Man's sin is so vile and heinous in the eyes of God that no angel nor creature whatsoever was able to appease the wrath of God for the least offence. But the Son of God Himself must come down from heaven and take man's nature on Himself. And not only that, but He must also suffer the most accursed death of the cross and shed His most precious heart blood to satisfy the justice of His Father on our behalf. If a father should be sick of such a disease that nothing would heal him but the heart blood of his own child, he would presently judge his own case to be dangerous, and would also vow, if ever he recovered, to use all means whereby he might avoid that disease. So likewise, seeing nothing could cure the deadly wound of our sin but a plaster made of the heart blood of Christ, it must make us acknowledge our pitiful case and the heinousness of the least of our sins, and stir us up to newness of life.

Again, considering the end of the redemption wrought by Christ was to deliver us from our evil conversation in sin and unrighteousness, we are not to continue and (as it were) lie bathing ourselves in sin. For that would be as if a prisoner, after he had been ransomed and had his bolts taken off and was put out of prison to go whither he would, should return again and desire to lie in the dungeon still.

Motive 2

The second motive is that God has made a promise to such as truly repent. First, of remission of sins. "Wash you, make you clean, take away the evil of your works from before mine eyes: cease to do evil.… Though your sins were as crimson, they shall be made as white as snow: though they were red like scarlet, they shall be as wool" (Isa. 1:16, 18). And, "Seek the Lord while he may be found, call upon him while he is near. Let the wicked forsake his ways, and the unrighteous his own imaginations, and return unto the Lord, and he will have mercy on him, for he is very plentiful in forgiving" (Isa. 55:6–7). Second, of everlasting life. "I will not the death of a sinner, but rather that he repent and live" (Ezek. 18:32). And, "Thus saith the Lord unto the house of Israel, Seek ye me, and ye shall live" (Amos 5:4). Third, of mitigating or removing temporal calamities. "Stand in the court of the Lord's house and speak unto all the cities of Judah…. If so be they will hearken and turn every man from his evil way, that I may repent me of the plague which I have determined to bring upon them, because of the wickedness of their works" (Jer. 26:2–3). And, "If we would judge ourselves, we should not be judged" (1 Cor. 11:31), that is, afflicted with temporal punishments.

I join with the removing of temporal calamities the mitigating of them, because they are not always taken away when the party repents. After David's repentance, the child dies and the sword departs not from his house [2 Sam. 12:14]. And the prophet Micah brings in the people humbling themselves before God under a temporal punishment, saying, "I will bear thy wrath, because I have sinned against thee" [Micah 7:9]. And it is God's pleasure that that chastisement shall remain after the party is reconciled to Him that he may by that means be admonished of his sin and be an example to others.

As God has made these merciful promises to penitent sinners, so He has faithfully performed them so soon as they have but begun to repent. *Examples.* Of David: "Then David said unto Nathan, I have sinned against the Lord. And Nathan said to David, Thy sin is forgiven thee" (2 Sam. 12:13). Of Manasseh: "When he was in tribulation he prayed unto the Lord his God, and humbled himself greatly before the Lord God of his fathers, and prayed unto him: and God was intreated of him, and heard his prayer" (2 Chron. 33:12). Of the publican: "The publican…smote his breast, saying, O Lord God, be merciful to me a sinner: I tell you, this man departed justified to his house, rather than the other" (Luke 18:13). Of the thief: "He said unto Jesus, Lord, remember me, when thou comest to thy kingdom. Then Jesus said unto him, Verily, I say unto thee, today shalt thou be with me in paradise" (Luke 23:42–43).

Having such notable promises made to repentance, no man is to draw back from the practice of it because of the multitude of his sins, but rather to do it. The Pharisees said to Christ's disciples: "Why eateth your master with publicans and sinners? When Jesus heard it, he said unto them, The whole need not the physician, but they that are sick…. I came not to call the righteous, but sinners to repentance" [Matt. 9:11–13]. And, "Verily I say unto you, that publicans and harlots shall go before you into the kingdom of God" [Matt. 21:31].

Chapter 10

The Time of Repentance

The time of repentance is the time present, without any delay at all, as the Holy Spirit says, "Today if ye will hear his voice" [Heb. 3:7], and, "Exhort one another daily, while it is called today: lest any of you be hardened through the deceitfulness of sin" [Heb. 3:13]. [The] reasons hereof are these.[1]

First, life is uncertain, for no man knows at what hour or moment and after what manner he shall go forth of this world. "Be ye also prepared therefore, for the day will come at an hour when ye think not" [Luke 12:40]. This one thing should make a man to hasten his repentance, and the rather because many are dead who purposed with[in] themselves to repent in time to come, but were prevented by death, and shall never repent.

Second, the longer a man lives in any sin, the greater [the] danger, because by practice sin gets heart and strength. Custom is of such force that that which men usually do in their lifetime, the same they do and speak when they are dying. One had three pounds owing to him to be paid three several years; when he was dying, nothing could be got of him but "three years, three pounds." Again, by deferring repentance, men treasure up wrath against the day of wrath [Rom. 2:5]. If a malefactor for his punishment should be appointed to carry every day a stick of wood to a heap to burn him twenty years later, it must needs be an exceeding great punishment and misery. And this is the case of every sinner who, neglecting repentance from day to day, does thereby employ himself in heaping up the coals of God's wrath to burn his soul in hell when the day of death comes.

Third, the more the time is prolonged, the harder it is to repent. The longer a man goes in his sickness without physic, the harder is the recovery. And where the devil dwells long, he will hardly be removed. The best way to kill a serpent is to crush it in the head when it is young.

Fourth, it is as meat and drink to the devil to see men live in their sins, deferring repentance. As on the contrary, there is great joy among the angels of God in heaven when a sinner does repent.

---

1. The paragraph breaks in this chapter are not in the original.

Fifth, late repentance is seldom (or never) true repentance. For if a man repents when he cannot sin as in former time (as namely in death), then he leaves not sin but sin leaves him. Wherefore, the repentance which men frame to themselves when they are dying is to be feared lest it dies with them. And it is very just that he should be condemned by God in his death, who condemned God in his life. Chrysostom says that the wicked man has this punishment on him, that in dying he should forget himself, who, when he was living, did forget God.

Sixth, we are with Abel to give unto God in sacrifice even the fat of our stock. Now they who defer repentance to the end do the contrary. Late repenters offer the flower of their youth to the devil, and they bring the lame and broken sacrifice of their old age to God.

Chapter 11

Certain Cases in Repentance

The Case of Revolt

Whether a man, who has professed Christ and His religion, yet afterwards in persecution denies Christ and forswears his religion, may repent and be saved? *Answer*. It is a grievous estate, yet a man may come to repentance afterwards. Manasseh fell away to idolatry and witchcraft, and yet [he] was received to mercy [2 Chron. 33:13]. So did wise Solomon, and yet [he] no doubt recovered, and is received to everlasting life. My reason is because God vouchsafed him to be a pen-man of some parts of Holy Scripture, and the Scriptures were written, not by such as were men of God only, but by such as were "holy men of God" [2 Peter 1:21]. Peter denied knowledge of Christ against his own conscience, and that with cursing and banning, and yet came to repentance afterwards, as appears by the testimony of Christ: "I have prayed for thee that thy faith fail not: therefore when thou art converted strengthen thy brethren" (Luke 22:32).

Objection 1. "Whosoever shall deny me before men, him will I deny before my Father which is in heaven" (Matt. 10:33). *Answer*. This place is only to be understood of such a denial of Christ which is final.

Objection 2. "It is impossible that they which were once lightened, and have tasted of the heavenly gift…if they fall away should be renewed by repentance" (Heb. 6:4). And, "If we sin willingly after that we have received the knowledge of the truth, there remains no more sacrifice for sin" (Heb. 10:26). *Answer*. These places must be understood of sin which is to death, in which men of desperate malice against Christ universally and wholly fall away from religion. For the Holy Spirit says not, "if they fall," but "if they fall away" [Heb. 6:6]. And it is added that "they crucify the Son of God, and make a mock of him," [and] that "they trample underfoot the Son of God," that "they account the blood of the new testament an unholy thing," [and] "they despise the Spirit of God" [Heb. 10:29]. And the word translated "willingly" [v. 26] imports somewhat more, namely, to sin because a man wills (that is, willfully). The same answer is to be given to the question whereby it is demanded whether men overtaken with the unnatural sins mentioned in Romans 1:24–26 may come to repentance afterwards or not? Namely, that although the sins are heinous and capital, yet the grace of repentance is not denied, as appears in the example of the Corinthians (1 Cor. 6:9–11).

The Case of Recidivation[1]

Whether the child of God, after repentance for some grievous sin, does fall into the same again, and comes to repentance the second time? *Answer.* The case is dangerous, as we may see by the comparison in the body. If one falls into the relapse of an ague (or any other strong disease) it may cost him his life. And the recovery will be very hard. Christ said to the man, who had been sick thirty-eight years, after He had healed him, "Behold, thou art whole, sin no more, lest a worse thing befall thee" [John 5:14]. And the unclean spirit, returning, "takes to him another seven spirits worse than himself" [Luke 11:26]. Indeed, we find no particular example of recovery after a relapse in the Scriptures, yet no doubt a recovery may be. [The] reasons are these. First, promise is made of remission of sins in Christ [Acts 10:43] without any term of time, without any limitation to any number or kinds of sin, save only the blasphemy against the Holy Spirit. Therefore, there may be repentance and salvation after a relapse. Second, Christ tells Peter that he must forgive not till seven times only (which peradventure he thought to be very much) but seventy-seven times [Luke 17:4], and that in one day, if one returns seventy-seven times, and says, "I repent." Now if we must do this, who have not so much as a drop of mercy in us in comparison of God, [then] He will no doubt often forgive, even for one sin, if men will return and say, "I repent," considering that with Him is "plentiful redemption" [Ps. 130:7] and He is "much in sparing" [Isa. 5:17].[2]

The Case of Restitution

Whether he who repents is to make restitution if he has taken anything wrongfully from his neighbor? *Answer.* Yes. Zacchaeus, when he repented and received Christ, gave half of his goods to the poor, and if he had "taken anything by forged cavillation, he restored it fourfold" [Luke 19:8]. It is but a bad practice when a man on his deathbed will very devoutly bequeath his soul to God, and his goods evil gotten (as his conscience will often cry in his ear) to his children and friends without making either restitution or amends.

Question. But what if a man is unable to restore? *Answer.* Let him acknowledge the fault, and God will accept the will for the deed. As Paul says in the like case: "If there be a willing mind, it is accepted according to that which a man hath, and not according to that which he hath not" (2 Cor. 8:12).

---

1. *Recidivation:* backsliding.
2. It is unclear what Scripture reference Perkins intends.

Question. When a man by restoring shall discredit himself, how shall he restore and keep his credit? *Answer.* Let him (if the thing to be restored is of small moment) make choice of some faithful or honest friend who may deliver the thing on the behalf of the party, concealing his name.

Question. How, if the parties are dead? *Answer.* Let him restore to the heirs and successors. If there are none, let him restore to God, that is, to the church and the poor.

The Case of Tears

Whether repentance does always go with tears or not? *Answer.* No. For very pride and hypocrisy will draw forth tears. And some there are who can weep for their sins in the presence of others, whereas, being alone, they neither will nor can. Some again are of that constitution of body that they have tears at command. And a godly man with dry cheeks may mourn to God for his sins, and entreat for pardon, and receive it. Yet, in all occasions of deeper grief for sin, tears will follow, unless men have stony and flinty hearts. And yet again, though the greatest cause of sorrow is offered, the softest heart that is, sheds not tears at the first, but afterwards it will. When the body receives a deep wound, at the first you shall see nothing but a white line or dint made in the flesh, without any blood. Stay but a while, then comes blood from the wound in great abundance. So at the first the mind is astonished and gives no tears, but after some respite and consideration tears follow.

The Case of Death

Whether the repentant sinner can always show himself comfortable on his death bed? *Answer.* Though the comfort of God's Spirit shall never be abolished from his heart, yet he cannot always testify it. For he may die of a burning ague. And by reason of the extremity of his fits, [he may] be troubled with idleness of head and break out into raving speeches and blasphemies. Likewise, he may die of a sickness in the brain, and be troubled with grievous convulsions, so as his mouth shall be writhen[3] to his ears, his neck turned behind him, and the very place where he lies shall shake through his trembling, as daily experience will testify. Neither is any to think this strange, for Solomon says, "All things (in outward matters) come alike to all: and the same condition is to the just and to the wicked: to the good and to the pure, and to the polluted, and to him that sacrificeth, and to him that sacrificeth not" (Eccl. 9:2).

---

3. *Writhen:* twisted or contorted.

Chapter 12

The Contraries to Repentance

Contrary to repentance is impenitency, whereby men continue in one estate, neither sorrowing for sin nor turning from it.

It is one of the most grievous judgments that is, if it is final. For as a sick man is most sick when he feels the least sickness, and says he is well, so miserable man is in most misery when he feels no misery and thinks himself in [a] good estate.

This sin befalls them who judge themselves righteous, needing no repentance, as the Pharisees in the days of Christ, the Catharists in the primitive church, and the Anabaptists in our age. Add unto these such as have hardened their hearts so as they cannot discern between good and evil, nor tremble at God's judgments, but rather fret and rage against them, till God in His wrath either destroys them or casts them to final despair, as it befell Julian the apostate, who died blaspheming and casting his own blood into the air.

Between the two extremes [of] repentance and impenitency is placed counterfeit repentance. For the wicked nature of man can dissemble and counterfeit God's grace. As the Lord complains of the Jews: "Her rebellious sister Judah hath not returned unto me with her whole heart, but feignedly, saith the Lord" (Jer. 3:10).

Counterfeit repentance is either ceremonial or desperate.

Ceremonial

Ceremonial [repentance is] when men repent in outward show but not in truth of heart, as Saul: "Then said Saul to Samuel, I have sinned: for I have transgressed the commandments of the Lord, and thy word: because I feared the people and obeyed their voice. Now therefore I pray thee take away my sin, and turn again with me, that I may worship the Lord" (1 Sam. 15:24). Again, "I have sinned, but honor me, I pray thee, before the elders of my people" (v. 30). Of Ahab: "When Ahab heard these words, he rent his clothes and put on sackcloth, and fasted, and went softly. And the word of the Lord came to Elijah, saying, Seest thou how Ahab is humbled before me?" [1 Kings 21:27–29].

Dissembling repentance may be discerned because men after a time return to their old bias again. Pharaoh, king of Egypt, said unto Moses and Aaron: "Pray unto the Lord that he may take away the frogs from me and from my people" (Exod. 8:8). And, "When Egypt was smitten with hail, he said, I have now sinned: and the Lord is righteous: but I and my people are wicked: Pray ye unto the Lord, that there be no more mighty thunders and hail" (Exod. 9:27). Again, troubled with grasshoppers, he said, "I have sinned against the Lord your God, and against you, and now forgive me my sin only this once" (Exod. 10:16–17). Now mark the issue of all: "When Pharaoh saw that he had rest given him, he hardened his heart, and hearkened not unto them, as the Lord had said" (Exod. 8:15). This is the ordinary and common repentance that most men practice in the world.

Desperate

Desperate repentance (commonly called penitence) is when a man, having only God's judgments before his eyes, is smitten with horror of conscience, and wanting assurance of God's mercy, despairs finally. This was Judas's repentance, who when he "had brought again the thirty pieces of silver, confessed his fault, and went and hanged himself" (Matt. 27:3).

Chapter 13

Corruptions in the Doctrine of Repentance

The Church of Rome at this day has corrupted the ancient doctrine of repentance, being one of the special points of religion. The corruptions are specially six.

The first [is] that they make repentance (or penance) to be a sacrament, which cannot be, because it wants an outward sign. And though some say that the words which the priest rehearses in absolution are the sign, yet that cannot be, because the sign must be not only audible but also visible.

The second [is] that a sinner has in him a natural disposition which, being stirred up by God's preventing grace, he may and can work together with God's Spirit in his own repentance. But, indeed, all our repentance is to be ascribed to God's grace wholly. The soul of man is not weak but stark dead in sin (Eph. 2:1). And, therefore, it can no more prepare itself to repentance than the body, being dead in the grave, can dispose itself to the last resurrection.

The third corruption [is] that contrition in repentance must be sufficient. A thing impossible, for sin does so greatly offend God's majesty that no man can ever mourn enough for it.

The fourth [is] that contrition does merit remission of sin. An opinion that does derogate much from the all-sufficient merits of Christ.

The fifth [is] that he who repents must confess all the sins that he can remember, with all their circumstances, to his own priest or one in his stead, if he will receive pardon. This kind of confession is a mere forgery of man's brain: (1) There is neither precept nor example of it in the Scriptures. (2) David and others have repented and have received remission of their sins without confessing of their sins in particular to any man [Ps. 32:3; 2 Sam. 12:13].

The last [is] that the sinner, by his works and sufferings, must make satisfaction to God for the temporal punishment of his sins. A flat blasphemy. The Scriptures mention no other satisfaction but Christ's [1 John 1:7; 2:2]. And if His is sufficient, ours is needless. If ours [is] needful, His [is] imperfect. Papists write that both may stand together. Christ's satisfaction (they say) is as a plaster in a box unapplied; man's satisfaction as a means to apply it, because it prepares us to receive it. Ah, good divinity! For even in common sense the satisfaction of Christ must first be applied to the person of man that it may please God, before the works (which they term satisfaction) can [in] any way be acceptable to God.

To conclude, the Romish doctrine of repentance is the right way to hell. For when a sinner shall be taught that he must have sufficient sorrow for his sin, and withal that he must not believe the remission of his own sins particularly, when sorrow comes upon him and he wants sound comfort in God's mercy, he must needs fall into desperation without recovery. Therefore, the papists in the hour of death (as we have experience) are glad to leave the trumpery of human satisfactions and to rest only for their justification on the obedience of Christ.

Laus Deo

The Combat of the Flesh and Spirit

"For the flesh lusteth against the spirit, and the spirit against the flesh: and these are contrary one to another, so that ye cannot do the things which ye would" (Gal. 5:17).

The apostle Paul, from the beginning of this chapter to verse 13, exhorts the Galatians to maintain their Christian liberty. And from thence to the end of the chapter, he persuades them to other special duties of godliness. In verse 13, he stirs them up to be serviceable one to another by love. In verse 15, he dissuades them from contentions and doing of injuries. In verse 16, he shows the remedy of the former sins, which is to walk according to the spirit. In verse 17, he renders a reason of the remedy, the force whereof is this: the flesh and the spirit are contrary, wherefore if you walk according to the spirit, it will hinder the flesh, that is, [the flesh] shall not carry you forward to do injuries and live in contentions, as otherwise it would.

In this verse we have to observe five points. The first [is] that there is a combat between the flesh and the spirit, in these words: "The flesh lusteth against the spirit, and the spirit against the flesh." The second is the matter of this combat, which stands in the contrary lusting of the flesh and the spirit. The third is the cause of the combat, in these words: "and these are contrary." The fourth is the subject or person in whom this combat is, noted in these words: "So that ye," [that is,] the Galatians. The last is the effect of the combat, in the last words: "that they cannot do, etc."

Point 1
Touching the combat itself, divers points are to be considered.

The first [is] what these two are which make combat (namely, the flesh and the spirit). They have divers significations. First of all, the spirit is taken for the soul, and the flesh for the body. But so they are not taken in this place, for there is no such combat between the body and the soul, both [of] which agree together to make the person of one man. Second, the spirit signifies natural reason, and the flesh the natural appetite or concupiscence. But they cannot be so understood in this place, for the spirit here mentioned does fight even against natural reason, which, though it serves to make a man without excuse, yet it is an enemy to the spirit. Third, the spirit signifies the Godhead of Christ, and the flesh the manhood. But it must not be so taken here, for then every regenerate man should be deified. Lastly, the spirit signifies a created quality of holiness, which by the Holy Spirit is wrought in the mind, will, and affections of man; and the flesh [is] the natural corruption or inclination of the mind, will, and affections to that which is against the law. In this sense these two are taken in this place.

Second, it is to be considered how these two, the flesh and the spirit, can fight together, being but mere qualities. And we must know that they are not severed asunder, as though the flesh were placed in one part of the soul and the spirit in another. But they are joined and mingled together in all the faculties of the soul. The mind (or understanding part) is not one part flesh and another spirit, but the whole mind is flesh and the whole mind is spirit, partly one and partly the other. The whole will is partly flesh and partly spirit. The flesh and the spirit (that is, grace and corruption) [are] not severed in place, but only in reason to be distinguished. As the air in the dawning of the day is not wholly light or wholly dark as at midnight and at noon day, neither is it in one part light [and] in another part dark, but the whole air is partly light and partly dark throughout. In a vessel of lukewarm water, the water itself is not only hot or only cold, or in one part hot and in another part cold, but heat and cold are mixed together in every part of the water. So is the flesh and the spirit mingled together in the soul of man. And this is the cause why these two contrary qualities fight together.

Third, in this combat we are to consider what equality there is between these two combaters, the flesh and the spirit. And we must know that the flesh is usually more in measure than the spirit. The flesh is like the mighty giant Goliath, and the spirit is little and small like young David. Hence it is that Paul calls the Corinthians, who were men justified and sanctified, "carnal." "I could not," says he, "brethren, speak unto you as unto spiritual, but as unto carnal, as unto babes in Christ" (1 Cor. 3:1). And none can come to be tall men in Christ according to the age of the fullness of Christ [Eph. 4:13] till after this life. And the speech which is used of some divines, that the regenerate man "has but the relics of sin in him," must be understood warily, else it may admit an untruth. As for the measure of grace, it can be but small in respect, whereas we do receive but the "first fruits of the Spirit" [Rom. 8:23] in this life, and [we] must wait for the accomplishment of our redemption till the life to come.[1]

---

1. This paragraph break is not in the original.

For all this, the power and efficacy of the spirit is such that it is able to prevail ordinarily against the flesh. For the flesh receives its deadly wound at the first instant of a man's conversion, and continually dies after by little and little, and therefore it fights but as a maimed soldier. And the spirit is continually confirmed and increased by the Holy Spirit, and it is lively and stirring, and the virtue of it is like musk, one grain whereof will give a stronger smell than many ounces of other perfumes. Some may say that the godly man does feel the flesh more than the spirit, and therefore that the flesh is every way more than the spirit. I answer that we must not measure our estate by feeling, which may easily deceive us. A man shall feel a pain which is but in the top of his finger more sensibly than the health of his whole body, yet the health of the body is more than the pain of a finger. Second, we feel corruption, not by corruption, but by grace. And, therefore, the more men feel their inward corruptions, the more grace they have.

Point 2

Thus much of the combat itself. Now let us come to the manner of this fight. It is fought by "lusting." To lust in this place signifies to bring forth and to stir up motions and inclinations in the heart, either to good or evil.

Lusting is twofold: the lusting of the flesh, and the lusting of the spirit.

The lusting of the flesh has two actions. The first is to engender evil motions and passions of self-love, envy, pride, unbelief, anger, etc. Saint James says that men "are enticed and drawn away by their own concupiscence" (James 1:14). Now this enticing is only by the suggestion of bad cogitations and desires. This action of the flesh made Paul say that he was "carnal, sold under sin" (Rom. 7:14).

The second action of the flesh is to hinder, quench, and overwhelm the good motions of the spirit. Paul found this in himself, when he said, "I see another law in my members rebelling against the law of the mind, and leading me captive to the law of sin" (Rom. 7:23). By reason of this action of the flesh, the man regenerate is like one in a slumber troubled with the disease called ephialtes (or the mare) who thinks that he feels something lying on his breast as heavy as a mountain, and would fain have it away, whereupon he strives and labors by hands and voice to remove it, but for his life [he] cannot do it.

On the contrary, the lusting of the spirit contains two other actions. The first is to beget good meditations, motions, inclinations, and desires in the mind, will, and affections. Of this David speaks: "My reins teach me in the night season" (Ps. 16:7), that is, my mind, affection, and will, and my whole soul, being sanctified and guided by the Spirit of God, do minister unto me considerations of the way in which I ought to walk. Isaiah, prophesying of the church of the New Testament, says, "When a man goeth to the right hand or to the left, he shall hear a voice, saying, Here is the way, walk ye in it" (Isa. 30:21). This voice is not only the outward preaching of the ministers, but also the inward voice of the spirit.

The second action of the spirit is to hinder and suppress the bad motions and suggestions of the flesh. Saint John says, "He that is born of God sinneth not, because his seed remaineth in him" (1 John 3:9); that is, grace wrought in the heart by the Holy Spirit, which resists the rebellious desires of the flesh.

That the manner of this fight may more clearly appear, we must examine it more particularly. In the soul of man there are two special parts: the mind and the will.

The Combat in the Mind

In the mind there is a double combat.

The first is between knowledge of the Word of God, and natural ignorance or blindness. For seeing we do in this life know but in part, therefore knowledge of the truth must needs be joined with ignorance in all who are enlightened. And each of these being contrary to another, they strive to overshadow and overcast each other.

Hence, we may learn the cause why excellent divines do vary in divers points of religion, and it is because in this combat natural blindness, yet remaining, prevails more or less. Men who are dim-sighted and cannot discern without spectacles, if they are set to descry a thing afar off, the most of them would be of divers opinions of it. And men, enlightened and regenerate in this life, do but see "as in a glass darkly" [1 Cor. 13:12]. Again, this must teach all students of divinity often to suspect themselves in their opinions and defenses, seeing in them who are of soundest judgment the light of their understanding is mixed with darkness of ignorance. And they can in many points see but as the man in the gospel, who, when our Savior Christ had in part opened his eyes, saw men walking, not as men, "but in the form of trees."[2] Also, this must teach all that read the Scriptures to invocate and call upon the name of God, that He would enlighten them by His Spirit, and abolish the mist of natural blindness. The prophet David was worthily enlightened with the knowledge of God's Word so as he excelled the ancients and his own teachers in wisdom. Yet, being privy to himself touching his own blindness, [he] often prays, "Enlighten my eyes that I may understand the wonders of thy law" (Ps. 119:18).

By reason of this fight, when natural blindness prevails, the child of God, truly enlightened with knowledge to everlasting life, may err not only in lighter points but even in the very foundation of religion, as the Corinthians and

---

2. Mark 8:24.

the Galatians did. And as one man may err, so a hundred men may also, yea, a whole particular church. And as one church may err, so a hundred more may. For in respect of this combat, the estate and condition of all men is alike. Whence it appears that the church militant upon earth is subject to error. But yet, as the diseases of the body are of two sorts, some curable and some incurable (which are to death), so likewise errors are. And the church, though it is subject to sundry falls, yet it cannot err in foundation to death. The errors of God's children are curable. Some may here say, "If all men and churches are subject to error, then it shall not be good to join with any of them, but to separate from them all." I answer [that], though they may and do err, yet we must not separate from them as long as they do not separate from Christ.

The second combat in the mind is between faith and unbelief. For faith is imperfect and mixed with the contrary: unbelief, presuming, doubting, etc. As the man in the gospel says, "Lord, I believe, help mine unbelief" [Mark 9:24].

By reason of this fight, when unbelief prevails, the very child of God may fall into fits and pangs of despair, as Job and David did in their temptations. For David,[3] once considering the prosperity of the wicked, broke out into this speech: "Certainly I have cleansed mine heart in vain, and washed mine hands in innocency" (Ps. 73:13). Yea, this despair may be so extreme that it shall weaken the body and consume it more than any sickness. No man is to think this strange in the child of God. For though he despairs of his election and salvation in Christ, yet his desperation is neither total nor final. It is not total, because he does not despair with his whole heart, faith even at that instant lusting against despair. It is not final, because he shall recover before the end of his life.

The Combat in the Will

To proceed, the combat in the will is this: the will partly wills and partly nills that which is good at the same instant, and so likewise it wills and nills that which is evil, because it is partly regenerate and partly unregenerate. The affections likewise, which are placed in the will, partly embrace and partly eschew their objects: as love partly loves and partly does not love God and things to be loved; fear is mixed and not pure (as schoolmen have dreamed) but partly *filial* [and] partly *servile*, causing the child of God to stand in awe of God not only for His mercies, but also for His judgments and punishments. The will of a regenerate man is like him who has one sound leg, the other lame, who, in every step which he makes, does not wholly halt or wholly go upright, but partly goes upright and partly halts. Or, like a man in a boat on the water,

---

3. *David*: that is, Asaph.

who goes upward because he is carried upward by the vessel, and at the same time goes downward because he walks downward in the same vessel at the same instant. If any shall say that contraries cannot be in the same subject, the answer is [that] they cannot, if one of them is in its full strength in the highest degree.[4] But if the force of them both is delayed and weakened, they may be joined together.

By reason of this combat, when corruption prevails against grace in the will and affections, there arises in the godly a certain deadness or hardness of heart, which is nothing else but a want of sense or feeling. Some may say that this is a fearful judgment, but the answer is that there are two kinds of hardness of heart. One possesses the heart and is never felt. This is in them who have their consciences seared with a hot iron, who by reason of custom in sin are past all feeling [Eph. 4:19], who likewise despise the means of softening their hearts [Zech. 7:11]. And, indeed, this is a fearful judgment. There is another hardness of heart which is felt, and this is not so dangerous as the former. For as we feel our sickness by contrary life and health, so hardness of heart, when it is felt, argues quickness of grace and softness of heart. David often complained of this in the Psalms. The children of Israel speak of this when they say, "Why hast thou hardened our hearts from thy ways?" [Isa. 63:17].

The Issue
Thus much of the manner of the combat in particular. Before we proceed any further, let us mark the issue of it, which is to prevail against the flesh. The spirit prevails against the flesh at two times: in the course of a man's life, and at his end, but yet with some foils received.

I say the spirit prevails not in one instant, but in the whole course of a man's life. So Saint John says, "He which is begotten of God sinneth not: for he preserveth himself" [1 John 5:18]. The grace of God [is] in his heart, ordinarily prevailing in him. And Paul makes it the property of the regenerate man "to walk according to the Spirit" [Rom. 8:4], which is not now and then to make a step forward, but to keep his ordinary course in the way of godliness. As in going from Barwick to London, it may be a man now and then will go amiss, but he speedily returns to the way again, and his course generally shall be right.

Again, the spirit prevails in the end of a man's life. For then the flesh is utterly abolished, and sanctification accomplished, because no unclean thing can enter into the kingdom of heaven.

This further must be conceived, that when the spirit prevails, it is not without resistance and striving. As Paul testifies, "I do not the good which I would,

---

4. In the margin: *In gradibus remissis non in summis.*

but the evil which I would not, that do I" [Rom. 7:19]. This place is not to be understood only of thoughts and inward motions (as some would have it), nor of particular offences, but of the general practice of his duty or calling through the whole course of his life. And it is like the practice of a sick man, who having recovered from some grievous disease, walks a turn or two about his chamber, saying, "Ah, I would fain walk up and down but I cannot," meaning not that he cannot walk at all, but signifying that he cannot walk as he would, being soon wearied through faintness.

I add further that this prevailing is with foils. A foil is when the flesh for the time vanquishes and subdues the spirit. In this case, the regenerate man is like a soldier who with a blow has his brain-pan[5] cracked, so as he lies groveling, astonished, not able to fight. Or, [it is] like him who has a fit of the falling sickness, who for a time lies like a dead man. Hence, the question may be moved, whether the flesh prevailing does not extinguish the spirit, and so cut off a man from Christ, till such time he is engrafted again? The answer is this: there are two sorts of Christians. The [first is] one who does only in show and name profess Christ, and such a one is not otherwise a member of Christ's mystical body than a wooden leg set to the body is a member of the body. The second is he who in name and deed is a lively part and member of Christ. If the first falls, he cannot be said to be cut off, because he was never engrafted. If the second falls, he may be and is cut off from Christ. But mark how: he is not wholly cut off, but in some part, namely in respect of the inward fellowship and communion with Christ, but not in respect of conjunction with Him. A man's arm, taken with the dead palsy, hangs by and receives no heat, life, or sense from the rest of the members or from the head, yet for all this, it remains still united and coupled to the body, and may again be recovered by plasters and physic. So, after a grievous fall, the child of God feels no inward peace and comfort but is smitten in conscience with the trembling of a spiritual palsy for his offence. And yet, indeed [he] still remains before God a member of Christ in respect of conjunction with Him, and [he] shall be restored to his former estate after serious repentance.

And God permits these foils for weighty causes. First, that men might be abashed and confounded in themselves with the consideration of their vile natures and learn not to swell with pride because of God's grace. Paul says, that after he had been rapt into the third heaven, the "angel of Satan was sent to buffet him" [2 Cor. 12:7], and (as we say) to beat him black and blue, so that he might not be exalted out of measure. The second [is] that we may learn to deny ourselves and cleave unto the Lord from the bottom of our hearts. Paul

---

5. *Brain-pan:* skull.

says that he was sick to death, "that he might not trust in himself, but in God who raiseth the dead" [2 Cor. 1:9].

Point 3

Thus much of the manner of the combat. Now follows the cause of it.

The cause is the contrariety that is between the flesh and the spirit. As Paul says, "The wisdom of the flesh is enmity to God" [Rom. 8:7].

Hence, we are taught that, since the fall, there is no free will in man in spiritual matters concerning either the worship of God or everlasting life. For flesh is nothing else but our natural disposition, and man is nothing else but flesh by nature. For the spirit comes afterward by grace, and the flesh is flatly contrary to the spirit which makes us do that which is pleasing unto God. Wherefore, the will naturally is a flat bond-slave unto sin.

Again, hence we may learn [that] it is not an easy matter to practice religion, which is to live according to the spirit, to which our natural disposition is as contrary as fire to water. Wherefore, if we will obey God, we must learn to force our natures to the duties of godliness; yea, even sweat and take pains therein.

Lastly, here we may learn the nature of sin. The spirit is not a substance but a quality; and, therefore, the flesh, which is nothing else but original sin and is contrary to the spirit, must also be a quality. For such as the nature of one contrary is, such is the other. There is in every man the substance of body and soul. This cannot be sin, for then the spirit also should be the substance of man. There is also in the substance the faculties of body and soul. And they cannot be sin, for then every man should have lost the faculties of his soul by Adam's fall. Lastly, in the faculties there is a contagion or corruption which carries them against the law. And that is properly sin and the flesh, which is contrary to the spirit.

Point 4

The fourth point is touching the persons in whom this combat is. Paul shows who they are when he says, "So that ye cannot, etc." Here it appears that such as have this combat in them must be as the Galatians, men justified and sanctified. And yet, not all such, but only they that are of years. For the infants of the faithful, howsoever we must repute them to belong to the kingdom of heaven, and therefore to be justified and sanctified, yet because they do not commit actual sin, they want this combat of the flesh and spirit, which stands in action. As for those who are unregenerate, they never felt this fight. If any say that the worst man in the world, when he is about to commit any sin, has a strife and fight in him, it is true indeed. But that is another kind of combat, which is between the conscience and the heart. The conscience on the one part terrifying the man for sin, the will and the affections hauling and pulling him thereunto. The will and the affections wishing and desiring that sin were no sin, and God's commandment abolished, whereas contrariwise the conscience with a shrill voice proclaims sin to be sin. This fight was in Pilate, who by the force of his conscience feared to condemn Christ, and yet [he] was willing and yielded to condemn Him that he might please the people.

Furthermore, this combat is in the regenerate but during the time of this life. For they who are perfectly sanctified feel no strife. If any shall say that this combat was in Christ when He said, "Father, if it be thy will let this cup pass from me, yet not my will but thine be done" [Luke 22:42], indeed here is a combat. But [it is] of another sort, namely the fight of two divers desires: the one was a desire to do His Father's will in suffering the death of the cross; [and] the other a natural desire (which was no sin but a mere infirmity of human nature) whereby He in His manhood desires (as the manner of nature is to seek the preservation of itself) to have the cursed death of the cross removed from Him.

Point 5

The fifth point is the effect of this combat, which is to make the regenerate man "that he cannot do the things which he would." And this must be understood in things both good and evil.

And first, he cannot do the evil which he would for two causes. First, because he cannot commit sin at whatever time he would. Saint John says, "He that is born of God sinneth not, neither can he sin, because he is born of God" [1 John 3:9], that is, he cannot sin at his pleasure or when he wills. Joseph, when he was assaulted by Potiphar's wife to adultery, because the grace of God abounded in him, whereby he answered her, saying, "Shall I do this, and sin against God?"—he could not then sin. Lot, because his righteous heart was grieved in seeing and hearing the abominations of Sodom, could not then sin as they of Sodom did. Hence it appears that such persons as live in the daily practice of sin against their own consciences (though they are professors of the true religion of Christ) have no soundness of grace in them.

Second, the regenerate man cannot sin in what manner he would. And there are two reasons thereof. First, he cannot sin with full consent of will or with all his heart, because the will, so far forth as it is regenerate, resists and draws back. Yea, even then when a man is carried headlong by the passions of the flesh, he feels some contrary motions of a regenerate conscience. It is a true rule that sin does not reign in the regenerate. For so much grace as is wrought in the mind, will, and affections, so much is abated proportionally of the strength of the flesh. Wherefore, when he commits any sin, he does it partly willingly and partly against his will. As the mariners in the tempest cast Jonah into the sea willingly, for else they had not done it, and yet against their wills too, which appears because they prayed and cast their goods out of the ship and labored in the rowing against the tempest, and that very long before they cast him out. And herein lies the difference between two men committing one and the same sin, the one of them being regenerate [and] the other unregenerate. For the latter sins with all his heart and with full consent, and so the first does not. Second, though he falls into any sin, yet he does not lie long in it, but speedily recovers himself by reason of grace in his heart.

Hence, it is manifest that sins of infirmities are committed only of such as are regenerate. As for the unregenerate man, he cannot sin of infirmity whatsoever some falsely think. For he is not weak, but stark dead in sin. And sins of infirmity are such only as rise from constraint, fear, hastiness, and such like sudden passions in the regenerate. And though they often sin of weakness by reason of this spiritual combat, yet they do not always, for they may sin against knowledge and conscience of presumption.

To come to the second point: the regenerate man cannot "do the good which he would" because he cannot do it perfectly and soundly according to God's will as he would. Paul says, "To will is present with me, but I find no means perfectly to do that which I would" [Rom. 7:18]. In this point the godly man is like a prisoner who is gotten forth of the jail, and that he might escape the hand of the keeper, desires and strives with all his heart to run a hundred miles in a day. But because he has strait and weighty bolts on his legs, [he] cannot for his life creep past a mile or two, and that with chafing his flesh and tormenting himself. So, the servants of God do heartily desire and endeavor to obey God in all His commandments, as it is said of king Josiah: "That he turned to God with all his heart, with all his soul, with all his might, according to all the laws of Moses" [2 Kings 23:25]. Yet because they are clogged with the bolts of the flesh, they perform obedience both slowly and weakly with divers slips and falls.

The Use

Thus much of the combat. Now let us see what use may be made of it.

First of all, by it we learn what is the estate of a Christian man in this life. A Christian is not one who is free from all evil cogitations, from rebellious inclinations and motions of will and affections, from all manner of slips in his life and conversation. For such a one is a mere device of man's brain, and not to be found upon earth. But, indeed, he is the sound Christian who, feeling himself laden with the corruptions of his vile and rebellious nature, bewails them from his heart, and with might and main fights against them by the grace of God's Spirit.

Again, here is overthrown the popish opinion of merit and justification by works of grace, in this manner: such as the cause of works is, such are works themselves. The cause of works in man is the mind, will, and affections sanctified, in which, the flesh and the spirit are mixed together, as has been shown before. Therefore, works of grace, even the best of them, are mixed works, partly holy and partly sinful. Whereby it is evident to a man, who has but common sense, that they are not answerable to the righteousness of the law, and that therefore they can neither merit life or [in] any way justify a man before God. If any reply that good works are the works of God's Spirit, and for that cause perfectly righteous, I answer [that] it is true indeed. They come from the Holy Spirit who cannot sin, but not only or immediately, for they also come from the corrupt mind and will of man, and in that respect become sinful, as sweet water, issuing out of a pure foundation, is by a filthy channel made corrupt.

Third, we do hence learn that concupiscence (or original sin) is properly and indeed sin after baptism, though it pleases the Council of Trent to decree otherwise. For after baptism it is flatly contrary to the spirit, and rebels against it. Papists object that it is taken away by baptism. *Answer.* Original sin (or the flesh) is taken away in the regenerate thus. There are three things in it: the guilt, the punishment, [and] the corruption. The first two are quite abolished by the merit of Christ's death in baptism. The third (that is, the corruption) remains still. But mark in what manner: it remains weakened, it remains not imputed to the person of the believer.

Lastly, hereby we are taught to be watchful in prayer. "Watch and pray," says Christ, "for the spirit is ready, but the flesh is weak."[6] Rebekah, when two twins strove in her womb, was troubled and said, "Why am I so?" (Gen. 25:22). Wherefore, she went to ask the Lord, namely by some prophet. So, when we feel this inward fight, the best thing is to have recourse to God by prayer, and to His Word, that the spirit may be strengthened against the flesh. As the children of Israel, by compassing the city of Jericho seven days, and by sounding ram horns, overturned the walls thereof, so by serious invocation of God's name, the spirit is confirmed, and the turrets and towers of the rebellious flesh battered.

1. The voice of carnal man:

    Evil. "I do that which is evil, and I will do it."

    Good. "I do not that which is good, and I will not do it."

---

6. Matt. 26:41.

2. The voice of regenerate man:

> Evil. "I do the evil which I would not."
>
> Good. "I do not the good which I would."

3. The voice of the glorified man:

> Evil. "I do not that which is evil, and I will not do it."
>
> Good. "I do that which is good, and I will do it."

Laus Deo[7]

---

7. Praise be to God.

A Treatise of Man's Imaginations

Showing:
His natural evil thoughts
His want of good thoughts
The way to reform them

Framed and Preached

by
M. William Perkins

"Either make the tree good, and his fruit good,
or else make the tree evil, and his fruit evil" (Matt. 12:33).

Printed by John Legate,
Printer to the University of Cambridge
1607

The Epistle Dedicatory

To the Right Worshipful S. Thomas Holcroft, Knight, with the virtuous Lady Elizabeth, his wife, grace and peace.

That weighty charge of Solomon (Right Worshipful) to every son of wisdom, for the "keeping of his heart above all watch and ward" [Prov. 4:23], may well persuade us that some matters of great importance depend thereon. Among many (because my gates may not be great before so small a city) I will touch one. There is a strange desire, not of earthly, but of spiritual powers, after the possession of man's heart. God says, "My son, give me thy heart" [Prov. 23:26]. And, indeed, the right belongs to Him; yet, through man's transgression, Satan has got such [a] hold thereof that, unless it is by divine power, he will not be kept out. And though we hear not Satan's voice, yet his dealing [see Acts 5:3; Luke 22:3] bewrays[1] his meaning, that above all things in man he desires the heart. Once he "strove about a dead man's body" [Jude 9],[2] but doubtless his purpose therein was to have set up an idol for himself in the hearts of the living. But what is man's heart that it should be so desired? Surely, in substance [it is] little, but for employment [it is] almost infinite. It is a treasure out of which man brings all his actions, good or evil [Matt. 12:35]. It is a temple wherein is placed either the ark of God or Dagon for the devil.[3] Yea, it is a palace[4] wherein dwells, and a throne whereon sits, either Christ or Satan, the "king of glory" [Ps. 24:7] or the "prince of darkness" [Eph. 6:2]. And "he that keeps possession will there exercise dominion."[5] Neither may we think that one heart will suffer both these. "No man can serve two masters" [Matt. 6:24]. God will have all or none. "If any part is shared from Him, in high displeasure He leaves the rest, and so the whole falls to the devil."[6] Now since the case stands thus with

---

1. *Bewray:* reveal.

2. In the margin: Moses's body.

3. In the margin: *Hinc fons boni, & peccandi origo.* Hieron. ad Demetriad.

4. In the margin: Aug. in Ps. 24:8.

5. In the margin: *Qui possedit ipse imperabit ib.* Aug.

6. In the margin: *Quia sit ibi pars aliqua Diabolo, discedit Deus iratus, & possidet totum Diabolus.* August. in Job.

man's heart, does it not nearly concern everyone to know his own estate in this behalf? To wit, what kind of treasury, whose temple, whose palace and throne, is his heart? If all is well, he may rejoice, and so keep it for the Lord. If otherwise, then [he may] seek redress betimes.

To this purpose serves this present treatise. Herein, as in a glass, may first be seen the fearful state of man's natural heart.[7] [It is] fully fraught with evil thoughts, void of good consideration, and so most fit for Satan. Then after do those blessed means appear whereby man's natural heart may be reformed to become the temple of God, the seat of grace, and a "bed of spices for the well beloved to feed upon" [Song 6:2]. And these are points of such importance that whosoever neglects them may say farewell [to] grace, and bid adieu to God Himself, for in the heart, if at all in man, just these are seated.

Now the publishing hereof being committed unto me, I present the same unto your Worships, and under your protection desire to commend it to the church of God. It would too much enlarge my gates to annex the manifold reasons which move me to this choice on your behalf. Only this I pray: that (seeing it is the firstfruits of my labors in this kind wherein I had full power of free choice in my dedication) it may intimate to you both my unfeigned heart's desire of that everlasting good I wish unto your souls, and also testify in part my thankful mind for your manifold favors to me and mine who depend upon you.

Now God Almighty bless your Worships with your children and family, according to your several necessities of His mercy and goodness, for soul and body in this life and forever.

Your Worships' in the Lord,
Thomas Pierson
Cambridge, August 20, 1606

---

7. In the margin: The sum of this treatise.

To the Reader

Know (good reader) that for my furtherance in the publishing of this tractate, I had the author's own draft of the platform of it, beside two perfect copies of all his sermons. I have for plainness' sake divided it into chapters and sections. For the better effecting whereof, I was constrained to transpose two of the uses, otherwise I doubt not but [that] everyone who heard it preached will judge me to have dealt faithfully with the godly author. The Lord bless it to your good.

The Contents

Chapter 1. The unfolding of the text whereon the treatise is grounded.

Chapter 2. The illness of man's natural thoughts, and how they may be known.

Chapter 3. Man's natural evil thoughts concerning God.

Chapter 4. Man's natural thoughts concerning his neighbor.

Chapter 5. Man's natural thoughts concerning himself.

Chapter 6. Man's natural want of good thoughts or consideration, with the fruit thereof.

Chapter 7. The use of the doctrine of man's natural imaginations.

Chapter 8. Rules for the reformation of evil thoughts.

Chapter 9. Of spiritual considerations concerning God.

Chapter 10. Of spiritual considerations concerning ourselves.

The Unfolding of the Text

"And the Lord said in his heart, I will henceforth curse the earth no more for man's cause: for the imagination of man's heart is evil even from his youth" (Gen. 8:21).

In the former part of this chapter, Moses has faithfully related the drying of the waters after the flood, and Noah's sacrificing unto God with God's acceptance thereof. Now in this verse and the next, he records such laws and decrees as God made with Noah touching the restoration of nature perished by the flood, as well for the sparing of the creatures from such like destruction, as for the continuance of His providence in needful times and seasons, meet for their future preservation. These words contain the first of these laws, wherein we may observe three points: (1) Moses's preface to this law; (2) the law itself; and (3) the reason thereof.

The Preface

"And the Lord said in his heart." These words must not be taken properly, for God has not a heart as man has, neither speaks He as man does. But hereby is meant that God determined and set down with Himself this law and decree.

In this phrase of speech note this one thing: if it had pleased Him, God could have spoken to man by a voice, the hearing whereof would have confounded him. But as we here see, He does abase Himself and (as it were) lay aside His honor and might, and speaks unto us after the manner of men, even to the capacity of the simplest. This teaches us that it is the good will and pleasure of God that not only the learned, but even the unlettered and most ignorant, should know and understand the holy Scriptures. For else He would never have penned them in a phrase and style that does so well accord to the capacity of the simple.

The Decree

"I will henceforth curse the ground no more for man's cause." This is the peremptory law of God touching the restoration of nature, wherein are contained two things: first, what God has done; [and,] second, what God will not do hereafter.

Point 1

The thing that God has done is "the cursing of the earth," for He says, "I will curse no more," implying that He once cursed it.

In this observe that God may truly be said to be a cause of curses, and to curse His creatures, not only because He does ordain and decree all curses but also because He inflicts them upon the creatures, yet so as the same is always most justly deserved by sin before it is inflicted by the Lord. And so must God's "cursing of the earth" be understood in this place, as a fruit of His wrath for the sin of man. Accordingly, God is said directly to "create evil" (Isa. 45:7) because whatsoever afflictions, curses, and punishments are in the world, they are ordained and inflicted by God upon the creatures for the sin of man.

This plainly confutes the common opinion of ignorant people, who hold that all good things (as peace, wealth, joy, and felicity) come from God, but all evil (as affliction, calamity, curses, and judgments) come from the devil, and God only suffers them. This is a most erroneous and blind concept, which fills many a soul with much anguish and impatience. For what comfort can he have in the time of trouble, who is persuaded it comes wholly from the devil, and the hand of God is not therein? We, therefore, must learn to reform this opinion, and know that crosses and troubles come from God. David knew this well and, therefore, when Shimei cursed him and railed on him, he forbade Abishai to touch him because (says he) "what if (or, it may be) God hath bid him curse David" (2 Sam. 16:10). So Joseph tells his brethren, who most traitorously sold him into Egypt, that "the Lord sent him before them" (Gen. 45:5).

Second, here consider the impulsive cause that moved God to curse the earth by a flood. It was not in the earth, but in men. "I will henceforth curse the earth no more for man (that is, for man's sins)." In the New Testament there are two special sins recorded for which God sent this curse. [The] first [is] carnal security. They were choked with worldly cares and drowned in earthly pleasures. "In the days of Noah, they did eat, and drink, marry, and give in marriage" (Matt. 24:38). [The] second [is] the contempt of the gospel in the ministry of Noah, who preached 120 years unto them while [he] was building the ark. But they were disobedient, as Saint Peter says, following their own pleasures and delights [1 Peter 3:20]. Whereby it appears that these two sins, security and contempt of the gospel, are most grievous sins. For these brought destruction, not only upon all mankind (Noah and his family excepted), but even upon all creatures that lived by breath.

Now look, as these sins were in the old world, even so are they rife in this last age, according to the prophecy of our Savior Christ: "As it was in the days of Noah, so shall it be in the days of the Son of man" (Luke 17:26). And as this is the state of the whole world, so it is the state of our church. Most men are drowned in the pleasures of this world and choked with the cares thereof. For howsoever they will hear the gospel preached, yet few apply their hearts to believe the same, showing forth the power thereof by repentance from dead works and amendment of life in new obedience. But we must know that if these two sins brought a curse, even destruction, upon the old world, then no doubt they will bring a fearful curse upon this age, though not by water yet some other way that shall countervail the flood. And, therefore, we must lay these things to our hearts, that unless we abandon security and worldly lusts and withal do repent and believe at the preaching of the gospel, we shall see that God's heavy curse will fall upon us. For if we match the old world in sin, we must not look to come behind them in judgments.

Point 2
The second thing in this decree is what God will not do hereafter, namely, "curse the earth anymore." This must be understood of that particular curse which the Lord laid on the earth by waters, when He drowned the world. For the general curses that were laid upon the ground and on mankind for Adam's sin remain still, and [they] shall not be taken quite away till the end of the world. So that, the meaning of this law is that the Lord will no more drown the whole earth for the sin of man by a flood.

Here then we see the cause why the sea, being as raging and stirring as it ever was, does notwithstanding keep itself within its bounds and not overflow the world, and why the clouds, being as full of water as they ever were, do not pour down more floods upon the earth to destroy it. Surely, it is by virtue of this particular law and decree of God, whereunto the sea and clouds become obedient: "I will henceforth curse the earth no more." And here we have just occasion to take knowledge and view of our own wretched and damnable estate, how we are sold under sin. For howsoever we were created blessed and happy, yet by our fall in Adam we are become far worse than any earthly creature. For each creature in its kind (as the sun, moon, stars, sea, clouds, and all others) obeys the commandment of God. But man of all creatures, having laws given him by God to keep, rebels in breaking the same. And to him it is meat and drink by nature to live in the transgression of God's commandments. Thus, by comparing ourselves with the brute creatures, we may learn to humble ourselves and to be abashed when we see them, which were made to serve us, to go before us in obedience to the laws of our Creator.

The Reason

The reason of God's decree [is] in these words: "for the imagination of man's heart is evil, even from his youth." At the first, this reason may seem very strange: that God should no more curse the earth for man because the imagination of his heart is evil. In all likelihood, God should have said the contrary: "I will still curse the earth because the imaginations of man's heart are evil." For so He says in Genesis 6:5–6, that seeing all "the imaginations of the thoughts of man's heart were only evil continually, therefore he would destroy the man from the earth, and from man to beast, and every creeping thing." How can both these stand together? *Answer.* In chapter 6, the Lord says He will "once" destroy the world by water because of the wickedness of the imaginations of man's heart. And here He says, "he will not proceed to curse the earth again and again" by the same punishment because the imaginations of man's heart are evil even from his youth. [It is] as if He should say, "I have once drowned the world for the wickedness of man's inventions, but if I should thus proceed to deal with man according to the wicked imaginations of his heart, I must bring every year a new flood upon the earth because I see the frame of man's heart is evil continually."

Here then observe that God in the preservation of mankind does temper and moderate His justice by mercy. For if He should deal according to man's deserts, He should every day bring curses upon him; yea, so soon as a man is born he should be destroyed. But God deals not so rigorously. He mingles mercy with justice, whereby the whole frame of heaven and earth, the state of man and all societies, do stand. That which Habakkuk prayed for, "in justice, or wrath, remember mercy" [Hab. 3:2], the Lord has performed ever since the flood, yea, since the fall of Adam.

There are three great and weighty causes which moved God to temper justice with mercy for the preservation of mankind and other creatures. First, that hereby He might "show his patience and long-suffering toward the vessels of wrath" [Rom. 9:22], that is, toward such as will not repent, that at the last day they may be most justly condemned. Second, that there may be a company of men upon earth who may worship God. For God has special care of His own glory among men, and therefore tempers justice with mercy in their preservation that they might glorify Him. "There is mercy, or pardon, with thee, that thou mayest be feared" (Ps. 130:4). That is, whereas (O Lord) Thou mightest in justice throw all men to hell suddenly, yet in mercy Thou pardonest the sins of some for this end that they might worship Thee (fear being put for worship and obedience). Third and principally, that the elect and chosen of God might be gathered. For God in His eternal counsel and decree has appointed and set down a certain number of men unto whom He will give eternal life, and for their cause does He spare the whole world from daily destruction. But when that number shall be accomplished, then shall heaven and earth go together, and the world shall be no more.

And here, by the way, this third cause of the continuance of nature must teach us our duty; to wit, that, seeing it pleases God in mercy to give us liberty to live a space of time in this world (some twenty, thirty, forty, or fifty years), and that for this end that herein we might be fitted for His kingdom, when as in the rigor of His justice He might have cast us to hell in our mother's womb or so soon as we were born, we therefore must be careful not to despise this long-suffering and patience of God. But rather, [we must] labor in the fear of God, so that it may become "salvation unto us" [2 Peter 3:15] by our conscionable endeavor in all such means unto the end as He has sanctified for the working of the graces of life in the hearts of His children.

And thus much for the reason in general.

Chapter 2

The Idleness of Man's Natural Thoughts

Section 1

The idleness of man's natural cogitations.

That we may the better perceive in this reason the state of man in respect of his natural imaginations, the words are more particularly to be unfolded. "For the imaginations of man's heart, etc."

The "heart" in Scripture is taken sundry ways: (1) sometimes for that fleshy part of man in the middle of the body, which is the fountain of vital blood; (2) sometimes for the soul of man; (3) sometimes for the faculties of the soul; and (4) sometimes for the middle of anything, as "the heart of the sea" [Ps. 46:2], "the heart of the earth" [Matt. 12:40], that is, the middle thereof. Here it is taken for the understanding faculty of the soul, whereby man uses reason, which Saint Paul calls "the spirit of the mind" [Eph. 4:23].

By "imaginations," he means the frame (or framing) of the heart. And this is taken two ways. Some [take it] for the natural disposition of the understanding after the fall of man. Others [take it] for that which the mind and understanding (by thinking) frames, plots, and devises, that is, for the effect thereof. We may take it both ways, yet I rather approve the latter, for the Lord says He will once destroy all flesh, and [He] gives this reason: "for the frame and thought of man's heart is evil continually" (Gen. 6:5). By "thoughts" or "imaginations" nothing else can be meant but that which is devised and plotted in the thoughts of man's heart. So Solomon, speaking of a "heart which God hateth," says, "it is framing or thinking thoughts of wickedness" (Prov. 6:18).

By "man's heart," we must not understand the heart of some particular persons, as of those who lived in the old world alone, but of all men generally, "man" being put for whole mankind.

"Is evil," that is, it imagines and thinks that which is against the law of God. "From his childhood," that is, so soon as he begins to think, reason, or conceive of anything, so soon does he imagine and conceive that which is evil.

So that, the whole meaning is this: the mind and understanding part of man is naturally so corrupt that as soon as he can use reason, he does nothing but imagine that which is wicked and against the law of God. The words thus explained contain in them two main points touching the frame of man's heart by nature. The first is this: the imagination and conceit of every man is naturally evil. This appears not only in this place, but elsewhere. "The wisdom of the flesh is (not an enemy, but) enmity against God" (Rom. 8:7). Again, such as the fountain is, such are the streams that flow thence. But our mind and understanding, the fountain of our thoughts, is by nature sinful. "To the impure their minds and consciences are defiled" [Titus 2:15]. And again, "Of ourselves we are not able to think a good thought" [2 Cor. 3:5]. And, therefore, the thoughts that come from thence must needs also be corrupt. Man's imagination stands in thoughts. The understanding devises by thinking. And these thoughts of the imagination are all naturally wicked. "From the heart," says Christ, "proceed evil thoughts" [Matt. 15:19]. And Solomon says, "The thoughts of the wicked (as all men are by nature) are an abomination to the Lord."[1]

Section 2

How the natural thoughts of man may be known.

Seeing that natural imagination is practiced by evil thoughts, we must consider something of the natural thoughts of man, and herein handle these two points: first, whether the thoughts of man may be known; [and,] second, what the natural thoughts of man are.

For the first, there are two ways to know man's thoughts: either directly without means, or indirectly by means. The first way is proper to God alone, for no creature in heaven or earth can immediately and directly know the thoughts of man. Solomon confesses this in his notable prayer to God: "Thou only knowest the thoughts of all the children of men" (1 Kings 8:39). "The heart is deceitful and wicked above all things; who can know it?" (Jer. 17:9). "I the Lord search the heart, and try the reins" (v. 10).

The second way to know men's thoughts is indirectly and by means. There are three: by instinct from God; by revelation from the Scripture; and by signs.

First, by an extraordinary instinct. So did Elisha "disclose the king of Syria's counsel to the king of Israel" [2 Kings 6:9, 12]. And by the same means he told his servant Gehazi what he did behind his back, when he took "gifts of Naaman the Assyrian" [2 Kings 5:20]. And so did Peter tell Ananias and Sapphira of their false conveyances with the money that they took for their possession [Acts 5:3]. And yet, here we must understand that when God revealed these secret thoughts to men, it was only in some things at some times and for some special causes. Whereupon Nathan was fain to revoke his counsel, which he gave to David for the building of the house of God, when he knew the will of

---

1. Prov. 15:26.

God more perfectly [1 Chron. 17:2, 4]. And so was Elijah deceived when he said "he was left alone, of all Israel that served God." For "God told him he had reserved seven thousand, that never bowed the knee to Baal" [1 Kings 19:18], which Elijah knew not.

Second, men's thoughts may be known by revelation from Scripture. For therein the Spirit, who knows the frame of the heart, speaks evidently. And hence it is that in the ministry of this word "the thoughts of natural men, are made manifest" [1 Cor. 4:2, 5].

Third, man's thoughts are known by signs, as speeches and actions. Thus, Peter knew the heart of Simon Magus [Acts 8:21], and Paul the heart of Elymas [Acts 13:10]. And thus, any man may know the thoughts of another, even as he may know the tree by its fruit and the fountain by its stream.

Besides these three there are two other means added whereby to know men's thoughts: one by the papists and another by the astrologers. The papists say [that] the saints in heaven know men's thoughts, not directly by themselves, but by reflection in the glass of the Trinity. But this is a mere forgery of their own, which Isaiah never knew, saying thus of the saints departed: "Abraham is ignorant of us, and Israel knoweth us not, but thou Lord art our redeemer" [Isa. 63:16]. And the saints under the altar cry, "How long Lord, how long wilt thou not judge and avenge our blood on them that dwell on the earth?" [Rev. 6:10], giving us to understand that they are not so sharp sighted as by the glass of the Trinity to see into the day of the last judgment, and therefore not into the thoughts of men's hearts. So that, there are only three ways to know the thoughts of men, and so they may be known.

Chapter 3

Man's Natural Thoughts Concerning God

Having found that the thoughts of man may be known, we come now to see what the natural cogitations of every sinful man are. Although they are almost infinite in themselves, yet they may be reduced to three heads. They either concern God, a man's neighbor, or a man's own self.

Touching God, there are in man four capital evil thoughts.

Thought 1

Of this thought: There is no God.

The first [is] that there is no God. As it is first in order, so it is the most notorious, vile, and damnable thought that can be in a natural man. And that this is one of the natural thoughts of man appears by the express testimony of God Himself, who knows the thoughts of man better than man does. "The wicked thinketh always there is no God" [Ps. 10:4]. And again, "The fool hath said in his heart, there is no God" [Ps. 14:1].

Touching this thought, observe these four points: first, in whom it is; second, how a man by thinking should deny God; third, what is the fruit of this thought; and, fourth, the examination of our hearts touching this thought.

Point 1

For the first,[1] we must not think that this wicked thought is only in some notorious and heinous sinners, but [that] it is in the corrupt mind and imagination of every man who comes of Adam naturally, no one excepted save Christ alone. So, the "fool," of whom David speaks [Psalms 10; 14], must be taken not for some special sinner but for every man who lives uncalled and without repentance, howsoever civil his life is [in] other ways. Though some shame restrains his tongue from uttering it, yet by nature his corrupt heart is prone to think "there is no God." This is made evident by Saint Paul who, going about to prove that all men are sinners by nature, alleges for his proof divers testimonies of Scripture and particularly out of these two psalms before cited [Romans 3].

---

1. In the margin: In whom this thought is.

Whereby he gives us to understand that the "fool," there mentioned, must be understood of every natural man. But it will be said that it is engrafted in man's nature to hold and think there is a God, and therefore every man does not deny God in his heart. *Answer.* We must know that these two thoughts, "there is a God" and "there is no God," may be (and are) both in one and the same heart. The same man, who by the light of nature thinks there is a God, may by that corruption and darkness of mind that came by Adam's fall think there is no God. For two contraries, being not in the highest degree, may be in one and the same subject, as light and darkness in the same house [and] heat and cold in the same body.

Point 2

How does a man by thinking deny God in his heart?[2] *Answer.* Two ways. First, by turning the true God into an idol of man's brain. Second, by placing somewhat that is not God in the room of the true God.[3]

For the first, the imagination of every man naturally, without further light from the Word of God, does turn the true God into an idol. And, therefore, Paul says of the Galatians, that before their vocation, "they did service to them which were no gods" [Gal. 4:8]; and of the Ephesians, "that they were without God in the world" [Eph. 2:12]; even because they did not in their minds conceive of God aright, and accordingly worship Him, though the wiser sort among them did acknowledge one God, the Creator of heaven and earth. And, therefore, David says plainly that "all the gods of the Gentiles are idols (or vanities)" [Ps. 96:5]; nay, as the apostle says, "devils." "That which the Gentiles sacrifice, they sacrifice unto devils and not unto God" (1 Cor. 10:20).

Now man's mind turns the true God into an idol by three notorious thoughts, which are the root of many damnable sins in this life. First, by thinking that God is not present in all places, whereby God is robbed of His attribute of omnipresence, for the true God, being infinite, must be in all places. When the heart of man denies this, it imagines God to be such a one as He is not, and so [it] turns Him into an idol. And that man naturally thinks thus of God, the Scripture is plain. Wicked men are brought in, speaking of God as though He were shut up in heaven and had nothing to do in the world: "Is not God on high in the heaven? And behold the height of the stars how high they are. How should God know? Can he judge?" (Job 22:12–13). So the psalmist expresses the thoughts of the wicked in their practice of sin: "God hideth away his face, and will never see: and the Lord shall not see" (Ps. 94:7). Yea, they who seek

---

2. In the margin: How a man by thinking denies God.
3. This paragraph break is not in the original.

the deep to hide their counsel from the Lord, whose works are in darkness, say, "Who seeth us? who knoweth us?" (Isa. 29:15).[4]

Second, by thinking there is no providence of God whereby He orders and disposes all things in the world particularly. The psalmist shows plainly that this is another natural thought [by] bringing in the wicked man, saying thus of God: "God hath forgotten, he hideth his face, and he shall not see." And the prophet Zephaniah brings in the sinner speaking thus of God, that "he doth neither good, nor evil."[5]

Third, by thinking there is no justice in God. This is done when men imagine with[in] themselves that albeit they proceed in the practice of sin, yet God will not punish them according to the threatening of His Word. If we doubt whether such an imagination is in man's heart, read Deuteronomy 29:19–20, where Moses directly forbids the people to say in their hearts, "I shall have peace though I walk in the stubbornness of my heart." This is that blessing of a man's self in sin which David charges upon the covetous and wicked [Ps. 10:3]. Thus they sin who "put far away the evil day," and say, "the evil shall not come" [Amos 9:10; 6:3]. Hereby God is robbed of His justice, and [He is] made a God all of mercy, such a one as will not punish sin, and so indeed is made an idol of man's brain.

The second way whereby a man denies God in thought is by placing in the room of the true God an idol of his own brain. Men do this by thinking some other thing besides the true God to be their chiefest good. Thus, voluptuous men make their belly their god [Phil. 3:19] and covetous men make riches their god [Col. 3:5] by placing their felicity in pleasure and riches. For look, what a man thinks to be the best thing in the world for him, that is his God, though it is the devil himself or any other creature. And for this cause is the devil called "the god of the world" [2 Cor. 4:4], because the men of this world judge their own courses, wherein they serve the devil, the best thing in the world for them, yea, far better than the service of God, and therefore give their hearts thereto. For affection follows opinion, and that which a man affects most, he must needs think best of. And, therefore, what a man affects most, he makes it to become his god, so that judging other things besides the true God to be best for him he must needs place them in the room of the true God, and so in his imagination deny God.

---

4. This paragraph break is not in the original.
5. Zeph. 1:12. This paragraph break is not in the original.

Point 3

What is the fruit of this thought?[6] For thereby we shall best judge what a cursed thing this is, to think there is no God. This thought brings forth the most notorious sins that can be, even atheism itself, which is a sin whereby men deny God [in] sundry ways. And it is twofold, either in practice or in judgment.

Atheism in Practice

Atheism in practice is that sin whereby men deny God in their deeds, lives, and conversations, and so declare this thought. This is a most horrible sin, and a huge burden to the whole earth. And yet, many that live in the bosom of the church are foully tainted herewith. This atheism in practice has three special branches: hypocrisy, epicureanism, and witchcraft. Hypocrisy is a sin whereby men worship the true God, but yet in a false manner, giving unto God the outward action, and [they] hold back from Him the true worship of the heart. Epicureanism is a sin whereby men condemn God and give themselves wholly to their pleasures, spending their time in eating, drinking, and other delights, and not seeking or fearing God. And this is the sin of the richer sort in this age. Witchcraft (or magic) is that sin whereby men renounce the true God and betake themselves to the aid, counsel, and help of the devil, either by himself or in his instruments. This is a large sin, and a great part of atheism, and many are tainted with this sin, either because they are practitioners of witchcraft or else do seek help of such.

Atheism in Judgment

Atheism in judgment is that sin whereby men deny God in opinion and persuasion of heart. And this likewise has three degrees. First, when men hold (and accordingly worship) the true God, Creator of heaven and earth, but yet so as they conceive of [Him] and worship Him otherwise than He has revealed Himself in His Word. To this first degree we must refer the three great religions of the Turk, the Jew, and the papist. For as they stand at this day, they are three great parts of atheism.

First, the Turk worships God, the Maker of heaven and earth, and likewise reverences Christ as man, acknowledging Him to be a prophet, yea, a worthier prophet than his Muhammed. And yet, his religion is atheism, for he conceives of God out of the Trinity, and so worships nothing but an idol.

Second, the religion of the Jews at this day is a part of atheism. For howsoever they hold one God and acknowledge the books of the Old Testament for the Scriptures of God, yet they worship not that God in Christ, and so, instead

---

6. In the margin: The fruit of this thought.

of the true God, [they] frame an idol in their own brain. For as Christ says, "Whosoever denieth the Son the same hath not the Father" [1 John 2:23]. So that, they, wanting Christ and by consequent the Father also, indeed and truly have no God, but, as Christ told the Samaritans: "they worship they know not what" [John 4:22].

Third, the religion of the papists at this day is a part of atheism. We must indeed distinguish it from the former two, for in word they acknowledge the Trinity in unity and unity in Trinity, and their doctrine of the union of Christ's two natures in one person is according to the Scripture. But yet, if we mark the drift and sequel of their doctrine in other points, we shall find it to be close [to] atheism, as may be proved by two reasons.[7]

First, because the true God, who is the Creator of heaven and earth, is infinite in justice and mercy. But, according to the doctrine of the papists, God is not infinite in justice and mercy. And, therefore, to them [He] is not the true God. For (1) God's justice according to them is not infinite, for they teach that a man by his own proper works of penance (which are finite and imperfect) may truly satisfy God for the guilt of temporal punishment.[8] (2) They make the mercy of God imperfect by piecing[9] up the same with man's merits in the work of redemption.[10] For God's mercy is either every way mercy or no mercy, as Paul says, "If it be of grace it is no more of works, or else were grace no more grace, and if it be of works it is no more grace, or else were work no more work" [Rom. 11:6].[11]

Second, the Christ of the papists is a false Christ. This will appear by plain reason out of their doctrine. For (1) they spoil Christ of His true manhood by their doctrine of real presence, wherein they hold that Christ's body is not only in heaven but really and substantially in all places where the sacrifice of the mass is offered. Thus, they make it omnipotent, and so quite take away the nature of a body. (2) They degrade Christ from the three offices of His mediatorship. First, from His kingly office, by placing the pope in His room and stead as His deputy in Christ's presence.[12] For they give power to the pope to rule the Catholic Church, and to make laws to bind men's consciences, which are things proper to Christ alone. Wherein they do as much as if they should take the crown from Christ's head, and set it on the pope's [head]. For to claim regency in the presence of the lawful prince is to proclaim rebellion against the prince,

---

7. This paragraph break is not in the original.
8. In the margin: Bellar. lib. 7. de pænit. c. 7.
9. *Piecing*: patching.
10. In the margin: Rhem. on Rom. 8:17. sect. 4.
11. This paragraph break is not in the original.
12. In the margin: Rhem. on Eph. 1:22. sect. 5.

for commission of vice-regency ceases in the presence of him who appoints it. Now Christ is always present with His church (Matt. 28:20). And, therefore, the pope by his claim must needs thrust Christ out of His office. Second, from His priestly office, which consists in satisfaction and intercession. They nullify Christ's satisfaction by joining therewith the satisfaction of men's works,[13] for thereby they make it imperfect. And they rob Him of His intercession by communicating the same to saints.[14] Yea, they exalt the virgin Mary far above Christ in this work, for they pray [to] her to ask the Father to command Christ her son by the authority of a mother, to do thus and thus for them.[15] And so [they] make Christ her underling. Third, from His prophetical office, by making the pope the infallible judge of all controversies, avowing that "they rather desire to know the ancient institution of Christian religion from the pope's mouth than from holy writ."[16] Now, thus robbing Christ of His offices, they make Him a false Christ. And so, wanting the Son, they cannot have the Father, for "he that hath not the Son hath not the Father" [1 John 2:23]. And, therefore, popish religion, wanting the Father and the Son, cannot be a true religion but mere colored atheism in judgment.

The second degree of atheism in judgment is when men place some idol in room of the true God, holding the same for their god. Thus did the Gentiles sin in worshipping the sun, moon, stars, and other creatures.

The third degree is when a man does avouch, hold, and maintain that there is no God at all. This is the highest degree of atheism and the most notorious sin that can be. And all such persons as maintain this cursed thought are unworthy [of] the common breath of men. For if that man shall die the death, and that worthily, who shall avouch his lawful prince to be no prince, how much more ought he to die the death, though he had a thousand lives that shall affirm the true God, to be no God? Thus, we see the fruits of this evil thought whereby the heinousness of it does plainly appear.

Point 4
[The last point is] the examination of our own hearts touching this thought, whether it may be found among us or not.[17] Doubtless, everyone will labor to clear himself hereof. And the reason wherewith many do soothe up themselves is this: because they never felt in themselves any such conceits as this, that there is no God. But we may easily deceive ourselves herein, for a man cannot always

---

13. In the margin: Rhem. on Rom. 8:17. sect. 4.
14. In the margin: Rhem. on 2 Cor. 1:11. sect. 3.
15. In the margin: *In officio beatæ Maria.*
16. In the margin: In annot. sup. dist. 40. c. si papa Edit. Greg.
17. In the margin: Examination of this thought.

discern what are the thoughts of his own heart. There are in man two kinds of cogitations or (as one may say) reasons.[18]

The first is a single cogitation whereby a man simply thinks, knows, or judges this or that. And this is properly called the mind. The second is a reflex cogitation (or reason) whereby a man judges that he knows or thinks this or that. And it is commonly called conscience. Now, since Adam's fall, the conscience is corrupt by original sin, as are all other powers of man's soul. Whence it comes to pass that conscience cannot do its duty in giving true testimony concerning man's imaginations. But a man may think evil, and yet his conscience not tell him. And, therefore, we may not say [that] because we feel not these evil thoughts in us, therefore we have them not or we are free from them.

But that we may the better examine our hearts, we must come to the signs whereby this evil thought is best discerned.[19] In Psalm 14 David sets down three signs hereof: first, a disordered life (vv. 2, 3); second, not calling on the name of God by prayer (v. 4); [and,] third, condemning them who put their trust in God (v. 6). Look where these are to be found, [and] there is this evil thought that "there is no God." Now if we examine ourselves by these signs, we shall find this wicked thought to be among us.

For first, many indeed are content to hear God's Word. But where is that man who reforms his life according to what he hears? Certain it is, as their conscience can witness, few turn unto God unfeignedly, few do break off their course in sinning. Now this unreformed life is an infallible token of this damnable thought.

Second, the exercise of prayer and invocation on the name of God is rare among men. No doubt many a touched heart does every day unfeignedly call on God for grace. But yet generally this is true: men go on from day to day, and from year to year, and never pray unto God for supply of grace. Indeed, men plead for themselves that they do pray, for they say the Lord's Prayer, the Creed, and the Ten Commandments. But we must know that with many this practice is nothing but a vain repetition of words. For prayer is an action of the heart and not the labor of the tongue and lips only. So, to say the Lord's Prayer is not to pray, for the words thereof may be repeated with the heart of an atheist.

Third, the contempt of them who put their trust in God is rife among us. For who is so much scorned and reproached as he who makes profession of religion? Now may that complaint be justly taken up by the servants of God: "Behold, I, and the children whom the Lord hath given me, are as signs and wonders" (Isa. 8:18). And, "He that refrains from evil, makes himself a prey" to

______

18. This paragraph break is not in the original.
19. In the margin: Three signs of this thought.

the evil tongue (Isa. 59:15). Yet let these scoffers know, whatever they are, that seeds of atheism do possess their souls.

To come yet more particularly to the trial of this thought in ourselves: whosoever denies the presence of God denies God. Now let the conscience answer whether we are not afraid to sin in the presence of many mortal men, and yet in the presence of God [we] do make no bones thereof [as long as] the eyes of men are turned from us. Now what is this but either flatly to deny the presence of God or (at least) to yield more fear and reverence to men than we do unto God? Again, what is the cause why men use oppression, injustice, deceit, and lying in their worldly affairs? Is it not because this thought of atheism does possess their hearts, that God regards not these outward things? Durst men directly sin against God in seeking these outward blessings for natural life, if they did rightly rely upon God's providence, knowing every good gift to come from His bountiful hand? Lastly, let your conscience speak; does not your heart, while you go on in sin, say thus unto you: "God is merciful, I will hereafter repent, and so I shall escape punishment"? If a man does well observe his own heart, he shall find therein this vile thought, which directly overturns the infinite justice of God, making Him a God all of mercy, when as indeed He is a God of justice as well as mercy. By all which it is more than evident that this vile thought runs naturally in man's heart: "There is no God."

The Use
Hereby, then, we must learn to see what vile, miserable, and wretched sinners we are in ourselves. Though we had no actual outward sins, yet this damnable thought makes us accursed. If a man "curse the king in his heart" [Eccl. 10:20], the sin is so great and heinous that "the souls of heaven shall disclose it." How horrible then is this sin, for a man in his thought to curse God, the King of kings and Lord of lords? This, therefore, must humble us in ourselves before the Lord.

Again, hereby we must be admonished to use all good means whereby we may come to see and know, not only the gross actual sins of our lives, but especially this damnable thought of our hearts. There are few who do see it and, therefore, we must be earnest with ourselves in searching our own hearts to find out this and such like abominations that are in us.

And thus much for the first evil thought.

Thought 2
Of this thought: The Word of God is foolishness.
The second damnable thought of man's natural heart concerning God is this: the Word of God is foolishness. This thought must principally be understood

of the gospel, as Saint Paul declares, saying, "It hath pleased God by the foolishness of preaching to save them that believe" [1 Cor. 1:21]. Here he calls the gospel of Christ "foolishness," not that it was so indeed but because the unconverted Corinthians and other Grecians judged the preaching of Christ crucified [to be] the most foolish thing in all the world (v. 23). And in the next chapter, he says, "the natural man (that is, he who is not effectually called) perceiveth not the things of the Spirit of God" [1 Cor. 2:14], to wit, that a man must repent of his sins and believe in Christ for the pardon of them if he would be saved. They are foolishness unto him. Nicodemus's answer to Christ makes this plain, esteeming "regeneration (without which Christ said no man could enter into the kingdom of heaven) to be a man's return into his mother's womb," and a birth from thence again [John 3:4].

This wicked thought must be understood of the law of God also. The heart of man by nature judges the threatenings of the law to be untruths, and so foolishness. Hence, the Lord by Moses forbade the people, when they heard the threatenings and curses of the law denounced against them, "to bless themselves in their hearts, saying, We shall have peace" [Deut. 29:19]. Hereupon He denounces a woe to them who deride His threatened judgments, and say, "Let him make speed, let him hasten his work that we may see it, etc." [Isa. 5:19]. As if they should say, "We do not believe that any such things shall come to pass." [They are] like the mockers of whom Peter prophesies, "who walk after their lusts, and say, Where is the promise of his coming?" [2 Peter 3:3–4].

Now that this is a most damnable thought may appear by the cursed fruits thereof.[20] For, first, hence arises that devilish and carnal opinion of sundry men who think and hold religion to be but human policy to keep men in awe, and so use it as a political device to exercise men's brains, to keep them from sedition, treachery, and rebellion.[21] Second, hence springs all apostasy and departing from the faith.[22] The Galatians were a worthy church planted by the apostle Paul, yet even in his time they began to fall away to another gospel, which made him to marvel. And the reason was this: "they were not contented with that simplicity which is in Christ" [Gal. 1:6], but would join with Him the observation of legal ceremonies. The like we may say of those famous eastern churches, as those seven churches of Asia, planted by the apostles. The truth flourished in them for a while, but not long after the apostles' times they fell into many damnable heresies as Arianism and such like. Yea, about six hundred years after Christ, they embraced the damnable religion of Muhammed. In the west parts also, worthy and famous churches were planted by the apostles and their

---

20. In the margin: Fruits of this thought.
21. In the margin: Machiavellism.
22. In the margin: Apostasy.

successors, as in Italy, France, Germany, Spain, and England. About the same time of six hundred years after Christ, [they] fell to papism, which spread itself over all Europe and further (some few churches of Greece excepted). In which religion men abandon the gospel of Christ and betake themselves to another gospel by adjoining their own devices to the truth of Christ. And this papism has reigned ever since, till now of late. And so, apostasy has taken place in those churches which the apostles planted.[23]

The cause whereof was in the wicked and sinful heart of man, judging the gospel foolishness, whereupon men were contented to yield themselves to any other religion rather than to that simplicity of truth which is in Christ Jesus. We now, in England, by God's special mercy, hold and teach the Word of God. But if God should alter our religion with the times, the greatest part of men among us would forsake the truth and cleave to any other religion, and that only upon this ground, because they judge the gospel [to be] foolishness. Let any man among us broach an error or heresy, and it shall have patrons at the first (be it ever so vile and absurd) and protectors afterwards. When that brutish heresy of the "family of love"[24] took shipping in[25] Germany and arrived in England (though it is an opinion void of common sense) yet it had applause among us, and [it] was received by many. And [it] would have spread itself further if the preaching of the Word, with the care of the magistrate, had not suppressed it. And the reason hereof is this: man's mind by nature is full of darkness. He cannot, without God's special grace, perceive the things of God. And so, he judges the gospel foolishness, and embraces error rather than the truth, yea, [he] "loveth darkness, rather than the light, because his deeds are evil" (John 3:19).

For the examination of our hearts touching this bad thought,[26] after due trial we shall find that the minds of most among us are possessed herewith. For we are indeed content to come into the assemblies where God is worshipped, and we do submit ourselves to the ministry of the Word, to be taught and instructed. Therein we have our own personal sins displayed and reproved, and withal very fearful and terrible curses of the law denounced against us for the same; both judgments in this life [and] judgments in death, and also eternal judgments after this life. Now let the conscience answer, what is the cause, when we hear these things, that we are not moved? Why are not our hearts touched with grief and sadness, when we hear God's judgments due unto us for our sins daily denounced against us? There are indeed some whose hearts tremble at the Word, but small is that number. If a man runs through the streets, and

---

23. This paragraph break is not in the original.

24. *Family of love*: a religious sect of Dutch origin, also known as Familists.

25. *In*: from.

26. In the margin: Examination for this thought.

cries, "fire, fire," our hearts are suddenly struck with great fear. But the minister of God may stand and cry "fire, fire," the fire of hell which is "kindled by the breath of the Lord like a river of brimstone," as the prophet speaks [Isa. 30:33], and yet men's hearts are nothing moved. What is the cause that we should be so affected with the burning of an old house by temporal fire, and not be afraid at the voice of God which proclaims unto us eternal burning with the fire of God's wrath? Surely, the cause is this: our hearts are forestalled with this false imagination that the curses of the law are foolishness, and that there are no such torments as the world denounces. It will not sink into the heart of a natural man that his sins are so heinous and God's judgments so terrible against them as the Word makes them. And till such time as this damnable thought is taken away, men's hearts will never be touched with the threatenings of the law. This is a bar to stop the way to all such passions as the law would work.

Again, when the minister of God speaks of the pardon of sin and of eternal life by Christ, who has his heart melting for joy in regard of this salvation? Though men are daily taught the doctrine of salvation, yet who learns the same? Though men are called upon to come into the kingdom of heaven, yet few strive to enter in. Though we are daily exhorted to repent, yet few turn to the Lord. All these are branches of the gospel, but men believe them not because their hearts are filled with this damnable thought: the gospel of Christ is foolishness. When the Israelites were restored from captivity in Babylon, it was as "a dream unto them" [Ps. 126:1]. Now if that temporal deliverance seemed a dream, what a dream will this spiritual deliverance from the captivity of hell and death seem to be to the liberty of the sons of God in grace and glory? And, indeed, to a natural man it seems foolishness that God should become man, and that Christ by death should free men from death, and by suffering the curse of the law should take away the same from us, and by His righteousness should justify us unto life. All these notwithstanding are points of the gospel. This also is the cause why after long teaching there is little turning or faithful obedience yielded unto the gospel. Neither will it be better with men, while this evil thought abides in them.

The Use

First, if this is a truth, that every natural man thinks the Word of God to be foolishness, then we must learn this lesson of the apostle: "He that seems to be wise in this world, must become a fool that he may be wise" [1 Cor. 3:18]. That is, he must reject his own natural reason, and stop up the eyes of his natural mind like a blind man, and suffer himself wholly to be guided by God's Spirit in the things of God, that thereby he may be made wise unto salvation.

Second, we must hereby learn to make earnest prayer unto God for the opening of our eyes [Ps. 119:18], so that we may be able to understand the gospel of Christ and know the right meaning of that Word of salvation. For of ourselves we can never understand it, unless the Lord instructs us by His Spirit. Christ says, "No man cometh unto me (that is, believes) except it be given him of my Father" [John 6:65], but "everyone that hath heard, and learned of the Father, cometh unto me" [v. 45].

Thus much of this second evil thought.

Of this thought: I will not obey God's Word.

From the former arises another most vile thought in the heart of every natural man, as a branch of the same; namely, because the Word of God is foolishness, therefore I will not perform obedience thereunto. Job teaches plainly that this is the natural thought of man, for he brings in the wicked (that is, every sinner), saying thus to God: "Depart from us, we will not the knowledge of thy ways" [Job 21:14]. The wicked man says this, not with his mouth, for none is so far past all shame that [he] dares thus blasphemously speak against God, but thus he says in his heart. His affections speak it when he purposes with[in] himself to cast off the yoke of God and to live after his own lusts. And, therefore, they say further, "Who is the Almighty that we should serve him?" [v. 15]. As if one should say, "It is a disgrace to me to abase myself to serve God. I will not do it." The prophet Jeremiah brings in the Lord, saying thus to His people: "Stand in the ways, and behold, and ask for the old way, which is the good way, and walk therein, and ye shall find rest for your souls" [Jer. 6:16]. But in the same place the Jews answer, "We will not walk in thy ways." Shall we think that they durst thus impudently answer the Lord with open mouths? No surely, but in these words the prophet sets down the purpose of their hearts, who hardened the same obstinately against the Word when they were exhorted to repentance and obedience before the Lord.[27]

Our Savior Christ compares Himself to a noble man who goes into a far country. Now, when he is gone, the citizens of his country send messengers after him to tell him "that they will not have him to reign over them" [Luke 19:14]. Though it is properly to be understood of the nation of the Jews, who did indeed say so to our Savior Christ, yet it may also be extended to all impenitent sinners who say in their hearts: "Christ shall not reign over us." For so long as a man is uncalled, he carries a purpose to live in sin, some in this sin and some in that, and so doing [he] says in his heart: "God shall not be my God. I will not submit myself unto His laws. Christ shall not reign over me." This is plain

---

27. This paragraph break is not in the original.

and manifest by men's behavior when they are reproved for their sins. Tell the covetous man of his avarice, the swearer of his blasphemy, and the drunkard of his drunkenness, etc. Will he humble himself in conscience of his sin? Nothing less, but his heart will swell against you as his fury and impatience will soon bewray. And the reason is because he never thinks of his own estate, how by creation he owes homage unto God as to his Creator. For his purpose is to go on in sin, and when he is reproved for the same, his desire is crossed, which he cannot abide, and therefore [he] rages, showing thereby manifestly that in his heart he says [that] he will not obey God's commandments.

For the examination of our hearts touching this thought, whether we did ever think thus with ourselves: "I will not obey God's commandments"?[28] Doubtless, every man will answer for himself that he abhors this thought. And yet, after just trial, it will appear that generally this thought is rife among us. For though we hear the Word and receive the sacraments, the pledges of our salvation, and [we] will be counted the members of Christ, yet what is the cause that there is so little knowledge of God and obedience to His Word? And why do men in their callings show forth so small love, so little mercy, justice, and good conscience? The truth is that, though some have these things in them in some measure, yet the body of our people is generally void of these good virtues and fruits of the Spirit. He who has but half an eye may see it. For where is that religious keeping of the Sabbath that should be? Where is that serious performing of worship unto God which ought to be? All which argue that the heart is corrupt and deceivable and says indeed to God: "I will not obey Thy Word. Lord, depart from me!" What man almost is there that says with[in] himself, "Oh miserable man, what have I done?"

The Use
By this wicked imagination we may see how hard a thing it is truly and soundly to convert a sinner unto God, and how easily a man may deceive his own soul and beguile the world by hypocrisy. For a man by long exercise in the Word may have a great measure of knowledge, and withal good wit and memory, and with them utterance, and by a common gift of the Spirit be able to teach the Word truly, and to conceive prayer to good purpose, and withal have a cankered heart toward God, poisoned with this damnable thought: "I will not obey the Word of God." For every man who has inwardly in him a purpose to live, though but in one sin, his heart is not upright with God, neither are God's graces (as faith and repentance) found in his heart. For true repentance is a purpose and resolution to leave all sin, and to please God in all things.

---

28. In the margin: Examination for this thought.

Thought 3

Of this thought: It is a vain thing to worship God.

The third wicked imagination of man's heart concerning God is this: it is a vain thing to worship God. Job shows this to be true, bringing in the wicked man, saying, "What profit shall I have if I pray unto God?" [Job 21:15]. We must not think that he said thus with his mouth, but in his heart. And the prophet Malachi brings in the Jews, saying, "It is a vain thing to serve God, and what profit is it that we have kept his commandment, and that we walked humbly before the Lord of hosts" [Mal. 3:14]. Yea, righteous David,[29] a man after God's own heart, was overtaken with this evil thought when he said, "Certainly I have cleansed my heart in vain, and washed my hands in innocency" [Ps. 73:13]. Whereby it is plain that this is a natural evil thought in every man.

Yet here we must remember that this evil thought comes not into the mind of man at all times but only at such time when occasion is offered, as namely when a man is called on to the service of God, which upon some occasion he is desirous to omit, then will his mind range about for liberty from God's service, and so he will bethink himself of the wicked man's estate who never served God and yet is in [a] better case outwardly than the godly man is. And hereupon he begins to say in his heart, doubtless, "It is a vain thing to serve God."

For the examination of our hearts touching this thought, after just trial it will be found among us, as will declare the state of all sorts of families.[30] Among the poorer sort you shall see men labor from morning to evening, and take great pains to provide for the world, but in the meantime, where is the worship and service of God? Where is prayer and thanksgiving, morning and evening? Surely, it is neglected. And the reason is because they think thus in their heart: "So that I may have provision for the world, it is no matter whether I serve God or not." Come to the rich man's house, and there you shall see them spend their time in eating, drinking, gaming, and such delights. But the worship of God is not regarded, for thus they think with[in] themselves: if they may have their pleasure all is well. Come and reason with ordinary men, and exhort them to use the means of salvation, and show forth love unto religion sincerely. Their answer is [that] they will do as they have done and as their forefathers did before them. They trust their souls are as good to God-ward as the best, and for ought they see, none are worse than those who have so much preaching. And, therefore, they hope to be saved though they do not follow it so much. And this also comes from this evil thought: it is in vain to serve God.[31]

---

29. *David*: that is, Asaph.

30. In the margin: Examination for this thought.

31. This paragraph break is not in the original.

Mark also in those places where the gospel is preached, if any seems to make more conscience of sin and of serving God than others, they are made a by-word and a mocking stock, and their profession is turned to their reproach. This argues plainly that man's thought is this: it is a vain thing to serve God. Nay, take a view of the whole world, and you shall see everywhere [that] men give themselves to will-worship. No nation is so barbarous as to deny unto God all worship. But do they give Him that which He commands in His Word? Nothing less: it is either the mere invention of men or altogether stained therewith. This is most evident with the Turk, Jew, and papist. Yea, our common sort of Protestants have their will-worship, for generally they content themselves with mumbling over the words of the Creed, the Lord's Prayer, and Ten Commandments, persuading themselves that by the bare rehearsal of the words they have sufficiently served God. Now would we know the cause hereof, as also why men are so slack and cold in prayer, so careless and irreverent in hearing God's Word? Surely, it is nothing but this vile imagination bewitching our souls, that it is a vain thing to serve God. This quenches the Spirit and hinders all good motions that are in our hearts.

Thought 4

Of men's thoughts of distrust.

The fourth evil thought concerning God is a thought of distrust, thus framed in the mind: God does not regard me, God will not help me, God will not be merciful unto me. This thought made entrance unto the fall of our first parents. For first Eve looked upon the fruit and saw that it was beautiful, and then a thought of distrust entered into her heart after this manner: it may be [that] it is not true what God has said concerning the use of this fruit, and it may be [that] God regards us not as we think He does, in that He denies us this fruit. Hereupon her will and her affections were carried to the breaking of God's commandment, and so she sinned by disobedience, and Adam also sinned.[32]

When the people of Israel murmured in the wilderness, Moses "sinned" a sin for [which] he was debarred entrance into the land of Canaan [Num. 20:12]. Now what was Moses's sin, for both he and Aaron prayed to the Lord, and checked the people, saying, "Hear, oh ye rebels" [vv. 6, 10], and at God's commandment he brought water out of the rock? Surely, his sin was secret, even inward unbelief and distrust in God's promise. For when he smote the rock, he might think thus with[in] himself: "It may be that God will not now give water out of the rock." And this seems the more probable because he went beyond

---

32. This paragraph break is not in the original.

his commission in smiting thrice upon the rock, when God bade him only to "speak unto it" [v. 8].[33]

This evil thought takes hold of religious David also: "I said in mine haste I am cast out of thy sight" [Ps. 31:22]. As though he should say, "Heretofore I have found favor with God, but now in my adversity I am utterly rejected." Again, "I said in my fear, all men are liars" [Ps. 116:11]; that is, when fear of death took hold of me, then I thought that Samuel lied unto me when he said I should come to the kingdom over Israel.[34]

The children of Israel did often bewray this thought of distrust. When they were pinched with hunger and famine in the wilderness, they say, "Can God provide a table for us in the wilderness? Can he give bread and flesh for his people?" [Ps. 78:19–20]. As if they should say, "We think He cannot nor will not."[35]

Yea, the apostle Peter was not free from this thought, for when Christ, walking on the waters, commanded Peter to come unto Him, he came out boldly and walked toward Jesus. But when "he saw a mighty wind he began to sink" [Matt. 14:30]. Whence came this? Surely, from a thought of distrust which he had in his heart to this effect: "It may be God will not support me in my walking." And that this or some such thought was in his heart appears by Christ's answer to him, saying, "O thou of little faith, why didst thou doubt?" [v. 31].[36]

By all this it is evident that this is [a] natural thought in the mind of man, which at some time troubles the most righteous man who is.

Now touching this thought of distrust, two things are to be scanned: first, the time when it takes place in man's mind; and, second, the danger of it.

Point 1

For the time, this thought does not always take place in the mind of man, but only in the time of some danger, affliction, and temptation, and especially in the time of sickness and in the pangs of death.[37] Thus, in his grievous affliction righteous Job was troubled with this thought of distrust, for then he complained that "God did hate him and gnash upon him with his teeth, and as his enemy, sharpened his eyes against him" [Job 16:9], yea, "that he made him as his butt and mark to shoot at" [v. 12]. And David, in a grievous trouble of mind, thus complained: "Will the Lord absent himself forever? And will he show no more favor? Is his mercy clean gone forever? Doth his promise fail forevermore? Hath God forgotten to be merciful?" [Ps. 77:7–9]. Whereby [it] appears

---

33. This paragraph break is not in the original.
34. This paragraph break is not in the original.
35. This paragraph break is not in the original.
36. This paragraph break is not in the original.
37. In the margin: Time of this thought.

that in his affliction he was greatly troubled with this distrustful thought. And there is no man living, but when trouble and affliction comes, he shall feel in himself these thoughts of distrust. Indeed, while peace and ease continue, presumptuous thoughts possess the mind. But when the days of peace are gone, and troublesome times approach, then presumptuous thoughts give place, and thoughts of distrust come in their room and stead.

Point 2

The danger of these thoughts of distrust is very great, as the fruits thereof declare.[38] For hence arise, first, all horrors and terrors of conscience, all fears and astonishments of the heart. For when the mind says (though falsely), "God does not regard me, God will not save me," then the trembling heart is full of horror and dread. Second, hence comes desperation itself, whereby men confidently avouch that God has forsaken them and cast them off, and that there is no hope of life, but present death remaining for them. This thought troubles the mind of the wicked and of the repentant person also, for desperation is nothing but the strength of this thought of distrust. Third, this weakens the foundation of our salvation, which stands in the certainty of God's promises. For this thought of distrust denies credit to God's promises and makes them uncertain. Among all other evil thoughts this does most directly hinder salvation, for it is flatly against faith, as water is to fire. For true faith makes a man say with good conscience, "Christ died and shed His blood for me, God the Father will be merciful unto me, and save me" [Gal. 2:20]; but this distrustful thought causes a man to say the clean contrary, "Christ died not for me, God will not save me." So that, where this thought prevails, true faith is not. Neither can [it] take place.

The Use

Considering the danger of this distrustful thought is so great, we must be admonished in the fear of God to use all good means, while the days of peace do last, that it takes no place with us in the day of trouble and temptation. The means to repress it are the preaching of the Word and the sacraments of baptism and the Lord's Supper.[39]

For the first, the Word of God preached is a special means ordained by God for the true applying of God's promises of mercy to our own souls. And, therefore, [it is] a most sovereign remedy against this thought of distrust. For when the promises of mercy in Christ are offered unto God's people in the preaching of the Word by a lawful minister, it is (by virtue of God's ordinance) as much

---

38. In the margin: Fruit of this thought.
39. In the margin: Means against distrust.

as if Christ Himself in His own person should speak unto them. If God from heaven should say to any man [that] mercy belongs to him, he would believe. If God says to Cornelius, "Believe you, and My mercy belongs to you," Cornelius will believe. If He says to Peter, "Believe you, and My mercy belongs to you," Peter will believe. And if He says so to Mary Magdalene, she will believe. Lo here, when the minister of God, out of God's Word, says to any man, "Believe you, and repent you, and God's mercy belongs unto you," it is as much as if the Lord should call him by name particularly, and say unto him, "Believe you, and repent, and My mercy belongs unto you." Yea, it is all one as if God Himself should say, "I am your Father and you are my child, if you will repent and believe."

The second means, which is also very effectual to cut off this thought of distrust, is baptism. If any earthly prince gives a pardon to any man and puts the man's name in the pardon and his own broad seal unto it, the man will never doubt of his pardon, but believe it. Behold, in baptism God enters covenant with miserable wretched man, and herein makes promise of life unto him; yea, He puts the man's name in the covenant, sealing the same with His own seal. And, therefore, the baptized party must believe against this thought.

The third means is the Lord's Supper rightly administered and received. For therein the bread and wine, given to the hand of every communicant by the minister, are particular pledges and tokens unto them of special mercy in Christ. These are the means which we must use with all good conscience in the days of peace, so that when troubles come this thought of distrust may not prevail against us.

And thus much of man's natural evil thoughts against God. Many others might be added hereunto, but these being the principal, I omit the rest.

Chapter 4

Man's Natural Thoughts Concerning His Neighbor

Now we come to the evil thoughts of man's natural heart against his neighbor. And to find them out we must have recourse to the second table of the moral law, which was penned with respect to the corrupt estate of man [Gal. 3:19], forbidding that which man's corrupt heart thinks naturally against his neighbor. For every commandment thereof is spiritual, forbidding not only the wicked actions, evil words, and gestures, but all corrupt affections, yea, all evil imaginations of man against man.

The thoughts of man against his neighbor are of two sorts: (1) without consent; or (2) with consent. Thoughts without consent are the very evil motions of the mind which a man conceives against his neighbor, to which the will never gives consent. And these are forbidden in the tenth commandment: "Thou shalt not lust." Thoughts with consent of will are such as a man, conceiving in his mind, does withal desire or purpose in his heart to practice. And these are forbidden in the fifth, sixth, seventh, eighth, and ninth commandments. By reason whereof they may fitly be reduced to five heads. They are either thoughts of dishonor against the fifth commandment, thoughts of murder against the sixth, thoughts of adultery against the seventh, thoughts of theft against the eighth, or thoughts of disgrace against the ninth commandment.

Section 1
Of thoughts of dishonor.
First, a thought of dishonor is any thought that tends to the contempt and abasing of the person of our neighbor in respect of ourselves. And it is then conceived in our minds when we think thus of all other men beside ourselves: "Such and such a man is far inferior unto me, a base and contemptible fellow in regard of me." We have [an] example hereof in the Pharisee, a man strict in profession and zealous in his religion, who comes to the temple to pray with the publican. Now mark what he says: "Oh God, I thank thee, that I am not as other men are, or as this publican" [Luke 18:11]. These words proceed from such a proud thought as this: "Lord, I thank Thee [that] all other men are far inferior unto me. I do far surpass the common sort. This publican is a base fellow and

nobody [in comparison] to me." If any shall imagine that this thought is not in every man, but in some few proud persons, I answer [that] it is by nature in every person living without grace. And, therefore, Saint Paul gives this commandment, "That every man in meekness should esteem others better than himself" [Phil. 2:3], giving us to understand that by nature all men think best of themselves and esteem others far worse than themselves.

The Use

If this thought of dishonor is in all men's hearts, then behold what a palace of all satanical and damnable pride the heart of man is naturally. It is like unto the table of Adoni-bezek, at which he sat in a chair of estate, and made others (even kings) to eat meat like dogs under his feet, with their thumbs cut off [Judges 1:7]. Such a one is every man by nature. He lifts up himself, saying, "I am the man." And [he] treads his brother under his feet as nobody unto him. And this is the cause of much strife and hurt in all human societies. This causes many jars, much scorning, and great contempt among men in word and deed.

Now that we may reform this thought in us, we must learn to say as Job did, after he had been afflicted and came to see his sins, "Behold, I am vile" [Job 40:4]; and with Abraham, "I am but dust and ashes" [Gen. 18:27]; and with David, "I am a worm, and no man" (Ps. 22:6); yea, we must labor with Paul to see our misery by reason of sin [Rom. 7:24]. And that will help to pull down the pride of our hearts.

Section 2

Of murdering thoughts.

The second evil thought of man (with consent) against his neighbor is a thought of murder or of anything that tends thereto. We have particular examples of this in Scripture. The Lord forbids the Jews to have this murdering thought in their hearts: "I will not relieve the poor, I will not do good unto them" (Deut. 15:9). This gives us to understand that this was the common thought of the Jews, or else He would not have forbidden it. Yea, the Lord does there set out this thought by two signs: first, "an evil eye" when a man turns his countenance from the poor or looks on them without compassion; [and,] second, "unmerciful dealing" when a man will not help the poor by gift according to his ability. And because all actions proceed from thoughts, the heart being the fountain of our deeds, hence it appears that this murdering thought against the poor is rife in this age. For where is the man who does pity the poor, and does good to them according to his ability? Nay, the Lord's complaint against the Jews may be fitly applied to our times in regard of cruelty and oppression: "The spoil of the poor is in your houses: what have ye to do, that ye beat my people to pieces, and grind the faces of the poor?" (Isa. 3:14–15).

The second example of a murdering thought is concerning God's church, and it is this: "I will do some spite or hurt to them who worship God." For proof hereof, read Psalm 74:8. David brings in the Babylonians, Edomites, etc., saying thus one to another against God's people, the Jews: "Let us destroy them all together." And, "Let us cut them off from being a people, and let the name of Israel be no more in remembrance." (Ps. 83:4). Now as this was their thought, so it is the thought of all men naturally. For that which was the disposition of Babel, Edom, Moab, and Ammon against God's church, is the disposition of all men naturally. For look how general the hatred of man is, so general is the purpose of mischief against those who profess religion. For all men by nature are haters of God's church and people. So, Christ says to His disciples: "Ye shall be hated of all nations for my name's sake" [Matt. 24:9]. Yea, "Whosoever killeth you shall think that he doth God good service" [John 16:2]. And, therefore, this thought of doing mischief is as general even in the mind of every man by nature.[1]

This further appears by the continual persecution that has ever been raised against God's poor church, since the beginning of the world. It began at Abel, soon after the giving of the covenant of grace to our first parents. And [it] has continued to this day, and [it] shall abide unto the end. So that, if carnal men could look into their own hearts, they should there behold this murdering thought against God's people. This murdering thought comes from another wicked imagination, set down by Saint Peter, who brings in the wicked of this world, who think it a strange thing that God's children do not as they do, and run not with them unto all excess of riot, living in drunkenness, fornication, and such other abominations [1 Peter 4:3–4]. For this cause, they do conceive hatred and purpose mischief against God's people, and so [they] will continue [to do] till God give them grace to repent. If any shall say this thought is not general, for Nebuchadnezzar, a heathen man, "showed favor to Daniel, and highly advanced him" [Dan. 2:48], I answer [that] it is true he did so, but that was a work of God's special providence, who procured him favor and disposed the king's heart to affect him as He did also the heart of the chief "eunuch" [Dan. 1:9]. Otherwise, Nebuchadnezzar did nothing naturally but intend mischief against God's church, as his rage against the three children did evidently bewray (Dan. 3:19).

A third example of this murdering thought I add, which every minister of God's Word may observe by daily experience, and it is this, when men's faults

---

1. This paragraph break is not in the original.

are particularly rebuked in the ministry of the Word, and the quick (as it were) touched by applying the Word to the conscience, then will the heart of a natural man thus conceive of the minister who reproves sin: "This man means me. He has some spite and malice against me, that he thus reproves my particular faults." When as the minister knew them not to be his personal sins, but it is the power of the Word that ransacks the sinful heart. This is the fault of all carnal hearers, who will hear quietly till their faults are rebuked, but then they think maliciously of the preacher. Herod dealt thus with John [the] Baptist. He heard him gladly for a while (Mark 6:20), but when he was rebuked for his "brother Phillip's wife, then he cast John in prison" (Luke 3:19–20). And if conscience might be judge, many a hearer would be found to have a Herod's heart toward God's minister.

Section 3

Of thoughts of adultery, theft, and disgrace.

The third thought of man touching his neighbor is the thought of adultery, which is the thought with consent to any unchastity. Judah had such a thought concerning Tamar, his daughter-in-law, when he judged her [to be] a whore and desired to lie with her (Gen. 38:15–16). And Amnon's heart was so sore vexed with such thoughts that he fell sick for his sister Tamar (2 Sam. 13:2). This makes a man an adulterer in heart before God, though actually he commits not the act (Matt. 5:28).

The fourth is the thought of theft, which is the thought with consent of beguiling or wronging another in his goods or substance. This is that imagining of iniquity and working of wickedness upon their beds in coveting of fields, against which Micah pronounces a "woe" (Micah 2:1). And this thought also possesses the hearts [of those] who, with the wicked Israelites, wish the time were come wherein they "might make the ephah small and the shekel great (that is, lessen the measure and enhance the price), and falsify the weights by deceit" (Amos 8:5).

The fifth evil thought is a thought of disgrace which some way tends to the reproach and debasing of our neighbor's good name. As, when a thing is well done, to think and judge it to be ill done; or, when a thing is amiss, to judge it worse than it is. Thus Eli thought disgracefully of Hannah, deeming her to be drunk, saying, "Put away thy drunkenness" (1 Sam. 1:14), when she prayed devoutly from a "troubled soul to the Lord" (v. 15). Thus Eliab, David's eldest brother, thought disgracefully of David when he showed himself willing to encounter with Goliath who reviled the host of the living God, saying, "I know the pride and malice of thine heart that thou art come to see the battle" (1 Sam. 17:28), when as indeed the Spirit of God put that motion into his heart to take away the shame from Israel, as the happy event declared plainly. So, when our Savior Christ spoke most comfortably to the sick of the palsy, saying, "Be of good comfort, thy sins are forgiven thee" [Matt. 9:2], then the cursed hearts of the wicked Pharisees thought thus in themselves: "This man blasphemeth" (v. 3). And when the gift of the Holy Spirit was sent upon the apostles, causing them to speak strange tongues to the great admiration of men of divers nations, then some of the "malicious Jews thought they were drunk," saying scoffingly, "they were full of new wine" (Acts 2:13). And this thought of disgrace is in every man, naturally bringing forth continually the fruits of disgrace as envy, strife, emulations, dissensions, and debates. For "love thinketh not evil,"[2] but naturally true love is wanting in all men. And, therefore, they cannot but think evil of others.

We see the five evil thoughts of man's natural heart against his neighbor. Touching this, two things are yet further to be scanned, to wit, (1) when these evil thoughts do arise in the mind, and (2) in whom they are.

For the first, it is true that they do not at all times arise in men's minds, but then only when occasion is given, at which time they arise so soon as it is given. For man's heart is like tinder or dry wood, which burns not of itself, but so soon as fire is put to it, then presently it kindles. When you come to talk with a natural man, it may be for the present he thinks not to lie. But give him occasion to lie, and then he soon bethinks himself thereof, and will spare to utter it if it may make for his advantage. And the like we may say of malice, adultery, theft, disgrace, or any other sin against our neighbor. Do but minister occasion there about to the natural heart of man, and he thinks of them, and without God's grace, restraining or renewing him, [he] will bring forth the same in action.

The second point: In whom are all these evil thoughts? *Answer.* In all men naturally without exception, till they are renewed by God's special grace. Yea, the truth is [that] these thoughts do everywhere abound. For look what men do practice, that first of all they think, for the thought is the beginning of every action. But in the world all sins against the second table do abound, as the practice of dishonor, murder, adultery, thefts, and disgraces, and therefore these evil thoughts, from whence these actions come, must needs be common.

The Use

By this we may see what a huge mass of corruption the natural heart of man is without God's special grace. For thoughts of dishonor make a man's heart a palace of pride like the table of Adoni-bezek. Also, thoughts of cruelty make man's heart a slaughter house. Thoughts of adultery make it a most filthy

---

2. 1 Cor. 13:5.

stewes. Thoughts of theft make it to become a den of thieves, wherein all manner of fraud and bad dealing is plotted and devised. And, lastly, thoughts of disgrace make it a fountain of backbiting, debate, slander, and reviling. And, therefore, howsoever the outward life may be ordered civilly, yet without God's grace, man's heart is most vile. And those who plead their good nature and good meaning are here confuted, for naturally the heart thinks all evil against his neighbor.

Chapter 5

Man's Natural Thoughts Concerning Himself

The third kind of man's natural evil thoughts are such as concern himself, and they are principally four.

Section 1

Man's proud thoughts of his own excellency.

The first may fitly be termed a thought of pride, whereby every man naturally thinks himself most excellent and far to exceed all other men whatsoever. Thus, the prophet Isaiah brings in Babylon, speaking in her heart, that is, thinking, "I will ascend into heaven, and exalt my throne above (or besides) the stars of God" [Isa. 14:13]. As if she should think with[in] herself: "I am far more excellent than any other whatsoever, and therefore I am to be exalted from the earth to heaven, and to be matched with God Himself." And the prophet Zephaniah brings in Nineveh, speaking thus in her heart: "I am, and there is none besides me" [Zeph. 2:15]. And so, the proud Pharisee in his private and secret prayer to God, says, "I thank thee, Lord, that I am not as other men" [Luke 18:11], meaning that he is more excellent. And the whore of Babylon[1] is brought in, saying of herself: "I sit as a queen, and am no widow, and shall see no mourning" [Rev. 18:7].[2]

All these places show this to be the nature of man: to exalt himself in his own heart above all others. If any shall say [that] hereby no more can be proved but that this thought is in some proud and insolent persons, I add, therefore, that as our first parents in the beginning did learn that proud lesson of the devil, "Ye shall be as gods," so we, being in their loins when they sinned, and descending from them by ordinary generation, do together with our nature receive that corruption from them whereby we think thus proudly of ourselves, that we far excel others and are as little gods on earth in respect of others. Indeed, most will say for themselves: "We abhor this proud thought. Neither did we ever find it to be in us." But we must know that the lesser we discern it in

---

1. In the margin: The heretical Church of Rome.
2. This paragraph break is not in the original.

ourselves, the more it reigns in our hearts. And the more we discern and bewail it, the lesser place it takes in us.

Now touching this thought of pride, two things must be observed: (1) the danger; and (2) the highest degree of it.

Point 1

For the danger of this thought,[3] the outward affecting of strange fashions in apparel is a wonderful pride, but the vilest and most wretched pride of all is that spiritual pride of the heart whereby a man despises all others in regard of himself and thinks himself far better than any. I manifest this by sundry reasons, as first, from the fruits of this inward pride.[4] For hence do flow many damnable sins in men's lives and conversations. First, ambition, whereby men are not content with that estate wherewith God has blessed them but do seek by all means to be advanced to higher dignity and estate. Second, presumption, whereby men dare enterprise things beyond their calling and above their power, taking upon them more than they are able to do. Third, boasting, whereby a man speaks of himself more than is seemly and extols himself above his desert. Fourth, hypocrisy, when a man pretends he has that grace and religion which indeed he has not, or else makes show of more grace than is truly in him. Fifth, obstinacy, when a man persists in an error, and will not yield to the truth, though it is manifested unto him. Sixth, contention, whereby men strive one against another in word or deed, without relenting. And lastly, affectation of novelties, especially in outward attire, for when a man conceives so highly of himself, then withal he thinks no manner of attire good enough to beautify and adorn his body, and so [he] begins to devise and affect strange and foreign attire.

Second, the danger hereof appears hence, that where this thought of pride reigns (as it does in all men naturally) there the Spirit of grace dwells not. In her song, Mary says well, "God scattereth the imaginations of the proud" (Luke 1:51); that is, those who have this conceit of their own excellency above others. And Saint James [says,] "God resisteth the proud, and giveth grace to the humble" (James 4:6). Yea, "Thus says he that is high and excellent, he that inhabiteth eternity, whose name is the holy one: I dwell in the high and holy place, with him also that is of a contrite and humble spirit, to revive the spirit of the humble" (Isa. 57:15). But "he who lifts up himself, his mind is not upright in him" (Hab. 2:4).

Third, such is the danger of this sin that when all other sins die in a man, this thought of pride dies not. Nay, when other sins are mortified and God's

____

3. In the margin: The danger of this thought.
4. In the margin: Fruits of inward pride.

graces come instead thereof, yet this will then revive and make the graces of God matter whereof to work. As when an ignorant person attains to some knowledge, this pride will take occasion from that gift of God to puff up the heart. Yea, when a man in true humility of heart shall renounce the actions of pride, yet then pride will be working, for this is a fruit of pride to think well of ourselves because we are not proud.

Point 2

The highest degree of this pride is when a man thinks himself to be equal with God.[5] This is a most notorious, nay an abominable, height of pride. And yet, the truth is [that] some men have come hereunto. The king of Babel thought of himself thus when he said in his heart: "I will ascend above the height of the clouds and will be like the most high" (Isa. 14:14). It may seem strange that men should think thus of themselves, but we must know that men may do it [in] two ways.[6]

First, when they think they have power of themselves whereby they are able to match or countervail the power of God. Nebuchadnezzar thought so when he said, "Who is that God that can deliver you out of my hand?" (Dan. 3:15). Such a thought had proud Pharaoh in his heart when he said to Moses and Aaron: "Who is the Lord that I should hear his voice, and let Israel go?" (Exod. 5:2).[7]

Second, when they take to themselves the honor of God, and think it to be due to them. Herod did thus when by silence he approved the blasphemous voice of the people, who cried unto him, "the voice of God, and not of man" [Acts 12:22]. And thus antichrist, sitting in the temple of God, "exalts himself above all that is called God, or worshipped" (2 Thess. 2:4). Now that man of sin is the pope of Rome, for howsoever in word he humbles himself and calls himself the servant of servants, yet indeed, through the pride of his heart, he sits as God, taking unto himself that honor which is proper to God. For he claims power to prescribe new rules of God's worship, to forgive sins, to make laws to bind the conscience properly, yea, to open and shut heaven, and to dispose at his pleasure of earthly kingdoms.[8] He takes upon himself to dispense with the moral law and with apostolic constitutions, all which belong to God alone. And no-one dares claim [that they] belong unto him but he who matches himself with God. And this is the highest degree of pride.

---

5. In the margin: The height of this thought.
6. This paragraph break is not in the original.
7. This paragraph break is not in the original.
8. In the margin: Bell. de Rom. Pontif. lib. 4.

The Use

By this every man may see what he is of himself, what a cursed and proud nature he carries about with him. For every man naturally, when occasion is offered, thinks highly of himself and basely of others in regard of himself. Let us, therefore, take notice of this satanical pride that is in our nature, and strive against it. For who would not be ashamed to say with the proud Pharisee, "I thank thee Lord, I am not as other men," or with the arrogant Jews, "Stand apart, touch me not, I am holier than thou" (Isa. 65:5).

Section 2

Man's thought of his own righteousness.

The second evil thought concerning a man's self is this: "I am sufficiently righteous, and I need no repentance." That this is the thought of every man naturally appears by the Lord's commandment to the people of Israel, forbidding them to say in their hearts, when they were placed in the promised land, that "for their righteousness the Lord brought them in to possess it" (Deut. 9:4). Whereby He gives us to understand two things. First, as the Jews did there, so every man thinks himself to be righteous. Second, he thinks that God does give His blessings unto him for his own righteousness, for the Lord does not forbid such a thought as men naturally have not in them.[9]

So, in like manner, when Jeremiah rebuked the people for their sins, they said, "They were innocent and guiltless…they had not sinned" (Jer. 2:35). And the church of Laodicea says thus of herself: "I am rich and need nothing" (Rev. 3:17); that is, "I abound in spiritual graces." This is the thought of the proud Pharisee "who trusts in himself that he is just" (Luke 18:9–10), and, therefore, brags unto God that he is not such and such, but he does this and that, he fasts, gives alms, pays tithes, etc. And in plain terms his heart says thus: "I am righteous, I need no repentance." For Christ spoke of such when He said, "He came not to call the righteous but sinners to repentance" (Matt. 9:13). And again, "I say unto you, that joy shall be in heaven for one sinner that converteth, more than for ninety and nine just men which need no amendment of life" (Luke 15:7). Here, we must observe that Christ means not that there are indeed some so righteous that they need no amendment, but [that] He speaks according to the opinion which some have of themselves, to wit, that they are righteous, and need no repentance. By all this it is more than manifest that this is a natural thought of a man concerning himself.

____

9. This paragraph break is not in the original.

This evil thought reigns in our age and time as all the former do.[10] For come to an ignorant man who has not been instructed in religion, reason with him touching his estate, and ask him whether he can keep the law of God or not, he will answer [that] he can, [and that] he loves the Lord his God with all his heart and his neighbor as himself. Ask him how he looks to be saved, his answer is by his own righteousness and for his own goodness. If due examination were made, this would be found to be the thought of many who live in the church among us. And there is none by nature free from this thought.

Hereby then we may see that the thoughts of every man, be he what he will, are plain papistry, for popery is natural. One chief pillar and ground thereof is justification and salvation by works. Every man brings this opinion with him from his mother's womb. And so it is in the point of merit, men naturally think they receive the good things which they have from God for their own righteousness.

Second, hence it appears that it is a matter of great difficulty to bring a man thoroughly to renounce his own righteousness, and soundly and heartily to embrace true religion and the righteousness of Christ by faith. This is no less than the change of nature. And yet, this must every man do who will be saved. He must become nothing in himself, that he may be all in Christ Jesus. This is as impossible to nature as to change water into fire, and therefore men had need to beware how they put off the time and neglect the means in which God shows His power in working this change in the hearts of His elect.

Third, hence we see the evident cause of that preposterous course of the world which most men take in spending their wit and strength, some for riches, others for honors and pleasures, and in the meantime, they can spare no time for religion, to seek God's favor in Christ and the graces of the Spirit. It might be [that] they will afford a good word unto religion, but yet they regard it not in respect of other things. And this is the behavior, not of some few, but of all sorts and degrees of men naturally. Now the cause hereof is this cursed evil thought whereby men persuade themselves [that] they are righteous and need no repentance. And till this thought is rooted out of [a] man's heart, he will never value the Word and religion of God according to the worth thereof, so as, with the good merchant, "he will part with all that he hath, rather than he will be frustrated of this pearl" (Matt. 13:45–46).[11]

Indeed, men usually plead thus for themselves: "We confess ourselves to be sinners, and therefore we cannot think such a wicked thought [as] that we need no repentance." But we must know that both these may well stand together in

---

10. In the margin: Examination for this thought.
11. This paragraph break is not in the original.

the wicked heart of man. He may confess himself to be a sinner, and yet think that he is righteous. For is not this the common practice to make great sins little sins, and little sins no sins? Do not men clothe vice in virtue's robe, and turn out virtue in the rotten rags of vice? Is not drunkenness counted good fellowship and kind neighborhood? Is not swearing made the token of a brave mind, pride counted [as] decency, fornication but a trick of youth, and covetousness esteemed good thrift and carefulness? On the other side, is not the more sincere profession of religion termed preciseness, Puritanism, hypocrisy, and such like? Does not he who refrains [from] the common sins of the time make himself a prey to the mouths of the ungodly? Now, where these things are, though the mouth says "I am a sinner," yet the heart thinks "I am righteous." And so, it is apparent [that] this thought is common among us.

Section 3

Man's thought of security in the day of peace.

The third evil thought concerning a man's self is a thought of security. In the time of peace and prosperity, men say thus in their hearts: "I am free from all God's judgments. I am in no danger of hell, death, or damnation, but sure enough of salvation." It may be thought that none is so bewitched of the devil as to have this conceit of himself. But the Scripture is most plain in the proof hereof: "The wicked man (such as is every man by nature, as we showed before) saith in his heart, I shall never be moved nor be in danger" (Ps. 10:6). And the prophet Isaiah brings in wicked men, saying, "We have made a covenant with death, and with hell we are at agreement" (Isa. 28:15). This must not be understood as done indeed (for death and hell will make league with none), but only in men's wicked imagination, persuading themselves that they are in no danger of hell or of the grave, for so much the next words import, that "though a scourge run over and pass through, yet it shall not come at us." Yea, righteous David was overtaken herewith, for in his prosperity he said in his heart, "I shall never be moved" (Ps. 30:6). Much more then is it the thought of every natural man to say with the rich fool upon the increase of outward blessings: "Soul, soul, take thine ease, thou hast enough, nothing can hurt thee" (Luke 12:19).

The Use

By this we may come to the knowledge of a thing, which falls out in all ages, worth our diligent observation. It has pleased God from time to time to send His prophets and ministers to call His people to repentance. Thus did Isaiah, Jeremiah, Joel, Amos, and the rest; yea, "The Lord himself," as Zephaniah says, "riseth every morning, and bringeth his judgments to light (which should turn men from their sins), he faileth not, and yet the wicked will not learn to be ashamed" (Zeph. 3:5).

To come to our own times. It has pleased God to stir up many worthy ministers unto us, who spend their time and strength in laboring to bring men to repentance and salvation. But yet, who is he who almost turns from his sins? Yea, the Lord Himself, as in former times, so now does preach from heaven by His judgments, as famine, plague, etc. And yet, by lamentable experience we see that the body of our people remain secure. They are "settled on their lees" (Jer. 48:11) and "frozen in their dregs" (Zeph. 1:12). No man stirs up himself to say, "What have I done?" (Jer. 8:6). Now the cause hereof is nothing else but this cursed thought of security, whereby a man says thus in his heart: "I am free from God's judgments." Read Matthew 24:37–39, "As it was in the days of Noah," says our Savior Christ, "so shall it be in the days of the coming of the Son of man: they did eat, drink, marry wives, and give in marriage, and knew nothing till Noah entered into the ark, and the flood came and took them all away."[12]

Question. How could it be that they should know nothing, seeing Noah had preached unto them of the flood a hundred and twenty years before? *Answer.* Surely it was as if they had known nothing, for they would not believe him. It would not sink into their heads, much less settle in their hearts, that God would destroy all the world by water. And so it may be said of these times. We know nothing. Though we are called to repentance by the ministry of the Word, yet we will not repent. And though we hear of God's judgments, we think ourselves free from them, and [we] will not believe till the besom[13] of His wrath sweeps us all away, as the flood did the old world.

Wherefore, to redress among us this damnable thought of security, let us consider our grievous sins in particular, and set before our eyes the curse of God, both temporal judgments and eternal death, due unto us for the same.[14] It is the applying of God's heavy wrath that must make us shake off this secure thought, which the rather we must do, though it is grievous to the flesh and as a pang unto death in a natural man, because till this thought is removed, the saving graces of God's Spirit will not take root in our hearts.

Section 4
Man's faint thoughts in time of distress.
The fourth and last evil thought of man's heart touching himself is this: in times of misery he says [that] his crosses are greater and worse than indeed they

---

12. This paragraph break is not in the original.
13. *Besom:* a broom made of twigs tied around a stick.
14. In the margin: Remedy.

are. So, Job complains in his affliction, that "his grief and misery was heavier than the sand of the seashore" [Job 6:2–3]. And the church in great affliction calls thus to passengers:[15] "Behold, and see if there be any sorrow like unto my sorrow which is done unto me" [Lam. 1:12]. And that it is the thought of every man's heart naturally appears by experience. For let a man be in distress outwardly, or else touched in conscience for his sins, when you shall labor to minister comfort unto him according to God's Word, he will answer that never any was in like case to him, so grievously tormented and afflicted as he is. And, indeed, it is the property of man's natural heart to esteem little crosses to be exceeding[ly] great [Jonah 4:8–9], yea, oftentimes to deem that to be a cross which is none at all. The reason is the want of judgment rightly to discern the state of their affliction, and the want of strength to support it as it is. "For if thou be faint in the day of adversity thy strength is small" [Prov. 24:10].

For the remedy of this evil thought, first we must seek to rectify the imagination by bringing the mind to a right conceit of the affliction. This is a special course to be observed in dealing with them who are oppressed with any distress. For a strong conceit of a man's own misery does many times more hurt than the misery itself. Therefore, be sure the judgment is well informed, and then the cure is half wrought and the cross half removed. This done, the afflicted party may well consider the desert of sin in the endless torments of the damned, which the Lord prevents in His children by temporal chastisements in this life. "For when we are judged we are chastened of the Lord, that we might not be condemned with the world" [1 Cor. 11:32]. And so, laboring to be humbled for sin and to lay hold on God's mercy in Christ, through whom all things (even afflictions) work together for the best, no doubt he will be able to say, "I will bear the wrath of the Lord, because I have sinned against him" [Micah 7:9]. "And why art thou cast down oh my soul, why art thou disquieted within me? Wait on God; for I will yet give him thanks; he is my present help, and my God" [Ps. 43:5].

Thus much of man's evil thoughts concerning himself.

---

15. *Passengers*: passers-by.

Chapter 6

The Want of Good Thoughts

Section 1

Good thoughts about temporal things be much wanting.

Having spoken of man's natural evil thoughts concerning God, his neighbor, and himself, we come to the second point to be observed in the text; to wit, that there is a want of good thoughts and consideration in every man naturally. For the Lord here says, "his thoughts are evil from his youth," and in Genesis 6:5, "they are only evil every day." Now look, where evil is only and continually, there good must needs be wanting altogether.

This want must be considered either in respect of temporal or spiritual things. By temporal things I mean such worldly affairs and actions as concern man's natural life, wherein though good consideration is not taken quite away, yet we must know that the same is corrupt, very weak, and imperfect, even as reason is. And there is much want in every man in this behalf. "There is one alone," says Solomon, "and there is not a second: which hath neither son nor brother, yet there is no end of his travail, neither can his eye be satisfied with riches; neither doth he think, for whom do I travail?" [Eccl. 4:8]. Behold here a notable example of this want of good consideration about earthly things, that a man should spend both his wit and strength in heaping up riches and knows not to whom he shall leave them. But we need not be inquisitive for examples, for we may daily observe in ourselves and others, apparent want of good consideration in these worldly affairs. This must not seem strange unto us, seeing that reason itself, the ground of consideration, is greatly blemished through the corruption of nature about these earthly things.

Section 2

Good thoughts in matters spiritual be altogether wanting.

In spiritual things, which concern the kingdom of God, there is in our nature an absolute want of good consideration, herein of ourselves we have no good thoughts. "We are not of ourselves," says Paul, "sufficient to think anything (that is, any good thing) as of ourselves" [2 Cor. 3:5]. The whole body of the gospel is therefore called a "mystery" because the things therein contained and revealed are such as "never came into man's heart to think" [1 Cor. 2:9]. We may observe this want especially in four things: in respect of (1) God's presence and providence, (2) God's judgments, (3) our sins, [and] (4) our duty to God.

First, man by nature does not think of (or consider) God's presence and providence, to behold and to remember all his ways in thought, word, and deed.[1] Hereof the Lord complains against Ephraim and Samaria, saying [that] they have dealt falsely, and they "consider not in their hearts that I remember all their wickedness" [Hos. 7:1–2]. And the same is the state of every natural man, being left to himself, for all by nature are equally corrupt with original sin, and so are destitute of this good thought. This may yet appear the plainer by this, that naturally man's heart is possessed of the clean contrary, to wit, God shall not see, God will not regard, as has been shown before. And, indeed, it is a work of grace to have the heart rightly affected with this thought: "God beholds all my ways. He considers and remembers everything I do." Flesh and blood cannot attain unto it.

Second, a man by nature does not consider (or think of) the judgments of God, temporal and eternal, due unto sin.[2] This thought was wanting in the men of the old world. Though Noah preached unto them [for] a hundred and twenty years of the general deluge, yet the consideration of it took no place in their hearts. And, therefore, it is said, "They knew nothing till the flood came and took them all away" (Matt. 24:38–39). From the want of this thought it came to pass that "Lot's sons-in-law thought their father had but mocked, when he told them that God would destroy Sodom" (Gen. 19:14). Hence it was that the rich fool blessed himself in his heart, saying, "Soul, soul, take thine ease." And [he] never thought [of] himself [in] any danger till it was said unto him: "O fool, this night will they fetch away thy soul" (Luke 12:19–20). And shall we think this thought is now wanting at this day, seeing Christ has said, "As it was in the days of Noah, so shall it be at the coming of the Son of man" (Matt. 24:37)?

Third, a man naturally does never bethink himself of his own sins.[3] He has no purpose of heart seriously to examine his past life, or to repent of such sins as he finds in him. This appears by the Lord's own complaint against the Jews, who were so far from turning from their sins that not one would say in his heart, "What have I done?" (Jer. 8:6). Nay, when they had committed most sottish idolatry, "in making an idol god of one part of a tree, with the other part thereof they had roasted their meat and warmed themselves, yet they considered not this in their hearts, neither had they knowledge or understanding to say, I have burnt half of it in the fire, I have baked bread upon the coals thereof;

---

1. In the margin: The first good thought wanting.
2. In the margin: The second good thought wanting.
3. In the margin: The third good thought wanting.

I have roasted flesh, and eaten it, and shall I make the residue thereof an abomination?" (Isa. 44:16–17, 19–20).

Fourth, a natural man does not consider what duty and service he owes unto God.[4] His mind is wholly bent to his own ways, but the "Lord's talent lies hid in the ground wrapped up in a napkin" (Matt. 25:18). Hereof the Lord complains against the Jews, "that they said not in their hearts, Let us fear the Lord our God" (Jer. 5:24). Hence it was that the "foolish virgins" did content themselves with the blazing lamp of an outward profession, and never thought of that oil of grace which God requires in all those who would enter with Christ into His bride-chamber, till it was too late (Matt. 25:8). And the sleight serving of God at this day declares the general want of this consideration.

Section 3
The fruit of this want of good thoughts.
Here further, we must know that this want of good consideration is a grievous evil and a mother sin, from whence (as from a fountain) streams of corruptions and transgressions (both of heart and life) do issue forth. First, hereby we are disabled from yielding unto God that obedience of heart which His law requires. For how can we "love the Lord with all our thought and mind; and our neighbor as ourselves" (Luke 10:27), as God commands, when as our hearts are naturally void of all good thoughts toward God and toward our neighbors? Again, whence comes sinning with a high hand, when men sin and will sin? Whence comes it that men bless themselves in their sins and flatter themselves in their own eyes, while they go on in sin, but from want of consideration of God's presence and of God's judgments? Abraham knew this well, and therefore said of the people of Gerar: "Because they wanted the fear of God (that is, all consideration of God's presence and of God's judgments), therefore they would kill him for his wife's sake" (Gen. 20:11). Whence also comes that sensuality whereby men addict themselves wholly to the profits, pleasures, and honors of this world, never minding heaven or hell, but from want of consideration of their duty to God? If men did call themselves to account for their sins, or did set before their eyes the judgments of God due unto them, it could not be that there should be such want of contrition toward God, or of compassion toward their brethren, as everywhere abounds. And the like might be said of many other capital sins, all which proceed from the want of good consideration. Where, by the way, we may observe that our common people do far deceive themselves in this persuasion of themselves: that by nature they have good hearts and good meaning. If you charge them with the sins of their lives, they will straightway

---

4. In the margin: The fourth good thought wanting.

plead their good intention, and say [that] though they sometimes fail in action, yet they always mean well. But the truth is [that] naturally well meaning and good consideration in spiritual things is altogether wanting. And, therefore, while men do soothe up themselves in their good meaning, they deceive their own hearts through ignorance of their natural estate. And they must know that they can never come unto Christ that they might have life till they are quite gone out of themselves in regard of such conceits.

Chapter 7

The Use of the Doctrine

Having seen what evil thoughts are in every man naturally and what good thoughts are wanting in him, it now follows to make some use of this doctrine concerning man's natural imaginations.

Section 1
That the Scripture is the Word of God.
The first use shall be against all atheists who think the Scripture to be mere policy, devised by man to keep men in awe. But we are to know that the holy Scripture is no device of man, but the very Word of the ever-living God. I demonstrate this out of the former doctrine: the Scripture says in general that all the imaginations of every natural man are evil and that continually. Now it does not only affirm this in general but declares it also in particular. For elsewhere it shows what those particular evil thoughts are which man's natural mind frames concerning God, his neighbor, and himself. Again, the same Scripture says in general that good thoughts and considerations are naturally wanting in every man, and elsewhere it declares in particular what those good thoughts are which enter not into the mind of a natural man. Both these have been plainly shown out of the Word of God. Now hereupon it does necessarily follow that the Scripture is the Word of God. For let the cunning atheist show whence it is that the Scripture does declare man's thoughts. He cannot say, "of man," for no man knows the thoughts of another; nay, he cannot find out his own thoughts. Neither can he ascribe it to any angel, good or bad, for the mind of man is hidden from them. They know not man's thoughts. It remains, therefore, that as God alone is the searcher of the hearts, so that Scripture, which declares unto man what are his thoughts, is the only Word of the same God. Indeed, God used man for His instrument in the penning and delivery of the Scripture, but He Himself by His Spirit is the sole Author thereof.

Section 2

That man has no free will to [do] good by nature.

The second use shall be against the papists who ascribe to man's will a natural power to that which is truly good, as by itself to co-work with God's grace in the first act of man's conversion.[1] But the charge of evil here laid upon the frame of man's natural heart by God Himself does teach us otherwise. For look, how far the frame of the mind, which is the principal part of the soul, is corrupt for thoughts and imaginations, so far is the will, the inferior part of the soul, corrupt in willing. But the mind is naturally so corrupt that it cannot think a good thought, and therefore answerably the will, by nature, is so corrupt that it cannot will that which is truly good. If it is said that man has liberty of will in human actions and in civil duties, I answer [that] he has, but yet such actions, proceeding from a corrupt fountain, are sins in every natural man, howsoever for the matter of the works they may be called good, being such as God Himself ordained.

Section 3

Of the timely preventing and suppressing of wicked imaginations.

The third use shall be for admonition unto them to whom is committed the education of youth, as parents, masters, tutors, etc. Seeing the imaginations of man's heart are evil from his youth, therefore they must all join hand in hand betime[s] to stop up (or, at least, to lessen) this corrupt fountain. Parents must sow the seeds of grace into the minds of their young children, [so] that if it were possible, even at their mother's breasts, they might be nourished in the faith. Lois and Eunice dealt thus with their young Timothy, for Paul says, "he learned the holy Scriptures of an infant"[2] [2 Tim. 3:15]. Then, as their children grow in discretion and use of reason, they must be nurtured in religion [Eph. 6:4] and have the grounds thereof by often repetition driven into their hearts. For this is the best means to free their minds, though not altogether from natural imaginations, yet from the force and poison thereof. For "folly is bound to the heart of a child, but the rod of teaching (that is, instruction with correction) will drive it away from him" [Prov. 22:15]. Yea, when as the "child set at liberty makes his mother ashamed" [Prov. 29:15], yet will "the son that is well instructed, give his father rest, and yield delight unto his soul" [v. 27].[3]

Further, where parents leave, there masters and tutors must take hold, building up that good foundation which is laid to their hand, that by them also the stream of man's natural imaginations may be stopped. Yea, though parents

---

1 In the margin: Bellarm. de grat. & lib. arbit. libr. 16. c. 15. sect. 10.

2. In the margin: ἀπὸ Βρέφουζ.

3. This paragraph break is not in the original.

should neglect this duty toward their own children, as too many do at this day, yet each godly master, if he desires to have God's church in his house, must instruct his family, as Abraham did [Gen. 18:19], and labor for circumcision of heart both to his children and servants, even as Abraham "did circumcise not only those that were born in his family, but also those that were bought for money" [Gen. 17:23].[4]

Both parents and masters are careful to prevent diseases and to break off sickness at the beginning in their children and servants, which by continuance might bring bodily death. Oh, then, how careful ought they to be to stop betimes the course of natural imaginations in them who, without the special grace of God, will bring eternal condemnation both to soul and body? And the rather must this course be taken in youth, and that betimes, because custom (whether in good or evil) is a second nature. For "teach a child in the trade of his way, and when he is old he will not depart from it" [Prov. 22:6]. But "can the black moor change his skin, or the leopard her spots? Then may he also do good that is accustomed to do evil" [Jer. 13:23]. Herein the vices of the mind are like the diseases of the body. By longer continuance they grow more incurable. Yea, all that study and read the Scriptures, either for their own private or for the public good, must seek by prayer to God for the sanctification of their minds from this evil corruption, lest being left unto themselves they become vain in their imaginations. David, a man according to God's own heart, prayed at least ten times in one Psalm for the teaching of God in the understanding of His law [Psalm 119]. Oh, then, what great cause have we so to do, whose "minds are naturally set in evil works" [Col. 1:21], being blind in the things of God, "not able to perceive them" [1 Cor. 2:14], but on the contrary, wholly prone to invent and to embrace that which is evil.

Section 4

Of repentance for evil thoughts.

The fourth and last use shall be for practice to every child of God. For if the imaginations of man's heart are evil from his youth, then there must be repentance for secret thoughts which never come into action; yea, though we never give consent of will thereto. When Joel proclaimed a fast, and called the people to humiliation, he bids them "rend their hearts, and not their garments" [Joel 2:13]. And Peter said to Simon Magus, "Repent of thy wickedness, and pray God that if it be possible, the thought of thy heart may be forgiven thee" [Acts 8:22]. Both of these places do plainly show that true repentance is not outward, in change of speech or attire, but inward, in the change of the thoughts of the

---

4. This paragraph break is not in the original.

mind and affections of the heart. And hence it is that Paul prays for the Thessalonians "that they may be sanctified throughout, in soul, and body, and spirit" [1 Thess. 5:23], that is, in the mind where is the framing of the thoughts. Now if sanctification is required in the mind, then there must be repentance of the sins that are therein. The Lord Himself vouchsafes to teach this duty, and therefore we must make conscience to learn and practice it, if we would be truly turned to the Lord. And to move us hereunto, consider the following reasons.

First, the curse of God, even the pangs and torments of the damned, both in this life and after death, are due to the person of man for his wicked thoughts.[5] For "cursed is every one," says Moses, "that continueth not in all things that are written in the law to do them" [Deut. 27:26]. So that, he who breaks the law but once, and that in thought only, is accursed, because he has not done all things that are written therein. Now wicked thoughts are a breach of the law, for Solomon says, "Do not they err that imagine evil?" [Prov. 14:22]. And again, "The thoughts of the wicked are an abomination to the Lord" [Prov. 15:26]. Yea, the want of good thoughts is a breach of the law, for Christ says, "Thou shalt love the Lord thy God with all thy thought" [Mark 12:30]. And, therefore, wicked thoughts must needs deserve this curse. The fall of the devils was most fearful and irrecoverable, and (though it is not certain, yet) most divines agree in this, that their sin was first in thought. And therefore, wicked thoughts are deadly evils. Also, to show the wickedness of evil thoughts, God has set this brand upon them since the fall of Adam, that by them, not only man's body, but also his mind and memory, are far sooner confounded than by outward accidents. This was not so by creation, and therefore it is the heavy curse of God upon them.

Second, these wicked thoughts are the root and beginning of all evil in gesture, word, and deed.[6] There cannot be an action before there is a thought, for this is the order whereby our actions are produced.[7] First the mind thinks, then that thought delights the affection, and from that comes consent of will. After consent of will comes execution of the action. After execution comes trade and custom by often practice. And upon custom (if the work is evil) comes the curse, which is eternal death. How great a cause, therefore, have we to repent of the wicked imaginations of our hearts? The old world indeed was drowned for their actual abominations, but no doubt the Lord had great respect in that judgment to their wicked thoughts, which were the root of all. And, therefore, He mentions them as a cause of the flood (Gen. 6:5).

---

5. In the margin: Reason 1.
6. In the margin: Reason 2.
7. In the margin: Order of producing actions.

In this repentance three things are required. First, a due examination of our heart concerning these imaginations,[8] which we may take by the knowledge of those points before handled of man's natural thoughts concerning God, his neighbor, and himself. And to further us herein we must remember that all the evil thoughts before mentioned are in us naturally, so as if we are left to ourselves, when occasion is offered, we will conceive them in our minds; as that there is no God, that the Word of God is foolishness, etc. Again, we must hear God's Word preached attentively, and apply, not only our outward senses, but our minds also thereto, so that it may enter into our hearts. For the Word of God, working in the heart, will discover unto a man what are his thoughts: "This word," says the Holy Spirit, "is mighty in operation, and sharper than any two-edged sword, it entereth through even to the dividing asunder of the soul and the spirit, the joints and the marrow, and is a discerner of the thoughts and intents of the heart" [Heb. 4:12]. At the preaching of this Word the secrets of the heart of an infidel are discovered. "If all prophesy," says Paul, "and there come in an infidel, or one unlearned, he is rebuked of all men, and judged of all, and so are the secrets of his heart made manifest, whereupon he falleth down, and worshippeth God, saying plainly, God is in the prophets indeed" [1 Cor. 14:25].[9]

Second, after examination, we must pray for the pardon of our evil thoughts.[10] Peter gives a plain commandment of this duty to Simon Magus: "Pray to God that the thought of thine heart may be forgiven thee" [Acts 8:22]. And, undoubtedly, he who has not grace to pray for the pardon of his evil thoughts, has not true repentance in his heart.[11]

Third, we must seek to reform our mind of evil thoughts.[12] This is a further matter than reformation of life, and it is expressly commanded by the Holy Spirit. "Be ye renewed in the spirit of your minds" (Eph. 4:23), that is, in the most inward and secret part of your souls, even where the thoughts and imaginations are framed and conceived. This duty must be remembered, for Christian religion consists not in outward shows and behavior (though thereby we may give comfortable testimony of God's inward graces) but it stands principally in the mind and in the heart, which must therefore be reformed with the powers and faculties thereof.

---

8. In the margin: Examination of evil thoughts.
9. This paragraph break is not in the original.
10. In the margin: Prayer for pardon of them.
11. This paragraph break is not in the original.
12. In the margin: Reformation of evil thoughts.

Chapter 8

Rules for the Reformation of Our Evil Thoughts

[Our thoughts must be brought into obedience to God. For the reformation of our thoughts, sundry rules must be observed.]

Rule 1

Our thoughts must be brought into obedience to God.

First, that we bring all our thoughts into the obedience of God.[1] Every man will grant that words and actions must be in subjection. But I say further, [that] every thought in the mind must be conceived in obedience to God, and not otherwise. Solomon says, "Establish thy thoughts by counsel" (Prov. 20:18), which may admit this meaning: that a man must not conceive a thought in his mind unless he has counsel and warrant from the Word of God so to think. And Saint Paul says, "The weapons of our warfare (speaking of the preaching of the gospel) are not carnal but mighty through God to throw down holds, casting down the imaginations, and every thing that is exalted against the knowledge of God, and bringing into captivity every thought to the obedience of Christ" (2 Cor. 10:4–5). [He] gives us to understand that those who submit themselves to the ministry of the Word must be of this mind, not only to be conformable thereunto in word and action, but in every thought of their mind, even those must bow the knee to Christ. Howsoever with men we say, "thought is free," yet with God it is not so. And, indeed, he who has effectually received the grace of Christ will endeavor to yield obedience in thought as [well as] in word and action. "Whatsoever things are true," says Paul, "whatsoever things are honest, whatsoever things are just, pure, and pertain to love; whatsoever things are of good report, if there be any virtue, if there be any praise, (he says not only, 'do these things,' but) think on these things" (Phil. 4:8–9). Here the commandment is plain, that a man's thoughts must be "holy," "pure," "just," and of such things as are "praiseworthy" and "of good report," so that they may be conceived in obedience to God.

---

1. In the margin: Rule 1.

Rule 2

Of the guarding of our hearts.

The second rule for the reformation of our thoughts is given by Solomon: "Keep (or counterguard) thy heart above all watch and ward" [Prov. 4:23];[2] that is, guard and keep your heart more than anything that is watched or guarded, whether city, house, treasure, or such like. And the adjoined reason shows the necessities of the rule: "for out of it come the issues of life."

In the right guarding of the heart, three duties must be performed.[3] First, we must covenant with our outward senses, resolving fully with[in] ourselves by God's grace that none of them shall be the instruments, the beginning, or [the] occasion, of any sin in heart or life. This "covenant Job made with his eyes, not to look upon a maid," to lust after her [Job 31:1]. And David prayed "the Lord to direct and keep his eyes from beholding vanity" (Ps. 119:37). Now look how these holy men dealt with their eyes, so we must proportionately deal [with] all the outward senses of our body, binding them all, after their example, from being the means of provocation to any sin. This duty is most necessary, for the outward senses are the doors and windows of the soul, and unless good care is had thereto, the devil will enter in by them and fill the soul with all corruption.

Second, we must observe our evil thoughts and, at their first arising, stop and restrain them, not suffering them to take any place in our hearts. This is a special means to preserve and guard the heart, for from the thoughts proceed all bad desires, corrupt affections, evil words and actions. The mind must first conceive before the will can desire, or the affections be delighted, or the members of the body practice anything, so that whatsoever is of a loose life and bad behavior, it comes from the profaneness of his heart in evil thoughts. Neither can it be hoped that any man should reform his life that will not guard his heart and keep his mind from wicked imaginations. The devil cannot work his will upon man's affections or prevail over man's will but by thoughts, and therefore it is necessary that the first motions of evil in the mind are restrained at the beginning.

Third, we must, with all care, cherish and maintain every good motion of God's Spirit that is caused in us by the ministry of the Word or by the advice of God's children. For these are the sparks and flames of grace which Paul means when he says, "Quench not the Spirit" (1 Thess. 5:19).

---

2. In the margin: Rule 2.
3. In the margin: Three things in the guarding of the heart.

Rule 3

Of the elevation of the heart to God.

Third, for the reformation of our thoughts we must often use [the] elevation of mind and heart to heaven, where Christ sits at the right hand of His Father.[4] Thus David did: "Unto thee, oh Lord, do I lift up my soul" (Ps. 25:1). And Paul [did], saying of himself and other Christians, "that they had their conversation in heaven" (Phil. 3:20). [He] signifies thus much, that not only their studies and meditations but also their dealings in the world were heavenly. Saint James bids us: "Draw near to God" (James 4:8). Now which way should a poor wretch here below draw near to God but by lifting up his heart to the throne of grace in heaven, so that God in mercy may draw near unto him by grace?[5]

The Lord has instituted in His church the use of His last supper, wherein the giving and receiving of bread and wine does represent and seal up unto us our communion and participation of the body and blood of Christ given for our redemption. Now the principal action on our behalf therein required is this elevation of the heart unto God for the contemplation of God's infinite mercy in Christ and of Christ's endless love to us, as well as for the application of His merits to our own souls by the hand of faith, as also for the spiritual resignation of ourselves in souls and bodies by way of thankfulness to Him who has redeemed us.[6]

Further touching this elevation, we must remember that it ought to be our continual and ordinary action unto God. For as it is with him who keeps a clock, unless he does every day wind up the weights which are always going downward, the clock will stand, so it fares with us. Our hearts are ever drawing toward the earth and the things here below by reason of that "body of sin which hangeth on so fast, and presseth down" (Heb. 12:1). And, therefore, we must endeavor by God's grace continually to lift them up to heaven. The apostle bids us, "Pray continually" (1 Thess. 5:17), not that we should do nothing else but pray, but his meaning is that we should every day, and every part of the day as often as just occasion is offered, lift up our hearts unto God. But of all other, there are three special times wherein we must use this heavenly elevation. First, in the morning by prayer, thanksgiving, or both, before the cogitations of any earthly affairs come into our minds, so that we may give unto God the first-fruits of our thoughts every day. Second, in the evening before we lay down our bodies to rest, for who knows, when he lays himself down to sleep, whether he shall ever rise again alive? Third, at any other time of the day wherein we receive any blessing from God, temporal or spiritual, or do feel ourselves to

---

4. In the margin: Rule 3.

5. This paragraph break is not in the original.

6. This paragraph break is not in the original.

stand in need of any of His gifts or graces. For seeing every good gift comes from Him, is it not reason we should give this glory to His name, to lift up our hearts to His throne of grace, whenever we receive or expect the same from His bountiful hand?

Rule 4

Of the assurance of our particular reconciliation with God.

Fourth, for the reformation of our thoughts, we must labor to be assured in our hearts by God's Spirit of our particular reconciliation with God in Christ.[7] This is that "knowledge of the love of God which passeth knowledge," for which Paul "bowed his knees unto the Father of our Lord Jesus Christ, in the behalf of the Ephesians" (Eph. 3:14, 19). In regard hereof, Paul "esteemed all things loss, yea to be dross and dung" (Phil. 3:8). Now when this assurance is settled in our hearts, it will purify not only the will and affections but also the first motions and thoughts of our minds. "He that hath in himself this hope," says Saint John, "purifieth himself as God is pure" [1 John 3:3]. For when a man shall be truly persuaded in his heart, that of a vile sinner, even the child of wrath, he is made the child of God and a vessel of honor acceptable to God, enjoying His love and favor in Christ, then he will reason thus with himself: Has God of His endless mercy vouchsafed to receive me into His grace and favor, who otherwise should have been a firebrand of hell for evermore? Oh then, how should I suffer my mind, will, and affections, to be any longer the instruments of sin, whereby I shall displease so gracious a God, and cast myself out of His love and favor? Nay, but I will employ my soul, which He has redeemed with all the powers and faculties thereof, as weapons of righteousness for the advancement of His glory.

Rule 5

Of spiritual consideration.

Lastly, if we would reform our thoughts, we must give ourselves to spiritual consideration or meditation.[8] By spiritual consideration I mean any action of the mind, renewed and sanctified, whereby it does seriously think on those things which may further salvation. This consideration I call spiritual to distinguish it from earthly plotting care whereby natural men show themselves wise and provident for the things of this life, though in the matters of God which concern salvation they are blind and ignorant. Also, I add [that] it must be an action of a mind renewed and sanctified, because the "natural man perceiveth

---

7. In the margin: Rule 4.
8. In the margin: Rule 5.

not the things of the Spirit of God" (1 Cor. 2:14). They seem foolishness unto him and therefore he cannot give his mind unto them.

Now the excellent use of this rule will plainly appear by the fruitful practice of it in the prophet David. For what was more usual with him than spiritual and heavenly meditation? Sometimes "upon God himself" [Ps. 119:55], sometimes "on the works of God" [Ps. 119:27], sometimes "on his own ways" [Ps. 119:59], and "continually on God's word" [Ps. 119:98]. Now sanctifying this duty by prayer, as it is plain he did continually, "Let the meditation of my heart, oh Lord, be acceptable in thy sight" (Ps. 19:14), hence it came to pass that he professed "a hatred unto vain inventions" (Ps. 119:113), which are the proper effects of an unreformed mind. And, on the contrary, by this godly practice "he got more understanding than his teachers" (Ps. 119:99). Yea, he attained to this excellent state of renewed mind that "his reins (whereby he means the most secret part of his soul) taught him in the night season" (Ps. 16:7). And in reason we may perceive the truth hereof, for seeing contraries do mutually expel one another, what can be more effectual to purge the mind of evil thoughts than to exercise the same with spiritual considerations? For when through the blessing of God these shall take place, the other must needs be gone. In regard whereof, it shall not be amiss somewhat to insist in the handling of them.

Chapter 9

Spiritual Considerations Concerning God

Spiritual considerations, serving for the reformation of our thoughts, do either concern God or ourselves. That which concerns God contains many branches, but I will insist in four especially.

Section 1

Of the consideration of God's presence.

First, touching God's presence whereby a man does think and so resolve himself that, wherever he is, he stands before God, and that all his thoughts, words, and deeds are naked in God's sight. David's heart was filled with this consideration when he penned Psalm 139, for that whole psalm, from the beginning to the end, serves to express this holy cogitation of God's presence. We must labor to have the like impression in our hearts touching God's presence, for it is the most notable means to cleanse the heart from evil thoughts, to restrain the will and affections from wicked delights, and to keep in order the whole man, causing him to stand in the awe of God's commandments. David says, "The fear of the Lord is clean" (Ps. 19:9). [He] means thereby that the man, who has the fear of God in his heart arising from this consideration of God's presence, has a clean and pure heart. This consideration is also a notable means of comfort in the time of trouble and danger. Hence, David says, "Though I walk through the valley of the shadow of death, I will fear none evil: for the Lord is with me" (Ps. 23:4). And hence it was that "he would not be afraid for ten thousand of the people that should rise up against him" (Ps. 3:6).

Section 2

The consideration of God's judgments.

The second consideration touching God is of His judgments, not only those which were done of old and are recorded in the Scripture or other histories, but even His late judgments which we behold or hear to fall upon kingdoms, towns, particular houses and persons, we must carefully lay unto our hearts. The Lord complains of the want hereof among His people, saying, "The whole land lieth waste, because no man setteth his mind on it" (Jer. 12:11). [He] gives us to understand that the neglect of due consideration of God's judgment brought desolation to the whole land, and therefore the want thereof is a main and grievous sin, bringing further judgments with it.

God has [at] sundry times sent His judgments among us, generally by plague and famine, and particularly on sundry families and persons. But who regards them? Wherefore, unless we will double God's judgments upon us, let us remember our duty and seriously think upon them. And that this consideration may be profitable unto us, we must do three things. First, we must carefully observe, mark, and remember them. "I remember thy judgments of old, O Lord" (Ps. 119:52). The Lord's people were much wanting therein (Ps. 78:11, 42).[1]

Second, we must apply them to our own person in particular so as the thought thereof may make us afraid though they befall others. When Habakkuk in a vision saw the judgments of God which were to come upon the Chaldeans, the consideration thereof was so powerful with him that it "made him tremble and quake" (Hab. 3:16). In a family, when the father beats his servant, the child fears, and when one child is beaten, then all the rest cry. Even so, when God our Father pours down His judgments, though upon the heathen, yet we must fear. But when any of His children are afflicted, it must strike sore to our hearts.[2]

Third, we must make use of God's judgments that light upon others by applying them to ourselves. When certain men brought news to our Savior Christ of a heavy judgment upon some Galileans, "whose blood Pilate had mingled with their own sacrifices" (Luke 13:1–3), our Savior immediately labors to bring them, who told Him, to make use thereof for their own good, saying, that thereby they ought to be moved to repentance. For they who were slain were no greater sinners than the rest. And, therefore, "except they" who told that news "did amend their lives, they should also perish." So that, whenever we see or hear of any judgment of God upon others, we must thereby be moved to repent. And thus doing, we shall come to a right consideration of God's judgments.

Section 3

The considerations of God's Word.

The third consideration concerning God is of His Word. David makes it the property of a "blessed" man to "meditate in the law of God day and night" (Ps. 1:2). And he professes of himself that "it was his meditation continually" (Ps. 119:97). Yea, oftentimes he promises to "meditate in God's precepts" [v. 15] [and] to "delight in God's statutes" [v. 16]. This is Mary's praise, that "she kept

---

1. This paragraph break is not in the original.
2. This paragraph break is not in the original.

in her heart sundry things which Jesus spoke" [Luke 2:51]. And so, every child of God (high or low) ought daily and continually to meditate in the Word of God. But, alas, this duty is little known and less practiced. Men are so far from meditating in God's Word that they are ignorant of it. Among many families you shall scarcely find the book of God, and such as have it (for the most part) do little use it. The statutes of the land are by very many searched out diligently, but in the meantime the statutes of the Lord are little regarded. Oh, that men knew the sweet "comfort of the scriptures" (Rom. 15:4)! Then certainly they would account their meditation therein "the joy and rejoicing of their heart" (Jer. 15:16).

Now the right consideration of God's Word consists in three things. First, we must observe the true sense and meaning of that which we hear or read. Second, we must mark what experience we have had of the truth of the Word in our own persons, as in the exercises of repentance and invocation of God's name, and in all our temptations. This is a special point in this meditation, without which the former is nothing. Third, we must consider how far forth we have been answerable to God's Word in obedience, and wherein we have been defective by transgressions. Again, in the Word of God, there are both commandments and promises. The consideration of God's commandments is a notable means to direct and moderate, not only our words and deeds, but also our secret thoughts and desires. For if before we think, before we will or speak anything, we would first consider that God commands us to think, will, and speak thus and thus, this would mightily stay and suppress in us all corrupt thoughts and desires, all evil words and actions. The promises of God likewise duly considered would greatly further us in good thoughts, for "to them that think on good things, shall be mercy and truth" (Prov. 14:22). The cause, then, why many who know the will of God so much fail in particular obedience is because that with their knowledge they do not join this serious consideration of God's commandments and promises and apply the same to their occasions.

Section 4

The consideration of God's works.

The fourth consideration concerning God is of His works, for as David says, "The works of the Lord are great, and ought to be sought out of all that love him" (Ps. 111:2). This consideration binds us to enquire and search what are the works of God toward us: His work of creation, providence, preservation, with all His other works of mercy and justice in us and upon us, whether ordinary or extraordinary. The prophet Isaiah denounces "a woe" against those who had the harp, viol, timbrel,[3] pipe, and wine in their feasts, "and regarded not the work of God, nor considered the work of his hands" (Isa. 5:11–12). Whereby we may see that the neglect hereof is a grievous sin, and yet it is the common sin of this age.

Now for the better performance of this duty, we must thus proceed. First, we must consider our creation, how the Lord gave us being when we were nothing, and how He made us reasonable creatures and not brute beasts. Yea, He created us in His own image when as He might, if it had so pleased Him, have made us toads and serpents. Second, we must consider His good providence over us, how He has preserved our life from time to time and saved us from many dangers. And His great patience must not be forgotten, how He has spared us from the righteous judgments of our sins. He might have cast us into hell in our mother's womb, or so soon as we were born, for our original sin, but He has given us a large time of repentance. Here also we must consider His exceeding favor in the time and place of our birth and life. He might have suffered us to have been born among infidels, but behold we were born in the bosom of God's church. He might have deprived us of the means of our salvation, His holy Word and sacraments, but in His tender mercy He has vouchsafed them unto us to bring our souls to life. He might have "hardened our hearts against his fear, and blinded our eyes against his light" (Isa. 63:17; Rom. 11:8), but yet He has enlightened our minds to know His truth, and softened our hearts, causing us to cry unto Him for the pardon of our sin. He might have "given us up to a reprobate sense" (Rom. 1:28), when we swerved from His testimonies and regarded not the knowledge of His will, but lo, as a loving Father, He has often "chastened us for our profit, that we might be partakers of his holiness" (Heb. 12:10). He might have left us comfortless under the reproach of the wicked, but He has vouchsafed us His Spirit for our everlasting Comforter.[4]

Thus, we must duly consider all these wonderful works of God toward us, and not, like the men of this world, think on nothing but pastimes, honors, and commodities. This will be a notable means to keep our hearts from evil thoughts. For whose heart will not relent toward his God, that has tasted [in] so many ways of His bounty toward him? Yea, this consideration will be an exceeding stay and comfort to our souls in the day of trouble and distress. So, Solomon says, "Behold the work of God, and in the day of affliction consider" (Eccl. 7:14–15). A natural man cannot [do] away with trouble. If sorrows increase upon him, he is ready to make away [with] himself, which comes of this, that he cannot consider the works of God. For he who can rightly meditate

---

3. *Timbrel:* tambourine.
4. This paragraph break is not in the original.

on God's goodness toward him in all His works shall be able with patience to support his soul under the greatest cross. We may see a practice hereof in David who, being in a most grievous temptation so as he cried out, "Is the Lord's mercy clean gone? Hath he forgotten to be merciful?" (Ps. 77:8), did yet recover himself by the "consideration of God's former works of mercy, and of his wonders of old, whereof he hath experience in his own person" (vv. 11–12).

Of Spiritual Considerations Which Concern Ourselves

The considerations which respect ourselves are six.

Section 1

The consideration of our own personal sins.

First, we must consider our own personal sins: the corruptions of our hearts as well as the actual transgressions of our lives. This was David's practice: "I considered my ways and turned my feet unto thy testimonies" (Ps. 119:59). The Jews likewise, in their great affliction, stirred up themselves to this duty, saying one to another, "Come let us search, and try our ways, and turn again unto the Lord" (Lam. 3:40).

In this consideration of our sins, we must do three things First, [we must] seriously call to mind in what manner we have sinned, whether of ignorance or of knowledge, of weakness through infirmity or of willfulness through presumption. Second, we must duly weigh the greatness of our particular sins, even of the least of them, remembering this, that by every sin we commit, God's infinite majesty is displeased and His justice [is] violated. Third, we must consider the number of our sins. We shall nearest attain unto this by searching out our thoughts, wills, and affections, our words and actions, all which, being diligently observed, will make us cry out that they are in number as the hairs of our head and the sands by the seashore.[1]

Question. But what if a man has truly repented of his sins? Must he still use this consideration of them? *Answer.* Yes, verily, although he is assured of the pardon of them. So did David after Nathan told him, "your sins are forgiven," he penned Psalm 51. And when he was high in God's favor, he prayed still for the "pardon of the sins of his youth" (Ps. 25:7). For howsoever God in mercy put our sins out of His remembrance upon our true repentance, yet we must never put them out of our remembrance, so long as we live in this world, because the consideration of them, though they are pardoned, is a notable means both to

---

1. This paragraph break is not in the original.

move us to renew our repentance and also to make us watchful against sin in time to come.

Section 2

Of man's misery through his sins.

Second, we must consider the misery into which everyone is plunged by nature through Adam's fall, and his own sins. This was Job's meditation, saying, "Man that is born of a woman, hath but a short time to live, he is full of misery" (Job 14:1). And he goes on so, most notably describing the misery of man. Yea, this was Solomon's consideration in the whole book of Ecclesiastes, from the beginning to the end.

Now that this consideration may take place in our hearts, we must enter into a particular view of our natural misery,[2] the principal branches whereof are these: First, a separation from all fellowship with God, for as Isaiah says, "Our sins have separated between God and us" (Isa. 59:2). And this is the special part of man's misery. Second, society and fellowship with the damned spirits, the devil and all his angels, standing in this, that man by nature bears the image of the devil, and withal performs service unto him in the practice of lying, injustice, cruelty, and all manner of sin. Third, all manner of calamities in this life, as ignominy in good name, pains and diseases in the body, losses, and damages in friends and in all temporal blessings whatsoever. Fourth, the [dis]honor of a guilty conscience, which is in itself the beginning of hell torments. For it is our accuser unto God, our judge to give sentence against us, and the very hang-man of our souls to condemn us eternally. Fifth, the second death, which is the full apprehension of the eternal fury of God's wrath, both in body and soul, eternally. This consideration must be often used of every man to move him to repentance, and it is very effectual thereunto, for if we do but consider how a man for the pain of one tooth will be so grieved that he could wish with all his heart to be out of the world so that his pain were ended, oh then, how great shall we think the apprehension of the full wrath of God to be, seizing not upon one little member, but upon the whole man both body and soul, and that forever? No tongue can express, nay no heart can conceive, the greatness of this terror, and therefore it must be an occasion both to begin and increase true repentance in us daily.

Section 3

Of our own particular temptations.

Third, we must consider our own particular temptations wherewith we are most assaulted through the malice of Satan and our own corruption. "Be sober and

---

2. In the margin: Man's natural misery branched out.

watch," says Peter, "for your adversary the devil goeth about like a roaring lion, seeking whom he may devour" (1 Peter 5:8). This was Paul's practice toward the incestuous man, whom he had enjoined to be excommunicated, for after he heard of his repentance, he gave direction that he should be received "into the church again, lest he were swallowed up of over much heaviness, and so Satan should circumvent them…for we are not ignorant of his enterprises" (2 Cor. 2:7, 11). If foreign enemies should seek the invasion of our land, not only our magistrates, but every ordinary man well affected to his country would bethink himself what coast were the weakest, that thither present defense might be sent to keep out the enemies. Even so, seeing the devil does assault us daily, we must enter into serious consideration of our thoughts, will, and affections, and see in what part we are most weak, and in what inclination Satan may most easily prevail against us, which we shall best espy by observing the sins of our lives. And this will make us arm ourselves against him by God's grace, even in the weakest parts, that he breaks not into our hearts to the ruin of our souls.

This consideration concerns all men, not only the dissolute and sinful, but even those who have received most grace. It would be infinite to go through all the temptations of Satan. Consider this one for all, whereby he kills many a soul.[3] Through the whole course of men's lives, he labors to fill their hearts with carnal security, and so bring them to neglect the ordinary means of salvation. This done, he seeks to keep them in this estate all their life long. But in the end he takes another course, for when death approaches, then he seeks to strike their minds with oblivion of God's mercies, and to fill their souls with terrors in regard of their sins and of God's judgments due unto them, so that, bereaving them of all hope of mercy, he may bring them to final despair. We, therefore, being forewarned of his deadly fraud, must seriously bethink ourselves of this temptation, and cast with ourselves every day how to avoid it. This we shall do if we shake off carnal security and negligence in the means of our salvation, and provide betimes for the assurance of God's love and favor, that when death shall come, we may be free from the terror of an evil conscience, and have strong hope and consolation in Christ Jesus.

Section 4

Of our particular end.

Fourth, we must consider our particular end. The Lord complains of the want hereof in His own people: "Oh that they were wise, then would they consider this; they would consider their latter end" (Deut. 32:29). In this consideration three points must be observed: first, that the time of death is uncertain, no man

---

3. In the margin: An ordinary and yet most dangerous temptation.

knows when he must die; second, that the place is uncertain, no man knows where he must die; [and,] third, that the manner of his death is uncertain, no man knows by what death he shall glorify God. And, therefore, that we may not deceive ourselves, we must think that most fearful and grievous ends may befall us, in regard of the bodily pain and torment, even then when we little fear or suspect any such thing. This consideration will be a notable means to stir up our hearts either to begin or renew our repentance. When wicked Ahab heard of his fearful end, he was humbled (1 Kings 21:27). And the Ninevites, being told of their sudden destruction, repented in "sackcloth, and ashes, and turned to the Lord" (Jonah 3:5–6).

Section 5

Of our strait account at the last day.

Fifth, we must often consider with[in] ourselves, and that most seriously, of that strait account and reckoning of all our thoughts, words, and actions, which we must make unto God at the last day of judgment. This is the principal consideration of all, and the want hereof a fearful sin, arguing great negligence, ignorance, blindness of mind, and hardness of heart. If a traveler comes into an inn, having but one penny in his purse, and calls for all manner of dainty fare and provision, spending sumptuously, will not all men judge him void of all consideration, since he has nothing to pay when his account is to be made? Lo this, or worse, is most men's case, who in this life pursue their profits and pleasures with all eagerness. They care not how, never regarding that reckoning which they must make unto God at His terrible day of accounts with all the world. And, therefore, though the former considerations will not, yet let this take place in our hearts to move us to a daily forehand reckoning with God in the practice of true repentance, and to employ the good gifts and blessings we receive from God, like good servants, unto the best advantage of His glory, that when this account is to be made, we may give it with joy and not with fear. And that this consideration is effectual to this purpose, Solomon teaches, in using it as his farewell with dissolute youth, with which otherwise he has little hope to prevail, saying, "Rejoice, thou young man, take thy pleasure in thy youth; yet know, that for all this thou must come to judgment" (Eccl. 11:9). But how powerful it is with God's child, we may see in Paul, who professes of himself that in "regard of this account, he endeavored to have always a clear conscience towards God, and towards men" (Acts 24:16).

Section 6

Of our present estate toward God.

Lastly, we must seriously consider of our present estate toward God, whether we are in the state of sin or in the state of grace; whether we belong to the kingdom of darkness or are true members of the kingdom of Christ. It is not enough to be in the church, but we must be sure [that] we are of the church. For many wolves and goats are in God's fold. "They went out from us," says Saint John, "but they were not of us" (1 John 2:19). And, therefore, Paul advises to this consideration, saying, "Prove yourselves, whether you be in the faith or not" (2 Cor. 13:5). The want hereof was the fearful sin of the "foolish virgins" (Matt. 25:3), who contented themselves with a show of religion, having the blazing lamps of outward profession, and labored not for that oil of true grace which might enlighten their souls to the fruition of God's glory. Yea, this is the common sin of this age. Men bless themselves in their good meaning, saying they hope well, and do not thoroughly search whether they are true members of God's church or not. Now if after trial it appears that true faith and repentance are wanting in us, which are the seals of adoption in God's children, then with all good conscience we must use the means appointed of God to obtain these graces for our assurance. The comfort whereof will be so precious unto our souls that we shall abhor to admit such wicked imaginations into our minds as any way tend to deprive us of it.

These are the considerations which respect ourselves. If we give our minds thereunto in a constant course, as also to the former which concern the Lord, observing withal the rules before prescribed, through God's blessing upon our endeavor, we shall undoubtedly find by good experience that evil thoughts shall not prevail against us, but being reformed in our cogitation we shall send out of our minds as from a cleansed fountain such streams of good words and works through the whole course of our lives as shall redound to the glory of our God, the good of our brethren, and the consolation of our own souls, through Jesus Christ our Lord, to whom with the Father and the Holy Spirit be praise in His church for evermore. Amen.

FINIS

A Direction
for the Government of the Tongue
According to God's Word

Printed by John Legate,
Printer to the University of Cambridge
1600

To the Reader

Christian Reader, lamentable and fearful is the abuse of the tongue among all sorts and degrees of men everywhere. Hence, daily arise manifold sins against God and innumerable scandals and grievances to our brethren. It would make a man's heart to bleed to hear and consider how swearing, blaspheming, cursed speaking, railing, backbiting, slandering, chiding, quarrelling, contending, jesting, mocking, flattering, lying, dissembling, [and] vain and idle talking overflow in all places, so as men who fear God had better be anywhere than in the company of most men. Well then, are you a man who has made little conscience of your speech and talk? Repent seriously of this sin and amend your life, lest for the abusing of your tongue you cry with Dives in hell: "Send Lazarus that he may dip the tip of his finger in water and cool my tongue" [Luke 16:24]. And if you are one who has had care to order yourself in speech and silence according to God's Word, oh, do it more! For what a shame is it that men with the same tongue wherewith they confess the faith and religion of Christ should by vain and ungodly speech utterly deny the power thereof? And for your better help therein, I have penned the following few lines concerning the government of the tongue. Use them for your benefit, and, finding profit thereby, give glory to God.

December 12, 1592
William Perkins

Chapter 1

The General Means of Ruling the Tongue

The government of the tongue is a virtue pertaining to the holy usage of the tongue according to God's Word. And for the well ordering of it two things are requisite: (1) a pure heart, and (2) skill in the language of Canaan.

Point 1
The pure heart is most necessary because it is the fountain of speech, and if the fountain is defiled, the streams that issue thence cannot be clean [Matt. 15:19]. And because the heart of man by nature is a bottomless gulf of iniquity, two things are to be known: first, how it must be made pure; and, [second,] how it is always afterward to be kept pure.

The way to get a pure heart is this: First, you must seriously examine your life and your conscience for all your past sins. Second, with a heavy and bleeding heart [you must] confess them to God, utterly condemning yourself. Third, with deep sighs and groans of spirit [you must] cry unto heaven to God the Father in the name of Christ for pardon. I say, for pardon of the same sins, as it were for life and death, and that, day and night, till the Lord sends down from heaven a sweet certificate into your perplexed conscience by His Holy Spirit, that all your sins are done away. Now at the same instant in which pardon shall be granted, God likewise will once again stretch forth that mighty hand of His, whereby He made you when you were not, to make you a new creature, to create a new heart in you, to renew a right spirit in you, and to establish you by His free Spirit. For whom He justifies, them also at the same time He sanctifies.

The purified heart appears by these signs: First, if you feel yourself to be displeased at your own infirmities and corruptions, and to droop under them as men do under bodily sickness. Second, if you begin to hate and to fly [from] your own personal sins. Third, if you feel a grief and sorrow after you have offended God. Fourth, if you heartily desire to abstain from all manner of sin. Fifth, if you are careful to avoid all occasions and enticements to evil. Sixth, if you travail and do your endeavor in every good thing. Seventh, if you desire and pray to God to wash and rinse your heart in the blood of Jesus Christ.

When the heart is pure, to keep it so is the special work of faith, "which purifieth the heart" [Acts 15:9]. Faith purifies the heart by a particular applying of Christ crucified with all His merits. "Elisha, when he went up and lay upon the dead child, and put his mouth on his mouth, and his eyes upon his eyes, and his hands upon his hands, and stretched himself upon him, the flesh of the child waxed warm" [2 Kings 4:34]. "Afterward Elisha arose and spread himself upon him the second time: then the child sneezed seven times and opened his eyes" [v. 35]. So must a man by faith even spread himself upon the cross of Christ, applying hands and feet to His pierced hands and feet, and his wretched heart to Christ's bleeding heart, and then he shall feel himself warmed by the hcat of God's Spirit, and sin from day to day crucified with Christ, and his dead heart quickened and revived. And this applying, which faith makes, is done by a kind of reasoning which faith makes thus: Has God of His tender mercy given His own Son to be my Savior, to shed His blood for me? And has He of His mercy granted unto me the pardon of all my sins? I will, therefore, endeavor to keep my heart and my life unblameable, so that I do not offend Him hereafter in word or deed, as I have done heretofore.

Point 2

The language of Canaan is whereby a man, endued with the Spirit of adoption, unfeignedly calls upon the name of God in Christ, and so consequently does (as it were) familiarly talk and speak with God [Isa. 19:18; Rom. 1:5–6]. This language must needs be learned, so that the tongue may be well governed. For man must first be able to talk with God before he can be able to talk wisely with man. For this cause, when men are to have communication with one another, they are first of all to be careful that they often make their prayers to God that He would guide and bless them in their speeches, as David did: "Set a watch, O Lord, before my mouth, and keep the door of my lips" (Ps. 141:3). And again, "O Lord, open thou my lips, and my mouth shall show forth thy praise" (Ps. 51:15). Here we may see that the mouth is (as it were) locked up from speaking any good thing until the Lord opens it. And Paul, having the gift of ordering his tongue in wonderful measure, yet desires the Ephesians "to pray for him, that utterance might be given him" [Eph. 6:19]. And [for] good reason: "because God ruleth the tongue" [Prov. 16:1].

Chapter 2

The Matter of Our Speech

The government of the tongue contains two parts: holy speech and holy silence. In holy speech we must consider its matter and manner.

The matter is commonly one of these three: God, our neighbor, or ourselves.

Concerning God, this caveat must be remembered: that the honorable titles of His glorious majesty never be taken into our mouths unless it is upon a weighty and just occasion, so as we may plainly see that glory will redound to Him thereby. And for this cause the third commandment was given, that men might not "take up the name of God in vain" (Exod. 20:7), that is, rashly and lightly.

And, therefore, lamentable and fearful is the practice everywhere. For it is a common thing with men to begin their speech, and to place the titles of God's most high majesty in the forefront of almost every sentence, by saying, "O Lord! O God! O good God! O merciful God! O Jesus! O Christ!" If a man is to say anything, he will not say, "Yea" or "Nay," but, "O Lord, yea" or "O Lord, nay." If a man is to reprove his inferior, he will presently say, "O Lord, have mercy on us, what a slow back are you, what a lie is this, etc." An earthly prince, if he should have his name so tossed in our mouths at every word, would never bear it. And how shall the ever-living God suffer it? Nay, how can He suffer it? I say no more, but you with yourself think how. For in the third commandment the punishment is set down: "He will not hold him guiltless that taketh his name in vain." And the angels in reverence to God's majesty cover their faces (Isa. 6:2).

Concerning our neighbor, we are to consider whether the thing which we are about to speak is good or evil.

This being weighed, if it is good and so commendable, then we are readily and cheerfully, and that upon every occasion, to utter it, especially in his absence, whether he is a friend or a foe. As Saint John writes of Demetrius: "Demetrius hath good report of all men, and of the truth itself: yea, and we ourselves bear record, and ye know that our testimony is true" [3 John 12].

As for the evil which any man shall know [of] his neighbor, he is in no wise to speak of it, whether it is an infirmity or a gross sin, unless in his conscience he shall find himself called of God to speak.

A man is called to speak in three cases. First, when he is called before a magistrate, and is lawfully required to testify the evil which he knows [of] another. Second, when any is to admonish his brother of any fault for his amendment. Third, when the hurt or danger that may arise of the evil is to be prevented in others. As a man may say to one well disposed: "Take heed of such a man's company, for he is given to such or such a vice."

To this end, they of the "house of Chloe" do certify Paul of the disorders in Corinth [1 Cor. 1:11]. And Joseph "certified his father of his brethren's slanders" [Gen. 37:2]. In this case all treasons are to be revealed as tending to the ruin of the whole commonwealth. Thus, Elisha reveals the secret of the king of Syria [2 Kings 6:8].

And if it shall be thought convenient to mention the evil which we know by any man, it must be done only in [a] general manner: the person, and all circumstances which will descry the person, concealed.

Concerning things which are secret in our neighbor, we are not to be suspicious, but to suspend both speech and judgment. "Love suspecteth no evil" [1 Cor. 13:5]. "Judge nothing (says Paul) before the time, until the Lord come, who will lighten things that are hid in darkness, and make the counsels of the heart manifest" [1 Cor. 4:5]. Augustine has a good and special rule to this purpose, that there are three things of which we must give no judgment: God's predestination, the Scriptures, and the estate of men uncalled.[1]

As touching a man's self, he is neither to praise nor dispraise himself. As Solomon says, "Let another praise thee, and not thine own mouth: a stranger, and not thine own lips" [Prov. 27:2]. Yet, other whiles[2] the times do fall out that a man may use a holy kind of boasting, especially when the disgrace of the person is the disgrace also of the gospel, religion, and God Himself, as Paul did: "But wherein any will use boldness (I speak foolishly) I will use boldness. They are Hebrews, so am I" (2 Cor. 11:21–22).

---

1. In the margin: Aug. lib. 10. confess. 13.
2. *Other whiles:* occasionally.

Chapter 3

The Manner of Our Speech:
Before We Speak

Thus much of the matter of our speech; now follows the manner. In the manner of our speaking three things are to be pondered: what must be done (1) before we speak, (2) in speaking, and (3) after we have spoken.

Before we speak, consideration must be used of the thing to be spoken, and of the end. James requires that men "should be slow to speak, and swift to hear" [James 1:19]. Solomon says, "He that answereth a matter before he hear it, it is folly and shame to him" [Prov. 18:13]. The mind is the guide of the tongue; therefore, men must consider before they speak. The tongue is the messenger of the heart and therefore, as oft as we speak without meditation going before, so oft the messenger runs without his errand. The tongue is placed in the middle of the mouth, and it is compassed in with lips and teeth as with a double trench, to show us how we are to use heed and pre-consideration before we speak.[1] And, therefore, it is good advice to keep the key of the mouth not in the mouth, but in the cupboard of the mouth. Augustine says well that as in eating and drinking men make choice of meats, so in manifold speeches we should make choice of talk.[2]

Here are condemned idle words, that is, such words as are spoken to little or no purpose. And they are not to be esteemed as little sins, when as men "are to give account of every idle word" (Matt. 12:36).

---

1. In the margin: Chry. hom. 22. ad pop. Antioch.
2. In the margin: Lib. de nat. & grat.

Chapter 4

The Manner of Our Speech:
While We Speak

When we are in speaking, two things are to be practiced: care must be had of the speech that (1) it is gracious, [and] (2) it is uttered with convenient bonds of truth.

The speech is gracious when it is so uttered that the graces of God [Col. 4:6], wrought in the heart by the Holy Spirit, are (as it were) pictured and painted forth in the same, for speech is the very image of the heart.

Contrary to this is "rotten speech" [Eph. 4:29],[1] that is, all such talk as is void of grace, which is the heart and pith[2] of our speech.

And by this it appears that no vice can be named but with disliking [Eph. 5:3; Ps. 16:4]. And hereupon, when by occasion a vice should be named in Scripture, in token of a loathing thereof, the name of the vice is omitted, and the name of the contrary virtue used in the room thereof, as in these words: "For Job thought, It may be that my sons have sinned and blessed (that is, blasphemed) God" [Job 1:5]. This being true, then by proportion the visible representation of the vices of men in the world, which is the substance and matter whereof plays and interludes are made, is much more to be avoided [1 Kings 21:10, 13].[3]

God's graces, which we are to show forth in our communication, are these: wisdom, truth, reverence, modesty, meekness, sobriety in judgment, urbanity, fidelity, care of others' good name. And let us consider of them in order.

Wisdom

Wisdom in our speech is a goodly ornament. The apostles, when they waited for the Holy Spirit in Jerusalem, it descended upon them in the form of fiery tongues. And then it is said that "they spoke as the Holy Ghost gave them utterance in *apophthegms* (or wise sentences)" [Acts 2:4].[4] And he who governs his

---

1. In the margin: σαπρὸσ.
2. *Pith:* core or essence.
3. The relevance of this Scripture reference is unclear.
4. In the margin: ἀποφθέγγεσθαι.

tongue wisely "addeth doctrine to the lips" [Prov. 6:23], that is, [he] so speaks as that others are made wise thereby.

This wisdom is then shown when a man can in judgment apply his talk, and (as it were) in good manner make it fit to all the circumstances of persons, times, places, things. "A fool poureth out all his mind, but a wise man keepeth in till afterward."⁵ "A word spoken in his place, is like apples of gold with pictures of silver" [Prov. 25:11].

Now he who would have his speech to be wise must first of all become a wise man. And the wise man, of whom the holy Scriptures speak, is a godly man, and such a one as fears God, because this fear of God is the "beginning and head of wisdom" [Prov. 1:7; Eccl. 12:13]. As on the contrary, the fool, whereof the Scripture often speaks, is the ungodly person who makes no conscience of any sin (Pss. 14:1; 38:5; Gen. 34:7). And, indeed, such a one is the most senseless fool of all. He who shall ever and anon be casting himself into the fire and water, and run upon dangerous places to break his legs, arms, neck, and further shall take pleasure in doing all this, is either a fool or a mad man. Now the ungodly man as often as he sins, he endeavors as much as in him lies to pitch his soul into hell, and whereas he takes pleasure in sin, he sports himself with his own destruction.

Furthermore, the man fearing God must have two things in his heart: a persuasion of God's presence, and awe.

The persuasion of God's presence is [that] whereby a man is continually resolved that, wheresoever he is, he stands before God who does see even into the secrets of his heart. This was in Cornelius. "Now therefore," says he, "we are in God's presence to hear all things that are commanded thee of God" (Acts 10:33).

Awe in regard of God is that whereby a man behaves himself reverently because he is in God's presence. Awe [is] either in regard of sin or in regard of chastisements.

Awe in respect of sin is when one is afraid to sin, fearing not so much the punishment as sin itself because it is sin. For he fears God indeed who is of this mind, that if there were no judge to condemn him, no hell to torment him, no devil nor conscience to accuse him, yet he would not sin because God's blessed majesty is by it offended and displeased. And if he had it in his choice whether he would sin or lose his life, he had rather die than willingly and wittingly sin against God. This awe, being in Joseph, was the cause that moved him not to commit folly with Potiphar's wife. "How then," says he, "can I do this great wickedness, and sin against God?" (Gen. 39:9).

---

5. Prov. 29:11.

Awe in chastisements is when one humbles himself under the mighty hand of God with all meekness and patience, when God lays His hand on him more or less. When Shimei came forth and cursed David, and flung stones at him, what did he? Truly he stood in awe of God, and therefore said, "What have I to do with you, ye sons of Zeruiah? For he curseth, even because the Lord hath bidden him curse David, who dare then say, Wherefore hast thou done so?" (2 Sam. 16:10).

When a man is thus made wise (that is, righteous and fearing God), he is so guided by the spirit of fear that he cannot but speak wisely. Solomon says, "The lips of the righteous know what is acceptable: but the mouth of the wicked speaketh froward things" (Prov. 10:32). And again, "The heart of the wise guideth the mouth wisely."[6]

Contrary to this is fond and foolish talk. An example hereof we have in Luke 23:14–16, where Pilate, wanting the fear of God, says, "I find no fault in Christ: let us therefore chastise him, and send him away." Whereas he ought to have reasoned thus: "I find no fault in Him; therefore, let us send Him away without chastisement."

---

6. Prov. 16:23.

Chapter 5

Truth and Reverence

Truth

Truth of speech is a virtue whereby a man speaks as he thinks, and so, consequently, he speaks as everything is, so far forth as he possibly can. It is made a note of a righteous man, "to speak the truth from the heart" [Ps. 15:2]. "And they that deal truly are God's delight" [Prov. 12:22].

This is always required in all our doctrines, accusations, defenses, testimonies, promises, bargains, counsels, but especially in judges and magistrates sitting on [the] judgment seat [Prov. 17:7], because then they stand in God's stead, who is truth itself.

To this place belongs *apology*, which is when a Christian called before a magistrate, and straightly examined of his religion, confesses Christ boldly and denies not the truth [Matt. 10:32].

Contrary to this is lying, cogging,[1] glossing, smoothing, [and] dissembling. As, for example, Gehazi, after he had received money and garments from Naaman, the Syrian, against Elisha's will, he went and stood before his master, who said unto him, "Whence comest thou, Gehazi?" [2 Kings 5:25]. He made it nothing to lie for [his] advantage, smoothed it over finely, and said, "Thy servant went no whither." To the like effect and purpose, report is made of a rich man who had two chests: the one whereof he calls "all the world" [and] the other he calls his "friend." In the first he puts nothing. In the second he puts all his substance. When his neighbor comes to borrow money, he answers, "Truly I have never a penny in all the world (meaning his empty chest), but I will see what my friend can do." [He] looks thereby for interest by the money of his other chest.

This vice is very common, and it is a rare thing to find a man who makes a conscience of a lie.

Lying is when a man speaks otherwise than the truth is, with a purpose to deceive. Here note that there is great difference between these two speeches: "It is an untruth," and "It is a lie." The first may be used when a man speaks

---

1. *Cog*: deceive or defraud.

falsehoods. But, in using the second, we must be heedy[2] and sparing. For when a man is challenged for a lie, three things are laid to his charge: (1) that he speaks falsely; (2) that he is willing to do so; and (3) that he has a desire and purpose to deceive.

Question. Whether a man may not lie if it is for the procuring of some great good to our neighbor or to the whole country where we are?

Answer. No. [The] reasons are these: First, lying is forbidden "as an abomination to the Lord" [Prov. 12:22]. Second, "We are not to do any evil that good might come thereof" [Rom. 3:8]. Third, he who lies, in so doing, conforms himself to the devil who is a liar and the father thereof [John 8:44].

Objection 1. Such lying is for our neighbor's good and not against charity. *Answer*. No, for "charity rejoiceth in the truth" [1 Cor. 13:6].

Objection 2. The holy Scriptures have mentioned the lies of the patriarchs. *Answer*. We must not live by examples against [the] rules of God's Word.

Objection 3. Rahab, in preserving the spies, and the midwives of Egypt, in preserving the Israelites' infants, used lying. And [they] are commended for their acts. *Answer*. They are commended for their faith, not for their lying. The works which they did, were excellent works of mercy, and therefore to be allowed. And the doers failed only in the manner of performing them.

Reverence

As truth is required in speech, so also reverence to God and man.

To God

Reverence to God is when we do speak of God and use His titles, that we show reverence ourselves and move reverence in others. "If thou wilt not keep," says the Lord, "and do all the words of this law (that are written in this book), and fear the glorious and fearful name, THE LORD THY GOD, then the Lord will make thy plagues wonderful" (Deut. 28:58).

Here take heed of all manner of blaspheming, which is when men use such speeches of God as do either detract anything from His majesty or ascribe anything to Him not beseeming Him. [This is] a sin of all others to be detested. *Reasons*. First, a blasphemer is worse than the rest of the creatures, for they praise God in their kind and show forth His power, goodness, and wisdom, but he dishonors God in his wretched speech. Second, he is the mad dog that

---

2. *Heedy*: careful.

flies in his master's face, who keeps him and gives him bread. Third, custom in blasphemies shows a man to be a child of the devil, and no child of God as yet.[3]

A father, lying on his death bed, called the three children to him, whom he kept, and told them that only one of them was his own son, and that the rest were only brought up by him. Therefore, he gave unto him all his goods. But which of these was his natural son he would in no wise declare. When he was dead, every one of the three children pleaded that he was the son and, therefore, that the goods were his. The matter, being brought before a judge, could not be ended. But the judge was constrained to take this course: he caused the dead corpse of the father to be set up against a tree, and commanded the three sons to take bows and arrows, and to shoot against their father, and to see who could come nearest the heart. The first and second did shoot at their father and hit him, [but] the third was angry with the others, through natural affection of a child to a father, and refused to shoot. This done, the judge gave sentence that the first two were not sons, but only the third, and that he should have the goods. The like trial may be used to know who are God's children. Such persons with whom blaspheming is rife are very devils incarnate, and the children of the devil, who do rend God in pieces, and shoot Him through with their darts, as it is said of the Egyptian when he blasphemed, that he "smote or pierced through God's name" [Lev. 24:10].[4] Magistrates and rulers severely punish such as shall abuse their names, and they do it justly. How much more then should blasphemers of God's name escape without great punishment?

Again, here we must be warned to take heed of that customable swearing and also of perjury. It is a very strange sin, for the perjured person does not only sin himself, but withal he endeavors to entangle God in the same sin with himself.

Further, take heed lest you do either make or recite the jests which are contrived out of the phrases of Scripture, which are very many and usually rehearsed in company. The oil, wherewith the tabernacle and the ark of the testament and the priests were anointed, was holy [Exod. 30:31–32]; and, therefore, no man might put it to any other use, as to anoint his own flesh therewith, or to make the like unto it. Pilate, a poor paynim,[5] when he heard the name of the Son of God, [he] "was afraid" [John 19:8]. And we ought to tremble much more at the Word of God, not to make ourselves merry with it. And, therefore, the scoffing of Julian the apostate is very fearful, who was wont to reach Christians [with] boxes on the ear, and withal bid them turn the other, and obey their Master's commandment: "Whosoever shall smite thee on the right cheek, turn

---

3. This paragraph break is not in the original.
4. In the margin: ααιικκοβη.
5. *Paynim:* pagan or heathen.

to him the other also" (Matt. 5:39). And he denied pay and like reward to his soldiers who were Christians, because he said he would make them fit for the kingdom of heaven, considering that Christ had said, "Blessed are the poor in spirit: for theirs is the kingdom of heaven" (Matt. 5:3).

Here also men must learn to take heed of all manner of charms and enchantments, which commonly are nothing else but words of Scripture (or such like), used for the curing of pains and diseases both in men and beasts. As, for example, the first words of Saint John's Gospel, "In the beginning was the word, and the word was with God," are written in a paper and hung about men's necks to cure agues. But the truth is [that] such kind of practices are devilish. Patrons of charms hold that in such words, as are either divine or barbarous, is much efficacy. But whence is this efficacy? From God? From men? Or from the devil? If it shall be said from God, we must know that the Word used in [a] holy manner is the instrument of God to convey unto us spiritual blessings, as faith, regeneration, [and] repentance. But it does not serve to bring unto us corporal health.[6]

Well, then, belike[7] words take virtue from the speaker, and are made powerful by the strength of his imagination. Indeed, some physicians are of this opinion, [such] as Avicenna[8] and Paracelsus,[9] who think that fantasies are like the sun, which works on all things to which its beams do come, and the latter that by imagination miracles may be wrought.[10] But this opinion is fond, and the reasons alleged for it are without weight. For imaginations are not things, but shadows of things. And as an image of a man in a glass has no power in it, but only serves to resemble and represent the body of a man, so it is with the fantasy and conceit of the mind, and not otherwise. And if imagination has any force, it is only within the spirits and humors of a man's own body. But it cannot give force to work in the bodies of others, no more than the shadow of one body can ordinarily cure the body of another on which it lights. Wherefore, words used in the way of bodily cure, be they in themselves ever so good, are no better than the devil's sacraments. And when they are used by blind people, it is he who, coming under hand, works the cure, and by turning himself into an angel of light, deludes them. But it would be better for a man to die a thousand times than to use such remedies, which, in curing the body, destroy the soul.

---

6. This paragraph break is not in the original.

7. *Belike:* perhaps.

8. Avicenna (c. 980–1037) was a Persian physician, astronomer, philosopher, and author. He belonged to the Islamic Golden Age. Some consider him to be the father of early modern medicine.

9. Paracelsus (c. 1493–1541) was a Swiss physician, alchemist, and astrologer.

10. In the margin: Parac. lib. de Tartaro.

Lastly, avoid all imprecations and cursing, either against men or other creatures. For God, in judgment to punish such cursed speaking, often brings to pass such imprecations, as may appear in the Jews who, at the arraignment of Christ, cried, saying, "His blood be upon us and upon our children" (Matt. 27:25). This imprecation is verified upon them till this day. At Newburg in Germany, a certain mother cursed her son, saying, "Get you away! I would you might never come again alive."[11] The very same day he went into the water and was drowned. Again, a mother brought her child to the University of Wittenberg because he was possessed with an unclean spirit. Being demanded how it came to pass, she answered in the hearing of many, that in her anger she said, "The devil take you," and thereupon presently the child was possessed.[12] And in our country men often wish the plague, the pox, the pestilence to their children, their servants, [or] their cattle. And often it falls out accordingly.

In the days of King Edward, certain English soldiers (as I am certainly informed by a witness then present), being by a tempest cast upon the sands on the coast of France, gave themselves to prayer, and commended their souls to God, as in so great a danger it was meet. But one among the rest, desperately minded, went apart and cried out, saying, "O gallows claim your right, gallows claim your right." Now the said party among the rest (as God would have it) escaped safe to land, and afterwards, living some space of time in France, returned again to England, where he was hanged for stealing horses. And thus, according to his desire, the gallows claimed its right.

To Man

Reverence to man is in two respects: because he is created after the image of God; or, because he is above us in age, gifts, [or] authority.

In the first consideration, men must have care to give such names to children as are proper and fit, usual and known, the signification whereof may admonish them of the promises of God, of godliness, or of some good duty. And there are four allowed ends of giving names: (1) To preserve the memory of something by the name given, as Adam, Israel, [and] Isaac. (2) To signify something to come, as Evah,[13] Abraham, John, [and] Peter. (3) To preserve the name and memory of parents and kindred, which was used in the birth of John [the] Baptist. This custom may still be retained, if there is any good example in the ancestors that the child may follow. (4) That the life and profession of good men may be revived in the renewing of their names.

---

11. In the margin: Lonicerus theat. hist. precept. 4.
12. In the margin: Idem.
13. *Evah*: Eve.

Here we must take heed in no wise to give to children the proper names or titles of God, as Jesus, Immanuel, etc.

Neither are the professors of the gospel to be entitled by the names of such as have been famous instruments in the church, as to be called Calvinists, Lutherans, etc. "Now this I say, that every one of you saith, I am Paul's, I am Apollos's, I am Cephas's, and I am Christ's. Is Christ divided? or was Paul crucified for you? either were ye baptized in the name of Paul?" [1 Cor. 1:12–13].

And it is a bold part of the pestilent generation of papists who take to themselves the name of Jesuits, whereas the like name of "Christian" was given to the disciples at Antioch, not by the devise of man, "but by divine oracle" [Acts 11:26; Rom. 1:4].[14]

As the changing of the name given in baptism is not to be allowed, so the varying of it according to the variety of languages (if neither hurt nor fraud to any is intended thereby) is not unlawful. Upon this ground Saul is called Paul, and Christ calls Simon, His disciple, Cephas at times [and] Peter at other times. And very worthy divines in this age, that their writings might be read by the adversaries, have in like sort without offence varied their names. Melanchthon calls himself *Dydimus Faventinus* and *Melangæus*; Bucer entitles himself *Aretinus Felinus*; and Theodore Beza once called himself *Nathaniel Nezechius*.

Reverence to man as he is superior is in using fit titles of reverence. Sarah is commended in Scriptures for obeying her husband and "for calling him sir" [1 Peter 3:6]. But excess must here be avoided when titles of honor proper to God are given to men, as "head of the Catholic Church" to the pope, [and] "Lady and Queen of heaven" to the mother of Christ. Christ reproved this fault in the young man, saying, "Why callest thou me good, there is none good but God" [Matt. 19:17].

---

14. In the margin: χρηματίσαι.

Chapter 6

Modesty and Meekness

Modesty

Modesty in speech has divers caveats. First, if a man speaks anything of himself, that is, in his own commendation, let him alter the person and speak of himself as of another. "I know a man," says Paul, speaking of himself, "in Christ above fourteen years ago…which was taken up into paradise, and heard words which cannot be spoken" [2 Cor. 12:2]. And John says of himself, "When Jesus saw his mother and the disciple whom he loved, standing by…" [John 19:26]. Take heed of boasting whereby men imitate the devil who said, "All this power will I give thee, and the glory of those kingdoms: for that is delivered unto me, and to whomsoever I will give it" [Luke 4:6].

Again, when a man shall have occasion to speak of his own faults and corruptions, let him speak the uttermost against himself, as Paul called himself "the first of all sinners" [1 Tim. 1:13, 15]. But if he is to mention anything of himself that may minister matter of commendation, let his speech incline to the defect rather than to the excess, as Paul says, "I am least of the apostles, which am not meet to be called an apostle, because I persecuted the church of God" [1 Cor. 15:9].

Second, in the mentioning of things which move blushing, we are to use as seemly words as may be chosen. "Afterward Adam knew Eve his wife, which conceived and bare Cain" (Gen. 4:1). "And when he came to the sheep coats by the way where there was a cave, Saul went in to cover his feet," that is, to do his easement (1 Sam. 24:3).

Meekness

Meekness is also required in communication, which is when a man uses courteous and fair speech. "Put them in remembrance…that they be courteous, showing all meekness to all men, for we ourselves also were in times past unwise, disobedient" (Titus. 3:1–3).

Meekness and gentleness show themselves in salutations, answers, and reproofs.

Salutations

For the first, daily experience shows that it makes much for the maintaining of love to call men by their proper names or surnames. And this was a sign of special favor that God called Moses by his proper name. Yet more convenient it is to salute our betters by names of honor or office. Thus, the disciples call our Savior Christ "Rabbi." And it was the usual manner among the Jews to call their betters *adon* (that is, lord or sir).

The forms of salutations are to be after the order practiced in Scripture. An angel saluted Gideon thus: "The Lord be with thee thou valiant man" [Judg. 6:12]. And Boaz came to Bethlehem, and said to the reapers, "The Lord be with you" [Ruth 2:4]. And they answered, "The Lord bless thee." And the angel saluted Mary, "Hail, freely beloved, the Lord is with thee" [Luke 1:28]. Christ, coming among His disciples, said, "Peace be among you."[1] And He taught them, coming to any house, to say, "Peace be to this house" [Matt. 10:11–13]. By this it appears that our common forms of salutations are commendable. These are of divers sorts: as when one meets another, "God save you"; when one goes away, "God be with you"; in the morning, "God give you a good morning"; in the afternoon, "God give you a good evening"; when one is going on his journey, "God speed your journey"; when one is working, "God speed you"; in eating, "much good do it you"; when one has a new office, "God give you joy of your office"; when one is sick, "God comfort you"; etc.

And it is a seemly thing when children salute their fathers and mothers after this manner: "I pray you, father, bless me; I pray you, mother, bless me." For God has made parents to be the instruments of blessing to their children, in nurturing them and praying for them, as the fifth commandment says, "Honor thy father and thy mother, that they may prolong thy days." Now they prolong the children's days by praying to God for blessings on them, and by such like duties.

It is a use in all places to salute a man when he sneezes by saying, "Christ help you." But there is no cause why the words should then be used more than at another time. The reasons are [these]: (1) It is an old custom fetched from the Gentiles before Christ, and [it] has no ground at all, for with the like words they used to wish men health because they thought sneezing to be a sacred and holy thing, and because some take it to be a sign of unhappy and evil success, which indeed is otherwise.[2] (2) If there is any danger in the brain before sneezing, when a man has sneezed the danger is past, as learned physicians teach. Therefore, there is no cause to use such words then, more than at coughing.

---

1. John 20:19.

2. In the margin: Arist. De hist. animal. l. 1. c. 10 & Probl. sect. 33. Plin. l. 28. c. 2.

Against the practice of saluting each other, some things may be objected: (1) "If there come any unto you, and bring not this doctrine, receive him not to house, neither bid him God speed" (2 John 2:10). *Answer.* This place does not forbid common civility and courtesy of man to man, but only familiarity and acquaintance with heretics, yea, such acquaintance and familiarity as many seem to give approbation and applause to their bad proceedings. (2) Elisha, sending Gehazi his servant to lay his staff on the dead child of the Shunamite, bade him if he met any not to salute them, and if they spoke to him not to answer them (2 Kings 4:29). And when our Savior Christ sent His disciples to preach in Judea, He bade them "to salute no man by the way" (Luke 10:4). *Answer.* The intent of these two places is not to forbid men to salute others, but rather to enjoin Gehazi and the disciples of Christ only to omit for that time the practice of the duties of common courtesy, so far forth as they might hinder or delay the performance of weightier affairs.

Answers
Our answers must be soft, so that anger is neither kindled nor increased. "A soft answer putteth away wrath, but grievous words stir up anger" [Prov. 15:1]. By churlish language Nabal provoked David to wrath, but Abigail by the contrary appeased him [1 Sam. 25:10, 24]. Gideon "spoke gently to the men of Ephraim" [Judg. 8:3], when they were angry against him, and appeased them. For the text says, "When he had thus spoken, then their spirits abated towards him." Therefore, Solomon says well, "A joy cometh to a man by the answer of his mouth, but how good is a word in due season" [Prov. 15:23].

Now if any shall rail on us, our duty is not to rail again. "Bless them that persecute you, Bless, I say, and curse not" [Rom. 12:14]. "Be courteous, not rendering evil for evil, neither rebuke for rebuke, but contrariwise bless, knowing that ye be thereunto called, that you should be heirs of blessing" (1 Peter 3:9). This thing was notably practiced by David: "For my friendship they were mine adversaries, but I gave myself to prayer" (Ps. 109:4). And, therefore, in this case either silence is to be used or at the most only a just and manifest defense of our innocency to be made. Hezekiah commanded the people to be silent, and not to say anything to the speech of Rabshakeh, now flattering, now threatening [2 Kings 18:36]. When Eli spoke hardly[3] of Hannah, and bade her put away her drunkenness, she answered, "Nay, my lord; I am a woman troubled in spirit, I have neither drunk wine nor strong drink, but have poured out my soul before the Lord" [1 Sam. 1:15]. Thus, Joseph clears himself, saying, "I have done nothing wherefore they should put me in the dungeon" [Gen. 40:15]. And Daniel to

---

3. *Hardly*: harshly.

Nebuchadnezzar:[4] "Unto thee, O king, have I done no hurt" [Dan. 6:22]. And when the Jews said unto our Savior, "Say we not true, that thou art a Samaritan and hast a devil?" He answered, "I have not a devil, but I honor my Father, and ye have dishonored me" (John 8:48–49). And Paul, making an apology for himself, begins thus: "Men and brethren, I have in all good conscience served God till this day" [Acts 23:1].

Now when a man has thus cleared himself, though his own word in his own behalf takes no effect, yet let him patiently commit his cause to God who in time will manifest the truth and bring it to light, as David did: "Judge me, O God," says he, "for I have walked in mine innocency" [Ps. 26:1]. And again, "The wicked watcheth the righteous, and seeketh to slay him: but the Lord will not leave him in his hand, nor condemn him when he is judged" [Ps. 37:32–33].

Reproofs

Meekness in reproof is when any shall admonish his brother of any fault for his amendment, with the like moderation that surgeons use, who being to set the arm or leg that is forth of joint, handle it so tenderly that the patient shall scant feel when the bone falls in again. Paul gives this counsel: "Brethren, if any man be fallen by occasion into any fault, ye which are spiritual, restore such a one (or set him in joint again) with the spirit of meekness" [Gal. 6:1]. This was practiced by Abraham toward Lot, when their herdsmen were at variance, saying, "Let there be, I pray thee, no strife between thee and me, neither between my herdsmen and thine: for we are brethren" [Gen. 13:8–9].

And this is done [in] four ways. First, when we reprove a man generally, as Nathan did David by a parable [2 Samuel 12].

Second, when we put an exhortation in the room of a reproof, in the exhortation insinuating an oblique reproof, as when a man shall swear in his talk. I shall not always need to say, "You do very ill to swear, and so to dishonor God." But I will lap it up in the form of an exhortation, as pills are lapped in sugar, by saying, "Yea and nay, yea and nay shall serve among us." "Rebuke not an elder, but exhort him as a father, and young men as brethren," says Paul to Timothy [1 Tim. 5:1].

Third, when the reproof is propounded in a man's own person, as though he were faulty. Paul practiced this: "Now these things, brethren, I have figuratively applied to mine own self and Apollos for your sakes, that ye might learn by us, that no man presume above that which is written" [1 Cor. 4:6].

Fourth, when the fault is directly reproved, but yet partly with prefaces that we do it of love, that we wish well to the party, that we speak as considering

---

4. *Nebuchadnezzar*: that is, Darius.

ourselves, that we also are in danger of the same fault [Gal. 6:1], and partly by framing the reproof out of the Word of God, so that the party may see himself to be reproved by God rather than by us. After this manner the inferior may admonish his superior, especially when there is no other way of redress. And he is to listen, yielding himself tractable. Naaman is advised by his servant, who said, "Father, if the prophet had commanded thee a great thing, wouldest thou not have done it: how much rather then, when he saith to thee, Wash, and be clean? Then went he down and washed himself seven times in Jordan" [2 Kings 5:13–14].

When any in this manner is admonished of a fault, they are to yield themselves tractable and thankful and heartily glad of so good a friend. Notable is the speech of the psalmist: "Let the righteous smite me, it is a benefit: and let him reprove me, it is the chief ointment, let it not be wanting to my head" [Ps. 141:5]. And Solomon says, "A reproof entereth more into him that hath understanding, than a hundred stripes into a fool" [Prov. 17:10]. And, "Open rebuke is better than secret love" [Prov. 27:5].

Chapter 7

Sobriety, Urbanity, Fidelity, and Care
of Our Neighbor's Good Name

Sobriety

Sobriety in judgment is when a man either suspends his opinion of his neighbor's sayings or doings or else speaks as charitably as he can by saying as little as may be (if the thing is evil) or by interpreting all in better part (if the speech or action is doubtful). Therefore, do thus: despise not your neighbor, but think yourself as bad a sinner and that the like defects may befall you. If you cannot excuse his doing, excuse his intent, which may be good. Or, if the deed is evil, think it was done of ignorance. If you can [in] no way excuse him, think some great temptation befell him, and that you would be worse if the like temptation befell you. And give thanks to God that the like as yet has not befallen you. Despise not a man [as] being a sinner, for though he is evil today, he may turn tomorrow.

Here is condemned all heady and rash judgment [Matt. 7:1] whereby men make things either worse than they are or else they take and turn all things to the worse part. Thus, the devil dealt with Job, saying, "Doth Job fear God for naught…but stretch out thine hand now and touch all that he hath, to see if he will not blaspheme thee to thy face" [Job 1:9, 11]. Such was the dealing of Doeg with David. "I saw the son of Jesse," says he, "when he came to Abimelech the son of Ahitub, who asked counsel of the Lord for him, and gave him victuals, and he gave him also the sword of Goliath the Philistine" [1 Sam. 22:9]. Here the backbiter conceals the necessary circumstances whereby Abimelech might have been excused, as that David, bring hungry, asked [for] bread, and that he told not Abimelech that he was out of Saul's favor. But he turns all his speech to this end: to bring the priest into suspicion with Saul.

Thus the Pharisees dealt. "John came neither eating nor drinking, and they say he hath a devil. The Son of man came eating and drinking, and they say, Behold, a glutton, and a drinker of wine, and a friend of publicans and sinners" [Matt. 11:18–19].

Contrary to this sobriety is flattery, whereby, for hope either of favor or gain, men (and especially such as are of dignity and place) are soothed up in their sins, and extolled above measure, even to their faces. As when Herod, arrayed in royal apparel, sat on the judgment seat and made an oration, the people gave a shout, saying, "The voice of a god, and not of a man" [Acts 12:22]. But mark what Solomon says: "He that praiseth his friend with a loud voice, rising early in the morning: it shall be counted to him for a curse" [Prov. 27:14]. One, being asked which was the worst of all beasts, answered, "Of wild beasts, the tyrant; of tame beasts, the flatterer." And another said that flatterers are worse than crows, for crows eat only dead carrion but these [flatterers] feed on living men.

And of all kind of flattery, it is the worst when a man shall speak fair to his neighbor's face, and praise him, but behind his back [he] speaks his pleasure, and even cuts his throat. David complains of his familiar friend, that "the words of his mouth were softer than butter, yet war was in his heart" [and] that "his words were more gentle than oil, yet they were swords" [Ps. 55:21]. The Pharisees, behind Christ's back, took counsel how they might entangle Him in talk. But before His face they say, "Master, we know that thou art true, and teachest the way of God truly, neither carest thou for any man: for thou considerest not the person of men" [Matt. 22:16].

Urbanity

Urbanity is a grace of speech whereby men in seemly manner use pleasantness in talk for recreation, or for such delight as is joined with profit to themselves and others. The preacher says, "There is a time to laugh, and a time to weep" [Eccl. 3:4]. "When the Lord brought again the captivity of Sion, we were like them that dream. Then was our mouth filled with laughter, and our tongue with joy" [Ps. 126:1–2].

Now this mirth must be joined with the fear of God, otherwise Solomon says well, "I have said to laughter, thou art mad: and of joy, what is that thou doest?" [Eccl. 2:2]. And Christ says, "Woe to you that now laugh, for ye shall weep" [Luke 6:25]. Second, [it must be joined] with compassion and sorrow for God's people in affliction and misery. "They drink wine in bowls, and anoint themselves with chief ointments, but no man is sorry for the affliction of Joseph" [Amos 6:6]. Third, it must be sparing and moderate. Paul condemns such as are "lovers of pleasures more than of God" [2 Tim. 3:4]. Fourth, it must be void of the practice of sin. Moses is commended that "he refused the pleasures of sin" [Heb. 11:25].

The usual time of mirth is at meats. And here Samson's practice may be followed. At his marriage feast [he] propounded a riddle or hard question to his friends [Judg. 14:12]. And Ambrose thinks that he did this to stop the mouths of talkers and to occupy their wits.

Withal it must be remembered to be a Christian duty, even at the table, to maintain talk of religion and duties of godliness, after the practice of our Savior Christ [Luke 11:37; 14:1; 22:15], though many upon little ground think otherwise. Tertullian records of the Christians of his time that in their love-feasts they used to talk together, as considering with themselves that they had God Himself as an ear-witness to them. Chrysostom on this point saith well, "I would to God that in taverns, and [at] feasts, and at baths, men would talk and dispute of hell, for the remembering of hell would hinder a man from falling into hell."[1] And it was the manner of the primitive church at dinner and supper to use the reading of the Scriptures. "When you come to the table," says Augustine, "hear that which is read according to custom, without any stir or striving, so that your mouths may not only receive the meat, but your ears may hunger after the Word of God."[2] And this ancient custom is to this day retained in the colleges of the University of Cambridge.

And this holy rejoicing at meats is especially to be used with such as are godly. As Solomon says that he who "eateth at the covetous man's table, shall vomit his morsels, and shall lose his sweet words" [Prov. 23:8]. The faithful at Jerusalem did break bread "together, with gladness and singleness of heart" [Acts 2:46].

Question. Whether jesting is tolerable in any sort or not?

Answer. That jesting which stands in quips, taunts, and girds, which serves only for the offence of some, with the delight of others, is not tolerable, because "all speech must edify, and minister grace to the hearers" [Eph. 4:29]. Neither does it agree with Christian gravity and modesty. But two kinds of jesting are tolerable. The first is moderate and sparing mirth in the use of things indifferent, in convenient season, without the least scandal of any man, and with profit to the hearers. The second is that which the prophets used when they jested against wicked persons, yet so, as withal they sharply reproved their sins. "At noon Elijah mocked them, and said, Cry aloud, for he is a god: either he talketh or pursueth his enemies, or is in his journey, or it may be he sleepeth and must be awaked" (1 Kings 18:27; 2 Kings 2:23; Isa. 14:10–11).

As for laughter, it may be used, otherwise God would never have given that power and faculty unto man. But the use of it must be both moderate and seldom, as sorrow for our sins is to be plentiful and often. We may learn this from Christ's example, of whom we read that He wept three times: at the destruction of Jerusalem, at the raising of Lazarus, and in His agony (Luke 19:41;

---

1. In the margin: Hom. 2 in 2 Thess. 2.
2. In the margin: Aug. epist. 109.

John 11:35; Heb. 5:7). But we never read that He laughed. And especially remember the saying of Chrysostom: "*Si risus in ecclesia, diaboli opus est*"; that is, To move laughter in the church is the work of the devil.

Fidelity

Fidelity is constancy in all our lawful sayings and promises.

A promise is to be made with this condition, "if God will," and then if a man is prevented by death, or by any like means, he is not to be blamed [James 4:15; 1 Chron. 13:2]; otherwise, a man's lawful word and promise binds him according to the will and pleasure of him to whom it is made [2 Chron. 27:23].[3]

Now if afterwards it is hurtful to him that made it, he may crave to be free from his promise. And liberty being granted, [he may] take it. But a promise bound with an oath is to be kept [Ps. 15:4], though private hindrances follow, yet so as the magistrate may order the matter, and proceed in equity, that the damage may be the less.

Care of Our Neighbor's Good Name

The last grace which is to be used in speech is care of our neighbor's good name, which is far "better to him than great riches" [Prov. 22:1].

Here is condemned the tale-bearer, who of an evil mind tells a thing of another to bring him into hatred, or to revenge himself, or to get something which otherwise he could not obtain.

This tale-bearing is of divers sorts (Rom. 1:30). One is when men whisper abroad secretly the fault of another, whereas they should rather admonish the party, as Ham when he had seen his father's nakedness, ran straight and told his brethren [Gen. 9:22].

The second [is] when they add to or change the thing said or done, as it serves their purpose. Some of the witnesses, which came against Christ, charged Him to say, "I will destroy this temple which is made with hands, and in three days build another without hands." Where, first, they change His meaning, for Christ spoke of the temple of His body. Second, they add to the words. For Christ said not, "I will destroy this temple," but "destroy ye this temple" [Matt. 26:60–61]. Therefore, the Holy Spirit notes them with the name of "false witness bearers."

The third [is] when men surmise and tell that which was never done. When Jeremiah was going out of Jerusalem to the land of Benjamin, and was in the gate of Benjamin, Irijah took him and said, "Thou fleest to the Chaldeans"

---

3. The relevance of this Scripture is unclear.

[Jer. 37:13]. Then Jeremiah said, "That is false, I flee not to the Chaldeans." But he would not hear him.

The fourth is the colored tale-bearing, when one speaks evil of another with fine prefaces and preambles, feigning that he is very sorry that his neighbor has done such or such a thing, that he speaks it not of malice but of a good mind, that he is constrained to speak but he speaks not all he could speak, [and] that the party to whom the tale is told must keep it secret. Luther writes of this fault very well: "This vice whereby we tell abroad the things which we hear of others, and take them in worse part is very rife, and of great force to sow discords; the rather because it often shows itself under the pretense and name of counsel and good advice. And it is a notable vizard[4] for a tale-bearer to transform himself into an angel of light, and under zeal of God's glory to accuse his neighbor of heresy, error, and wicked life."[5]

Therefore, the prophet's meaning is that we should conceal the evils that are in our neighbor, and not speak them to others, though he is an enemy and deserves it at our hands, and only speak of those good things in him which seem to preserve concord. For this we would that men should do unto us. Yea, and let us take heed that we judge not or condemn any man's saying or doing rashly. Augustine says that this was the care which his mother had toward her enemies.[6] To do this is a notable point of just dealing, but indeed there is no man utterly without this fault in this life. Such is our wretched estate in this world. For though some are of this mind, that they desire not to have other men's wants told them, and will not take all in worse part, yet if they are told and take in worse part of others, they can willingly hear them, neither will they check the teller, but suffer bad surmises to take place with them. But Gedaliah, the son of Ahikam, excelled in the contrary virtue, who chose to hazard his life rather than suspect evil of Ishmael [Jer. 40:14].

This tale-bearing is the common table talk in England. And it is wonderful to see how those who are otherwise godly are overtaken with it. But men must learn to stand more in awe of God's commandment, and also to consider that the same thing a man speaks of another comes home again by his own door. Such as use tale-bearing and backbiting are by God's just judgment paid home in the same kind. And hereupon Christ says, "Judge not that ye be not judged, for with what judgment ye judge, ye shall be judged" [Matt. 7:1]. Wherefore, when men shall enter any evil communication of others, we are to interrupt it by other talk, as not regarding it.

---

4. *Vizard*: disguise.

5. In the margin: Upon Psalm 15:3.

6. In the margin: Confess. l. 9.

Here remember that when governors and magistrates shall use hard words, not in the way of defamation, but for the reproving of a vice, it is not to slander, as, "O foolish Galatians" [Gal. 3:1]; [and] "O generation of vipers" [Matt. 3:7]. And Christ terms Herod [a] "fox."[7]

---

7. Luke 13:32.

Chapter 8

The Bonds of Truth

Thus much of grace in speech; now follows the bonds of truth whereby the truth of our talk is testified and confirmed. There are three: (1) a simple assertion; (2) an asseveration; [and] (3) an oath.

A simple assertion is either a simple affirmation (as "yea, yea") or a simple negation (as "nay, nay"). And they are to be used only in our familiar and common talk. "Let your communication be yea, yea: nay, nay: and whatsoever is more cometh of evil" [Matt. 5:37].

If the truth which we affirm or deny is doubtful or contingent, then such clauses as these ("It is so" or "It is not so as I think, as I remember, as I take it") are to be added. If one shall say, "It is so," and afterwards it proves otherwise, he receives discredit because he spoke an untruth. But he if shall say, "I think it is so," though it falls out otherwise, yet he saves his credit because he deceives not, but only is deceived.

An asseveration is a form of speech whereby one does vehemently affirm or deny anything, as when a man shall say, "Verily, in truth, in very truth, without all doubt, etc." These and such like are not to be used at every word, but then only when a truth of greater importance is to be confirmed. When the false prophets among the Jews and the priests would not believe that Jeremiah was sent of God, what saith he? Not simply, "The Lord hath sent me," but "In truth the Lord hath sent me" [Jer. 26:15]. Our Savior Christ, when He used to speak any weighty matter used to say, "Amen, amen, Verily, verily." This is a plain asseveration, for "amen" is more than a simple affirmation, and is less than an oath, as the very sense of the word does import, which is no more but "truly, certainly."

The third is an oath, which must not be made by anything in heaven or earth, but only by the name of God alone. It must be used as the last refuge and remedy of all. For when any truth of great importance is to be confirmed, and all signs, evidences, proofs, [and] witnesses fail among men on earth, then we may lawfully fetch the Lord as a witness from heaven, who is the Knower of all truth. And in this case an oath may be taken, either publicly before a magistrate, or privately among private persons, if it is done with reverence and consideration, as it was between Jacob and Laban [Gen. 31:53].

Chapter 9

The Manner of Our Speech:
After We Speak

After a man has spoken his mind, very few words are to be added. He who has knowledge spares his words. "In many words there cannot want iniquity: but he that refraineth his lips is wise" [Prov. 10:19].

He who speaks many words speaks either false things or superfluous [things] or both. As when a river overflows, the water gathers much slime, so many words [gather] many faults. When a vessel, being smitten, makes a great noise, it is a token that it is empty. And so, the sound of many words shows a vain heart. The Gentiles have said that God gave a man one tongue and two ears that he might hear more and speak less. Valerius Maximus reports of Xenocrates that, being in the company of some who used railing speeches, held his tongue. And, being asked why he did so, [he] answered, "That it had repented him that he had spoken, but it never repented him that he had held his peace." And the proverb is: "He that will speak what he will shall hear what he would not." To the framing of our speech Ambrose requires three things: a yoke, a balance, and a metwand:[1] a yoke to keep it in stayed gravity; a balance to give it weight of reason; [and] a metwand to keep it in measure and moderation.[2]

This rule must be practiced carefully for the avoiding of chiding, brawling, and contending. "Let nothing be done by contention" (Phil. 2:3). Let students and scholars learn to practice this. For what shall another man's opinion hurt you, though in reasoning he is not of your mind in every point?

Take heed of the spirit of contradiction whereby some, by thwarting and contradicting every man, at length prove either obstinate heretics or lewd atheists, and make no bones to contradict the Holy Spirit, and to call the Scriptures in[to] question, and dispute that there is no God.

Now if a man speaks necessary things, though he continues his speech till midnight, as Paul did [Acts 20:7], it cannot be called immoderate or superfluous talk.

---

1. *Met-wand:* measuring rod.
2. In the margin: Offic. lib. 1.

Chapter 10

Writing

All this which is set down concerning speech must as well be practiced in writing as in speaking. Whereby are condemned ballads, books of love, all idle discourses and histories, being nothing else but enticements and baits unto manifold sins, fitter for Sodom and Gomorrah than for God's church. And it must be followed as well in speaking of Latin or any good tongue, as English, which students have not marked. For whereas they will not swear in English, yet in Latin they make no bones of it, saying, *Mehercule*,[1] *medius fidiùs*,[2] ædipol, *per deos immortales.*[3] And whereas they hold but one God in judgment, yet in their Latin exercises they speak of Jupiter and of the immortal gods, after the manner of the heathen. What a shame is this, that a Christian (and that in Christian schools) should either be ashamed to speak, or not used to speaking, as a Christian but as atheists do? If you have many tongues and know not how to use them well, he who has but his mother tongue, ordering it aright, is a better linguist than you.

---

1. By Hercules.
2. By heaven.
3. By the immortal gods.

Chapter 11

Silence

Wise and godly silence is as excellent a virtue as holy speech, for he knows not how to speak who knows not how to hold his tongue. The rule of our silence must be the law of God. By means of which wise consideration must be had whether the thing which we have in mind is for God's glory and our neighbor's good; which done, we are answerably to speak or to be silent.

Here must be considered the things for which silence must be used, and the persons before whom [it must be used].

Point 1
The things are many.

First, if any truth is to the hindrance of God's glory or of the good of our neighbor, it must be concealed. The concealing of the truth is either in whole or in part.

[It is] in whole, when the speaking of the least word is hurtful. As, for example, the father and the son are both sick at once. The son dies first. The father asks whether the son is dead or not. If it is said no, an untruth is told. If yea, then the father's grief is increased and his death hastened. Therefore, silence is the best.[1] In days of persecution holy martyrs have chosen rather to suffer death than to reveal their brethren who have been of their private assemblies with them.

The concealing of a thing in part is when a man speaks a little of the truth and conceals the rest. This is warranted in all good and lawful proceedings which manifestly tend to the glory of God. When Samuel is sent to anoint David, he answers the Lord and says, "How can I go? For if Saul hear of it he will kill me. Then the Lord answered, Take a heifer with thee, and say, I am come to do sacrifice to the Lord: and call for Jesse to sacrifice, and I will show thee what thou shalt do, and thou shalt anoint unto me him whom I shall name unto thee" [1 Sam. 16:1–3]. When Jeremiah had shown king Zedekiah how he might escape death, then the king said unto him: "Let no man know of these

---

1. In the margin: Aug. lib. ad Conser.

words…but if the princes understand that I have talked with thee, and they come unto thee, and say unto thee, Declare unto us what the king hath said unto thee…then shalt thou say unto them, I humbly besought the king that he would not cause me to return to Jonathan's house to die there" [Jer. 38:24–26]. And afterwards he so answered, and the matter was not perceived. The like was practiced by Paul (Acts 23:6).

Second, you are to conceal your own secrets. Samson, revealing his own secret, overthrows himself (Judges 14). If you desire ease by revealing, then tell them to but few, and to such as are faithful.

That which you would not have known, tell no man. For how shall another keep your counsel, when you cannot do it? Keep your friend's secret likewise, if it is not hurtful. And let ministers conceal the sins and wants that trouble the conscience of such as are dying. Let magistrates conceal things done in the senate, especially concerning war, lest they are revealed to the enemy.

If God brings any strange thing to pass, speak not boldly of it, but rather in silence wonder. At the consideration of God's majesty in His works, Job says, "Behold, I am vile: what shall I answer thee? I will lay my hand upon my mouth" [Job 40:4]. Nadab and Abihu, for offering incense with strange fire before the Lord, were both destroyed with fire, which being done, Moses told Aaron that God would be sanctified in them who come near Him, and be glorified before all the people. And then the text says, "but Aaron held his peace" (Lev. 10:3). When Peter had taught the Gentiles, and after returned to Jerusalem, they of the circumcision contended with him. He then renders a reason for his act, which being made, they were silent. For so the text is: "When they heard these things, they held their peace, and glorified God" (Acts 11:18). When God's judgments befall men among us, if we speak anything we must judge charitably. "Blessed is he that judgeth wisely of the poor, the Lord shall deliver him in the time of trouble" (Ps. 41:1).

Third, the infirmities and sins of our neighbors are always to be concealed, unless it is in the case before named, that we find ourselves called of God to speak. "He that covereth a transgression seeketh love" (Prov. 17:9). If God in mercy covers his sins, why should you reveal them? Solomon says, "It is the glory of a man to pass by an infirmity" (Prov. 19:11).

Fourth, all unseemly matters, all things unknown, things which concern us not, things above our reach, are in silence to be buried.

Point 2

The persons, before whom silence must be used, are these. First, malicious enemies of religion: "Give not that which is holy unto dogs: neither cast your pearls before swine" [Matt. 7:6]. This was (among the rest) one cause of the silence of

Christ before Caiaphas and Pilate [Matt. 27:14]. Second, before magistrates in their open courts, where such as come before them are not to speak till they are bidden. "Then Paul after that the governor had beckoned unto him that he should speak, answered" [Acts 24:10]. Third, in the presence of our elders and betters, who must have leave and liberty to speak first, and must of others be heard with silence [Ecclesiasticus 32:8].[2] This practice was in Elihu to Eliphaz and Bildad [Job 32:6]. A company of men (as some say) is like the alphabet in which [there] are vowels, half vowels, and mutes [Eccl. 7:5, 11]. Vowels are old men: learned, wise, expert. Half vowels are young men and women, who are then only to speak when they are asked. Mutes are the same parties who, being not occasioned, are in silence to hear their betters. And here all servants and children must remember when they are justly reproved, to be silent, and not to answer anything again [Titus 2:9]. Fourth, fools and prattlers are not to be answered, unless it is to let them see their folly.

---

2. Cf. Eccl. 3:7.

Chapter 12

An Exhortation to Keep the Tongue

Thus, I have in part set down how the tongue is to be governed. And I heartily desire that all Christians would put these rules in practice.

Reasons

First, "If any man seem to be religious, and refrain not his tongue, he deceiveth himself, and his religion is in vain" [James 1:26].

Second, the man of an evil tongue is a beast in the form of a man, for his tongue is the tongue of a serpent [Ps. 140:3], under which lies nothing but venom and poison. Nay, he is worse than a serpent. For it cannot hurt unless it is present to see a man, or to bite him, or to strike him with his tail, but he who has not the rule of his tongue hurts men [who are] absent as well as present. Neither sea nor land nor anything can hinder him. And again, his throat is like a grave that has a vent in some part, and therefore sends forth nothing but stink and corruption.

Third, as the holy men of God, when they preached, had their tongues (as it were) touched with a coal from the altar of God [Isa. 6:6], and as godly men, when they speak graciously, have their tongues inflamed with the fire of God's Spirit [Matt. 3:11], so contrariwise when you speak evil, your tongue is kindled by the "fire of hell" [James 3:6]. And Satan comes from thence with a coal to touch your lips, and to set them on fire to all manner of mischief. Chrysostom says that when men speak good things, their tongue is the tongue of Christ, but all manner of ungodly and cursed speaking is the devil's language.[1]

Fourth, the moderating of the tongue is a matter of great difficulty. Saint James says, "The whole nature of beasts and of birds, and of creeping things… but the tongue can no man tame: it is an unruly evil" [James 3:7–8]. Pambus, one without learning, came to a certain man to be taught a psalm. When he had heard the first verse of Psalm 39, "I said, that I will keep my ways that I offend not in my tongue," [he] would not suffer the next verse to be read,

---

1. In the margin: Chrysostom. 79 in Matt.

saying, "This verse is enough, if I could practice it."[2] And when his teacher blamed him because he saw him not for six months after, he answered that he had not yet done the verse. And one who knew him many years after, asked him whether he had yet learned the verse. "I am forty years old," says he, "and I have not learned to fulfill it." Now then, the harder it is to rule the tongue, the more care is to be had therein.

Fifth, the strange judgments of God for the abuse of the tongue, especially in blasphemies and perjuries, are many and fearful.[3]

Example 1. Three men conspired together against Narcissus, bishop of Jerusalem, a man who led a godly and blameless life. And they charged him with a most heinous crime. All three affirmed their accusation by oath.[4] The first wished, if it were not so, that he would be burned. The second, that he would die of the jaundice. The third, that he would lose his eyes. Afterwards, in process of time, the first had his house set on fire in the night and he with all his family was burned. The second had the jaundice from the head to the sole of the foot, and died thereof. The third, seeing what was befallen these two, repented and confessed the conspiracy against Narcissus. And yet for all that he lost his eyes.

Example 2. In the days of Queen Mary, as James Abbes was led by the sheriff for execution, divers poor people stood in the way and asked their alms.[5] Not having any money to give them, he did pull off all his apparel save his shirt, and gave it unto them, to some one thing, to some another. In the giving whereof he exhorted them to be strong in the Lord and to stand steadfast in the truth of the gospel. While he was thus instructing the people, a servant of the sheriff's going by, cried out aloud, and blasphemously said, "Believe him not, good people. He is a heretic and a mad man out of his wit. Believe him not, for it is heresy that he says." And as the other continued in his godly admonitions, so did this wicked wretch blow forth his blasphemous exclamations, until they came unto the stake where he should suffer. But immediately after this martyr was bound to the stake and fire put to him, such was the fearful stroke of God's justice upon this blasphemous railer that he was there presently in the sight of all the people stricken with a frenzy wherewith he had before railingly charged that good martyr of God.

---

2. In the margin: Hist. Tripar.
3. In the margin: God's judgment for the abuse of the tongue.
4. In the margin: Euseb. l. 6. c. 8.
5. In the margin: Fox. Act. Mon.

In this furious rage and madness, [he] cast off his shoes and the rest of his clothes, cried out unto the people, and said, "Thus did James Abbes, the true servant of God, who is saved, but I am damned." And [he] thus ran about the town of Bury, still crying that "James Abbes was a good man and saved, but I am damned."

Example 3. Children, sitting in company together, fell into communication of God, and to reason what God was. [6] And some said one thing [and] some another. Among the rest one said, "He is a good old Father." To which another, named Denis Benfield, replied with a most outrageous blasphemy: "What, He is an old doting fool." But shortly after this young girl was so stricken that all the one side of her was black, and she became speechless, and died.

Example 4. One Leaver, a ploughman, railing, said that he saw the evil-favored knave Latimer when he was burned, and also in spite [he] said that he had teeth like a horse.[7] At which time and hour, as near as could be gathered, the son of the said Leaver most wickedly hanged himself.

Example 5. In the time of King Edward, a young gentleman of Cornwall, being in company with other gentlemen together with their servants, being about the number of twenty horsemen, among whom this lusty younger entered into talk, and began withal to swear and use ribald speech.[8] Being gently reproved, the young gentleman took snuff, and said to the reprover: "Why take you thought for me? Take you thought for your winding sheet." "Well," quoth[9] the other, "Mend, for death gives no warning. For as soon comes a lamb's skin to the market as an old sheep's skin." "God's wounds," said he, "care you not for me." Raging still in this manner worse and worse in words, till at length passing on their journey, they came riding over a great bridge, standing over a piece of an arm of the sea, upon which bridge this gentleman swearer spurred his horse in such sort as he sprang clean over with the man on his back, who as he was going, cried, saying, "Horse and man and all to the devil."

Example 6. There was a serving man in Lincolnshire, who had still in his mouth a use to swear, "God's precious blood," and that for very

---

6. In the margin: Act. Mon. Fox.
7. In the margin: Idem.
8. In the margin: Idem.
9. *Quoth:* spoke.

trifles.[10] Being often warned by his friends to leave the taking of the Lord's blood in vain, [he] did notwithstanding still persist in his wickedness until, at the last, it pleased God to cite him first with sickness, and then with death. During this time of the Lord's visitation, no persuasion could move him to repent [of] his foresaid blaspheming. But, hearing the bell to toll, [he] did most hardly in the very anguish of his death, start up in his bed, and swore, "By God's blood the bell tolls for me." Whereupon immediately the blood abundantly from all the joints of his body (as it were) in streams did issue most fearfully from mouth, nose, wrists, knees, heels, and toes, with all other joints, not one left free, and so died.

These and such like judgments must be as warnings from heaven to admonish us, and to make us afraid of the abuse of the tongue, especially when it tends to the dishonor of God. And we are to imitate the example of Polycarp, the martyr, who when he was bidden to take his oath and curse Christ, answered, "Fourscore and six years have I been His servant, yet in all this time He has not so much as once hurt me. How then may I speak evil of my King and Sovereign Lord, who has thus preserved me?"

Sixth, God has honored your tongue with the gift of speech and utterance. And the great excellency of this gift you should perceive, if you were stricken dumb for a time. Therefore, let your tongue be applied to the honoring of God and to the good of your neighbor.

FINIS

---

10. In the margin: Peter Stubbe's book, printed 1581.

A Discourse of the Damned Art of Witchcraft

So far forth as it is revealed in the Scriptures,
and manifested by true experience.

Framed and delivered by M. William Perkins,
in his ordinary course of preaching,
and published by Thomas Pickering, Bachelor of Divinity,
and Minister of Finchingfield in Essex.

Printed by Cantrel Legge,
printer to the University of Cambridge.
1608

The Epistle Dedicatory

To the Right Honorable, Sir Edward Cooke, Knight, Lord Chief Justice of his Majesty's Court of Common Pleas; grace and peace.

Right Honorable. The Word of God, that only oracle of truth, has pointed out the enemy of mankind by his proper characters in sundry places. Our Savior terms him "the prince of this world" [John 12:31] and "a murderer from the beginning" [John 8:44]. Peter compares him to "a roaring lion" that ranges abroad in the earth, "seeking whom he may devour" [1 Peter 5:8]. His attempts, in regard of their quality, are called νοήματα [2 Cor. 2:11], subtle and deep devices, yea, μεθοδείας [Eph. 6:11], plots exquisitely contrived and orderly framed (as it were) in method. The meaning of the Holy Spirit, in these and such like attributes, is to express that measure of policy and power which Satan has reserved unto himself even in the state of his apostasy, improved by long experience, and instantly practiced upon the sons of men, that he might set up in the world a spiritual regiment of sin as a means to encounter[1] the kingdom of grace, and, if it were possible, to bring the same to ruin. To forbear instances of open force made against God and His church by other courses for the compassing of his desires, how skillfully he works his own advantage by secret opposition in the exercise of that cursed art (which is the subject of the present discourse) is a point not unworthy your honorable consideration.

The power of this prince of darkness, being above the might of all sensible creatures, and every way seconded by the greatness of his knowledge and experience, manifests itself herein, for the most part, by works of wonder, transcendent in regard of ordinary capacity, and diversely dispensed by his chosen instruments of both sexes, sometimes in matter of divination, sometimes by enchantment, sometimes by rare sleights and delusions; at other times by hurting, curing, raising tempests, speedy conveyance and transportation from place to place, etc.; and all to purchase unto himself admiration, fear, and faith, from the credulous world which is usually carried away with affectation

---

1. *Encounter*: counter.

and applause of signs and wonders. His policy appears in a wise and exquisite manner of framing and conceiving both his practices and grounds; the one to procure credit and entertainment; the other that he may not fail of his purpose but proceed upon certainties.

Touching the manner of his practice. He stands resolved that the world has taken notice of him to be "a liar, and the father thereof" [John 8:44]; and, therefore, if he should offer to speak in his own language, or inform an art by rules of his own devising, he might haply[2] incur suspicion of falsehood. Hereupon he composes his courses, μιμητικως, by way of counterfeit and imitation, not of the actions and dealings of men, but of the order of God's own proceeding with His church, holding it a sure principle in policy that actions will be much more effectual when they are framed unto the best precedents than when they are suited to the direction of meaner examples. To this purpose, as God has made a covenant with His church, binding Himself by promise to be their God, and requiring of them the condition of faith and obedience, so does Satan indent[3] with his subjects by mutual confederacy, either solemnly or secretly, whereby they bind themselves on the one part to observe his rules, and he on the other to accomplish their desires. Again, God gives His Word (the interpreter of His will) and His sacraments (the seals of His promises), to which, being rightly administered and received, He has tied His own presence and the work of His grace in them who believe. Answerable to this, the devil gives a word of direction to his instruments, and adds unto it charms, figures, characters, and other outward ceremonies, at the use whereof he has bound himself to be present, and to manifest his power in effecting the thing desired. Furthermore, God has revealed His will to the patriarchs, prophets, and apostles by familiar conference [Gen. 18:17], dreams [Num. 12:6], inspiration [Amos 3:7], [and] trances [Acts 10:10]. In the same manner, Satan has his diviners and soothsayers, his Pythonesses,[4] his Cassandras,[5] his Sibyls,[6] to whom he makes known things to come by familiar conference, dreams, etc. To conclude, in the Old Testament, God had His temple at Jerusalem, yea, His oracle (Exod. 25:22; Num. 7:89), from where He spoke and gave the answer unto Moses; so, of ancient times the devil erected his temple at Dodona and Delphos,[7] where he gave his answers

---

2. *Haply*: by chance.

3. *Indent*: enter into an agreement with someone by means of a contract.

4. In Greek mythology, Pythoness was a priestess of Apollo at Delphi.

5. In Greek mythology, Cassandra was a princess of Troy, who possessed the gift of prophecy.

6. The Sibyls were ancient oracles, who allegedly prophesied at holy sites throughout Greece.

7. The ancient cities of Dodona, in northern Greece, and Delphos (or Delphi), in southern Greece, were known for their temples of Zeus and Apollo respectively. They were also famous for their oracles.

for the satisfaction of the superstitious heathen.[8] Yea, and at this day, as the ministers of God do give resolution to the conscience in doubtful and difficult matters, so the ministers of Satan, under the name of wise men and wise women, are at hand by his appointment to resolve, direct, and help ignorant and unsettled persons in cases of distraction, loss, or other outward calamities.

Now the grounds whereupon he builds his proceedings for certainty are cunningly gathered from the disposition of man's heart by natural corruption, and that in three special instances. First, he knows that man, naturally out of the light of grace, has but a mere soul [1 Cor. 2:14],[9] endued only with some general and confused notions. And as for matters of deeper apprehension touching God and heavenly things, there is a veil of ignorance and blindness drawn over the eyes of his mind. Whereupon, though he is apt to know and worship God and learn His will, yet for want of information by the Word, he is prone to err in the practice of his notion. Here Satan applies himself to man's measure, and at his own will, draws the mind into error by his delusions and impostures. This made the Samaritans in the Old Testament [2 Kings 17:29; John 4:22], and the superstitious Athenians in the New [Acts 17:23], to worship "an unknown god," that is, the devil [1 Cor. 10:20]. Hence it was that the greatest clerks of Greece, Thales, Plato, and the rest, for want of a better light, sought unto the wizards of Egypt, whom they called prophets, men instructed by Satan in the grounds of divination.[10] And Jannes and Jambres, mentioned in the Scriptures [2 Tim. 3:8], were of this sort. Hence, it was also that the ancient heathen, having "no law and testimony from God" [Isa. 8:19–20], inquired at soothsayers and murmuring enchanters. Others betook themselves in matters of doubt and difficulty to the old oracles of Jupiter Ammon in Libya,[11] Jupiter Dodonæus at Dodona in Epirus,[12] Apollo at Delphos,[13] Jupiter Trophonius in Boeotia,[14] and the rest. Here the devil gave the answer, sometimes one way and sometimes another.[15]

Second, Satan by observation perceives that man, upon a weak and ignorant mind,[16] is prone superstitiously to dote upon the creatures, attributing some divine operation or virtue to them without any ground from God's Word or common understanding; and consequently [man is] disposed to worship

---

8. In the margin: Herodot. Euterpe.

9. In the margin: ψυχικος.

10. In the margin: Diog. Laert. lib. 1 in Thaletis epist. ad Pherecid. & l. 3. Strabo Geogr. l. 17.

11. In the margin: Diod. Sic. l. 17. Plin. l. 5. c. 5.

12. In the margin: Herodot. Euterpe. Strabo Geogr. l. 16. ex Hom. Odyss.

13. In the margin: Pausan. in Phocicis. Herodot. Euterpe. Strabo Geogr. lib. 9. & lib. 16.

14. In the margin: Pausan. in Bœoticis. Strabo Geogr. lib. 9.

15. This paragraph break is not in the original.

16. In the margin: *Omnis superstitio imbecilli animi atque anilis est.* Cic. de Divin.

God in some work of man, or to join to the same worship the inventions of man, which He has not commanded. Upon which ground he made the heathen to dote upon their wise men, "to regard soothsayers, and them that wrought with spirits" [Lev. 19:31]. [He made] the Chaldean philosophers, renowned for their superstitions and magical courses, to make the heavens, *fatalium legum tabulam*, ascribing that to the virtue of the stars which was known and done by satanical operation.[17] [He made] the magicians of Persia to admit of corruptions in their ancient good learning, and to give themselves, upon reading the fabulous writings of the Chaldean sorcerers, to the study of unlawful arts invented by himself, both before and after the times of Daniel the prophet [Dan. 2:2; Matt. 2:1]. Lastly, [he made] the ancient Romans, upon a superstitious dotage, never to undertake any business of weight, *nisi auspicato*, unless they had lucky consent and warrant from the colleges of their augurors[18] erected by Romulus.[19]

Third, there is a natural distemper in the mind of man, showing itself in these particulars: that he cannot endure to stand in fear of imminent danger; that he swells in a high conceit of his own deserts, especially when he is in a lower estate than he would be; that he will not bear a wrong done without revenge; [and] that he rests not satisfied with the measure of knowledge received, but affects the searching of things secret and not revealed. When the mind is possessed with these troubled passions with care to help itself, then comes the devil, and ministers occasion to use unlawful means in the general, and forces the mind by continual suggestion to determine itself in particular upon his own crafts. It was the case of Saul [1 Sam. 28:7] and Nebuchadnezzar [Dan. 2:1–2]. It caused many of the heathen philosophers to go from Athens to Memphis, from Greece to Syria, from men on earth to wicked spirits in hell, to get more illumination at the hands of the prince of darkness. It moved sundry malcontented priests of Rome[20] to aspire unto the chair of supremacy by diabolical assistance; yea, to exercise magical arts when they were popes[21] and thereby to manifest indeed that they were not the true successors of Simon Peter, but heirs of the virtues of Simon Magus who bewitched the people of Samaria, and professed to do that by the great power of God which he wrought by the aid and assistance of the devil [Acts 8:9].

If any do think it strange that Satan should in this sort oppose himself to the kingdom of God, and maintain his own principality by such ungodly arts and exercises, they must know that this and all other evils come to pass even by

---

17. In the margin: Clem. Al. ϛραμ lib. 6. Strabo Geogr. l. 15.

18. An augur was a priest in classical Rome. His main role was to interpret the will of the gods.

19. This paragraph break is not in the original.

20. In the margin: Platina in Sylv. 2. &c. Fascic. temporum.

21. In the margin: Benno Cardinal de Sylvest. 3. and Gregor. 6.

the will of God,[22] who has justly permitted the same to punish the wicked for their horrible sins, as Saul for his wickedness [1 Samuel 28]; to avenge Himself upon man for his ingratitude [2 Thess. 2:10–12], who, having the truth revealed unto him, will not believe or obey it; to waken and rouse up the godly who are sleeping in any great sins or infirmities; lastly, to try and prove His people whether they will cleave to Him and His Word or seek unto Satan and wicked spirits [Deut. 13:3].

Now from the consideration of the premises, we conclude it a necessary thing for the church and people of God to be acquainted with the dealing of Satan in this kind, that knowing his subtle devices they may learn to avoid them. For which purpose this treatise was first framed, and now exhibited to your lordship. The just commendation whereof, above others formerly divulged touching this argument, appears herein, that it serves to the full opening and declaration of Satan's method in the ground and practices of witchcraft. Wherein among many other remarkable points, it may please you to take special notice of these particulars.[23]

First, they do grossly err who either in express terms deny that there are witches or, in effect, and by consequent, avouch that there is no league between them and the devil, or affirm [that] they can do no such miraculous works as are ascribed to them. The former issues plainly out of the body of the discourse. And for the latter; that there is a covenant between them, either explicit in manner and form, or implicit by degrees of superstitious proceeding in the use of means insufficient in themselves, is plainly taught and confirmed in the same. That witches may and do work wonders is evidently proved; howbeit not by an omnipotent power (as the gainsayer[24] has unlearnedly and improperly termed it) but by the assistance of Satan, their prince, who is a powerful spirit, but yet a creature as well as they. And the wonders wrought by them are not properly and simply miracles,[25] but works of wonder, because they exceed the ordinary power and capacity of men, especially such as are ignorant of Satan's ability, and the hidden causes in nature whereby things are brought to pass.

Second, the witch truly convicted is to be punished with death, the highest degree of punishment, and that by the law of Moses, the equity whereof is perpetual; yea, even the better witch of the two in common reputation, because both are equally enemies to God and all true religion. And it is well

---

22. In the margin: August. Enchirid. cap. 95 and 96.
23. This paragraph break is not in the original.
24. In the margin: Reginald Scot. epist. ad Lectores.
25. In the margin: *Mira vel miranda, non miracula.*

known by true experience that all professed sorcerers are guilty of many most monstrous impieties.[26]

Third, the miracles of the popish church at this day are indeed either no miracles or false and deceitful works. Touching corporal presence in the sacrament, which they affirm to be by miracle, if it were true, then miracles are not yet ceased, but should still be as ordinary in the church as are the sacraments—a point not only confuted in the latter part of this treatise, but also by the testimony of purer antiquity. Augustine says that "miracles were once necessary to make the world believe the gospel, but he who now seeks a sign that he may believe, is a wonder, yea, a monster in nature."[27] Chrysostom concludes upon the same grounds that "there is now in the church no necessity of working miracles," and [he] calls him "a false prophet," who now takes in hand to work them.[28] Again, if there is a miracle in the sacrament, it is contrary to the nature of all those who were wrought, either by Moses and the prophets or by Christ and His apostles. For they were apparent to the eye, but this is insensible and, therefore, neither of force to move admiration nor to convince the mind of man and make him to believe. As for those which are pretended to be wrought by saints in that church, if we make recourse to the primitive times wherein God gave the gift to breed faith in the Gentiles, we shall find that the power of producing such works was never actually inherent in the apostles but dispensed by them "in the name of Christ" [Acts 3:12, 16]. Neither was it in their liberty to work miracles when they would, but when it pleased God upon special cause to call them thereunto. And if neither the power nor the will was in them, much less is it likely to be found in any of the saints. And for their relics, of whatsoever name, so greatly magnified and resorted unto, we deny there is any such virtue in them. For they may not be thought to be more effectual than the hem of Christ's garment, from which the power of healing the woman did not proceed but "from himself" [Luke 8:46], or the napkin of Paul, which did not cure the sick, but "the power of God" only, dispensed "by the hands of Paul" [Acts 19:11–12]. Miracles, therefore, avouched by them to be wrought at the tombs and statues of saints, and by their relics and monuments, are but mere satanical wonders, serving to maintain idolatry and superstition, and are in truth no better than the wonders of the Donatists in Saint Augustine's time: "*Aut figmenta mendacium hominum, aut portenta fallacium spirituum.*"[29]

---

26. This paragraph break is not in the original.

27. In the margin: Lib. de Civ. Dei. 22. c. 8.

28. In the margin: Homil. 19. oper. imperfect.

29. "Either the fictions of lying men or the illusions of deceiving spirits." In the margin: Aug. lib. de unitat. eccl. cap. 16.

Fourth, the light of the gospel purely preached is a sovereign means to discover and confound the power and policy of Satan in witchcraft and sorcery. The Word of God preached is the "weapon" of the Christian's "warfare" and "is mighty through God to cast down strongholds" [2 Cor. 10:4]. At the dispensation of it by the disciples of Christ, "Satan fell from heaven as lightning" [Luke 10:18]. After the ascension of Christ into heaven, in the times of Claudius Caesar, the devil stirred up sundry persons, who in regard of the admirable works which they did, by the help of magic and sorcery, were accounted as gods, and their statues erected and worshipped with great reverence.[30] Among the rest, one Simon, called by a kind of eminency, Magus, practicing his trade with success, to the admiration of the multitude, was held to be "the great power of God" [Acts 8:10]. His dealing was first discovered by the light of the Word, shining in the ministry of the apostles, and [he] himself [was] convicted with such evidence of truth to be an instrument of Satan that he was forced at length to fly out of Samaria into the western parts, as Eusebius records in his ecclesiastical history.[31] By this, Christ, the true Angel of the covenant, locked "and bound up Satan for a thousand years" [Rev. 20:2] after His ascension, that he might not be so generally powerful in seducing the Gentiles as he had been before His incarnation. But toward the expiration of those years, when corruption began to creep into the papacy, when the bishops affected that sea, and aspired unto it by diabolical arts, when the canons, decrees, sentences, synodals, decretals, clementines, [and] extravagants, with other laws and constitutions, prevailed above the Scriptures, then Satan began again to erect his kingdom, and these works of iniquity to be set abroach.[32]

These points together with the whole work ensuing, I humbly commend to your honorable patronage, that under your protection they may freely pass to the common view of the world. Wherein if I seem over bold, thus to press upon your lordship unknown, my answer is at hand: that all by-respects set apart, I have been hereunto induced many ways. First, upon a reverent opinion of those rare gifts of knowledge and piety wherewith God has beautified your person, and thereby advanced you to a high place and estimation in this commonwealth, whereof your grave and judicious speeches, even in the weightiest matters touching God and Caesar, as also those many learned writings, have given large testimony. From which has issued the greatness of your name, both in the present judgment of the world and in future expectation. Next, out of a resolved persuasion of your honorable disposition, as in general to the whole house of Levi, so particularly to those whose labors have fruitfully flowed out

---

30. In the margin: Just. Mart. Apol. ad Anton.

31. In the margin: Euseb. Eccl. hist. lib. 2. cap. 12.

32. *Abroach*: let out or put in circulation.

of the schools of the prophets, among whom the author of this book, in his time, was none of the meanest. Lastly, by the consideration of the argument, arising out of a judicial law, agreeable to the calling and quality of a judge. A penal law in regard of the offence, and therefore suitable to his proceedings, whose office is to hear with favor, to determine with equity, to execute justice with moderation. A law of the highest and greatest weight, immediately concerning God and His honor, and therefore appertaining to him who "sits in the place of God," to maintain His right, "that he may be with him, in the cause and judgment" [Deut. 1:16; 2 Chron. 19:6].

By such motives, I have encouraged myself, under assurance of your lordship's pardon, to present you with that wherein you are most deservedly interested, further entreating your favorable interpretation and acceptance, both of the quality of the work and of the pains of the publisher. And thus, heartily wishing to your lordship increase of grace and honor, with a daily influence of blessing and direction from heaven, upon your grave consultations and employments, I humbly take my leave, and commend you to the grace of God "by whom do rule all the judges of the earth" [Prov. 8:16].

Your Lordship's in all Christian duty to be commanded,
Thomas Pickering

Finchingfield, October 26, 1608

Table of Contents

The entrance into the discourse.

Chapter 1: Of the Nature of Witchcraft
    Witchcraft is an art.
    Witchcraft is a wicked art.
    The end of witchcraft: to work wonders.
        The grounds of working wonders: discontentment and curiosity.
    Wonders are wrought by Satan's assistance.
        The sorts of wonders.
    True wonders are wrought only by God.
    Lying wonders are wrought by Satan and his instruments.
        Satan is able to do extraordinary works by the help of nature.
    The sorts of lying wonders:
        Illusions of the senses and mind.
        Real works.
            Satan cannot change one creature into another.
    God's permission of the practices of witchcraft.
        Why He permits them.
        Satan cannot go beyond His permission.

Chapter 2: Of the Ground of all the Practices of Witchcraft
    There is a league between Satan and the witch.
    This league is twofold: open and secret.

Chapter 3: Of the Parts of Witchcraft: Divination
    How Satan, being a creature, reveals things to come.
    Divination by means which are the true creatures of God.
        By the flying and noise of birds.
        By the entrails of beasts.
        By the stars.
            Predictions by the stars are unlawful.
            The observation of the sign.

The observation of days.
By dreams: divine, natural, diabolical.
Notes of difference to know them from each other.
By lots.
Divination by counterfeit means: necromancy.
Whether that which was raised by the witch of Endor was truly Samuel.
Divination without means: by immediate assistance of a familiar spirit.
Practiced in two ways:
When the spirit is within the witch.
When he is out of the witch.
The difference between trances divine and diabolical trances.

Chapter 4: Of the Working of Witchcraft
The parts of it.
Enchantment: what it is.
What a charm is.
Whether the charm is in itself effectual to work wonders.
Particular practices referred to enchantment.
Juggling: consisting in delusion and sleight.
The wonders done by the sorcerer of Egypt before Pharaoh were juggling sleights, and not true and real works.

Chapter 5: Of Witches
What a witch is.
How many sorts of witches
The bad witch.
The good witch.
That the word ςαρμακευς (used by the seventy) signifies a witch.

Chapter 6: Of the Punishment of Witches
Why witches are (and ought) to be punished with death.

Chapter 7: Of the Application of the Doctrine of Witchcraft to the Present Times
Whether the witches of our times are the same as those who are condemned by the law of Moses.
Reasons proving that they are.
Allegations to the contrary answered.

How we may be able in these days to discern and discover a witch.

    The means of discovery are two:

        Examination upon presumptions.

        Conviction upon proofs.

    The causes moving Satan to further their discovery.

    Why all witches are not speedily detected by Satan's means.

What remedy may be used to prevent or cure the hurts of witchcraft.

    Remedies are of two sorts:

    Lawful.

        Preservative.

            Concerning persons.

                Whether the child of God may be bewitched or not.

            Concerning places.

         Restorative

            How whole countries may be cured.

            How particular persons may be cured.

    Unlawful remedies prescribed by the Church of Rome.

        General.

            The gift of casting out of devils.

            That there is no such gift in the Church, since the days of the apostles.

        Particular.

            The name Jesus.

            The use of relics.

            The sign of the cross.

            The hallowing of creatures.

            Exorcisms.

Whether the witches of our times are to be punished with death, and that by virtue of the law of Moses.

    Reasons proving that they ought.

    Objections answered.

A Discourse of Witchcraft

"Thou shalt not suffer a witch to live" (Exod. 22:18). This text contains one of the judicial laws of Moses touching the punishment of witchcraft. I have chosen to entreat of this argument for these causes:

First, witchcraft is a rife and common sin in our days, and very many are entangled with it, being either practitioners thereof in their own persons, or at the least yielding to seek for help and counsel of such as practice it.

Second, there are sundry men who receive it for a truth that witchcraft is nothing else but a mere illusion, and witches nothing but persons deluded by the devil. And this opinion takes place not only with the ignorant but is held and maintained by such as are learned, who do avouch it by word and writing that there are no witches; but as I said before.

Upon these and such like considerations, I have been moved to undertake the interpretation of this judicial law, as a sufficient ground of the doctrine which shall be delivered. In handling whereof, two things are distinctly to be considered: First, what is a witch. Second, what is her due and deserved punishment. And both these being opened and handled, the whole meaning of the law will the better appear.

For the first. To give the true description of a witch is a matter of great difficulty, because there are many differences and diversities of opinions touching this point. And, therefore, that we may properly and truly define a witch, we must first pause a while in opening the nature of witchcraft so far forth as it is delivered in the books of the Old and New Testaments and may be gathered out of the true experience of learned and godly men.

Touching witchcraft, therefore, I will consider three points: (1) what witchcraft is; (2) what is the ground of the whole practice thereof; and (3) how many kinds and differences there are of it.

Chapter 1

The Nature of Witchcraft

To begin with the first, according to the true meaning of all the places of holy Scripture which treat of this point, it may be thus described: witchcraft is a wicked art, serving for the working of wonders, by the assistance of the devil, so far forth as God shall in justice permit.

Section 1

I say it is *an art* because it is commonly so called and esteemed among men, and there is reason why it should be thus termed. For as in all good and lawful arts, the whole practice thereof is performed by certain rules and precepts, and without them nothing can be done, so witchcraft has certain superstitious grounds and principles whereupon it stands, and by which alone the feats and practices thereof are commonly performed.

If it is demanded what those rules are, and whence they had their beginning, considering that every art has reference to some author by whom it was originally taught and delivered, I answer that they were devised first by Satan, and by him revealed to wicked and ungodly persons of ancient times, as occasion served, who receiving them from him, became afterward, in the just judgment of God, his instruments to report and convey them to others from hand to hand.

For manifestation whereof, it is to be considered that God is not only in general a sovereign Lord and King over all His creatures, whether in heaven or earth, none excepted, no, not the devils themselves, but that He exercises also a special kingdom, partly of grace in the church militant upon earth, and partly of glory over the saints and angels, members of the church triumphant in heaven. Now in like manner the devil has a kingdom, called in Scripture the kingdom of darkness, whereof [he] himself is the head and governor, for which cause he is termed "the prince of darkness" [Eph. 6:12] and "the god of this world" [2 Cor. 4:4], ruling and effectually working in the hearts of the children of disobedience.

Again, as God has enacted laws whereby His kingdom is governed, so has the devil his ordinances whereby he keeps his subjects in awe and obedience, which generally and for substance are nothing else but transgressions of the very law of God. And among them all, the precepts of witchcraft are the very chief and most notorious. For by them especially he holds up his kingdom, and therefore [he] more esteems the obedience of them than of others. Neither does he deliver them indifferently to every man, but to his own subjects, the wicked; and not to them all, but to some special and tried ones, whom he most entrusts with his secrets, as being the fittest to serve his turn, both in respect of their willingness to learn and practice, as also for their ability to become instruments of the mischief, which he intends to others.

If it is here asked, whence the devil did fetch and conceive his rules? I answer, out of the corruption and depravation of that great measure of knowledge he once had of God, and of all the duties of His service. For that being quite depraved by his fall, he turns the same to the inventing and devising of what he is possibly able, against God and His honor. Hereupon, well perceiving that God has expressly commanded to renounce and abhor all practices of witchcraft, he has set abroach this art in the world, as a main pillar of his kingdom, which notwithstanding is flatly and directly opposed to one of the main principal laws of the kingdom of God, touching the service of Himself in spirit and truth [John 4:24].

Again, the reason why he conveys these ungodly principles and practices from man to man is because he finds in experience that things are far more welcome and agreeable to the common nature of mankind, which are taught by men like unto themselves, than if the devil should personally deliver the same to each man in special. Hereupon, he takes the course at first to instruct some few only, who, being taught by him, are apt to convey that which they know to others. And hence in probability this devilish trade had its first original and continuance.

Section 2

In the second place, I call it *a wicked art*, to distinguish it from all good and lawful arts, taught in schools of learning, which as they are warrantable by the Word of God, so are they no less profitable and necessary in the church. Again, to show the nature and quality of it, that it is a most ungracious and wicked art, as appears by the Scriptures. For when Saul had broken the express commandment of God in sparing Agag and the best things, Samuel tells him that rebellion and disobedience is as the sin of witchcraft, that is, a most horrible and grievous crime, like unto that wicked, capital, and mother sin (1 Sam. 15:23).

Section 3

Third, I add, *tending to the working or producing of wonders*, wherein is noted the proper end of this art, whereby I put a further difference between it and others that are godly and lawful.

Now if [the] question is moved, why man should desire by witchcraft to work wonders? I answer, the true and proper cause is this: the first temptation, whereby the devil prevailed against our first parents, had enclosed within it many sins. For the eating of the forbidden fruit was no small or single offence, but, as some have taught, contained in it the breach of every commandment of the moral law. Among the rest, Satan labored to bring them to the sin of discontentment whereby they sought to become as gods, that is, better than God had made them, not resting content with the condition of men. This sin was then learned, and could never since be forgotten, but continually is derived from them to all their posterity, and now is become so common a corruption in the whole nature of flesh and blood that there is scarce a man to be found who is not originally tainted therewith as he is a man.

This corruption shows itself principally in two things, both of which are the main causes of the practices of witchcraft.

First, in man's outward estate. For being naturally possessed with a love of himself and a high conceit of his own deserving, when he lives in a base and low estate whether in regard of poverty or want of honor and reputation, which he thinks by right is due unto him, he then grows to some measure of grief and sorrow within himself. Hereupon, he is moved to yield himself to the devil to be his vassal and scholar in this wicked art, supposing that by the working of some wonders he may be able in time to relieve his poverty and to purchase to himself credit and countenance among men.

It is easy to show the truth of this by examples of some persons who by these means have risen from nothing to great places and preferments in the world. Above all, it appears in certain popes of Rome (as Sylvester II, Benedict VIII, Alexander VI, John XX, John XXI, etc.), who for the attaining of the popedom (as histories record) gave themselves to the devil in the practice of witchcraft, that by the working of wonders they might rise from one step of honor to another, until they had seated themselves in the chair of the papacy.[1] So great was their desire of eminency in the church that it caused them to dislike meaner conditions of life, and never to cease aspiring, though they incurred thereby the hazard of good conscience, and the loss of their souls.

---

1. In the margin: Platina de vit. Pont. in vita Silv. 1. Baleus in Act. Rom. Pont. lib. 5 and lib. 6.

The second degree of discontentment is in the mind and inward man, and that is curiosity,[2] when a man rests not satisfied with the measure of inward gifts received, as of knowledge, wit, understanding, memory, and such like, but aspires to search out such things as God would have kept secret. And hence he is moved to attempt the cursed art of magic and witchcraft as a way to get further knowledge in matters secret and not revealed, that by working of wonders he may purchase fame in the world, and consequently reap more benefit by such unlawful courses than in likelihood he could have done by ordinary and lawful means.

Section 4

Fourth, it is affirmed in the description that witchcraft is practiced *by the assistance of the devil*, yet the more fully to distinguish it from all good, lawful, and commendable arts. For in them experience teaches that the arts-master is able by himself to practice his art, and to do things belonging thereunto, without the help of another. But in this it is otherwise. For here the work is done by the help of another, namely, the devil, who is confederate with the witch. The power of effecting such strange works is not in the art, neither does it flow from the skill of the sorcerer, man or woman, but is derived wholly from Satan, and is brought into execution by virtue of mutual confederacy, between him and the magician.

Now that this part of the description may be more clearly manifested, we are to proceed to a further point, to show what kind of wonders they are which are ordinarily wrought by the ministry and power of the devil. Wonders, therefore, are of two sorts: either true and plain, or lying and deceitful.

Section 5

A true wonder is a rare work, done by the power of God simply, either above or against the power of nature, and it is properly called a *miracle*. The Scripture is plentiful in examples of this kind. Of this sort was the dividing of the Red Sea and making it dry land by a mighty east wind, that the children of Israel might pass through it (Exod. 14:21). For though the east wind is naturally of great force to move the waters and to dry the earth, yet to part the sea asunder, and to make the waters to stand as walls on each side, and the bottom of the sea as a pavement, this is a work simply above the natural power of any wind, and therefore is a miracle. Again, such were the wonders done by Moses and Aaron before Pharaoh in Egypt, one whereof, in [the] stead of many, was the turning of Aaron's rod into a serpent, a work truly miraculous. For it is above

---

2. In the margin: August. confess. l. 10, c. 35.

the power of natural generation that the substance of one creature should be really turned into the substance of another, as the substance of a rod into the substance of a serpent. Of the like kind were the standing of the sun in the firmament without moving in its course for a whole day (Josh. 10:13), the going back of the sun in the firmament ten degrees (2 Kings 20:11), the preservation of the three men, Shadrach, Meshach, and Abednego, in the midst of the hot, fiery furnace (Dan. 3:25), and of Daniel in the lions' den (Dan. 6:22), the feeding of five thousand men, beside women and children, with five loaves and two fishes (Matt. 14:20–21), the curing of the eyes of the blind man with spittle and clay tempered together (John 9:6–7), etc.

Now the effecting of a miracle in this kind is a work proper to God only. And no creature (man or angel) can do anything either above or contrary to nature, but He alone who is the Creator. For as God in the beginning made all things of nothing, so He has reserved to Himself, as a peculiar work of His almighty power, to change or abolish the substance, property, motion, and use of any creature. The reason is, because He is the Author and Creator of nature, and therefore at His pleasure, [He] is perfectly able to command, restrain, enlarge, or extend the power and strength thereof without the help or assistance of the creature.

Again, the working of a miracle is a kind of creation, for therein a thing is made to be, which was not before. And this must needs be proper to God alone by whose power things that are were once produced out of things that did not appear. The conclusion therefore must needs be this, which David confesses, "God only doth wondrous things" (Ps. 136:4), that is, works simply wonderful.

But it is alleged to the contrary that the prophets in the Old Testament, and the apostles in the New, did work miracles. I answer, they did so. But how? Not by their own power, but by the power of God, being only His instruments, whom He used for some special purpose in those works, and such as did not themselves cause the miracle, but God in and by them. The same do Peter and John acknowledge when they had restored the lame man to the perfect use of his limbs: "that by their power and godliness, they had not made the man to go" (Acts 3:12).

Again, it is objected that our Savior Christ in His manhood wrought many miracles, as those before mentioned, and many more. *Answer.* Christ, as He was man, did something in the working of miracles, but not all. For in every miraculous work there are two things: the work itself and the acting or dispensing of the work. The work itself, being by nature and substance miraculous, considering it was above or against the order of natural causes, did not proceed from Christ as man, but from Him as God. But the dispensation of the same, in this or that visible manner, to the view of men, was done and performed by

His manhood. For example, the raising up of Lazarus out of the grave, having been dead four days, was a miracle. To the effecting whereof both the Godhead and the manhood of Christ concurred by their several and distinct actions. The manhood only uttered the voice, and bid Lazarus come forth, but it was the Godhead of Christ that fetched his soul from heaven, and put it again into his body, yea, which gave life and power to Lazarus to hear the voice uttered, to rise and come forth (John 11:43). In like manner, when He gave sight to the blind (Matt. 20:34), He touched their eyes with the hands of His manhood, but the power of opening them, and making them to see, came from His Godhead, whereby He was able to do all things. And in all other miraculous works which He did, the miracle was always wrought by His divine power only. The outward actions and circumstances that accompanied the same proceeded from Him as He was man.

Now, if Christ, as He is man, cannot work a true miracle, then no mere creature can do it, no not the angels themselves, and consequently not Satan, it being a mere supernatural work, performed only by the omnipotent power of God.

Section 6

The second sort of wonders are lying and deceitful, which also are extraordinary works in regard of man, because they proceed not from the usual and ordinary course of nature. And yet, they are not miracles, because they are done by the virtue of nature, and not above or against nature simply, but above and against the ordinary course thereof. And these are properly such wonders as are done by Satan and his instruments, examples whereof we shall see afterwards.

If any man in reason thinks it unlikely that a creature should be able to work extraordinarily by natural means, he must remember that though God has reserved to Himself alone the power of abolishing and changing nature, the order whereof He set and established in the creation, yet the alteration of the ordinary course of nature He has put in the power of His strongest creatures (angels and devils). That the angels have received this power and do execute the same upon His command or permission, is manifest by Scripture, and the proof of it is not so necessary in this place. But that Satan is able to do extraordinary works by the help of nature (which is the question in hand) shall appear if we consider in him these things:

First, the devil is by nature a spirit and, therefore, of great understanding, knowledge, and capacity, in all natural things of whatsoever sort, quality, and condition, whether they are causes or effects, whether of a simple or mixed nature. By reason whereof he can search more deeply and narrowly into the grounds of things than all corporal creatures that are clothed with flesh and blood.

Second, he is an ancient spirit, whose skill has been confirmed by experience of the course of nature for the space almost of six thousand years. Hence, he has attained to the knowledge of many secrets, and by long observation of the effects is able to discern and judge of hidden causes in nature, which man in likelihood cannot come unto by ordinary means, for want of that opportunity both of understanding and experience. Hereupon it is that whereas in nature there are some properties, causes, and effects, which man never imagined to be; some that men did once know, but are now forgot[ten]; some that men knew not, but might know; and thousands which can hardly (or not at all) be known. All these are most familiar unto him because in themselves they are no wonders, but only mysteries and secrets, the virtue and effect whereof he has at times observed since his creation.

Third, he is a spirit of wonderful power and might, able to shake the earth, and to confound the creatures inferior to him in nature and condition, if he were not restrained by the omnipotent power of God. And this power, as it was great by his creation, so it is not impaired by his fall, but rather increased and made more forcible by his irreconcilable malice, [which] he bears to mankind, especially the seed of the woman.

Fourth, there is in the devil an admirable quickness and agility, proceeding from his spiritual nature, whereby he can very speedily and in short space of time convey himself and other creatures into places far distant from one another.

By these four helps, Satan is enabled to do strange works. Strange, I say, to man whose knowledge since the fall is mingled with much ignorance, even in natural things; whose experience is of short continuance, and much hindered by forgetfulness; whose agility by reason of his gross nature is nothing, if he had not the help of other creatures; [and] whose power is but weakness and infirmity in comparison of Satan's.

Yet if there is any further doubt [as to] how Satan can by these helps work wonders, we may be resolved of the truth thereof by considering three other things: First, that by reason of his great knowledge and skill in nature he is able to apply creature to creature, and the causes efficient to the matter, and thereby bring things to pass that are in common conceit impossible.

Second, he has power to move them, not only according to the ordinary course, but with much more speed and celerity.

Third, as he can apply and move, so by his spiritual nature he is able, if God permits, to convey himself into the substance of the creature, without any penetration of dimensions. And, being in the creature, although it is ever so solid, he can work therein, not only according to the principles of the nature thereof, but as far as the strength and ability of those principles will possibly reach and extend themselves. Thus, it appears that the devil can in general work wonders.

Section 7
Now more particularly, the devil's wonders are of two sorts: illusions or real actions.[3]

Point 1
An illusion is a work of Satan whereby he deludes or deceives man. And it is twofold: either of the outward senses or of the mind. An illusion of the outward senses is a work of the devil whereby he makes a man to think that he hears, sees, feels, or touches such things as indeed he does not.[4] The devil can easily do this [in] divers ways, even by the strength of nature; for example, by corrupting the instruments of senses (as the humor of the eye, etc.), or by altering and changing the air which is the means whereby we see, and such like.

Experience teaches us that the devil is a skillful practitioner in this kind, though the means whereby he works such feats are unknown to us. In this manner Paul affirms that the Galatians were deluded, when he says, "O foolish Galatians, who hath bewitched you?" (Gal. 3:1). Here he uses a word[5] borrowed from the practice of witches and sorcerers who cast a mist (as it were) before the eyes, to dazzle them, and make things to appear unto them which indeed they do not see. And the ground of Paul's comparison is that which he takes for a granted truth, that there are such delusions whereby men's senses are and may be corrupted by satanical operation.

Thus, again, the devil by the witch of Endor deceived Saul in the appearance of Samuel (1 Samuel 28), making him believe that it had been Samuel indeed, whereas it was but a mere counterfeit of him, as shall appear hereafter. Again, the devil, knowing the constitutions of men, and the particular diseases whereunto they are inclined, takes the advantage of some, and seconds the nature of the disease by the concurrence of his own delusion, thereby corrupting the imagination and working in the mind a strong persuasion that they are become that which in truth they are not. This is apparent in that disease which is termed *lycanthropia*,[6] where some, having their brains possessed and distempered with melancholy, have verily thought themselves to be wolves, and so behaved themselves. And the histories of men in former ages have recorded strange testimonies of some who have been thus turned into wolves, lions,

---

3. This paragraph break is not in the original.
4. In the margin: Aug. de Civ. Dei. l. 18. c. 18.
5. In the margin: ἐβάσκανεν.
6. *Lycanthropia* is a compound term: *lykos* (wolf) and *anthropos* (human), hence werewolf.

dogs, birds, and other creatures, which could not be really in substance, but only in appearance, and fantasy corrupted, and so these records are true. For God in His just judgment may suffer some men so to be bewitched by the devil that to their conceit they may seem to be like these brute beasts, though indeed they remain true men still. For it is a work surmounting the devil's power to change the substance of any one creature into the substance of another.[7]

By this kind of delusion, the Church of Rome in the times of blindness and ignorance has taken great advantage and much increased her riches and honor. For there are three points of the religion of that church (to wit, purgatory, invocation of saints, and honoring of relics) whereby she has notably enriched herself. All these had their first foundation from these and such like satanical impostures. For the only way they have brought the common sort to yield unto them, both for belief and practice, has been by deluding their outward senses with false apparitions of ghosts and souls of men, walking and ranging abroad after their departure, and such like. Whereby simple persons, ignorant of their fetches and delusions, have been much affrighted, and caused through extremity of fear and dread to purchase their own peace and security by many and great expenses. And indeed, these were the strongest arguments that ever they had, and which most prevailed with the common people, as is manifest in stories of all nations and ages, where such deceits have taken place, though oftentimes by the just judgment of God they were taken in their craft and their feats revealed.

The second kind of illusion is of the mind, whereby the devil deceives the mind, and makes a man think that of himself which is not true. Thus, experience teaches that he has deluded men, both in former and later times, who have avouched and professed themselves to be kings or the sons of kings. Yea, some have held themselves to be Christ, some to be Elias, some to be John the Baptist, and some [to be] extraordinary prophets. And the like conceits have entered into the minds of sundry witches by the suggestion and persuasion of the devil. When they have wholly resigned their souls and bodies to him, they have been moved to believe things impossible touching themselves, as that they have indeed been changed into other creatures, as cats, birds, mice, etc. The inquisitions of Spain and other countries, wherein these and such like things are recorded touching witches really metamorphosed into such creatures, cannot be true, considering that it is not in the power of the devil thus to change substances into other substances. And those conversions recorded by them were only Satan's illusions, wherewith the minds of witches were possessed,

---

7. This paragraph break is not in the original.

and nothing else. Though they were extraordinary (as the rest of this kind are), yet they went not beyond the power of nature.

Point 2

The second sort of the devil's wonders are real works, that is, such as are indeed that which they seem and appear to be. These, howsoever to men who know not the natures of things, nor the secret and hidden causes thereof, they may seem very strange and admirable, yet they are no true miracles, because they are not above and beyond the power of nature.

If it is here alleged that the devil's works are not real and true actions because the Holy Spirit calls them "lying wonders" (2 Thess. 2:9), I answer that they are called "lying wonders," not in respect of the works themselves, for they were works truly done and effected, but in regard of the devil's end and purpose in working them, which is to lie unto men, and by them to deceive. The truth of which point will appear in the view of some particular examples.

Example 1. We read in the history of Job that Satan brought down fire from heaven, which burned up Job's sheep and servants, and [he] caused a mighty wind to blow down the house upon his children, as they were feasting, to destroy them (Job 1:16–19). Again, he smote the body of Job with botches and boils. All these were true and real works, very strange and admirable, and yet [they were] not miracles because they exceeded not the compass of nature. First, when he cast down the fire from heaven, he did not create the fire from nothing (for that is a work proper to God alone), but applied creature to creature, and thereof produced such a matter as was fit to make fire of. If it is demanded, how is he able to do this? We must remember that his knowledge in natural causes is great and, therefore, he was not ignorant of the material cause of fire, which being thoroughly known and found out, Satan brought fire unto it, and so putting fire to the matter of fire, he brought it down by his power and agility from heaven upon the cattle and servants of Job.[8]

Second, the wind which blew down the house, where his sons and daughters were eating and drinking, was not created by the devil, but he, knowing well the matter whereof winds are generated naturally, added matter to matter, and thence came the wind. Whereunto he joins himself, being a spirit of a swift and speedy nature, and so makes it, for his own purpose, the more violent and forcible. Third, he smote Job's body with sore boils from the crown of his head to the sole of his foot. Now this may seem strange that he should have such power over man's body as to cause such diseases to breed in it. Therefore, we

---

8. This paragraph break is not in the original.

are further to understand that his knowledge extends itself to the whole frame and disposition of man's body, whereby it comes to pass that the causes of all diseases are well known unto him, and he is not ignorant how the humors in the body may be putrefied, and what corrupt humors will breed such and such diseases, and by what means the air itself may be infected. Hereupon preparing his matter and applying cause to cause, he practiced upon the body of Job, and filled him with grievous sores.

Example 2. Another example of Satan's real works is this: By reason of his great power and skill, he is able to appear in the form and shape of a man, and resemble any person or creature, and that not by deluding the senses, but by assuming to himself a true body. His power is not so large as to create a body or bring again a soul into a body, yet by his dexterity and skill in natural causes he can work wonderfully. For he is able, having gathered together fit matter, to join member to member, and to make a true body, either after the likeness of a man or some other creature. And, having done so, [he is able] to enter into it, to move and stir it up and down, and therein visibly and sensibly to appear unto man. Though it is a strange work, and besides the ordinary course of nature, yet it is not simply above the power thereof.

Example 3. The devil is able to utter a voice in plain words and speech, answerable to man's understanding in any language. Not that he can take unto himself, being a spirit, an immediate power to speak or frame a voice from nothing without means, but, knowing the natural and proper causes and means by which men do speak, he frames by them in himself the voice of a man, and plainly utters the same in a known language. In this manner he abused the tongue and mouth of the serpent, when in plain words he tempted Eve to eat the forbidden fruit. Now it is to be remembered here that when the devil speaks in a creature, it must be such a creature as has the instruments of speech, or such whereby speech may be framed and uttered, not otherwise. For it was never heard that he spoke in a stock or a stone, or any created entity, that had not the means and power of uttering a voice, at least in some form. It is a work peculiar to the Creator to give power of utterance where it is not by creation. Again, when he frames a voice in a creature, he does it not by giving immediate power to speak, for that he cannot do, and the creature abused by him remains in that regard as it was before. But being naturally fitted and disposed to utter a voice, though not perfectly to speak as a man, he furthers and helps nature in it, and adds to the faculty thereof a present use of words, by ordering and ruling the instruments to his intended purposes. And to conclude this point, look [at] what strange works and wonders may be truly effected by the power of nature (though they are not ordinarily brought to pass in the course of nature). The devil can do those, and so far forth as the power of nature will permit, he is able to work true wonders, though for a false and evil end.

Here a question is moved by some: whether the devil can change one creature into another, as a man or woman into a beast? For some, notwithstanding the doctrine already taught, are of [the] opinion that he can turn the bodies of witches into other creatures, as hares, cats, and such like. *Answer.* The transmutation of the substance of one creature into another, as of a man into a beast of whatever kind, is a work simply above the power of nature, and therefore cannot be done by the devil or any creature. For it is the proper work of God alone (as I have said) to create, change, or abolish nature.

It is objected that such changes have been made, for Lot's wife was turned into a pillar of salt (Gen. 19:26). *Answer.* It is true, but that was done by the mighty power of God. Neither can it be proved that any creature, angel, or other, was ever able to do the like.

But it is further said that king Nebuchadnezzar was turned into a beast, and [he] did eat grass with the beasts of the field (Dan. 4:32). *Answer.* There is no such matter. His substance was not changed so as his body became the body of a beast indeed, but his conditions only were altered by the judgment of God upon his mind, whereby he was so far forth bereaved of human sense and understanding. Again, for his behavior and kind of life, he became altogether brutish for the time, and excepting only his outward form and shape, no part of humanity could appear in him. But that he still retained his human body is evident by his own words, when he says, "And mine understanding was restored to me" (v. 36). This argues plainly that the hand of God was upon him in some kind of madness and fury, and therefore that there was not a change of his body and substance, but a strange and fearful alteration in his mind and outward behavior. And though such a transmutation should be granted, yet it makes nothing for the purpose, considering it was the work of God only, and not of the devil.

And thus, we see what kind of wonders the devil can bring to pass. The meditation of which point may teach us two things.

First, that the working of wonders is not a thing that will commend man unto God, for the devil himself, a wicked spirit, can work them. And many shall allege this in the day of judgment that they have by the name of God cast out devils and done many great works, to whom notwithstanding the Lord will say, "I never knew you, depart from me ye workers of iniquity" (Matt. 7:22–23). It behooves us to get unto ourselves the precious gifts of faith, repentance, and the fear of God, yea, to go before others in a godly life and upright conversation, rather than to excel in [the] effecting of strange works. When the seventy disciples came to our Savior Christ with joy, and told Him that "even the devils were subdued unto them through his name," He counsels them not to rejoice in this, that wicked spirits were subdued unto them, but rather because their names were written in heaven (Luke 10:17, 20).

Indeed, to be able to work a wonder is an excellent gift of God and may minister matter for rejoicing when it proceeds from God. But, seeing the devil received this power by the gift of creation, our special joy must not be therein, but rather in this, that we are the adopted sons of God, in which privilege the devil has no part with us. And, therefore, the apostle, making a comparison of the gifts of the Spirit (as of speaking divers tongues, prophesying, and working miracles) with love, in the end wishes men to labor for the best gifts which are faith, hope, and love (1 Corinthians 13), because by these we are made partakers of Christ, on whom we ought to set our hearts, and in whom we are commanded always to rejoice (Phil. 4:4).

Second, we learn from hence not to believe or receive a doctrine now or at any time because it is confirmed by wonders. For the devil himself is able to confirm his errors and idolatrous services by strange and extraordinary signs, by which he usually labors to avouch and verify the grossest points of falsehood in matter of religion. On the contrary, we must not reject or condemn a doctrine because it is not thus confirmed. This was a main fault in the Jews, who would not receive the word preached by Christ, unless He showed them a sign from heaven. Indeed, in the primitive church it pleased God to confirm that doctrine which the apostles taught, by great signs and miracles, but now that gift is ceased, and the church has no warrant to expect any further evidence of the religion it professes and enjoys by arguments of that kind; yea, rather, it has cause to suspect a doctrine taught for the wonders' sake whereby men labor to avouch it.

Section 8

The last clause in the description is this: *so far forth as God in justice suffers*. I add it for two causes.[9]

Cause 1

First, to show that God, for just causes, permits the arts of magic and witchcraft, and the practices thereof.[10] Now this He does in His providence, either for the trial of His children or for the punishment of the wicked.

---

9. This paragraph break is not in the original.
10. In the margin: August. de Trin. l. 3, c. 7.

First, God permits these wicked arts in the church to prove whether His children will steadfastly believe in Him and seek unto His Word or cleave unto the devil by seeking to his wicked instruments. Moses plainly forewarned the church of God of this in his time: "If there arise among you a prophet, or a dreamer of dreams, and give thee a sign or wonder, and the sign and wonder which he hath told thee, come to pass, saying, 'Let us go after other gods, which thou hast not known, and serve them,' thou shalt not hearken to the words of that prophet" (Deut. 13:1–3).

Second, God suffers them for the punishment of unbelievers and wicked men. For oftentimes God punishes one sin by another, as the antecedent sins by the consequent. Paul plainly shows this (speaking of the days of antichrist): that "because men received not the love of the truth, therefore God would send upon them strong illusions, that they should believe lies" (2 Thess. 2:10–11). And we may resolve ourselves that for this very cause God suffers the practices of witchcraft to be so rife in our days, to punish the ingratitude of men who have the truth revealed unto them, and yet will not believe and obey the same, but tread it under their feet, "that all they might be condemned which believed not the truth, but took pleasure in unrighteousness" (v. 12).

Cause 2

Second, this last clause is added to show that in the practices of sorcery and witchcraft, the devil can do only as much as God permits him, and no more. Doubtless, his malice reaches further, and consequently his will and desire. But God has restrained his power in the execution of his malicious purposes, whereupon he cannot go a whit further than God gives him leave and liberty to go. The magicians of Egypt did some wonders in show like unto the miracles wrought by Moses and Aaron, and that for a time, by changing a rod into a serpent and water into blood, and by bringing frogs through the sleight and power of the devil (Exodus 7–8). But when it pleased God to determine their practices, and give them no further liberty, they could not do that which in likelihood was the meanest of all the rest, the turning of the dust of the land into lice. And [they] themselves gave the true reason thereof, saying, "That this was the finger of God" (Exod. 8:19). When the devil went out and became a false spirit in the mouth of all Ahab's prophets, to entice him to go to fall at Ramoth Gilead, he went not of his own will, but by the authority of God, who commanded him to go to entice Ahab, and suffered him to prevail (1 Kings 22:22). And the act was not the act of Satan, but of God, whose instrument he was. And, therefore, the Holy Spirit says by Micaiah: "The Lord hath put a lying spirit in the mouth of all these thy prophets, and the Lord hath appointed evil against thee" (v. 23). Hence also it was that the devils, being cast out of the man who had an unclean spirit, asked leave of Christ to enter into the herd of swine, and could not enter till He had permitted them (Mark 5:12–13). And we read oftentimes in the Gospels that our Savior cast out many devils by His word only, thereby showing that He was absolute Lord over them and that without His permission they could do nothing.

And thus much touching the general nature of this art.

Chapter 2

The Ground of All the Practices of Witchcraft

The ground of all the practices of witchcraft is a league or covenant made between the witch and the devil, wherein they do mutually bind themselves to each other. If any shall think it strange that man or woman should enter [a] league with Satan (their utter enemy), they are to know it for a most evident and certain truth that may not be called into question. And yet, to clear the judgment of anyone in this point, I will set down some reasons in way of proof.

First, the Holy Scripture does intimate so much unto us in Psalm 58:5, where (howsoever the common translation runs in other terms), the words are properly to be read thus: "which heareth not the voices of the murderer joining societies cunningly." And in them the psalmist lays down two points. First, the effect or work of a charm, muttered by the enchanter: that it is able to stay the adder from stinging those who shall lay hold on him or touch him. Second, the main foundation of the charm: societies or confederacies cunningly made, not between man and man, but (as the words import) between the enchanter and the devil. The like we read in Deuteronomy 18:11, where the Lord charges His people when they come into the land of Canaan, that among other abominations of the heathen they should beware lest any were found among them who joined society (that is, entered into league and compact) with wicked spirits.

Second, it is the practice of the devil to offer to make a bargain and covenant with man. He dealt thus with our Savior Christ in the third temptation wherewith he assaulted Him, promising to give unto Him all the kingdoms of the earth and their glory (which he showed Him in a vision) if Christ for His part would fall down and worship him (Matt. 4:9). The offer was passed on the behalf of Satan, and now to make a perfect compact between them there was nothing wanting but the free consent of our Savior unto the condition propounded. Whereby it is manifest that the devil makes many covenants in the world, because he finds men and women, in the most places, fitted for his turn in this kind, who will not let to worship him for a far less matter than a kingdom. And it is not to be doubted that thousands in the world, had they been offered so fair [a kingdom] as Christ was, would have been as willing to have yielded upon such conditions as the devil to have offered.

Third, the common confession of all witches and sorcerers, both before and since the coming of Christ, does yet more fully confirm the same. For they have confessed with one consent that the very groundwork of all their practices in this wicked art is their league with the devil. And hence it appears how and whereupon it is that sorcerers and witches can bring to pass strange things by the help of Satan, which other men ordinarily cannot do; namely, because they have entered a league with him, whereby he has bound himself to them for the effecting of rare and extraordinary works, which others, not joined with him in the like confederacy, are not able either by his help or any power or policy of their own to bring to pass. Hereupon it was that the witch of Endor showed unto Saul the appearance of Samuel, which neither Saul himself nor any in all his court could do. There was no great virtue in the matter or frame of her words, for she was ignorant and had no learning. By power she could not effect it, being a weak woman. Neither was it likely that she had more cunning and policy than any of the learned Jews in those times had for such purposes. The main reason was her league made with Satan, by virtue whereof she commanded him to appear in the likeness of Samuel, which neither Saul nor any of his company could do by virtue of such covenant which they had not made.

The end why the devil seeks to make a league with men may be this: it is a point of his policy not to be ready at every man's command to do for him what he would except he is sure of his reward, and no other means will serve his turn for taking assurance hereof but this covenant. And why so? That hereby he may testify both his hatred of God and his malice against man. For since the time that he was cast down from heaven, he has hated God and His kingdom, and greatly maligned the happy estate of man, especially since the covenant of grace made with our first parents in Paradise. For he thought to have brought upon them by their fall eternal and final confusion, but perceiving the contrary by virtue of the covenant of grace then manifested, and seeing man by it to be in a better and surer estate than before, he much more maligned his estate, and bears the ranker hatred unto God for His mercy bestowed upon him.

Now that he might show forth this hatred and malice, he takes upon him to imitate God and to counterfeit His dealings with His church. As God, therefore, has made a covenant with His people, so Satan joins in league with the world, laboring to bind some men unto him, so that (if it were possible) he might draw them from the covenant of God and disgrace the same. Again, as God has His Word and sacraments, the seals of His covenant unto believers, so the devil has his words and certain outward signs to ratify the same to his instruments, as namely, his figures, characters, gestures, and other satanical ceremonies, for the confirmation of the truth of his league unto them. Yea, further, as God in His covenant requires faith from us to the believing of His promises, so the devil in his compact requires faith from his vassals to put their affiance in him and rely on him for the doing of whatsoever he binds himself to do. Lastly, as God hears them who call upon Him according to His will, so is Satan ready at hand upon the premises, endeavoring to the utmost of his power (when God permits him), to bring to pass whatsoever he has promised.

And so much of the league in general. More particularly, the league between the devil and a witch is (1) expressed and open, or (2) secret and close.

Open League

The express and manifest compact is so termed because it is made by solemn words on both parties. And it is not so expressly set down in Scriptures as in the writings of learned men, who have recorded the confessions of witches. And they express it in this manner: First, the witch for his part, as a slave of the devil, binds himself unto him by solemn vow and promise to renounce the true God, His holy Word, the covenant he made in baptism, and his redemption by Christ, and withal to believe in the devil, to expect and receive aid and help from him, and at the end of his life to give him either body or soul or both. And for the ratifying hereof, he gives to the devil for the present either his own handwriting or some part of his blood as a pledge and earnest penny to bind the bargain. The devil, on the other side, for his part promises to be ready at his vassal's command, to appear at any time in the likeness of any creature, to consult with him, to aid and help him in anything he shall take in hand for the procuring of pleasures, honor, wealth, or preferment to go for him, to carry him whither he will; in a word, to do for him whatsoever he shall command. Many sufficient testimonies might be alleged for the proof hereof, but it is so manifest in daily experience that it cannot well be called into question.

But yet, if it seems strange unto any that there should be such persons in the world, who make such fearful covenants with the devil, let them consider but this one thing, and it will put them out of doubt. The nature of man is exceeding impatient in crosses, and outward afflictions are so tedious unto mortal minds, and press them with such a measure of grief, that some could be contented with all their hearts to be out of the world if thereby they might be released of such extremity. And hereupon they care not what means they use, what conditions they undertake, to ease and help themselves. The devil, finding men in these perplexities, is ready to take his advantage. And, therefore, perceiving them now fitted for his purpose to work upon, he insinuates and offers himself to procure them ease and deliverance if they will use such means as he shall prescribe for that purpose. And to a natural man there is no greater means than this to make him join society with the devil. He, therefore, without any further doubting or deliberation, condescends to Satan so as he may be eased and relieved in these miseries.

Again, we are to consider that in these cases the devil gets the greater hold of man, and moves him to yield unto his suggestions the rather, because that which he promises to do for him is present and at his command and, therefore, certain; whereas the thing to be performed on the behalf of the party himself, as the giving of body and soul, etc., is to come sundry years after, and, therefore, in regard of the particular time, uncertain. Now the natural man, not regarding his future and final estate, prefers the present commodity before the loss and punishment that is to come afar off, and thereby is persuaded to yield himself unto Satan. And by these and such like antecedents are many brought to make open league with the devil.

Secret League

The secret and close league between the witch and Satan is that wherein they mutually give consent each to other, but yet without a sworn covenant conceived in express words and conference. Of this there are two degrees.

First, when a man uses superstitious forms of prayer wherein he expressly requires the help of the devil without any mention of solemn word or covenant going before. It is plain that this is a kind of compact, because herein there is a mutual under-hand consent between the party and the devil, though it is not manifest. For when a man is content to use superstitious forms of invocation for help in time of need, by the very using of them his heart consents to Satan, and he would gladly have the thing effected. When, therefore, the devil has notice of them, and endeavors to effect the thing prayed for, therein also he gives consent, so as, though there are no express words of compact outwardly framed on both parts, yet the concurrence of a mutual consent for the bringing to pass of the same things makes the covenant authentic. For according to the received rules of equity and reason, mutual consent of party with party is sufficient to make a bargain, though there is no solemn course or form of words to manifest the same to others.

The second degree is when a man uses superstitious means to bring anything to pass, which in his own knowledge have no such virtue in themselves to effect it without the special operation of the devil.

Superstitious means I call all those which, neither by order of creation nor by the special appointment and blessing of God since, have any virtue in them to bring to pass that thing for which they are used. For example, a charm, consisting of set words and syllables (rude, barbarous, and unknown), used for the curing of some disease or pain, is a superstitious means, because it has no virtue in itself to cure, either by the gift of God in the creation or by any special appointment afterward in His Word, or otherwise. And, therefore, when this means is used by man, which he knows has no such virtue in it, for the effecting of that work for which it was used, there is a secret league made with the devil.

Yet, here I add this clause, *in his own knowledge*, to put a difference between men who use superstitious means to bring some things to pass. For some there are who, when they use them, know they are merely superstitious, yea, weak and impotent, having no virtue in themselves for the purpose whereto they are used, as the repeating of [a] certain form of words, the using of signs, characters, and figures, which in effect are mere charms, no whit effectual in themselves, but so far forth as they serve for watchwords unto Satan without whose aid nothing is done by thcm, a plain argument that the user hereof has in his heart secretly indented with Satan for the accomplishment of his intended works. A second sort there is who uses them for some special end, being persuaded that there is virtue in the means themselves to bring the thing to pass, and yet not knowing that either they are superstitious or have their efficacy by the power and work of the devil. Such persons have made as yet no league with Satan, but they are in the highway thereunto. And this course is a fit preparation to cause them to join with him in covenant. I show it by an example. A man is fallen into some extremity and finds himself bewitched. His pain is great, and he desires with all his heart to be cured and delivered. Hereupon he sends for the suspected witch. Being come, he offers to scratch him or her, thinking by this means to be cured by the witchcraft.[1] His reason is no other than a strong persuasion that there is simply virtue in his scratching to cure him, and discover the witch, not once suspecting that the help comes by the power of the devil but from the action itself. This doing, he may be healed. But the truth is he sins and breaks God's commandment. For the using of these means is plain witchcraft, as afterward we shall see. And yet for all this, the party cannot be said in present to have made a league with Satan, because he thought that, though he yielded to the use of superstitious means for his curing, yet there had been in the said means a virtue of healing without any help or work of the devil.

---

1. In Perkins's day, drawing blood by means of scratching was a common practice. It was based on the belief that it was possible to find relief from physical affliction by scratching the witch who had caused it. If the affliction subsided after the act of scratching, it was confirmation of the witch's guilt.

Chapter 3

The Kinds of Witchcraft: Divination

Witchcraft is of two sorts: divining or working. For the whole nature of this art consists either in matter of divination and conjecture or in matter of practice. And in both these it is to be remembered that nothing can be effected unless the party has made a league with the devil, express or secret, or (at the least) a preparation thereunto by a false and erroneous opinion of the means.

Section 1

Divination is a part of witchcraft whereby men reveal strange things (past, present, or to come) by the assistance of the devil.

If it is here demanded how the devil, being a creature, should be able to manifest and bring to light things past or to foretell things to come, I answer, first generally, that Satan in this particular work transforms himself into an angel of light, and takes upon him the exercise of these things in an ambitious (though false) imitation of divine revelations and predictions, made and used by God in the times of the prophets and apostles. And this he does (as much as in him lies) to obscure the glory of God, and to make himself great in the opinion of ignorant and unbelieving persons. Again, though Satan is but a creature, there are sundry ways whereby he is able to divine.

First, by the Scriptures of the Old and New Testaments wherein are set down sundry prophecies concerning things to come. Many prophecies concerning the state of God's church are recorded in the Old Testament, from the first age of the world till the coming of Christ. Likewise, others are recorded in the New Testament, touching the same thing from the coming of Christ in the latter days to the end of the world. Now the devil, being acquainted with the history of the Bible, and having attained unto a greater light of knowledge in the prophecies contained therein than any man has, by stealing divinations out of them he is able to tell of many strange things that may in time fall out in the world, and answerably may show them ere they come to pass.

For example, Alexander the Great, before he made war with Darius king of Persia, consulted with the oracle (that is, with the devil), touching the event and issue of his enterprise. The oracle answered him thus: "Alexander shall be a conqueror."[1] Upon the prediction of the oracle, Alexander waged war with Darius and invaded Asia. And having conquered him, [he] translated the empire from Persia to Greece, according as the oracle had said. Now if question is made how the devil knew the event of this war and consequently made it known to Alexander? The answer is by the help of a prophecy in the Old Testament. For this thing was particularly set down beforehand by the prophet Daniel, where he says "that a mighty king shall stand up, and shall rule with great dominion, and do according to his pleasure" (Dan. 11:3).[2] And this was Alexander the Great. Satan, therefore, knowing the secret meaning of the angel's words unto Daniel, framed out of them a true and direct answer, whereas he was not able by himself to divine certainly of the event of things to come in particular.

The second means whereby the devil is furnished for his purpose is his own exquisite knowledge of all natural things, as of the influences of the stars, the constitutions of men and other creatures, the kinds, virtues, and operations of plants, roots, herbs, stones, etc. His knowledge of this goes many degrees beyond the skill of all men, yea, even of those who are most excellent in this kind, as philosophers and physicians. No marvel, therefore, that out of his experience in these and such like he is able afore-hand to give a likely guess at the issues and events of things which are to him so manifestly apparent in their causes.

A third help and furtherance in this point is his presence in most places. For some devils are present at all assemblies and meetings, and thereby are acquainted with the consultations and conferences both of princes and people; whereby, knowing the drift and purpose of men's minds, when the same is manifested in their speeches and deliberations, they are the fitter to foretell many things which men ordinarily cannot do. And hence it is apparent how witches may know what is done in other countries, and whether one nation intends war against another, namely, by Satan's suggestion, who was present at the consultation, and so knew it, and revealed it unto them. But how then comes it to pass that the consultations and actions of God's church and children are not disclosed to their enemies? Even by the unspeakable mercy and goodness of God, who though for special causes sometimes suffers Satan by this means to bring things to light, yet He has restrained his liberty, and subjected it unto His own will, so as He keeps him out of such meetings or compels him to conceal; whereas, otherwise, his malice is so great that not a word could be spoken but it should be carried abroad to the hurt and disturbance both of churches and commonwealths.

---

1. In the margin: Plutarch. in vita Alex.
2. In the margin: Chap. 8. potius.

The fourth way is by putting into men's minds wicked purposes and counsels. For after the league [is] once made, he labors with them by suggestions, and where God gives him leave, he never ceases persuading till he has brought his enterprise to pass. Having therefore first brought into the mind of man a resolution to do some evil, he goes and reveals it to the witch, and by force of persuasion upon the party tempted, he frames the action intended to the time foretold, and so finally deludes the witch (his own instrument), foretelling nothing but what [he] himself has compassed and set about.

The fifth help is the agility of Satan's nature whereby he is able speedily to convey himself from place to place, yea, to pass through the whole world in a short time. For God has made him by nature a spirit, who by the gift of his creation has attained the benefit of swiftness, not only in dispatching his affairs but also in the carriage of his person with great expedition for the present accomplishment of his own desires.

Lastly, God has often used Satan as His instrument for the effecting of His intended works and the executing of His judgments upon men. And in these cases [He] manifests unto him the place where, the time when, and the manner how, such a thing should be done. Now all such things as God will have effected by the devil, he may foretell before they come to pass because he knows them beforehand by revelation and assignment from God. Thus, by the witch of Endor he foretold to Saul the time of his death and of his sons, and the ruin of his kingdom, saying, "Tomorrow shalt thou and thy sons be with me, and the Lord shall give the host of Israel into the hands of the Philistines" [1 Sam. 28:19]. This particular event, and circumstances appertaining, he did truly define, not of himself, but because God had drawn away His good spirit from Saul and had delivered him to be guided by the devil, whom He also appointed as a means and used as an instrument to work his overthrow. The Scripture indeed makes not particular mention of the time of Saul's death. It only records the manner thereof, and that which followed upon his death, the translating of the kingdom to his neighbor David after him. And yet, because God used Satan as an instrument to bring this to pass, hereupon he was able to foretell the particular time when the will of God should be wrought upon him.

And these are the ordinary means and helps whereby the devil may know and declare strange things, whether past, present, or to come.

Neither may this seem strange that Satan by such means should attain unto such knowledge, for even men by their own observations may give probable conjectures of the state and condition of sundry things to come. Thus, we read that some by observation have found out probably, and foretold the periods of families and kingdoms; for example, that the time and continuance of kingdoms is ordinarily determined at five hundred years, or not much above; and that great families have not gone beyond the sixth and seventh generation. And as for special and private things, the world so runs (as it were) in a circle, that if a man should but ordinarily observe the course of things, either in the weather or in the bodies of men or otherwise, he might easily foretell beforehand what would come after. And by these and such like instances of experiences, men have guessed at the alterations and changes of estates and things in particular. Now if men, who are but of short continuance and of a shallow reach in comparison, are able to do such things, how much more easily may the devil, having so great a measure of knowledge and experience, and being of so long continuance, having also marked the course of all estates, be able to foretell many things which are to come to pass? Especially considering what the wise man has set down to this purpose: "that which hath been, shall be; and that which hath been done, shall be done; and there is no new thing under the sun" (Eccl. 1:9).

If it is here alleged that divination is a prerogative of God Himself and a part of His glory incommunicable to any creature (Isa. 41:23), I answer [that] things to come must be considered [in] two ways: either in themselves or in their causes and signs, which either go with them or before them. To foretell things to come, as they are in themselves, without respect unto their signs or causes, is a property belonging to God only, and the devil does it not by any direct and immediate knowledge of things simply considered in themselves, but only as they are present in their signs or causes. Again, God foretells things to come certainly without the help of any creature or other means out of Himself. But the predictions of Satan are only probable and conjectural. And when he foretells anything certainly, it is by some revelation from God (as the death of Saul) or by the Scripture (as Alexander's victory) or by some special charge committed unto him for the execution of God's will upon some particular places or persons, as before has been showed.

Thus much for the causes of divination. Now follow the parts and branches thereof. Divination is of two sorts: (1) by means, or (2) without means. Divination by means is likewise of two sorts: (1) by such as are the true creatures of God, or (2) by those which are merely counterfeit and forged.

Section 2

Divination by the true creatures of God is distinguished according to the number of creatures into five distinct kinds, whereof four are mentioned in the Scriptures.

Birds

The first is by the flying and noise of birds. Sorcerers among the heathen used to observe fowls in their flight; for example, whether they did fly on the right hand or on the left, above them or below them, whether cross and overthwart or directly against them. In like manner they observed the noise and sound of the fowl. And both these ways, sometimes by the noise and sometimes by the flight, they divined of things to come, both public and private, of good and bad success in man's affairs, of the state of kingdoms, towns, families, and particular persons. Now this kind of divination is condemned by Moses: "Let none be found among you that is a diviner of divinations (that is, as some interpret it, a marker of the flying of fowls), or a charmer, or a consulter with spirits, or a soothsayer" (Deut. 18:10–11); that is, such a one as takes upon himself to foretell good or bad success by observing the flying and noise of fowls.

Beasts

The second kind of creatures used for divination are the "entrails of beasts," of which mention is made in Ezekiel 21:21, where Nebuchadnezzar, being to make war both with the Jews and the Ammonites, and doubting in the way which enterprise to undertake first, he offers a sacrifice to the idol gods, and opening the belly of the sacrifice, looks upon the liver, and by the signs therein found he judges what should be the issue of the war. Nebuchadnezzar did this thing according to the usual practice of the heathen, who, when they were to make war or to attempt any business of importance, were wont to offer sacrifice to their gods, and to pry into the entrails of the beast sacrificed (for example, the heart, stomach, spleen, kidneys, but specially the liver), and by certain signs appearing in those parts, the devil was wont to reveal unto them what should be the success of their affairs they had in hand. It would be easy to exemplify both these sorts of divination by sundry particulars out of the heathen writers, but seeing the Scripture has manifested that there are such, and experience shows the same, I will forebear that labor, and proceed.

But here it is demanded, why should both [of] these kinds of divination be condemned in Scripture, considering they had so great applause among the heathen? I answer, because the flying of birds and the disposition of the inward parts of creatures are no true signs either of good or bad success. For that which is a true sign of a future event must have the virtue and power whereby it signifies from God Himself, either by creation in the beginning, or by His special ordinance and appointment afterward. Now it cannot be shown that God in the creation infused any such virtue into the natures and motions of these creatures whereby they might signify such things. Neither is there any apparent testimony in the whole book of the Scriptures whereby it may be proved that since the creation they were appointed by God to serve such uses and ends. And, therefore, howsoever they were esteemed of the heathen, yet the Word of

God has justly censured them as no true and proper causes of divination sanctified by God, but merely diabolical.

It is alleged that Joseph divined by his cup, as may appear both by his steward's speech as also by his own (Gen. 44:5, 15), and yet that cup received no power from God, either the one way or the other, to be a cause or mean of divination. The answer anciently and commonly made is this, that Joseph's steward spoke not as the thing was indeed, but as the common received opinion was among the Egyptians, who esteemed Joseph to be a man of great skill and wisdom, able by sundry means to divine and prophesy. To this I add a second answer, that the steward spoke not as he thought, but his purpose was in those words to conceal the knowledge of Joseph his master from his brethren, that thereby they might not discern who he was, but take him to be an Egyptian. Third, the words may not unfitly admit this interpretation, as if the steward had said, "Know you not that this cup which I find in the sack's mouth of your youngest brother is that whereby my master will easily prove what manner of men you are?" This answer is also ancient, and may well be received.

It is further objected that our Savior Christ by His speech unto the Pharisees seems to approve of divining by creatures (as by winds and cloud). "When you see a cloud rising out of the west, straight way you say, a shower cometh, and so it is: and when you see the south wind blow, ye say, that it will be hot, and it cometh to pass" (Luke 12:54–55). *Answer.* There are some kinds of predictions that are (and may be) lawfully used because they are natural, of which sort are those that are made by physicians, mariners, and husbandmen, touching the particular alterations and dispositions of the weather. And these, being agreeable to that order which God has set in nature from the beginning, by them a man may probably gather the state of the weather, whether it will be fair or foul. And of these natural signs our Savior Christ speaks, not of diabolical [signs], which have no warrant, either from the common course of nature created or by any special appointment from God. So that whatsoever can be said in their defense, this yet remains certain, that the flying and noise of birds, and the state of the entrails of beasts, are no true signs ordained by God, but invented by the devil and his instruments, and therefore all divination by them is justly condemned as wicked and devilish.

Whence it appears what judgment may be given by those common signs of divination, which are observed in the world, especially of the more ignorant sort. For example, a man finds a piece of iron, [and] he presently conceives a prediction of some good luck unto himself that day. If he lights on a piece of silver, then he stands contrarily affected, imagining some evil will befall him. Again, when a man is taking his journey, if a hare crosses him in the way, all is not well; his journey shall not be prosperous; it presages some mischief toward him. Let his ears tingle or burn, he is persuaded he has enemies abroad, and that some man either then does or presently will speak ill of him. If the salt fall toward a man at the table, it portends (in common conceit) some ill news. When a raven stands upon some high place, look what way he turns himself and cries—thence, as some think, shall shortly come a dead corpse. Albeit, this sometimes may be true by reason of the sharp sense of smelling in the raven. These and sundry other of the like sort are merely superstitious. For the truth is they have no virtue in themselves to foreshow anything that is to come, either in nature or by God's ordinance. Therefore, whatsoever divination is made by them must needs be fetched from satanical illusion. And though we cannot say they are soothsaying, or term the users and favorers of them soothsayers, yet we may safely refer them to this kind of divining, being such as no Christian may warrantably use, though some of them are not so gross and palpable as those that are condemned in the Scriptures.

Stars

The third kind of creatures used to divine by are the stars. Divination by stars is commonly called judicial astrology, of which we may read in Deuteronomy 18:10–11, where the Holy Spirit does of purpose reckon up all those kinds of devilish arts whereby men have dealings and society with Satan, either in divining or practicing, among which this is the second.

The word there used may carry a double sense,[3] for it signifies either him who observes times (under which acceptation astrology is comprehended), or him who observes the clouds. And howsoever the best learned interpreters do dissent about the notation of it, yet all agree in this, that this profession of divining by the stars is there condemned. And that it is to be numbered among the rest expressed in the prohibition may further appear by other places of Scripture, as in Isaiah 47:13–14, where the Lord threatens the same judgments against diviners by the stars that He doth against soothsayers and magicians. Again, in Daniel 2:2, enchanters, astrologers, and sorcerers are joined together, as being all sent for about the same business, namely, to expound the king's dream. Now if the Lord Himself has allotted the same punishment to the astrologer which He has to the soothsayer and magician, and accounts them all one, it is manifest that divining by the stars ought to be held as a superstitious kind of divination.

Here, if it is thought strange that predictions, by so excellent creatures as the stars are, should carry both the name and nature of diabolical practices,

---

3. In the margin: *Megnonen*.

which can be done by none but such as are in league with Satan, I answer, the reasons hereof are these:

Reason 1

First, it must be considered that the drift and scope of this art is to foretell the particular events of things contingent, as the alteration of the states of kingdoms, the deaths of princes, good or bad success of men's particular affairs from the hour of their birth to the day of their death. And from this all men may judge what the art itself is. For the foretelling of things to come, which in their own nature are contingent, and in regard of us casual (I say not in regard of God, to whom all things are certainly known), is a property peculiar to God alone, and not within the power of any creature, man, or angel, a point that is plainly taught by Isaiah in chapters 4 to 48 of his prophecy. The scope whereof is to prove that it is a prerogative appropriated to the Deity, and not communicable to the creature, to foreshow the events of things to come, which in our understanding and reach may either be or not be, and which when they are, may be thus or otherwise. It remains, therefore, that divinations of this kind, taking from God His right and robbing Him of His honor, are justly censured of impiety, and are in themselves wicked and abominable.

It is alleged that stars in the heavens are the causes of many things happening in the world, and therefore to practice by them in this manner deserves no such imputation. *Answer.* It cannot be denied that they are causes of some things, but I demand what causes? Not particular of particular events, but general and common, that work alike upon all things. And no man can divine of a particular event by a general cause, unless he also knows the particular causes subordinate to the general and the particular dispositions and operations of them. For example, let twenty or thirty eggs of sundry kinds of birds be taken, and set under one and the same hen to be hatched. It is not possible for any man, only upon the bare consideration of the heat of the hen, which is the general cause of hatching the eggs, to set down certainly what kind of bird each egg will bring forth, unless he knows what the eggs were particularly. For a general and common cause does not immediately produce a particular effect, but only moves and helps the particular, immediate, and subordinate causes. Therefore, the heat of the hen does not make one egg to send forth a chicken, another egg a duck, a third a swan, etc., but only helps it forward by sitting and crouching upon them. In like manner, the stars are general causes of natural things, as the heat of the hen is of the hatching of the eggs, and by them no man can rightly divine of particular events. And, therefore, divination by the stars, whereby are foretold particular contingent events in kingdoms, families, or particular persons, is but a forged skill, that has no ground in nature from the virtue of the stars for any such purpose.

Reason 2

A second reason is this: all the rules and precepts of astrology set down by the most learned among the Chaldeans, Egyptians, and other astrologers, are nothing else but mere dotages and fictions of the brain of man. For the rules and conclusions of all good and lawful arts have their ground in experience, and are framed by observation, whereupon they are called axioms (or positions of art), so generally and undoubtedly true that they cannot deceive. But these rules are of a contrary nature, having no foundation in experience at all. For if they had, this must needs follow, that the position of the heavens, and the course of all the stars, must needs continue one and the same. For the principles of art ought to be immutable. But neither the position of the heavens, nor the course of all the stars, is always one and the same. Again, he who would make sound rules of art by observation must know the particular estate of all things he observes, but no man knows the particular estate of all the stars, and consequently none can gather sound rules of art by them. Third, no man knows or sees all the stars, and though they might be all discerned, yet the particular virtues of those which are seen cannot be known because their influences in the air and upon the earth are confused. And, therefore, by observation of them no rules can be made whereby to judge of particular events to come that are contingent.

But experience teaches (some may say) that if a man addicted to this course shall practice the rules of astrology, it will fall out that the most things he foretells shall be true and come to pass accordingly, which being verified in experience it should seem that these principles are not uncertain. For how is it possible that upon false grounds should proceed true predictions? To this objection, learned divines have framed [an] answer thus: that in this there is a secret magic at the least, if not an open league with Satan. For look what is wanting to the effect of the stars, the devil makes supply of it by his own knowledge in things that are to come to pass. And this is the judgment of them who have known this art, which was also received for true in the days of the apostles.

Reason 3

The man who repairs to the astrologer upon the particular case for his help and counsel must believe that he can and will do for him; otherwise, if he comes doubting of his ability, or in way of tempting him, he cannot help him. Now, in common understanding, if the diviner brings the thing to pass, here must needs be more than art. For he who is master of a lawful art can work by his rules, whether a man believes that he can or not; yea, though all the men in the world should doubt, his rules would be effectual. The art itself, therefore, is the old superstitious art of the Chaldeans, which they, being idolaters, first fetched from the devil and his oracles; yea, the practice thereof is nothing but superstitious sorcery, and the undertakers [are] no better than sorcerers. If any man doubts hereof, their writings are sufficient testimonies, and they themselves avouch it. For it is a rule and maxim among them in all kinds of sorcery that the learner must come credulous, and not doubting, or to tempt; otherwise no answer can be given.

But notwithstanding all these reasons alleged for the proof of this point, sundry things are opposed to the contrary.

First, it is said that the sun, moon, and stars were created "for signs" (Gen. 1:14), and therefore that it is lawful to divine by them, seeing that in so doing we do but use them to the end for which God made them. *Answer.* The reason is of no force. The stars indeed by this ordinance do serve for "signs," but of what? Not of all things, but (as the text plainly shows) of days, weeks, months, and years; yea, of the seasons of the year, as of spring, summer, autumn, and winter; yea further, of the alterations of the weather in general. But all this makes nothing to ratify divination of particular events in things contingent, which are to fall out in the state of kingdoms, families, and persons. For they are not causes, but "signs" and that of some general things only, not of particular.

Second, it is said that Moses and Daniel, two famous prophets, are commended for their skill in this art. It is said of Moses that "he was learned in all the wisdom of the Egyptians" (Acts 7:22), and of Daniel that [he was learned] "in all the wisdom of the Chaldeans" (Dan. 1:17, 20). And we know that the Egyptians and Chaldeans were the masters of divination, and eminent above all others in matter of astrology. *Answer.* It cannot be proved out of those places that Moses and Daniel were trained up in this art. And though it should be granted they were, yet it follows not that they were practicers of it, at least continually. For albeit, being children and of tender years in the courts of Pharaoh and Nebuchadnezzar, they had been trained up by their governors in this knowledge, it may not thence be concluded that they finally submitted themselves to the practice thereof, considering that a man may learn that when he is young which afterwards upon better judgment and consideration he may utterly disclaim. And so, we are to think of them, that after God had called them they did forever lay aside all such wicked and devilish practices, forbidden by God and yet in use among the Egyptians and Chaldeans.

Third, it is objected [that] the stars are admirable creatures of God, and the causes of many strange effects in the air, in the waters, and upon the earth also, in the bodies of men and beasts. It may seem, therefore, not unlawful to divine by them. *Answer.* We grant that the stars, and especially the sun and moon, have great virtue and force upon the creatures that are below, partly by their light and partly by their heat. But hence it will not follow that they are (or may be) lawfully used for divination. For whereas it has been shown that the grounds of all good arts are gathered by observation and experience, it is not possible for any man, truly and certainly, to observe all particular events brought forth by the stars, whereupon he might ground his rules. And for proof hereof, suppose there were a heap of all kinds of herbs growing upon the earth gathered together, which should be all strained into one vessel, and the liquor brought to the most skillful physician that is (or ever was). Can we think him able, by tasting or smelling thereof, to distinguish the virtues of the herbs, and to say which is which? To do this, when all is severed from each another, is a hard matter, yet possible, considering they have their several natures and operations. But in this confused mixture, to discern the several is a thing passing the skill of man.

The same may be said of the particular virtue of every star. For they all have their operation in the bodies of men and other creatures, but their virtues being all mixed together in the subject whereon they work, can no more be known distinctly than the virtues of a mass of herbs of infinite sorts beaten together. For this is an undoubted truth in nature: that the virtues of celestial bodies in their operations are mingled with the qualities of the elements in the inferior bodies, and the virtues of them all do so concur that neither the heat or light of the stars, nor the virtue of the elements, can be severed one from another. And, therefore, though there is notable virtue in the stars, yet in regard of the mixture thereof in their operation, no man is able to say by observation that this is the virtue of this star, and this of that. The seven planets, being more notable than the other lights of the heaven, especially the sun and moon, have their operations and effects plainly and perfectly known. As for the other, there was never any man who could either feel their heat or certainly determine of anything by them.

There being then some stars whose virtues are unknown, how can their operations and effects be discerned in particular? Therefore, no rules can be made by observation of the virtues of the stars in their operations, whereupon we may foretell particular events of things contingent, either concerning men's persons, families, or kingdoms.

Reason 4
All stars have their work in the qualities of heat, light, cold, moisture, and dryness. As for the secret influences which men dream of, coming from them besides the said qualities, they are but forged fancies. The Scripture never mentions any such, neither can it be proved that the sun has any efficacy upon

inferior bodies, but by light and heat. Because they are mixed with other qualities, they afford no matter of prediction touching particular events. For what if the celestial bodies do cause in the terrestrial, heat and cold, drought and moisture? Does it therefore follow that these effects do declare beforehand the constitution of man's body? The disposition of men's minds? The affections of men's hearts? Or finally, what success they shall have in their affairs, touching wealth, honor, and religion? Hence, I conclude that divining by them in this sort is mere superstition and a kind of sorcery, for which cause in Scripture astrologers are justly numbered among sorcerers.

Now that which has been said touching this point, may serve for special use. First, it gives a caveat to all students, that they have care to spend their time and wits better than in the study of judicial astrology, and rather employ themselves in the searching out of such things as may most serve for the glory of God and the good of His church. It is the subtlety of Satan to draw men into such meditations, and to make this study so pleasant that it can hardly be left when it is once begun. But let them take heed betimes. For assuredly these vain and superstitious practices are not the builders and furtherers but the hinderers and destroyers of religion and the fear of God.

Second, this must admonish them who suffer any losses not to seek for help or remedy at the hands of astrologers, commonly called figure casters. For their directions in the recovery of lost or stolen things comes not by the help of any lawful art, but from the work of the devil, revealing the same unto them. And it would be better to lose a thing finally, and by faith to expect till God makes supply another way, than in this manner to recover it again. Yea, the curse of God hangs over the head of him who uses diabolical means to help himself. For put the case a thing of great value is lost, and again restored by the help of Satan, yet God in His justice, for the use of these unlawful means, may take from the consulter twice as much (or at least His grace) and so give him up to a reprobate sense to believe the devil to his utter perdition.

Third, it serves to admonish us of some other vanities that accompany astrology, especially of two.

The first, is the observation of the sign in man's body, wherein not only the ignorant sort, but men of knowledge, do far overshoot themselves, superstitiously holding that the sign is especially to be marked, an opinion in itself fantastical and vain, not grounded in nature, but borrowed from astrology. For the astrologers, for better expressing and establishing thereof, have devised new spheres in the heavens, more than indeed there are, to wit, the ninth and the tenth. And in the tenth, commonly called the first moveable,[4] [they] have

---

4. In the margin: *Primum mobile.*

placed an imaginary sphere which they term the zodiac, and in the zodiac twelve signs (Aries, Taurus, Gemini, and the rest) which they imagine to have power over the twelve parts of man's body, as Aries the head and face, Taurus the neck and throat, etc. But these are only twelve imaginary signs, for in the heavens there is no such matter as a ram, bull, etc. And how can it stand with reason that in a firmament, feigned by poets and philosophers, a forged sign, which indeed is nothing, should have any power or operation in the bodies of men?

Again, the very order of the government of these signs in man's body is fond[5] and without show of reason. For according to this platform, when the moon comes into the first sign (Aries), she rules in the head. And when she comes into the second sign (Taurus), [she rules] in the neck. And so, [she] descends down from part to part, in some part ruling two [days], in some three days, etc. Where observe that the moon is made then to rule in the cold and moist parts when she is in hot and dry signs. When, as in reason, a more consonant order were this: that when the moon is in hot and dry signs (as Aries, Leo, and Sagittarius), she should rule in hot and dry parts of the body; and when she is in cold and moist signs, she should rule in the cold and moist parts of the body; and so still govern those parts which in temperature come nearest to the nature of the signs wherein the moon is.

Besides this, some learned physicians have upon experience confessed that the observation of the sign is nothing material, and that there is no danger in it for gelding of cattle or letting of blood. Indeed, it prevails oftentimes by an old conceit and strong imagination, of some unlettered persons, who think it to be of force and efficacy for restoring and curing. And yet the vanity of this conceit appears in the common practice of men who commonly upon Saint Stephen's day let blood, be the sign where it will, though it is in the place where the vein is opened. But the truth is the sign in its own nature is neither way available, being but a fancy, grounded upon supposed premises, and therefore [it] ought to be rejected as a mere vanity.

The second thing belonging to astrology, which ought to be eschewed, is the choice and observation of days. Curious diviners do set apart certain days, whereof some are (as they say) lucky [and] some unlucky. And they appoint these to be observed for the beginning of ordinary works and businesses, as to take a journey, to begin to lay the foundation of a building, to plant a garden, to wean a child, to put on new apparel, to flit[6] into a new house, to traffic into other countries, to go about a suit to a prince or some great man, to hunt and use exercises, to pare the nails, to cut the hairs; in a word, to attempt anything

---

5. *Fond*: foolish.
6. *Flit*: move.

in purpose or action which is not done every day. The effect and force of these days is not grounded either in art or in nature, but only in superstitious conceit and diabolical confidence, upon a wicked custom, borrowed from the practice of diviners. And the danger of such confident conceits is this, that the devil by them takes the vantage of fantastical persons and brings them further into league and acquaintance with himself, unless they leave them. And all such persons as make difference of days for this or that purpose are in express words plainly condemned (Deut. 18:10–11).

Dreams

The fourth kind of divination by true means is the prediction of things to come by dreams. In the Old Testament we read that sorcerers and false prophets used to foretell strange events by revelations which they had in their dreams. Such diviners were among the Jews. And for that cause the people of God were expressly forbidden to hearken unto "dreamers of dreams" (Deut. 13:3). And the Lord Himself by the prophet Jeremiah taxes the false prophets, who broached false doctrine in His name by this devilish means, saying, "I have dreamed, I have dreamed" (Jer. 23:25).

Yet here it is to be remembered that foretelling of future things by dreams is not simply to be condemned, but only in part. For there are three sorts of dreams: divine, natural, and diabolical. Divine [dreams] are those which come from God; natural proceed from a man's own nature and arise from the quality and constitution of the body; [and] diabolical are caused by the suggestion of the devil.

Divine Dreams. Touching divine dreams, that there are (or, at least, have been) such is evident. For these are the words of God: "If there be a prophet of the Lord among you, I will be known unto him by a vision, and will speak unto him by a dream" (Num. 12:6). And Job says that "God speaketh in dreams and visions of the night, when sleep falleth upon men, and they sleep upon their beds" (Job 33:15). Now these divine dreams were caused in men either immediately by God Himself, as the former places show, or by means of some good angel. In this latter kind Joseph was often admonished in dreams what to do by the ministry of an angel (Matt. 1:20; 2:13, 19). And divining by such dreams is not condemned, for by them the worthiest prophets of God have revealed God's will in many things to His church. Thus, Joseph by a dream had notice given him of his own advancement (Gen. 37:7, 9), and by Pharaoh's dreams, which were sent from God, he also foretold the state of the kingdom of Egypt touching provision for seven years dearth (Gen. 41:25). By the same means the prophet Daniel prophesied of the flourishing and fading of the chief monarchies of the world from his time to the coming of Christ (Dan. 9). These, therefore, being one of the extraordinary means whereby God has manifested His will unto man in times past, more or less, divination by them is not to be censured as unlawful, but rather to be honored and esteemed as the ordinance of God.

Natural Dreams. For the second sort, which are natural, arising either from the thoughts of the mind or the affections of the heart or the constitution of the body. As they are ordinary in all men, in some more [and] in some less, so they vary according to the diversity of men's thoughts, affections, and constitutions. And by them a man may probably conjecture of sundry things concerning the state and disposition, partly of his body and partly of his mind.

First, he may guess in likelihood what is his constitution, as the learned in all ages do constantly avouch. For when his mind in dreaming runs upon wars, contentions, fire, and such like, it argues his complexion is choleric. When he dreams of waters and inundations, it betokens abundance of phlegm. When his fantasy conceives heavy and doleful things, full of grief, fear, and horror, it betrays a melancholic constitution. When his dreams are joyful and pleasant (as of mirth, pastimes, and delightful news), his complexion is judged to be sanguine.

Second, by natural dreams a man may guess at the corruption of his own heart and know to what sins he is most naturally inclined. For look what men do ordinarily in the day time conceive and imagine in their corrupt hearts, for the most part they do corruptly dream of the same in the night. And this is the rather to be observed because, though the wicked man shuts his eyes and stops his ears and hardens his heart, and will not take notice of his enormities by the light of the law, yet even by his own dreams in the night his wickedness shall be in part discovered, and his conscience thereby convinced, and he himself left in the end inexcusable before God. Now albeit a man may give a probable conjecture of the premises by natural dreams, yet no divination of things to come, whether public or private, good or bad, can be made by them, either concerning persons, families, or kingdoms. Therefore, the common observations of dreams in the world, whereby men imagine things to come to pass, and accordingly foretell them by those means, are vain and superstitious, and justly so condemned in the places before named (Deuteronomy 13; Jeremiah 23).

Diabolical Dreams. Concerning the third kind of dreams which are caused by the devil, it has been granted in all ages for a truth that Satan can frame dreams in the brain of man, and by them reveal his divinations. And it is plainly manifested by the continual observation of the Gentiles before the coming of Christ.

For when oracles (that is, answers from the devil) were in force, men that used to consult with them, and desired to be resolved in matters of doubt, were to lay them down and sleep beside the altar of Apollo, where they had offered their gift, and sleeping they received in a dream the answer for which they came. And this dream was framed in the brain of him that slept by the devil, and in it the answer was delivered by him speaking at or in the oracle.[7]

So likewise, in the primitive church, since the coming of Christ, though oracles then ceased, which were the greatest and strongest delusions that ever Satan had, yet he has by dreams and visions wrought in the heads of many men most strange and curious conceits for the raising up of heresies, to the great disturbance of the peace of the church. For we read in ecclesiastical stories that the Manicheans had their damnable opinions first inspired into them and then confirmed by dreams. And in this age the first authors of the sect of the Anabaptists had their curious conceits of revelation, partly in dreams [and] partly in visions. Likewise, the Family of Love have their revelations in dreams. For he who desires to become one of that sect must ascend thereunto by degrees before he can come to perfection to be an illumined elder or a deified man, to which estate when he is once come he has for his confirmation strong illusions, both waking and sleeping in visions and dreams. Histories of latter times and woeful experience show this to be true, the devil prevailing so strongly that many have fallen away by this means, being corrupted by a doctrine merely carnal, howsoever maintained with pretense of great holiness. Again, as the good angels may cause divine dreams from God, and therein reveal unto men His will and pleasure concerning things to come, so no doubt the evil spirits may cause in men diabolical dreams, and therein reveal unto them many strange things, which they by means unknown to men may foresee and know. By all which it is evident that there are (and may be) diabolical as well as divine dreams.

The conclusion then is this, that as divining by the second sort is superstitious, having no ground from God's Word, so foretelling by this third sort is flat witchcraft, directly condemned in the places afore-named, where men are forbidden to prophesy by them or to regard them.

Yet forasmuch as dreams are of sundry kinds, as has been said, it shall not be amiss to set down some notes of difference between them, whereby they may be known and distinguished from each other. Which point indeed has long ago been handled in the primitive church, but hardly determined. For the learned of that age have avouched it a very hard matter, considering that the devil in these, as well as in other things, can transform himself into an angel

---

7. This paragraph break is not in the original.

of light. But howsoever the case is hard, and the devil politic, yet by light of direction from the Word of God there may be some true differences set down between them, as namely these.

First of all, divine dreams have always had their preeminence above others, that generally they have concerned the weightiest matters in the world, as the coming and exhibiting of the Messiah, the changes and alterations of kingdoms, the revealing of antichrist, and the state of the church of God. And this may plainly appear by those which Joseph expounded unto Pharaoh, and Daniel unto the kings of Babel and Persia. But in the other sort it is otherwise. For if there is anything represented more than ordinary in those that be natural, it proceeds merely from fancy and imagination. And as for diabolical, they are not of so weighty matters, nor so hard to foretell. For though the devil has great power and skill, yet it is above his reach to determine of such things as these are, or to foretell them without help from God.

Second, divine dreams are always plain and manifest, or if they are obscure, yet they have a most evident interpretation annexed unto them. Of the plainer sort were the dreams of Joseph, the husband of Mary (Matthew 1). Of the other sort were Pharaoh's dreams, very dark and hidden, but God raised up Joseph to give them an easy interpretation upon the instant (Genesis 41). Nebuchadnezzar's dreams were full of obscurity, and many matters were contained in them, so as his spirit was troubled and he forgot them, but God stirred up Daniel and revealed to him the secret, so as he remembered it to the king, and declared the true meaning thereof (Dan. 2:1, 28, 36). Lastly, Daniel's dreams of the four beasts, etc., were of like difficulty, but the angel Gabriel was presently sent to make him understand them (Dan. 8:16). Now those that are caused by the devil, as they are obscure and intricate, so the interpretation of them is ambiguous and uncertain, because he himself cannot infallibly determine how things shall come to pass, and thereupon is constrained to give doubtful answers by dreams. And such were not only the ancient oracles among the heathen, where he gave the resolution, but the modern prophecies given by him to some of his instruments in the latter time.

Third, the dream that comes from God is always agreeable to His revealed will, and represents nothing contrary to the same, in whole or in part. Whereas those that proceed from nature do savor of nature, and are agreeable to man's corruption, which is repugnant unto God's will. And those that are suggested by Satan are of the same nature; the general scope whereof is to cross the will of God, and to withdraw the heart from obedience thereunto.

Fourth, divine dreams aim at this end, to further religion and piety, and to maintain true doctrine. But the devil, an enemy of God, works in his dreamers the subversion of true religion and the worship of God, that in the room thereof he may set up idolatry and superstition. For so much we learn in Deuteronomy 13, where the false prophet brings his dream and utters it, yea, and confirms it by a wonder. But mark his end: it was to draw men to apostasy. "Let us go after other gods, which thou hast not known, and let us serve them" (v. 2). Answerable to which was the practice of the false prophets afterwards, who caused the people to err by their lies and flatteries (Jer. 23:32).

To conclude this point, it must be here remembered that howsoever there are (and have been) distinct sorts of dreams, yet those which are from God were only in ordinary use in the Old Testament and in the church of the New, [and] are ceased and take not place ordinarily. Whereas, therefore, men in their sleeps have dreams, they must take them commonly to be natural, and withal know that they may be diabolical, or mixed partly of the one kind [and] partly of the other. And howsoever there may be some use of the natural, as has been said, yet commonly they are not to be regarded. And for the other which are from Satan, or mixed, they are not to be received, believed, or made means whereby to foretell things to come, lest by this use of them we grow into familiarity with the devil, and before God be guilty of the sin of witchcraft.

Lots

The fifth and last kind of divination by true means is by lots, when men take upon them to search out fortune (as they speak), that is, good or bad success in any business by casting of lots, whether it is by casting a die or opening of a book, or any such casual means. I mention this the rather because among the ignorant and superstitious sort such practices are common and in great account. The lot is an ordinance of God, appointed for special ends and purposes, but when it is thus applied, it ceases to be lawful, because it is abused to other ends than God by His Word and ordinance has allowed.

That we may the better know the abuse of a lot in this kind, we must remember there are three sorts of lots: the civil, the sporting, and the divining.

The civil use of lots is when they are used for the ending of controversies, the dividing of lands and heritages, the disposing of offices among many that are equally fit, the trying of the right in doubtful things, or lastly the discovering of a malefactor hid among many suspects. By this use of the lot was Saul chosen to be king over Israel (1 Sam. 10:21), the scapegoat separated from that which was to be sacrificed (Lev. 16:8), the land of Canaan divided among the children of Israel (Josh. 14:2), the trespass of Achan found out (Josh. 7:15), and Matthias chosen to be one of the twelve (Acts 1:26). And of this lot Solomon says, "The lot causeth contentions to cease, and maketh partitions among the mighty" (Prov. 18:18). Hereupon the civil use of lots has its warrant in God's Word, so it is lawfully used in case of necessity, with invocation of the name of

God, and with expectation of the event from God, by whose hand and immediate providence it is disposed. "For the lot," says Solomon, "is cast into the lap, but the whole disposition thereof is from the Lord" (Prov. 16:33).

The sporting lot is that which is commonly used for some vain and unnecessary end, as to set up bankrupts or such like. This has no warrant in the Word of God whereupon men should use it, and therefore [it] is no better than an abuse of God's ordinance, to speak no more of it.

Now the divining lot, performed by the opening of a book or the casting of a die or such like, thereby to declare good or bad success, cannot be done without confederacy with Satan, either explicit or implicit. For the plain cast of a die, or the opening of a book, without believing, can do nothing for discovering of future contingents. And what is there in the nature of these actions to produce such effects? Or where, or when, did God give this virtue to them, certainly to determine of things hidden from man, and known only to Himself? Divination, therefore, by them is to be held as a practice not only savoring of superstition but proceeding from the art of witchcraft and sorcery.

And thus much of divination by means of the creatures, and the several kinds thereof.

Section 3

The second kind of divination is by counterfeit and forged means, which are none of the creatures of God, whereof only one kind is mentioned in Scripture, namely, when Satan is consulted within the shape of a dead man. This is commonly called necromancy (or the black art) because the devil, being sought unto by witches, appears unto them in the likeness of a dead body. And it is expressly forbidden (Deut. 18:11), yea, condemned by the prophet Isaiah, who says in plain terms that God's people ought not to go "from the living to the dead, but to the law and to the testimony" (Isa. 8:19–20). A memorable example hereof is recorded in 1 Samuel 28, the observation whereof will discover unto us the chief points of necromancy. Saul [was] about to encounter the Philistines. Being forsaken of God who refused to answer him by dreams, urim, or prophets, [Saul] inquired for one who had a familiar spirit. And hearing of the pythoness[8] at Endor, [he] went unto her by night, and caused her to raise up Samuel to tell him of the issue of the war. Now the witch, at his request, raised up the devil, with whom she was confederate, in Samuel's likeness. He gave Saul [an] answer concerning his own overthrow and the death of his sons. This example declares plainly that there is a kind of divination whereby witches and

---

8. *Pythoness*: a female soothsayer.

sorcerers reveal strange things by means of the devil appearing unto them in the shapes or shadows of the dead.

Touching the truth of this example, two questions may be moved. The first is whether that which appeared was truly Samuel or not? Some say it was Samuel indeed. Others (who hold that there are no witches) deny that it was Samuel or the devil. [They] affirm it to be some other counterfeit coming in Samuel's attire to deceive Saul. Both of these opinions are false, and here to be confuted.

Opinion 1

First, I prove that the opinion which says that true Samuel appeared unto Saul is a flat untruth by these reasons:

First, before this time God had withdrawn His Spirit from Saul, as [He] Himself confesses, and [He] denied to answer him any more by ordinary means in such sort as before He had done. Hereupon I gather that it was not probable that God would now vouchsafe him the favor to suffer Samuel to come unto him extraordinarily and tell him what should be the end of his war with the Philistines. And to this purpose it is affirmed twice in that chapter that God had taken His good spirit from Saul.

Second, the souls of the faithful departed are in the hands of God and do rest in glory with Him, and their bodies are in the earth and rest in peace there. So says the voice from heaven: "Blessed are the dead that die in the Lord: for they rest from their labors, and their works (that is, the reward of their works) follow them immediately (or, at the heels, as the word signifies)" (Rev. 14:13). Now suppose the devil had power over Samuel's body, yet to make true Samuel he must have his soul also. But it is not in the power of the devil to bring again the souls that are in heaven unto their bodies, and so to cause them to appear unto men upon earth, and to speak unto them. The devil's kingdom is in hell and in the hearts of wicked men on earth; yea, while the children of God are in this world, he usurps some authority over them by means of their own corruption. But heaven is the kingdom of God and His saints, where Satan has nothing to do, considering that there is no flesh or corruption to make him entrance or yield him entertainment. Neither can it be proved by Scripture that the devil can disturb either the bodies or souls of them who die in the Lord. And, therefore, the witch with all her power and skill could not bring Samuel's rotten body (for so no doubt it was [by] now) and soul together.

Third, this shape which appeared suffered Saul to adore and worship it, whereas the true Samuel would never have received adoration from Saul, the king, though it had been in civil manner only. Whom then did Saul adore? *Answer.* The devil himself, who being an enemy to the glory of God, was content to take to himself that honor which a king in duty is to perform to God Himself.

Fourth, if it had been true Samuel, he would certainly have reproved Saul for seeking help at witches, contrary to God's commandment and that doctrine which he had taught him from God in his life time. But this counterfeit reproved him not, and therefore it is not likely to be the true prophet of God, but Satan himself, framing by his art and skill the person and shape of Samuel.

But it is alleged to the contrary that Samuel, after his sleep, prophesied of the death of Saul. "After his sleep also he told of the king's death" (Ecclesiasticus 46:20). *Answer.* That book penned by Jesus the son of Sirach is a very worthy description of Christian ethics, containing more excellent precepts for manners than all the writings of heathen philosophers or other men, but yet it is not Scripture. Neither did the church ever hold and receive it as canonical. Yea, the author himself insinuates so much in the beginning thereof, for in the preface he disables himself to interpret hard things, and after a sort craves pardon for his weakness, which is not the manner of the men of God, who were penmen of Scripture. For they were so guided by God's Spirit in their proceedings that nothing could be hard unto them. No ordinary man has assurance of this privilege, and therefore this author, writing upon his own private motion, was subject to error. And no doubt this speech of his, being contrary to that which is recorded in the canonical Scriptures, is a flat untruth.

Second, it is objected that the Scripture calls him Samuel, who appeared unto Saul. *Answer.* The Scripture does often speak of things, not as they are in themselves, but as they seem to us. So, it is affirmed that God made two great lights, the sun and the moon (Gen. 1:16). Whereas the moon is lesser than many stars, yet because in regard of her nearness to the earth, she seems to us greater than the rest, therefore she is called a "great light." In like manner, idols in the Scripture are called gods, not that they are so indeed (for an idol is nothing (1 Cor. 8:4), but because some men do so conceive of them in their minds. In a word, the Scripture oftentimes does abase itself to our conceit, speaking of things not according as they are, but after the manner of men. And so, in this place [it] calls counterfeit Samuel by the name of the true Samuel because it seemed so unto Saul.

Third, that body which appeared prophesied of things that come to pass the day after, as the death of Saul and of his sons. These indeed so fell out, and at the same time, therefore [it] was like to be Samuel. *Answer.* There is nothing there said or done which the devil might not do. For when the Lord uses the devil as His instrument to bring some things to pass, He does beforehand reveal the same unto him. And look what particulars the devil learns from God, those he can foretell. Now the truth is [that] Satan was appointed by God to work Saul's overthrow, and it was made known unto him when the thing should be done and by what means. And by none other the devil was enabled to foretell the death of Saul. Where (by the way) observe that in this case the devil can reveal things to come certainly, to wit, if he is appointed God's immediate instrument for the execution of them or knows them by light of former prophecies in Scripture.

Fourth, dead men do often appear and walk after they are buried. *Answer.* It is indeed the opinion of the Church of Rome, and of many ignorant persons among us, but the truth is otherwise. Dead men do neither walk nor appear in body or soul after death. For all who die are either righteous or wicked; the souls of the righteous go straight to heaven, and the souls of the wicked to hell, and there remain till the last judgment. And, therefore, of the just it is said that they are "blessed when they die, because they rest from their labors" (Rev. 14:13). But how do they rest, if after they are dead they wander up and down in the earth?

If it is said that Moses and Elijah appeared when Christ was transfigured in the mount, and that Lazarus rose again, and at Christ's resurrection many dead bodies rose again and appeared, I answer [that] there were two times when God suffered the dead to be raised up again, either at the planting of His church or at the restoring and establishing of it when it was razed to the foundation. Thus, at the restoring of religion in Elijah's and Elisha's times, the son of the Shunamite woman (2 Kings 4:34) and the widow's son at Zarephath (1 Kings 17:21) were raised. Again, when God would restore His church, which was fallen to idolatry about the death of Elisha, He caused the like miracle to be wrought in the reviving of a dead man by the touching of Elisha's dead carcass in the grave, thereby to assure the people of their deliverance, and to cause them to embrace the doctrine of the prophet after his death, which in his life they had condemned. In like manner at the establishing of the gospel in the New Testament, it pleased Christ to raise up Moses and Elijah, and to make them known to His disciples by extraordinary revelation, that they might believe that the doctrine which He preached was not new, but the same in substance with that which was recorded in the law and the prophets, both which were represented by Moses and Elijah. So also, He wrought the miracle upon Lazarus, the widow's son, and Jairus's daughter, thereby to show the power of His Godhead, the truth of His calling, [and] the testimony of His doctrine. And lastly, to make known the power of His resurrection, He caused some to rise and appear to others when He Himself rose again. But out of these two times we have neither warrant nor example that God suffered the dead to be raised up. Wherefore, those instances will not any way confirm Samuel's appearing, which indeed was not true, but counterfeit and forged by the devil himself.

Opinion 2

Now for the opinion of those who deny that there are any witches, and thereupon hold that this was a mere cozenage[9] of the witch, suborning[10] some man or woman to counterfeit the form, attire, and voice of Samuel, thereby to delude Saul. [This opinion] is also untrue. For he who spoke foretold the ruin of Saul, his sons, and his army, yea, the time also wherein this was to come to pass. Whereas in likelihood no man or woman in all Israel could have foretold such things beforehand by themselves. It was not then any cozenage (as is affirmed), but a thing effected by the devil, framing to himself a body in the likeness of Samuel, wherein he spoke.

If, therefore, it is manifest that by counterfeit apparitions of the dead witches and sorcerers can foretell things to come, hence sundry points of witchcraft may be observed.

First, that there is a league between the witch and the devil. For this was the cause which moved Saul to seek to witches, because neither [he] himself nor any of his servants could raise up Satan in Samuel's likeness, as the witch of Endor did. But Saul, being a king, might have commanded help from all the wise and learned men in Israel, for the effecting of such a matter. Why then would he rather seek to a silly woman than to them? The reason was because she had made a compact with the devil, for the using of his help at her demand, by virtue whereof he was as ready to answer as she to call him. Whereas Saul and the learned Jews, having made no such league, neither he by his power, nor they by their skill, could have performed such a work.

Second, the devil will be ready at the call and command of witches and sorcerers when they are intending any mischief. For here the witch of Endor no sooner spoke but he appeared, and therefore the text gives her a name that signifies one having rule and command over *Pytho* (that is, the familiar spirit). Yet when he is commanded, he yields not upon constraint, but voluntarily, because he builds upon his own greater advantage the gaining of the soul of the witch. Where, by the way, let it be observed what a precious thing the soul of man is; the purchasing whereof can make the proud spirit of Satan so far to abase itself as to be at the command of a silly woman. Again, what an inveterate malice Satan bears to man, which for the gaining of a soul will do that which is so contrary to his nature. It may teach man what to esteem of his soul, and not to sell it for so base a price.

Third, by this, the great power of the devil in the behalf of the sorcerer is made manifest. For he was presently at hand to counterfeit Samuel, and did

---

9. *Cozenage:* trickery.
10. *Suborn:* bribe or induce.

it so lively and cunningly, as well in form of body as in attire and voice, that Saul thought verily it was the prophet. This may be a caveat unto us, not easily to give credit to any such apparitions. For though they seem ever so true and evident, yet such is the power and skill of the devil that he can quite deceive us, as he did Saul in this place.

Section 4

Hitherto I have shown the first kind of divination by means, both true and forged. Now follows the second: practiced without means.

Divination without means is the foretelling and revealing of things to come by the alone and immediate assistance of a familiar spirit. This kind is mentioned and expressly forbidden: "Ye shall not regard them that work with spirits" (Lev. 19:31). Again, if any turn "after such as work with spirits, to go a whoring after them, I will set my face against that person, and will cut him off from among his people" (Lev. 20:6). [Again,] let none be found among you "that consulteth with spirits" (Deut. 18:11). In these places the Holy Spirit uses the word *ob*, which more properly signifies a spirit or devil, in which sense it is taken in Leviticus 20:27 and 1 Samuel 28:8. And by reason of the league which is between the witch and the devil, the same is also given to the witch who works by the devil. And, therefore, the Pythoness at Endor is both called *ob* (1 Sam. 28:9) and she who rules *ob* (vv. 7–8).

Now this kind of divination is practiced two ways: (1) inwardly, when the spirit is within the witch; or, (2) outwardly, when being forth of the witch, he does only inspire him or her.

The Scripture affords an example of the former way [in] Acts 16:16. A woman at Philippi, who had a spirit of Pytho, got her master much advantage with divining. And this spirit, whereby she divined, was within her. For Paul, being molested, said to the spirit, "'I command thee in the name of Jesus Christ, that thou come out of her,' and he came out the same hour" (v. 18). And because the devil is not wont in this kind to speak out of the throat and breast (or belly) of the witch possessed, hereupon learned men have thought that this name (*ob*) is given to the devil because he speaks out of the witch as out of a bottle or hollow vessel, for so the word *ob* properly signifies.

Second, this may be practiced when the devil is forth of the witch, and then he either inspires her or else casts her into a trance, and therein reveals unto her such things as she would know.

Of this kind, though we have no example in Scripture, yet the histories of the heathen do afford unto us many instances of experience therein. One of the principal is the history of the ten Sibylles of Greece, who were most famous witches, and did prophesy of many things to come. Some [of these things] were true concerning Christ and His kingdom, which the devil stole out of the Bible, and some were false. And they received all of them by revelation from the devil in trances.

But it will be said [that] if the devil reveals unto his instruments strange things in trances, then how shall a man discern between diabolical revelations and the true gift of prophecy which God in trances reveals unto His prophets? *Answer.* In this point Satan is (as it were) God's ape. For as He in old times raised up holy prophets to speak unto the fathers for the building up of His church, so has Satan inspired his ministers and furnished his instruments with prophetic inspirations from time to time for the building up of his own kingdom. And hereupon he has notably counterfeited the true gift of prophecy received first from God Himself. And yet, though in many things they are alike, there is [a] great difference between them.

First, divine trances may come upon God's children either when the soul remains united with the body or else when it is severed for a time. Paul insinuates as much when he says of himself that he was rapt up (as it were in a heavenly trance) into the third heaven, but whether in the body or out of the body he knew not (2 Cor. 12:2). But in all diabolical ecstasies, though the body and senses of the witch are (as it were) bound or benumbed for the time, yet their souls still remain united to their bodies, and [are] not severed from them. For though the devil by God's permission may kill the body, and so take the soul out of it forever, yet to take it from the body for a time, and to reunite them again, is miraculous and, therefore, beyond the compass of his power.

Second, in divine trances the servants of God have all their senses, yea, all the powers of soul and body, remaining sound and perfect. Only for a time the actions and operations are suspended and cease to do their duty. But in ecstasies that are from Satan, his instruments are cast into frenzies and madness, so as reason in them is darkened, understanding obscured, memory weakened, the brain distempered; yea, all the faculties are so blemished that many of them never recover their former estate again. And they who scape[11] best do carry their blemishes, as the devil's scars, even unto their grave. Satan is so kind to his friends that he will leave his tokens behind him, wherever he comes in this sort. The servants of God receive no such blemish, but rather a further good and a greater measure of illumination of all the powers of the soul.

Third, divine ecstasies tend always to the confirming of the truth of the gospel and the furtherance of true religion and piety. Such was Peter's (Acts 10:11), which served to assure him of his calling to preach the gospel to the Gentiles, and to inform his judgment in this truth, that there was no exception

---

11. *Scape*: escape.

of persons with God and that to them of the New Testament all things were clean and nothing polluted. But the scope of them who are from Satan is principally the suppressing and hindrance of religion, the drawing of the weak into errors, the ratifying and confirming of them who are fallen thereinto, and the general upholding of the practices of ungodliness. And by these and such like particular differences has God pulled off the devil's visor and made him better known and discerned by true Christians.

And thus much concerning divination, the first part of witchcraft.

Chapter 4

The Kinds of Witchcraft: Operation

The second part is that which consists in operation and is, therefore, called operative or working witchcraft. Witchcraft in operation is that which is employed in the practice and real working of strange things or wonders, and it has two parts: enchantment and juggling.

Section 1

Enchantment is the working of wonders by a charm. The Lord expressly forbids it: "Let none be found among you, that is a charmer" (Deut. 18:11). In this description, two points are to be considered: (1) what things may be done by enchantment, namely wonders, for I say it is the practice of wonders; [and] (2) by what means these wonders are wrought, that is, by a charm.

The Work of Enchantment: Wonders
For the first, the wonders done by enchanters are: (1) the raising of storms and tempests, winds and weather, by sea and by land; (2) the poisoning of the air; (3) the blasting of corn; (4) the killing of cattle, and annoying of men, women, and children; (5) the procuring of strange passions and torments in men's bodies and other creatures, with the curing of the same; [and] (6) the casting out of devils. Enchanters can do these and such like things by their charms. And for proof hereof we have the uniform consent of all ages with the records of witches' confessions to manifest the same, besides the testimony of experience in this age, so as the man who calls it into question may as well doubt of the sun shining at noon day.

Yet for the further declaration thereof, we will allege what the Scripture says on this point. Solomon says, "If the serpent bite when he is not charmed, no better is a babbler" (Eccl. 10:11). The words are thus in our English translation, but they may better be thus read according to the original: "If the serpent bites before he is charmed, what profit has the master of the tongue (that is, the charmer) thereby?" And so, they bear this sense: if the enchanter is bitten before the serpent is charmed, then he has no benefit by his charm. For in that place Solomon gives us to understand what power enchanters have and what they may do by their charms if they come in time, namely, stay the poison of the serpent so as it cannot hurt either by biting or stinging.[1]

When Balak intended evil against Israel, he hired Balaam to curse them (Num. 22:6). Now this Balaam was an enchanting witch, for though he is called a prophet, yet this was only in the reputation of the world, for his practice was to enchant by charms of words. And to that purpose he was hired to curse God's people, that is, to bring mischief upon them by charming. When he had often and many ways assayed to do this thing, and could no way prevail, but that it pleased God contrary to his endeavors to bless Israel, then he breaks out into these words: "There is no sorcery against Jacob, nor soothsaying against Israel" (Num. 23:23). As if he should have said, "I know well that sorcery is powerful in many things and of force to bring much mischief upon men, yet it can take no place against the people of God because He has blessed them, and whom He blesses, them no man can hurt by cursing." Enchanters, therefore, may upon God's permission work strange things, as appears by these places, to name no more.

The Means of Enchantment: Charms
The second point to be observed is the means whereby these wonders are practiced. These are counterfeit and supposed means, not ordained and sanctified by God, which are commonly called charms. A charm is a spell or verse, consisting of strange words, used as a sign or watchword to the devil to cause him to work wonders.

First, I say it is a spell consisting of strange words because in these enchantments certain words or verses are secretly uttered, which in regard of the common forms of words are strange, and wherein there is thought to be a miraculous efficacy to bring some extraordinary and unexpected thing to pass. [This] point [is] of itself evident and needs no further proof, considering it is not unknown to the more ignorant sort who are better acquainted with these [words] than with the Word of God. And these words are not all of one and the same kind. But some are rude and barbarous, neither known nor conceived (or understood), of which the more ancient sort of charms were wont to be made especially, and some later. Again, some are plain and known terms which may be understood, [such] as the names of the Trinity, words and sentences of Scripture as *in principio erat verbum*,[2] etc. Again, charms that consist of words are not all of one sort, but some are imprecations, wishing some evil. Others in show have the form of praises and blessings whereby the witch either

---

1. This paragraph break is not in the original.
2. "In the beginning was the Word" (John 1:1).

flatteringly commends or favorably wishes some good. Again, others are made in [the] form of prayer and petition. And they all are sometimes plainly conceived, sometimes in ruder and more unknown words, as those well know, who have heard them or read them where they are to be found.

Second, I add that the charm is used for a sign and watchword to the devil, to cause him to work wonders. Herein stands the nature and proper end of a charm: the nature, in that it is a diabolical sign; the end, to cause the devil to work a wonder. It is hereby distinguished from all other speeches of men, for they commonly carry the nature of the thing whereof and whereabout they are made. But the charm does not always follow the nature of the words, but has another nature in regard of the immediate relation it has to the devil, to whom it is a sign. Again, the pronounced charm does not the wonder, but the devil admonished by it as by the watchword to do the feat.

Now because some are of [the] opinion, in regard of the ordinary production of strange effects by these means, that the spell has in itself some virtue and power to such and such purposes whereunto it is used, I will stand a little in the proof of the contrary: that a charm is only a diabolical watchword, and has in itself no such effectual power or possibility to work a wonder. My reasons are these:

First, this must be taken for a main ground: that as there is nothing in the world that has being but from God, so nothing has in it any efficacy but by His ordinance. Now whatsoever efficacy is in any creature from God, it received the same into itself either by creation or since the creation by some new and special institution, appointment, and gift of God. For example, the bread in the sacrament, by a natural power given unto it in the creation, serves to nourish the body; and the same bread, by God's special appointment in His Word, feeds the soul, in that by His ordinance it is made to us a sign and seal of the body of Christ broken for us. And so it is in every creature. If the effect is ordinary and natural, it has it by creation. If [it is] extraordinary and supernatural, it has that by divine ordination. So that whatever comes to pass by any other means is by satanical operation. Now charms and spells, standing of set words and syllables, have no power in them[selves] to work wonders, either by the gift of nature in the creation or by God's appointment since the creation. And, therefore, they have in them no power at all for any such purpose. This latter part of the reason, being the assumption or application of the ground to the present instance, consists of two parts, which I will prove in order.

Part 1
First, then, I affirm that by the gift of nature no words of charms have power in them to work wonders. And I prove it in this manner.

First, all words made and uttered by men are in their own nature but sounds framed by the tongue, of the breath that comes from the lungs. And that which is only a bare sound, in all reason, can have no virtue in it to cause a real work, much less to produce a wonder. The sounds of bells and many musical instruments, and the voices of many brute creatures, are far more strong and powerful than the voice of a man. Yet, who knows not that none of these is available to such purposes. Indeed, they have power to affect the mind by their sweetness or otherwise, but they are not able to bring to pass a real work, either by the inflicting of hurts and harms or by the procuring of good. I conclude, therefore, that the voice of man by nature has no power to work any wonders.

Second, everything which hurts or affects another must necessarily touch the thing which it hurts or affects. For it is a granted rule in nature that every agent works upon the patient by touching.[3] But words uttered in charms are commonly made of things absent, and therefore though it should be granted that they had the power of touching a substance (which they cannot have) yet of themselves they are not available[4] to bring upon things absent either good or evil.

Third, moreover, if words conceived in charms and spells have any such power as is pretended, why should not every word that any man speaks have the same power, inasmuch as all words are of the same nature, being only sounds framed in the breast and uttered by the tongue in letters and syllables? But experience teaches that the same word spoken by another has not the same virtue. For the charm uttered by the charmer himself will take effect, but being spoken in the same manner by another man (that is, no enchanter) [it] makes to no purpose, for nothing is effected by it.

Fourth, that which is in nature nothing but a bare signification cannot serve to work a wonder, and this is the nature of all words. For as they are framed of man's breath, they are natural, but yet in regard of form and articulation they are artificial and significant, and the use of them in every language is to signify that which the author thereof intended. For the first significations of words depended upon the will and pleasure of man who framed and invented them. Being, therefore, invented only to show or signify something, it remains that neither in nature nor proper use can they be applied to the producing of wonderful and strange effects. Thus, the former part of the assumption is cleared.

---

3. In the margin: *Omne agene, agit per contactum.*
4. *Available*: able.

Part 2

In the second place I affirm that the words of charmers have not this power in them by any special gift, blessing, or appointment of God, since the creation. This is the other part of the assumption. And I show it thus: whatever is powerful and effectual to any end or purpose by God's gift, blessing, or appointment, the same is commanded in His Word to be used. And [it] also has a promise of blessing annexed to the right use thereof. To use the instance before made for explanation's sake: The bread in the Lord's Supper has this power and property given it by Christ, to seal and signify unto every believing receiver, the body of Christ. And by this property given it, it is available to this purpose, though it is a thing above the common and natural use of bread. And thereupon we have warrant from Christ's own commandment, ordinance, and example so to use it. But in the whole body of the Scripture, there is not the like commandment to use the words of charms for the effecting of wonders, much less the like promise of blessing upon the same so used. Therefore, the conclusion is that God has given no such power unto them in special.

If it is asked then, what they are and for what they serve? I answer, they are no better than the devil's sacraments and watchwords, to cause him to do some strange work. For the enchanter has relation in his mind to the devil, whose help he has at hand by covenant, either open or secret, or at least some superstitious opinion of the force of the words which is a preparation to a covenant.

The truth of this doctrine, howsoever it is thus made manifest, finds not general entertainment at all men's hands. For there are (and have been) some learned men in all ages who maintained the contrary both by word and writing; and namely, that there is great virtue and power in words pronounced in time and place to effect strange things. For proof whereof, they allege these reasons:

First, that the bare conceit and imagination of man is of great force to do strange things and, therefore, words expressed much more. *Answer.* The ground of the reason is naught. Imagination is nothing else but a strong conceit of the mind touching anything, whatsoever it is. And by reason of the communion that is between the body and soul, being together, it is of great force to work within the man who imagines diversely, and to cause [an] alteration in himself, which may tend either to the hurt or to the good of his own body. But yet imagination has no force out of a man to affect or hurt another. A man (conceiving desperately of his own estate) by the strength of imagination may kill himself. But the same conceit, be it ever so strong, cannot hurt his neighbor. For it is no more than Caesar's image upon his coin, which serves only to represent Caesar. So, imagination is nothing but the representation of something in the mind by conceit. And, therefore, as the person of Caesar is nothing hurt, though his image is defaced, so when we conceive of men in our minds, though ever so badly and maliciously, yet all is of no force to hurt or annoy them, either in person or state.

Second, they allege that witches by malicious and wry looks in anger and displeasure may (and do) hurt those upon whom they look, whether they are men or other creatures. And it is an old received opinion that in malicious and ill-disposed persons noisome and malignant spirits proceed out of the eye with the beams. [These] infect the air, and do poison or kill, not only them with whom they are daily conversant, but others also whose company they frequent, of whatsoever age, strength, and complexion they are. *Answer.* But the opinion is as fond as it is old. For it is as much against nature that such virtue should proceed out of the eye, or such spirits break out of the nerves to the hated party, as it is for the blood of the body (of itself) to gush out of the veins.

Yet, for the ratifying of this opinion, they allege that which is written in Genesis 30:37, where Jacob laid speckled rods before the sheep in their watering troughs, and that by God's appointment, for this end, that they might bring forth partly colored lambs. I answer that this was not a work of sight, but a special and extraordinary work of God's providence upon Jacob in his necessity, as we may plainly see in the next chapter; yea, it was taught Jacob by God Himself (vv. 9–11). And if it had been an ordinary work, doubtless the gains thereof being so good, Jacob would have done it again afterward. But we never read that he did it again. And be it granted it were a natural work, yet it cannot prove witching by sight, because the sheep received into their eyes the species and resemblance of the rods, which is according to nature. Whereas in fascination, or bewitching by sight, malignant spirits should not be received in, but sent forth from the eye, which is against nature.

Yea, but the basilisk or cockatrice[5] does kill man and beast with his breath and sight, yea, the wolf takes away the voice of such as he suddenly meets withal and beholds. And why may not wicked men or women do the like? *Answer.* Indeed, it is a thing received by common error, and held of some for a truth, but no experience of any man has yet been brought for the proof thereof, and therefore it is to be reputed as fabulous. Thus much in probability may be thought (if the allegation should be true) that the basilisk, being possessed of a thick poison, may by his breath send forth some gross venomous vapors, and thereby infect the air and poison the thing that is near unto him. Again, that the sudden and unexpected beholding of the venomous cockatrice or the ravenous wolf (being creatures in their kind fearful, especially to those who are not acquainted with them) may cause present astonishment, and consequently peril of death. But that this should be done by the eyes of these creatures, in

---

5. The basilisk and cockatrice were mythical creatures, hybrids from a rooster and a serpent.

manner aforesaid, is not credible. And, therefore, authors have upon good ground denied it as being confirmed neither by reason nor experience.

Third, they reason thus: enchanters by [the] whispering of words in charms can stay the stinging and poisoning of serpents, for so David in effect speaks, that the voice of the charmer charms the serpent (Ps. 58:5). It may seem, therefore, that there is no small force in words for the effecting of strange works. *Answer.* It must be granted that the charmer may enchant the serpent. But how? Not by virtue of the words in the charm, but by the power of the devil who then is stirred up, when the charm is repeated, to do the thing intended. The truth of this answer appears by the words of the text, as they are read in the original, that the enchanter "joineth societies very cunningly," namely, with the devil. Now these societies between Satan and the charmer are the very ground of the work upon the serpent. This work, upon confederacy formerly made, is done by the devil. And the words of the charm are no more but the enchanter's item or watchword to occasion him thereunto. And let any other man repeat the same words a thousand times, that either is not thus confederate with Satan, or has not a superstitious opinion of charms, and all his labor will be in vain.

Fourth, the Word of God is of great force in the hearts of men to convert and change them, as it is uttered by the mouth of mortal man. And this force is not in the man by whom it is spoken. Where then should it be but in the words? And if in the words, why may not other words be of like efficacy, being uttered by man?

Answer 1. The power of God's Word comes not from this, that it is a word, and barely uttered out of the mouth of a man, for so it is a dead letter. But it proceeds from the powerful operation of the Spirit, annexed by God's promise thereunto, when it is uttered, read, and conceived. If this operation were taken away, the Word might be preached a thousand years together without any fruit or effect, either to salvation or condemnation.

Answer 2. The Word of God is powerful by the concurrence of the work of the Spirit, not in all things (as, for example, in raising winds and tempests, infecting the air, killing and annoying men or other creatures), but in the conversion of sinners, gathering the elect, and confirming those who are called. And it has this power also by His special blessing and appointment.

Answer 3. Furthermore, the same Word is not of power when it is barely read, heard, or spoken, unless it is also conceived in the understanding, received with reverence, treasured up in the memory, and mingled with faith in the heart. Whereas the bare reading and muttering over the words of a charm by an enchanter, though in an unknown tongue, in rude and barbarous words, is sufficient to procure the working of wonders.

Now, though the Word of God is in itself pure and serves to excellent purpose, as has been said, yet by the way we may remember that, as it is with all things that are most precious, nothing is so excellent in its kind which may not be abused. So it is with this heavenly Word, for it is (and may be) made a charm [in] two ways. First, when some part of it is indeed used for a charm. Thus, many texts of Scripture, both in Latin and other languages, have been abused by enchanters, as might easily be shown. Second, when it is heard, read, recited, or made a matter of prayer without understanding. And thus, the ignorant man, as much as in him lies, makes it a charm. For in his ordinary use thereof, he neither conceives nor takes care to understand it, as lamentable experience teaches. Yet in neither of these is the very bare repeating of the Word effectual. For as when a man hears or reads it, unless the Spirit of God enlightens his heart, it is to no purpose, so when it is made the matter of a spell, nothing will be effected unless the devil either by confederacy or superstitious conceit is drawn to confer his help in the point for his own advantage.

Of all enchantments, these, which are made of the Scriptures, are the most dishonorable to God, most acceptable to Satan, and most hurtful to the charmer. For beside the sin of witchcraft in the charming, this inconvenience ensues, that Satan procures more credit to one of these than to twenty others, because the words are Scripture. Hereby [he] cloaks his mischievous practices under the color of holiness, and so confirms the truth of that which the Holy Spirit says, that when he works most deceitfully "he transforms himself into an angel of light" (2 Cor. 11:14). He knows well that ordinary words seem nothing to some men, therefore he teaches and suggests phrases and sentences out of the Word, for such ungodly ends, that even the grace of them fetched from the Scriptures may make them seem powerful. Wherefore, let everyone who is endued with grace and knowledge, duly consider this with himself: God's Word cannot be effectual, when it is used to edification, unless the work of His own Spirit accompanies the same. Then, surely, it is impossible that the same which is holy, being used to an evil end, should be powerful except the devil affords his help for the effecting thereof.

To conclude, therefore, let men say what they will, the truth is this, that words of enchantment, be they ever so holy or profane, either by way of cursing or blessing, have no power of themselves to the producing of strange works. But [they] are (as has been said) only diabolical signs, admonishing the devil of some wickedness intended and desired, which he through his power must cause to be done.

And thus much of enchantment standing upon the practice of wonders by a charm. To this head of enchantment sundry other practices of witches are to be referred, the chief whereof are these:

First, the using and making of characters, images, or figures, especially the framing of circles, for this end, to work wonders by them; as to draw the picture of a child, man, other creature in clay or wax, and to bury the same in the ground, or to hide it in some secret place, or to burn it in the fire, thereby intending to hurt or kill the party resembled; again, to make an impression into the said picture by pricking or gashing the heart or any other place with intent to procure dangerous or deadly pains to the same parts. This is a mere practice of enchantment, and the making of the image and using it to this end is in virtue a charm, though no words are used. For the bare picture has no more power of itself to hurt the body represented than [do] bare words. All that is done comes by the work of the devil, who alone by the using of the picture in that sort is occasioned so or so, to work the party's destruction.

Second, hither we may refer the using of amulets, that is, remedies and preservatives against enchantments, sorceries, and bewitching, made of herbs or some such things, and hung about the neck for that end.

Third, the using of exorcisms; that is, certain set forms of words used in way of adjuration for some extraordinary end. [It is] a practice usual in the Church of Rome, whereby the priest conjures the salt, holy water, cream, spittle, oil, palms, etc., all which are in truth mere enchantments. For howsoever the Council of Trent has ratified them by their decrees, and so commended them to general use within the compass of the popish church,[6] yet they have in them no power or ability of blessing or cursing, either by nature or God's appointment.

Fourth, in this number we reckon the using of the name "Jesus" to drive away the devil or to prevent witchcraft—a common practice among the ignorant. Wherein the wonderful malice of Satan bewrays[7] itself in making the ignorant people think that Christ is a conjurer, and that there is virtue in the naming of His name to do some strange thing. Whereas the truth is he cares neither for this name nor for all the names of God, if a man goes no further than the bare repeating of them. But [he] rather delights to see them so abused and disgraced. And hereupon it is that in all conjurations, when he is raised by the sorcerer, he is willing to be adjured by all the holy names of God that are in the Scripture, to the end that he may the more deeply seduce his own instruments, and make them to think that these holy names will bind him and force him to yield unto their desires in the particular, when indeed there is no such matter. This point, thoroughly considered, may admonish us to take special heed of these cunning glosses[8] and devilish insinuations, whereby he intends

---

6. In the margin: Council. Trid. sess. 23. cap. 2.
7. *Bewray:* reveal.
8. *Gloss:* disguise.

to delude us, always remembering that the apostles themselves, to whom the power of working miracles was given, did never acknowledge the work to be done by the name of Jesus, but as Saint Peter affirms, "through faith in his name" (Acts 3:6, 16).

Fifth, the crossing of the body, to this end, that we may be blessed from the devil; a thing [that is] usual, even of latter times, especially in popery, wherein the cross carries the very nature of a charm, and the use of it in this manner, a practice of enchantment. For God has given no such virtue to a cross, either by creation or special privilege and appointment.

Sixth, the scratching of a witch to discover the witch. For it is a means which has no warrant or power thereunto, either by the Word of God or from nature, but only from the devil. If he yields either at crossing or scratching, he does it willingly, and not by compulsion, that he may feed his instrument with a false faith and a superstitious conceit, to the dishonor of God, and their own overthrow. In a word, look whatsoever actions, gestures, signs, rites, and ceremonies are used by men or women to work wonders, having no power to effect the same, either by creation and nature or by special appointment from God, they must all be referred to this head, and reckoned for charms.

The Use

Now, considering that all kinds of charms are the devil's watchwords to cause him to work the wonder, and [that they] have no virtue in them, be the words wherein they are conceived ever so good, hereby we must be admonished to take heed of the use of them and all other unlawful ceremonies, both in respect of their forms, be they praises or prayers or imprecations, as also in regard of their ends, be they ever so good in outward appearance. But alas! the more lamentable is the case, charming is in as great request as physic, and charmers more sought unto than physicians in time of need. There are charms for all conditions and ages of men, for divers kinds of creatures, yea, for every disease, as for headache, toothache, stitches, and such like. Nevertheless, howsoever some have subjected themselves to such base and ungodly means, yet the use hereof by the mercy of God has not been universal. And those who have sought for help are to be advised in the fear of God, to repent of their sin, and to take a better course. Let them rightly consider that they have hitherto depended upon Satan for help, and consequently have dishonored God, and renounced lawful means sanctified by Him, which should not have been done in case of the greatest worldly gain. For no man may do evil that good may come of it.

But they who use the help of charmers, and consult with witches, are wont to allege something in defense or excuse of their practice.

First, that they for their part mean no hurt. They know no evil by the man whom they seek to. They only send to him, and he does them good, how and in what manner they regard not. *Answer.* Indeed, many are ignorant of the enchanter's courses. But in cases of loss and hindrance, men ought not only to inquire [into] the means, but weigh and consider the warrant thereof, otherwise they do not what they do of faith, and so are guilty of sin before God (Rom. 15:2).[9] Put the case [that] they themselves mean no hurt, yet in this action they do hurt to themselves, by reposing trust in things which upon better consideration they shall find to be dishonorable and, therefore, hateful to God.

Second, they allege, we go to the physician for counsel, [and] we take his recipe, but we know not what it means. Yet, we use it and find benefit. If this is lawful, why may we not as well take benefit by the wise-man, whose courses we are ignorant of? *Answer.* (1) Physic used in time and place is a worthy ordinance of God and, therefore, being rightly used, God gives His blessing to it. But enchantment was never sanctified by God and, therefore, [it] cannot be used in any assurance of His blessing. (2) The physician's recipe, being a composition and mixture of natural things, though a man knows it not, yet he takes it into his stomach, or applies it to his body, and sensibly perceives the virtue and efficacy thereof in the working. Whereas the charmer's course consists of words, which neither are known in themselves nor are manifest in their use to sense or understanding. And hereby it is plain [that] there is not the same reason of physic and charms: the one having a sensible operation by virtue given it of God; the other insensible and wrought above ordinary means by the work of Satan.

Third, they allege [that] God is merciful, and He has provided a salve for every sore. They have used other means, but they have not succeeded. And what should they do more? May they not in extremity repair to the enchanter, and see what he can do for them, rather than [that] their goods and cattle should be lost and spoiled? *Answer.* (1) It would be better for you to bide by the loss, yea, to live and die in any sickness, than to tempt God by seeking help at [the] charmer's hands. For their help is dangerous and comes from the devil, whereupon if you rest yourselves, you join league with him, and so hazard eternally the safety both of bodies and souls. (2) Use good means allowed of God, and when they have been used often without success, proceed not to other courses, but refer yourselves to God, and say with Job: "The Lord hath given, and the Lord hath taken away; blessed be the name of the Lord" (Job 1:21).

And thus much of enchanting, the first part of operative witchcraft.

---

9. Cf. Rom. 14:23.

Section 2

The second part is juggling. Juggling is the deluding of the eye with some strange sleight done above the ordinary course of nature. In this description there are two points necessarily required in the point of juggling: (1) delusion of the eye, and (2) extraordinary sleight.

Delusion is then performed when a man is made to think he sees that which indeed he sees not. And this is done by the operation of the devil diversely, but especially [in] three ways: (1) by corrupting the humor of the eye, which is the next instrument of sight; (2) by altering the air, which is the means by which the object (or species) is carried to the eye; [and] (3) by altering and changing the object, that is, the thing seen (or whereon a man looks).

This deluding of the sense is noted by Paul in Galatians 3:1, "O foolish Galatians, who hath bewitched you?" Here the Spirit of God uses a word[10] borrowed from this kind of sorcerer, which in full meaning signifies thus much: "Who has deluded your eyes, and caused you to think you see that which you see not?" As if he should have said, "Look, as the juggler by his devilish art deludes the outward eye and makes men think they see that which indeed they do not, even so the false apostles by their erroneous doctrine have deluded the eyes of your minds, and have caused you, Galatians, to judge that to be the Word of God which is not, and that to be truth which is error and falsehood." Paul gives us to understand, by the very phrase used, that there is such a kind of juggling as is able to deceive the eye, for otherwise his comparison would not hold.

The second thing required in juggling is a sleight done above the order and course of nature. This is the point which makes these conveyances to be witchcraft. For if they were within the compass of nature, they could not be rightly termed and reputed sorceries, considering that divers men, by reason of the agility of their bodies and sleight of their hands, are able to work divers feats which seem strange to the beholders, and yet not meddle with witchcraft. Again, some by the lawful art of the optics may show strange and admirable things by means of light and darkness, and yet may be free from imputation of magical works, because they keep themselves wholly within the power and practice of nature. But sleights done in juggling, over and above delusion, must pass the ordinary bounds and precincts of nature, and so are made points of witchcraft. One memorable example, for the clearer manifestation of this point, we have in the Scripture, where Moses and Aaron wrought wonders before Pharaoh, turning the rod into a serpent, and water into blood, with many other such like (Exodus 7–9). Now Jannes and Jambres (for so Paul calls them in

---

10. In the margin: ἐβάσκανεν.

2 Timothy 3:8), the magicians of Egypt, did work the same miracles which Moses and Aaron had done. But here was the difference: Moses made true creatures and wrought true miracles, whereas they did all in appearance and outward show. For theirs were not truly real actions, but only magical illusions, wrought by the sleight and subtlety of the devil in the practice of juggling.

And because some think that the serpents and frogs, caused by the magicians, were true creatures, and all their other works as really and truly done as those which Moses and Aaron did, I will here stand a little to show and prove the contrary, that they were only in show and appearance, and not in deed and truth.

First, then, if the frogs and serpents caused by Jannes and Jambres were true creatures indeed, and their other sleights true and real works, then they were made and caused either by the devil or by God Himself (for no man of himself can make a rod to become a true serpent). But this was done neither by the devil nor by God, as shall appear in the sequel.

They were not done by the devil because the devil cannot make a true creature, either serpent or frog. How does that appear? *Answer.* To make a true creature of any sort by producing the same out of the causes is a work serving to continue the creation and is indeed a kind of creation. Now the devil, as he cannot create a thing at the first, so he is not able to continue the same by a new creation; that being a property belonging to God only. For better conceiving hereof, we must know that God creates [in] two ways: (1) primarily in the beginning when He made all things [out] of nothing (Gen. 1:1); or (2) secondarily in the government of the world when He produces a true creature in a true miracle, yet not making it [out] of nothing (as He did in the beginning) but producing it by ministering and informing the matter immediately by Himself without the aid of ordinary means and instruments appointed after the creation. The former is creation properly called; the latter [is] a continuance thereof. God has reserved both of these to Himself, as incommunicable to any creature. As for the succession and propagation of creatures in their kinds (as of men, beasts, birds, fish, etc.), it is only a continuation of the creatures in their kinds, and is wrought by ordinary means of generation; but [it] is no continuance of the work of creation. And the devil by his power may make counterfeits of the true creatures of God, but neither by creating them nor by continuing their creation. These two works are peculiar and proper to the Deity alone.

Again, if the devil could turn a rod into a true serpent and water into blood indeed, then his power should be equal to the power of the Son of God Himself. For the first miracle that He wrought was the turning of water into wine (John 2). And that was no greater a work than the turning of water into blood or a rod into a serpent. But this were most horrible blasphemy, to match the devil with the Son of God, and his finite power with the power of the Godhead by which miracles are wrought. And the truth is [that] Satan can work no true miracles. Neither does the text import that the magicians did that which they did by miracle, but by enchantment and sorcery (Exod. 7:11, 22; 8:7).

In the second place, I affirm that God did not create these creatures, or cause the works of the magicians to be effected. And this is proved by the words of Paul, who says that Jannes and Jambres (who did these works) withstood Moses and Aaron, whom God had sent, and by whom He wrought (2 Tim. 3:8). If then God had wrought with the magicians also, He should have been against Himself; yea, He should have wrought both ways (for Himself and against Himself) and consequently should have impeached His own glory, for the manifestation whereof He wrought miracles by Moses and Aaron. We may not once think [this] of God. Seeing, therefore, that these serpents (if they were true creatures) were not created either by Satan (because he could not) or by God Himself (because He would not), it must needs remain that they (and all of the magicians' other works) were mere illusions, and not otherwise.

Yet for the further clearing of the matter in hand, the text itself yields sundry reasons to prove that these acts of the sorcerers were but appearances and not things really produced.

First, they who cannot do a lesser thing cannot possibly do a greater. Now Moses shows that the Egyptian enchanters could not do a lesser thing than the turning of rods into true serpents, or [the] waters into blood. For they could not by all their power and skill preserve themselves from the plagues of Egypt, as the boils and other judgments (Exod. 9:11), which was an easier thing than making or changing a creature. Nay, they were not able to bring forth lice by their enchantment, which seemed to be the least miracle, but acknowledged that to be the finger of God (Exod. 8:18–19).

Second, the text says that Aaron's serpent devoured their serpents (Exod. 7:12); hence, it follows that theirs could not be true creatures. For in all likelihood they were all of the same kind, and of like quantity, at least in show. And it was never seen that one creature should receive into itself another creature of equal bigness with preservation of itself. Neither has it been observed ordinarily that one creature should devour another of the same kind. It was, therefore, a work of God's secret power in the true serpent whereby He would show that the others were not true and real, but formal and imaginary.

Third, if the magicians had been able to have made true frogs and serpents, then by the same power they might have removed those which Moses brought, for the like ability is required in both, yet this they could not do, but were fain to entreat Moses to pray for their removal. So says the text, "Then Pharaoh called for Moses and Aaron, and said, Pray…" (Exod. 8:8).

Lastly, the frogs which Moses caused, when they were removed, being gathered on heaps, caused great corruption, and the whole land stank of them (Exod. 8:14). Again, the water turned into blood made the fish in the river to die, and the water to stink, so that the Egyptians could not drink of the water of the river (Exod. 7:21). But we read of no such effect of the frogs and waters of the enchanters, which doubtless would have followed as well as the other, if both had been true and real creatures. It remains, therefore, that these were but mere appearances and juggling tricks, and the sorcerers themselves jugglers, yea, all their works but sleights caused by the power and subtlety of Satan, and no true works, as has been said.

Thus, I have declared the whole nature, grounds, and kinds of this damnable art.

Chapter 5

Witches

Having in the former part of this treatise opened the nature of witchcraft, and thereby made way for the better understanding of this judicial law of Moses, I come now to show who is the practicer hereof, whom the text principally aims at, namely, the witch, whether man or woman.

A witch is a magician who either by open or secret league, wittingly and willingly, consents to use the aid and assistance of the devil in the working of wonders.

Point 1

First, I call the witch a magician to show what kind of person this is; to wit, such a one as does profess and practice witchcraft. For a magician is a professor and practicer of this art, as may appear in Acts 8:9 where Simon, a witch of Samaria, is called *Magus*, or Simon the magician.

Again, in this general term I comprehend both sexes (or kinds) of persons, men and women, excluding neither from being witches. A point the rather to be remembered because Moses in this place, setting down a judicial law against witches, uses a word of the feminine gender (*mecashepha*), which in English properly signifies a woman witch. Whereupon some might gather that only women were witches. Howbeit, Moses, in this word, exempts not the male, but only uses a notion referring to the female for good causes, principally for these two:

First, to give us to understand that the woman, being the weaker sex, is sooner entangled by the devil's illusions with this damnable art than the man. And in all ages it is found true by experience that the devil has more easily and more often prevailed with women than with men. Hence it was that the Hebrews of ancient times used it for a proverb, "The more women, the more witches." His first temptation in the beginning was with Eve, a woman, and since [then] he pursues his practice accordingly, as making most for his advantage. For where he finds easiest entrance and best entertainment, thither will he most often resort.

Second, to take away all exception of punishment from any party that shall practice this trade, and to show that weakness cannot exempt the witch from death. For in all reason, if any might allege infirmity, and plead for favor, it would be the woman who is weaker than the man. But the Lord says that if any person of either sex among His people is found to have entered covenant with Satan, and become a practicer of sorcery, though it is a woman and the weaker vessel, she shall not escape, she shall not be suffered to live, she must die the death. And though weakness in other cases may lessen both the crime and the punishment, yet in this it shall take no place.

Point 2

The second point in the description is: consenting to use the help of the devil, either by open or secret league, wittingly and willingly. Wherein stands the very thing that makes a witch to be a witch: the yielding of consent upon covenant. By which clause two sorts of people are expressly excluded from being witches. First, such as be tainted with frenzy or madness, or are through weakness of the brain deluded by the devil. For these, though they may be said after a sort to have society with Satan, or rather he with them, yet they cannot give their consent to use his aid truly, but only in imagination. It is far otherwise with the true witch. Second, all such superstitious persons, men or women, as use charms and enchantment for the effecting of anything upon a superstitious and erroneous persuasion, that the charms have virtue in them to do such things, not knowing that it is the action of the devil by those means, but thinking that God has put virtue into them, as He has done into herbs for physic.[1]

Of such persons we have (no doubt) abundance in our land, who though they deal wickedly and sin grievously in using charms, yet because they intend not to join league with the devil, either secretly or formally, they are not to be counted witches. Nevertheless, they are to be advertised[2] in the meantime that their estate is fearful. For their present ungodly practices have prepared them already to this cursed trade and may bring them in time to be the rankest witches that can be. Wherefore, I advise all ignorant persons who know not God nor the Scriptures to take heed and beware of this dangerous evil, the use of charms. For if they are once convinced in their consciences, and know that God has given no power to such means, and yet shall use them, assuredly they do in effect consent to the devil to be helped by him, and thereupon are joined in confederacy with him in the confidence of their own hearts, and so are become witches.

---

1. This paragraph break is not in the original.
2. *Advertised*: advised.

Point 3

The third and last thing in the description is the end of witchcraft: the working of wonders. Wonders are wrought three ways (as has been shown): by divination, enchantment, or juggling. All feats and practices of witchcraft are to be referred to one of these three heads.

Now if any man doubt whether there are such witches indeed as have been described, let him remember that beside experience in all ages and countries, we have also sundry examples of them even in the Scriptures.

In the Old Testament we read of Balaam (Numbers 23) who, though he is called a prophet because he was so reputed of men, yet indeed he was a notorious witch, both by profession and practice, and would have showed his cunning in that kind upon the Israelites, if God had not hindered him against his will. Of the same kind were the enchanters of Egypt (Exodus 7), the witches of Persia (Daniel 2), and the pythoness of Endor, known as a renowned sorcerer over all Israel, and therefore Saul's servants, being asked, could presently tell of her (1 Samuel 28).

In the New Testament, mention is made of Simon, whose name declared his profession. His name was Magus, and the text says that he used witchcraft and bewitched the people of Samaria, calling himself a great man (Acts 8:9). Whence it was that, after his death, there was a statue set up in Rome in honor of him, in the days of Claudius Caesar, with this inscription, *Simoni Deo sancto*.[3] And it is not unlikely [that] Bar-jesus, the false prophet at Paphus, was a man addicted to the practices of witchcraft, and for that cause was called by a kind of excellency, "Elymas the magician" (Acts 13:6–8), that is, the great or famous sorcerer.[4] Lastly, the Pythoness at Philippi, "that gat her master much advantage by divining" (Acts 16:16). And all these used the help of the devil for the working of wonders.

There are two sorts of witches: the bad witch and the good witch. For so they are commonly called.

The bad witch is he or she who has consented in a league with the devil to use his help for the doing of hurt only, as to strike and annoy the bodies of men, women, children, and cattle with diseases and with death itself, so likewise to raise tempests by sea and by land, etc. This is commonly called the binding witch.

The good witch is he or she who, by consent in a league with the devil, does use his help for the doing of good only. This cannot hurt, torment, curse, or kill, but only heal and cure the hurts inflicted upon men or cattle by bad witches. For as they can do no good but only hurt, so this can do no hurt but good only. And this is that order which the devil has set in his kingdom, appointing to

---

3. In the margin: Just. Mart. Apolog. ad Anton. Pium.

4. In the margin: ὁ μάγος.

several persons their several offices and charges. And the good witch is commonly termed the unbinding witch.

Now howsoever both these are evil, yet of the two the more horrible and detestable monster is the good witch. For look in whatsoever place there are any bad witches who only hurt, there also the devil has his good ones, who are better known than the bad, being commonly called wise men or wise women. This will appear by experience in most places in these countries. For let a man's child, friend, or cattle be taken with some sore sickness, or strangely tormented with some rare and unknown disease, the first thing he does is to bethink himself and inquire after some wise man or wise woman, and thither he sends and goes for help. When he comes, he first tells him the state of the sick man. The witch then, being certified of the disease, prescribes either charms of words to be used over him, or other such counterfeit means, wherein there is no virtue, being nothing else but the devil's sacraments to cause him to do the cure, if it comes by witchcraft. Well, the means are received, applied, and used, the sick party accordingly recovers, and the conclusion of all is the usual acclamation: "Oh happy is the day that ever I met with such a man or woman to help me!"

Here observe that both have a stroke in this action: the bad witch hurt him [and] the good healed him. But the truth is the latter has done him a thousand-fold more harm than the former. For the one did only hurt the body, but the devil by means of the other, though he has left the body in good plight, yet he has laid fast hold on the soul, and by curing the body has killed that. And the party thus cured cannot say with David, "the Lord is my helper," but "the devil is my helper," for by him he is cured. The present law of Moses must be understood of both these kinds of witches.

This point well considered yields matter both of instruction and practice.

Of instruction, in that it shows the cunning and crafty dealing of Satan, who afflicts and torments the body for the gain of the soul. And for that purpose [he] has so ordered his instruments that the bad witch gives the occasion by annoying the body or goods, and the good [witch] immediately accomplishes his desire by entangling the soul in the bands of error, ignorance, and false faith. Again, this shows the blindness of natural corruption, especially in ignorant and superstitious people. It is their nature to abhor hurtful persons, such as bad witches are, and to count them execrable. But those who do them good, they honor and reverence as wise men and women, yea, seek and sue unto them in times of extremity, though of all persons in the world they are most odious. And in them Satan seems the greatest friend, when he is most like himself and intends greatest mischief. Let all ignorant persons be advised hereof in time, to take heed to themselves, and learn to know God and His Word, that by light from thence they may better discern of the subtle practices of Satan and his instruments.

For matter of practice, hence we learn our duty to abhor the wizard as the most pernicious enemy of our salvation, the most effectual instrument of destroying our souls and of building up the devil's kingdom, yea, as the greatest enemy to God's name, worship, and glory, that is in the world, next to Satan himself. Of this sort was Simon Magus, who by doing strange cures and works, made the people of Samaria to take him for some great man, who wrought by the mighty power of God, whereas he did all by the devil. He, therefore, being a good witch, did more hurt in seducing the people of God than Balaam (a bad one) could with all his curses. And we must remember that the Lord has set a law upon the witch's head, "he must not live," and if death is due to any, then a thousand deaths of right belong to the good witch.

But the patrons of witches endeavor to delude the true interpretation of that law. For by a witch (say they) we must understand a poisoner, and they allege for that purpose the seventy interpreters who translated the original word (*mecashepha*) by φαρμακευς, which signifies a poisoner. I answer, first, the word used by the seventy interpreters signifies indeed so much, yet not that only but also a witch in general, as may appear in sundry places of Scripture. The apostle, reckoning up witchcraft among the works of the flesh [Gal. 5:20], uses the Greek word φαρμακεια, not for poisoning, but for all magical arts, as Jerome testifies upon the place. And that it must necessarily be so translated is evident, because in the next verse "murder" is termed another work of the flesh, under which poisoning and all other kinds of killing are comprehended. And the same word is used in the like sense in Revelation 21:8 and 22:15.

Second, the word (*mecashepha*), which Moses uses, is ascribed to the enchanters of Egypt (Exodus 7–9) and to the wise men of Babel (Daniel 2), who are also called φαρμακευς in the translation of the seventy. And both sorts of them were witches and sorcerers. The kings of Egypt and Babylon used these *mecashephim* for sundry purposes and made them of their council. And if they had been, according to this allegation, poisoners, it is not likely they would have so fitted the humors of these two princes, Pharaoh and Nebuchadnezzar, much less that they would have so ordinarily required their presence and assistance in the business there mentioned.

Third, there is a peremptory law against the willful murderer, that he should be put to death, and that no recompense should be taken for his life (Num. 35:31). In which place all poisoners are condemned because they are willful murderers. Now, if here in Exodus, by *mecashepha* we should understand a poisoner, then there should be one and the same law twice propounded for the same thing, which is not likely. And, therefore, the word used by Moses in this text signifies not a poisoner properly, but a witch.

Chapter 6

The Punishment of Witches

Hitherto I have treated of the nature of witchcraft, both in general and particular, and [I] have also shown what witches are, both good and bad. And now I proceed to the second point considered in this text, the punishment of a witch, and that is death.

In the judicial laws of Moses (whereof this is one) the Lord appointed sundry penalties, which in quality and degree differed one from another, so as according to the nature of the offence was the proportion and measure of the punishment ordained. And of all sins, as those were the most heinous in account which tended directly to the dishonor of God, so to them was assigned death, the greatest and highest degree of punishment. He who despised the law of Moses died without mercy under two or three witnesses (Heb. 10:28), the punishment of the thief was restitution four-fold (Exod. 22:1), but the murderer must be put to death (Num. 35:31), the idolater and seducer were commanded to be slain (Exod. 22:20; Deut. 13:5), [and] the blasphemer must be stoned (Lev. 24:16). And the witch is numbered among these grievous offenders, therefore his punishment is as great as any other. For the text says he might[1] not be suffered to live (Exod. 22:18).

But why should the witch be so sharply censured? And what should move the Lord to allot so high a degree of punishment to that sort of offenders? *Answer.* The cause was not the hurt which they brought upon men in body, goods, or outward estate. For there are sundry that never did harm, but good only. We read not of any great hurt that was done by the enchanters of Egypt, or by the Pythoness of Endor, or by Simon Magus in Samaria. And those divining witches, who have taken upon themselves to foretell things to come, hurt not any but themselves. Yet they must die the death. This, therefore, is not the cause. But what if these do hurt or kill, must they not then die? Yes, verily, but by another law, the law of murder, and not by the law of witchcraft. For in this case, he dies as a murderer, and not as a witch, and so he should die, though he were no witch.

---

1. *Might*: must.

The cause then of this sharp punishment is the very making of a league with the devil, either secret or open, whereby they covenant to use his help for the working of wonders. For by virtue of this alone it comes to pass that witches can do strange things in divining, enchanting, and juggling. Now let it be observed of what horrible impiety they stand guilty before God, who join in confederacy with Satan. Hereby they renounce the Lord who made them, they make no more account of His favor and protection, they do quite cut themselves off from the covenant made with Him in baptism, from the communion of the saints, from the true worship and service of God. And on the contrary, they give themselves unto Satan, as their god, whom they continually fear and serve. Thus, they are become the most detestable enemies to God and His people that can be. For this cause, Samuel told Saul that rebellion was as the sin of witchcraft; that is, a most heinous and detestable sin in the sight of God. The traitor who does no hurt to his neighbor, but is willing and ready to do him the best services that can be desired, is notwithstanding, by the law of nations, no better than a dead man, because he betrays his sovereign, and consequently cannot be a friend unto the commonwealth. In like manner, though the witch were in many respects profitable, did no hurt, but procured much good, yet because he has renounced God, his King and Governor, and has bound himself by other laws to the service of the enemy of God and His church, death is his portion justly assigned him by God, [and] he may not live.

Chapter 7

The Application

Having thus delivered the true sense and interpretation of this judicial law, both concerning the sin of witchcraft and the persons by whom this sin is practiced, it remains now that I should make some use thereof by way of application to the witches of our times. In doing whereof, four particular questions of moment are to be handled. First, whether the witches of our times are the same with those who are here condemned by the law of Moses? For some there are (and those men of learning and members of God's church) who hold [that] they are not. Second, if they are the same (as it shall appear they are), then how may we in these days be able to discern and discover a witch? Third, what remedy may be used against the hurt of witchcraft? Fourth, whether our witches are to be punished with death, and that by virtue of this law of Moses?

Section 1

Question. Whether the witches of our times are the same with those who are here condemned by the law of Moses?

Answer. If we do well consider the quality and condition of the witches of our days, we shall easily see that they are the same. For experience shows that whether they are men or women, but especially aged women, they are such persons as do renounce God and their baptism, and make a league with the devil (either secretly or openly) in which the devil binds himself to teach them certain rites and ceremonies whereby they may be able to work wonders, as to stir up tempests, reveal secrets, kill or hurt men and cattle, or cure and do good, according to the tenor of their covenant.

The confessions of witches, recorded in the chronicles of countries through all Europe, do with common consent declare and manifest this point.[1] So that howsoever our witches may differ in some circumstances from those in the time of Moses, as either in the instruments and means used, or in the manner and form, or in some particular ends of their practices, yet in the substance and

---

1. In the margin: Joan. Fr. Pic. Mirand. de prænot. l. 1. c. 2. Nicol. Remigius, Dæmonolatr. c. 1. c. 5.

foundation of witchcraft they agree with them. For both of them have made a covenant with the devil one way or another, and by virtue thereof have wrought wonders above the order of nature. Agreeing therefore in the very foundation and form of witchcraft, which is the league, and in the proper end, the working of wonders, they must needs be in substance and effect the same with the witches mentioned by Moses. And yet this point is denied by some, and the witches of these days have their patrons, who use reasons to prove that now we have none such as we speak of. Their reasons are especially three.

Reason 1
First, they labor to take away the form of witchcraft, affirming that there can be no confederacy made between the witch and the devil, and that for four causes.

First, in every league and contract the parties must be mutually bound to each other. Now there can be no bond made between a man or woman and the devil, and though there could, yet man is bound in conscience to God, to renounce the bond of obedience to Satan, and to break the covenant.

Answer. There are two sorts of leagues: lawful and unlawful. In all lawful leagues it is true that there must be a mutual bond of both parties to each other, which may not be dissolved. But in unlawful compacts it is otherwise. And no man can say that this league between a witch and the devil is lawful, but wicked and damnable, yet being once made, howsoever unlawfully, it is a league and compact. This, therefore, proves not that there can be no covenant at all, but that there can be no lawful covenant between them, which no man will deny.

Second, Satan and the witch are of divers natures. He is spiritual [and] they are corporal substances; therefore, there can be no league made between them.

Answer. The reason is not good. For even God Himself, who is of nature most simple and spiritual, made a covenant with Adam, renewed the same unto Abraham, Isaac, and Jacob, and continues it with His church on earth from age to age. Hence it appears that diversity of nature in the parties cannot hinder the making of a covenant. And, therefore, if man may make a covenant with God Himself, who is most spiritual, then he may likewise come in league with the devil, whose substance is not so pure and spiritual. Again, we must remember that in making of a covenant, it is sufficient that the parties consent and agree in will and understanding, though other circumstances and rites, which are but signs of confirmation, are wanting. Be it then that Satan has not a bodily substance as man has, yet considering that man is endued with understanding to conceive of things as the devil does, and [that he] also has will to yield consent and approbation thereunto (though in a corrupt and wicked manner), there may pass a confederacy, and a covenant may be made and stand in force between them.

Third, whatsoever the devil does in this compact, he does it in fraud and deceit, never meaning in his promises as man does. And when both parties mean not one and the same thing, how can they grow to agreement in any kind?

Answer. Suppose this is true, yet it only proves that the covenant made between them was deceitful and unlawful. But what of that? It still remains a bargain howsoever, for it fails only in the circumstance, [but] the substance (which is the consent of the parties) was not wanting.

Fourth, witches of our times (say they) are aged persons, of weak brains, and troubled with abundance of melancholy, and the devil takes advantage of the humor, and so deludes them, persuading that they have made a league with him when they have not, and consequently moving them to imagine that they do (and may do) strange things, which indeed are done by himself and not by them.

Answer. This reason is a mere melancholic conceit without ground. And the contrary is a manifest truth, that they are not so (as is affirmed) parties deceived by reason of their humors. For first, our witches are as wise and politic, yea, as crafty and cunning in all other matters, as other men are. Whereas brainsick persons troubled with melancholy, if their understanding is distempered in one occasion, it will be faulty likewise in others, more or less.

Second, our witches know that they sin in their practices of witchcraft, and therefore they use subtle means to cover them, and he who would convict them must have great dexterity to go beyond them. Now if they were persons deluded through corruption of any humors, look what humor caused them to do a thing, the same would urge them to disclose it.

Third, they are also of the same stamp, they take the same courses in all their practices, their consent in word and action is universal. Men of learning have observed that all witches through Europe are of like carriage and behavior in their examinations and convictions. They use the same answers, refuges, defenses, [and] protestations. In a word, look what are the practices and courses of the witches in England in any of these particulars, the practices of the witches in Spain, France, Italy, Germany, etc., are the same. Wherefore, the case is clear, they are not deluded by Satan through the force of humor, as is avouched. For such persons, according as they are diversely taken, would show themselves diversely affected, and vary in their speeches, actions, and conceits, both public and private.

Fourth, our witches are wont to communicate their skill to others by tradition, to teach and instruct their children and posterity, and to initiate them in the grounds and practices of their own trade, while they live, as may appear by the confessions recorded in the courts of all countries. But if they were persons troubled with melancholy, their conceits would die with them. For conceits and imaginary fancies, which rise from any humor, cannot be conveyed from party to party, no more than the humor itself.

Lastly, if this sleight might serve to defend witches under pretense of delusion through corrupted humors, then here is a cover for all manner of sins. For example, a felon is apprehended for robbery or murder, and is brought before the judge. Upon examination he confesses the act. Being convicted, the law proceeds to condemnation. The same man's friends come in, and allege before the judge in this manner: This man has a crazy brain, and is troubled with melancholy, and though he has confessed the act, yet the truth is [that] it was not him but the devil who himself committed the murder, and made him think he did it when he did it not, and hereupon he has confessed. Would any man think that this was a reasonable allegation, and a sufficient means to move the judge to acquit him? Assuredly, if it were, upon the same ground might any sin be laid upon the devil's back, and all good laws and judicial proceedings be made void.

Therefore, howsoever the patrons of witches are learned men, yet they are greatly deceived in fathering the practices of sorcery upon a melancholic humor.

But for the further ratifying of their assertion, they proceed, and use this argument: they who confess of themselves things false and impossible must needs be parties deluded, but our witches do this when they are examined or consulted with, as that they can raise tempests, that they are carried through the air in a moment from place to place, that they pass through keyholes and clefts of doors, that they be sometimes turned into cats, hares, and other creatures, and, lastly, that they are brought into far countries to meet with Herodias, Diana, and the devil, and such like. All which are mere fables and impossible things.

Answer. We must make a difference of witches in regard of time. There is a time when they first begin to make a league with Satan, and a time also after the league is made and confirmed.

When they first begin to grow in confederacy with the devil, they are sober and their understanding [is] sound. They make their match waking, and as they think wisely enough, knowing both what they promise the devil and upon what conditions, and therefore all this while it is no delusion. But after they are once in the league, and have been entangled in compact with the devil (considerately as they think for their own good and advantage) the case may be otherwise.

For then reason and understanding may be depraved, memory weakened, and all the powers of their soul blemished. Thus, becoming his vassals, they are deluded, and so intoxicated by him that they will run into thousands of fantastical imaginations, holding themselves to be transformed into the shapes of other creatures, to be transported in the air into other countries, yea, to do many strange things, which in truth they do not.

Reason 2

I come now to their second reason. The witches of our age (say they) were not known in the days of Moses nor of Christ, therefore the law concerns them not. To this I answer two ways.

First, that their argument is naught, for by the same reason the papists might avouch the lawfulness of the images of saints (as of Peter, Paul, and others, yea, of Christ Himself) because they were not known in the days of Moses, and therefore could not be condemned in the second commandment. Whereas contrarily the Spirit of God has so framed and penned the laws, moral and judicial, which concern man, as that they fetch within their compass all sins of all ages, and condemn them. And, therefore, whatsoever is against the law of God written by Moses, though it were not known nor heard of, either when the law was made or afterward, is yet condemned by the same law.

Again, I answer that our witches are the same that were in Moses's time and, therefore, by their own reason must needs be condemned by this judicial law. For by the records of ancient writers it is proved that about 1,200 years before Christ's birth, shortly after the Trojan war, which was a hundred years and upward before the building of the temple by Solomon, there were the same witches that are now, as the Circes and Syrenes, and such like, mentioned in the narration of that war, as is manifest to them that know the story.[2]

Again, five hundred years before Christ, when the Romans made their twelve tables,[3] which comprised all the laws whereby that famous commonwealth was governed, they made one expressly against witches, even the same with these of our time, for practicing the same things, as blasting of corn, hurting of cattle, men, women, and children, etc. And for the time of Christ, though there is no particular mention made of any such witches, yet thence it follows not that there were none. For all things that then happened were not recorded. And I would fain know of the chief patrons of them, whether those parties possessed with the devil and troubled with strange diseases, whom Christ healed,

---

2. In the margin: Homer. Odyss. lib. 10 and 12.

3. In the margin: Sub tit. de injur. aliisq; delict. c. 9. Senec. lib. Nat. Quest. 4. Qui fruges excantassit, etc.

and out of whom He cast devils, were not bewitched with some such people as our witches are? If they say no, let them (if they can) prove the contrary.

Reason 3

The third and last reason is this: Christ abolished all sin at His coming, and therefore miracles and witchcraft then ceased also. The apostle says "that he spoiled principalities and powers, and triumphed over them upon the cross" (Col. 2:15).

Answer. This argument is frivolous, serving as well to justify the traitor, the thief, and the murderer, as the witch. For whereas it is alleged that Christ abolished all sin, we must understand how. Not simply, so as sin should be no more, but only in part, in this life, reserving the final destruction thereof to the last judgment. Again, sin is not abolished, no not in part unto all, but only to the members of Christ. Whereupon the apostle says, "There is no condemnation to them, that are in Christ" (Rom. 8:1), because no sin is imputed unto them. But unto witches, and all the enemies of Christ, sin is imputed and not abolished.

To conclude, howsoever much is said in their defense, yet the first part is clear affirmatively, that the witches of our time are the same with the witches that were in Moses's time, in truth and substance. And so much for the first question.

Section 2

Question. How may we be able in our days to discern and discover a witch?

Answer. The discovery of a witch is a matter judicial, as is also the discovery of a thief and a murderer, and belongs not to every man, but is to be done judicially by the magistrate, according to the form and order of law. He, therefore, is set apart for such ends, and has authority both to discover and to punish the enemies of God and His church. Now for the magistrate's direction in this business, we are to know that in the discovery of a witch two things are required: examination and conviction.

Examination

Examination is an action of the magistrate, making special enquiry of the crime of witchcraft. This action must have the beginning from occasions and presumptions. For the magistrate, though he is a public person, and stands in the room of God for the execution of justice, yet he may not take upon him[self] to examine whom and how [he] himself wills, of any crime. Neither ought he to proceed upon the sleight causes, as to show his authority over others, or upon sinister respects, as to revenge his malice, or to bring parties into danger of suspicion. But he must proceed upon special presumptions.

I call those presumptions which do at least probably and conjecturally note one to be a witch. And these are certain signs whereby the party may be discovered. I will touch some few of them.

The first in order is this: if any person, man, or woman, is notoriously defamed for such a party. Notorious defamation is a common report of the greater sort of people, with whom the suspected party dwells, that he or she is a witch. This yields a strong suspicion. Yet the magistrate must be wary in receiving such a report. For it falls out oftentimes that the innocent may be suspected, and some of the better sort notoriously defamed. Therefore, the wise and prudent judge ought carefully to look that the report be made by men of honesty and credit. If it is, he may then proceed to make further inquiry of the fact.

Second, if a fellow witch or magician gives testimony of any person to be a witch, either voluntarily, or at his or her examination, or at his or her death. This is not sufficient for conviction or condemnation, but only a fit presumption to cause strait examination of the party to be made.

Third, if after cursing there follows death, or at least some mischief. For witches are wont to practice their mischievous acts by cursing and banning. This also is a sufficient matter of examination, not of conviction.

Fourth, if after enmity, quarrelling, or threatening, a present mischief does follow. For parties devilishly disposed, after cursing, do use threats. And that also is a great presumption.

Fifth, if the suspected party is the son or daughter, the manservant or maidservant, the familiar friend, near neighbor, or old companion of a known and convicted witch. This may be likewise a presumption. For witchcraft is an art that may be learned and conveyed from man to man, and often it falls out that a dying witch leaves some of the forenamed heirs of her witchcraft.

Sixth, some do add this for a presumption: if the suspected party is found to have the devil's mark. For it is commonly thought [that], when the devil makes his covenant with them, he always leaves his mark behind him, whereby he knows them for his own. Now if by some casual means, such a mark is descried[4] on the body of the suspected party, whereof no evident reason in nature can be given, the magistrate in this case may cause such to be examined, or take the matter into his own hand, that the truth may appear.

Lastly, if the examined party is inconstant, or contrary to himself in his deliberate answers, it argues a guilty mind and conscience which stops the freedom of speech and utterance and may give just occasion to the magistrate to make further enquiry. I say not if he or she is timorous and fearful. For a good man may be fearful in a good cause, sometimes by nature, sometimes in regard

---

4. *Descry:* catch sight of something.

of the presence of the judge, and the greatness of the audience. Again, some may be suddenly taken, and others naturally want the liberty of speech, which other men have. And these are the causes of fear and astonishment, which may befall the good as well as the bad.

Touching the manner of examination, there are two kinds of proceeding: (1) by a single question; or, (2) by some torture. A single question is when the magistrate himself only makes enquiry, what was done or not done, by bare and naked interrogations. A torture is when, besides the enquiry in words, he uses also the rack or some other violent means to urge confession. This course has been taken in some countries and may no doubt lawfully and with good conscience be used, howbeit not in every case, but only upon strong and great presumptions going before, and when the party is obstinate.

And thus much for examination. Now follows the conviction.

Conviction

Conviction is an action of the magistrate, after just examination, discovering the witch. This action must proceed from just and sufficient proofs, and not from bare presumptions. For though presumptions give occasion to examine, yet they are no sufficient causes of conviction. Now in general the proofs used for conviction are of two sorts: some are less sufficient, [and] some are more sufficient.

The less sufficient proofs are these. First, in former ages, the party suspected of witchcraft was brought before the magistrate, who caused red hot iron and scalding water to be brought and commanded the party to put his hand in the one, or to take up the other, or both. And if he took up the iron in his bare hand without burning, or endured the water without scalding, hereby he was cleared, and judged free. But if he did burn or scald, he was then convicted, and condemned for a witch. But this manner of conviction has long ago been condemned for wicked and diabolical, as in truth it is, considering that thereby many times an innocent man may be condemned, and a rank witch escape unpunished.

Second, our own times have afforded instances of such weak and insufficient proofs. As first, scratching of the suspected party, and present recovery thereupon. Second, burning of the thing bewitched, if it is not a man (as a hog, ox, or such like creature), is imagined to be a forcible means to cause the witch to discover herself. Third, the burning of the thatch of the suspected party's house, which is thought to be able to cure the party bewitched, and to make the witch to betray herself.

Third, beside these, in other countries they have a further proof justified by some that are learned. The party is taken, and bound hand and foot, and cast cross ways into the water. If she sinks, she is counted innocent, and escapes. If she floats on the water, and sinks not, she is taken for a witch, convicted, and accordingly punished.

All these proofs are so far from being sufficient, that some of them, if not all, are after a sort, practices of witchcraft, having in them no power or virtue to detect a sorcerer, either by God's ordinance in the creation, or by any special appointment since. For what virtue can the scratching of a witch have to cure a hurt? Where do we find it in any part of the Word of God that scratching should be used? Or what promise of recovery upon the use thereof?

But how then comes it to pass that help is often procured by these and such like means? *Answer*. It is the sleight and subtlety of the devil, upon scratching the witch, to remove such hurts, as [he] himself has inflicted, that thereby he may inure men to the practice of wicked and superstitious means. And what I say of scratching, the same may be enlarged to all other proofs of this kind before named. God has imprinted no such virtue in their natures to these purposes or added the same unto them by special and extraordinary assignment. That, therefore, which is brought to pass by them when they are used, comes from the devil.

And yet to justify the casting of a witch into the water, it is alleged that, having made a covenant with the devil, she has renounced her baptism, and hereupon there grows an antipathy between her and water. *Answer*. This allegation serves to no purpose, for all water is not the water of baptism, but that only which is used in the very act of baptism, and not before nor after. The element out of the use of the sacrament is no sacrament but returns again to its common use.

To go yet further, another insufficient proof is the testimony of some wizard. It has been the ordinary custom of some men, when they have had anything ill at ease, presently to go or send to some wise man or wise woman, by whom they have been informed that the thing is bewitched. And to win credit to their answer, some of them have offered to show the witch's face in a glass. Whereof the party, having taken notice, returns home, and detects the man or woman of witchcraft. I grant this may be a good presumption to cause strait examination, but a sufficient proof of conviction it cannot be. For put the case the grand jury at the assizes goes on a suspected party, and in their consultation the devil comes in the likeness of some known man and tells them the person in question is indeed a witch, and offers withal to confirm the same by oath. Should the inquest receive his oath or accusation to condemn the man? Assuredly not. And yet, that is as much as the testimony of another wizard, who only by the devil's help reveals the witch. If this should be taken for a sufficient proof, the devil would not leave one good man alive in the world.

Again, all other presumptions commonly used are insufficient, though they may minister occasion of trial. For example, if a man in open court should affirm before the judge [that] such a one fell out with me and cursed me, giving me threatening words, that I should smart for it, and some mischief should light upon my person or goods, ere it were long. Upon these curses and threats, presently such and such evils befell me, and I suffered these and these losses. The magistrate thus informed may safely proceed to inquire into the matter, but he has not from hence any sure ground of conviction. For it pleases God many times to lay His hand upon men's persons and goods without the procurement of witches. And yet experience shows that ignorant people, who carry a rage against them, will make strong proofs of such presumptions, whereupon sometimes jurors do give their verdict against parties innocent.

Lastly, if a man, being dangerously sick and likely to die, upon suspicion will take it on his death, that such a one has bewitched him, it is an allegation of the same nature which may move the judge to examine the party, but it is of no moment for conviction. The reason is because it was but the suspicion of one man, and a man's own word for himself, though in time of extremity, when it is likely he will speak nothing but the truth, is of no more force than another man's word against him.

And these are the proofs which men in place and time have ordinarily used for the detecting of such ungodly persons. But the best that may be said of them is that they are all either false or uncertain signs, and unavailable for the condemnation of any man whatsoever.

Now follow the true proofs and sufficient means of conviction, all which may be reduced to two heads.

The first is the free and voluntary confession of the crime made by the party suspected and accused after examination. This has been thought generally of all men, both divines and lawyers, a sufficient proof. For what needs more witness, or further enquiry, when a man from the touch of his own conscience acknowledges the fault.

And yet the patrons and advocates of witches except against it, and object in this manner: that a man or woman may confess against themselves an untruth, being urged thereto either by fear or threatening, or by a desire upon some grief conceived to be out of the world, or, at least, being in trouble, and persuaded it is the best course to save their lives and obtain liberty, they may upon simplicity be induced to confess that which they never did, even against themselves. *Answer.* I say not that a bare confession is sufficient, but a confession after due examination taken upon pregnant presumptions. For if a man, examined without any grounds or presumptions, should openly acknowledge the crime, his act may be justly suspected as grounded upon by-respects. But when proceeding is made against him at the first upon good probabilities, and hereupon he is drawn to a free confession, that which he has manifested thereby cannot but be a truth. Other points of exception urged by them are of small moment and may easily be answered out of the grounds before delivered, and therefore I omit them.

Now if the party held in suspicion is examined and will not confess, but obstinately persists in denial, as commonly it falls out, then there is another course to be taken by a second sufficient means of conviction, which is the testimony of two witnesses of good and honest report, avouching before the magistrate, upon their own knowledge, these two things: either that the accused party has made a league with the devil; or [that he] has done some known practices of witchcraft. And all arguments that do necessarily prove either of these, being brought by two sufficient witnesses, are of force fully to convince the party suspected. For example:

First, if they can prove that the suspected party has invocated and called upon the devil or desired his help. For this is a branch of that worship which Satan binds his instruments to give unto him. And it is pregnant proof of a league formerly made between them.

Second, if they can give evidence that the party has entertained a familiar spirit and had conference with it in form or likeness of a mouse, cat, or some other visible creature.

Third, if they affirm upon oath that the suspected person has done any action or work which necessarily infers a covenant made, as that he has shown the face of a suspected man (being absent) in a glass, or used enchantment, or such like feats. In a word, if they both can avouch upon their own proper knowledge that such a suspected man or woman has put in practice any other actions of witchcraft as to have divined of things afore they came to pass, and that peremptorily, to have raised tempests, to have caused the form of a dead man to appear, or the like. Standing either in divination or operation, it proves sufficiently that he or she is a witch.

But some may say, if these are the only strong proofs for the conviction of a sorcerer, it will then be impossible to put anyone to death, because the league with Satan is closely made, and the practices of sorcery are also very secret, and hardly can a man be brought, who upon his own knowledge can aver[5] such things.

I answer, howsoever both the ground and practice are secret and to many unknown, yet there is a way to come to the knowledge thereof. For it is usual with Satan to promise anything, till the league be ratified. But when it is once

---

5. *Aver*: attest.

made, and the party entangled in society with him, then he endeavors nothing more than his or her discovery and uses all means possible to disclose them. So that whatsoever end the witch propounds to herself in the league, he intends nothing else but her utter confusion. Therefore, in the just judgment of God, it often falls out that those who are true witches indeed shall either by confession discover themselves, or by true testimony be convinced. The causes which move the devil not only to effect, but to hasten this discovery, are two, principally.

The first is his malice toward all men in so high a degree that he cannot endure [that] they should enjoy the world or the benefits of this life (if it were possible)[6] so much as one hour. Though, therefore, by virtue of the pre-contract, he is cock-sure of his instruments, yet his malice is not herewith satisfied till the party is brought to light and condemned to death. Which may be a caveat to all ill-disposed persons, that they beware of yielding themselves unto him.

The second is his insatiable desire of the present and full possession of them whom he has got within the bounds of the covenant. For though he has good hope of them, yet he is not certain of their continuance. The reason is because some united with him in confederacy, through the great mercy of God [and] by careful usage of holy means and faith in Christ, have been reclaimed and delivered out of his bondage, and so at length freed from his covenant, so as he has eternally left them. Hence it is that he labors by might and main to keep them in ignorance and to prevent the usage of means effectual to their conversion by laying a plot for their discovery. But how then comes it to pass that all such persons are not speedily detected, but some live long and others die without any man's privity?[7] *Answer.* The reasons hereof may be divers.

First, because some one or more of them may belong to God's election. And, therefore, albeit for causes best known to Himself, He suffers them for a time to be held in the snares of Satan, yet at length in mercy He reclaims them. And in the meantime [He] suffers not the devil to exercise the depth of his malice in discovering them to their confusion. Again, for others, the Lord may in justice and anger suffer them not to be disclosed, that living under the means where they might be reclaimed, and willfully condemning the same, they may live to fill up the measure of their iniquities, and thereby be made finally inexcusable, that they may receive their more just condemnation.

Second, the devil suffers some to live long undisclosed, that they may exercise the greater measure of his malice in the world; especially if they are[8] parties maliciously bent to do hurt to men and other creatures.

---

6. From here to footnote 77, the text is taken from *Works* (1631), 3:645, because pages 215–17 are missing from the original text.

7. *Privity:* discovery.

8. From footnote 75 to here, the text is taken from Works (1631), 3:645.

Third, some witches do warily agree with the devil for a certain term of years, during which time he binds himself not to hurt them but to be at their command. And Satan is careful, especially in [the] case of his own advantage, to keep touch with them, that they may the more strongly cleave unto him on their parts.[9]

But if the case so stands that neither the suspected party confesses nor yet sufficient witnesses can be produced who are able to convict him or her either of these two ways, we have no warrant out of the Word, either in general or in special, to put such a one to death. For though presumptions are ever so strong, yet they are not sufficient proofs for conviction, but only for examination.

I would, therefore, wish and advise all jurors, who give their verdict upon life and death in courts of assizes, to take good heed that as they are diligent in zeal in God's glory and the good of His church in detecting of witches by all sufficient and lawful means, so likewise they would be careful what they do, and not to condemn any suspected party upon bare presumptions without sound and sufficient proofs, so that they are not guilty through their own rashness of shedding innocent blood.

Section 3

Question. Whether a man may prevent the danger of witchcraft, and if he may, then what remedies may he lawfully and effectually use against it?

Answer. To this question we answer affirmatively that a man may. And for the manifestation of this point, the remedies of witchcraft are to be considered. In the handling whereof, I will proceed in this order: first, to set down the true, lawful, and effectual remedies allowed and prescribed in the Word; [and,] second, [to set down] the unlawful and superstitious means prescribed and practiced in the Romish church.

Lawful

Lawful remedies of witchcraft are of two sorts: preservative and restorative.

Preservative. The preservatives are those which keep a man from the hurt of witchcraft. And these are of two sorts: either such as keep safe the persons of men, or such as preserve the places of men's abode.

For the persons of men, there is one sovereign preservative, and that is to be within the covenant of grace, made and confirmed in the gospel by the blood of Christ, and that not outwardly in profession only, as all those are which are within the compass of the church, but truly and indeed as all the elect are. And

---

9. This paragraph break is not in the original.

a man is then in the covenant when God, of His grace in the use of the means, gives him a true knowledge of the nature of it and of conditions required in the same on both parts, and withal gives him a true and lively faith to apprehend and apply to himself the promise of God in Christ, touching remission of sins and life everlasting; yea, further, to show forth his faith by the fruits of true repentance and new obedience. When a man in this manner comes to be brought within the covenant, and is in Christ, he then receives assurance of God's favor, and to him belong the promises depending thereupon, to wit, not only of the comfortable presence of God's Spirit, but of the presence and special protection of His holy angels, to pitch their tents about him, to keep him safe in soul and body from the power and malicious practices of Satan and his members. The ground of this assurance is laid down in the Word: "He shall give his angels charge over thee" (Ps. 91:11). And the speech of Balaam confirms the same, who, when he was hired by Balak to curse God's people, and had oftentimes assayed to do it but could not, at last broke out into this confession: "There is no witchcraft against Jacob, nor sorcery against Israel" (for so the words are to be read, according to the true meaning and circumstances of the text).[10] As if he should have said, "I was of your opinion (O Balak) that Israel might be cursed, but after trial made, I found by good experience that I could do that people of God no hurt by my enchantments."

Howbeit we must here remember that the promise of protection made unto God's children is not absolute, but admits [an] exception, as all other promises of temporal blessing do. And that in this manner: "You shall be partaker of this or that blessing, and this or that curse shall be removed, if it is expedient for you. But if for special causes to try your faith and to exercise your patience, I make denial, you must rest yourself contented in My good will and pleasure."

By warrant of this doctrine, a question commonly moved may be resolved: Whether the servant and child of God may be bewitched or not?

Out of that which has been said, I answer, he may. And that is plain by the Word. For by God's permission the holy body of Christ Himself was by Satan transported from place to place (Matthew 4). Righteous Job was miserably afflicted in his body by the power of the devil, and his children, who no doubt were God's servants, and brought up in His fear, as their father was, were slain by the same power. Yea, Christ Himself testifies that "a daughter of Abraham (that is, of the faith of Abraham) had been troubled eighteen years with a spirit of infirmity" (Luke 13:16). The devil caused this by bowing her body together, so as she could not lift herself up (v. 11). And, therefore, whereas some men are of this mind that their faith is so strong that all the witches in the world, and

---

10. Num. 23:23.

all the devils in hell, cannot hurt them, they are much deceived. Their faith is but a fond presumption and no true faith. For no man in the earth can absolutely assure himself of safety and protection from the devil. And if any could, it would be the child of God. But Solomon says that "all outward things may come alike both to the good and to the bad" (Eccl. 9:2).

Howbeit in this case there is great difference between the servant of God and an unrepentant sinner. Though the godly man is not exempt from witchcraft, yet he is a thousand-fold freer from the power thereof than other men are. For there is only one case, and no more, wherein the devil has any way power to hurt him, and that is when it pleases God by that kind of cross to make trial of his faith and patience, and out of this case he is always free from the annoyance of the vilest witches in the world.

If then this is the only sovereign preservative to keep a man safe and sure from the power of witches and of the devil, to have part in the covenant of grace, to be made partaker of Christ by a true faith, testified by dying unto all sin and living unto God in newness of life, [then] we must not content ourselves with a formal profession, as many in the visible church do, who wanting the life of faith, do not live in Christ; but [we must] strive to go further and to adorn our profession by framing our lives according to the Word, that we may have our portion in this excellent privilege of preservation from the power and malice of the enemies of God and all ungodly persons.

Preservatives of the second sort are such as concern the places of men's abode. For Satan contents not himself to have manifested his malice in afflicting men's persons, but he also enlarges the same to the molestation of the places where they dwell, by infecting the air and such like. The only effectual means to remedy this evil is the sanctification of the places of our habitation. Look, as we are wont to sanctify our meat and drink by God's Word and by prayer, and thereby procure His blessing upon His own ordinance for our refreshing, so in like manner we may sanctify the places of our abode, and thereby both procure the blessing which we want and also avoid many curses and dangers which otherwise would fall upon us.

If any shall think the consecration of houses and places in this sort to be a mere device of man's brain, let them remember that in the Old Testament, besides the dedication of the temple, allowed by all, there was a law prescribed to the Jews for the special dedication of every man's house: "If any hath built a new house," says Moses, "and hath not dedicated it, let him return again, etc." (Deut. 20:5). As who should say, he has omitted a necessary duty. Now this dedication was nothing else but the sanctification of them by word and prayer, wherein they made acknowledgement that they became theirs by the free gift and blessing of God, and further desired a free and lawful use of the same to

His glory and their mutual good. A duty which has been performed by the servants of God in ancient times.

The first thing that Abraham did when he came from Ur of the Chaldeans to the land of Canaan, which God gave him to possess, was the building of an altar for the worship of God, his sacrificing thereon, and calling upon the name of the Lord (Gen. 12:8). Before him, Noah did the same at his first coming out of the ark after the flood (Gen. 8:20). After him, Jacob [did the same] in Bethel. And they were all moved hereunto because they knew their comfortable abode in those places came not by their own endeavor, but from the blessing of God. When the good king, Hezekiah, kept the Passover in Jerusalem, his principal care was that the priests and all the people might first be sanctified. And, therefore, he prayed unto God to be merciful to them who were not sanctified (2 Chron. 30:18). And as he behaved himself in his kingdom, so should every master of a family behave himself in his house where he dwells, laboring to sanctify the same, that it may be comfortable to him and his, lest for neglect thereof he pulls upon himself, and those who belong unto him, the heavy hand of God in plagues and punishments.

Restorative. The second kind of remedies are restorative, which serve to deliver men from witchcraft by curing the hurts of witches in the bodies of men or other creatures. In the handling whereof, first, we will consider how whole countries, and then how every private man, may be cured and delivered. Whole countries and kingdoms are freed and cured especially by one means: the publishing and embracing of the gospel. When our Savior Christ had sent the seventy disciples to preach in Jewry, at their return He gave this testimony of the effect of their ministry: "He saw Satan fall down from heaven like lightning" (Luke 10:18). His meaning was this: as lightning is suddenly and violently sent out of the cloud, and (as it were) cast down to the earth by the crack of the thunder, even so Satan, the prince of the world who rules in the hearts of the disobedient, was cast down, and his kingdom ruinated by the power of the gospel preached. In the times of ignorance, the devil triumphed freely without controlment, but the mist and darkness of his delusions cannot possibly abide the bright beams of God's glorious will revealed by preaching. The Lord of ancient times commanded His people not to do according to those nations, among whom they dwelt in Canaan, by practicing witchcraft or following after sorcery (Deut. 18:9). And that they might be able to obey this commandment, Moses prescribes unto them this restorative: "the reverent and obedient hearing of the Lord's prophets" (v. 18). In our church, if we would be healed of our wounds, and banish Satan from among us, who greatly annoys a great number of our people by his delusions and damnable practices of sorcery, the only way to bring it to pass is the maintaining of a learned ministry, the advancing of prophets, by whose labors the gospel may flourish. For the faithful dispensation thereof is the Lord's own arm and scepter, whereby He beats down the kingdom of darkness, and confounds the works and enterprises of the devil.

The second sort of restoratives serve for the cure of particular persons. For howsoever the gift and power of casting out devils, and [the] curing witchcraft, are ordinarily ceased since the apostles' times, it being a gift peculiar to the primitive church, and given to it only during the infancy of the gospel, yet there may be means used (and that effectual) for the easing of any person who is bewitched by Satan's instruments. Those, therefore, who are in these days tormented in this kind must do three things.

First, they must enter into a serious examination of themselves, and consider the cause for which it pleases God to suffer Satan to exercise them with that kind of cross. And here, upon diligent enquiry, they shall find that their own sins are the true and proper causes of these evils. When Saul was disobedient to the commandment of God, the Lord sent upon him an evil spirit to vex him (1 Samuel 15). Hymenaeus and Alexander, for their pestilent errors, were both cast out of the church, and given up also to Satan, that they might learn not to blaspheme (1 Tim. 1:20). In the same manner was the incestuous person dealt withal (1 Cor. 5:5).

Second, after this examination, the same parties must show forth their faith whereby they depend on the free favor and mercy of God for their deliverance. How may this be done? By hearty prayer unto God, joined with fasting that the same may be more earnest. In [this] prayer the main desire of the heart must be absolutely for the pardon of their sins, and then for deliverance from the hurts and torments of diabolical persons, yet not absolutely (as for the other) but with this condition: so far forth as it stands with God's glory and their own good. For these are the bounds and limits of all temporal good things. The Lord makes no absolute promise of them, but with these conditions and qualifications.

Third, the bewitched parties must patiently bear the present annoyance, comforting themselves with this, that it is the Lord's own hand, by whose special providence it comes to pass, and who turns all things to the good of His chosen. Again, they are to remember that He, being a most wise God and loving Father in Christ, will not suffer them to be tried above what they are able to bear, but in His good time [He] will grant a joyful issue. Now when the bewitched shall thus submit themselves unto God in the cross, be it that He (upon some causes) defers their deliverance, yet they shall not finally be deceived of their hope. For either in this life at the appointed time, or in the end of this life by death, they shall be eternally delivered and put in present possession of everlasting ease and happiness.

Thus much of the true remedies against witchcraft.

Unlawful

In the next place we are a little to examine the false and superstitious remedies prescribed and used by them of the popish church.

The most learned papists of this age do teach and avouch that there is in God's church an ordinary gift and power whereby some men may cast out devils and help annoyances that come by witches. The Protestant is of a contrary judgment and holds according to truth that there is now no such ordinary gift left to the church of God since the days of the apostles.

[The] reasons of this opinion may be these:

First, [the] casting out of devils and curing such annoyances are extraordinary and miraculous works. For Christ accounts [the] handling of serpents without hurt, speaking with new tongues, curing of diseases by imposition of hands (all which are things of less moment) to be miracles (Mark 16:18–19). But all these lesser works (yea, the ordinary power of working them) is ceased, for it was only given to the apostles in the primitive church as a means to confirm the doctrine of the gospel to unbelievers who never heard of Christ before. So, Paul says "strange tongues (that is, the gift of speaking strange languages without ordinary teaching) are for a sign, not to them that believe, but to them that believe not" (1 Cor. 14:22). And for the same end were all extraordinary gifts then given. Seeing, therefore, the doctrine of the gospel has been already established, and the truth thereof sufficiently confirmed by miracles in the primitive church, the same gift must needs cease unto us. For if it should still continue, it would call into question the effect of the apostolic preaching, and imply thus much, that the gospel was not well established nor sufficiently confirmed by their extraordinary ministry and miracles accompanying the same. Again, if the gift of working miracles should remain, then the promise of God for His special and extraordinary assistance therein should yet continue. For the gift and promise go together; so long as the promise is in force, so long is the gift also. But the promise made by Christ, "in my name shall they cast out devils, and speak with new tongues" (Mark 16), was in force only in the persons and ministry of the apostles, and those who had [an] extraordinary and immediate calling from God, and it ceased when they and their calling ceased. Therefore, if ministers should now lay their hands on the sick, they would not recover them. If they should anoint them with oil, it would do them no good, because they have no promise.

Howbeit the papists stand stiffly in defending the continuance of these gifts.

First, they say [that] the church of the New Testament is nothing inferior to that of the Old. The Jewish church, before the coming of Christ, was the church of the Old Testament, and had the power and gift of casting out devils. So says our Savior Himself: "If I through Beelzebub cast out devils, then by whom do your children cast them out?" (Matt. 12:27). In these words He ascribes this gift unto the Jews; therefore, it should seem the same remains still in the church.

Answer. That place of Scripture is diversely expounded. Some, by "children" there mentioned, understand the apostles who were Jews by birth, and had received from Christ this gift and power to cast out devils. If this is so, it makes not for them, because they had it extraordinarily. But I rather think that by "children" are meant the exorcising Jews before Christ's time, who did cast out devils among them, pretending an ability to do this work in the name of God, whereas in truth they were all flat sorcerers, and did it by virtue of a league and compact made with the devil. This practice has been of long continuance and is at this day common and usual among the popish sort. And that there were such exorcists among the Jews is evident. For such were those vagabonds which came to Ephesus and took upon them to cast out devils by the names of Jesus and Paul (Acts 19:13). But the man, in whom the evil spirit was (so soon as they had adjured the spirit), ran upon them and mightily prevailed against them (v. 16). Now if they had done this great work by the power of God (as they pretended), the Holy Spirit would not have called them exorcists and vagabonds. Neither could the evil spirit possibly have overcome them, as he did.[11]

Again, in the histories of the Jews many practices of such as exercised this power among them are recorded. Raphael, the angel, tells Tobias that a perfume made of the heart and liver of a fish will help a man vexed with an evil spirit (Tob. 6:7).[12] This counsel is flat magic, for there is no such virtue in the liver of a fish. And in other histories,[13] we read that one Eleazar, a Jew, by the smell of a certain root, put to the nose of a man possessed with a devil, caused the devil to come out of his nostrils and forsake him. This thing was done in [a] public place before Vespasian and others. This also was effected by mere conjuration. For what virtue can there be in any root or herb in the world, available to command and enforce Satan to depart from a man possessed? And yet such feats were played by sundry magicians among the Jews. Whereupon I conclude that the meaning of our Savior, in the place alleged, is in effect thus much, "If I by the power of Beelzebub, etc.," that is, you have among you sundry

---

11. This paragraph break is not in the original.
12. Perkins is here quoting the apocryphal Book of Tobias (or Tobit).
13. In the margin: Joseph. Antiquit. Judaic. l. 8. c. 2.

magicians and exorcists who pretend and exercise the gift of casting out devils, and you think they do it by the power of God, why then do you not carry the same opinion of me also?

Their second reason is grounded on the promise of Christ: "These tokens shall follow them that believe, in my name they shall cast out devils" (Mark 16:17). They gather from this that there shall always be some in the church who shall have [the] power to cast forth devils, if they believe.

Answer. That promise was made by Christ unto His church, to be fulfilled immediately after His ascension. It did not extend to all times and persons, so long as the world endures, but only to the times of the primitive church and to such as then lived. For to them only the doctrine of the gospel was to be confirmed by signs and miracles. And this lasted about two hundred years after Christ's ascension. During this time, not only the apostles and ministers, but even private men and soldiers, wrought many miracles.

The third reason is taken from experience, which (as they say) in all ages from the apostles' times to this day shows that there have been always some in the church who have had this gift of casting out devils and curing the hurts of witchcraft.

Answer. This gift continued not much above the space of two hundred years after Christ, from which time many heresies began to spread themselves. And then shortly after popery, that mystery of iniquity beginning to spring up, and to dilate itself in the churches of Europe, the true gift of working miracles then ceased, and instead thereof came in delusions and lying wonders by the effectual working of Satan, as it was foretold by the apostle (2 Thess. 2:9). Of which sort were (and are) all those miracles of the Romish church whereby simple people have been notoriously deluded. These indeed have continued from that time to this day. But this gift of the Holy Spirit, whereof the question is made, ceased long before.

To proceed yet further, we are here to consider the particular remedies which they of the popish church have prescribed against the hurts that have come by witchcraft. And they are principally five.

The first is the name of Jesus. We must grant that any Christian may lawfully call upon the name of Jesus in prayer, for the help and deliverance of those who are possessed and bewitched, but yet with the caveat and condition before specified, if it is the will of God, and if their recovery may make for His glory, the benefit of the church, and the good of the diseased parties.

But the papist, by the use of this name, intends a further matter, to wit, that the very name uttered in so many letters and syllables is powerful to cast out devils and to help those who are bewitched. For when it is uttered, then (they say) the authority of Christ is present, that the work may be done. [This is] a flat untruth and a practice full of danger. For let this be well considered, whatsoever any man does in this case, he must do it by virtue of his calling, and have also his warrant for the doing thereof out of the Word. If he lacks this, and yet undertakes such a work, he may justly fear the like event that befell the vagabond Jews who were exorcists (Acts 19:13). Now the church of Christ has no warrant in the Word to use this name of Christ for any such purpose. Neither has any ordinary Christian a special calling from God so to do. Therefore, he may not do it.

And they would bear men in hand that the said name, of all the names of Christ and above all other things, is of most special virtue, though it is used even by a man that wants faith, because the apostle says, "At the name of Jesus every knee shall bow, both of things in heaven, in earth, and under the earth" (Phil. 2:10), and by things "under the earth" are meant the devils. But we must know that their allegation is weak, and that they greatly abuse the place. For there the name Jesus is not only a title of Christ, but withal signifies the power, majesty, and authority of Christ, sitting at the right hand of the Father, to which all creatures in heaven, earth, and hell are made subject. And by that power indeed (if they had it at command) they might be able to cure the hurts of witchcraft.

The second special remedy is the use of saints' relics, as their books, bones, apparel, staves, or such like. Being but touched by the vexed parties, [they] are excellent means to recover them.

Answer. The use of these things, to the purposes aforesaid, is a mere superstitious practice. For, first, they have not the true relics of the saints, as would plainly appear if a true inventory were taken of all such as they say are to be found in their monasteries and churches. Second, though they had them, yet they have no warrant (or calling) to use them to this end. For in all the Word of God there is neither commandment to warrant the use, nor promise to assure any man of a blessing upon use of them. Albeit they would seem to have some warrant, and therefore they allege that which is written of a dead man who, being for haste thrown into the sepulcher of Elisha, so soon as he touched the bones of Elisha, revived and stood upon his feet (2 Kings 13:21). To this also they add the examples of cures done by Peter's shadow (Acts 5:15), and of sundry diseases healed by Paul's handkerchiefs (Acts 19:12). *Answer.* These things indeed are true, but they serve nothing to their purpose. For, first, the quickening of the dead soldier came not from any virtue in the corpse of Elisha. But it was a miracle, which it pleased God then to work by means of a corpse, so that the Jews at that time might be confirmed in the truth of that doctrine which Elisha had taught them from God, and which before his death they had neglected (as I have shown before). And it was a thing only then done, and never since. It cannot, therefore, be a ground for the ordinary use of relics. Again, touching the other examples, I answer that both Peter and Paul had the gift of working miracles, and having the gift, they might use such means for the present to cure diseases. But the papists are not able to show that God has given them the like gift, whereby they might be warranted for the use of the like means. Neither can they assuredly hope for success, although they should undertake to use them.

The third remedy is the sign of the cross made upon the body of the tormented party. Behold to what a height of impiety they are grown, ascribing that to the creature which is proper to the Creator! For the power of working miracles is proper only to the Godhead. The prophets and apostles in their times did not work them of themselves, but were only God's passive instruments in this manner: when the Lord intended by them to work any miracle, they received from Him at the same time an extraordinary and special instinct whereby they were moved to attempt the work. They, therefore, yielded themselves to the present motion of God's Spirit to be His instruments only in the dispensation of the work. But the sole Author and Producer of the miracle was God Himself. And in this case the very manhood of our Savior Christ, considered apart from His Godhead, had no power of itself, but was only the instrument of His Godhead, whenever it pleased Him in that kind to manifest the same. Wherefore, to ascribe this virtue to the cross, being a creature or the work of a creature, is to communicate the incommunicable power of the Creator to it, which is plain blasphemy.

The fourth remedy is the using of hallowed things, as hallowed grains, salt, water, bread, images, especially the image of *agnus dei*.

Answer. Hallowed creatures are in truth unhallowed superstitions. For every creature is sanctified by the Word and prayer (1 Tim. 4:4); by the Word, when God in His Word commands us to use it for some end; and, by prayer, when we give thanks for giving the creature and withal desire His blessing in the use thereof. Now let any papist show me one letter or syllable in all the Book of God commanding the use of a creature for any such end.

They affirm indeed that Elisha wrought miracles by hallowed salt, for by it he cured the bitter waters (2 Kings 2:21). But the prophet used not hallowed, but common salt, and that not ordinarily, but only then as a means whereby to work a miracle. It was, therefore, powerful in his hands because, for the doing thereof, he had power and warrant from God extraordinarily. And it cannot be so in any other who has not the same gift.

The fifth and last remedy is exorcism, which is an adjuring and commanding the devil in the name of God to depart from the possessed party and to cease to molest him anymore. This means was used by our Savior Christ Himself, and after Him by His apostles and other believers in the time of the primitive church when the gift of working miracles was in force. But in these days (as I said before) that gift is ceased, and also the promise of power annexed to the use of adjuration, and therefore the means thereof must needs cease. And for an ordinary man now to command the devil in such sort is mere presumption and a practice of sorcery.

Section 4

Question. Whether the witches of our age are to be punished with death, and that by virtue of this law of Moses?

Answer. I doubt not but in this last age of the world, and among us also, this sin of witchcraft ought as sharply to be punished as in former times. And all witches, being thoroughly convicted by the magistrate, ought according to the law of Moses to be put to death. For proof hereof, consider these reasons.

Reason 1

First, this law of Moses flatly enjoins all men in all ages, without limitation of circumstances, not to suffer the witch to live. And hereupon I gather that it must stand the same, both now and forever to the world's end.

Patrons of witches except against[14] this, holding that it was a judicial law which continued but for a time, and concerned only the nation of the Jews, and is now ceased. But I take the contrary to be the truth, and that upon these grounds:

First, those judicial laws whose penalty is death, because they have in them a perpetual equity and do serve to maintain some moral precept, are perpetual. The Jews indeed had some laws of this kind, whose punishments were temporal, and they lasted only for a certain time. But the penalty of witchcraft being death by God's appointment, and the inflicting of that punishment serving to maintain the equity of the first three moral precepts of the first table (which cannot be kept unless this law is put in execution), it must necessarily follow

---

14. *Except against*: object to.

that it is in that regard moral, and binds us, and shall in like sort bind all men in all ages, as well as the Jews themselves, to whom it was at that time personally directed.

Second, every judicial law that has in it the equity of the law of nature is perpetual. But this law of punishing the witch by death is such. For it is a principle of the law of nature, held for a grounded truth in all countries and kingdoms, among all people in every age, that the traitor, who is an enemy to the state and rebels against his lawful prince, should be put to death. Now the most notorious traitor and rebel that can be is the witch. For she renounces God Himself, the King of kings. She leaves the society of His church and people. She binds herself in league with the devil. And, therefore, if any offender among men ought to suffer death for his act, much more ought she, and that of due desert.

Reason 2

The second reason for the proof of the point in hand is this: according to Moses's law, every idolater was to be stoned to death. "If there be found any among you, that hath gone and served other gods, as the sun, the moon, or any of the host of heaven: if the thing upon enquiry be found to be true and certain, thou shalt bring them forth unto thy gates, whether it be man or woman, and shalt stone them with stones till they die" (Deut. 17:3–5). Now this is the very case of a witch. She renounces the true God and makes choice to serve the devil. She is, therefore, a gross idolater, and her punishment must be suitable. It is alleged by the favorers of the contrary part that Peter denied Christ, and yet was not put to death. I answer, there is great difference between Peter's denial of Christ and witches' denying of God. Peter's denial was upon infirmity and in haste. The witch denies God upon knowledge and deliberation, wittingly and willingly. Again, Peter did not upon the denial betake himself to the devil, but turned unto Christ again, which he testifies by his hearty and speedy repentance. But witches deny God and betake themselves to the devil of their own accord, as is manifest even by their own confessions at their arraignments.

Reason 3

Every seducer in the church, whose practice was to draw men from the true God to the worship of idols, though it were a man's own son or daughter, wife or friend, by the peremptory decree and commandment of God, was at no hand to be spared or pitied. But the hand of the witness first, and then the hands of all the people, must be upon him, to kill him (Deut. 13:6, 9). If this is so, no convicted witches ought to escape the sword of the magistrate, for they are the most notorious seducers of all others. When they are once entangled in the devil's league, they labor to inure their dearest friends and posterity in their cursed and abominable practices, that they may be the more easily drawn into the same confederacy wherewith they themselves are united to Satan. I might here allege that they deserve death because many of them are murderers, but I stand not upon that instance because I hold in the general that witches are not to be suffered to live, though they do no hurt either to man or other creatures, and that by virtue of Moses's law, only for their league's sake whereby they become rebels to God, idolaters, and seducers, as now has been shown.

Yet notwithstanding all that has been said, many things are brought in defense of them by such as are their friends and well-willers.[15]

First, it is said that the hurt that is done comes not from the witch but from the devil. He deserves the blame because it is his work. And she is not to die for his sin.

Answer. Let it be granted that the witch is not the author of the evil that is done, yet she is a confederate and partner with the devil in the act, and so the law takes hold on her. See it in a familiar comparison. A company of men conspire together in a robbery. By common consent some stand in [an] open place to spy out the booty and to give the watchword. Others are set about the passage, privily to rush upon the man and to spoil him of his goods. What says the law in this case? The parties who gave the watchword, though they did nothing to the man, yet being accessories and abettors to the robbery by consent, they are thieves, and liable to condemnation and execution, as well as the principals. Even so stands the case with the witch. In the working of wonders, and in all mischievous practices, he or she is partaker with the devil by consent of covenant. The witch only uses the watchword in some charm or otherwise and does no more. The devil, upon notice given by the charm, takes his opportunity and works the mischief. He is the principal agent, but the other yields help, and is rightly liable to punishment. The reason is because if the devil were not stirred up and provoked by the witch, he would never do so much hurt as he does. He would never have appeared in Samuel's likeness had he not been solicited by the witch of Endor. He would not have caused counterfeit serpents and frogs to appear in Egypt but for Jannes and Jambres and other enchanters. And in this age, there would not in likelihood be so much hurt and hindrance procured unto men and other creatures by his means but for the instigation of ill-disposed persons who have fellowship and society with him.

Second, they object that witches convicted either repent or repent not. If they repent, then God pardons their sin. And why should not the magistrate as well

---

save their bodies and let them live, as God does their souls? If they do not repent, then it is a dangerous thing for the magistrate to put them to death, for by this means he kills the body and casts the soul to hell.

Answer. All witches, judicially and lawfully convicted, ought to have space of repentance granted unto them wherein they may be instructed and exhorted, and then afterward executed. For it is possible for them to be saved by God's mercy, though they have denied Him. Second, the magistrate must execute justice upon malefactors lawfully convicted, whether they repent or not. For God approves the just execution of judgment upon men without respect to their repentance. Neither must their impenitence hinder the execution of justice. When the people of Israel had committed idolatry in worshipping the golden calf, Moses did not expect their repentance and in the meantime forebear the punishment, but he and the Levites presently took their swords and slew them. And the Lord approved their course of proceeding (Exod. 32:28). When Zimri, an Israelite, had committed fornication with Cozbi, a Midianite woman, Phinehas in zeal of God's glory executed judgment upon them both without any respect unto their repentance (Num. 25:8), and [he] is therefore commended (Ps. 106:30). Wars are a worthy ordinance of God, and yet no prince could ever attempt the same lawfully if every soldier in the field should stay the killing of his enemy upon expectation of his repentance. And whereas they say that by executing an impenitent witch, the magistrate casts away the soul, we must know that the end of execution by the magistrate is not the damnation of the malefactor's soul, but that sin might be punished, that others may beware of the like crimes and offences, and that the wicked may be taken away from among God's people.

But there are some witches who cannot be convicted of killing any. What shall become of them?

Answer. As the killing witch must die by another law, though he were no witch, so the healing and harmless witch must die by this law, though he kills not, only for covenant made with Satan. For this must always be remembered as a conclusion, that by witches we understand not only those who kill and torment, but all diviners, charmers, jugglers, wizards, commonly called wise men and wise women; yea, whosoever does anything (knowing what they do) which cannot be effected by nature or art. And in the same number we reckon all good witches who do no hurt but good, who do not spoil and destroy but save and deliver. All these come under this sentence of Moses because they deny God and are confederates with Satan. By the laws of England, the thief is executed for stealing, and we think it just and profitable. But it would be a thousand times better for the land if all witches, but especially the blessing witch, might suffer death. For the thief by his stealing, and the hurtful enchanter by charming, bring hindrance and hurt to the bodies and goods of men. But these are the right hand of the devil, by which he takes and destroys the souls of men. Men do commonly hate and spit at the damnifying[16] sorcerer as unworthy to live among them, whereas the other is so dear unto them that they hold themselves and their country blessed that have him among them. They fly unto him in necessity. They depend upon him as their god. And by this means thousands are carried away to their final confusion. Death, therefore, is the just and deserved portion of the good witch.

FINIS

---

16. *Damnifying*: cursing.

A Resolution to the Country Man

Proving It Utterly Unlawful to Buy or Use Our Yearly Prognostications

Written long since by W. Perkins

"Stand now among thine enchanters, and in the multitude of sooth-sayers (with whom thou hast wearied thyself from thy youth), if so be thou mayest have profit, or if so be thou mayest have strength. Thou art wearied in the multitude of thy counsels: let now the astrologers, the star-gazers, and prognosticators stand up, and save thee from these things that shall come upon thee. Behold, they shall be as stubble: the fire shall burn them, they shall not deliver their own lives from the power of the flame: there shall be no coals to warm at, nor light to sit by" (Isa. 47:12–14).

London
Printed by John Haviland, for James Boler

1631

Not convenient to have prognostications

Reasons:

1. Concerning the buyer:
    1. Immoderate care joined with distrust in God
    2. Contempt of the providence of God, in not reverently regarding it

2. Concerning the maker:
    1. His inability in prognosticating, proved:
        1. By the true end of the heavens
        2. By want of good experience
        3. By ignorance of particular causes
    2. His manifold untruths
    3. His impieties, profane speeches, actions, not seeming a Christian
    4. His tricks of deceit

A Resolution to the Country Man, Proving It Utterly Unlawful to Buy or Use Our Yearly Prognostications

Good reader, I have thought it convenient (for some special causes) in this short treatise to disclose a part of my mind unto you, concerning the making of prognostications, and if it might be, to persuade you not to spend your money in buying any of them. I have long studied this art, and [I] was never quiet until I had seen all the secrets of the same. But at length it pleased God to lay before me the profaneness of it, nay, I dare boldly say, idolatry, although it is covered with fair and golden shows. Wherefore, that which I will speak with grief, the same I would desire you to mark with some attention. My reason shall partly concern you [and] partly the prognosticator himself.

The Buyer

First, on your behalf, I reason thus.

Reason 1: Immoderate Care

As a man does see the blessings of God upon him, so he must also labor with a careful diligence to maintain the state of this life. But because the affection of man is carried headlong unto a greedy covetousness, this desire to overmuch carping and caring must be bridled with two strong bits: First, all our care must extend itself no further than the present day [Matt. 6:11]. Second, in caring we must not trust unto ourselves, but fix all our confidence in the mercy and providence of God who blesses all, and without whose goodness nothing can come to pass, do what we will.[1]

As touching the first, we have the direction of our Savior Christ, who teaches us to pray in this way: "Give us this day our daily bread." Whereby we are given to understand that we are only to seek for the present time, resting with this persuasion that He who has blessed us this day will also tomorrow and the next day show His like goodness unto us. Again, in the same place, our Savior Christ speaks in this way: "Care not thou for the morrow; for the morrow shall care for itself: the day hath enough with its own grief" [Matt. 6:34]. By

---

1. This paragraph break is not in the original.

this we learn that God will provide all things necessary for every day, though we do not increase the present grief with caring and casting in our heads how we shall live in the time to come.

Now tell me what is the cause that yearly you do buy a prognostication, and one of those which tells the strangest things? Is it because you have a delight to read the style of prognostications? Or because you would learn to prognosticate? Or because the pictures and characters which they make delight your minds? It would be folly to be persuaded of this, seeing the very cause itself is manifest. Your whole desire is to fill your coffers, and to heap up wealth. You are afraid lest you should become poor, therefore you greedily buy the prognostications, and continually search all the corners of them to see the state of the year to come, even reasoning in mind with yourself thus: "I can never be quiet nor take my sleep until such time as I have known the state of the ensuing year, that I may frame my business accordingly." "There will be much rain next year; it will rot [the] corn upon the ground; it will be spoiled; I will keep my corn until the next year." "I find that corn will be dear about half a year hence; I will not sell my corn now, but keep it so that I may have plenty of money for it, and sufficient beside to maintain my house." "The sea and land are calm and quiet this year; the next year many shipwrecks and troubles will fall in many countries; now I will fraught[2] my ships that then I may be quiet."[3]

These imaginations are lively arguments of your diffidence and despair in the goodness and loving-kindness of God. If you fear God, love God, put your whole trust in God, you are content to refer your whole preservation unto the hands of God. Now these proling[4] and reigning conceits of the time to come argue that either you never think on God or, at the least, persuade yourself that either He will not or cannot help you. And if you in your covetous mind pray unto God, you cannot pray according to the institution of Christ without hypocrisy: "Give us our daily bread this day." Wherefore, seeing the having of prognostications comes from so wicked causes, as is the greedy desire of prosperity and wealth, and argues some kind of diffidence in God, when you read my words, examine your own heart. If you find my sayings [are] true (as certainly you shall), never hereafter desire to know the state of the year beforehand, except it is for the seasons of the year, which I am persuaded you may know in some part without any skill, even by your own experience.

---

2. *Fraught*: fill.

3. This paragraph break is not in the original.

4. *Proling*: prowling.

Reason 2: Neglect of God's Providence

Concerning the contempt of God's providence, I say thus much: the prognosticator, if he is asked whether he confesses the providence of God, he will with all his heart confess it, but by his deeds he does deny it. For all things whatsoever which can happen in a whole year he attributes them to the stars, and so he publishes his predictions always mentioning stars, never or very slenderly[5] making any signification of the power, justice, mercy, and everlasting wisdom of God. And surely, even for the very paring of your nails, cutting of your hair, putting on of your shoes, taking a journey two or three miles from your house, obtaining at God's hands your request, making your bargain with your neighbor, for all your actions (be they ever so small), these wise men (if you will ask their advice) will give you counsel from the stars.[6]

Now when their irreligious predictions shall be had in your bosom and read by you daily, you, being a man unlearned and worldly given, never hearing any mention of the special providence and hand of God in everything, but long discourses of the virtues of planets and signs, do never think upon the wonderful and most infinite power of God, working after a special manner in every matter, but [you] are drawn straight ways into an admiration of the astrologer and a great fear of the constellations of heaven. An experience of this I found in you about two years ago. A learned man (yet in this case far deceived) wrote an astrological discourse of the conjunction between Jupiter and Saturn, wherein he showed of great alteration in everything to fall. You were sore aghast at this. Your mind was encumbered with settling your goods to set them in order against that day. Your song for half a year was nothing else but the conjunction. The day being come, what staring was there and gazing into heaven, to see the meeting of those two planets! Now all this while where was God's providence? Where was that trust and rejoicing in Him? Where was that praising of His name for all things whatsoever should come to pass? Where was that meditation of His infinite and unsearchable wisdom? These things were never thought nor heard of, yea, by reason of your earthly affections they took no place in your heart.[7]

Your dealing is like unto the folly of that man who, having a costly clock in his bosom, never extolls or thinks on the wit and invention of the clock-maker, but is continually in admiration of the spring or watch of the clock, by whose means all the wheels have their swifter or slower, their backward or forward, motions, and by which the whole clock keeps its course. Wherefore, I think that in a Christian commonwealth only those books should be published, for your

---

5. *Slenderly*: seldomly.

6. This paragraph break is not in the original.

7. This paragraph break is not in the original.

use, which might beat into your head, and make you every hour and moment to think on the providence of God. This being once settled in your mind, the consideration of the means which God uses will follow of itself. Contrariwise, to tell you the means which God does use, to thunder out the aspects and constellations of stars, and seldom to mention His providence, makes you to fear, admire, and love the means, quite forgetting the work of God in the means.[8]

This fault was very rife among the Israelites, who came yearly unto astrologers and wise men. Wherefore, that which is spoken by Jeremiah unto them is also spoken unto you: "Hear ye the word of the Lord, that he speaketh unto you, O house of Israel. Thus saith the Lord, Learn not the way of the heathen, and be not afraid for the signs of heavens, though the heathen be afraid of such" [Jer. 10:1–2]. In like sort, God forbids His people of England to give credit or fear the constellations and conjunctions of stars and planets, which have no power of themselves but are governed by Him. And their secret motions and influences are not known to man, and therefore can be no certain judgment thereof. If you will not hear and follow this which I say, see what will ensue. You see that the greatest matters which these diviners and prognosticators foretell, fall out flat otherwise than they say, to their perpetual shame. Truly, I am persuaded that it is the judgment of God upon them (although they cannot see it) who makes them, when they think they are most wise, to be most fools. For so the Lord used the wise men and astrologers of Chaldea, as He speaks by His prophet Isaiah: "I am the Lord that made all things, that spread out the heavens alone, and stretched out the earth by myself; I destroy the tokens of soothsayers, and make them that conjecture fools, and turn their wise men backward, and make their knowledge foolishness" [Isa. 44:24–25]. Do you then, O careless and miserable man, think to escape the same or greater punishment, being a cause of this fault? For if none desired to know what is to come, none would busy themselves in that vanity. Wherefore, read the Word of God: "When thou shalt come," says the Spirit of God, "into the land which the Lord thy God giveth thee, thou shalt not learn to do after the abominations of those nations" [Deut. 18:9]. In the following words Moses numbers nine abominations:

1. To make his child go through the fire.
2. To use witchcraft.
3. To regard times (this is your fault).
4. To mark the flying of fowls.
5. To be a sorcerer.
6. To be a charmer.

---

8. This paragraph break is not in the original.

7. To counsel with spirits.

8. To be a soothsayer.

9. To ask counsels at the dead.

All these horrible abominations being rehearsed, mark what follows: "For all that do such things are an abomination unto the Lord. And because of their abominations, the Lord your God does cast them out before you" [Deut. 18:12]. Now, seeing most of these abominations (and especially the third) are used by us, why should we not fear the like judgments upon us unless we repent, and that with speed?

The Maker

The reasons which concern the prognosticator, and may avail to the persuading of you not to buy any more of their unprofitable books, are these which follow: first, their inability in prognosticating: second, their manifest untruths: third, their impieties; [and,] fourth, their tricks of deceit.

Reason 1: Their Inability

What, can they not foretell that which is to come? Can they not make conjectures of that which is like[ly] to ensue? No surely. And I will use arguments to confirm it unto you.

Argument 1: The Use and End of the Heavens

The true use of the heavens consists in many points. First, to declare the glory of God. "The heavens," says David, "declare the glory of God, and the firmament showeth the work of his hands" [Ps. 19:1]. It is an alphabet written in great letters, in which is described the majesty of God, and that by these four special points: (1) the majesty of the work itself; (2) the infinite multitude of stars; (3) the wonderful variety of stars; [and] (4) the greatness of the stars.

Second, it makes sinners and wicked men inexcusable before the judgment seat of God. "For the invisible things of him," says Paul, "that is, his eternal power and Godhead, are seen by the creation of the world, being considered in his works to the intent that they should be without excuse" [Rom. 1:20].

Third, they serve to the appointing of times (as day, night, month, [and] year), which are both measured and described by the course of the sun, moon, and other stars [Gen. 1:14]. And so, the feasts of the Israelites, and the computation of the year in our church, depends thereupon, and without them there would be great confusion both in the commonwealth and church.

Fourth, they serve to be signs, that is, to foretell things to come. And they are signs either of extraordinary things or things which are ordinary.

When they are signs of extraordinary things, then there is (and appears) in them some extraordinary work of God, as appears in these examples which follow. At the suffering of Christ, not only [was] "the veil of the temple rent, and the dead rose forth of their graves," but also the sun was wholly eclipsed, the moon being in the full [Matthew 27]. At which sight, Dionysius [the] Areopagite,[9] a good astronomer, spoke these words: "Either the frame of the world is destroyed or the God of nature suffers." The prophet Ezekiel, being commanded by God to prophesy the destruction of Egypt, first puts down extraordinary signs: "And when I will put thee out, I will cover the heaven, and make the stars thereof dark: I will cover the sun with a cloud, and the moon shall not give her light. All the lights of heaven will I make dark for thee, and bring darkness upon the land, saith the Lord" [Ezek. 32:7–8]. Before the second coming of our Savior Christ, there shall be signs in the sun, moon, and stars. Lastly, the extraordinary going back of the sun signified the lengthening of the life of king Hezekiah.

Second, the stars are signs of general things which happen ordinarily every year in nature among us.

1. Approaching and declining of (1) spring, (2) summer, (3) harvest, (4) winter.
2. Ordinary weather in these quarters.
3. Ebbing and flowing of the sea.
4. Seasons of (1) plowing, (2) sowing, (3) setting, (4) planting, (5) cutting, (6) felling, (7) reaping.

I say, general, because the particular estate and affairs of men can in no way be fore-signified by the stars. I say, ordinary, because the things which fall out seldom, and are besides the common course of nature (as plenty of all things, famine, plague, war, invasions of kingdoms, etc.), do not depend upon the stars. For the confirming of this, I have three reasons.

First, in Genesis 1, God says He "made the lights to be signs" [Gen. 1:14–15], and yet the same God says He "will destroy the signs of them which divine" [Isa. 47:13–14], flatly forbidding us to use stars as means to judge of anything to come, saving only of those of which they are expressly made signs of God in the creation; all which are put down before.[10]

---

9. **Dionysius the Areopagite** is mentioned in Acts 17:34. A writer assumed this name in the sixth century, and produced a series of letters and treatises with the purpose of uniting Neoplatonic philosophy and Christian theology. His writings include *On the Divine Names, On Mystical Theology, On the Celestial Hierarchy*, and *On the Ecclesiastical Hierarchy*.

10. This paragraph break is not in the original.

Second, this is manifest by the order of the creation: "The third day God created upon the earth herbs and trees, and the earth brought forth fruits and was fertile: the fourth day God commanded lights to be made in the firmament of heaven, to separate the day and the night, and to be for signs and for seasons, and days, and months, and then it was so, and then God saw it was good" [Gen. 1:13–14]. Out of this I gather that it cannot be a sign causing famine, or plenty and fertileness, because fertility went before the creation of the host of heaven. Also, wars and plagues, and the particular estates of men, can be no signs because man was not yet created, and yet even then they were signs. Some will say, they were not signs of those matters in the creation, but now they may be and are. No, for the works which God created He now preserves, neither increasing nor diminishing anything in them. Philo Judaeus,[11] in his book *De opificio mundi*, says, "He was persuaded that God, foreseeing the minds of men given to search strange matters to come, did in this order create the heavens, to confute and disprove their imaginations."[12]

Third, the heavens and stars were made for the use of man, and man is their end, so that it is absurd to imagine they have any force in the affairs of man. Now then, prognosticators, if they will foreshow of strange things to come, they must undo the work of their Creator, and give new uses unto it; otherwise, they shall not be able to prognosticate as they yearly do.

Argument 2: The Providence of God

The providence of God is His decree by which He appoints how everything shall come to pass. The continual execution of this decree is ordinarily by means, but often without means. The means which God uses are either general or special.

General [means] are those by which He governs all the whole world, and every particular thing which concerns this life. Unto this kind are referred spiritual creatures called angels, by whom the philosophers say the heavens are governed, and we see that whole kingdoms, provinces, and cities have been kept and defended by them, as also consumed and destroyed. Again, the stars and heavenly bodies are used by God to govern and order things here below, as it is in Psalm 19, "Nothing is hid from the heat of the sun." And by the prophet Hosea, the Lord speaks thus: "I will hear the heavens, the heavens shall hear the earth, the earth shall hear the corn, the corn shall hear Israel."[13] But this instrument is only a general instrument, and [it] has its work in ordinary matters of nature. Besides these means, there are many others by which God

---

11. Philo Judaeus (also known as Philo of Alexandria) (c. 20 BC – 50 AD) was a Hellenistic Jewish philosopher.

12. This paragraph break is not in the original.

13. Hos. 2:21–22.

rules the world. In the beginning He set man over the whole world that he might have rule over fishes, fowls, beasts, and all other things. He appointed husbands to govern their wives. He set the firstborn before their brethren (as Cain before Abel), princes and tyrants over cities, kingdoms, commonwealths, and therefore by reason of their dignity calls them gods. There are also governors of families over their families, fathers over their children, masters over their servants.[14]

Yet, God has a more near care in preserving and governing His chosen, as appears in Isaiah 43, "Thus saith the Lord God that created thee, O Jacob: and he that formed thee, O Israel: Fear not, for I have redeemed thee, I have called thee by thy name, thou art mine: when thou passest through the waters, I will be with thee, and through the floods, that they do not overflow thee. When thou walkest through the very fire, thou shalt not be burnt, neither shall the flame kindle upon thee, for I am the Lord thy God, the holy one of Israel, thy Savior." This is also manifested by that sympathy which is in the Lord when His children are afflicted, as appears in Zechariah 11, "He which toucheth you, toucheth the apple of mine eye." And [it appears] in Acts 9, "Saul, Saul, why persecutest thou me (that is, My elect)?" Wherefore, there are also special means by which He more carefully governs the elect. [They include] angels, whom Paul calls "ministering spirits" (Hebrews 1). It is certain they defend every one of the elect particularly. Hitherto may be referred the preaching of the Word of God [and] the ministering of the sacraments. Besides this, God uses the devils, wicked men, and tyrants to exercise the faith of His elect and to confirm them in patience, whereby they are called the servants of the Lord, axes, hammers, saws, and swords in the land[15] of God, as [in the case of] Pharaoh, Nebuchadnezzar, and Sennacherib.

Moreover, the means by which He works upon the wicked are also many: (1) good and evil angels (Exodus 14); (2) friends and familiars (Jer. 13:14; Amos 7:1); (3) wild beasts (Jer. 8:17); (4) heaven above (Deut. 11:17); (5) diseases and plagues (Exod. 15:16); (6) famine (Hos. 9:3); (7) fire (Hos. 8:14); (8) fury (Hos. 7:9); (9) hardness of heart (Rom. 1:28); and (10) captivity (Jer. 15:2).

God's providence uses all these means: first, that He might show His goodness toward us; second, that He might be known to be the Lord over all; [and,] third, that we might be thankful because He not only governs us but also makes His creatures to serve our turns.

Marry,[16] this must be noted (as I said before) that in all these secondary causes, beside their natural work which God has given them, there is also

---

14. This paragraph break is not in the original.
15. Hand?
16. *Marry*: indeed.

shown the special work of God's special hand. God works not by second causes as magistrates govern their commonwealths by their inferior officers. For they so govern by them that they do nothing (or very little) themselves, and peradventure never know what is done. God governs not the world so, but in every particular work He has His particular stroke. It is the general providence of God that the thunder burns, moves, [and] hurts. But it is the special providence of the same God that it burns or hurts this or that man, on this or that part, in this or that manner. The Lord has shown His special providence in one excellent example: "If the hatchet," says God, "fall forth of the hand of him which loppeth the tree, and kill a man in the way, I the Lord have killed him."[17]

God also governs the world immediately, and His providence works without means, and many things He brings to pass against all means, which is manifest by that of Matthew: "Man liveth not by bread only, but by every word which proceedeth out of the mouth of God."[18] For example, without means, the Spirit of God did move upon the waters, and cover them in the creation immediately. The first garment, which was made, was of leather, and God alone without means made it. Noah in the ark was preserved by God alone a whole year, against the force of the waters. Without means He did keep the shoes and garments of the Israelites whole forty years. He alone justifies, sanctifies, and converts a sinner. Against the course of nature, He made the sea to divide itself, the sun to go backward, the fire not to burn the three children, [and] the lions not to devour Daniel. The causes of this are these: (1) that we may know [that] when God works by causes, He does it by no necessity, but freely; (2) that we might know [that] when God uses means, He is not idle, but works all in all; [and,] (3) that if means want, nay, if means be against us, yet we should not despair of God's providence.[19]

Now to come to our prognosticators and moon-prophets, how shall they be able to know what will come to pass hereafter? For first, the heavens, being only one particular instrument of God's providence among many, they cannot certainly and truly say [that] this thing or that thing proceeds from the heavens. Second, they cannot determine whether God in extraordinary matters (as plague, famine, barrenness, distempered weather, earthquakes, wars, etc.) does work immediately or with means. If with means, they cannot determine whether the heavens, or angels, or men, or any other things are the means of His providence. Third, if they were able to know what the heavens work naturally, yet they were never the better. For God, beside the power of the heavens, has in all things His particular working providence, altering, framing, and

---

17. Deut. 19:5. This paragraph break is not in the original.

18. Matt. 4:4.

19. This paragraph break is not in the original.

bending as wax His instruments to His good will. Truly by this consideration, a Christian man will be brought to leave off seeking what event the works of God shall have before they come to pass. If a man shall come into a joiner's shop, can he, by knowing the use of all his tools, tell what things he has made in his shop? No. What is the cause of that? He uses not only his tools in his work but thereunto adjoins his own hand, by which he handles and turns the tool to his own pleasure, and so makes divers kind of works with the same instruments. The same may be said of our prognosticators, which I would to God they would somewhat consider.

Argument 3: Their Lack of Experience

If our prognosticators have any means to foretell things to come, they have those means either without experience or with experience. If they have them without experience, then you must account all which they do to be foolish dreams and deceit. For all kinds of human learning, which is profitable and useful in the life of man, is taken from often observations and experience. If it is said that they have their directions in prognosticating from experience, and that of all times, I will convince them thus. True experience of the causes of things is an often observing of the effects of the same causes, with this ground that they can proceed from no other thing. The physician says rhubarb does purge choler. Well, how knows he this? He has often tried this and that in old men, young men, [and] children. And [he] has found that, in the bodies of all men, the cause of purging this humor could be ascribed to nothing else. Wherefore, he may peremptorily conclude [that] rhubarb purges choler. Our prognosticators can have no such experience in the heavens, for they cannot observe often the same position of stars in the heaven. The order and cause of the fixed stars and planets, which we find in the heavens this day, the next day will be changed, and never the like again. They will say indeed [that] although the same position of the whole heavens never happens, yet the same conjunctions of notable stars, the same risings and settings, and the same constellations of the chief stars, are often marked. I say again that when these eclipses and great conjunctions happen, the rest of the stars, being otherwise affected than they were before, and having new positions, may either increase and diminish their effects, or else hinder them and quite take them away. As we see when the sun, casting its beams into a chamber, the light of candles, torches, and fires do make it shine dim, yet these being absent, it will shine bright.[20]

Again, they are not able to say that constellations, which they have marked, are causes of those effects which follow, as wars, diseases, distempered weather,

---

20. This paragraph break is not in the original.

earthquakes, famine, etc. For in those things which happen together, the one is not the cause of the other. When Nero played upon his harp, Rome was on fire. Yet Nero's playing on the harp was no cause of the burning of Rome. Also, these effects may have causes in the heavens other than those which they mark; they may come immediately from God [or] they may come only from the will of man. Wherefore, seeing that they cannot assure themselves that those eclipses and conjunctions are the works of such effects upon earth, and they cannot have often observation of the course of heaven, their rules of predictions are feigned and supposed, and not built upon true experience.[21]

Let a man who knows not one herb, take all kinds of herbs, and put them into a great vessel, yet so that there are more of some herbs and less of others. Let him beat them all together and make a compound virtue of all their virtues. Can he now tell the nature and operation of every particular herb? Can he divide and sever by any help the virtue of one herb from another? No indeed. The same thing may be said of the stars of heaven. All their lights and all their influences (as they term it) are in the lower bodies. More plainly, every earthly body has in it all the secret powers and working of every particular star, so that they make (as it were) a compound operation rising from all, or from the most of their virtues joined together. For the astrologers hold that although the light may be hindered by the thickness of the body, yet the heavenly influence pierces through all. Therefore, they are not able to sever and learn the nature of these stars, except they can stop the influence of what stars they list and bring them into what compass they will.[22]

Yet thus much I will grant them, that they may have a little knowledge of the virtue of the sun and moon and some other stars, as we see those herbs in the former composition, whose virtues be the chiefest, though not fully, yet somewhat do represent their nature, and show themselves above the rest. But what is this to the purpose? If I confess the operations of the sun and moon, if I shall grant that Saturn is in nature cold and dry, Jupiter warm and moist, Mars hot and dry, Venus cold and moist, Mercury in nature mixed, the notable fixed stars in the Zodiac to be of the nature of planets and to have manifest operations, as the rising of the dog[23] to make heat and tempestuous seas, the rising of Arcturus to make rain and showers, Pleiades to be of the nature of Mars and the moon, etc., what will all this suffice to make a prognostication? For seeing all stars have their own powers, and peradventure also the least stars, which we make no account of, have great effects among us (as one grain of musk in the

---

21. This paragraph break is not in the original.

22. This paragraph break is not in the original.

23. This is likely a reference to Sirius (the Dog Star), which is the brightest star in the constellation Canis Major.

apothecary's shop makes a greater smell than all other powders, be they ever so many), the knowledge of the operation of some stars will prevail nothing, the rest being not known and never regarded. They will say they have some experience, but yet imperfect. I have shown how they have no true experience at all, and their imperfect experience makes them perfect liars.

Argument 4: Their Ignorance of Causes
A man who will judge rightly of any matter by the causes must not only consider the common causes but he must also with them confer the particular causes of all things which happen among us; so he shall judge aright. In [the] heavens the stars are common causes of all things among us, because they show their virtue on every matter, one way or another. The same things have their peculiar efficients and matters and forms by which, and not by the heavens, they are made that, whatsoever they are. These proper causes, because their natures are unknown unto us, I cannot see how the prognosticator is able to foretell anything to come in [a] good and convenient manner, laying aside all deceiving and forging of untruths.[24]

To make this plainer, I will use this similitude. Suppose a hen [were] to sit upon many eggs, some of her own [and] some of divers other fowls. She imparts her heat equally unto them. At length she hatches, and some of her chickens are cocks, some hens, some crows, some partridges, some doves, some black, [and] some white. Some live, some [are] dead, some are killed by the kite, [and] some are roasted. No man, I think, will profess so much skill as to say that he, by the considering of the hen and her heat, which is a common cause of the chickens and all that befalls them, is able to tell why of this egg came a partridge [and] of that a crow, why this egg had no chicken, why that had a dead chicken, etc., except he does therewithal adjoin the consideration of the particular effects.[25]

The heaven is (as it were) a hen fostering under her wings all earthly things, imparting its virtue and heat unto all. Can our prognosticator, by the erecting of figures, by considering the disposition of every planet in their houses, and the significations of everything, judge why this man is wealthy [and] that man [is] a beggar, why this noble man dies this year [but] none the next year, why it is naught to travel this way [and] good to travel that way, why these diseases abound and not others, why corn shall be dear this quarter [but] not the next, why this week is fair and temperate [and] that week [or] month [is] unseasonable and tempestuous? Truly, it is a thing flatly impossible. They must hereunto adjoin the particular nature of the country, the particular causes both in men's

---

24. This paragraph break is not in the original.
25. This paragraph break is not in the original.

minds and bodies (as education, place, honesty, birth, blood, sickness, health, strength, weakness, meat, drink, liberty of mind, learning, etc.), and all other special circumstances. They never do this, as we may see in their prognostications. And if they would do it, yet they could not. Wherefore, I must needs say this, that their folly is great in publishing their prognostications, and you also [are] greatly to be blamed which by your greedy desire give them great occasion to be so unprofitably occupied.

To show more briefly and plainly of their inability in prognosticating, although I grant the stars have great force, yet I say they cannot judge of things to come [Hosea 2]. And there are six impediments.

The first impediment is imbecility of wit, for man's eye from the earth, beholding the heavens and the stars, perceives them not in their just quantity but as very small lights. For indeed the sun is 136 times bigger than the earth, Saturn [is] 90 [and] Jupiter 96. Mars [is] one and a half, the moon is the thirty-ninth part of the earth. The biggest fixed stars contain the earth 107 times, the stars of the second magnitude 90 times, the third 70 times, the fourth 54 times, the fifth 35 times, the sixth 18 times. So, the weakness of man's understanding is not able to conceive and learn the things which the heavens do bring to pass on earth.

The second impediment [is] the infinite number of stars, which (no doubt) all have great power, although we do not find it. For the prognosticator only marks 1,028 stars, and he only takes heed unto a very few of these. Which is as though a man should judge the power of an army by the power of one or two soldiers and captains, not by the power of the whole company.

The third impediment is the infinite varieties of the virtues of stars and the parts of heaven, which astrologers grant to be. Yet they do not know them. Touching the nature of the fixed stars, they know nothing but by the color (which is red, leady, white, pale, etc.) resembling some planet. And because they know not the virtue of all stars and every part of heaven, they are not able to judge anything but to their own shame, no more than the physician is able to know the nature of a compound medicine without the knowing of every simple[one].

The fourth impediment [is] the manifold and daily change of the motions, positions, and configurations of the stars. For if a man could tell both the number and nature of stars, yet the variety of positions breeds trouble and hinders right judgment, because by this means the powers of stars are increased, diminished, and changed. And these rules, which served for ancient times to foretell things, will not serve us because all the fixed stars have changed their places, and the rest are daily changed.

The fifth impediment [is] the infinite variety of inferior things, which do hinder, pervert, change, receive, or not receive the virtue and predictions of stars, as the nature of the soil, the natural disposition of air, orders and constitutions of the commonwealth, occasions, education, institutions, kinds of meat and drink, etc.

The sixth impediment [is] the will of man, which freely in common matters chooses this and refuses that. There are many things which are caused without any work of stars, only by the will of man, and study, as we may see in Socrates, Demosthenes, and others.

Thus much shall suffice to show that they cannot prognosticate of things ensuing.

Reason 2: Their Untruths

Now follow their manifold untruths and most false rules. In disclosing them I will keep the same order they use in their almanac. In the first or second leaf of their books, you shall find a picture of man's body with the twelve signs round about it. They call it the anatomy of man's body, showing how the twelve signs have government of the same. For the moon (or any other indicator[26] of anything), being in the sign, they say that it is dangerous to box, to fear that part, or to let blood in it, which is subject to the dominion of that sign. All these are nothing but vain fables, as I will manifestly prove.

Whereas they call it an anatomy, I think it is a butcherly anatomy; nay, that of the butcher is far better for they join head and appurtenance together. These men, being sparing, give Aries the head, Leo and Cancer the heart and lungs. As for the liver, I know not which sign has it, peradventure in old times men have no livers. At the anatomy of a carrion, crows deal friendly, for everyone has somewhat, but in the division of man's body, signs play foul play, for Capricorn has got nothing but a pair of knees. It is like that the signs, scrambling for their portions, Capricorn being slow got nothing. Hereupon, compassion being had, there was a gathering made, and Sagittarius gave the lower part of the thigh, Aquarius the higher part of the leg, which both together make the knee. But to deliver you out of all doubt, mark these reasons which follow.[27]

First, the signs cannot have any such dominion over [a] man's body. I make it manifest thus. There is no corporal heaven indeed above the firmament, yet because the firmament or eighth sphere has many motions, to give reasons of those motions, the astronomers have feigned two heavens above the firmament: the Christaline heaven; and the first moveable or tenth sphere, which

---

26. In the original the term is *significator*.

27. This paragraph break is not in the original.

they divide into twelve parts, which parts they call signs. Now I pray you, tell me, is it possible to conceive that an imagined part of any imagined heaven void of all stars shall either have in itself, or give unto other stars, power to govern the parts of [a] man's body? More reasonable was that man who, being asked what was the cause of the sands in Sandwich haven,[28] answered, the building up of Tenterton steeple.[29]

Second, the government of the signs in the body is not taken from experience in nature, but feigned long ago by some drowsy pate,[30] and now because it has a cloak of antiquity, it is allowed. More natural was this kind of way that hot signs should govern hot parts, cold signs cold parts, earthly signs earthly parts.[31] So Aries should govern the heart and the vital blood, not the head, and the rest of the signs those parts which are of their nature and disposition.

Third, [the] great experience of many men confutes this rule daily. For many learned physicians and expert surgeons have by infinite examples found that if a man is let blood in the sign, or lanced, or boxed, or seared, no harm ensues; nay, they have given testimony that the patients have found even then great comfort. Wherefore, let not these things trouble your mind any more, but let them be numbered even among vain and unprofitable fables.

Next after follow elections of days and hours necessary for all matters, as follows: [There are] special days to (1) prepare humors; (2) let blood; (3) purge with vomit, electuaries, potions, and pills; (4) cut hair; (5) comfort the virtue (attractive, digestive, retentive, expulsive); (6) bathe; (7) put children to school; (8) travel; (9) marry; (10) hunt, hawk, fish; (11) plant; (12) geld cattle; [and] (13) lay foundations.

Here, I pray you, mark their naughty dealings, how they abuse your ignorance to make themselves skillful, and to do more than they can do. For if the judgments of the best astrologers may be taken, certainly most of these elections cannot be prescribed to you, unless they know beforehand the figure of your nativity. For all election, which concerns your person, must be moderated (to speak as plainly as their toys will suffer me) by the direction of the root of your nativity, and by the monthly and diurnal[32] progressions of your present revolution. If any of these portend some evil, the particular election may be a means to increase and to bring it to pass. For example, suppose you, being a man toward marriage, you find in the almanac a good day noted by

---

28. The town of Sandwich is located on the southeast shore of England, not far from Dover.

29. Allegedly, the funds which should have been used to repair the sea-wall in Sandwich were diverted to the building of a nearby church.

30. *Pate:* head.

31. In the margin: The twelve signs feigned.

32. *Diurnal:* daily.

the prognosticator to marry in. You take your opportunity. After a while, you are weary of your life. The first day of your marriage was the last day of your joy. What is the cause of this? All the planets, which were signifiers of your marriage in your nativity were then evilly affected, and peradventure also, when you were first born, they received some disgrace. So then, you may lay all blame partly upon yourself for believing and partly upon the prognosticator who deceived you.[33]

But to come unto particulars, the elections of days to purge the body with any kind of purgation, and to comfort the same, are most ridiculous. Why do they not also prescribe hours of eating meat? Why do they not appoint the kinds of meats and drinks which we must eat and use daily? If you see that God does daily bless the enterprises of those physicians who never regard those elections in ministering to their patients, [and] never esteem of them, let them go as lies to the devil from whence they came. Concerning the elections of days to sow, to set, to plant, to lop, they are also foolish. The general observation of the season of the year in which these things are to be done is sufficient. And Saint Augustine, in his book *de civitate Dei*,[34] laughs at the folly of them who choose particular days to do their husbandry, as though some certain positions of stars had some special influence to the things which are sown then. His reason is because many grains of corn, being cast into the ground together and ripening all at one time, yet some of them are blasted, some are eaten by birds, some are trodden down under foot, some stand and are never touched.[35]

The rest of the elections, and especially that of laying foundations, is most absurd. They say that if a house, a city, [or] a town has its foundation when the stars are well affected, the inhabitants shall have [a] prosperous and quiet living. If, when the stars are evil disposed, then trouble and disquietness. They have no experience of this, but that only which is most false, for they know not the foundations of cities and towns, neither the positions of the stars, when they were built. Let Rome and Venice be examples, because these are most alleged of astrologers; the time in which they were built is uncertain, and the planets are falsely set in the figure of the foundation of Rome, because Mercury is contrary to the sun, a thing flat impossible. Again, the folly of this is thus manifest, that a house, or city, or commonwealth, may remain, the people being gone, as it is in the time of plague, and banishment, and conquests by princes. And the inhabitants also may be safe and remain, the building quite ransomed and beaten down, as we may see in Carthage, the people and commonwealth remained, the city quite defaced. That all elections are unlawful, Saint Augustine, writing

---

33. This paragraph break is not in the original.
34. *The City of God.*
35. This paragraph break is not in the original.

unto Januarius, proves it forth out of Galatians 4 by these words: "to observe months and times and years." Therefore, let us not observe days, years, months, and times, lest we hear this of the apostle: "I am afraid lest I have taken labor in vain with you." For he rebukes them who say, "I will not go because the moon is thus or thus moved, or I will take my journey that I may have good success because there is such a position of stars. I will not do my business this month because such a star governs this month, or I will do my business this month because such a star rules."[36]

What then shall a man do not to break the Word of God? Are you a man who desires to lead a Christian life? Then, take the example of Paul as a pattern to govern all the actions of your life. "Without ceasing," says he, "I make mention of you in my prayers: beseeching that by some means, one time or other I might have prosperous journey by the will of God to come unto you" [Rom. 1:10]. So, you, if you have any business in hand, any journey to take, anything to buy or sell, or any other matter, never regard the constellations of heaven. Commit yourself alone to the providence of God, in whom you have your life and motion and being. He directs all your steps. Pray unto Him privately with[in] yourself to bless you and all your actions, that they may tend to His glory [and] your welfare. You shall find that all your enterprises will have better success than if the whole host of heaven, and all the prognosticators of England, had promised ever so much prosperity.[37]

Now let us show their absurd folly in prognosticating of the state of the year, of which their predictions are either general for the whole year or special for every day. In their general predictions are considered either the grounds of them or the matters which they foretell.

The Grounds

Their grounds are especially two: (1) the figure of the revolution of the year, erected when the sun enters into the first minute of Aries; [and] (2) the figure celestial for the time of the eclipse of the sun and moon. For upon these two, say they, depends the whole estate of the year. In their celestial figures they consider the erecting of them and the finding of the lord of the figure. The erecting of the figure contains very many absurdities.

First, they follow that way which Regiamontanus[38] invented. [It] as yet has never been proved by any experience, and [it] flatly differs from those ways which were used by ancient astrologers and [those that] were invented by

---

36. This paragraph break is not in the original.

37. This paragraph break is not in the original.

38. Johannes Regiamontanus (1436–76) was an important mathematician, astronomer, and astrologer.

Gazulus[39] and Campanus.[40] Nay, oftentimes it makes the planet (or fixed star) to signify a flatly contrary thing to that which the other two do.

Second, the casting of the heavens into twelve distinct kinds of matter is ridiculous, because it, being imagined and void of stars, can have no force. Yet (some will say) other stars, being in those places, may have and signify such or such effects. I answer, that if stars of divers natures, coming to such a house, always signify one kind of thing, then the house must of necessity give some force unto the planet. And so it shall have not only an augmenting, but also an effectual working power which astrologers deny, and no reason can prove.

Third, they make the twelfth and eleventh houses, being higher above the horizon than the first, to be of less force than it. And [they make] the fourth house to be of greater power than any above the horizon not cardinal. And [they make] the end of the ninth to be more in power than the beginning of the eleventh house. All which are against reason because a planet, the more perpendicular its beams are, the more is its force. They answer, although the force of the light is greater, yet the secret influence is less, and the first house has more forcible influence than the twelfth or eleventh. If the influence is secret, how can they know it? Again, they can by no good experience show that those houses have more influence than the rest. This influence makes against them. I say they cannot prognosticate because they know not one star's virtue. For whereas they say that the sun, moon, and planets have most force, I answer that it is by reason of their light, not their influence, which is small. And there is far greater [influence] in the smallest fixed stars. So that the fixed stars, although they have no light or very small light perceived, yet they have [the] most influence. And so these men must needs dream because they judge by wrong causes. Well, their figure being framed and distinguished with fair characters, then they go on to find the lord of the figure, that is, that planet which has most dignities in the figure.

The dignities of the planets are found out by these means especially: (1) houses of planets; (2) exaltation; (3) triplicity; (4) terms; (5) stars; (6) houses; (7) freeness from combustion; (8) directions; (9) velocity of course; (10) sazimi;[41] and (11) some aspects of other planets.

These toys are so foolish that a reasonable man would not vouchsafe to refute them, yet a word or two. If the houses of the planets shall be battered and pulled down, all the rest of their worship and dignity will lie in the dust. Aries

---

39. Johannes Gazullus (1400–65) was a famous astronomer and mathematician.

40. Likely a reference to Campanus of Novara (c. 1220–96), a renowned Italian physician, mathematician, astronomer, and astrologer.

41. *Sazimi*: cazimi. This term is used to describe a planet whose center is within 17 minutes of the arc of the sun's center.

and Scorpius are appointed the houses of Mars; Taurus and Libra, the houses of Venus; Gemini and Virgo, the houses of Mercury; Cancer, the house of the moon; Leo, the house of the sun; Sagittarius and Pisces, the houses of Jupiter; Aquarius and Capricornus, the houses of Saturn. What reason do they give of this? Leo and Cancer, say they, are the houses of the sun and moon because they resemble the nature of these planets, and because they come most near our heads. Such reason they give to the rest. What feeble grounds are these? As in the north part of the world Cancer and Leo resemble the nature of the sun, so in the south part, in the contrary climates, Capricornus and Aquarius do resemble their natures. Also, in every country some divers signs are either vertical or else come near the top of the country, and so all signs shall be the houses of the sun and moon. Now then, the sun being displaced, I cannot find how the rest of the planets can keep their hold.[42]

To go further, the exaltations of planets in like manner are very dreams. They suppose exaltations are those degrees in which the planets were in the beginning of the world. But why should those places give more force than any other? And if they could give more force, yet they have falsely assigned them. For the sun was not in Aries when it was created by God, but was placed in Libra, which I prove by this reason. God created man and beast in perfect age, giving unto them all kinds of fruits being then ripe, so that in the beginning was the time of the year which we call harvest. Now, because God never afterwards changed the seasons, and we find that in the time of ripeness the sun is always in Libra, we must needs also say that its place in the creation was in Libra. In Exodus 23, God commanded that the feast of tabernacles should be celebrated in the end of the year, when the Israelites had gathered their fruits out of the fields. Wherefore, it must needs be that harvest was in the beginning of the year (the beginning and ending being both together) and so by counting backwards we shall find that the sun was in Libra in the beginning of the world. To this agrees Josephus,[43] Rabbi Eleazar,[44] and Rabbi Abraham.[45]

The rest of the dignities of the planets consist of principles weaker than water. First, what is more unreasonable to a reasonable man than this, that swift motion should give unto a planet two dignities, and slow motion two debilities? It seems to be plainly contrary. For a swift course hinders the force of the planet, a slow course helps the same. And the stations of any planet make an effectual and sensible operation. A coal of fire in a man's hand, if it is shaken about very much, heats very little. If it is shaken more slowly, it heats more. But

---

42. This paragraph break is not in the original.
43. In the text: De Antiquit. Lib. 1. cap. 3.
44. In the text: Upon Genesis.
45. In the text: Aben Ezra upon Daniel 7.

if it lies still, it burns violently. Beside this, experience also confirms my assertion. In the year of our Lord 1513, the sun entering into Pisces was almost in trine aspect with Saturn stationary, a little while after, there was a great frost and snow continuing many days. And when Saturn began again to be direct, the weather was indifferently warm. In the year 1518, in April, Jupiter almost in *secunda statione*, beholding Saturn in *statione prima*, caused a great heat, considering the time of the year. In the year 1520, Saturn (as I said before), being stationary, made such a cold that spoiled the grapes and made wine dear. Upon these examples and many others, I may conclude that the work and influence of planets is most felt when they are stationary, because their virtue is fixed (as it were) in one place by reason of the slow motion.

Combustion is in like sort a feigned thing. What reason can astrologers give why it should give unto a star five debilities? They talk [of] how experience teaches them that planets, being under the beams of the sun, do lose a great (nay, some say, all their force). It is a manifest untruth. For Mercury, being of the nature of that planet with which it is conjoined, if it goes from conjunction with Saturn unto the sun, it gets no debilities thereby, but rather losing the feeble and unfortunate nature of Saturn, receives a more strong and fortunate nature of the sun. If any man says against me that Mercury's combust has no force, he deceives himself. For if it is not hindered, it naturally will cause winds. Being combust, it not only engenders winds but causes tempestuous winds and foul weather. In Aries, Taurus, [and] Cancer, it makes tempests. In Virgo and Scorpius, [it makes] raging seas. In Sagittarius, Capricornus, Aquarius, and Pisces, [it makes] rain and snow. Again, when there has been fair weather [for] many days together, the sun, if it comes to be in conjunction or any other aspect with Saturn, makes very foul weather, and therefore the aspects of the sun and Jupiter are called *apertiones portarum pro pluvia*.[46] This could not come to pass if Saturn had its force diminished by the beams of the sun.

A planet, also being in sazimi (that is, being within 16 minutes of the sun's middle), has thereby five dignities, which cannot well be if that combustion gives five debilities. For the planet is in the middle of its combustion, and the sun casts its beams and force very vehemently upon it. These things show how absurd a dream combustion is. Yet if it were a good and sound principle of astrology, and gave unto every planet five debilities, yet it could not be proved that liberty from combustion should give five dignities, being only a mere absence and privation of the other. Magnes,[47] at the presence of the adamant,[48]

---

46. The opening of the doors for rain.

47. Magnets?

48. Historically, the word *adamant* applied to actual stones (and other substances) believed to be impenetrable. In the 17th century, it was used as a synonym of diamond.

is hindered from drawing iron. Yet, if the adamant is away, the attractive virtue of the magnes is not increased. Here I might with ease confute the triplicities of planets, directions, aspects, applications, preventions, refrenations,[49] with many such like, but my intent at this time is only to show you some untruths of our prognosticators.

The Matters

Thus much of the grounds of their predictions; now follow the matters of which they prognosticate. And they are very many; nay, there is almost no matter of which they will not give their verdict. But I will briefly make manifest unto you how they do this, so that their lies and their un-Christian dealing may be more loathed by you.

First, they foretell of comets, earthquakes, famines, plagues, etc., but they do it as the blind man who casts his staff he knows not where. No man as yet ever knew the true causes of these. As for comets and blazing stars, they do not rise from the influence of any stars, neither are they any earthly things, but [they] are in heaven, most commonly far above the moon, as by geometrical and astronomical demonstrations may be proved. How this comes to pass, the Lord only knows. And surely, they do you great injury, who when (as no doubt) God does lighten them, and sends the rest extraordinarily, as threatening tokens of His sore displeasure, yet they will rock you asleep in the cradle of security by telling [you] that such tokens came from the ordinary course of the heavens.

Second, they foretell all things which happen in civil affairs among men, as are these which follow: love and hatred of kinsfolk; marriages; increase of farms and livings; injuries and quarrels; raising of rents; exacting of subsidies by officers; false rumors; imprisonments; hard entreating of ecclesiastical persons; buying, selling, undermining; the studying of sciences; friends fall out for trifles; solemn progresses; favor of noble men; men shall fall, body and goods, into the prince's hands; merchandise unprofitable; etc.

These and such like proceed only from the will of man. The constellations of stars are neither signs nor causes of them. Some will say, *Non imponere necessuatem, sed inclinare stellas* (that is, stars do not constrain but only incline the minds of men). [This is a] most wicked saying, although most commonly spoken of and defended. For the inclining of the will of man is only the work of God, as the Holy Scriptures do teach us. "The heart of man," says Solomon, "purposeth his ways, but the Lord directeth his steps" [Prov. 16:9]. "O Lord," says Jeremiah the prophet, "that the way of man is not in himself, neither is it

---

49. *Refrenation*: the act of refraining or restraining.

in man to walk and direct his steps" [Jer. 10:23]. He speaks this because Nebuchadnezzar purposed to have made war against the Moabites and Ammonites, but hearing of Zedekiah's rebellion, he turned his power to go against Jerusalem. Therefore, the prophet says that whereas he had otherwise purposed, yet this was the Lord's inclination and direction. Again, in the Proverbs, we read thus: "That the heart of the king is in the hands of the Lord, as the rivers of water, he directeth it whither he will" [Prov. 21:1].[50]

It will be said that although God properly and immediately inclines the will of man, yet also some small inclination must be given unto the stars, and that immediately. For, say some, "Constellations work upon the elements by the four first qualities. Elements work upon and alter the compound bodies and humors. Compound bodies by their qualities change the senses. The senses, being altered, the understanding is altered. The understanding lastly alters and inclines the will of man. Therefore, constellations incline the will."

This reason is not much unlike that which the drunken man makes, serving as well for the defense of his vice as the former for approving of truth in divination. "He who drinks well sleeps well. He who sleeps well thinks no harm. He who thinks no harm is a good man. Therefore, he who drinks well is a good man."

The deceits and untruths which are in their reasons are very many.

First, the stars work upon men's bodies, yet so that the nature of the country and soil, the meats and drinks, have most commonly greater force. Why are the bodies of gentlemen of England and poor laboring men of divers dispositions? Are they not both in one country? Do not the stars show their force in them alike? Yes, truly, but the kind of life and diet prevail. In the same region, why are they, who dwell upon hills, of other temperatures than they who dwell upon plain and champion ground? Why do not the same influences of stars make them of like natures? Is it not because the nature of the soil prevails? So then, when as there are many causes effectual and differing in altering men's bodies, to build an argument upon one cause is most unreasonable.

Second, the stars work upon the elements (earth, water, air) by making heat, cold, moisture, [and] dryness. How do the elements work on men's bodies? They will also say by making heat, cold, moisture, [and] dryness. This is most untrue. For the hotter and drier the elements are, the colder and moister by nature are men's bodies. According to that saying of Empedocles,[51] nature placed a hot body in a cold country, and a cold body in a hot country.

---

50. This paragraph break is not in the original.

51. Empedocles (c. 494–434 BC) was a Greek pre-Socratic philosopher, who is best known for his theory of the four classical elements.

Third, the philosophers say that all causes are either *per se*[52] or *per accidens*.[53] Now, the heavens, being causes of the alteration of the senses *per accidens*, they must not be causes of the inclination of the will, either *per se* or *per accidens*, but *per accidentis accidens*, which is most ridiculous.

Fourth, this long chain by which they link the will of man to the stars, if it shall be applied unto particulars, must needs break. For the actions of the will in buying, selling, travelling, lying, heaping up wealth, murdering, spreading false rumors, offering of discourtesies, hating of kinsfolks, and such like, which our heaven-gazers foretell, have no coherence with the first qualities (heat, cold, moisture, dryness). Neither can they [in] any way proceed from them. And therefore the stars cannot be [the] causes of them, for they work only by these qualities.

Fifth, this reason is nothing to their purpose. For, because they grant that a man may freely resist the inclination of the stars, and [that] he may hinder that unto which the stars bend his will, how dare they presume to say this or that will come to pass? The heathen men gave up themselves to their own lusts and vanities and followed every little and vain inclination. And of them, in this order, did ancient astrologers among them divine that this or that time, such actions, such vices, such enterprises, such affairs should be among them. In like manner our English wise men speak of us as though we were beasts, not reasonable men, as though we never had heard the blessed gospel of God, never tasted of the grace of God, never learned what is good and what is bad, never labored to subdue our lusts and affections, always turned to and fro with the blast of any influence working very slenderly in us.

Thus much of civil affairs. They also make mention yearly of the diseases which shall reign. But the way they follow is taken forth from the barren and uncertain rules of the old astrologers, who do so ascribe unto every planet certain diseases that, if need shall require, they may refer the same diseases unto many significators. In the plague, the putrefaction of humors is attributed unto Jupiter, the sharp fever unto Mars, the madness which follows unto Mercury, the whole plague unto Mars. In the pleurisy, the inflammation of the blood between the skin (called pleuritis) and the ribs is attributed unto Jupiter, the suppuration[54] of the blood unto Saturn, and the whole pleurisy unto Jupiter. In the jaundice, the inflammation and corruption of humors [are attributed] unto Jupiter, the yellow humor in the gall unto Mars, the obstruction of the parts unto Saturn, the whole jaundice, being white, unto Mars, being black,

---

52. By itself; i.e., that which is intended.
53. By accident; i.e., that which is unintended.
54. *Suppuration:* festering.

unto Saturn. And so, in every disease, they use this inconstancy and ambiguity in prognosticating.[55]

It is a rule among the astrologers that if the planets' signifiers of diseases are well affected, then there shall be no diseases but health. If they are evilly affected, then diseases follow. Our prognosticators never mark this rule, but howsoever the planets are affected, they straight away pronounce that such diseases shall reign. For example, the last winter quarter, it was said by one of them that the diseases which should afflict men's bodies were rhewmes,[56] coughs, cold laskes,[57] swelling of the face and throat, falling of the colmell,[58] sore eyes, deafness, the stone, gout, dropsy, green-sickness, madness, quartern fevers,[59] etc. And all the planets' signifiers of diseases in that quarter werc indifferent[ly] well affected. Wherefore, you have not one cause to fear their threatening, but rather to be sorry for their continual deceits, wishing them minds that they may one day see their own folly.

Concerning the time when the constellations take their effects, our prognosticators say that some take their effects the same year, some not the same year, but long after, as great conjunctions and eclipses. For they say if the moon is eclipsed one hour, it works its effect a month after; if two hours, two months after. And the sun, for every hour it is eclipsed, takes its effect a whole year after. Truly this rule which they follow must needs be against all reason. For why should not all conjunctions and oppositions of the sun and moon defer their effects as well as those conjunctions and oppositions in which the sun and moon are eclipsed? If they show forth their power immediately after, why should not these also do the same? Moreover, epignostical[60] astrologers, who have conferred the course of the heavens with histories, show very manifestly that eclipses do not defer the time of working their spite upon the earth.

In the year of our Lord 1419, the sun was eclipsed in Aries, and presently after showed all its force. There was [a] great sedition in Prague that year. In Paris [there was] an uproar between them of the city and the university, and two thousand scholars were slain. Then also Wenzeslaus, king of Bohemia, being in a great palsy, died. In the year 1524, there was a conjunction of Saturn and Jupiter in Scorpius, and also a great eclipse of the sun in June, which took their effects the same year. Charles, king of France, [was] driven forth of

---

55. This paragraph break is not in the original.
56. *Rhewmes:* catarrh or head-cold.
57. *Laskes:* diarrhea.
58. *Colmell:* meaning unknown.
59. *Quartern fever:* a fever that recurs every fourth day.
60. *Epignostical:* meaning unknown.

his country. [There was] war between the Danes and the men of Sleswicke.[61] There was a great plague in Germany, civil dissention among the princes of the empire and them who took the part of John Huss. In 1452, [there was] an eclipse of the sun in Sagittarius. Its effects began presently, and lasted a great while; even then Constantinople was taken by the Turk. The Hungarians and Bohemians besieged Frederick the emperor. On April 27, 1473, the sun was eclipsed in Taurus, Mars being in Aries, and Jupiter in Sagittarius. The same year, in the summer, was such heat and dryness of weather that woods even withered and one might wade over deep rivers. In the years of our Lord 1476, 1460, 1469, 1486, 1502, 1518, and many years after, there were both great conjunctions and strange eclipses, which took their effects presently, not one or two or three years after (as our heaven-gazers bear you in hand). All these examples which I bring against them I have not feigned, but taken forth of those books which they have in [the] greatest estimation. And [I] could, if need should serve, bring a hundred more all to show their lies when as they commonly say thus, "There shall be an eclipse this year, marry I will not here determine its effects, but reserve them to be declared in my prognostication one year or two years hence when it will take place."

To know where the effects of the stars shall take place, they have appointed certain countries unto every sign. They have set the fiery triplicity over Europe, the airy triplicity over the oriental and northern parts of Asia, the watery triplicity over Africa, [and] the early triplicity over the southern parts of Asia. And so, every peculiar sign has its dominion over some parts of those. Now therefore, when a conjunction or eclipse is in any of these signs, the cities and countries subject unto them feel the force of that constellation especially. This is a most manifest untruth and may be confuted by many reasons.[62]

First, the nature of the signs is not the same now as it was in past times, and by the confession of the best learned have other effects now than they had in the days of King Ptolemy. Yet, we see the nature of countries and people to remain the same still, as may be seen by reading Tacitus, Pliny, Caesar, [and] Strabo.

Second, America, which is half the world, has no signs appointed over it. Why? It was found out of late. True it is, but this is an argument that [proves] the rules of astrology are absurd, and were the bare inventions and imaginations of idle brains. For there is no doubt but that America's parts and islands, as Brasilia, Peru, Pari, Terra Florida, Java Major, Java Minor, Puloana, Pavilonga, Subath, Massana, Mattan, Juvacana, Cozumella, Jamaica, etc., have felt the force of those constellations which they attribute to some parts of the

---

61. The Duchy of Schleswig was located on the current border between Germany and Denmark.

62. This paragraph break is not in the original.

old world. Because these countries are about the middle zone, and have both planets and signs full over them, and therefore if the stars threaten any strange thing to come, they must especially feel it.

Third, experience, the cause of all acts, is against them, as is manifest in these examples. Forty-seven years before the nativity of our Savior Christ, there was a conjunction of the higher planets in Scorpius, and then was civil war between Caesar and Pompey, and the change of the empire was in Europe. But, according unto the institution of astrologers, all these troubles should have been in Africa because Scorpius has its dominion there. In the year of our Lord 34, there was a great conjunction of planets in Leo, and then (says one very profanely) was the gospel preached through the world. But if he makes this conjunction to be a sign of the preaching of the gospel, then it should have been preached more in the parts of Europe than Asia, which is not true. In the years of our Lord 331 and 1127, there [were] great conjunctions in Virgo, and yet the countries subject to this sign felt no harm, but Italy was troubled with the pope's superstitions, and Arius's heresy was broached. There was a meeting of planets in Sagittarius 73 years after Christ, when as Otto, Galba, Vitellius, and Vespasian troubled the Roman Empire, yet there was nowhere a more grievous war than in Palestine, and no greater slaughter than of the Jews, who are subject unto Scorpius and not unto Sagittarius. In the year 1464, a conjunction of higher planets was in Pisces, under whose dominion, although Europe is not placed, yet it most felt the smart by troubles and civil wars. So, two eclipses of the sun [occurred in] 1576 and 1577, the one in Leo [and] the other in Capricorn, [and they] took their effects in Germany, when as Leo and Capricorn do not rule that country. It is vain to show the absurdity of this rule by more examples. These shall be sufficient.

This shall suffice to have spoken of their general predictions; now follow their special determinations of the state and temperature of the weather. Herein I will set forth, first of all, a most manifest and absurd contradiction, which most of them make, and that is this: they (as I have said) set down their judgments of the whole quarter, that it should be either moist, hot, cold, or dry; afterwards, judging particularly, they disprove by particular days that which they said before. In the year of our Lord 1581, one said that in the autumn quarter [there] should be a great drought, yet I, perusing his particular judgment upon the days of the quarter, find it should have plenty of rain. In the past year, another said [that] the summer should be so hot and dry that even wells and rivers should be dried up, and fishes be scarce, and cattle die for want of water. Yet the same party in his particular judgment of the weather makes twenty days of the same quarter, at the least rain and misting, and thirty other either temperate or very cold.

In one word, the judgments which are set down of the weather are more tolerable than the rest. Yet, as long as the world endures, no man shall be able to prognosticate truly what [the] weather shall be in every day of the year. The causes of this I have set down before and need not now to repeat. Wherefore, they might leave off any longer to busy themselves in this kind. And it shall be sufficient for the leading of a Christian life to know the general and ordinary estate of the parts and seasons of the year.

Reason 3: Their Impieties
Besides all this, the impious speeches and ungodly practices which these men use might move a Christian man to loath their predictions. First, some of them do foretell yearly whether men shall study and embrace or forget and neglect true religion. What a filthy and devilish thing is this, not to be suffered in a commonwealth where the gospel of Christ is preached. Every man naturally is the child of wrath, the unprofitable servant, dead in all kinds of sin. His understanding is enmity against God. His affections are rebellious against His will. None does good, no not one. Not one has any faculty to receive or keep true religion. We are as saws in the hands of God, as the prophet Isaiah speaks. How then become we religious? Only by the work of God. "No man can come to me," says Christ, "except the Father draw him" [John 6:44]. And as God draws us first unto true religion, so He also makes us continue in the professing of the same, as Saint Paul says, "he which hath begun a good work in you, will finish the same."[63] By what means does God do this? By the outward preaching of the law and the gospel, and by the inward working of His Holy Spirit. The Scripture never mentions other means. On the contrary part, if any man refuses the grace of God, and will not embrace the true religion, it proceeds from the hardness of his own heart and [his] willful rebellion. Seeing, therefore, the rebellion of man comes from his own will, and the embracing of true godliness from God alone, why dare they presume, without great impiety, to adjoin the constellations as adjuvants either unto man or God in this divine work?

Again, these predictions are very perilous, for if a man is wickedly given, they hinder him from the acknowledging of his sin, because they make him lay part of his faults upon the stars, when as all indeed come from his own soul. And if a man is a penitent sinner, and feels the grace of God, yet being weak in faith and conscience, they make him not to put his whole trust in God, and to love Him with all his soul, with all his strength. But [they] allure him in some part to attribute that unto the stars which is the only work of God and not of any creature.

---

63. Phil. 1:6.

Second, they foretell what vices shall reign, as in these examples: (1) there shall be much unlawful and secret whoredom; (2) great robbing by highway sides; (3) wanton and young men shall sit in their ladies' laps by reason of their goddesses' well-placing; [and] (4) many shall use deceit and cozening. By these and such like, lewd and dissolute people take occasions and are stirred up to live profanely and to follow those vices unto which the lusts of their nature carry them.

Reason 4: Their Tricks of Deceit

A juggler, who takes upon him to do strange things, must use many sleights, lest he is descried by the stander-by who sees his tricks of legerdemain, and all his former cunning turns to his shame. Our prognosticators, understanding this, have thought it convenient to use in their kind some tricks of deceiving jugglers. I can call them by no better name, for so they are indeed. First, publishing their predictions in your behalf, they use such absurd, unknown, and insolent words, as (I think) never the like were read or heard among us in England. As are these which follow:

1. A prognostication astrologically calculated for the pole arctic, for such a city whose longitude and latitude is thus.

2. Quartill revolution.

3. Rectified for the motions and aspects of the meridian and elevation.

4. Capricorn in quality cold and dry, melancholy, in taste bitter, nocturnal feminine, meridional, of the earthly trigon.

5. Mercurialists, Jovialists, Martialists. Hiemal Solstice, Aestival, Vernal, Autumnal.

6. Parstortura coupled with the dragon's tail.

7. Taurus a sign of the earthly trigonism naturally, cold in the sign horoscope, and Virgo of the same stamp the sign of the prevention preceding.

8. A sign of the same triangularity, Jupiter lord of this revolution resident with Venus *in domicilio deorsum ab augulo cadente*.

9. Planets retrograde.

10. Cardivalor a succedent position.

11. Lunary defect. In his dodecatimorian.

12. Names of strange authors, Proclus, Alchindus, Messahala, Zael, Albohazen, Haly, Albumacer, Albubater, Guido, Bonetus, Hispalensis, Firmius, Abraham, Avenezra, Trismegistus, with many other

wondrous doctors, having a great deal of small learning, and being far born, as in Chaldea, Persia, Arabia, Jewry.

You will say, what means all this? "Here is great learning." "No doubt, it passes my capacity." "Who would not have an almanac, if it were for nothing but for this, to see and hear how profound our prognosticators are?" You far deceive yourself! For they, perceiving well that their deceits and lies may be soon espied, have invented strange terms to color them, and to cast a mist before your eyes, that you may not see their naughty dealing. For any man, the truer and more honest he thinks his matter, the more desirous is he to speak plainly to the understanding of all.

It was a point of the knavery[64] of the devil, otherwise called Apollo, as the heathen men asked his counsel, to answer doubtfully because, when as he was ignorant of the event, yet [he] would not but seem to know as in this answer: "I tell you, Pyrrhus, the Romans may conquer." It is understood [in] two ways: either that Æacides might vanquish the Romans or the Romans [might vanquish] Æacides.[65]

Our prognosticators have chosen a very good pattern to follow. Their dealing with you is the same. When they doubt and cannot tell what to prognosticate, then they use two ways of foretelling: either they speak that which is true every way, or that which is true every year. For the first, among many examples, I will put one or two that you may see their dealing in true, not forged, examples.

1. The conjunction of Mars and Saturn threatens wars, but Jupiter will mitigate the same. As [if] a man should say, the prognosticator tells the truth except he tells a lie.

2. 1585. We shall have a very dry winter. If peradventure any floods and store of rain do fall, they shall proceed from former causes.

3. This summer quarter is like to be, for the greatest part, dry and whole, yet it is like neither to be too hot or too cold, but indifferent.

4. Neither fair nor foul, both together.

5. Fair and calm, but a little misting.

6. Clouds portending rain and snow.

Examples of those predictions which may agree to every year are common with them, as these:

1. This year artificers must take heed of too much straining their backs.

---

64. *Knavery:* dishonest dealing.
65. For the historical context, see *Plutarch's Lives of the Noble Greeks and Romans.*

2. Take heed of venturing in slippery places boldly, in building.

3. Old men shall die.

4. Death of sheep and other cattle this year shall be.

5. Sundry diseases are like to reign among many, which will sweep away many.

6. False rumors, imprisonments, tortures.

7. Brethren and sisters shall not love one another.

8. Sundry men and women shall be troubled with pains in their eyes.

9. Much strife among men and women.

10. Small love among kinsfolk.

11. Much unlawful lust this year, and secret fornication.

12. Some ecclesiastical person shall be in trouble, and some noble man shall die. This is ever at one place or other.

13. Many shipwrecks, and other stirs on the seas.

14. Many shall addict themselves to the study of necromancy.

Again, beside these ways, there is also a third, and that is this: they, fearing lest their prognostications should not be regarded because of their lies and that they might win men unto the using of them, have adjoined astronomical matters of the rising and setting of stars, of the aspects and motions of planets, which are [of] no profit to you. Here also they have annexed tables of all the fairs in the land, and of the chief highways, which, being of some price with you, make that which is naught of itself to be of some account.

Conclusion

Thus much (good reader) I hope shall be sufficient to persuade you of the vanity of prognostications. If not, I beseech you [to] accept of my simple endeavor, serving in some part unto your profit. For if you are a Christian man, you ought only to be content with knowing the times and ordinary seasons of the year, not regarding nor searching any secret and special predictions for which the Lord never gave any man warrant but in plain words has forbidden them. Nay, they who are ingrafted into Jesus Christ indeed are so far from searching what shall be hereafter that they lead a life which is a continual meditation of present death. The which the Lord, for Jesus' sake, grant unto us that we may in some measure behold our own vanities.

Trinuni Deo sit omnis honos, omnis gloria[66]

---

66. To the triune God be all honor and glory.

Scripture Index

OLD TESTAMENT
Genesis
1:1	367
1:13–14	415
1:14	338, 413
1:14–15	414
1:16	349
2:17	69
2:23	16
2:24	147
4	99
4:1	271
4:7	153
6:2	142
6:5	194, 229, 236
6:5–6	192
8:2	88
8:20	392
8:21	xix, 189
9:22	144, 279
12:8	392
13:8–9	274
17:23	235
18	99
18:17	296
18:19	235
18:27	216
19:14	230
19:26	320
20:11	231
21:9	145
25:22	179
30:37	360

31:9–11	360
31:53	282
34:7	263
37:2	260
37:7	342
37:9	342
38:15–16	218
39:9	263
40:15	273
41	345
41:25	342
42:21	133
44:5	334
44:15	334
45:5	190

Exodus
1	99
5:2	223
7	372
7–8	322
7–9	366, 374
7:11–12	368
7:21	369
7:22	368
8:7–8	368
8:8	166
8:14	369
8:15	166
8:18–19	368
8:19	322
9:11	368
9:27	166

Exodus (*continued*)
10:16–17	166
14	416
14:13	126
14:21	312
15:16	416
16:24	144
20:5	141
20:6	39
20:7	259
21:24	145
22:1	375
22:18	xxiii, 307, 375
22:20	375
23:1	149
23:13	142
25:22	296
30:31–32	267
32:6–8	142
32:28	402
34:21	144

Leviticus
6:3	148
10:3	286
16:8	346
18:22	146
19:16	149
19:26	143
19:31	298, 352
19:32	145
19:35	147
20:6	143, 352
20:27	352
24:10	267
24:16	143, 375

Numbers
7:89	296
12:6	296, 342
20:6	211
20:8	212
20:10	211
20:11–12	126
20:12	211

22:6	356
23	372
23:23	356, 390n10
25:8	402
30	145
35:31	374–75

Deuteronomy
1:16	302
9:4	224
11:17	416
12:28	142
12:23	143
13	343
13:1–3	322
13:2	346
13:3	299, 342
13:5	375
13:6	400
13:6–9	xxiii
15:9	216, 400
17:3–5	xxiii, 400
18:9	392, 412
18:10–11	333, 335, 342
18:11	143, 324, 347, 352, 355
18:12	413
18:18	392
19:5	417n17
20:5	391
22:22	146
23:17	147
23:21	144
25:2–3	145
27:26	236
28	115, 154
28:58	266
29:19	205
29:19–20	199
32:6	106n12
32:29	250
32:34	154

Joshua
7:15	346
10:13	313

14:2 346
24:15 137

Judges
1:7 216
6:12 272
8:3 273
14 286
14:12 277
15:18 5

Ruth
2:4 272

1 Samuel
1:14–15 218
1:15 273
2:23 145
2:25 115
10:21 346
15 393
15:23 310
15:24 165
15:30 165
16:1–3 285
17:28 218
22:9 276
24:3 271
25:10 273
25:24 273
28 299, 316, 347, 372
28:7 298
28:7–9 352
28:19 331

2 Samuel
12 274
12:13 144, 167
12:13–14 159
13:2 218
15–16 99
16:10 190, 264

1 Kings
5:20 195

6:9 195
6:12 195
8:29 195
17:21 350
18:21 142
18:27 278
19:18 196
21:10 262
21:13 149, 262
21:27 251
21:27–29 165
22:22–23 322

2 Kings
2:21 398
2:23 278
4:29 273
4:34 6, 350
4:34–35 258
5:13–14 275
5:25 265
6:8 260
13:21 6, 397
17:29 297
18:4 142
18:36 273
20:11 313
23:25 178

1 Chronicles
13:2 279
17:2 196
17:4 196
21:8 150

2 Chronicles
16:9 142
16:12 142
18:1 142
19:6 302
27:23 279
30:18 392
33:12 133, 159
33:13 162

Ezra

9:6	19, 150

Nehemiah

13:15	144

Job

1:5	262
1:9	276
1:11	276
1:16–19	318
1:21	126, 365
3:1	126
6:2–3	228
9:3	141
13:26	153
14:1	249
16:9	212
16:12	212
21:14–15	208
21:15	210
22:12–13	198
31:1	239
32:6	287
33:15	342
36:15	125
39:36	150
40:4	216, 286
42:6	73, 150

Psalms

1:2	244
1:3	44
3:6	243
6:1	126
6:8	126
10	197
10:3	199
10:4	197
10:6	226
10:17	126
14	197
14:1	197, 263
14:2–4	203
14:5	141
14:6	203
15:2	265
15:3	280n5
15:4	279
16:4	262
16:7	171, 242
16:10	68
16:11	76
19	415
19:1	413
19:9	243
19:12	141
19:14	242
22:6	216
23:4	243
24:7	183
24:8	183n4
25:1	240
25:7	153, 248
26:1	274
27:8	137
30:6	226
31:22	212
32	87
32:3	167
37:32–33	274
38:5	263
39	288
40:6–7	11
41:1	286
41:9–11	126
43:5	228
46:2	194
51	248
51:1–2	126
51:2	151
51:3–5	150
51:4–5	126
51:5	100n9
51:15	258
52:1–2	149
55:21	277
58:5	324, 361
58:6	143
59:7	56

73:13	173, 210
74:6–7	143
74:8	217
77:7–9	212
77:8	247
77:11–12	247
78:11	244
78:19–20	212
78:42	244
82:2	148
83:4	217
84:10	52
91:11	390
91:13	8
94:7	198
97	154
101	87
106:30	402
109:4	273
110:3	18
111:2	245
115:8	143
116:11	212
119	235
119:6	137
119:15–16	244
119:18	172, 208
119:27	242
119:30–31	137
119:35	137
119:37	239
119:40	151
119:52	244
119:55	242
119:57	137
119:59	140, 242, 248
119:71	133
119:97	244
119:98–99	242
119:106	137
119:112	137
119:113	242
126:1	207
126:1–2	277
130:4	192

130:7	163
132:3–4	143
136:4	313
139	243
140:3	288
141:3	258
141:5	275
143:2	35n5
143:10	151
147	106

Proverbs

1:7	263
1:32	154
4:23	xix, 183, 239
5:20–21	56
6:18	194
6:23	263
7:22	147
8:16	302
10:19	283
10:32	264
11:15	148
12:18	145
12:22	265–66
14:22	236, 245
15:1	273
15:23	273
15:26	195n1, 236
16:1	258
16:9	429
16:23	264n6
16:33	143, 347
17:7	265
17:9	286
17:10	275
17:18	148
18:13	143, 261
18:18	346
19:11	286
20:13	147
20:14	148
20:18	238
21:1	430
22:1	279

Proverbs (*continued*)

22:6	235
22:15	234
22:28	146
23:8	278
23:26	183
24:10	228
25:11	263
26:19	149
27:2	260
27:5	275
27:14	277
28:13	79
29:11	263n5
29:15	234
29:27	234

Ecclesiastes

1:9	332
2:2	277
3:4	277
3:7	287n2
4:8	229
7:5	287
7:11	287
7:14–15	246
9:2	164, 391
10:11	355
10:20	204
11:9	251
12:13	263

Song of Solomon

6:2	184

Isaiah

1:13	144
1:16	148, 158
1:18	158
1:23	148
3:14–15	217
4–48	336
5:11–12	246
5:17	163
5:19	205
6:6	288
7:12	142
8:18	203
8:19–20	297, 347
11:6	8
14:10–11	278
14:13	221
14:14	223
19:18	258
28:15	226
28:20	152
29:13	141–42
29:15	199
30:21	172
30:33	207
32:2	62
38	99
41:23	332
43	416
44:16–17	231
44:19–20	231
44:24–25	412
45:7	190
47:12–14	405
47:13	143
47:13–14	335, 414
49:4	84n8
53:11	5
55:6–7	159
57:15	222
58:13	144
59:2	130, 249
59:15	204
61:3	131
63:3	72
63:16	196
63:17	174, 246
64:6	35
64:7	143
65:5	224
65:17	69
66:2	143

Jeremiah

2:35	224

3:10	165
4:2	143
4:22	141
5:24	231
6:16	208
8:6	95n4, 149, 227, 230
8:17	416
10:1–2	412
10:23	430
12:11	243
13:14	416
13:23	235
15:2	416
15:16	245
17:9–10	195
22:21	154
23	343
23:6	58
23:25	342
23:32	346
26:2–3	159
26:15	282
31:18	132
31:19	129
32:40	44
37:13	280
38:24–26	286
40:14	280
48:10	146–47
48:11	227

Lamentations

1:12	228
3:20	133
3:22	93
3:39–40	140
3:40	90, 122, 248

Ezekiel

7:6	154
16:49	153
18:6–8	146
18:7	148
18:32	159
21:21	333
22:27	148
32:7–8	414
33:15	148
47:12	131

Daniel

1:9	8, 217
1:17	338
1:20	338
2	372, 374
2:1	345
2:1–2	298
2:2	335
2:28	345
2:36	345
2:48	217
3:15	223
3:19	217
3:25	313
4:32	320
4:36	320
5:6	152
6:22	274, 313
8:16	345
9	343
9:5–7	150
9:18–19	151
11:3	330

Hosea

2	421
2:18	8
2:21–22	415n13
5:15	133
7:1–2	230
7:9	416
8:14	416
9:3	416
11:1	71
14:1–2	151

Joel

2:13	141, 235

Amos

3:7	296
5:4	159
5:10	143
6:3	199
6:6	277
7:1	416
8:5	148, 218
9:10	199

Jonah

3:5–6	251
4:8–9	228

Micah

2:1	218
3:11	148
7:9	159, 228

Nahum

1:4–5	154
1:9	154

Habakkuk

2:4	32, 222
2:9	148
3:2	192
3:16	244

Zephaniah

1:12	199n5, 227
2:1	88
2:1–2	xvi, 79, 89–122
2:15	221
3:5	227

Zechariah

7:11	174
11	416
12:10	13, 51
13:3	149

Malachi

3:8	147
3:14	210

NEW TESTAMENT

Matthew

1	345
1:20	342
2:1	298
2:13	342
2:19	342
3:7	281
3:10	11
3:11	288
3:12	117n20
4	88, 390
4:4	417n18
4:7	142
4:9	324
5–7	88
5:3	268
5:10	72
5:20	139
5:22–23	145
5:23	143
5:24	151
5:28	146, 218
5:34–35	143
5:37	143, 282
5:39	268
6:11	409
6:24	183
6:33	142
6:34	409
7:1	149, 276, 280
7:6	286
7:12	148
7:13	77
7:22–23	320
7:23	33
9	37
9:2–3	219
9:11–13	159
9:13	224
10:11–13	272
10:28	141
10:32	265
10:33	162
10:38	142

11:18–19	276
11:29	13
12:27	395
12:33	181
12:35	183
12:36	261
12:40	68, 194
13:45–46	225
14:20–21	313
14:30–31	212
15:19	xxii, 195, 257
17	76
18:17	149
19:9	147
19:17	270
20:34	314
21:31	159
22:16	277
23:2	144
23:13	146
24:9	217
24:37	230
24:37–39	227
24:38	190
24:38–39	230
25:3	252
25:8	231
25:18	231
25:41	156n10
25:41–42	15
26:37–38	51
26:41	179n6
26:60	149
26:60–61	279
27	414
27:3	166
27:14	287
27:25	269
28:20	202

Mark

3:35	32
5:12–13	323
6:12	132
6:20	218
6:22	147
8:24	172
9:24	173
11:24	63
12:30	236
16	394
16:17	396

Luke

1:28	272
1:51	222
2:14	50
2:51	245
3:19–20	18
4:6	271
6:25	277
9:6	132
9:23	74
10:4	273
10:17	321
10:18	301, 392
10:20	321
10:27	231
10:42	120n22
11:26	163
11:37	278
12:19	226
12:19–20	230
12:40	160
12:54–55	334
13:1–3	244
13:11	390
13:16	390
13:27	32
13:32	281n7
14:1	278
14:19	143
15:7	224
15:18–19	150
16:19	145
16:24	255
17:4	163
17:8	144
17:26	191
18:9–10	224

Luke (*continued*)

18:11	32, 215, 221
18:13	xiv, 150, 159
19:8	163
19:14	208
19:41	278
21:36	56
22:3	183
22:15	278
22:32	162
22:42	177
23:14–16	264
23:42–43	159
24:25	62
24:47	69, 132

John

1:1	356n2
1:16	7, 43, 46
1:51	8
2	367
3:4	205
3:19	108n13, 206
3:34	46
4:22	201, 297
4:24	310
5:14	163
6:44	435
6:45	208
6:51–55	46
6:56	55
6:65	208
7:39	68
8:44	143, 266, 295–96
8:48–49	274
9:6–7	313
10:32	109
11:35	279
11:43	314
12:31	295
15:2	16
15:5	16
16:2	217
16:7	44
16:33	70

17:3	5, 53, 66
17:19	47
17:23	51
19:8	267
19:26	271
20:19	272n1
20:28	6n1
20:28–29	63

Acts

1:26	346
2:4	262
2:13	219
2:24	67n44
2:37	13, 134
2:46	278
3:6	364
3:12	300, 313
3:15	70
3:16	300, 364
3:21	76
4:19	144
5:3	148, 183, 195
5:15	397
7:22	338
8:9	298, 370, 372
8:10	301
8:21	196
8:22	141, 235, 237
9	416
9:4	15, 71
10:10	296
10:11	353
10:33	263
10:43	163
11:18	286
11:23	137
11:26	270
12:22	223, 277
13:6–8	372
13:10	196
14:22	73
15:9	258
16:16	352, 372
16:18	352

17:23	297
17:30	106
19:11–12	300
19:12	397
19:13	397
20:7	283
23:1	274
23:6	286
24:10	287
24:16	77, 137, 251
26:20	130

Romans

1:4	68, 270
1:5–6	258
1:10	425
1:16	132
1:20	413
1:24–26	162
1:28	246, 416
1:29	146
1:30	141, 144, 279
1:31	145, 148
1:32	154
2:4–5	149
2:5	160
3	197
3:2	105
3:8	266
3:22	57
3:24	25, 36, 59
3:25	57, 62
3:26	59
4:1	59
4:2–3	65
4:25	68
5:1	8
5:2	66
5:3	73
5:5	73
5:14	97
5:19	59
6:1	61
6:4	70
6:8	47
6:23	155
7:14	171
7:18	178
7:19	175
7:23	171
7:24	216
8	74
8:1	382
8:4	174
8:7	176, 195
8:11	69
8:15	134
8:23	170
8:28	44
8:34	68
8:35	77
9:22	192
9:29	12
10	37n15
10:3	32
10:5	57
11:6	41, 201
11:8	246
11:10	145
12:14	273
13:14	147
14:23	365n9
15:2	365
15:4	73, 245
16:25	50

1 Corinthians

1	37n14
1:11	260
1:12–13	270
1:21	205
1:23	205
1:30	xv, 46, 60
2:2	5
2:9	230
2:14	205, 235, 242, 297
3:1	170
3:18	207
3:22	9
3:23	15

1 Corinthians (*continued*)

4:2	196
4:4	38
4:5	196, 260
4:6	274
5:5	393
6:2	45
6:9	146
6:9–11	163
6:15	55
7:2	147
7:37	147
8:4	349
8:9	142
9:19	13
9:27	136
10:3	143
10:7	144
10:10	142
10:13	72
10:16	46
10:20	198, 297
11	74
11:1	11
11:31	150, 159
11:32	228
13	321
13:1–3	33n1
13:5	149, 219n2, 260
13:6	266
13:12	172
13:13	75
14:22	394
14:25	237
15:9	271
15:17	68
15:24	75
15:28	76
15:35	146
15:55–56	155

2 Corinthians

1:9	73, 176
1:11	202n14
2:7	250
2:11	250, 295
2:17	148
3:5	195, 229
3:7	132
4:4	153, 199, 309
4:6	22, 50
4:11	73
4:17	37
5:19	158
5:21	25, 60
7:10	130, 141
8:12	163
10:4	301
10:4–5	238
10:5	53
11:14	362
11:21–22	260
12	74
12:2	271, 353
12:7	175
12:9	73
13:5	252

Galatians

1:6	205
2:20	63, 213
2:21	35
3:1	18, 281, 316, 366
3:19	215
4	424
4:8	198
4:29	145
5:4	41
5:9	146
5:13	169
5:15–17	169
5:17	xviii
5:20	145, 374
5:24	12, 136
6:1	274–75
6:2	17n11
6:14	1, 5

Ephesians

1:3	7

1:17	7
1:22	201n12
2:1	167
2:6	67
2:9	38
2:12	198
3:14	241
3:17	55
3:18	51n17
3:19	241
4:13	170
4:18	130
4:19	174
4:21–22	52
4:22	11
4:23	141, 194, 237
4:24	11
4:28	148
4:29	262, 278
4:31	145
5:2	13
5:3	147, 262
5:4	149
5:5	142
5:14	71
5:18	147
5:30	16
6:2	183
6:4	234
6:9	145
6:11	295
6:12	76, 309
6:19	258

Philippians
1:6	435n63
1:21	54
1:29	62
2:3	216, 283
2:5	13
2:10	143, 397
3:3–8	29
3:7	23–78
3:7–8	29, 31
3:7–9	xiv

3:8	5, 11, 66, 241
3:9	57
3:10	11, 13, 66
3:19	199
3:20	12, 240
3:21	76
4:3	88
4:4	19n18, 321
4:8–9	238

Colossians
1:15	15, 50
1:22	235
1:24	71
2:3	7, 43
2:10	9n6, 48
2:15	382
2:23	142
3:1	12, 71
3:5	136, 199
3:10	25, 43
3:11	9n6, 22
3:15	8
3:22	145
4:6	262

1 Thessalonians
4:6	110n15, 148
5:6–7	141
5:17	240
5:19	239
5:23	147, 236
5:24	85

2 Thessalonians
2	278n1
2:4	145,
2:10–12	299, 322
2:11	52
3:10	148
3:11	147

1 Timothy
1:10	148
1:13	271

1 Timothy (*continued*)

1:15	20, 271
1:20	393
2:6	43
2:9	146
2:15	37
3:2	146
3:4	145
3:16	49
4:4	398
5:1	274
5:8	147
6:4	148
6:9	148
6:10	147

2 Timothy

1:7	77
1:12	75
2:11	73
2:21	136
2:25	132, 153
3:2	144
3:4	147, 277
3:5	142
3:8	297, 367–68
3:15	234

Titus

2:9	287
2:15	195
3:1–3	271

Hebrews

1	416
1:3	14, 25, 50
1:14	44
2:5	69
3:7	160
3:13	160
3:16	144
4:12	237
5:7	78, 279
5:8	73
6:4	162
6:6	162
6:18	63
9:12	25
9:14	25
10:20	55
10:26	162
10:28	375
10:29	149, 162
10:31	154
11	88
11:25	277
11:26	77
11:35	77
12:1	77, 240
12:4	73
12:7	73
12:10	246

James

1:14	77, 171
1:19	261
1:26	288
2:20	141
2:21–22	65
2:22	37
3:6–8	288
3:14	145
4:1	145
4:6	222
4:8	240
4:15	279
5:4	146
5:9	145
5:16	151

1 Peter

1:3	69
1:12	18
2:21	72
3:3	146
3:6	270
3:9	273
3:15	144
3:20	190
3:21	70

4:3–4	217
4:13–15	72
4:14	73
5:8	250, 295

2 Peter
1:4	76
1:21	162
2:20	142
3:3–4	205
3:15	193

1 John
1:7	167
2:2	167
2:19	252
2:23	201–2
3:3	12, 136, 241
3:9	172, 177
3:15	145
3:23	53, 63, 149
3:24	55
4:3	149
4:8	149
4:13	57
5:4	70
5:18	136, 174

2 John
10	273

3 John
12	259

Jude
9	183

Revelation
1–3	88
2:10	85, 141
3:16	143
3:17	224
6:10	196
14:13	348, 350
18:7	221
20:2	301
20:6	70
21:3	76
21:4	75
21:7	76
21:8	374
22:15	374
22:17	121n24

APOCRYPHA
Ecclesiasticus
46:20	349

Tobias
6:7	395

Subject Index

Aaron, 286, 312, 322, 366–69
Abbes, James, 289–90
Abigail, 273
Abimelech, 276
abodes, sanctifying of, 391–92
Abraham
    justification of, 59
    self-abasement of, 216
Abraham, Rabbi, 427
acceptance of everlasting life, 7–8
actual sins, 102, 140–41, 176
Adam
    fall in, 191
    headship of, 50
    member of, 18
    as public person, 96–97
    sin of, xvi, 59–60, 96–97, 100, 101
admonishment of a brother, 260
Adoni-bezek, 216, 219
adoption as children of God, 44
adorning profession by framing lives
        according to the Word, 391
adultery, 110, 146–47, 218, 219
adversity, 154
affections, xii–xiv, 6–7, 173
afflictions, 10, 11, 21, 73–74, 94, 133,
        190, 228
    impatience with, 326
Ahab, 251, 322
Ahithophel, 99
Alexander, 154, 393
Alexander the Great, 329–30
Ambrose, 37, 277, 283

America, no astrological signs
        appointed over, 433
Ammon, 217
amulets, 363
Anabaptists, 165, 344
Ananias and Sapphira, 195
anatomy (of prognosticators), 422
angels
    desire to look into the incarnation
        of Christ, 50
    ministry of, 44, 416
    peace with, 8
Annas, 19
Anselm, 40, 60
answers, meekness in, 273–74
antichrist, 223
Antiochus, 154
apology, 265
apostasy, 205
Apostles' Creed, 203, 211
application, xii–xiii, 6
Aquarius, 422, 427, 428
Arendt, Hannah, xxin50
Arianism, 205
Aries, 341, 422, 423, 425, 426–27, 428,
        432, 433
asseveration, 282
assurance, of reconciliation with
        God, 241
astrologers, 196, 335–38, 412, 419,
        421, 423, 425–28, 431–32
    vanity of, 340–42
atheism, 200–204

atheism (*continued*)
    in judgment, 200–202
    in practice, 200
    seeds of, 202–4
atheists, on Scripture, 233
Athenians, 297
Augustine, 40, 41, 60, 261, 278, 280, 300, 424
Augustinian voluntarism, xxn49
Avicenna, 268
awe
    in chastisements, 264
    in regard of God, 263
    in respect of sin, 263

Babel, 217
Babylonian captivity, 112, 207
backbiting, 220, 280
backsliding, 163
bad witch, 372–73
Balaam, 356, 372, 390
Balak, 356, 390
balance, in speech, 283
baptism, 214
Barabbas, 20
Basil, 37
basilisk, 360
beasts,
    as means of providence, 416
    used for divination, 333–35
beggars, 33
benefits of Christ, 6, 7, 64
Benfield, Denis, 290
Benhadad, 33–34
Bernard, 37, 59
Beza, Theodore, 270
birds, used for divination, 332–33
blasphemy, 110, 266–69, 289
boasting, 38
Boaz, 272
bondage under Satan, 100–101, 152–53, 388
born of God, 18
Bradford, John, 125
brawling, 283

briberies, 110
Brownists, 118
Bucer, Martin, 270
Burgensis, 41

Caesar, 433
Caiaphas, 19, 287
Cain, 99
calamities, 249
    become blessings, 44
    mitigating or removing of, 159
callings, in family, church, and commonwealth, 75
Calvin, John, xxn48
Calvinists, 270
Campanus of Novara, 426
Cancer, 422, 427, 428
Canisius, 88
Capricorn, 422, 427, 428, 434, 436
captivity, as means of providence, 416
Catharists, 165
causes, *per se* and *per accidens*, 431
ceremonial repentance, xviii, 165–66
certainty, of God's promises, 213–14
chaff, 89, 90, 95, 102–4, 116–18, 120
Chaldeans, 298, 337–38
charity, in judgment, 286
Charles, king of France, 432
charms, 268, 327, 356–65, 371
chiding, 255, 283
children, names of, 269–70
children of God, 267
child of wrath, 100
"Christ crucified," xii–xiv, xxii, 5–6, 9–10, 14–16, 17, 21–22, 54, 205, 258
Christian liberty, 169
Christians
    as lively part and member of Christ, 175
    in name and show only, 175
Chrysostom, 37, 156, 161, 278, 288, 300
church
    being and subsisting in Christ, 16

murderous thoughts against, 217
Church of England, 118
civil life, as abomination without
    grace, 139
cockatrice, 360
cogging, 265
Combat of the Flesh and Spirit (1593),
    xvii, xix, 169–80
comets, 429
comfort, from Christ's resurrection,
    69
comfort of Christ, 48
coming to Christ, 33–34
commandments of God, 245
common Protestants, knowledge of
    Christ, 17
compunction of heart, 134
concupiscence, 169, 171, 179
confession, to priest, 167
confession of sin to men, 151
confession of sin unto God, 150
confidence in Christ, 63
confidence in works, 32
conformity to Christ, 3, 11–12
    general, 12
    special, 12–14
conscience, 94, 134
    binding of, 201
    combat with the heart, 177
    examination of, 140–49
    seared, 174
    sin against, 177
    testimony of, 90, 98
    wounding of, 138, 177
consent to receive Christ, 53
consideration of Christ, xii–xiii, 5
contempt of the gospel, 108–9, 190
contending, 283
contradiction, spirit of, 283
contrition, 126
    as merit for remission of sin, 167
Cooke, Edward, 295
Cornelius, 214
corruption of sin, 102
    remaining in the believer, 179

Council of Trent, 179, 363
    defaces Christ crucified, 17
counterfeit apostles, 29
counterfeit repentance, xviii, 165
covenant of grace, 105, 107, 325,
    378–79, 389–91
covenant of works, 97
covenant with outward senses, 239
covetousness, 226, 409
cozenages, 93, 110
Crashaw, William, xxiv, 85, 88
creation, 246
    order of, 415
cross of Christ, 20–21
crosses
    as trials, 10, 11
    impatience with 326
crossing of the body, 364
crucifixes, 18
cruelty, 89
curiosity, 312
curse of God, 100
    on creation, 190
    due for sin, 91
cursing, 269, 362, 363, 383

daily bread, 409–10
Daniel, 8, 273–74
    in lions' den, 313
    prophecy of, 342–43, 345
Darius, 329–30
David
    confession of, 100
    distrust of God, 212
    and Goliath, 170, 218
    overtaken by prosperity, 226
    repentance of, 138, 159
    self-abasement of, 216
day of judgment, 55–56, 65, 251
days, observance of, 341
death, 250–51
    changed by death of Christ, 10
    and repentance, 164
death bed, 164
debtors to Christ, 16

Declaration of the True Manner of Knowing Christ Crucified (1596), xii–xiv, 1–22
decree, no more to curse the earth, 189–92
"decree come forth," xvi, 89, 113–14
deluding the eye, 366
Demetrius, 259
denial of Christ, 162
Denny, Edward, 25
Dent, Arthur, 125
deprecation (repentance), 151
despair, 173
desperate repentance, xviii, 166
devil
    as "god of the world," 199
    knowledge of natural things, 330, 331
    presence in most places, 330
    see also Satan
diabolical dreams, 343–44
Diana, 380
Dionysius the Areopagite, 414
Direction for the Government of the Tongue according to God's Word (1593), xxi–xxii
discontentment, 311–12
Discourse on the Damned Art of Witchcraft (1608), xxii–xxiv, 293–403
disease, 158, 168, 318–19, 373, 416, 431–32
disgrace, 220
dishonesty, 110
dishonor (against neighbor), 215–16
disordered life, 203
dissembling (speech), 265
distress, thoughts in time of, 227–28
distrust of God, 211–14
divination, xxiii, 329–54, 374
    by counterfeit and forged means, 347–52
    by means, 332
    by true creature of God, 332–47
    without means, 332, 352–54

divine dreams, 342–43, 345–46
Doeg, 276
Domitian, 154
Donatists, 300
double justification, 65, 66
drawing near to God, 240
dreams, used for divination, 342–46
drunkenness, 226
dung, 30, 35, 38
Durand, 41
duty to God, 231

earthly blessings, 9
earthquakes, 115, 119, 417–18, 429
Ecclesiastes, 249
Ecclesiasticus, as non-canonical, 349
eclipses, 432–33
Edom, 217
Egypt
    astrologers of, 337–38
    magicians of, 322, 366–69, 372, 374, 375
eighth commandment, 110, 147–48, 215
elders, silence before, 287
Eleazar, Rabbi, 427
elect, gathering of, 192
election of days and hours, 423–25
elements, 430
Elijah, appearance at transfiguration, 350
Elisha, 6, 258, 273
Elymas, 196, 372
Empedocles, 430
enchantments, xxiii, 268, 355–65, 374
endeavor in life (repentance), 136, 137
enemies, conquering of, 69, 70
England
    call to repentance, 115
    sins of, 107–11, 113
entrails of beasts, 333
epicureanism, 200
esteeming others, 216
eternal death, 101, 156
eternal fellowship with God, 76

eternal judgments, 230
eternal life, 76–77
Eunice, 234
Eusebius, 301
evening prayer, 240
everlasting life, 7–8, 159
"evil eye," 216
evil thoughts, 194–95, 233. *See also*
    natural thoughts
    reformation of, xix, 237, 238–42
    repentance for, 235–37
    as root of all evil, 236
evil tongue, 288
examination
    concerning imaginations, 237
    and pure heart, 257–58
    as restorative against witchcraft,
        393
    for seeds of atheism, 202–4
    for sins, 140–49
    on worship and service to God,
        210
    see also searching (repentance)
exorcisms, 363, 394–96, 399
experiential piety, xi–xii, xv
extortions, 110
extraordinary repentance, 138

faint thoughts, 227–28
faith
    brings forth fruits, 36
    combat with unbelief, 173
    as gift of God, 62–63
    as instrument, 36–37
    as instrument to receive benefits of
        Christ, 64–65
    and justification, 64–66
    purifies the heart, 258
    without the law, 65
faith and repentance, xviin33
Faithful and Plain Exposition Upon
    Zephaniah 2:1–2 (1606), xvi–
        xvii, 79–122
false faith, 64
false prophets, 342

false witness, 148–49
Familists (Family of Love), 206, 344
famine, 113, 115, 119, 227, 244, 417,
        419, 429
fanning of God's judgments, 117–19
fanning of God's law, 120
fanning of the last day, 116–19
fanning of the Word, 117–19
Father, love of, 3
fear, from distrust of God, 213
fear of God
    in speech, 263
    want of, 231
fear of nature, 77
fear ordered by faith, 78
fear without cause, 78
fellowship with Christ, 57, 66–74
    in His death, 66, 71–74
    in His resurrection, 66, 67–71
fellowship with damned spirits, 249
fidelity, in speech and promises, 279
Fiering, Norman, xxn49
fifth commandment, 144–45, 215, 272
figure casters, 340. *See also* astrology
filial fear, 173
fire, 207, 416
first commandment, 141–42
first death, 101
flattery, 276–77
flesh
    as body, 169
    as manhood of Christ, 170
    as natural appetite, 169
    as natural corruption, 170
    resistance and striving against
        spirit, 174–75
flesh and spirit, combat between,
        xviii–xix, 126, 169–80
flood, 191, 236
folk religion, xxiv
fool, natural man as, 197–98
foolish talk, 264
foolish virgins, 252
    parable of, 231
fools, not to be answered, 287

fornication, 226
fourth commandment, 144
fraud, 89
free will, 234
friends and familiars, as means of
    providence, 416
fruit worthy amendment of life, 131
fury, as means of providence 416
fury of God. *See* wrath of God

Gahazi, 265
gaining Christ, 30, 31, 43–78
    after death, 45
    in death, 45
    in this life, 43–44
Gazullus, Johannes, 426
Gedaliah, 280
Gee, William, 81
Gemini, 341, 427
general means (providence), 415–16
Gentiles, atheism of, 202
gentleness, 271
gentry and nobility, 9
Gideon, 272, 273
glory of God, 50
glossing, 265
God
    causes calamities, 190
    consent to give Christ, 53
    goodness and loving-kindness of,
        410
    judgments of, xvi–xix, 94–95,
        243–44
    justice of, 51, 115–16, 204
    knowledge of thoughts of man, 195
    moderates justice by mercy, 192
    patience of, 192, 246
    permits arts of magic and witch-
        craft, 321–22
    preservation of mankind, 192
    restraining hand of, 98
    use of Satan as instrument, 331
    vengeance of, 113
    wonders of, 312–13
    works of, 245–46

godliness, 126, 169, 278
    in speech, 263
godly sorrow, xviii, 13, 130, 135
Goliath, 170
good conscience, 38, 70, 73, 85
good thoughts, want of, 229–32
goodwill of God to the world, 50
good witch, 372–73
good works, xxii, 16
    as mixed works, 179
gospel
    called a "mystery," 229–30
    frees countries and kingdoms
        from witchcraft, 392–93
    instrument of repentance, 132
gospel foolishness, 205–7
grace, state of, 251–52
gracious speech, 262
great sins, 92
Gregory of Arimine, 41
guilt, of Adam's sin, 101
guilty conscience, 152, 249

Habakkuk, 244
hallowed things, as remedy against
    witchcraft, 398–99
Hannah, 273
hardness of heart, 174, 251, 416
heart, 183–84, 194
    elevation to God, 240
    guarding of, 239
    kept from evil thoughts, 246
heavens
    declare glory of God, 413
    made for the use of man, 415
hell, 154–55
    talk of, 156–57
herbs, 419
Herod, 13, 131, 154, 218, 223, 276–77,
    281
Herodias, 380
Hezekiah, 273
Hilary, 37
Holcroft, Thomas, 183
holiness, 12, 170

holy silence, 259. *See also* silence
holy speech, 259–60. *See also* speech
Holy Spirit
    as cause of repentance, 132
    cheering every good motion of,
      239
    as Comforter, 44
    giving of, 68
    inward working of, xx, 435
    and justification of Christ, 49
    and power of the Word, 361
    principal cause of godly sorrow,
      xviii
    and searching, 90–91
    as "Spirit of revelation," 7
    testimony of, xiii, 6, 7, 8, 63, 90
    and union with Christ, 55
humility, 13, 38
hungering after Christ, 48
Huss, John, 433
Hymenaeus, 393
hypocrisy, 164, 200, 209, 226

idleness, of imagination, 194
idle words, 261
idol, turning true God into, 198–99
idolatry, 89, 230, 300, 346
    witchcraft as, xxii, 375, 400, 401,
      402
    prognostication as, 409
Ignatius of Loyola, xiiin11
ignorance, of God's will and worship,
    108
illusion
    of mind, 317–18
    of outward senses, 316–17
image of *agnus dei*, as remedy against
    witchcraft, 398
image of God, 246
imaginations, 194
    as evil, 192
    as force, 268, 359–60
imitation of Christ, 11–12
impenitency, 165
imprecations, 269

imputation
    of disobedience of Adam, 59–60
    of obedience of Christ, 7, 43, 47
    of sins to Christ, 10, 49
in Christ, 54–57
inclination in will (repentance), 136,
    137
inquisition over heart and con-
    science, 94
intellectualism, xxn49, xxin50
Israel
    distrust of God, 212
    encounters with astrologers, 412
    failure to repent, 112–13
    as nation not worthy to be
      beloved, 105–7

Jacob, 360
James, on justification by works, 65
Jannes and Jambres, 297, 366–69
Jeremiah, 224, 279–80, 282, 285–86,
    342
Jerome, 37, 150
jesting, 278
jests, from phrases of Scripture, 267
Jesuits, 270
Jesus Christ
    agony in the garden, 18–19
    ascension of, 50
    burial of, 21
    death of, 10, 20–21, 71–74
    deity of, 45–46, 58
    estate of exaltation, 48, 73
    estate of humiliation, 48, 73
    example of, xii–xiiin9, 11–14, 18
    faith of, 12–13
    forsaken of the Father, 20
    headship of, 50
    humanity of, 38, 46
    humility of, 13
    incarnation of, 49
    intercession of, 44
    justification of, 49
    laughter never recorded, 279
    learned obedience, 73

Jesus Christ (*continued*)
   as Lord, 52
   love of, 13
   made sin, 60
   as Mediator, 58, 61–62, 75, 201
   meekness of, 13
   merits of, xiiin9, 7–10, 70
   miracles of, 313–14
   obedience of, 57, 58, 59, 61–62
   as our wisdom, righteousness,
      sanctification, and redemption,
      xv, 46–47
   passion of, 5, 20–21
   as pledge and surety, 6
   power of judgment, 69
   as Redeemer, 7
   resurrection of, 10, 67–73
   as satisfaction for the sins of the
      world, 68
   as Savior, 68, 69
   as second Adam, 18
   silence before Caiaphas and Pilate,
      287
   suffering of, 14, 20–21, 71–74
   temptation of, 324
   transfiguration of, 350
   true and perfect savior of the
      world, 68
   virgin conception of, 49
   virtue of, 10–11
   weeping of, 278–79
Jews
   atheism of, 200–201
   deny Christ, 32
   killed Jesus, 13, 16
   know not Christ, 16
   will-worship of, 211
Job, 212, 216, 228, 249, 276, 318–19
Jonah, 178
Joseph, 273, 334, 345
   speech to Potiphar's wife, 263
Joseph (husband of Mary), 345
Josiah, 178
joy, in repentance, 135
Judas, xviiin35, 13, 16, 99, 166

judgment, sobriety in, 276–77
judgments of God, 230
   for abuse of tongue, 289–91
judicial law
   as perpetual, xxiii
   on punishment of witches, 299,
      303, 375–76
juggling (deluding the eye), xxiii,
      366–69, 374
Julian the apostate, 99, 165, 267
Jupiter (god), 284, 297
Jupiter (planet), 411, 419, 421, 427,
      428, 431, 432, 436, 437
justice
   of the gospel, 58–59
   of the law, 58–59
justice of God, 51, 115–16, 204
   denial of, 199
justification, 38, 59
   and repentance, xviin33
   and resurrection of Christ, 68
justification by faith alone, 36
justification by works, 35–36

kingdom of Christ, true members of,
      252
kingdom of darkness, 252
knowing Christ, 49–53
   as lively, powerful, and operative
      knowledge, 5
knowing the natural thoughts of
      men, 195–96
knowledge
   of Christ crucified, 3–22
   of neighbors, 15
   required for repentance, 134
   of Word of God, 172
knowledge of God, 14–15, 50–51
knowledge of gospel, 134
knowledge of self, 15, 51

Lactantius, 37
language of Canaan, 257, 258
Larazus, raising of, 314
last day, 251
   fanning of, 116–19

last judgment, 155–56
late repentance, seldom true repentance, 161
Latimer, Hugh, 290
Latin, swearing in, 284
laughter, 277, 279
law, 51
    as no cause of repentance, 132
    searches the heart, 96
law and gospel, 58–59
Lazarus, raising of, 350
leagues, lawful and unlawful, 378
learning obedience, 73
Leo, 45
Leo (sign), 341, 422, 427, 434
lesser sins, 92
Libra, 427
life, uncertainty of, 160
lip-faith, 91
lip-repentance, 91
little sins, counted as no sins, 92–93
Lois, 234
Lord's Prayer, 203, 211, 409–10
Lord's Supper, 214, 240, 359
lots
    civil use of, 346–47
    used for divination, 346–47
Lot's wife, 320
love, 13
lust, 149
    of the flesh, xix, 171
    of the spirit, xix, 171
Luther, Martin, 280
Lutherans, 270
lycanthropia, 316
lying, 265–66
lying wonders, 314, 318–20

magicians, 335, 370
magicians of Egypt, 322, 366–69, 372, 374, 375
magistrate
    and conviction of witch, 384–89
    and examination of witch, 382–84
    reproving a vice, 281
    silence before, 287

Manasseh, 159, 162
Manicheans, 344
Mars, 419, 421, 427, 431, 433, 437
Mary, Roman Catholic Church on, 17, 202, 270
Mary Magdalene, 214
means (providence), 415–16
mecashephim, 374
meditation, 171, 241–42
meekness
    of Christ, 13
    in speech, 271–75
Melanchthon, Philipp, 270
Mercury, 419, 424, 427, 428, 431
mercy of God, 51
merit, 32, 38–39, 42. *See also* Jesus Christ, merits of
merit of condignity, 40
metwand, in speech, 283
mind
    combat in, 172–73
    as principal part of the soul, xx
miracles, 300, 312–13
mirth, 277, 278
misery
    ceasing of, 75
    of hell-fire, 154–55
    of impenitent sinner, 152–55
    on left hand, 154
    before man, 153
    of past sin, 153
    on right hand, 153–54
    of sin, 249
mistletoe, 49
Moab, 217
moderation, for worldly cares and affections, 33
modesty, in speech, 271
moon-prophets. *See* prognosticators
morning prayer, 240
mortification, xviin34, 10, 11, 44, 72, 125
Moses
    appearance at transfiguration, 350
    sinned in the wilderness, 211–12

Moses and Aaron, wonders in Egypt,
    312, 322, 366–69
Muhammed, 200, 205
Muller, Richard A., xxin50
murder, 145–46, 374
murdering thoughts (against neigh-
    bor), 216–18

Naaman, 275
Nadab and Abihu, 286
name of God, taken in vain, 259
name of Jesus, used against witch-
    craft, 363, 396–97
names
    given at baptism, 270
    given to children, 269–70
Nathan, 274
natural blindness, 172
natural dreams, 343
natural life, 18
    ceasing of, 75
natural man, repentance of, 139
natural misery, 249
natural reason, 207
natural thoughts
    concerning God, 196–214
    concerning neighbor, 215–20
    concerning the self, 221–28
    idleness of, 194–96
nature
    restoration of, 189
    signs from common course, 334
Nature and Practice of Repentance
    (1593), xvii–xviii, 123–68
Nebuchadnezzar, 153, 217, 320, 333,
    345, 374, 416
necromancy, 347
neighbors, infirmities and sins to be
    concealed, 286
neighbor's good name
    care of, 279–80
    debasing of, 218–19
newness of life, 70, 137, 151. *See also*
    vivification
new obedience, 126

Nicodemus, 205
Ninevites, 251
ninth commandment, 148–49, 215
Noah, 189–91, 227, 230

oath, 282
obedience, to Word of God, 208–9,
    245
obedience of heart, 231
open league (between devil and
    witch), 326–27, 371, 374, 375
ordinary repentance, 138
original sin, 97, 102, 140, 176, 179
    ceasing of, 75

Pambus, 288–89
papists
    atheism of, 201
    false Christ of, 201–2
    on free will, 234
    on merit, 32
    will-worship of, 211
    see also Roman Catholic Church
Paracelsus, 268
pardon of sin, 43, 151
parents
    as instrument of blessing to chil-
    dren, 272
    naming of children, 269–70
    suppress natural imaginations of
    children, 234–35
particular end, consideration of,
    250–51. *See also* death
passion of Christ, meditation on,
    xiii–xiv, 13–14, 15, 18, 21
patience
    against witchcraft, 393
    in suffering, 72–73
    under the cross, 247
Paul
    boldness in speech, 260
    certainty of losses, 38–41
    courage and fortitude of, 77
    on knowing Christ, 49–53
    losses after his conversion, xiv,
    34–38

losses before his conversion, xiv,
31–34
on misery of sin, 216
necessity of losses, 41–42
as Pharisee, 31, 32
on works of the law, 61
peace, 50
with all creatures, 8
with angels, 8
with enemies, 8
with God, 8
with self, 8
with those who fear God, 8
Pelagianism, 40
penitence, 134
perfection
in the highest degree, 137
in substance, 137
perjury, 267, 289
Perkins, William
experimental piety of, xi–xii, xxv
plain style of preaching, xviin31
persecution, 217
perseverance, 44
pestilence, 113, 115, 119, 125, 416
Peter
denial of Christ, 162, 400
distrust of God, 212
repentance of, 138
response to circumcision party,
286
Pharaoh, 374, 416
ceremonial repentance of, 166
cruelty of, 99
dreams of, 345
Pharisees, 32, 165
as civil, 139
pride of, 221, 224
as superficial searchers, 93
Phinehas, 402
physic, right use of, 365
Pickering, Thomas, 302
Pierson, Thomas, 184
Pilate, 13, 16, 177, 264, 267, 287
Pisces, 427, 428, 434

plague, 116, 227, 244, 433
hangs over England, 114, 125
as means of providence, 416, 417
prognosticators on, 429
as trial, 116
planets, 419, 420, 424, 431–32
dignities of, 426–29
Plato, 297
Pliny, 433
poisoner, 374
pollution of sin, 102
Polycarp, 291
poor, 15, 216–17
pope
as antichrist, 223
as head of Catholic Church, 270
and practice of witchcraft, 311
see also papists
practical syllogism, 134
prayer
for blessing, 240–41
continual, 240
for grace and strength, 151
for pardon of evil thoughts, 237
rare among men, 203
as restorative against witchcraft,
393
superstitious forms of, 327
watchfulness in, 179
preaching
foolishness of, 205
outward working of, 435
preparation for salvation, 33
presence of God, 230, 243
denial of, 204
persuasion of in speech, 263
present estate toward God, 251–52
pride, 32, 216, 219, 221–24, 226
danger of, 222–23
highest degree of, 223
will draw tears, 164
priority, temporal and causal, xxi
privileges outside of Christ, provide
no true comfort or happiness,
32–33

prodigal son, 32, 150

prognostications, xxiv, 409–38

prognosticators

    deceitful tricks of, 436–38

    ignorance of causes, 420–22

    impieties of, 435–36

    inability of, 413–20

    lack of experience, 418–20

    predictions of, 429

    untruths of, 422–25

promises of God, 245

prosperity, abuse of, 135

providence, 204, 230, 246, 411, 425

    denial of, 199

    as continual execution of decree, 415

    through means, 415–17

    without means, 417

Ptolemy, 433

publican, 159

pure heart, xxi–xxii, 257

Puritanism, 226

Puritan literature, xin2

purpose in mind (repentance), 136, 137

Pytho, 351, 352

Pythoness of Philippi, 352, 2372

quenching not the Spirit, 239

Radulfus Ardens, 40

Rahab, 266

ransom, 21

real works (wonders of the devil), 318–20

recidivation, and repentance, 163

reconciliation, 7–8, 18, 20

recreation, 9–10

redemption, 7, 18, 47, 158

reform, of mind of evil thoughts, 237

reformation of life, 14

regenerate

    cannot do the evil he would, 177

    cannot do the good which he would, 178

    cannot sin in what manner he would, 177

    repentance of, 139

    sins of infirmities of, 178

Regiamontanus, Johannes, 425

relics of saints, as remedy against witchcraft, 397–98

religion, as but a human policy, 205

remission of sins, 7–8, 158

repentance, xvi–xix, xxiv, 8, 14, 37, 89, 121–22

    ascribed to grace alone, 167

    in case of death, 164

    in case of recidivation, 163

    in case of restitution, 163–64

    in case of revolt, 162–63

    in case of tears, 164

    cause of, 132–33

    and consideration of sins, 248

    continues throughout believer's life, xviii

    contraries of, 165–66

    corruptions in doctrine of, 167–68

    deferring of, 160–61

    definition of, 129–31

    degrees of, 138

    evangelical motives to, 158–59

    for evil thoughts, 235–37

    legal motives to, 152–57

    limited time of, 111–13, 160–61

    parts of, 136–37

    practice of, 140–51

    and searching, 94

    as a work, 129

    as a work of grace, 129–30

    wrought in the heart, 134

    see also true repentance

reproofs, meekness in, 274–75

Resolution to the Country Man, Proving It Utterly Unlawful to Buy or Use Yearly Prognostications (1631), xxiv, 405–38

restitution, and repentance, 163–64

restraining grace, 98

resurrection of the body, 45, 57, 74–78

reverence
    to God in speech, 266–69
    to man in speech, 269–70
reviling, 220
revolt, and repentance, 162–63
rich man and Lazarus, 255
righteousness of Christ, 57–66
Roman Catholic Church
    as another gospel, 206
    on dead men walking and appear-
        ing, 350
    delusion of, 317
    on exorcisms, 363, 395
    false and deceitful miracles of, 300
    on justification, 61, 179
    knows not Christ, 16
    makes creature our gain, 52
    on Mary as "queen of heaven," 17
    on merit, 42, 48, 179
    on preparation for salvation, 33
    on repentance, 167
    on saints in heaven knowing men's
        thoughts, 196

Sabbath, 110, 209
sacraments, as seals of the promise,
    63
Sagittarus, 341, 422, 427, 428, 433,
    434
saints, Roman Catholic Church on,
    54, 202
salt, as remedy against witchcraft,
    398–99
salutations, meekness in, 272–74
saluting each other, 273
salvation by works, 38
Samaritans, 297
Samson, 5, 21, 277, 286
Samuel, 285
    counterfeit appearance of, 316,
        347–52
sanctification, 47, 236
    accomplishment of, 174
    no part of justification, 65
    and repentance, xviin33

Sandwich (town), 423
Satan
    agility of, 331
    bondage of, 152–53
    can do only what God permits,
        322
    can frame dreams, 343–44
    confederacy with (*see* witches, in
        league with the devil)
    as counterfeit and imitation, 296,
        325–26
    cunning and crafty dealing of, 373
    desires the heart, 183
    power of, 295–99
    power through witches, 299–301,
        387–89
    wonders of, 314–21
satisfaction of Christ, 167
Saturn, 411, 419, 421, 427, 428, 431–32
Saul
    ceremonial repentance of,
        xviiin35, 165
    deceived by witch of Endor, 316,
        325, 331, 332, 347–52
    disobedience of, 310, 376, 393
scorpion, 155
Scorpius, 427–28, 432, 434
Scotus, 41
scratching witches, 328, 364
Scripture
    reveals men's thoughts, 196
    as Word of God, 233
sea, ebbing and flowing of, 414
searching (repentance), 89–105, 121.
        See also examination
seasons, 414
secondary means, 416–17
second commandment, 142–43
second death, 101, 249
secret league (between devil and
        witch), 327–28, 371, 375, 376
secrets, concealing of, 286
security, thoughts of, 226–27
Sedulius presbyter, 60

seeds of all sins, in every man by nature, 97–98

self-denial, 11

self-examination. *See* examination; searching (repentance)

self-righteousness, 224–26

Sennacherib, 99, 153, 416

sensuality, 231

serpents, enchanted by charmers, 361

serpents and frogs, in Egypt, 367

service to God, 231

servile fear, 173

seven churches of Asia, 205

seventh commandment, 110, 146–47, 215

Shadrach, Meshach, and Abednego, 313

Shimei, 264

Shunamite woman, son of, 350

Sibylles of Greece, 352

"sight of angels," 50

sign of the cross, as remedy against witchcraft, 398

signs

    appointed over countries, 433

    of extraordinary things, 413–14

    of general things, 413, 414–15

silence, 259, 285–87

Simon Magus, 196, 235, 298, 301, 370, 374, 375

simple asseveration, 282

sin, sins

    as chaff, 95

    conscience of, 211

    as craggy rock, 90–91

    against the gospel, 149

    greatness of, 51, 248

    grievousness of, 15

    with a high hand, 231

    of infirmities, 178

    misery of, 249

    nature of, 176

    number of, 248

    practice of, 160

    state of, 251

ugliness of, 99

    want of thoughts on, 230–31

sixth commandment, 110, 146–47, 215

slander, 220

slavery under Satan, 152–53

"slow to speak," 261

smoothing (speech), 265

sneezing, 272

sobriety, in judgment, 276–77

Sodom, 115

Sodomites, lust of, 99

soft answer, 273

softness of heart, 174

Solomon, 162

soothsayers, 335

sorrow, in repentance, 135

Spanish inquisition, 93–94

special means (providence), 416

speech

    manner after we speak, 283

    manner before we speak, 261

    manner while we speak, 262–64

    meekness in, 271–75

    modesty in, 271

speech about God, 259

speech about neighbor, 259

speech about self, 260

speech before magistrate, 260

spirit

    as Godhead of Christ, 170

    as natural reason, 169

    as soul, 169

Spirit of adoption, 63, 258

spiritual ascension into heaven, 12

spiritual blessings, 240

spiritual bodies, 75

spiritual consideration, xix–xx, 241–42

    concerning God, 243–48

    concerning the self, 248–52

spiritual life, 10–11, 18, 44

spiritual matters, thoughts on, 229–31

spiritual oblation, 11

spiritual resurrection, 12
spiritual touching of Christ, 6
sporting lots, 347
Stapleton, Thomas, 40
stars, 421
    counsel from, 411
    and inclination of senses, 430
    used for divination, 335–42
stars in the heaven, 418–22
stealing, 147–48
sting of death, 155
stipulation of a good conscience, 70
Stourbridge Fair, xvi, 83
Strabo, 433
suffering, patience in, 72–73
superstition, xxiv, 297–98, 299, 344,
    371
superstitious means, 327–28
superstitious remedies against witch-
    craft, 394–99

table talk, 278, 280
Tacitus, 433
tale-bearing, 279–80
Tamar, 218
Taurus, 341, 427, 428, 433, 436
tears, and repentance, 164
temporal blessings, 9, 240
temporal judgments, 230
temporal things, thoughts of, 229
temptations, 21
    particular, 249–50
Ten Commandments, 120, 203, 211
tenth commandment, 149, 215
Tertullian, 278
testimony of the Spirit, 6, 7, 8, 63, 90
Thales, 297
theft, 218, 220
Theophylact, 60
thief on the cross, 159
third commandment, 143–44, 259
thirsting for Christ, 5
Thomas (apostle), 6
Thomas Aquinas, 40
thoughts, brought under obedience of
    God, xix

thoughts with consent, 215
thoughts without consent, 215
time of repentance, 110–13, 160–61
Timothy, 234
tongue
    abuse of, xxi–xxii, 255
    government of, 257–58, 259,
        288–91
torture, of witches, xxiiin59, 384
transgression of the law, 39
treason, punishable by death, xxiii
treasury of merit (Roman Catholic
    Church), 48
Treatise of Man's Imagination (1607),
    xix–xxi, 181–252
trials, 10, 11
Trinity, as charm, 356
true circumcision, 29
true faith, 64
*True Gain: More in Worth than All
    the Goods in the World* (1601),
    xiv–xv, 23–78
true repentance, 8, 51, 64, 82, 92, 132,
    161, 209, 235, 237, 248–49, 251,
    390. *See also* repentance
true wonders, wrought by God,
    312–13
truth
    bonds of, 282
    concealing of, 285
    speech within the bonds of, 262
truth of speech, 262, 265
Turks
    atheism of, 200
    deny Christ, 32
    know not Christ, 16
    will-worship of, 211
turning to God, 130
turning from sin, 130–31

union with Christ, xv, 54–57
unlawful ceremonies, 364
"unmerciful dealing," 216
urbanity (grace in speech), 277–79
usuries, 110

Valerius Maximus, 283
vanity, 9
Venus, 427, 429, 436
vessels of wrath, 192
vice, clothed in virtue, 226
Virgo, 427, 428, 434, 436
virtues of pilgrims, 75
visions from God. *See* divine dreams
vivification, xviin34, 69, 125
voluntarism, xxn49, xxin50

Waldensis, 41
walking in newness of life, 151
Warfield, B. B., xi
"watch and pray," 179
weather, 414, 434–45
Wenzeslaus, king of Bohemia, 432
wheat and chaff, 95, 103–4, 116–18
wicked imaginations, preventing and
　　suppressing, 234–35
widow's son at Zarephath, 350
will, combat in, 173–74
will-worship, 211
winnowing times, 116–19
wisdom, in speech, 262–64
witchcraft, xxii–xxiv, 200
　　as an art, 309–10
　　and assistance of the devil, 312
　　as deceitful art, 310
　　preservatives against, 389–92
　　restorative remedies against, 389,
　　　392–94
　　works wonders, 311
witch of Endor, 316, 325, 331, 347,
　　351–52, 372, 375, 401
witches, 370–74
　　casting into water, 385
　　of current time, 377–82
　　discerning and discovering of,
　　　382–89

in league with the devil, xxiii,
　　324–28, 371, 374, 375, 380
power of, 299–301
punishment of, xxiii, 299, 303,
　　375–76, 399–403
torture of, xxiiin59, 384
women, sooner entangled by devil's
　　illusions, 370–71
wonders, 312–13
　　of the devil, 314–21
　　by enchanters, 355–56, 372
　　lying and deceitful, 314
Word of God
　　consideration of, 244–45
　　experience of, 245
　　fanning of, 117–19
　　power from concurrent work of
　　　the Spirit, 361
　　regarded as foolishness, 204–9
　　true meaning of, 245
Word and sacraments, and knowl-
　　edge of Christ crucified, 18
works, as necessary for salvation, 35
works of grace, 34–35
works of nature, 34–35
world, conversion of, 50
worldly, xviii
worship of God, 209, 210–11
wrath of God, xviii, 20, 49, 91, 100,
　　102, 119, 134, 154, 156, 207, 249
writing, 284

Xenocrates, 283

yoke, in speech, 283

Zaccheus, 163
zodiac, 341, 419